Lecture Notes in Artificial Intelligence   1321

Subseries of Lecture Notes in Computer Science
Edited by J. G. Carbonell and J. Siekmann

Lecture Notes in Computer Science

Edited by G. Goos, J. Hartmanis and J. van Leeuwen

W0055298

Springer
Berlin
Heidelberg
New York
Barcelona
Budapest
Hong Kong
London
Milan
Paris
Santa Clara
Singapore
Tokyo

Maurizio Lenzerini (Ed.)

AI*IA 97:
Advances in
Artificial Intelligence

5th Congress of the Italian Association
for Artificial Intelligence
Rome, Italy, September 17-19, 1997
Proceedings

 Springer

Series Editors
Jaime G. Carbonell, Carnegie Mellon University, Pittsburgh, PA, USA
Jörg Siekmann, University of Saarland, Saarbrücken, Germany

Volume Editor

Maurizio Lenzerini
Università degli Studi di Roma "La Sapienza"
Dipartimento di Informatica e Sistemistica
Via Salaria 113, I-00198 Roma, Italy
E-mail: lenzerini@dis.uniroma1.it

Cataloging-in-Publication Data applied for

Die Deutsche Bibliothek - CIP-Einheitsaufnahme

Advances in artificial intelligence : Rome, Italy, September 17 - 19, 1997 ;
proceedings / Maurizio Lenzerini (ed.). - Berlin ; Heidelberg ; New York ;
Barcelona ; Budapest ; Hong Kong ; London ; Milan ; Paris ; Santa Clara ;
Singapore ; Tokyo : Springer, 1997
(... congress of the Italian Association for Artificial Intelligence, AIIA ... ; 5)
(Lecture notes in computer science ; Vol. 1321 : Lecture notes in artificial
intelligence)
ISBN 3-540-63576-9

CR Subject Classification (1991): I.2

ISBN 3-540-63576-9 Springer-Verlag Berlin Heidelberg New York

© Springer-Verlag Berlin Heidelberg 1997
Printed in Germany

Typesetting: Camera ready by author
SPIN 10545769   06/3142 – 5 4 3 2 1 0   Printed on acid-free paper

Preface

This book contains 37 scientific papers and 8 system description papers accepted for presentation at the Fifth Congress of the Italian Association for Artificial Intelligence (AI*IA). The Congress of the AI*IA is the most relevant Italian event in the field of Artificial Intelligence, and has been receiving much attention from many researchers and practitioners of different countries. The fifth congress, this year, is held in Rome, and is organized into 11 scientific sessions and one demo session.

The papers report on significant work carried out in the different areas of artificial intelligence, not only in Italy, but also in other countries both inside and outside Europe. Areas such as automated reasoning, knowledge representation, and planning continue to be thoroughly investigated. The collection also shows a growing interest in the fields of distributed artificial intelligence, perception, vision and robotics. The scientific papers on machine learning and natural language reflect a strong interest on these subjects, also confirmed by the large variety of approaches addressed by the various research groups. Finally, the Demo session reports on the work done on several protoype system, covering various important and interesting application domains.

In addition to the contributed papers collected in this book, the program of AI*IA 97 includes invited talks and tutorials covering advanced topics. The invited speakers are Georg Gottlob from the Technical University of Vienna (Austria), and Nicola Muscettola from the NASA AMES Research Center (USA), giving talks on "Complexity in artificial intelligence and knowledge representation," and "Automatic on-board planning for autonomous spacecraft," respectively.

Moreover, two workshops are scheduled with the purpose of illustrating significant applications in the field of artificial antelligence. The first one deals with the use of artificial intelligence in financial institutions, while the second one is devoted to an analysis of artificial intelligence techniques for improving the quality of public services for citizens. These workshops have mainly been conceived for potential users of artificial intelligence technologies so as to stimulate active interactions with them, and useful feedback to theoretical investigations.

Many people contributed in different ways to the success of the congress. First of all, the members of the program committee who efficiently handled the reviewing of the 88 submitted papers. They provided three reviews for each manuscript, by relying on the support of valuable additional reviewers. The members of the organizing committee, namely, Amedeo Cesta, Daniela D'Aloisi, Carlo Ficini, and Marco Schaerf, worked hardly for supporting all typical problems related to local arrangements. I thank them all very much for their support. In particular, I would like to thank Marco Schaerf, who chaired the organizing committee, and shared with me all the problems related to the arrangement of the various events. Without him, the congress would not have taken place.

I wish to thank Giovanni Soda, who chaired the past edition of the congress, and provided me with constant help in several aspects of the organization. Also, I am very grateful to Marco Cadoli and Andrea Schaerf, who were not formally involved in the organization, but provided valuable support especially in the organization of the tutorials and in the preparation of the proceedings.

The financial support by Consiglio Nazionale delle Ricerche (Comitato Scienze d'Ingegneria e Architettura, e Comitato Scienze e Tecnologia dell'Informazione) for partially covering the publication cost of this book, is acknowledged.

This book is dedicated to Domenico Catarci, who died a few days before the program committe meeting of the congress. Domenico Catarci was the father of my wife, and, above all, was one of the persons that I loved most in my life.

Rome, July 1997

Maurizio Lenzerini, AI*IA 97 Program Chair

Program Chair
Maurizio LENZERINI (Università di Roma "La Sapienza")

Program Committee
Francesco BERGADANO (Università di Torino)
Sonia BERGAMASCHI (Università di Modena)
Cristiano CASTELFRANCHI (CNR, Roma)
Amedeo CESTA (CNR, Roma)
Marco COLOMBETTI (Politecnico di Milano)
Luca CONSOLE (Università di Torino)
Francesco M. DONINI (Università di Roma "La Sapienza")
Floriana ESPOSITO (Università di Bari)
Salvatore GAGLIO (Università di Palermo)
Massimo GALLANTI (CISE, Milano)
Nicola GUARINO (CNR, Padova)
Leonardo LESMO (Univeristà di Torino)
Giannetto LEVIZZARI (Centro Ricerche FIAT, Orbassano, Torino)
Giancarlo MAURI (Università di Milano)
Daniele NARDI (Università di Roma "La Sapienza")
Roberto SERRA (Montecatini S.p.a., Ravenna)
Maria SIMI (Università di Pisa)
Giovanni SODA (Università di Firenze)
Oliviero STOCK (IRST, Trento)
Furio SUGGI LIVERANI (Illy Caffè, Trieste)
Carlo TASSO (Università di Udine)
Renato ZACCARIA (Università di Genova)

Organizing Committee
Marco SCHAERF (Università di Roma "La Sapienza") - Chair
Amedeo CESTA (CNR, Roma)
Daniela D'ALOISI (Fondazione Ugo Bordoni, Roma)
Carlo FICINI (Finmeccanica, Roma)

Referees

Table of Contents

Automated Reasoning

Knowledge Representation 1

Distributed Artificial Intelligence

Planning

Modelling Conceptual Change: An Interdisciplinary Approach

Filippo Neri*, Lorenza Saitta*, Andrée Tiberghien+

* Università di Torino
  Dipartimento di Informatica
  Corso Svizzera 185
  10149 Torino (Italy)
  {saitta, neri}@di.unito.it

+Equipe COAST de l'UMR GRIC
  CNRS - Université Lyon 2
  Ecole Normale Supérieure de Lyon
  46, Allée d'Italie
  69364 LYON Cedex 07 (France)
  atibergh@cri.ens-lyon.fr

Content Areas: cognitive modeling, machine learning, causality

Abstract

A computational approach to the simulation of cognitive models of conceptual change in children learning elementary physics is presented[1]. The student's mental model is inferred from a sequence of interviews collected along a period of eleven teaching sessions. Goal of the simulation is to support the cognitive scientist's investigation of learning in humans. The hypothesized cognitive models are based on a theory of conceptual change, derived from psichology results and educational experiences, which accounts for the evolution of the student's knowledge over a learning period. A Machine Learning (ML) system, able to handle domain knowledge (including a causal model of the domain), has been chosen as tool for the simulation of the cognitive models evolution. The system performs knowledge revision and provides causal explanation for its conclusions.

1 Introduction

People acquire, in their lifetime, models of the world that they use to interpret data, to explain phenomena and to make predictions. These models usually evolve when new information is gathered, and their evolution can be described as a particular aspect of learning, called *conceptual change* [Tiberghien, 1989, 1994; Vosniadou & Brewer, 1992, 1994; Caravita & Halldén,1994; Chi et al., 1994; Vosniadou, 1994]. The issue of conceptual change has been addressed from a variety of perspectives, but, even though quite a large body of experimental findings has been collected, still no single definition of conceptual change is universally accepted [White,1994].

In order to make a step ahead toward a deeper understanding of conceptual change, one possibility is to build models, which offer, at the very least, a mean to obtain predictions from tentative hypotheses. For what concerns conceptual change, models proposed in Cognitive Science have a descriptive nature: they describe mental models or knowledge states, but do not provide an account for the actual mechanisms of transition from a knowledge state to another.

---

[1] This work has been performed within the project "Learning in Humans and Machines", supported by the European Science Foundation

Rumelhart and Norman [1977] have categorized the type of transitions occurring as *Accretion, Tuning* or *Restructuration,* which are reminiscent of Piaget's *Assimilation, Accomodation,* and *Self-Regulation.* Accretion involves addition of new information to existing theories, and presents no problem when the new information does not contradict previous knowledge. When the new information is inconsistent with previous theories, tuning or restructuration may occur. However, when a contradiction emerges, also *failures in learning* may happen, taking the form of *inert knowledge* or *misconceptions.*

Conceptual change has been mainly studied in the context of learning Mathematics or Physics [Forbus & Gentner, 1986; diSessa, 1993; Vosniadou, 1994; Chi et al., 1994].

Starting from a descriptive model, a first step toward building a computational one consists in adding an operational definition of the mechanisms involved in conceptual change. One possibility is to simulate these mechanisms with a model sufficiently precise to be run as a program on a computer. The idea is to let the model (program) run in a set of situations comparable to a specific experimental setting, and to test the predictions from the model with the actual behaviour of human learners. In the Machine Learning literature, two approaches have been followed in modeling human learning: in the first one, a static snapshot of what a student knows at a given instant is inferred from his/her answers to a set of problems [Sleeman et al., 1990; Baffes & Mooney, 1996]. In the second approach the learning process is modeled as a sequence of knowledge states [Anderson et al., 1990; Klahr & Siegler, 1978; Sage & Langley, 1983; Newell, 1990; Schmidt & Ling, 1996; Shultz et al., 1994; Shultz et al., 1995]. An attempt to build up a computational model of the day/night cycle has been done in [Morik & Vosniadou, 1995], using the Machine Learning system MOBAL [Morik et al., 1993].

However, two aspects are overlooked in these models: the first is the strict interconnection between the heuristic knowledge in a specific domain (substantially the one modelled in the Machine Learning systems) and pre-existing deeper knowledge structures or theories [Murphy & Medin, 1985; Vosniadou, 1994, 1995; Tiberghien, 1994; Chi et al. 1994]. Several education and cognitive scientists have clearly pointed out that *misconceptions* and errors can be traced back to conflicts between taught concepts and this deeper layer, and suggest that education should be mainly directed toward this deeper level and not primarily toward the domain-specific one [Hestenes,1987; Vosniadou & Brewer, 1992, 1994; White, 1994; Caravita & Halldén, 1994].

The second aspect is the importance of *explanation.* Human learning is, to a great extent, a search for explanations; then, any model of human learning should provide an explanatory framework, allowing not only answers to questions to be predicted, but also reasons put forward in support of those answers to be formulated.

In this paper, a new approach to modeling human conceptual change, which is intended to extend current modeling practice and to overcome the said limitations, is presented. One of the main novelties is the differentiation between the pragmatic knowledge a student uses to answer questions and/or to interpret experimental results, and an *explanatory framework,* which the student uses to "make sense" of what he/she observes or is taught. A central hypothesis of the approach is that explanation corresponds to *causal* attribution. This hypothesis derives from a number of previous studies (for instance, [diSessa, 1993, 1996; Tiberghien, 1994]), and from the direct observation that children, even young ones, spontaneously use verbal constructs suggesting causality. The specific learning/teaching context envisages the task of acquiring basic concept in Physics, specifically *Heat* and *Temperature* concepts by middle school students. The computational model is grounded on an epistemological framework proposed by Tiberghien [Tiberghien, 1994].

As computational modeling tool it has been selected the Machine Learning system WHY, which acquires and/or revises a First Order Logic classification theory by exploiting a causal model of the domain and a set of examples [Saitta, Botta & Neri, 1993; Giordana et al., 1997].

2   The Learning Task: Educational/Cognitive Perspective

In Physics education research, results on students' conceptions show difficulties in learning Physics. For instance, students can solve rather difficult physics problems dealing with complicated mathematical relationships between physical quantities, but are not able to interpret or predict related events in practical situations [diSessa, 1996].

In [Tiberghien, 1994] a theoretical framework for interpreting such difficulties has been proposed. In this framework interpretation and prediction in Physics imply a modeling process articulated on three levels: "theory", "model" and "experimental field" of reference.

In [Tiberghien, 1994] no formal definition of these levels was given. In this paper we try to go further, adding tentative operational specifications for the involved elements.

In the proposed theoretical framework, Tiberghien assumes that when the learner is interpreting (or predicting) a material situation, s/he constructs a "model", where causality plays a crucial role, of the situation, which depends of his/her background theory and is also internally coherent. This assumption is basically shared by Vosniadou's approach [Vosniadou, 1994,1995].

The specific learning context [Neri et al. 1997; Saitta et al., 1997] considered here is the following: A group of secondary school students (12-13 years old, 6-5th grades), were exposed to a Physics course, outside normal teaching, consisting of 11 sessions, once a week, including experimentation, questions, discussions and explicit teaching. Content of the course were basic concepts and qualitative relations in the domain of *heat transfer* in everyday life situations.

The mentioned different types of learning, *accreation*, *tuning* and *restructuration*, have been observed in the experiments.

3   The Modeling Tool WHY

In this section a brief description of the functionalities of the learning system WHY is given. WHY learns and revises a knowledge base for classification problems using domain knowledge and examples. The domain knowledge consists of a *causal model* C of the domain, stating the relationships among basic phenomena[1], and a body of *phenomenological theory,* describing the links between abstract concepts and their possible manifestations in the world.

---

[1]   In general, C may contain any "deep" model of the domain, not necessarily a causal one.

The causal model C provides explanations in terms of causal chains among events, originating from "first" causes. The phenomenological theory P contains the semantics of the vocabulary terms, structural information about the objects in the domain, ontologies, taxonomies, domain-independent background knowledge (such as symmetry, spatial and temporal relations); finally, P contains a set of rules aimed at describing the manifestations of abstractly defined concepts in terms of properties, objects and events in the specific domain of application.

The causal model C is represented as a directed, labelled graph. Three kinds of nodes occur in the graphs: *causal* nodes, corresponding to processes or states related by cause-effect relations, *constraint* nodes, attached to edges and representing conditions which must be verified in order to instantiate the corresponding cause-effect relation, and *context* nodes, associated to causal nodes, representing contextual conditions to be added to the cause in order to obtain the effect.

The goal of WHY is to build up or revise a knowledge base KB of heuristic classification rules. A causal explanation (justification) of any KB revision is automatically provided.

It is important to clarify the relations between the causal model C and the heuristic knowledge base KB. The causal model could be used directly to obtain classifications. However, causal reasoning is slow, and the rules in KB act as shortcuts, compiled from C. On the other hand, the fact that the rules are justified by C (being derived from it according to the method described in [Saitta, Botta & Neri, 1993]) guarantees their validity and correctness (with respect to that of C) and also allows for explanations of the given classification in terms of the deep knowledge. On the other hand, KB and C may not be related at all, for instance in the case that KB is not derived from C but is directly "taught" by a teacher or acquired by the learner on a pure inductive basis. In this case, KB will give unjustified classifications (correct or not), for which no explanation exists with respect to C. Exploiting these different types of relations between KB and C, all the learning models emerged in the experimentation can be modeled. In the interplay between KB and C, the knowledge in P supplies the links between the general principles stated in C and the concrete experiments. The content of P contributes, as well, to enrich the modeling of students' misconceptions and conceptual change. Actually, it is in P, for instance, that ontological shift occurs.

4   The Modeling Methodology

As WHY learns knowledge for classification tasks, and provide explanations thereof, the task considered in this paper has to be mapped accordingly. We have chosen to follow the individual evolution of three students over two years (6th and 5th grades), because our goal was not to verify general hypotheses about learning, but rather to show how conceptual change in an individual can actually be modeled with WHY. In this paper we will show how the model can be built up and used through a specific example: the knowledge evolution of the student "David" with respect to learning in the 6th grade.

Before outlining the methodology used to implement the mapping reported in Table I, we will briefly describe the material available from the David's history:

$T_0 = $ <u>Before teaching</u>

Answers to Questionnaires Q_1 and Q_2 and their explanationAnswers to the initial Interview I_0 and their explanations. (Examples of the types of questions are reported in Appendix C)

T_i $(1 \leq 1 \leq 11)$ = <u>During teaching</u>

Answers to questions, predictions of outcomes from practical manipulations, and given explanations during the i-th teaching session.

T_f = <u>After teaching</u>

New answers to Questionnaires Q_1 and Q_2 and their explanations. Answers to the final Interview I_f and their explanations.

T_t = <u>Post test</u>

Answers to a test Interview I_t and their explanations, six months after the end of teaching.

The overall modeling methodology can be summarized as follows:

Step 0 – Using the blank questionnaires and interviews, and the available teaching material, define the teacher's bodies of knowledge C^*, P^* and $\mathcal{KB}^*$. Obviulsy, the encoded knowledge is strictly limited to, and highly constrained by, the teaching methods and materials, and by what the teacher has decided the students must learn. An excerpt of the teacher's knowledge is reported in Appendix A.

Step 1 – Using a protocol analysis of the material at time T_0, hypothesize the initial content (before teaching) of David's C_0, P_0 and $\mathcal{KB}_0$; the encoded knowledge must account for both the answers and their explanations given by David at this time. Part of this knowledge can be found in Appendix B.

For $i = 1$ to 11 **do**

Step i – During each lesson, students are required to make predictions and are then confronted with the true outcome of the experimentation: if this outcome contradicts the prediction, a change in the mental model should occur.

Using C_{i-1}, P_{i-1} and $\mathcal{KB}_{i-1}$, predict David's answers and compare the system's predictions with the actual answers. Build up C_i, P_i and $\mathcal{KB}_i$, and compare them with the previous ones.

Individuate possible changes, according to the definitions reported in Section 5.

Step f – Using a protocol analysis of the material at time T_f, hypothesize the final content (after teaching) of David's C_f, P_f and $\mathcal{KB}_f$. Compare this knowledge with C_0, P_0 and $\mathcal{KB}_0$, in order to assess global changes (if any) induced by the teaching.

Step t – Same as Step f, with the material at time T_t.

In order to use WHY to model David, each practical experiment is represented as an example, consisting of two parts: a description of the experimental setting and a question. The experimental setting corresponds to the description of the example, whereas the possible answers to the question are considered as alternative classes. Then, the process of predicting the outcome of an experiment is mapped onto the problem of predicting the correct answer. Examples of this mapping are given in Appendix C.

In the current experimentation, the various knowledge bodies C, P and $\mathcal{KB}$ have been manually constructed and encoded by the experimenters. WHY relies on a sophisticated algorithm for uncovering errors or incompletenesses in its knowledge.

This is actually the only part that has been run automatically, in the current experimentation, even though WHY can also make the changes from one step to the following automatically by using automatic induction as in [Sleeman et al., 1990; Baffes & Mooney, 1996].

5 Tentative Definition of Conceptual Change

In Section 2 we have outlined the main findings emerged from the experimentation. In order to obtain a computational model of conceptual change, we associate, as described in the following, each type of observed change to the application of one or more WHY's revision operators, in order to make possible the automatization of the change process.

Accretion

Learning by accretion *increases coverage,* in the sense that more experimental situations can be handled (independently of their correct interpretation/prediction). A rule is applicable to a situation when all the conditions specified by the rule's antecedent are defined, i.e. they have a "true" or "false" value. Accretion, then, affects both the *phenomenological theory* or the *heuristic knowledge base,* by adding to any of them a new rule. Accretion may also consists of addition of a property to an ontological node. In our approach, accretion is not considered conceptual change in a strict sense. Accretion can be implemented with the "adding rules" operator.

A typical situation in which accretion occurs is when a student memorizes, without explanation, a piece of information taught by the teacher. This information can be added, as a rule, to the student's knowledge, without checking for compatibility with previous knowledge. The rule can be accessed, on the basis of recency, for giving a correct answer for a while, until it is forgotten, or other pieces of knowledge, incorrect but supported by the student's deep beliefs, gain higher priority.

Tuning

Tuning *increases the number of correct predictions or explanations,* but does not modify the deep explanatory framework. It may affect the *heuristic knowledge base* or the *phenomenological theory,* by changing the preconditions in some rule or by adding new rules. Tuning may also involve the *causal model,* but only with addition/deletion in the constraint and context nodes (causal nodes and links between them cannot be changed). Tuning can be implemented with the operators that generalize or specialize rule antecedents, or add and delete rules. Also tuning is not considered here a conceptual change in a strict sense.

Restructuration

Restructuration affects the explanatory framework. It involves the *causal model,* via addition/deletion of causal nodes, or modification of causal links, and the *ontologies* of the domain, via addition/deletion of nodes or changing a node from one ontology to another. Restructuration is considered conceptual change.

As it can be seen, we have given a stricter definition of conceptual change than in some approaches (for instance, [Vosniadou, 1994, 1995]), but larger than in others (for instance, [Chi et al., 1994]).

In the appendices, examples of the above types of changes will be given for the specific case of David.

6 Conclusion

We have introduced a new way of interpreting learning in relation with teaching in the domain of physics. Our analysis is based on a type of knowledge processing which can be a relevant frame of reference from the points of view of both personal knowledge of a learner and "official" knowledge, such as that of Physics. Our framework allows us to establish an independence between analysis of the learner's acquisition and of Physics knowledge. Thus, it is possible to take into account the *coherence of the learner per se* , even if it is incompatible with Physics. The structuring of the analysis in terms of causal theory, phenomenological knowledge and field of applicability allows the learner's knowledge and Physics knowledge to be compared. This independence and this comparison are essential to the characterisation of different types of learning.

Moreover, WHY's articulated knowledge representation allows most of phenomena observed in children learning elementary physics to be modeled, notably their explanation in terms of simple causality, and the interdependence of "surface" heuristic knowledge and deep beliefs.

A   Teacher's knowledge

In this appendix excerpts from the teacher's knowledge are given, for the sake of exemplification.

A.1. Causal Model

In Fig. A.1, a part of the causal graph (which consists of three disconnected subgraphs) is reported.

A point to notice is the explicit mention to a state of "thermal equilibrium", which the teacher want the student to eventually acquire.

A.2. Phenomenological Theory

The teacher's phenomenological theory, which consists of 121 rules, contains taxonomies, i.e, rules of the type "gold(x) $\Rightarrow$ METAL(x)", information on measurements, such that "TEMP(x,T) $\wedge$ lower(T,θ_0) $\Rightarrow$ COLD(x)", abstractions, such as "person(z) $\wedge$ OBJ(x) $\wedge$ to-heat(z,x) $\Rightarrow$ TO-HEAT(x)", in which the person heating the object x is hidden, or general knowledge of the type "full-of(x,y) $\Rightarrow$ INSIDE(y,x)", which states the domain-independent information that if a container x is full of y, then y is insidex. The most important part of $\mathcal{P}$, however, is the definition of the phenomenology of the domain; for instance, the rule

CONTAINER(y) $\wedge$ INSIDE(x,y) $\wedge$ TO-HEAT(y) $\Rightarrow$ TO-HEAT(x)

states that if the material x is inside the container y, and y is heated, than also x will be heated; this rule provides an operational way of heating x.

Another example is the rule

SAME-TEMP(x,y) $\Rightarrow$ THERMAL-EQUILIBRIUM(x,y),

which explains what "thermal equilibrium" means.

The teacher has also a heuristic knowledge base of 23 rules, compiled from the causal net, which he uses to gives quick answers, without performing causal reasoning. For instance, the following rule

MATERIAL(x) $\wedge$ SOLID(x) $\wedge$ TO-HEAT(x) $\Rightarrow$ MELTING(x),

allows the teacher to decide that a solid body will melt if heated.

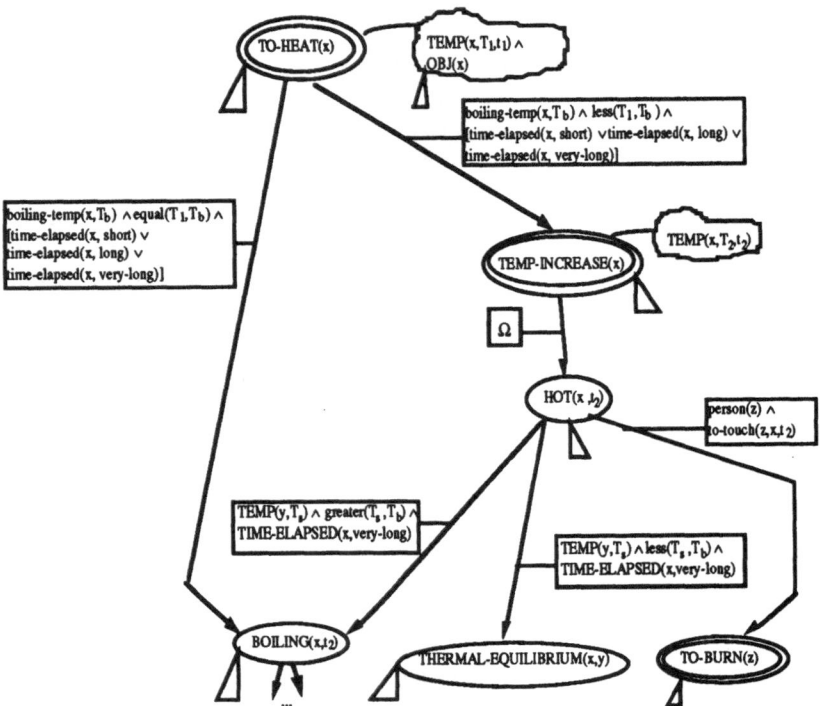

Figure A.1 – Part of the teacher's causal graph.

B   David's knowledge

In this appendix we give an example of David's knowledge. From his answers to the questionnaires and interview, David's initial causal network (before teaching) in reported in Fig. B.1. Also David's model has more than one part; we report the one that matches the teacher's in Appendix A. The reported graph provides exactly the same explanations given by David, and this fact has been considered a tentative validation of the model. A furher validation will come from the behaviour of the model under changes.

In David's causal model we may notice many interesting differences from the teacher's model, only some of which will be outlined here. First of all, there is no notion that an object x, if heated, may not change its temperature (if it is changing state, for instance). This incompleteness will be filled by David in the course of teaching, by accretion, when he will see boiling water with a stable temperature. The second difference, fundamental for the understanding of the involved phenomena and not remediable with accretion nor tuning, is the dependence of the outcome of heating from the substance of the heated object. We may notice David's everyday life experience (sugar becomes caramel, and so on). Moreover, the perceptive aspect of phenomena is still the primary one: David asserts that the water becomes hot because it boils; in fact, the way that David known to ascertain whether water is hot is from its boiling and not vice-versa, as it should be. In the course of learning, David will arrive

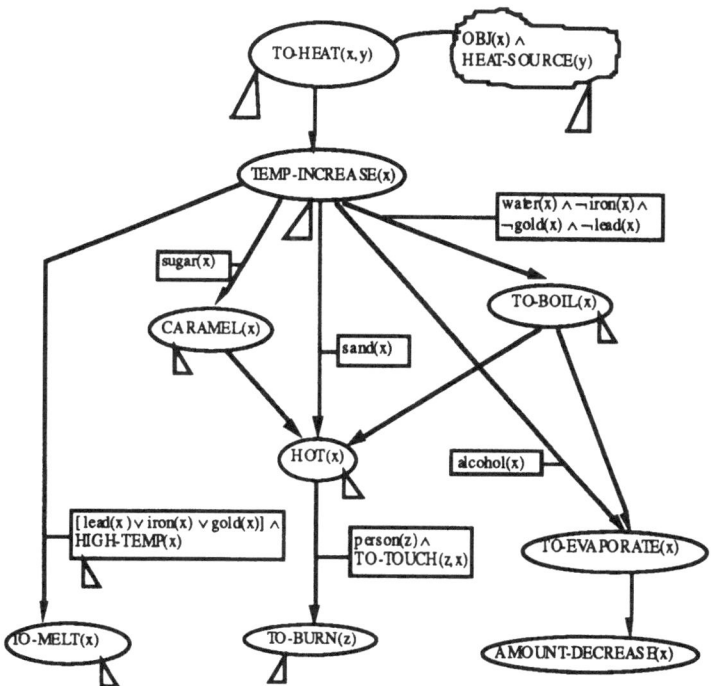

Figure B.1 -Hypothesized David's causal network before teaching.

at combining all the possibilities of becoming hot for the various substances into a unique node, very much as in the teacher's graph.

David's initial phenomenological theory contains 96 rules. As it can be seen, there is no substantial difference between David and the teacher in terms of number of rules, but the content is very different. Then David's knowledge is not a subset of the teacher's one. Just to give an example, let us consider the rule "feel-cold(x) $\Rightarrow$ COLD(x)", which parallels the one reported in Appendix A. The teacher knows that coldness is related to a given range of temperature, whereas David has a perceptive notion of it: an object is cold if it feels cold when touched.

As an example of the interplay between causal model and knowledge base, let us consider David's rule:

HEAT-SOURCE(y_1) $\wedge$ HEAT-SOURCE(y_2) $\wedge$
same-features(y_1,y_2) $\wedge$ TO-HEAT(x_1,y_1) $\wedge$ TO-HEAT(x_2,y_2) $\wedge$
$\wedge$ SAME-TIME-ELAPSED(y_1,y_2) $\wedge$ SAME-MATERIAL(x_1,x_2) $\wedge$
$\wedge$ GREATER-AMOUNT(x_1,x_2) $\Rightarrow$ GREATER-TEMP(x_2,x_1,final)

David uses this rule to answer correctly to the question of Appendix C, so he has an experiential knowledge of heat transfer. However, he cannot give a justification for his answer (he says "I do not know" for explanation); this behavior derives from the fact that the above rule cannot be derived from the graph in Fig. B.1. Then, David has only added this piece of information to his knowledge, without trying to understanding it.

C   Example of a Modelling Session

Question: "Two saucepans A and B, with thermometers inside, are put on two gas stoves g_a and g_b, which are equal (denoted by the predicate "same-feature"). A contains a smaller amount (a) of water than B does (b). The initial temperature of the system is 20 ºC. After a short time interval, the thermometer in A indicates 50 ºC.
1) Will the thermometer h_b in B indicate the same, a greater or a lower temperature than that h_a in A?
2) Please, explain your answer"
To answer the question is modeled as a classification problem, in which there are three classes
$\{$GREATER-THERMOM-READING(h_b,h_a,t_2),
SAME-THERMOM-READING(h_b,h_a,t_2),
LOWER-THERMOM-READING(h_b,h_a,t_2)$\}$,
among which David has to choose. Then, he is confronted with the actual outcome of the manipulation (In this case he answered correctly).

person(David) $\wedge$ saucepan(A) $\wedge$ saucepan(B) $\wedge$
$\wedge$ same-features(A,B) $\wedge$ water(a) $\wedge$ water(b) $\wedge$ thermometer(h_a) $\wedge$ $\wedge$ thermometer(h_b)
$\wedge$ same-features(h_a ,h_b) $\wedge$ gas-stove(g_a) $\wedge$
$\wedge$ gas-stove(g_b) $\wedge$ same-features(g_a,g_b) $\wedge$ ignited(g_a) $\wedge$
$\wedge$ ignited(g_b) $\wedge$ on(A,g_a) $\wedge$ on(B,g_b) $\wedge$ person(Tournesol) $\wedge$
$\wedge$ person(Tintin) $\wedge$ person(Haddock)
$\wedge$ to-put-inside(Tournesol,a,A) $\wedge$ amount(a,small) $\wedge$
$\wedge$ to-put-inside(Tournesol,b,B) $\wedge$ to-put-inside(Tournesol,h_a,A) $\wedge$
$\wedge$ to-put-inside(Tournesol,h_b,B) $\wedge$ amount(b,large) $\wedge$
$\wedge$ temp(a, 20,initial) $\wedge$ temp(b, 20,initial) $\wedge$ not-boiling(a,initial) $\wedge$
$\wedge$ not-boiling(b,initial) $\wedge$ time-elapsed(a,short) $\wedge$
$\wedge$ time-elapsed(b,short) $\wedge$ time-elapsed(g_a,short) $\wedge$
$\wedge$ time-elapsed(g_b,short) $\wedge$ thermom-reading(h_a,50,final)

References

Anderson J.R., Boyle C.F., Corbett A.T. and Lewis M.W. (1990). "Cognitive Modelling and Intelligent Tutoring", *Artificial Intelligence, 42*, 7-49.

Baffes P. T. and Mooney R. J. (1996). "A Novel Application of Theory Refinement to Student Modeling". *Proc. of Thirteenth National Conference on Artificial Intelligence* (Portland, OR), pp. 403-408.

Caravita S. and Halldén O. (1994). "Re-framing the Problem of Conceptual Change". *Learning and Instruction, 4*, 89-111.

Chi M. T. H., Slotta J. D. and de Leeuw N. (1994). "From Things to Processes: A Theory of Conceptual Change for Learning Science Concepts". *Learning and Instruction, 4*, 27-43.

diSessa A. (1993). "Toward an Epistemology of Physics". *Cognition and Instruction*, *10*, 105-225.

diSessa A. (1996). "What Do "Just Plain Folk" Know about Physics". In D. Olson N. Terrance (Eds.), *Handbook of Education and Human Development*, Blackwell Publ., pp. 709-730.

Forbus K.D. and Gentner D. (1986). "Learning Physical Domains: Toward a Theoretical Framework". In R. Michalski, J. Carbonell & T. Mitchell (Eds.), *Machine Learning: An Artificial Intelligence Approach, Vol. II*, Morgan Kaufmann, Los Altos, CA, pp. 311-348.

Gentner D. (1989). "The Mechanisms of Analogical Learning", in Vosniadou S. and Ortony A. (Eds.), *Similarity and Analogical Reasoning*, Cambridge University Press, pp.199-241.

Giordana A. and Neri F., Saitta L. and Botta M. (1997). "Integrating Multiple Learning Strategies in First Order Logics". *Machine Learning Journal*. (Special issue on Multi Strategy Learning), Kluwer Academic Publishers (Boston, MA). In Press.

Hestenes D. (1987). "Toward a Modelling Theory of Physics Instruction". *American Journal of Physics, 55*, 440-454.

Klahr D. and Siegler R.S. (1978). "The Representation of Children's Knowledge". In H.W. Reese and L.P. Lipsitt (Eds.), *Advances in Child Development and Behavior*, Academic Press, New York, NY, pp. 61-116.

Morik K. and Vosniadou S. (1995). "A Developmental Case Study on Sequential Learning: the Day-Night Cycle". In Reimann P. and Spada H. *Learning in Humans and Machines: Towards an Interdisciplinary Learning Science* , pp. 212-227.

Morik K., Wrobel S., Kietz J.-U. and Emde W. (1993). *Knowledge Acquisition and Machine Learning* , Academic Press, London,UK.

Murphy L.G. and Medin D.L. (1985). "The Role of Theories in Conceptual Coherence". *Psychological Review, 92*, 289-316.

Neri F., Saitta L. and Tiberghien A. (1997). "Modelling Physichal Knowledge Acquisition in Children with Machine Learning". Proc. of *19th Annual Conference of the Cognitive Science Society*, Stanford (CA), Morgan Kaufmann, in press.

Saitta L., Neri F. and Tiberghien A. (1997). "World Model Construction in Children during Physics Learning". Proc. of *International Symposium Methodologies for Intelligent Systems '97 (ISMIS 97)*, Lecture Notes in Artificial Intelligence series, Springer Verlag (Berlin, Germany), in press.

Newell A. (1990). *Unified Theories of Cognition*, Harvard University Press, Cambridge, MA.

Rumelhart D. E. and Norman D. A. (1977). "Accretion, Tuning and Restructuring: Three modes of Learning", in Cotton J. W. and Klatzky R. L. (Eds.), *Semantic Factors in Cognition* , Erlbaum (Hillsdale, NJ).

Sage S. and Langley P. (1983). "Modeling Cognitive Development on the Balance Scale Task". *Proc. 8th Int. Joint Conf. on Artificial Intelligence* (Karlsruhe, Germany), pp. 94-96.

Saitta L., Botta M., Neri F. (1993). "Multistrategy Learning and Theory Revision". *Machine Learning, 11,* 153-172.

Schmidt W.C. and Ling C.X. (1996). "A Decision-Tree Model of Balance Scale Development". *Machine Learning, 24,* 203-230.

Shultz T.R., Mareschal D. and Schmidt W. (1994). "Modeling Cognitive Developemnt on Balance Scale Phenomena". *Machine Learning, 16,* 57-86.

Shultz T.R., Schmidt W.C., Buckingam D. and Mareschal D. (1995). "Modeling Cognitive Development with a Generative Connectionist Algorithm". In T. Simon and G. Halford (Eds.), *Developing Cognitive Competence: New Approaches to Process Modeling,* Erlbaum, Hillsdale, NJ.

Sleeman D., Hirsh H., Ellery I. and Kim I. (1990). "Extending Domain Theories: two case Studies in Student Modeling". *Machine Learning, 5,* 11-37.

Tiberghien A. (1989). "Learning and Teaching at Middle School Level of Concepts and Phenomena in Physics. The Case of Temperature". In H. Mandl, E. de Corte, N. Bennett and H.F. Friedrich (Eds.), *Learning and Instruction. European Research in an International Context, Volume 2.1,* Pergamon Press, Oxford, UK, pp. 631-648.

Tiberghien A. (1994). "Modelling as a Basis for Analysing Teaching-Learning Situations". *Learning and Instruction, 4,* 71-87.

Vosniadou S. (1994). "Capturing and Modeling the Process of Conceptual Change". *Learning and Instruction, 4,* 45-69.

Vosniadou S. and Brewer W.F. (1992). "Mental Models of the Earth: A Study of Conceptual Change in Childhood". *Cognitive Psychology, 24,* 535-585.

Vosniadou S. and Brewer W.F. (1994). "Mental Models of the Day/Night Cycle". *Cognitive Science, 18,* 123-183.

White R. T. (1994). "Commentary Conceptual and Con-ceptional Change". *Learning and Instruction, 4,* 117-121.

Refining Numerical Terms in Horn Clauses

Marco Botta, Attilio Giordana and Roberto Piola

Dipartimento di Informatica, Università di Torino
corso Svizzera 185, 10149 Torino (TO), Italy
email: {*botta,attilio,piola*} @di.unito.it

Abstract. This paper presents an experimental analysis of a method recently proposed for refining knowledge bases expressed in a first order logic language. The method consists in transforming a classification theory into a neural network, called First Order logic Neural Network (FONN), by replacing predicate semantic functions and logical connectives with continuous-valued derivable functions. In this way it is possible to tune numerical constants in the original theory by performing the error gradient descent. The classification theory to be refined can be manually handcrafted or automatically acquired by a symbolic relational learning system able to deal with numerical features. The emphasis of this paper is on the experimental analysis of the method and an extensive experimentation is provided considering different choices for encoding the logical connectives, and different variants of the learning strategy. The experimentation is made on a challenging artificial case study and shows that FONNs converge quite fastly and generalize better than propositional learners do on an equivalent task definition.

1 Introduction

The use of First Order Logics (FOL) for encoding classification theories is appealing for two main reasons. First, FOL can face problems which cannot be reduced to propositional logics, such as data of unrestricted size, and recurrent structures. Second, even when a problem can be reduced to a propositional setting, the solutions found in FOL are more abstract and simpler than the corresponding ones in propositional logics. Nevertheless, a serious obstacle to the use of FOL in this sense in real world problems is represented by the numerical terms, such as thresholds and parameters, which are difficult to estimate for an expert. In the propositional framework many induction algorithms belonging to either the symbolic or the connectionist paradigm are capable of effectively learning numerical constants from data. On the contrary, in the FOL framework, few steps forward have been done, up to now.

A novelty is represented by a method, recently proposed by the authors [4], which learns numerical constants in FOL classification theories by combining the logic paradigm with the connectionist one. This is made by mapping a FOL classification theory into a network of elementary continuous-valued functions, corresponding to predicates and logical connectives, which can be refined by performing an error gradient descent algorithm [14]. Such a kind of network, called First Order logic Neural Networks (FONN), can be seen as an extension to FOL of KBANN [15] and of analogous methods, based on Radial Basis Function Networks (RBFNs) [1, 16, 7], developed for propositional logic.

In this paper, we further investigate FONN's properties and we discuss the problem of choosing the encoding functions for the logical connectives. An extensive experimentation performed using different kinds of functions is reported. Moreover, we analyze the performances reached by FONNs using several variants of the learning strategy and of the error measure.

The experimentation is performed on an artificial problem inspired to the well known *train-going-east* problem proposed by Michalski [10]. In the present case a set of continuous attributes has been added and a generation program which automatically builds trains according to user assigned probability distributions has been implemented. Trains are partitioned into positive and negative instances according to user defined criteria. In this way, learning problems of different complexity can be generated in order to challenge the learning algorithm.

2 Mapping First Order Logics to Continuously Valued Operational Networks

In order to make the paper self contained, in the following we will briefly overview FONN architecture. A more detailed description can be found in [4].

For the sake of simplicity, we will consider only flat classification theories consisting of set of rules having the following general form:

$$
\begin{aligned}
\forall y_1, \ldots, y_r [\exists x_1, \ldots, x_k \psi(x_1, \ldots, x_k, y_1, \ldots, y_r) \wedge \\
\wedge \varphi(x_1, \ldots, x_k, y_1, \ldots, y_r)] \rightarrow \omega(y_1, \ldots, y_r) \; ,
\end{aligned}
\tag{1}
$$

being $\psi(x_1, \ldots, x_k, y_1, \ldots, y_r)$ a conjunctive subformula containing only predicates stating conditions on non numerical terms, and $\varphi(x_1, \ldots, x_k, y_1, \ldots, y_r)$ a conjunctive subformula containing predicates stating conditions on numerical terms. As a special case either ψ or φ can be empty.

In order to verify such a kind of rule on a given universe U, containing a set of constants, one must find all the models of $\psi \wedge \varphi$ existing in U. In other words, $\psi \wedge \varphi$ must be checked on all possible substitutions of variables $y_1, \ldots, y_r$ in $\psi \wedge \varphi$ with constant names $a_1, \ldots, a_r$ in U. For each substitution $\theta_y = \{y_1/a_1, \ldots, y_r/a_r\}$ for variables $y_1, \ldots, y_r$ in φ, there might be many possible substitutions for variables $x_1, \ldots, x_k$ that should be taken into account. θ_y is a positive instance of ω if there exists at least one substitution θ_x for variables $x_1, \ldots, x_k$ such that $(\psi \wedge \varphi)\theta_x \theta_y$ is true.

This task can be accomplished by means of a four level architecture as shown in Fig. 1. For each formula φ, the first level (Unifier) generates all possible substitutions (compatible with constraints ψ) of the variables $x_1, \ldots, x_r$ with constants in the universe U represented by input data; the second level (α) evaluates the truth of the logical conditions stated by the classification rule, and the third level node (β) implements the existential quantifier semantics. For every substitution

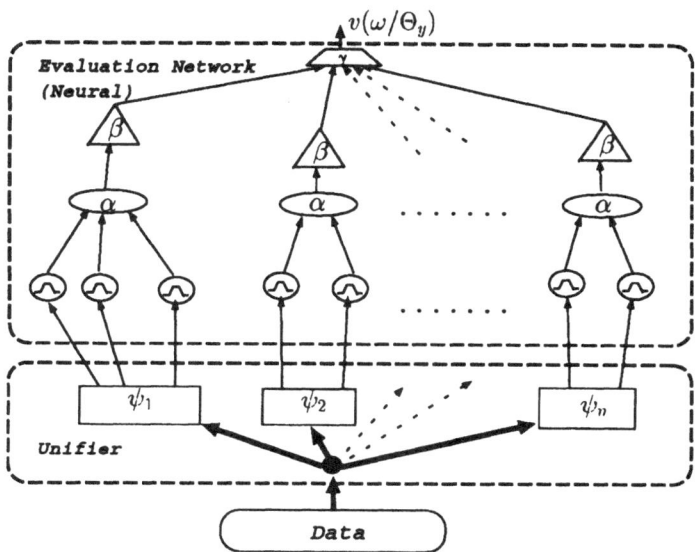

Fig. 1. FONN architecture: each branch from data up to γ represent a formula, each φ_n a logical constraint.

θ_y, the β operator collects the results obtained by evaluating φ on each corresponding substitution θ_x and asserts the consequent if at least one of them is "true". A fourth level (γ node) combines the assertions made by different rules.

On one hand, this architecture offers the possibility to deal with data (Universes) of unrestricted size, because the Unifier dynamically builds all the possible ground instances of a classification rule. On the other hand, the evaluation network in Fig. 1 is a static structure that can be translated into a neural network by defining α, β and γ as continuous derivable functions, in a similar way as done for the propositional case [1, 15].

In order to have a uniform mechanism for translating the predicates connected to α nodes into continuous valued units, the logic language has been restricted so that assertions about numeric properties can be made only by means of a special predicate having the syntactic form: $inside(f(x_1, \ldots, x_s), [a, b])$, being $f(x_1, \ldots, x_s)$ a real function defined on the input data, and $[a, b]$ a close interval in the real domain. The semantics of predicate $inside$ is defined as follows:

$$v(inside(f(x_1 \ldots, x_s), [a, b])) = \begin{cases} 1 \text{ if } f(x_1, \ldots, x_s) \in [a, b] \\ 0 \text{ otherwise} \end{cases} \quad (2)$$

Then, a positive literal $L_i = inside(f_i(x_1, \ldots, x_s), [a_i, b_i])$ will be translated into a Gaussian activation function of center $\mu_i = (b_i + a_i)/2$ and width $\sigma_i = (b_i - a_i)/2$. Other kind of activation functions are under study.

The choice of the activation functions for α, β and γ nodes needs special attention: most of our experiments have been performed by using the arithmetic product as α operator ($\wedge$), the so-called $softmax(S_M)$ as β operator ($\exists$), and a weighted sum followed by a sigmoid (perceptron) as γ operator ($\vee$). Therefore:

$$\alpha(v_1,\ldots,v_n) = \prod_{i=1}^{n} v_i \ , \qquad \beta(v_1,\ldots,v_m) = \frac{\sum_{i=1}^{m} v_i e^{\lambda v_i}}{\sum_{i=1}^{m} e^{\lambda v_i}} \ ,$$
$$\gamma(v_1,\ldots,v_s) = \frac{1}{1+e^{-\rho \sum_{i=1}^{s} w_i v_i + \xi}} \ . \tag{3}$$

The reason for this choice was due to the fact that the network obtained is a straightforward generalization of a Factorizable RBFN [12, 1], whose behavior has been widely investigated in the literature. In fact, the only difference is represented by the additional layer implementing the existential quantification. Anyhow, it is worth noting that this choice is in some sense arbitrary and in no way pretends to be considered as an optimal one. For instance, several alternative proposals can be found in the fuzzy logic controller literature [2, 17]. Here, we investigated the behavior of three different alternatives for the β operator (existential quantifier):

$$softmax(v_1,\ldots,v_m) = \frac{\sum_{i=1}^{m} v_i e^{\lambda v_i}}{\sum_{i=1}^{m} e^{\lambda v_i}}, \tag{4}$$

$$Max(v_1,\ldots,v_m) = \max_{i=1}^{m} v_i, \tag{5}$$

$$t_{max}(v_1,\ldots,v_m) = \begin{cases} v_1 & \text{if } m = 1 \\ v_1 + v_2 - v_1 * v_2 & \text{if } m = 2 \\ t_{max}(t_{max}(v_1,\ldots,v_{m-1}),v_m) & \text{otherwise} \ . \end{cases} \tag{6}$$

As shown in Section 4, an operator like Max preserves the symbolic readability of the refined knowledge base, while $softmax$ helps in having a smooth convergence curve. The t_{max} operator can be useful for implementing evidential reasoning strategies where a decision is taken on the basis of co-occurrence of several circumstantial symptoms.

The reason for keeping separate the evaluation of constraints ψ from the numeric part φ is simply due to complexity reasons. In fact, matching First Order formulae is per se a combinatorial problem [8]. Nevertheless, in many practical cases the complexity can be tamed by exploiting the knowledge gained during the matching process in order to avoid testing subformulae which depend upon conditions which are known to be false.

Moving to continuous valued semantics, every condition is always verified at a given extent so that the control strategies used to guide an inference engine in boolean logics do not work anymore.

Being n the number of items in the input data and k the arity of a formula, the number n_θ of substitutions which need to be tried is n^k. Then, when formulae have many variables and data consist of many items, the transformation into a continuous semantic evaluation network can produce an intractable algorithm.

The solution we propose consists in mapping into a continuous semantic network only literals related to numeric properties. Doing in this way, we achieve the goal of dealing with the inherent fuzziness of numeric properties, and keep the possibility of constraining the combinatorial explosion of the number of substitutions to evaluate.

As described in Fig. 1, the constraints part ψ_i of every rule r_i is used by the Unifier in order to send to the corresponding numerical part φ_i only substitutions satisfying ψ_i. The Unifier can be easily implemented by means of a simple theorem prover.

Since all activation functions in FONNs are continuous and derivable, the classical error gradient descent technique can be applied in order to finely tune the weights w_i, μ_j, σ_j and ξ .

3 The Train Check-Out Case Study

Many different aspects have been considered in designing the experimental setup: in this work, we are interested in showing properties of FONNs, such as convergence and flexibility, and studying their behavior. To this aim, data must be structured and described by both numerical and categorical features. Moreover, their classification must depend upon both type of features.

Being not aware of a standard benchmark showing the above mentioned characteristics (benchmarks in the UCI repository either are in a *propositional* form, or deal with symbolic values only), we decided to build a new dataset that provides the kind of features needed to test our claims [4] . Data are available from http://www.di.unito.it/~mluser/datasets.html .

Furthermore, artificial datasets offer the advantage that the learning task can be made arbitrarily complex by choosing the size of the data, the distribution of the attribute values and the rules for partitioning the learning events into positive and negative ones.

The *Train Check-Out Case Study* is an extension to the well-known *train-going-east* problem defined by Michalski [10]: trains are composed by a variable number of cars, each described by a vector of four continuous (width, length, height and weight) and four categorical attributes (the presence of lights and brakes, the load type, and whether a car is an engine or not). A procedure randomly generates instances of trains whose classification depends upon user defined criteria.

The general problem we chose is that of deciding whether a train cannot transit on a given line (check-out procedure followed by a railway inspector), according to the characteristics of the line (for instance, if there are bridges on the line, the train must not weigh more than the bridges can bear). Three instances of the problem, of different complexity, have been created by varying the number of cars and the kind of attributes (numerical and categorical) involved in the decision.

The first criterion is a simple disjunctive rule based on the value of a numerical attribute of a car: *a train cannot go if and only if it contains at least one car whose weight (height, length or width, respectively) exceeds a threshold.*

The second criterion classifies trains using rules based on both numerical and categorical attributes of two cars: *a train cannot go if it contains two near cars, both without brakes and heavier than a threshold we_1 or if it contains two near cars carrying special materials and heavier than $we_2 < we_1$.*

A third criterion classifies trains according to the total weight of the train: *a train cannot go if the sum of the weights of cars with no brakes exceeds a threshold* we_3.

The first two tasks have been used to verify the effectiveness of the learning algorithms and the convergence properties of the network, whereas the third task has been designed to test the behavior of the network using different semantic functions for the logical connectives.

In order to show that FONNs generalize well over the number of objects that constitute a learning instance (a train), we generated two learning sets $\mathcal{L}_{100}$ and $\mathcal{L}_{500}$ composed of 100 and 500 trains, whose length was randomly chosen between 2 and 8 cars; then, we built a first test set $\mathcal{A}$ containing 10000 trains whose number of cars was randomly chosen between 2 and 8, as for the learning sets, and a second test set $\mathcal{B}$ of 10000 trains composed by 2 to 15 cars.

4 FONN Experimental Analysis

Knowledge bases to be refined by FONNs can be either manually handcrafted or automatically learned by a relational learning system. Here, we report experiments based on manually handcrafted knowledge bases, whose rules are structurally correct (they resemble the ones used to classify the instances), but contain rough (or even wrong) approximations of numerical terms. Then, the relational learner SMART+[3], that is able to learn with reasonable approximation numerical terms in the form (2) has been used to generate knowledge bases to be refined by FONNs; for the experiments with SMART+ two settings were used: in the second one, we supplied SMART+ with a partial domain theory, consisting of the structural terms (constraints) of the rules, in order to constrain the search space. In both runs, we allowed SMART+ to produce partially inconsistent knowledge bases (some rules cover negative instances), differently than the first setting we used in [4]. Results with the two knowledge bases are identified as "SMART+(1)" and "(2)". There was no point in testing SMART+(2) on Task 1, since there is no constraint part in that simple task.

Finally, we used two propositional learners (C4.5 [13], CART [5]) on an equivalent propositional formulation of Tasks 1 and 2, where each train is represented by a vector of 135 features, nine per car; trains with less than 15 cars were represented by filling the vector with values out of range (-1).

Table 1 reports the sizes of the rule bases produced/used in our experiments, along with the sizes of the corresponding neural networks; the obtained accuracy, averaged over 5 runs, is reported in Table 2. Moreover, Table 3 shows results obtained by refining knowledge bases learned by SMART+ and Table 4 reports classification accuracies of the propositional learners used.

A first observation concerns the complexity of the knowledge bases: as we claimed in Section 1, a first order representation is more compact, especially with larger learning sets, and results in smaller networks, with respect to the propositional counterpart.

Table 1. Size of the rule bases and of the corresponding networks built by the various learners in 5 different runs.

	learning set size	Rules task 1	Rules task 2	Network units task 1	Network units task 2
handcrafted KB	—	4	2	9	7
SMART+ (1)	100	5–8	5–7	13–24	10–34
	500	2–6	8–14	5–29	26–54
SMART+ (2)	100		2–5		5–16
	500		8–15		22–42
C4.5	100	11–14	11–24		
	500	34–46	46–77		
CART	100	8–12	8–10	44–90	35–58
	500	25–31	31–40	174–248	200–307

Table 2. Accuracy results for the handcrafted knowledge base and refining for 1000 epochs.

	learning set size	Task 1 $\mathcal{L}$	Task 1 $\mathcal{A}$	Task 1 $\mathcal{B}$	Task 2 $\mathcal{L}$	Task 2 $\mathcal{A}$	Task 2 $\mathcal{B}$
handcrafted	100	67.0	69.4	74.7	91.6	90.8	89.6
knowledge base	500	68.0	69.4	74.7	91.0	90.8	89.6
handcrafted	100	85.6	87.8	89.2	98.2	96.9	96.3
KB + FONN ($\varepsilon = 0$)	500	88.8	85.8	88.4	97.5	97.4	96.7
handcrafted	100	98.0	94.3	95.9	98.4	96.9	96.3
KB+ FONN ($\varepsilon = 0.3$)	500	96.1	95.7	96.9	98.3	97.6	97.1
handcrafted KB + FONN	100	83.0	84.0	86.6	99.2	96.0	95.3
(Bernoulli error, $\varepsilon = 0.3$)	500	79.9	87.8	90.5	98.4	97.4	96.8

For what concerns accuracy results, it should be pointed out that performances of FONN do not degrade from test set $\mathcal{A}$ to test set $\mathcal{B}$, rather in some cases performances are better, whereas propositional learners cannot generalize as well on test set $\mathcal{B}$ (their performances are only slightly worse because a large part of the examples in test set $\mathcal{B}$ can be correctly classified by only looking at the initial part of a train).

The experiments clearly indicate that the refinement step performed by FONN usually increases accuracy on both learning and test sets. In particular, in order to improve learning speed and classification accuracy, to avoid overtraining, the error gradient descent technique has been performed on a pattern if the error is greater than a fixed threshold ε. By setting $\varepsilon = 0$, standard backpropagation is performed. This mechanism essentially resulted in a faster convergence, and in most cases it also reached slightly better performances (see Table 5).

Table 6 reports results obtained on Task 3 using a manually handcrafted knowledge based consisting of only one rule:

$$\exists x \, [\neg has\_brakes \, (x) \land inside \, (weight \, (x) \, , [50, 70])] \rightarrow train\_cannot\_go() \; .$$

Table 3. Accuracy results for the FOL learner SMART+. Backpropagation was applied for 1000 epochs.

	learning set size	Task 1 $\mathcal{L}$	$\mathcal{A}$	$\mathcal{B}$	Task 2 $\mathcal{L}$	$\mathcal{A}$	$\mathcal{B}$
SMART+ (1) classifier	100	80.0	71.2	66.9	79.8	65.3	65.0
	500	87.1	86.5	87.9	86.5	82.5	80.4
SMART+ (1) + FONN ($\varepsilon = 0.3$)	100	92.8	88.0	87.3	92.4	69.9	68.3
	500	88.6	83.6	86.6	88.9	83.2	81.8
SMART+ (2) classifier	100				87.6	82.2	79.2
	500				96.3	94.3	92.8
SMART+ (2) + FONN ($\varepsilon = 0.3$)	100				94.4	87.5	82.7
	500				98.9	96.1	95.4

Table 4. Accuracy results for the propositional learners C4.5 and CART.

	learning set size	Task 1 $\mathcal{L}$	$\mathcal{A}$	$\mathcal{B}$	Task 2 $\mathcal{L}$	$\mathcal{A}$	$\mathcal{B}$
C4.5	100	97.2	77.2	73.6	97.6	64.0	62.1
	500	98.5	89.3	86.5	97.9	71.4	68.8
CART	100	93.6	75.2	73.0	90.8	65.1	62.2
	500	98.2	93.1	90.7	92.9	73.0	66.9

The aim of this experiment is to show that the *softmax* and *max* combination functions have similar behaviors and can be used interchangeably when one wants to preserve the logical semantics of the existential quantifier, whereas the use of a strengthening combination function such as t_{max} for β helps overcoming the lack of feature constructors in the antecedent of the rule.

Table 8 presents another interesting result: we used the *softmax* as β operator, but only performed error backpropagation on the binding that activated the most: as can be noted, the classification accuracy is not significantly af-

Table 5. (Left) Results with various values of ε; they were obtained with the hand-crafted knowledge base on Task 2, learning set $\mathcal{L}_{100}$, in a single run lasted 1000 epochs.

Table 6. (Center) Results with different connectives for the β operator on Task 3, after 1000 refinement epochs.

Table 7. (Right) Average number of bindings effectively evaluated vs. total number of bindings.

ε	$\mathcal{L}$	$\mathcal{A}$	$\mathcal{B}$
0.0	97.0%	94.4%	93.7%
0.2	99.0%	95.8%	95.0%
0.3	99.0%	96.6%	96.1%
0.4	98.0%	96.6%	96.3%

	$\mathcal{L}$	$\mathcal{A}$
softmax	85.5%	86.44%
Max	86%	87.74%
t_{max}	92%	92.16%

set	Task 1	Task 2
$\mathcal{L}_{100}$	22.5/22.5	2.1/76.1
$\mathcal{L}_{500}$	21.2/21.2	2.0/69.0
$\mathcal{A}$	21.2/21.2	2.1/67.0
$\mathcal{B}$	33.8/33.8	3.6/182.9

Table 8. Accuracy results for a handcrafted knowledge base when backpropagating only on the maximum activated binding.

	learning set size	Task 1			Task 2		
		$\mathcal{L}$	$\mathcal{A}$	$\mathcal{B}$	$\mathcal{L}$	$\mathcal{A}$	$\mathcal{B}$
handcrafted KB + FONN	100	93.4	94.8	96.2	99.0	96.6	96.1
($\varepsilon = 0.3$)	500	93.8	94.2	95.8	98.6	97.7	97.2

fected, while the speed-up that can be obtained is proportional to the number of evaluated bindings. For instance, the number of evaluated bindings in Task 1 is 22 (see Table 7) on average (about 6 bindings per rule), therefore performing backpropagation on only one binding per rule results in a speed-up of 6 times.

Moreover, Table 7 shows the effectiveness of using symbolic constraints to further speed-up the learning process by comparing the number of effectively evaluated bindings (i.e.: filtered by constraints in the handcrafted knowledge base) versus the total number of bindings generated with an exhaustive approach; obviously the two numbers coincide for Task 1, where there are no constraints; the logical constraints help a lot in dominating the complexity, when the number of components of an instance grows (as is the case moving from test set $\mathcal{A}$ to test set $\mathcal{B}$) or when the number of variables grows: the number of bindings generated by a brute-force approach grows substantially faster than the number of bindings effectively evaluated by the network.

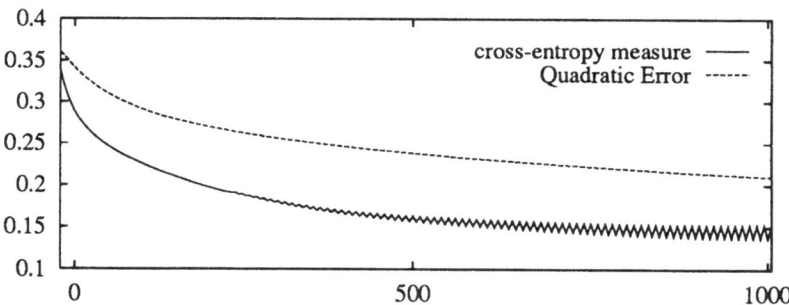

Fig. 2. Convergence curves of FONN when different error measures are used; the root mean square error is plotted against the number of learning epochs.

Figure 2 compares the behavior of the network when using the cross-entropy measure (also known as the Bernoulli error) and the mean square error as error functions: the error rate decreases more rapidly with the cross-entropy error measure, but it also starts oscillating earlier; it might be interesting to explore solutions which dynamically adjust learning rates.

5 Conclusions and Future Work

This paper present a method for mapping classification theories described in a restricted form of First Order Logics into evaluation networks (FONNs), which are an extension of Factorizable Radial Basis Function Networks. This allows to combine symbolic relational learning algorithms with connectionist algorithms in order to deal with numeric features in FOL. The experimental analysis shows that FONNs, working in a FOL setting, generalize much better than many other propositional learners do, when working in an equivalent setting in propositional logic.

Nevertheless, in spite of this initial successful implementation, we believe that FONNs still need much more investigation and are suitable of many improvements concerning both the learning algorithm and the operator semantics. On the one hand, operators such as min for α and max for β and γ preserve the semantics of the original classification theory and allow to reduce the cost of the matching algorithm because the answer comes from the hypothesis which maximally activates the network. In this case algorithms such as A^* can be exploited for guiding the matching process. On the other hand, operators such as t_{max} or the linear perceptron allow to learn evidential evaluation strategies, which can recover structural errors in the original classification theory. The drawback is that the logical semantics is blurred and that the matching process is necessarily more complex because all substitutions for the variables contribute in some way to construct the output.

A last point woth investigating is the relation between FONNs and the recurrent neural networks [9, 6, 11], which also have the capability of dealing with data of unrestricted size. From the expressiveness point of view FONNs relate to a restricted form of Horn clauses, while Recurrent NN relate to finite automata and regular grammars; it should be interesting to compare both models with respect to the expressiveness and to the learning capabilities (complexity and convergency).

References

1. C. Baroglio, A. Giordana, M. Kaiser, M. Nuttin, and R. Piola. Learning controllers for industrial robots. *Machine Learning*, 23:221–250, July 1996.
2. H.R. Berenji. Fuzzy logic controllers. In R.R. Yager and L.A. Zadeh, editors, *An Introduction to Fuzzy Logic Applications in Intelligent Systems*, pages 69–96. Kluwer, 1992.
3. M. Botta and A. Giordana. SMART+: A multi-strategy learning tool. In *IJCAI-93, Proceedings of the Thirteenth International Joint Conference on Artificial Intelligence*, pages 937–943, Chambéry, France, 1993.
4. M. Botta, A. Giordana, and R. Piola. FONN: Combining first order logic with connectionist learning. In *Proceedings of the 14th International Conference on Machine Learning ICML-97*, Nashville, TN, July 1997. Morgan Kaufmann.
5. L. Breiman, J.H. Friedman, R.A. Ohlsen, and C.J. Stone. *Classification And Regression Trees*. Wadsworth & Brooks, Pacific Grove, CA, 1984.

6. P. Frasconi, M. Gori, M. Maggini, and G. Soda. Representation of finite state automata in recurrent radial basis function networks. *Machine Learning*, 23:5–32, 1996.

7. L.M. Fu. Knowledge-based connectionism for revising domain theories. *IEEE Transactions on Systems, Man and Cybernetics*, 23(1):173–182, January 1993.

8. D. Haussler. Learning conjunctive concepts in structural domains. *Machine Learning*, 4:70–40, 1989.

9. R. Maclin and J.W. Shavlik. Using knowledge-based neural networks to improve algorithms: refining the Chou-Fasman algorithm for protein folding. *Machine Learning*, 11:195–215, 1993.

10. R. Michalski. A theory and methodology of inductive learning. In R. Michalski, J. Carbonell, and T. Mitchell, editors, *Machine Learning: An Artificial Intelligence Approach*, pages 83–134, Los Altos, CA, 1983. Morgan Kaufmann.

11. C.W. Omlin and C.L. Giles. Constructing deterministic finite-state automata in recurrent neural networks. *Journal of the ACM*, 43(6):937–972, 1996.

12. T. Poggio and F. Girosi. Networks for approximation and learning. *Proceedings of the IEEE*, 78(9):1481–1497, September 1990.

13. R.J. Quinlan. Induction of decision trees. *Machine Learning*, 1:81–106, 1986.

14. D. E. Rumelhart and J. L. McClelland. *Parallel Distributed Processing : Explorations in the Microstructure of Cognition, Parts I & II*. MIT Press, Cambridge, Massachusetts, 1986.

15. G. Towell and J.W. Shavlik. Knowledge based artificial neural networks. *Artficial Intelligence*, 70(4):119–166, 1994.

16. V. Tresp, J. Hollatz, and S. Ahmad. Network structuring and training using rule-based knowledge. In S.J. Hanson, J.D. Cowan, and C.L. Giles, editors, *Advances in Neural Information Processing Systems 5 (NIPS-5)*, pages 871–878, San Mateo, CA, 1993. Morgan Kaufmann.

17. L.A. Zadeh. Knowledge representation in fuzzy logic. In R.R. Yager and L.A. Zadeh, editors, *An Introduction to Fuzzy Logic Applications in Intelligent Systems*, pages 1–25. Kluwer Academic Publishers, 1992.

Handling Continuous Data in Top-Down Induction of First-Order Rules

Donato Malerba Floriana Esposito Giovanni Semeraro Sergio Caggese

Dipartimento di Informatica, Università degli Studi di Bari
via Orabona 4, 70125 Bari, Italy
{malerba | esposito | semeraro | caggese}@lacam.uniba.it

Abstract. Handling numerical information is one of the most important research issues for practical applications of first-order learning systems. This paper is concerned with the problem of inducing first-order classification rules from both numeric and symbolic data. We propose a specialization operator that discretizes continuous data during the learning process. The heuristic function used to choose among different discretizations satisfies a property that can be profitably exploited to improve the efficiency of the specialization operator. The operator has been implemented and tested on the document understanding domain.

1 Background and motivation

One of the most important research issues for practical applications of first-order learning systems is the handling of numerical information [7,18]. Indeed, in many applications, continuous data are predominant and should be treated suitably.

Image analysis and understanding is one of the widest application fields where the capability of handling both symbolic and numeric descriptors (that is, attributes and relations) is essential for the successful application of machine learning techniques. In a previous work [9] the authors proposed the application of machine learning techniques to the problem of document understanding, that is, identifying semantically relevant components in the layout extracted from document images. Preliminary results were encouraging, but not totally satisfying. One of the main issues seemed to be the *a priori* discretization of numeric attributes, such as height, width and position of a block. In fact, the first-order learning system used to automatically learn classification rules was not able to perform an on-line, autonomous discretization of numerical descriptors. As pointed out by Connel and Brady [4], both numeric and symbolic descriptions are essential to generate models of visual objects, since the former increase the sensitivity while the latter increase the stability of the internal representation of visual objects.

These considerations prompted the investigation of an extension of our first-order learning algorithm in order to handle numerical descriptors as well. Our goals are:

1. On-line discretization of numerical descriptors should be performed by a specialization operator, since the learning algorithm performs a general-to-specific (or top-down) search.

2. The operator should always guarantee to cover the *seed* example that guides the induction process.

3. The heuristic function used to choose among different discretizations should satisfy a property that reduces the computational complexity of the operator.

In this paper, we present a new specialization operator developed according to these goals. It can specialize a clause by adding literals of the type $f(X_1, \ldots, X_n) \in [a..b]$. An information-theoretic heuristic is used to choose among different discretizations. A property of such a heuristic is claimed and exploited to improve the efficiency of the closed interval selection. This operator has been embedded into a first-order learning system called INDUBI/CSL [20]. The application to the domain of document understanding proved the importance of handling both numeric and symbolic descriptions for this task.

2 The representation language

The inductive learning problem solved by INDUBI/CSL is the usual induction of a set of hypotheses $H_1, H_2, \ldots, H_r$ from a set E of training examples. Each hypothesis H_i is the description of a concept C_i, $i = 1, \ldots, r$.

The representation language adopted in the system is an evolution of the logic language VL_{21} [21], with two distinct forms of *literals* (also called *selectors*):

$f(t_1, \ldots, t_n) = \text{Value}$ *(simple literal)* and $f(t_1, \ldots, t_n) \in \text{Range}$ *(set literal)*

where f is an n-ary function symbol, called *descriptor*, t_i's can be either variable or constant terms, Value is the value taken by f when applied to $t_1, \ldots, t_n$, and Range is a set of possible values taken by f. Some examples of literals are the following: color(x_1)=red, height$(x_2) \in [1.1 .. 2.1]$, distance$(x_1, x_2) \in [0.0 .. 1.0]$, and ontop$(x_1, x_2)$=true.

The last example points out the lack of predicate symbols in this logic language. The literals $p(x_1,x_2)$ and $\neg p(x_1,x_2)$ will be represented as $f_p(x_1,x_2)$=true and $f_p(x_1,x_2)$=false, respectively, where f_p is the function symbol associated to the predicate p. Therefore, INDUBI/CSL can deal with *classical negation*, $\neg$, not with *negation by failure*, not [19].

Literals can be combined to form *definite clauses*, which can be written as:

$$L_0 :- L_1, L_2, \ldots, L_m$$

where the simple literal L_0 is called *head* of the clause, while the conjunction of simple or set literals $L_1, L_2, \ldots, L_m$ is named *body*. Definite clauses of interest for classification problems satisfy two different constraints: *linkedness* [15] and *range-restrictedness* [5].

Each training example is represented as a single ground, linked and range-restricted definite clause. On the contrary, a hypothesis H is a set of linked, range-restricted definite clauses, called *rule*, such that all clauses have the same head and no constant terms. Permitted literals in H can be either single-valued or range-valued. Each concept to be learned has its own *hypothesis language*, that is a set of function symbols used in the body and in the head of clauses defining the concept. Indeed, a peculiarity of INDUBI/CSL is the possibility of learning *multiple*, possibly dependent, concepts [20].

Regardless of the representation language used, a key part of the induction process is the search through a space of hypotheses. A generalization model provides a basis for organizing this search space, since it establishes when a hypothesis H entails or *covers* an observation and when an inductive hypothesis is more general/specific than another [3]. The generalization model adopted in INDUBI/CSL is θ_{OI}-subsumption [29], a variant of the well-known θ-subsumption [25]. Under this generalization model, a definite clause C is a generalization of another clause C', if it is obtained from C' by simply applying two distinct operators: *Drop-literal* and *turn-constants-into-variables*. The latter operator turns distinct constants into distinct variables, and replaces all occurrences of a constant t_i with the same variable X_i *(simple inverse substitution* [28]).

3   Learning a single concept

At the high level INDUBI/CSL implements a separate-and-conquer search strategy to generate a rule. The *separate* stage of the algorithm is a loop that checks for the completeness of the current rule and, if this check fails, begins the search for a new consistent clause. The search space for the separate stage is the space of rules. In contrast, the search space of the *conquer* stage is the set of clauses. The conquer stage performs a general-to-specific beam-search to construct a new consistent, linked and range-restricted clause. A thorough description is in [20].

The separate-and-conquer search strategy is adopted in other well-known learning systems, such as FOIL6.2 [27]. On the other hand INDUBI/CSL bases the conquer phase on the concept of *seed* example, whose aim is to guide the learning process. Indeed, if e^+ is a positive example to be explained by a hypothesis H, then H should contain at least one clause C that generalizes e^+. As mentioned above, this means that C is obtained from e^+ by applying the *drop-literal* and *turn-constants-into-variables* operators.

In the conquer stage, INDUBI/CSL starts with a seed example e^+ and generates a set *Cons* of at least M, if any, distinct range-restricted clauses which are consistent and cover e^+. The best generalization is selected from *Cons* according to a user-defined preference criterion, and the positive examples covered by such a generalization are removed from the set of examples to be covered. If there are still some positive examples to be covered, a new seed will be selected and a new set *Cons* will be generated. The M clauses are searched in the *specialization hierarchy* rooted into a definite clause with empty body,

$$f(X_1, \ldots, X_n) = \text{Value} :-$$

obtained by applying the operator *turn_constants_into_variables* to the head of e^+.

During the specialization process, INDUBI/CSL considers only a subset of N literals in the example: They are chosen according to the associated cost of the main function symbol, so that the user can express a preference for some literals. Obviously, literals that cause the partial clause to become unlinked are not considered at all. All specialized clauses, which cover e^+ and possibly other positive examples, are ranked according to a preference criterion. The first P generalizations are selected for the next specialization step. Consistent generalizations are copied into *Cons*.

The problem of finding a definite clause consistent with a sequence of positive and negative examples is a generalization of the problem of finding a consistent conjunctive existential concept [14]. Indeed a definite clause with a nullary predicate in the head:

$$L_0 :- L_1, L_2, \ldots, L_m$$

can be reformulated as:

$$L_0 :- \exists * L_1 \wedge L_2 \wedge \ldots \wedge L_m$$

where $\exists * L_1 \wedge L_2 \wedge \ldots \wedge L_m$ is an existential conjunctive concept. Haussler proved that learning consistent conjunctive existential concepts is an NP-complete problem, under the assumption that the number of parts of each example is upper bounded. Thus, under the same assumption, the general problem of finding a consistent definite clause is NP-complete as well. However, when only one example e^+ is positive, while the others are negative, it is possible to find a consistent clause, if any, in a polynomial time. This is done by turning all contants in e^+ into variables and then by checking whether the generated clause still covers a negative example. Obviously we are more interested in finding general consistent clauses than in covering only e^+, thus it is necessary to perform a search through the space of all clauses that cover the seed example (*seed covering problem*).

In the case of symbolic descriptors, it can be easily shown that the size of this space is exponential in the number of literals of the seed.[1] Indeed, all clauses in the specialization hierarchy can be obtained by adding a (possibly emply) set of literals to

$$f(X_1, ..., X_n) = \text{Value} :-$$

Since literals used in the specialization process must be generalizations of literals in $body(e^+)$, obtained by turning constants into variables, the number of clauses is $2^{|body(e+)|}$.

Nevertheless, INDUBI/CSL explores only a polynomially bounded portion of this space. More precisely, during the first step at most N clauses will be considered. At worst, $N = | body(e^+) |$. Soon afterwards, P of them are selected for the next specialization step. During the second step each selected hypothesis can be specialized in at most $| body(e^+) | - 1$ different ways. In general, at the ith step, each selected hypothesis can be specialized in at most $|body(e^+)| - i - 1$ different ways. To sum up, the number of generated clauses is:

$$\left|body(e^+)\right| + \sum_{i=1}^{\left|body(e^+)\right|-1} P \cdot i = \left|body(e^+)\right| + \frac{P}{2}\left|body(e^+)\right| \cdot \left(\left|body(e^+)\right| - 1\right)$$

This analysis confirms the efficiency of the system while searching for a consistent clause, since the number of tested hypotheses is polynomial in the beam of the search and in the maximum number of literals of a training example. Neither the arity of the function symbols nor the number of variables in any learned clause affect the cost of the beam-search in INDUBI/CSL, which happens with other well-known learning systems, such as FOIL. Indeed, a theoretical analysis of FOIL performed by Pazzani and Kibler [22] showed that the number of tested hypotheses depends on the maximum number of variables in any clause of the learned rule. Such a number grows exponentially with the largest arity of considered predicates.

To sum up, at worst INDUBI/CSL solves as many seed covering problems as the number of positive examples. In this way it bypasses the NP-complete problem of learning a consistent clause, if any, that covers all positive examples.

Finally, it is worth noting that the consistent clause efficiently found by INDUBI/CSL in the conquer stage is not (probabilistically) guaranteed to perform well on further random examples drawn from the instance space according to the same fixed distribution used to build the training set. The algorithm used in the conquer stage is not Probably Approximately Correct (PAC) [31], that is, there is no guarantee that, using only polinomial computation time and polynomial sample size, it will find a consistent clause, if any, with error at most ε with probability at least 1-δ. Haussler [14] has already shown that existential conjunctive concepts are not PAC-learnable unless RP=NP, where RP is the class of problems that have randomized polynomial time algorithms. Thus it is strongly suspected that no PAC algorithm exists for the more general problem of learning a definite clause.

---

1. Here we are not considering inductive biases such as linkedness and range-restrictedness. In general, the introduction of these constraints leads to smaller search spaces.

4   Specializing a clause

In order to specialize a clause G, INDUBI/CSL has to choose some literals to be added. Both numeric and symbolic data are handled in the same way (see Figure 1). The only difference is that numeric literals already present in G can be reconsidered later on. In this case, the best (sub-)interval is recomputed, since it may be influenced by the addition of further literals. All selected literals are generalizations of literals in the seed, e^+, obtained by turning distinct constants into distinct variables.

The computation of the interval for numerical literals is described in Figure 2. A table associated to the term $f(X_1, X_2, ..., X_n)$ is built by matching the specialized clause

$$G': \quad G, f(X_1, X_2, ..., X_n) \in [-\infty .. +\infty]$$

against positive and negative examples. Each example produces as many entries as the number of matching substitutions. More precisely, if G'' is the set of literals in the body of G', that contain some *local* variables not occurring in the head of G', then the number of matching substitutions is upper bounded by two combinatorial functions of the number of local variables and literals in G'', respectively. The table, initially empty, contains pairs $\langle Value, Class \rangle$, where *Class* can be either $+$ or $-$ according to the sign of the example e from which *Value* is taken. The *Value* is determined by considering the literal of the example e that matches with $f(X_1, X_2, ..., X_n) \in [-\infty .. +\infty]$.

Then the problem is finding the interval that best discriminates positive from negative examples. Any threshold value α lying between two consecutive distinct values defines two disjoint intervals: The left interval $[l_1, l_2]$ and the right interval $[r_1, r_2]$. The lower bound l_1 of the left interval is the smallest value in the table with a $+$ sign, while the upper bound l_2 is the largest value in the table that does not exceed the threshold α. On the contrary, the lower bound r_1 of the right interval is the smallest value in the table that exceeds α, while the upper bound r_2 is the largest value with a $+$ sign. When one of the two intervals contains no positive value, then it is set to *undefined*. However, at least one of the two intervals must be defined, since the table contains at least one $+$ value corresponding to the Seed_value. Not all definite intervals are to be considered, since the specialized clause $G, f(X_1, X_2, ..., X_n) \in$ Range for a given Range might no longer cover the

---

```
procedure choose_best_linked_literals(N,e⁺,G,E⁺,E⁻)
List_linked := ∅
foreach literal Lit in e⁺ do
    [f(X₁, X₂, ..., Xₙ)=Value] := turn_constants_into_variables(Lit, G, e⁺)
    if [f(X₁, X₂, ..., Xₙ)=Value] is linked to G then
        if the descriptor f is numeric then
            Set_literal := determine_range([f(X₁, X₂, ..., Xₙ)=Value],e⁺,G,E⁺,E⁻)
            if  Set_literal ≠ nil then add Set_literal to List_linked endif
        else
            if [f(X₁, X₂, ..., Xₙ)=Value] is not in G then add [f(X₁, X₂, ..., Xₙ)=Value] to List_linked endif
        endif
endforeach
    sort List_linked on cost
return the first N literals in List_linked
```

Figure 1. Algorithm for the choice of the best linked literal

```
procedure determine_range([f(X₁, X₂, ..., Xₙ)=Seed_value],e⁺,G,E⁺,E⁻)
  initialize table T[f(X₁, X₂, ..., Xₙ)]
  foreach example e in E⁺ do
    foreach substitution θ such that  G,f(X₁, X₂, ..., Xₙ)∈[-∞ .. +∞] covers e do
      select the literal [f(X₁, X₂, ..., Xₙ)=Value]θ of e
      add the tuple ⟨Value ,+⟩ to the table T[f(X₁, X₂, ..., Xₙ)]
    endforeach
  endforeach
  foreach example e in E⁻ do
    foreach substitution θ such that  G,f(X₁, X₂, ..., Xₙ)∈[-∞ .. +∞] covers e do
      select the literal [f(X₁, X₂, ..., Xₙ)=Value]θ of e
      add the tuple ⟨Value ,-⟩ to the table T[f(X₁, X₂, ..., Xₙ)]
    endforeach
  endforeach
  sort table T[f(X₁, X₂, ..., Xₙ)] on the Value field
  Cut := determine_all_cut-points(T[f(X₁, X₂, ..., Xₙ)])
  MaxIG := -∞
  foreach cut-point α in Cut do
    determine the left and right intervals [l₁,l₂], [r₁,r₂] with l₂<α<r₁
    if Seed_value∈[l₁ .. l₂] then Admissible_interval := [l₁, l₂] else Admissible_interval := [r₁, r₂] endif
    IG := information_gain(T[f(X₁, X₂, ..., Xₙ)], Admissible_interval)
    if  IG > MaxIG then
      Best_interval:=Admissible_interval
      MaxIG := IG
    endif
  endforeach
  if Max IG ≠ -∞ then return [f(X₁, X₂, ..., Xₙ)∈Best_interval] else return nil endif
```

Figure 2. Choice of the best range for numerical descriptors.

seed example e^+. Those definite intervals that include the Seed_value are said to be *admissible*, because they guarantee that the corresponding specializations still cover e^+.

The best admissible interval is selected according to an information-theoretic heuristic, the *information gain*, which is an entropic measure commonly used in decision tree induction [26] and in relational learning [27]. By looking at the table as a source of messages labelled + and –, the expected information on the class membership conveyed from a randomly selected message is:

$$info(n^+, n^-) = -\frac{n^+}{n^+ + n^-}log_2\frac{n^+}{n^+ + n^-} -\frac{n^-}{n^+ + n^-}log_2\frac{n^-}{n^+ + n^-}$$

where n^+ and n^- are the number of values in the table with a positive and a negative sign, respectively. If we partition the table into two subsets, S_1 and S_2, the former containing $n_1^+ + n_1^-$ values falling within an admissible interval and the latter containing the remaining values, the information provided by S_1 will be close to zero when almost all cases have the same + or – sign. Although the information prefers partitions that cover a large number of cases of a single class and a few cases of other classes, we must bias such a preference towards intervals with a high number of positive cases, as well. The following *weighted entropy*:

$$E(n_I^+, n_I^-) = \frac{n_I^-}{n_I^+} \, inf \, o(n_I^+, n_I^-)$$

penalizes those admissible intervals with a low percentage of positive cases. The quantity

$$gain(n^+, n^-, n_I^+, n_I^-) = \, inf \, o(n^+, n^-) - E(n_I^+, n_I^-)$$

measures the information gained by replacing the table with S_I. A heuristic would be choosing the admissible interval that maximizes the information gain, i.e., that minimizes $E(n_I^+, n_I^-)$. This heuristic differs from that adopted in other well-known learning systems. In particular, ID3 [26] does not weight the entropy, while FOIL uses only the information content of the positive class.

As a concrete illustration of the procedure determine_range, consider the table below.

Value	0.5	0.7	0.9	1.0	1.5	1.5	1.5	1.7	2.5	2.5
Sign	+	-	-	-	-	-	+	+	-	+

There are four possible cut points that generate the following intervals:

α	0.60	1.25	1.60	2.10
[l1, l2]	[0.50 .. 0.50]	[0.50 .. 1.00]	[0.50 .. 1.50]	[0.50 .. 1.70]
[r1, r2]	[0.70 .. 2.50]	[1.50 .. 2.50]	[1.70 .. 2.50]	[2.50 .. 2.50]

Let us suppose that Seed_value equals 1.50. Then only those intervals including 1.50 are admissible. The weighted entropy for each of them is

Adm. interval	[0.70 .. 2.50]	[1.50 .. 2.50]	[0.50 .. 1.50]	[0.50 .. 1.70]
E	1.836592	1.000000	2.157801	1.590723

Thus, the best interval is the second one, with weighted entropy equal to 1.0.

Note that cut points 0.80 and 0.95 have not been considered. Indeed, only those between two consecutive distinct values with a different sign (*boundary points*) are considered. This choice is due to the following

Theorem. If a cut-point α minimizes the measure $E(n_I^+, n_I^-)$, then α is a boundary point. The proof can be obtained electronically from http://lacam.uniba.it:8000/pagine/proof.html.

This result helps to discard several computations of the gain by considering only boundary points, so improving the efficiency of the procedure *determine_range*. Actually, the theorem above is similar to that proved by Fayyad and Irani [12] for a different measure, namely the "unweighted" class information entropy computed in some decision tree learning systems.

5   Other approaches

The first attempt to deal with continuous-valued attributes in first-order systems that learn classification was made by Bergadano and Bisio [1], who proposed a method to automatically set some parameters of predicate "schemes" with a parametric semantics.

Later on, a two-step approach was implemented in the system ML-SMART [2]: First, a tentative numerical parameter is learned, and then a standard genetic algorithm is applied to refine the numerical knowledge. On the contrary, the system Rigel [13] discretizes continuous data by applying the generalization operator called *consistent extending reference rule*, which extends the reference of a selector, that is the set of values taken by a function f. Values are added only if this increases the number of covered positive examples without covering negative ones. A different approach was proposed by Esposito *et al.* [8] who combined a discriminant analysis technique for linear classification with a first-order learning method, so that the numerical information is handled by linear classifiers, while the symbolic attributes and relations are used by the first-order learning system. A common characteristic of all these approaches is that they have been conceived for systems that can learn only rules with nullary predicates in the head, that is with predicates corresponding to propositional classes.

Dzeroski *et al.* [6] proposed transforming first-order representations into propositional form, in order to handle real numbers by means of techniques already tested in zeroth-order induction systems. Nevertheless, the transformation algorithm is applicable only when the background relations are determinate [17].

A different approach has been adopted in FOIL6.2 [27]. The system automatically produces comparative literals of type $V_i > k$, $V_i \leq k$, $V_i > V_j$, $V_i \leq V_j$, where V_i and V_j are numerical variables already present in other non-comparative literals and k is a numerical threshold. The selection of the threshold is based on an information-theoretic measure, which is different from that adopted in our system. Indeed, FOIL's specialization operator does not guarantee it will cover a specific positive example, the seed. Other differences between the two systems concern the top-down learning process (beam-search, seed-driven vs. hill-climbing, information-gain-driven), and the stopping criterion (at least M consistent hypotheses found vs. minimum description length).

Much related work can also be found in other contexts, such as qualitative and relational regression in inductive logic programming, and learning numerical constraints in inductive constraint logic programming. An updated review can be found in [18].

6   Application to document understanding

INDUBI/CSL has been applied to some zeroth-order learning problems involving both symbolic and numeric attributes [11]. In this paper we present the application to the field of document understanding. According to the ODA/ODIF standard [16], any document is characterized by two different structures representing both its internal organization and its content: The *layout* (or *geometrical*) structure and the *logical* structure. The former associates the content of a document with a hierarchy of *layout objects*, such as text lines, vertical/horizontal lines, graphic/photographic elements, pages, and so on. The latter associates the content of a document with a hierarchy of *logical objects*, such as sender/receiver of a business letter, title/authors of an article, and so on. The term *document analysis* denotes the extraction of the layout structure from the bitmap of a document, while the term *document understanding* denotes the process of mapping the layout structure of a document into the corresponding logical structure [30]. The document understanding process is based on the assumption that documents can be understood by means of their layout structures alone.

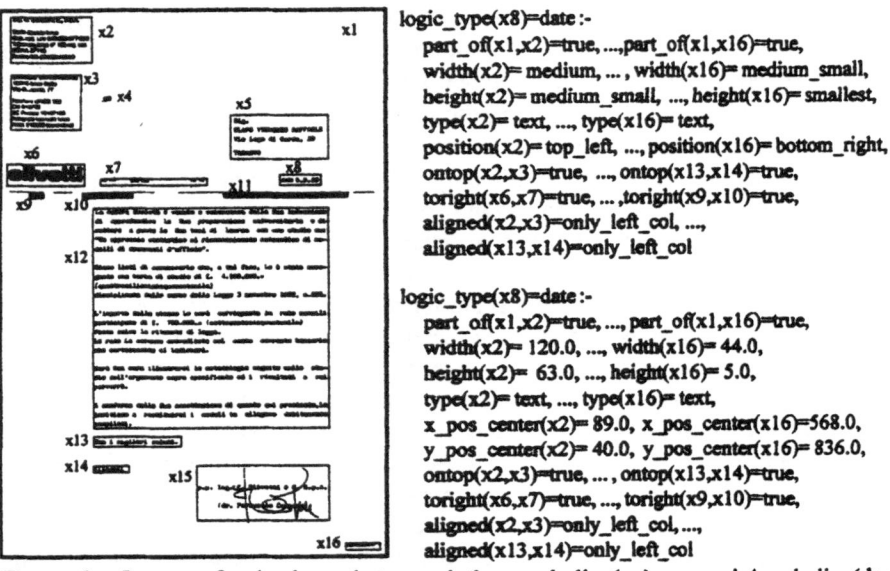

Figure 3. Layout of a business letter and the symbolic (up), numeric/symbolic (down) descriptions of the logical component *date*.

The mapping of the layout structure into the logical structure can be represented as a set of rules. Traditionally, such rules have been handcoded for particular kinds of documents [22], requiring much human tune and effort. We proposed the application of inductive learning techniques in order to automatically generate the rules from a set of training examples [9]. The user-trainer is asked to label some layout components of a set of training documents according to their logical meaning. Those layout components with no clear logical meaning are not labelled. Therefore, each document generates as many training examples as the number of layout components. Classes of training examples correspond to the distinct logical components to be recognized in a document. The unlabelled layout objects play the role of counterexamples for all the classes to be learned.

Each training example is represented as a definite ground clause, where different constants represent distinct layout components of a page layout. The choice of a representation language for the description of the layout of each document is very important. In previous experiments we used only symbolic descriptors by discretizing numeric attributes, such as height, width and position of a block (see Figure 3). Since the current release of INDUBI/CSL is able to handle numerical descriptors as well, we decided to organize an experiment to test the improvement of the generated rules in terms of accuracy, learning time and simplicity.

We considered a set of 30 business letters containing 364 layout objects. Each document was described with only symbolic descriptors or mixed numeric/symbolic descriptors. Experimental results for a 10-fold cross-validation are summarized below:

Average Number of Errors		p-value Wilcoxon signed ranks test	Number of Clauses		Average Learning Time	
symbolic	mixed		symbolic	mixed	symbolic	mixed
3.6	2.9	0.3114	28.0	11.5	20:24	19:17

logic_type(X₁)=date ← y-pos-centre(X₁) ∈[262.0..279.0], x-pos-centre(X₁) ∈[453.0 ..525.0]

logic_type(X₁)=date ← width(X₁)= medium_small, height(X₁)= very_very_small,
aligned(X₁,X₁)=both_rows
logic_type(X₁)=date ←position(X₁)= top_right, ontop(X₁,X₁)=true, toright(X₁,X₁)=true,
aligned(X₁,X₁)=both_rows, aligned(X₁,X₁)=only_left_col
logic_type(X₁)=date ← width(X₁)= medium, ontop(X₁,X₁)=true, aligned(X₁,X₁)=both_rows
logic_type(X₁)=date ← aligned(X₁,X₁)=both_rows, aligned(X₁,X₁)=only_lower_row,
aligned(X₁,X₁)=both_rows
logic_type(X₁)=date ← aligned(X₁,X₁)=both_rows, aligned(X₁,X₁)=only_lower_row
logic_type(X₁)=date ← toright(X₁,X₁)=true, aligned(X₁,X₁)=only_left_col,
aligned(X₁,X₁)=only_lower_row
logic_type(X₁)=date ← width(X₁)=small, ontop(X₁,X₁)=true,aligned(X₁,X₁)=only_right_col

Figure 4. Rule for the logic type *date* learned in one of the ten trials from mixed numeric-symbolic (up) and only symbolic descriptors (down).

The average number of errors made by the new release of INDUBI/CSL is decreased, although not significantly w.r.t. the non-parametric Wilcoxon signed-ranks test [23]. However, by decomposing the average number of errors into omission and commission errors we can conclude that rules generated from mixed descriptions made a significantly lower number of commission errors[2] (0.3 vs. 1.5, p-value=0.0277), and slightly increased the number of omission errors (2.6 vs. 2.1, p-value=0.7353). On-line discretization of numerical attributes increases the sensitivity of the learner, thus reducing commission errors, but increasing omission errors. Indeed, rules containing literals of the type $f(X_1, \ldots, X_n) \in [a..b]$ often miss the match with an instance because the value taken by f is either a little higher than b or a little lower than a. Although commission and omission errors are generally considered equally important, it is worthwhile to observe that in document processing systems omission errors are deemed to be less serious than commission errors, which can lead to totally erroneous storing of information. Moreover, we have also shown that a significant recovery of omission errors can be obtained by relaxing the definition of flexible matching between definite clauses [10].

As to the other parameters, we observed that the introduction of numerical descriptors simplified the classification rules (see an example of learned rules in Figure 4) and reduced the learning time. The latter result is somehow surprising since the symbolic description of a training instance is slightly simpler than the corresponding symbolic/ numeric description. This strengthened our opinion that the handling of numerical attributes was actually beneficial in this application.

As a final experiment, we compared INDUBI/CSL to FOIL6.2 on the mixed approach, since Quinlan's system has been often used as a yardstick for other empirical studies on first-order inductive learning. The results are summarized below.

Average Number of Omission/Commission Errors		Average Number of Errors		Number of Clauses	
INDUBI/CSL	**Foil6.2**	**INDUBI**	**Foil6.2**	**INDUBI**	**Foil6.2**
2.6/0.3	1.3/1.5	2.9	2.8	11.5	11.0

---

2. Omission errors are made when some examples of C_i are not classified as instances of C_i. Commission errors are made when some examples of C_i are classified into C_j, with $j \neq i$.

The average error rate, as well as the average number of clauses, is almost the same for both systems. The difference is in the type of errors made by the two systems. Foil6.2 discretizes into larger intervals than INDUBI/CSL, thus causing more commission errors than our system.

7   Conclusions

Handling both numeric and symbolic descriptors is an important issue for the successful application of first-order learning systems to real-world problems. In this paper we have presented a specialization operator for the on-line discretization of continuous data. Such an operator has been implemented in the learning system INDUBI/CSL and tested in the field of document understanding. In particular, we observed that the on-line discretization of numerical attributes increases the sensitivity of the learner, thus reducing commission errors and simultaneously increasing omission errors. A solution to this problem can come from a definition of flexible matching between definite clauses. Furthermore, the definition of a distance measure between examples can help to solve the problem of choosing the seed that guides the induction process.

Acknowledgments

The authors would like to thank Marzio Cristiano Rotondo for his valuable collaboration in conducting the experiments, Lynn Rudd for her help in re-reading the first draft of the paper, and the anonymous reviewers for their useful comments.

References

[1]   F. Bergadano, and R. Bisio. Constructive learning with continuous-valued attributes. In B. Bouchon, L. Saitta, and R.R. Yager (Eds.), *Uncertainty and Intelligent Systems.*, LNCS 313, Berlin: Springer-Verlag, pp. 54-162, 1988.

[2]   M. Botta, and A.Giordana. Learning quantitative features in a symbolic environment. In Z.W. Ras and M. Zemankova (Eds.), *Methodologies for Intelligent Systems*, LNAI 542, Berlin: Springer-Verlag, pp. 296-305, 1991.

[3]   W. Buntine. Generalized subsumption and its application to induction and redundancy. *Artificial Intelligence*, vol. 36, no. 2, pp. 375-399, 1988.

[4]   J.H. Connell and M. Brady. Generating and generalizing models of visual objects. *Artificial Intelligence*, vol. 31, no. 2, pp. 159-183, 1987.

[5]   L. De Raedt. *Interactive Theory Revision*. London: Academic Press, 1992.

[6]   S. Dzeroski, L. Todorovski, and T. Urbancic. Handling real numbers in ILP: A step towards better behavioural clones (Extended abstract). In N. Lavrac and S. Wrobel (Eds.), *Machine Learning: ECML95*, LNAI 912, Berlin: Springer, pp. 283-286, 1995.

[7]   S. Dzeroski, and I. Bratko. Applications of inductive logic programming. In L. De Raedt (Ed.), *Advances in Inductive Logic Programming*, Amsterdam: IOS Press, pp. 65-81, 1996.

[8]   F. Esposito, D. Malerba, and G. Semeraro. Incorporating statistical techniques into empirical symbolic learning systems. In D.J. Hand (Ed.), *Artificial Intelligence Frontiers in Statistics*, London: Chapman & Hall, pp. 168-181, 1993.

[9]   F. Esposito, D. Malerba, and G. Semeraro. Multistrategy learning for document recognition. *Applied Artificial Intelligence*, vol. 8, no. 1, pp. 33-84, 1994.

[10] F. Esposito, S. Caggese, D. Malerba, and G. Semeraro. Classification in noisy domains by flexible matching. *Proceedings of the European Symposium on Intelligent Techniques*, pp. 45-49, 1997.

[11] F. Esposito, S. Caggese, D. Malerba, and G. Semeraro. Discretizing continuous data while learning first-order rules. In M. van Someren & G. Widmer, *9th European Conference on Machine Learning - Poster Papers*, pp. 47-56, Edicní oddelení VŠE, Prague, 1997.

[12] U.M. Fayyad and K.B. Irani. On the handling of continuous-valued attributes in decision tree generation. *Machine Learning*, vol. 8, pp. 87-102, 1992.

[13] R. Gemello, F. Mana, and L. Saitta. Rigel: An inductive learning system. *Machine Learning*, vol. 6, no. 1, pp. 7-35, 1991.

[14] D. Haussler. Learning conjunctive concepts in structural domains. Machine Learning, col. 4, no. 1, pp. 7-40, 1989.

[15] N. Helft. Inductive generalization: A logical framework. In I. Bratko and N. Lavrac (Eds.), *Progress in Machine Learning - Proceedings of the EWSL87*, Sigma Press, pp. 149-157, 1987.

[16] W. Horak. Office document architecture and office document interchange formats: current status of international standardization. *IEEE Computer*, vol. 18, no. 10, pp. 50-60, 1985.

[17] N. Lavrac, and S. Dzeroski. *Inductive Logic Programming: Techniques and Applications*. Chichester: Ellis Horwood, 1994.

[18] N. Lavrac, S. Dzeroski, and I. Bratko, Handling imperfect data in inductive logic programming. In L. De Raedt (Ed.), *Advances in Inductive Logic Programming*, Amsterdam: IOS Press, pp. 48-64, 1996.

[19] J.W. Lloyd. *Foundations of Logic Programming*. Second Edition. Berlin: Springer-Verlag, 1987.

[20] D. Malerba, G. Semeraro, and F. Esposito. A multistrategy approach to learning multiple dependent concepts. In C. Taylor and R. Nakhaeizadeh (Eds.), *Machine Learning and Statistics: The Interface*, London: Wiley, pp. 87-106, 1997.

[21] R.S. Michalski. Pattern Recognition as rule-guided inductive inference. *IEEE Transactions on Pattern Analysis and Machine Intelligence*, vol. PAMI-2, no.4, pp. 349-361, 1980.

[22] G. Nagy, S.C. Seth, and S.D. Stoddard. A prototype document image analysis system for technical journals. *IEEE Computer*, vol. 25, no. 7, pp. 10-22, 1992.

[23] M. Orkin, and R. Drogin. *Vital Statistics*, New York, NY: McGraw Hill, 1990.

[24] M.J. Pazzani, & D. Kibler. The utility of knowledge in inductive learning. *Machine Learning*, vol. 9, no. 1, pp. 57-94, 1992.

[25] G.D. Plotkin. Automatic methods of inductive inference. PhD thesis, Edinburgh University, August 1971.

[26] R. Quinlan. Induction of decision trees. *Machine Learning*, vol. 1, pp. 81-106, 1986.

[27] J.R. Quinlan, and R.M. Cameron-Jones. FOIL: A midterm report. In P.B. Brazdil (Ed.), *Machine Learning: ECML-93*, Lecture Notes in Artificial Intelligence, 667, Berlin: Springer-Verlag, pp. 3-20, 1993.

[28] C. Rouveirol. Flattening and saturation: Two representation changes for generalization. *Machine Learning*, vol. 14, pp. 219-232, 1994.

[29] G. Semeraro, F. Esposito, and D. Malerba. Ideal refinement of Datalog programs. In M. Proietti (Ed.), *Logic Program Synthesis and Transformation*, LNCS 1048, Berlin:Springer-Verlag, pp. 120-136, 1996.

[30] Y.Y. Tang, C.D. Yan, and C.Y. Suen. Document processing for automatic knowledge acquisition. *IEEE Transactions on Knowledge and Data Engineering*, vol. 6, no. 1, pp. 3-21, 1994.

[31] L.G. Valiant. A theory of the learnable. *Communications of the ACM*, vol. 27, no. 11, pp. 1134-1142, 1984.

Inductive Inference of Tree Automata by Recursive Neural Networks

P. Frasconi[2], M. Gori[1], M. Maggini[1], E. Martinelli[1], and G. Soda[2]

[1] Dipartimento di Ingegneria dell'Informazione
Università di Siena
Via Roma, 56 - 53100 Siena (Italy)
[2] Dipartimento di Sistemi e Informatica
Università di Firenze
Via S. Marta, 3 - 50138 Firenze (Italy)

Abstract. Recurrent neural networks are powerful learning machines capable of processing sequences. A recent extension of these machines can conveniently be used to process also general data structures like trees and graphs, which opens the doors to a number of new very interesting applications previously unexplored.
In this paper, we show that when the problem of learning is restricted to purely symbolic data structures, like trees, the continuous representation developed after learning can also be given a symbolic interpretation. In particular, we show that a proper quantization of the neuron activation trajectory makes it possible to induce tree automata. We present preliminary experiments for small-size problems that, however, are very promising, especially when considering that this methodology is very robust with respect to accidental or malicious corruption of the learning set.

1 Introduction

The art of building intelligent systems and modeling cognitive processes has been hovering, pendululum-like, between symbolic artificial intelligence and subsymbolic models like neural networks, for over three decades. The resurgence of interest in connectionist models of the past decade, however, has generated many blind debates on the supposed "actual nature" of intelligence.

M. Boden [1] has recently given her view on these debates by a very colorful comparison of the two different approaches to intelligence with the color of the horse in the film *The Wizard of Oz*. Her conclusion is that, like in the film, "... the pretty creature was *visibly* the same horse, changing colour as it trotted along." That is, "AI is one beast, like the Wizard's pony." Somewhere located in this story, this paper faces the inductive inference of tree automata, a purely symbolic task, by adaptive computation, a processing scheme taking place in a continuous domain.

Inductive inference is nicely reviewed concerning both problem definition and methodology in seminal papers by D. Angluin [2] and K-S. Fu and T.L. Booth [3], who also reviewed the case of tree grammars, considered in this paper [4].

The idea that symbols can emerge from subsymbolic representations through proper quantization of the neuron activation trajectory is not new in its own. In particular, a number of papers have focused on the inductive inference of finite state automata by using different recurrent neural network architectures (see e.g. [5,6]). Although the complex nonlinear dynamics of neural networks often departs to some extent from the corresponding automata behavior, especially for long sequences, proper architectures and conditions can be identified in which, under the given state space quantization, the automata offer a perfect representation of the neural dynamics [7,8].

In this paper, we go one step further and face the problem of inducing the rule(s) that generate a given set of trees. This entails a new crucial step, namely the definition of connectionist models capable of processing data structures. Sperduti and Starita [9] have proposed a connectionist-based architecture, based on the concept of generalized recurrent neuron, for classifying data structures. These approaches to processing data structures, however, were not conceived for inductive inference of grammars, as their adaptive scheme acts by modifying the weights of a sort of cryptic black box.

In this paper, we propose two algorithms for the extraction of tree automata from the learned configuration. In particular, the second one produces tree automata with *don't care* conditions, thus simplifying the corresponding representation significantly. These algorithms are based on proper quantizations of the state trajectory of the recursive networks associated with the given training set. We also introduce *third-order recursive neural networks*, and show that they are very well-suited for processing binary trees and that they inherit the basic features of the recursive networks used to process strings. Our preliminary experimental results are very promising. In particular, we show the the rule hidden in the *traffic policeman problem*, a nice cognitive graphical test defined in this paper, can be inferred successfully from examples.

2   Recursive Networks for Processing of Data Structures

In this section, we review briefly the basic idea proposed in [9] concerning adaptive processing of DOAGs (Directed Acyclic Graphs) [10]. The recursive networks considered in this paper process data structures beginning from a fixed initial state. The examples can be regarded as a collection of pairs composed of DOAGs with their own targets. Formally, let d^-, $d^+ \in R$ be such that $[d^-, d^+] \subset [\underline{d}, \overline{d}]$ and define $\mathcal{D} \doteq \{(\mathcal{U}_l, d_l), \ l = 1, \ldots, L\}$, where $\mathcal{U}_l$ is a DOAG and $d_l \in \{d^-, d^+\}$ its corresponding target.

$\mathcal{U}_l$ is a directed acyclic graph, where the set of nodes leaving to a given node is ordered. For all DOAGs, there exists at least a special node, called *supersource* and denoted by $\mathbf{U}_{ls}$, that receives no inputs from other nodes.

Let o be the maximum outdegree of the given DOAGs. The dependence of node v from its children $ch[v]$ can be expressed by *pointer matrices* $A_r \in \mathcal{R}^{n,n}$, $r = 1, \ldots o$. Similarly, the information attached to the nodes can be propagated by weight matrix $B \in \mathcal{R}^{n,m}$. Hence, the parameters of the adaptive model are $\boldsymbol{\theta}_f \doteq \{A_1, \ldots, A_o\}$ and $\boldsymbol{\theta}_g \doteq B$. The state is updated according to

$$X_v = \sigma \left(\sum_{k=1}^{o} A_k \cdot q_k^{-1} X_v + B \cdot U_v \right), \qquad (1)$$

where q_k^{-1} is an operator which returns X_v's children and σ is a vectorial sigmoidal function. This equation is a straightforward extension of *first-order recurrent neural networks*, the only difference being in the generalized form of processing taking place in the "pseudo-time" dimension v. The output is determined by a general two-layer perceptron so as to generate any desired map of the state to the output according to

$$Y_v = \sigma \left(D\sigma \left(C X_v \right) \right). \qquad (2)$$

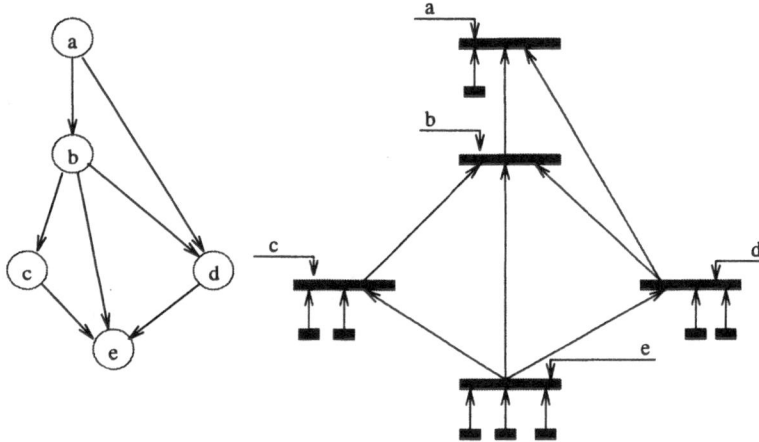

Fig. 1. A DOAG with the corresponding encoding network. Note that $\bar{o} = 2$ (graph outdegree), and that the nil pointers are represented by proper frontier (initial) states. The nodes must be presented according to a *topological sort*, e.g. e, c, d, b, a.

Fig. 1 is a pictorial representation of the computation taking place in the recursive neural network. In Fig. 1, all the recursive neurons are represented by the layer they belong to, whilst a proper notation is used to represent the nil pointer. Each nil pointer is associated with a *frontier state*, which is in fact an initial state that turns out to be useful to terminate recursive equation 1.

High-order neural networks, proposed mainly by Giles and associates for both static networks [11] and recurrent networks [12], are very interesting models especially for dealing with symbolic tasks. One can easily conceive high-order networks for processing data structure as an extension of second-order recurrent networks. For instance, in the special case of binary trees, one can introduce *third-order networks* based on $\boldsymbol{\theta} \doteq \{w_{ijkl}\}$ as follows

$$X_{i,v} = \sigma \left(\sum_{j,k,l} w_{ijkl} \cdot q_L^{-1} X_{j,v} \cdot q_R^{-1} X_{k,v} \cdot U_{l,v} \right). \tag{3}$$

In this equation q_L^{-1} and q_R^{-1} are operators which return $\boldsymbol{X}_v$'s left and right children, respectively. The extension to the general case of $(o+1)$-dimensional networks is straightforward. In the case $\bar{o} = 1$, commonly used in the literature to carry out sequence processing, these models reduce to second-order recurrent networks.

According to the classical connectionist learning optimization-based approach, the output-target data fitting is measured by means of the cost function. The process of learning the given data structures consists of determining the parameters of the defined adaptive models.

3 Extraction of Symbolic Rules from Tree Automata

The computation of recursive networks rely on on a set of real-valued state and input variables which are processed using a set of continuous operators such as multipliers, adders and sigmoidal functions. When a recursive network parses a symbolic data structure, its state vector $\boldsymbol{X}_v \in R^n$ describes complex trajectories that encode the network memory about the processed nodes. These trajectories are generated applying for each node the network transition function to the o-uple of state vectors produced while processing its descendants. The state transition function $\phi(\boldsymbol{X}_1, \ldots, \boldsymbol{X}_o, \boldsymbol{U}_v) : [R^n]^o \times R^m \to R^o$ depends on the node label $\boldsymbol{U}_v$. For symbolic tasks, the input alphabet is finite and can be encoded by a finite sets of vectors $\mathcal{U} = \{U_1, \ldots, U_K\}$, each corresponding to a symbol of the input alphabet. As a consequence, the network transition function defines a set of K different maps, which transform o vectors in R^n onto a point in R^n. This computation can be thought of as an extension of Iterated Function Systems (IFSs)[1].

The behavior resulting from the application of this set of non-linear maps may be very complex and may reveal a deep recursive structure. The generated trajectories may be much more complex than that of recurrent network analyzing time sequences because of the high dimensionality of the map input.

In order to give a *symbolic* interpretation of the continuous computation of the network, one can introduce an approximation based on the quantization of the continuous state trajectories. This process can be regarded as a *symbolic projection* of the regions of the continuous state space onto a set of discrete

---

[1] An IFS is defined as a set of S transformations $\boldsymbol{\Phi}_s$ on a metric space $\mathcal{X}$. For each time step we can pick up one of these transformations to map a point $x \in \mathcal{X}$ to $\boldsymbol{\Phi}_{s(t)}(x) \in \mathcal{X}$. The *attractor* of the IFS is the set $\mathcal{A} \subset \mathcal{X}$ such that $\forall a \in \mathcal{A}$ and $s \in \{1, \ldots, S\} \Rightarrow \boldsymbol{\Phi}_s(a) \in \mathcal{A}$.

states. In particular, because of the nature of the computation performed by recursive networks, we propose a method to approximate the network behaviour by means of *Frontier to Root Automata* (FRA).

Definition 1. (see e.g. [14])
A FRA $\mathcal{A}$ is a 5-uple $\{\Sigma, S, s_0, M, F\}$ where $\Sigma = \{\sigma_1, \ldots, \sigma_K\}$ is the input alphabet used to label the nodes, S is a finite set of q states, s_0 is the initial state used to label the frontier nodes, $M : \Sigma \times S^o \rightarrow S$ is the state transition function and F defines the set of accepting states.

The FRA computation is carried out starting from the leaves of the graph which are supposed to have frontier nodes labeled with state s_0 as descendants; then for any node the corresponding state is computed as $M(\sigma, s_1, \ldots, s_o)$ being σ the node label and $< s_1, \ldots, s_k >$ the states computed for the node descendants. Obviously the computation must take place following the ordering of the nodes by descending values of their depth.

The symbolic interpretation of a recursive neural network in terms of a FRA emerges by partitioning the state space into a set of regions that are associated to the finite set of states of the automaton. The choice of the number of regions is crucial, since it defines the amount of loss in the memory capacity with respect to that of the network.

The state space can be partitioned by using the K-MEAN algorithm for the points of the state space visited by the neural network, while parsing a given set of data structures. This technique defines convex regions in the state space and has the property of using the higher resolution in the regions that are mostly visited. The representative point of each region may be chosen as the centroid of the corresponding cluster. Possible measures of the resolution are the minimum distance between two centroids and the number of clusters. If we use more clusters to approximate the network trajectories, we obtain a more detailed description and, consequently, the extracted machine is likely to have a larger number of states. The extraction of a complete FRA from the associated recursive network $\mathcal{N}$ with training set set $\mathcal{D}$ can be carried out by the following algorithm:

Algorithm 1 FRA extraction
$\quad \mathcal{X} \leftarrow$ StateVectors($\mathcal{N}, \mathcal{D}$);
$\quad$ States $\leftarrow 2$;
$\quad$**repeat**
$\quad\quad \mathcal{C} \leftarrow$ GeneratePartition($\mathcal{X}$,States);
$\quad\quad s_0 \leftarrow$ GetRegion($X_0, \mathcal{C}$);
$\quad\quad$**for** $(< s_1, \ldots, s_o, \sigma > \in S^o \times \Sigma)$
$\quad\quad\quad X \leftarrow \phi(C(s_1, \mathcal{C}), \ldots, C(s_o, \mathcal{C}), U(\sigma))$;
$\quad\quad\quad s \leftarrow$ GetRegion($X, \mathcal{C}$);
$\quad\quad\quad M(s_1, \ldots, s_o, \sigma) \leftarrow s$;
$\quad\quad$**for** $(s \in S)$
$\quad\quad\quad$F(s) $\leftarrow$ GetNearestTarget($C(s, \mathcal{C})$);
$\quad\quad$Errors $\leftarrow$ CompareIO($\mathcal{N}, < \Sigma, S, s_0, M, F >, \mathcal{D}$);
$\quad\quad$States $\leftarrow$ States+1;
$\quad$**until** (Errors<>0)

This algorithm extracts FRAs with increasing number of states (i.e. memory capacity) until it finds a machine that produces a perfect approximation of the Input/Output behaviour of the recursive network on the set of examples used for the extraction process. The comparison (CompareIO) can be carried out for each node (full I/O equivalence) or only on those nodes for which an output target is provided (target I/O equivalence).

The algorithm computes the state space partition C (GeneratePartition) using the state trajectories points $\mathcal{X}$ obtained while processing the graphs of the learning set (StateVectors). The continuous transition function of the recursive network $\phi()$ is computed and quantized for any combination of the centroids of the partition regions ($C(s, C)$). The output corresponding to each state s is obtained by computing the network output when its state is initialized with the centroid $C(s, C)$ and by finding the nearest target defined on the leaning set (GetNearestTarget).

The previous algorithm produces a FRA in terms of its full state transition map that is represented by a table with $n^o K$ entries. The number of entries becomes huge when the number of states increases and can make the extraction process impractical. Moreover, most of these transitions are not contained in the training examples; this is often due to constraints in the data structure that make some combinations of states and inputs impossible.

In order to reduce the computational complexity of the extraction process, Algorithm 1 can be modified so as to produce *don't care* conditions for certain entries in the FRA state transition table. In many cases this choice corresponds to a drastic reduction of the valid transition rules, thus obtaining simpler solutions. The algorithm extracts only those state transitions that are activated while processing the data graphs in the learning set. The extraction algorithm turns out to be updated as follows:

Algorithm 2 FRA extraction (*don't cares*)

    $\mathcal{X} \leftarrow$ StateVectors($\mathcal{N}, \mathcal{D}$);
    States $\leftarrow$ 2;
    repeat
        $C \leftarrow$ GeneratePartition($\mathcal{X}$,States);
        $s_0 \leftarrow$ GetRegion(X_0,C);
        for ($Graph \in \mathcal{D}$)
            for ($Node \in Graph$)
                $< s_1, \ldots, s_o > \leftarrow < State(Node.child[1]), \ldots, State(Node.child[o]) >$
                $X \leftarrow \phi(C(s_1), \ldots, C(s_o), U(Node.\sigma))$;
                $s \leftarrow$ GetRegion(X,C);
                $M(s_1, \ldots, s_o, \sigma) \leftarrow s$;
        for ($s \in S$)
            F(s) $\leftarrow$ GetNearestTarget($C(s)$);
        Errors $\leftarrow$ CompareIO($\mathcal{N}$,$< \Sigma, S, s_0, M, F >$,$\mathcal{D}$);
        States $\leftarrow$ States+1;
    until (Errors<>0)

The main difference between the two algorithms resides in the loops where the transition extraction is performed. In the case of Algorithm 2 only the transitions in the learning set $\mathcal{D}$ are considered, while all the others are set to *don't care*.

4 Inference of Tree Automata: Experimental Results

In this section we show the experimental results we found when using recursive networks and the FRA extraction algorithm to infer tree automata. The first two experiments concern binary trees, while the third one involves a graph with a higher outdegree, but a fixed number of nodes. In all these experiments the network weights were initialized with random values in the interval [-0.5,0.5]. Input symbols were coded by unitary vectors (i.e. vectors having an entry equal to 1 and all other entries equal to 0). The learning and the test sets were generated randomly. Table 1 reports the complete setup for the three experiments. The rules used to generate the examples are the following:

1. **No b** : Given a set of binary trees with nodes whose labels are in the alphabet $\{a, b\}$, positive trees are those with no b labels, regardless of the the tree structure.
2. **f(a,b)** : Given a set of binary trees with nodes whose labels are in the alphabet $\{a, b, f\}$, positive trees are those containing sub-term $f(a, b)$ and following the rule: labels a and b can be found only in leaves, while term f must have two children. An example for this class of trees is the "expression" $f(f(b, a), f(a, f(a, b)))$ that corresponds to a tree with depth 4.
3. **The traffic policeman problem:** It is related to a cognitive task in which a traffic policeman can stop a car depending on his gestures (see Fig. 2). The policeman *stops* the car when he raises one of his arms or when he holds the red sign in one of his hands. The policeman can be represented by a graph which is constructed by inspection of the relative positions of its body components and colors. An empty position results in a nil pointer assigned to the corresponding direction link for the node. Thus the rule can simply be translated into the graphical formalism: one of the pointers NW or NE from the root node (1) must not be nil or one of the hand labels (nodes 7,9,10,11 if linked) must be r.

Table 2 summarizes the results for these experiments. In all the experiments all the training examples were learned perfectly. From the last column, the advantage of using the *don't care*-based extraction algorithm is clear, especially for the traffic policeman problem.

Figure 3 shows the extraction process for the *No-b trees* problem. The plot shows the states generated while parsing the 50 examples of the training set. Although the state distribution is quite complex, a simple partition into 3 regions turns out to be sufficient for extracting a FRA that has the same I/O behaviour as the network on the root nodes (the only nodes with targets). The resulting FRA has three states: s_0 is the initial state, s_2 codes the presence of the b symbol,

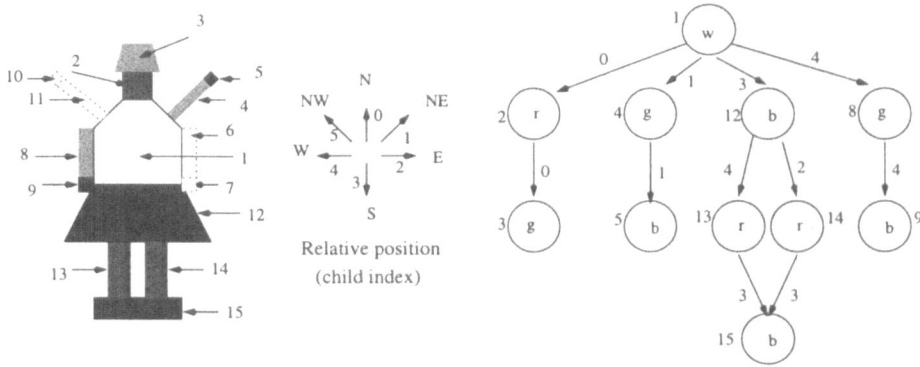

Fig. 2. The traffic policeman problem: Each component of the figure can be labeled with one out of four colors ([b]lack, [g]reen, [r]ed, [w]hite).

Problem	Network	Symbols	Learning	Test	Depth	Nodes
No b	3rd 2-21	{a/*,b/*}	13-27	32-68	[4,6]	[10,33]
f(a,b)	3rd 2-21	{a/0,b/0,f/2}	18-32	75-125	[2,5]	[3,15]
Policeman	1lr 2-37	{b/-,g/-,r/-,w/-}	193-207	243-257	[4,4]	[11,11]

Table 1. Experimental setup. The first column reports the problem rule; the second column specifies the neural network architecture used for the experiments reporting the network model (3d = third-order, 1lr = feedforward with one layer), the number of state neurons and the number of learnable parameters; the third column reports the symbols used to label the nodes and the constraints on the number of required descendants (* = no constraint, - = depends on node position); the fourth and fifth columns report the number of positive and negative graphs contained in the learning and test sets; the last two columns show the ranges for the depth and the number of nodes of the examples.

Problem	Learning	Test	States	Transitions
No b	100%	100%	3	18/18
f(a,b)	100%	100%	8	40/192
Policeman	100%	100%	5	64/62500

Table 2. Experimental results. The first two columns report the accuracy of the inferred rule on the training and test sets, respectively; the third column reports the number of states of the extracted FRA; the last column represents the number of extracted transitions with respect to the total entries in the FRA state table.

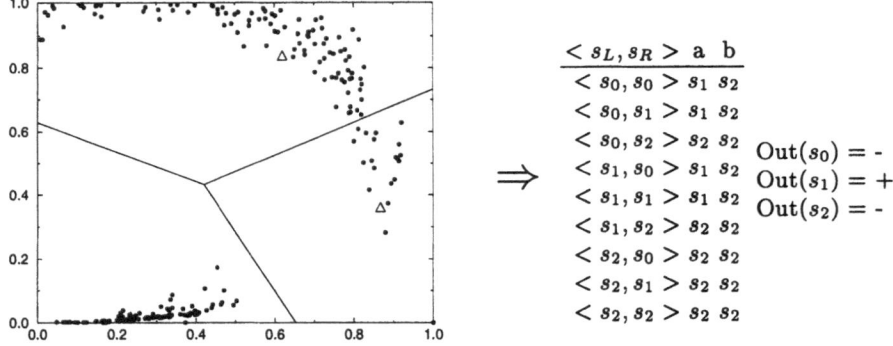

Fig. 3. FRA extraction for the No-b problem. The plot shows the state vectors, the state space partitions and the corresponding centroids. The table reports the FRA transition rules and the state/output map.

s_1 is the accepting state. The FRA state becomes s_2 whenever symbol b is read in a tree node.

For the $f(a, b)$ experiment, the extracted FRA is more complex. Only the transitions that are compatible with the term constraints are present. In particular, from the initial state only the transitions with symbols a and b are defined, while from all the other states only transitions with symbol f are extracted. The 8 state FRA can be minimized to an equivalent 4 state FRA that implements exactly the classification rule. The four states represent a leaf containing symbol a, a leaf labeled with b, an internal node having a sub-tree containing term $f(a, b)$, and an internal node which has no subtree containing $f(a, b)$. In Fig. 4 it is shown that 8 regions are required by the automata extraction process, since the extraction with 7 clusters is not successful, as the two states near the origin are not equivalent.

Figure 5 reports the extraction results for the traffic policeman problem. The extraction is performed using 5 regions. It is easy to see that the classification rule was extracted successfully by inspection of the developed state transitions. Because of the fixed structure of the graphs, it can be seen that transitions 1 through 5 are always applied to the root node. Transitions 1 and 2 deal with a raised arm (s_{NW} and s_{NE} not nil, i.e. s_0); transitions 4 and 5 correspond to the case of a red sign in the hand with both arms down (respectively in the left and right hand); transition 3 represents a *non-stopping* policeman (state s_2 is not accepting). Transition 6 says whether the color of a leaf is red (s_3). Transition 7 (8) is used to propagate the presence (absence) of a red sign in a hand to the root node when the arm is down (through the s_S link). The other transitions are necessary to manage the other nodes and reflect the independence on the component color.

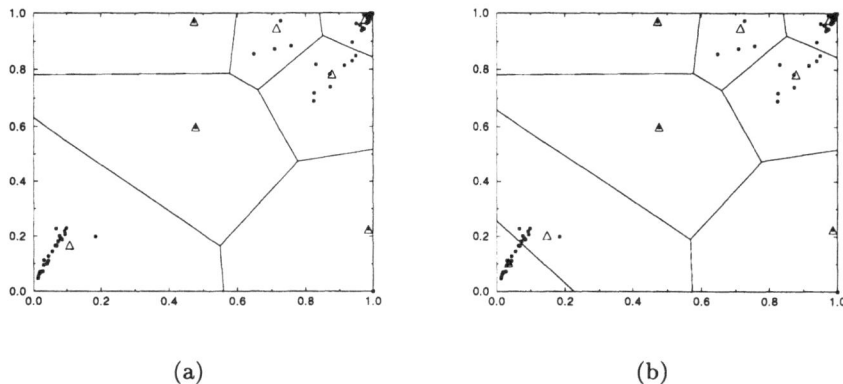

(a)   (b)

Fig. 4. FRA extraction for the $f(a, b)$ problem: (a) state space partition using 7 states. This resolution is not sufficient to satisfy the network-FRA I/O equivalence condition. (b) State space partition using 8 states. The network I/O behaviour is exactly approximated by the extracted FRA.

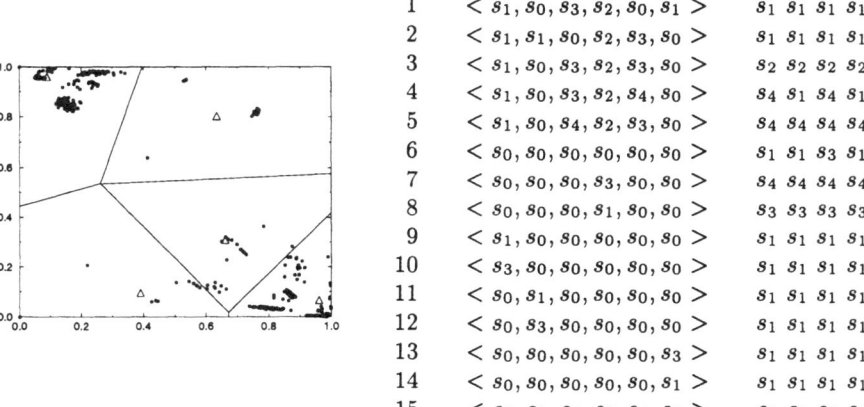

	$< s_N, s_{NE}, s_E, s_S, s_W, s_{NW} >$	b	g	r	w
1	$< s_1, s_0, s_3, s_2, s_0, s_1 >$	s_1	s_1	s_1	s_1
2	$< s_1, s_1, s_0, s_2, s_3, s_0 >$	s_1	s_1	s_1	s_1
3	$< s_1, s_0, s_3, s_2, s_3, s_0 >$	s_2	s_2	s_2	s_2
4	$< s_1, s_0, s_3, s_2, s_4, s_0 >$	s_4	s_1	s_4	s_1
5	$< s_1, s_0, s_4, s_2, s_3, s_0 >$	s_4	s_4	s_4	s_4
6	$< s_0, s_0, s_0, s_0, s_0, s_0 >$	s_1	s_1	s_3	s_1
7	$< s_0, s_0, s_0, s_3, s_0, s_0 >$	s_4	s_4	s_4	s_4
8	$< s_0, s_0, s_0, s_1, s_0, s_0 >$	s_3	s_3	s_3	s_3
9	$< s_1, s_0, s_0, s_0, s_0, s_0 >$	s_1	s_1	s_1	s_1
10	$< s_3, s_0, s_0, s_0, s_0, s_0 >$	s_1	s_1	s_1	s_1
11	$< s_0, s_1, s_0, s_0, s_0, s_0 >$	s_1	s_1	s_1	s_1
12	$< s_0, s_3, s_0, s_0, s_0, s_0 >$	s_1	s_1	s_1	s_1
13	$< s_0, s_0, s_0, s_0, s_0, s_3 >$	s_1	s_1	s_1	s_1
14	$< s_0, s_0, s_0, s_0, s_0, s_1 >$	s_1	s_1	s_1	s_1
15	$< s_0, s_0, s_4, s_0, s_4, s_0 >$	s_2	s_2	s_2	s_2
16	$< s_0, s_0, s_3, s_0, s_3, s_0 >$	s_2	s_2	s_2	s_2

Fig. 5. FRA extraction from the traffic policeman problem. The plot shows the state vectors, the state space partitions, and the corresponding centroids. The table reports the FRA transition rules. States s_1 and s_4 are accepting.

5 Conclusions

In this paper we have shown that recursive neural networks, used for processing data structures, can be given an intriguing symbolic interpretation in terms of tree automata. On the basis of the experience gained from some preliminary experiments, we have shown that proper quantization algorithms can be conceived that make it possible to infer tree automata from examples. It is worth mentioning that, at the moment, we do not have evidence to state that the proposed methodology can challenge symbolic approaches to inductive inference. Our own feeling is that the proposed adaptive model can in fact hardly compete in a purely symbolic domain, like the inductive inference of tree automata. On the other hand, unlike most symbolic approaches to inductive inference, the one we propose is likely to be very robust with respect to accidental or malicious modifications of the training set, since the optimization process on which learning relies is inherently robust. Finally, Boden's moral on artificial intelligence, mentioned in the introduction, seems to suggest that the new "color" emerging from connectionist models could play his own role, particularly in the case of noisy examples: "when lighting conditions change, the Wizard's pony could trot along with this new color.

Acknowledgements

We thank Alessandro Sperduti (Dipartimento di Informatica, Università di Pisa) for fruitful discussions on recursive neural networks and their links with tree automata.

References

1. M. Boden, "Horses of a different colour?," in *Artificial Intelligence and Neural Networks* (V. Honavar and L. Uhr, eds.), pp. 3–19, Academic Press, 1994.
2. D. Angluin and C. Smith, "Inductive inference: Theory and methods," *Computing Surveys*, vol. 15, no. 3, pp. 237–269, 1983.
3. K.-S. Fu and T. Booth, "Grammatical inference: Introduction and survey - part i," *IEEE Transactions on Systems, Man, and Cybernetics*, vol. 5, pp. 95–111, January 1975.
4. K.-S. Fu and T. Booth, "Grammatical inference: Introduction and survey - part ii," *IEEE Transactions on Systems, Man, and Cybernetics*, vol. 5, pp. 409–423, May 1975.
5. R. Watrous and G. Kuhn, "Induction of finite-state languages using second-order recurrent networks," *Neural Computation*, vol. 4, no. 3, pp. 406–414, 1992.
6. C. Giles, C. Miller, D. Chen, G. Sun, H. Chen, and Y. Lee, "Learning and extracting finite state automata with second-order recurrent neural networks," *Neural Computation*, vol. 4, no. 3, pp. 393–405, 1992.
7. P. Frasconi, M. Gori, M. Maggini, and G. Soda, "Representation of finite state automata in recurrent radial basis function networks," *Machine Learning*, vol. 23, pp. 5–32, 1996.

8. C. Omlin and C. Giles, "Constructing deterministic finite-state automata in recurrent neural networks," *Journal of the ACM*, vol. 43, no. 6, pp. 937–972, 1996.

9. A. Sperduti and T. Starita, "Supervised neural networks for classification of structures," *IEEE Transactions on Neural Networks.* to appear.

10. M. Arbib and Y. Given'on, "Algebra automata i: Parallel programming as a prolegomena to the categorical approach," *Information and Control*, vol. 12, pp. 331–345, 1968.

11. C. Giles and T. Maxwell, "Learning, invariance, and generalization in high-order neural networks," *Applied Optics*, vol. 26, no. 23, p. 4972, 1987.

12. C. Miller and C. Giles, "Experimental comparison of the effect of order in recurrent neural networks," *Int. Journal of Pattern Recognition and Artificial Intelligence*, 1993. Special Issue on Applications of Neural Networks to Pattern Recognition (I. Guyon Ed.).

13. E. Sontag and H. Sussman, "Backpropagation separates when perceptrons do," in *International Joint Conference on Neural Networks*, vol. 1, (Washington DC), pp. 639–642, IEEE Press, June 1989.

14. J. Thatcher, "Tree automata: An informal survey," in *Current Trends in the Theory of Computing* (A. Aho, ed.), pp. 143–172, Prentice-Hall, Inc.

A Computational Model of Misunderstandings in Agent Communication*

Liliana Ardissono, Guido Boella and Rossana Damiano

Dipartimento di Informatica - Università di Torino
Corso Svizzera n.185 - 10149 Torino - Italy
E-mail: {liliana, guido}@di.unito.it
Fax: +39-11-751603; Phone: +39-11-7429111

Abstract. In this paper, we describe a plan-based model for the treatment of misunderstandings in NL cooperative dialogue: an utterance is considered coherent if it is related to some of the interactants' intentions by a relation of goal adherence, goal adoption or plan continuation. If none of them is fully satisfied, a misunderstanding is hypothesized and the goal of realigning the interactants' interpretation of the dialogue is adopted by the agent detecting the problem. This goal makes the agent restructure his own contextual interpretation, or induce his partner to do that, according to who made the mistake.

1 Introduction

We describe a plan-based model of misunderstandings within an agent architecture supporting cooperative NL communication. In a dialogue, a misunderstanding occurs when an interactant chooses an interpretation for some turn which is complete and coherent from his point of view, but it is not the one intended by the speaker [21]. A wrong interpretation of one or more turns can cause a misalignment of the speakers' dialogue contexts, with the eventual production of a turn perceived as incoherent by its hearer. At this point, however, either the speaker or the hearer might have constructed separately an erroneous dialogue context, so it is necessary to exploit the incoherent turn to identify the responsible for the mistake.

We model the treatment of misunderstandings as a goal-directed, rational behavior: our notion of coherence in communication is based on the idea that the goals identified when interpreting a turn have to be related with the previously expressed or inferred goals of the interactants [2, 8]. When an agent receives an incoherent turn (or a turn which only partially matches his expectations), he adopts the further goal of realigning the interactants' diverging interpretations. To do so, he reasons to understand which agent misunderstood the other one; then, he can restructure his own interpretation, or make the partner restructure

---

* We are indebted to Prof. Leonardo Lesmo and Prof. Carla Bazzanella for their fruitful discussions and hints to our work. This work has been supported by MURST and CNR, project "Pianificazione e Riconoscimento di Piani nella Comunicazione".

his accordingly. Repair turns are explained as cooperative subdialogues aimed at restoring the common interpretation ground; in fact, the maintenance of a correct dialogue context is a mutual goal of the interactants [10].

Incoherent turns are not always due to misinterpretations: also topic shifts and breakdowns in cooperation should be considered. Currently, we don't model topic shifts due to the initiation of new dialogues; however, as pointed out by many researchers [11, 17, 18], focus and topic shifts are usually marked by the presence of "cue" words. On the contrary, since we model cooperative dialogues, we exclude the hypothesis that a breakdown in communication can occur.

2 Background

Schegloff [24, 25] has analized misunderstandings with respect to the sequences of turns of a dialogue, in order to identify the mechanisms used by the interactants to defend the "intersubjectivity", i.e. the common set of beliefs necessary for an interaction to continue successfully. He points out that speakers monitor their partners' reactions and interpret them as displays of understanding / misunderstanding of the previous turns. [25] identifies different repairs to misunderstandings, according to their position in the dialogue and whether the agent performing them is correcting himself, or his partner.

In particular, in *"third position repair"*, the misunderstood agent realizes that the partner has a wrong interpretation and urges him to restructure it:

Example1 (translated from [14]):
    T0: B: *"Hello. I'd like to have an English book [...] for the American school. Is there a 10% discount?"*
    T1: A: *"Do you have the enrollment card?"*
    T2: B: *"Yes, I have it."*
    T3: A: *"No, you should show me your card."*
    T4: B: *"Oh I understand."*

Independently from the actual turn position, this corresponds to a repair accomplished by the misunderstood speaker in one of his own subsequent turns, i.e. a *"self-repair"*.

Instead, in *"fourth position repair"*, a speaker A realizes that he has misunderstood a turn $T1$ uttered by his partner only after having replied to it ($T2$) and having received back a turn $T3$ incoherent with respect to $T1$ and $T2$ ($T3$ is coherent with the partner's intended interpretation of $T1$). Typically, after having corrected his interpretation, A performs another type of repair, telling the partner that he has understood what he initially meant:

Example2 (from [25]):
    T1: Marty: *"Loes, do you have a calendar,"*
    T2: Loes: *"Yeah"* ((reaches for her desk calendar))
    T3: Marty: *"Do you have one that hangs on the wall?"*
    T4: Loes: *"Oh, you want one."*
    T5: Marty: *"Yeah"*

Since these repairs are typically accomplished by the interlocutor who has misunderstood in one of his turns, these turns are called *"other-repairs"*, referring to the agent they belong to.

3 Our agent model

The work presented in this paper extends our agent model to enable it to cope with misunderstandings in NL communication. Our agent architecture has a two-level plan-based representation of the knowledge about acting [4, 5]. At the metalevel, the Agent Modeling (AM) plan library describes the (precompiled) problem-solving recipes used by an agent to choose the actions for reaching his goals, and to execute them; at the object level, the Domain library describes recipes for obtaining domain goals (such as buying a book, see Example1), and the Speech Act Library describes the direct and indirect speech-acts [3]. The three libraries are composed of a Generalization Hierarchy and a Decomposition Hierarchy [16] and share the same representation formalism.

The AM actions take domain actions and speech-acts as objects: an agent performing a problem-solving activity can plan to perform domain and linguistic actions. In the AM actions, one parameter (*source*) denotes the beneficiary of the action that the modeled agent is performing: usually, *source* is bound to the agent of the AM action itself; however, it can be used to model cooperation between agents. There are two major actions in the AM library:

- "Satisfy(*agt, source, g*)" describes the behavior of an agent *agt*, who wants to satisfy a goal *g*; its body consists of looking for a feasible plan for *g* and executing it. If no feasible plan is found, the decomposition of "Satisfy" includes the notification to the *source* agent that the goal cannot be reached (see the notion of Joint Intention in agent cooperation [10]).
- "Try-execute(*agt, source, action*)" describes the execution of actions; it includes checking the preconditions of *action* and performing it (possibly expanding its decomposition, if it is complex). The decomposition of "Try-execute" also describes acknowledgements in agent cooperation: after a successful execution of *action*, if *agt* is collaborating with another *source* agent, he has to inform him that the action has succeeded; on the contrary, if the action could not be executed, he has to inform him of the problem.

The agent's behavior is ruled by an interpreter which loops on three phases, each one performed by means of a call to a "Satisfy" action: interpretation of the input (P1), decision of which goal to commit to (P2), and reaction (P3, where the agent acts to reach the chosen goal). The plan-based representation of knowledge supports a declarative representation style, that can be used both for interpreting and generating the agent behavior. A basic assumption of the recognition task is that all agents have equal plan libraries (on the contrary, we don't assume that agents have equal beliefs about the world state).

The agent interprets a dialogue incrementally: for each turn, he builds the semantic representation of the input sentence [6], finds the goal which the sentence is aiming at, and relates it with the dialogue context. The interpretation of each turn consists of a Context Model (CM), which contains the problem-solving actions (AM) referring to the linguistic (SAM) and domain-level (DM) actions observed (or performed) by the agent: the AM actions explain the reasons for performing the object-level actions. The local CM built during the interpretation of each turn is embedded into the dialogue context by identifying how the sentence contributes to the previous interaction: the context contains the sequence of interpretations (CMs) of the turns (properly interleaved), together with the relations existing among them, as explained in the following section.

4 Coherence and misunderstandings

We consider a new contribution coherent if a relation exists among the intentions underlying it and the previous pending intentions of the interactants, either expressed explicitly, or inferred by reasoning on their plans [9]. An utterance is coherent with the previous context if its receiver A can interpret it as a means of the speaker B to achieve a goal g such that:

1. *Goal adherence:* g is one of the goals previously expressed by A.
2. *Goal adoption:* g is one of the goals that B has inferred A is going to aim at; e.g. in:
   T1: A: *"I need a book. Where is the library?"*
   T2: B: *"It is over there, but it is closed."*
   B provides A with an extra-helpful information which satisfies his next goal of checking whether the library is open [2].
3. *Plan continuation:* g contributes to a plan that B is carrying on.[2] E.g:
   T1 B: *"Where is the library?"*
   T2 A: *"It's over there."*
   T3 B: *"Is it open today?"*

Goal adherence and adoption refer to a complete satisfaction of the hearer's pending intentions. So, when the partner satisfies only some of the goals that the hearer expects him to obtain, although a partial match exists, the analyzed turn is not considered coherent with the previous part of the interaction.[3]

---

[2] We assume that an agent continues the execution of his plans only when there aren't other goals of the partner to be achieved.

[3] Actually, it is not necessary to satisfy all the pending goals separately. In a CM, some goals strictly depend upon other ones, at a higher level. In that case, the satisfaction of the latter makes the former irrelevant, so that they can be considered as "closed". For example, if somebody asks a question, he expects that his partner acknowledges in some way the fact that he has understood the utterance. However, if the partner answers the question directly, this satisfies all the pending expectations and no other acknowledgement is required in order to be coherent.

Uncooperative replies (e.g. refusals) and subdialogues for solving interpretation problems are other types of coherent contributions. Although in this paper we do not take these phenomena into account, they have to be explained as related with some speaker's goal as well: respectively, the goal to know whether the hearer intends to cooperate, and that the hearer interprets the utterance.

The interpretation phase (P1) is performed by means of an elementary "Build-interpretation" action. Consider the basic interpretation of an input turn by its hearer A: "Do(B, Utterance-act(B, A, *"input-utterance"*))".[4] As the result of a successful execution of "Build-interpretation", the agent A has a new dialogue context where the last turn is related with the previous context by one of the three relations described above. In principle, the previous context can be:
- void (e.g. at the beginning of a dialogue);
- composed of an elementary uninterpreted CM, simply containing the execution of an utterance act ("Do(*agt*, Utterance-act(...))");
- a complex context, composed of the interpretations of the previous turns, properly linked by coherence relations.

The process of executing "Build-interpretation" is composed of a local and a global interpretation phase. In the description of these phases, we will represent the uninterpreted turns of the form "Do(*agt*, Utterance-act(...))" with the notation t_i. On the contrary, we will use the notation T_i to represent in a generic way either an uninterpreted turn or its local interpretation.

1. The local turn interpretation phase is called "upward-expansion", because it consists of an expansion of a CM along a path up in the plan libraries. In this phase, the possible (metalevel and object level) plan leading B to the execution of the turn is looked for, and the agent's current goals are identified.
2. In the global interpretation phase, the newly identified goals and their high-level plans are related with the participants' goals pending from the previous dialogue context. This is done by means of the "matching" and "focusing" functions, which model two different relations among turns:
   - The "matching procedure" succeeds when the top-level goal, recognized in the local interpretation phase as the reason for B's last turn T_n, corresponds to one of the (unsatisfied) goals ascribable to A. This goal has been expressed by A (see the notion of *goal adherence* above), or B can have inferred it during the interpretation of A's previous turns (*goal adoption*).
   - The "focusing procedure" succeeds when B's turn T_i is the continuation of an AM plan performed by B (and previously identified by A).[5]

In practice, these two phases are carried on together by a number of heuristic rules we have defined. The rules exploit the speaker and hearer's contextual

---

[4] In the CM, *"input-utterance"* is a string of characters.
[5] The continuation of an AM plan can correspond to the continuation of a domain or a communicative action [19].

Restructure $\equiv$

name: Restructure

roles: ((agent x)(partner y)(turns $[t_1, \ldots, t_n]$) (old-inter ctx)(intended-inter ctx_j))

var-types: ((person x y)(turn $t_1 \ldots t_n$)(context ctx ctx' ctx_j))

eff: inter(x, $[t_1, \ldots, t_j]$, ctx_j)

constr: inter(x, $[t_1, \ldots, t_n]$, ctx) $\wedge$ inter(y, $[t_1, \ldots, t_n]$, ctx') $\wedge$
          correct-subcontext(ctx_j,ctx,ctx') $\wedge$ agent(y,ctx_j[j])

Fig. 1. The "Restructure" action.

pending goals to guide the interpretation of the new contribution toward these goals, by pruning the non promising directions. The rules look for the paths in the plan library relating an object-level action (underlying the input utterance) with the object-level plan built in the interpretation of the previous turns. Since a rule searches for the shortest path linking the last turn to the previous context, "Build-interpretation" provides at each call a different result, with a progressive degree of complexity.

The hypothesis that a misunderstanding among the agents has occurred arises in the following situation: if, during the interpretation of an utterance, the "matching" and "focusing" procedures fail,[6] no relation is established between the turn and the dialogue context. In this case, the interpretation phase returns a context where the last turn remains unrelated. In principle, two hypotheses are possible: a focus shift has occurred or the cooperation between the speakers has broken down. If neither hypothesis is feasible, the lack of coherence can be interpreted as a display that a misunderstanding has occurred.

In this case, the agent (A) commits to the goal of realigning the interactants' subjective views of the dialogue; this is done by the execution of a "Satisfy" action on the goal that A's interpretation of the dialogue is the same as B's:

(i) Satisfy(A, B, (inter(A, $[t_1, \ldots, t_j]$, ctx_j) $\wedge$ inter(B, $[t_1, \ldots, t_j]$, ctx_j)))

The variables j and ctx_j occurring in the third argument of the "Satisfy" action are intended to be existentially quantified. The meaning of the complex formula containing them is that agents A and B have two equivalent interpretation contexts (ctx_j) for the part of the dialogue from turn t_1 to t_j. Although j and ctx_j are unbound when the "Satisfy" action is started by the agent, at the end of its execution they are bound respectively to the first turn which was misunderstood and to the correct interpretation context of subdialogue $[t_1, \ldots, t_j]$.

The execution of (i) starts with a planning activity, where A identifies the action which has a change of dialogue interpretation in its effects: "Restructure" (shown in Figure 1).[7]

---

[6] I.e. although the utterance is interpretable, at least, as a speech act, there is no interpretation of it such that the procedures above can find a contextual pending goal to which the turn can be related.

[7] The "Satisfy" action does not manage complex goals in a general way. It can however satisfy separately the subgoals of a conjunctive goal. In this particular formula, this is enough, because after the instantiation of "Restructure", variable ctx_j is bound

Reinterpret(agt, $[T_1, \ldots, T_n]$, ctx) ≡
begin i := n - 1; LC := ∅; RestC := ∅;
    while (i > 0 ∧ empty(LC)) do
    begin LC := Build-interpretation(agt, T_i, T_n, ctx);
        if empty(LC) then i := i - 1
        else begin RestC := Reinterpret(agt, $[T_1, \ldots, LC[1]]$, ctx);
                if RestC then
                    begin j := i + 1;
                        while (j < n) do
                        begin
                            RestC := Build-interpretation(agt, RestC, T_j, ctx);
                            j = j + 1;
                        end;
                        if empty(RestC) then LC := ∅ /*Try another local ctx*/
                end
                else LC := ∅ /*Try another local context*/
        end
    end;
   return(RestC) /* Return the reinterpreted context */
end.

Fig. 2. The "Reinterpret" algorithm.

In order to perform the "Restructure" action, its constraint must be true. The constraint of "Restructure" requires that:
- The agent x (who has to perform the action to correct his wrong interpretation) has an interpretation ctx of the whole dialogue, up to the last turn t_n.
- An alternative interpretation ctx' of the dialogue can be attributed to x's partner y.
- ctx_j is the coherent interpretation of the misunderstood speaker, up to the misinterpreted turn t_j $(j < n)$.
- The agent y corresponds to the speaker of the first turn that has been interpreted differently in ctx and ctx' (i.e. the last turn of ctx_j, denoted as $ctx_j[j]$ in Figure 1).

    In order to evaluate this constraints, the agent A must determine B's interpretation context ctx', alternative to A's one (ctx). He does this by executing a "Satisfy(A, B, Knowref(A, ctx', inter(B, $[t_1, \ldots, t_n]$, ctx')))".
The "Knowref(...)" goal is obtained by executing an action corresponding to the "Reinterpret" algorithm described below.

    If, after the execution of "Reinterpret", the first turn for which ctx and ctx' differ has been uttered by A, then he has to persuade B to restructure his dialogue context, by means of a linguistic repair. Otherwise, A executes "Restruc-

---

to the interpretation subcontext of one of the two speakers; so, it is not necessary to satisfy both the subgoals.

ture", changing his own interpretation to ctx_j (see the effect of "Restructure"); after that, they can continue the interaction from the reestablished interpretation context. In both cases, the recovery goal is shared among the speakers; when everything ends up well, the agent informs the partner about the success of their aims (see turns T4 in Example 1 and 2); otherwise, if no reconstruction is feasible, the agent warns his partner that the intersubjectivity cannot be recovered (as the last step of "Satisfy" prescribes).

We now describe the reinterpretation algorithm "Reinterpret", shown in Figure 2. The algorithm traces back the dialogue, turn after turn, and looks for a relation between the problematic turn T_n and some previous (misinterpreted) turn. "Reinterpret" has the following arguments: the agent (agt), a sequence of turns ($[T_1, \ldots, T_n]$) and the old context ctx (the agent's wrong interpretation of the dialogue). It tries to relate T_n to the alternative interpretations of a previous turn, in order to constrain the search for the correct interpretation of the dialogue and improve this search, with respect to a blind form of backtracking. It is worth noting that the agent executing the algorithm must consider the alternative interpretations of his own turns, beside those of the partner's turns.

When "Reinterpret" is called on a list of uninterpreted turns $[t_1, ..., t_n]$, it goes backward from the problematic last turn t_n, towards the beginning of the dialogue. It stops when it finds the most recent turn t_i for which "Build-interpretation" has found a new interpretation, coherent with t_n.[8] Then, "Reinterpret" propagates the new interpretation LC (*Local Context*) to the whole context, using the interpretation T_i of t_i in LC (which corresponds to the first component of this context, denoted by $LC[1]$) as a "pivot", backward by calling itself recursively, and forward by means of a loop of "Build-interpretation" on the remaining turns.

5 Example

We now sketch how our model works on Example1; Figure 3 shows the intended interpretation of the clerk's (A) turns.[9]

In order to sell a book with a discount as requested by B, A must check whether B has the enrollment card (action "Satisfy(A, B, Knowif(have(B, Card)))" in AM1). Cautiously, he decides to obtain that goal by making B show him this card. He has to request B to show him the card, but he adopts an indirect strategy to suggest B that he wants to *see* her card: in T1, he asks her whether "she has" the card (a precondition of action "Show").[10]

---

[8] Although "Build-interpretation" takes in input a context and a turn, there is no contradiction here, because a single turn is by itself an elementary context.

[9] The figure represents the Agent Modeling plans and the object level actions, linked by means of arcs.

[10] Although AM1 contains two equal occurrences of the "Satisfy" action, they do not lead to any loop. In fact, we constrain the search strategy in the AM library not to select any object-level action that the agent is already carrying on. In our example,

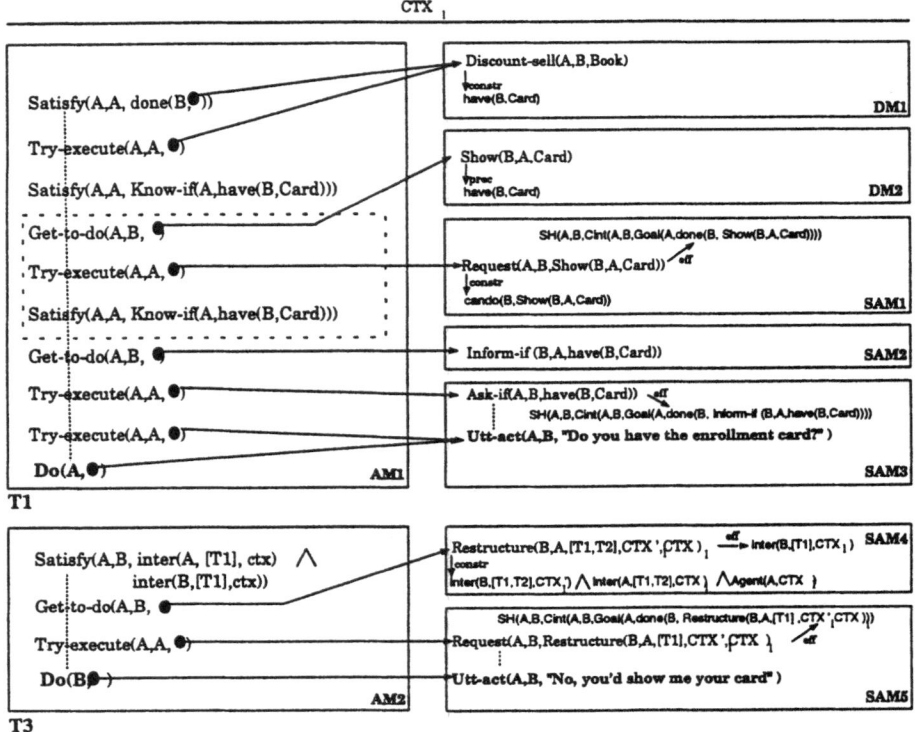

Fig. 3. Intended interpretation of the clerk's (A) turns in Example1.

In T2, B answers positively to the question; this is interpreted by A as a "Satisfy(B, A, done(B, Inform-if(B, A, have(B, Card))))", not shown in the figure.

However, T2 alone is not a coherent reply to T1, because it leaves unsatisfied A's implicit expectation that B shows him the card. This expectation corresponds to the formula "SH(A, B, Cint(A,B, Goal(A, done(B, Show(B, A, Card)))))"[11] which is the effect of A's request (in SAM1). So, A hypothesizes that a misunderstanding has occurred and commits to realigning the two interpretations, by performing action "Satisfy(A, B, inter(A, $[t_1,\ldots,t_j]$, ctx_j) $\wedge$ inter(B,$[t_1,\ldots,t_j],ctx_j$))".[12] A selects the "Restructure" action for obtaining his

---

the lower-level "Satisfy" for discovering the value of the constraint cannot be solved by another "Show" action.

[11] In the formula, the SH modal operator represents mutual beliefs; the $Cint$ modal operator, instead, represents communicative intentions, as defined in [1]. Finally, $Done$ maps an action on the (world) state where the action has been successfully executed.

[12] In this case, the dialogue $[t_1,\ldots,t_j]$ reduces to T1, since $j < n$ and $n = 2$: see AM2 in Figure 3.

goal, because the effect "inter$(x, [\ldots], ctx)$" matches the goal to be obtained (it can be used to change interpretation context).

As described in the AM library, before executing an action, its constraints must be evaluated.[13] So, A performs a "Satisfy" action (not reported in the figure) to know if the constraints of "Restructure" are true. This leads A to find an alternative interpretation context (CTX$_1$') to be ascribed to B, by means of the "Reinterpret" algorithm: in fact, T1 is ambiguous since A's question could be interpreted as a direct way of learning from B's answer whether she is enrolled. In this case, the ambiguity that misleads B is due to alternative reconstructions of the speaker's problem solving activity (in the figure, B's wrong interpretation of T1 can be derived from AM1 by ignoring the contents of its inner dashed rectangle). In this second interpretation, T2 would be a coherent reply to T1, since it does not leave any unsatisfied goal.

At this point, the misunderstood turn has been detected by A. Given that A is the misunderstood speaker, B should perform a "Restructure" action to correct her interpretation (to CTX$_1$). So, A performs a "Get-to-do" action[14] to induce her to do that: this leads A to plan a "Request" for "Restructure". The request would be expressed by making explicit his real intentions, which were implicit in T1.

6 Conclusions

We have described a plan-based agent model for a computational treatment of misunderstandings in dialogue. In this model, the coherence of a turn is evaluated by relating its underlying goals with the interactants' contextual pending goals. If a satisfactory relation cannot be found, a misunderstanding is hypothesized and the goal of reestablishing the intersubjectivity among the interactants is adopted. This goal leads the agent who has received the incoherent turn to reason on the previous context, to understand which agent has misunderstood the other one. The whole processes of interpretation and recovery are based on goal acquisition and the occurrences of self and other repairs are reduced to the same goal-based process. Moreover, by modeling linguistic and domain actions uniformly, we provide a general model of misunderstandings, not limited to linguistic interaction.

Our model takes into account the different types of ambiguity which may cause a misunderstanding: since the interpretation process is performed in a layered model of dialogue processing, at each level a misinterpretation is possible. So, we can analyze misunderstandings related with the syntactic or semantic interpretation of utterances (including references), with their illocutionary force and with the domain-level and AM plans underlying the speech-acts.

---

[13] See the description of "Try-execute" in section 3.

[14] The "Get-to-do" action has been introduced in the AM library to model the strategies adopted by an agent to induce another agent to perform an action for his own sake.

Other researchers have used abductive frameworks for managing the interpretation of utterances [22, 21] but they cover only a subset of the levels at which a misunderstanding can be identified in our approach (typically only the illocutionary one). Moreover, some of these works exploit contextual expectations to guide the interpretation process, but they are principally focused on linguistic expectations (e.g. [21]), so that they strictly depend on the occurrence of incoherent turns immediately after the misunderstood turn. For instance, in [21] and [12] only third and fourth *turn* repairs are analyzed, while our plan-based approach supports a more complex dialogue context, where both object level and problem-solving level expectations are considered; this allows us to analyze self and other-repairs, without imposing strict constraints on the distance between the first misunderstood turn and the repair turn. Our work also differs with respect to the others in that most of them do not consider collaboration aspects of dialogue to explain misunderstandings; so, they are resolved by means of strict recovery strategies, like metarules for restructuring the dialogue context [21, 13].

Currently, we don't generate agent behavior,[15] so we have not defined specific repair strategies; however, we can explain a linguistic repair as a behavior adopted by an agent after he instantiates a "Restructure" action (to realign the participants' dialogue contexts) and he realizes that his partner has misunderstood him. On the other hand, we can explain an uptake by an agent in a fourth turn repair (*"Oh, you meant ... "*) as a notification to his partner that he has corrected his own dialogue interpretation.

In a model for the treatment of communication problems, also speaker and hearer misconceptions should be dealt with, since they can cause breakdowns in the communication [20, 15, 23, 7, 13]. Note however that plan misconceptions have been implicitly reduced to the presence of different interpretation contexts in all the approaches based on the presence of *buggy plan libraries*. This suggests that a basic model of misunderstandings can be extended to the treatment of misconceptions, by considering also the buggy plans as alternatives.

The interpretation of dialogue by means of our plan-based agent model is implemented in Common Lisp and runs on SUN workstations.

References

1. G. Airenti, B. Bara, and M. Colombetti. Conversational and behavior games in the pragmatics of discourse. *Cognitive Science*, 17:197–256, 1993.
2. J.F. Allen. Recognizing intentions from natural language utterances. In M. Brady and R.C. Berwick, editors, *Computational models of discourse*, pages 107–166. MIT Press, 1983.
3. L. Ardissono, G. Boella, and L. Lesmo. A computational approach to speech acts recognition. In *Proc. 17th Cognitive Science Conference*, pages 316–321, 1995.
4. L. Ardissono, G. Boella, and L. Lesmo. Recognition of problem-solving plans in dialogue interpretation. In *Proc. 5th Int. Conf. on User Modeling*, pages 195–197, Kailua-Kona, Hawaii, 1996.

---

[15] In order to process dialogues, we type the input sentences to the system in the form of separate turns; so, the system plays alternatively the role of the two hearers.

5. L. Ardissono, G. Boella, and L. Lesmo. A plan-based formalism to express knowledge about actions. In *Proc. 4th ModelAge Workshop: Formal Models of Agents*, pages 255–268, Pontignano, Italy, 1997.

6. L. Ardissono, L. Lesmo, P. Pogliano, and P. Terenziani. Representation of determiners in natural language. In *Proc. 12th IJCAI*, pages 997–1002, Sydney, 1991.

7. R.J. Calistri-Yeh. Utilizing user models to handle ambiguity and misconceptions in robust plan recognition. *User Modeling and User-Adapted Interaction*, 1:289–322, 1991.

8. S. Carberry. *Plan Recognition in Natural Language Dialogue*. MIT Press, 1990.

9. C. Castelfranchi and D. Parisi. *Linguaggio, conoscenze e scopi*. Il Mulino, 1980.

10. P.R. Cohen and H.J. Levesque. Confirmation and joint action. In *Proc. 12th IJCAI*, pages 951–957, Sydney, 1991.

11. R. Cohen. Analyzing the structure of argumentative discourse. *Computational Linguistics*, 13:11–24, 1987.

12. M. Danieli. On the use of expectations for detecting and repairing human-machine misomunicaiton. In *AAAI 1996 Workshop: Detecting, Repairing and Preventing Human-Machine Miscommunication*, pages 87–93, Portland, 1996.

13. R.M. Eller. *A Plan Recognition Architecture for Ill-Formed Dialogue*. PhD thesis, University of Delaware, 1993.

14. Gavioli and Mansfield. *The PIXI corpora: bookshop encounters in English and Italian*. CLUEB, Italy, 1990.

15. B. Goodman. Repairing reference identification failures by relaxation. In *Proc. 23th Annual Meeting ACL*, pages 204–217, Chicago, 1985.

16. H. Kautz. A formal theory of plan recognition and its implementation. In R.J. Brachman, editor, *Reasoning About Plans*, pages 69–125. Morgan Kaufmann Publishers, 1991.

17. D. Litman and J. Allen. A plan recognition model for subdialogues in conversation. *Cognitive Science*, 11:163–200, 1987.

18. K.E. Lochbaum. The use of knowledge preconditions in language processing. In *Proc. 14th IJCAI*, pages 1260–1265, Montreal, 1995.

19. M.T. Maybury. Communicative acts for explanation generation. *Int. Journal of Man-Machine Studies*, 37:135–172, 1992.

20. K.F. McCoy. The ROMPER system: responding to object-related misconceptions using perspective. In *Proc. 24th Annual Meeting of the ACL*, pages 97–105, New York, 1986.

21. S.W. McRoy and G. Hirst. The repair of speech act misunderstandings by abductive inference. *Computational Linguistics*, 21(4):433–478, 1995.

22. K. Nagao. Abduction and dynamic preference in plan-based dialogue understanding. In *Proc. 13th IJCAI*, pages 1186–1192, Chambery, 1993.

23. M.E. Pollack. Plans as complex mental attitudes. In P.R. Cohen, J. Morgan, and M.E. Pollack, editors, *Intentions in communication*, pages 77–103. MIT Press, 1990.

24. E.A. Schegloff. Some sources of misunderstanding in talk-in-interaction. *Linguistics*, 25(1):201–218, 1987.

25. E.A. Schegloff. Repair after the next turn: The last structurally provided defense of intersubjectivity in conversation. *American Journal of Sociology*, 7(5):1295–1345, 1992.

Wide-Coverage Lexicalized Grammars*

Cristina Barbero and Vincenzo Lombardo

Dipartimento di Informatica - Università di Torino
corso Svizzera 185, 10149 Torino, Italy
E-mail: cris@di.unito.it, vincenzo@di.unito.it

Abstract. This paper proposes a hierarchical organization of the linguistic knowledge, that views grammar as an abstraction of item-dependent information (in particular, an abstraction of subcategorization frames into a hierarchy of classes). The formalism has been successfully applied to a classification of 105 Italian verbal frames, developed by analysing a corpus of about 500,000 words.
The proposed framework (expressed in a dependency approach) is of linguistic and computational interest. From a linguistic point of view, it is a clear, significant and non-redundant representation. From a computational point of view, structuring the grammar into a hierarchy allows to define a predictive component for parsing, exploiting the information at many levels of the hierarchy: this allows to reduce the ambiguity, a very big problem in large scale NLP systems.

1   Introduction

Most current linguistic theories (LFG [9], GPSG [5], HPSG [12], CCG [16], LTAG [8]) shift information from syntactic categories to lexical items and give lexical accounts of several phenomena. This trend originally arose in linguistics from the observation that the constraints expressed on syntactic categories were too general to explain facts about words (e.g. the relation between a verb and its nominalization, *"destroy the city"* and *"destruction of the city"*), or to account uniformly for a number of phenomena (e.g. passivization) across languages.

Grammar and lexicon come to coincide, and the subcategorization frames associated with each lexical item contribute necessarily to the well-formedness of a syntactic structure. A subcategorization frame is a specification of the number and the type of elements that a lexical item requires (*subcategorizes for*) in order to be complete. For example, different verbs require different numbers of nominal elements in order to form a complete sentence. An intransitive verb such as *dormire*, "sleep", subcategorizes for only one nominal element (the subject), while a transitive verb such as *baciare*, "kiss", subcategorizes for two nominal elements (the subject and the object). This contribution of subcategorization frames to well-formedness also has a computational importance. The constraints posed by the subcategorization frames can reduce remarkably the number of alternative structures computed by the parser.

---

* We are indebted to Paola Merlo and Leonardo Lesmo for their precious support.

Some researchers [8] [14] have provided a formal definition of grammar lexicalization and have demonstrated some general results. A lexicalized grammar is a grammar that includes a lexical item (called *anchor*) in each elementary structure it defines (a tree in a Tree-Adjoining Grammar, a production rule in a Context-Free Grammar, ...). Schabes [14] has proved that the lexicalized grammars defined in this way are finitely ambiguous, i.e. there is no sentence of finite length that can be analyzed in an infinite number of ways, [2] and that it is decidable whether or not a string is accepted by a lexicalized grammar. Also, the expressive power of lexicalized grammars remains unchanged with respect to their non-lexicalized counterparts.

These linguistic and mathematical advantages of lexicalized formalisms are useful in practical applications. Currently, most large scale NLP systems adopt CFG-like grammars, that have to face the problem of syntactic ambiguity, because the constraints expressed on the syntactic categories are too general to limit the huge hypothesis space generated by wide-coverage grammars. To reduce computation time, systems employ several methods (stochastic approaches, shallow parsing, structure compaction, psycholinguistic preferences). The immediate application of individual item information (including subcategorization knowledge) can save computational resources that maybe avoid the necessity for these methods. At present, rare examples of wide-coverage lexicalized grammars do exist (see e.g. [6], [4]).

In parsing lexicalized grammars, substantial information can only be extracted when the item governing a certain phenomenon is encountered. This leads naturally to define bottom-up parsing techniques. However, pure bottom-up parsers (as the CKY parser [19]) have some computational limits if they are not augmented with a predictive component, since they do not exhibit the *valid prefix property*, i.e. the capability of detecting whether a substring is a valid prefix for the language defined by the grammar. A predictive component improves the practical performance of the parser, cutting off as soon as possible the incorrect structures.

The formalism described in this paper supports the design of a parser with a predictive component. Syntactic knowledge consists in an abstraction over the subcategorization frames associated with the lexical items. The formalism is expressed in the dependency paradigm, that, as we see in the next section, is particularly suitable to define the grammar constraints in terms of subcategorization frames. The formalism (presented in section 2) uses hierarchical representations of more and more loose subcategorization frames that avoid redundancy. Then we support the validity of the formalism by showing a classification of a number of Italian verbal frames (see the section 3 and the appendix at the end of the paper). Although the amount of data is still modest, this is the first attempt, to our knowledge, to provide a systematic description of the behaviour of lexical items in the Italian language, by referring to a uniform syntactic framework. In section 4, we discuss some related work and parsing issues.

---

[2] There are no heavily ambiguous, infinitely ambiguous or cyclic lexicalized grammars (such as $S \to SS$; $S \to a$; $S \to \epsilon$; see [18]).

2 The formalism

The formalism is expressed in the dependency approach. Dependency grammars describe the structure of a sentence in terms of binary relations (*dependency relations*) on the words of the sentence. A dependency relation is an asymmetric relation between a word called *head* and a word called *dependent*. One special word does not play the role of the dependent in any relation, and it is named the *root*. The set of the dependency relations that can be defined on a sentence form a tree, called the *dependency tree*. Figure 1 shows the dependency tree for the sentence *Paolo ama una ragazza con gli occhi verdi*, "Paolo loves a green-eyed girl". The verb *ama*, "loves", is the root of the sentence; it has two dependents, *Paolo* and *ragazza*, "girl", playing the roles of subject (*Sogg*) and object (*Ogg*), respectively. The word *ragazza*, "girl", has a dependent playing the role of Determiner (*Det*), *una*, "a", and a dependent playing the role of prepositional modifier (*P-Mod*), *con*, "with". The word *con*, "with", has a dependent playing the role of prepositional object (*P-Obj*), *occhi*, "eyes". The word *occhi*, "eyes", has a dependent playing the role of Determiner (*Det*), *gli*, "the", and a dependent playing the role of attribute (*Attr*), *verdi*, "green".

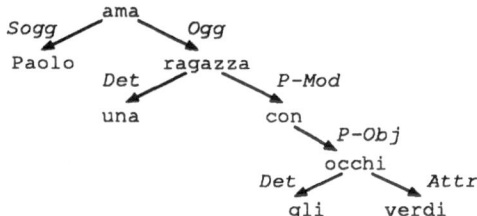

Fig. 1. Dependency structure of the sentence *Paolo ama una ragazza con gli occhi verdi*

A subcategorization frame associated with a lexical item x states which are the grammatical relations that must be necessarily realized in a well-formed dependency structure rooted by x. If we group subcategorization frames that are alike in one class, the whole grammar can be described in terms of successive abstractions over these classes. So, a class represents a syntactic category. In the rest of this section we give an informal description of the grammar, and an application of the formalism to the classification of 80 Italian verbal frames. Nouns, adjectives, prepositions have similar but less complex hierarchies. Formal descriptions and further empirical studies can be found in [2].

A dependency grammar is defined as a number of hierarchies of frame classes, plus a set of classes that can be the root of a dependency tree [3]. Frames are described by a finite number of parameters. Frames with the same restrictions on parameter values are in the same class; classes, in turn, form a hierarchy. A

---

[3] We refer to the context-free part of the grammar: we leave out phenomena that go beyond the context-free power.

class (figure 2) has a name (*ClassName*) and n dependents [4]. $r_1, \ldots, r_n$ are the names of the grammatical relations associated to the dependents, $I_1, \ldots, I_n$ the "ranges" of the relations (indicating the minimum and the maximum number of the possible instantiations), $S_1, \ldots, S_n$ the sets of categories that can instantiate the relations.

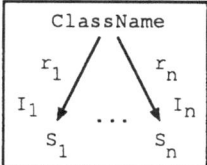

Fig. 2. The generic form of a subcategorization class.

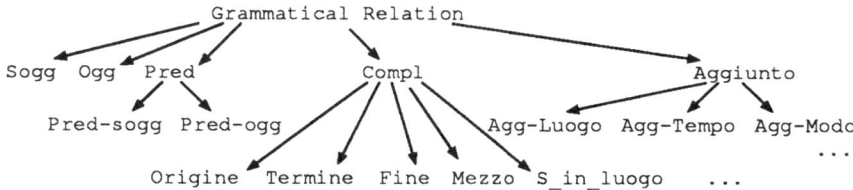

Fig. 3. Hierarchy of grammatical relations

Classes are organized in hierarchies, according to the values of the parameters. The class at the top of a hierarchy represents the loose constraints that can be abstracted over the totality of frame classes: it corresponds to the traditional notion of syntactic category. The constraints are inherited and progressively restricted in the subclasses of the hierarchy, including subcategorization frames that are described by more specific (restricted) parameter values. The (sub)classes down in the hierarchy can be termed as traditional subcategories. Restrictions on parameter values, that define the subsumption in the hierarchy, can occur in the following ways:

1. each grammatical relation r_i can be replaced by one of its "subrelations", if any, in reference to a hierarchy of grammatical relations. In the application to Italian verbal frames, the hierarchy of grammatical relations is sketched in figure 3. The names of the relations are written in Italian, as indicated in the Italian textbooks in linguistics [13], [1]. The main relations are: *Sogg* (subject), *Ogg* (direct object), *Pred* (predicative complement), *Compl* (complement), *Aggiunto* (Adjunct). The distinction between complements and

---

[4] The order between the dependents is kept free here: the Italian language allows, to a certain extent, free constituent order, even in written texts ([13], [17]).

adjuncts is not binary (central and peripheral elements of the predication), as we adopt a three-level distinction (see [15]): the complements are indicated as "obligatory" or "optional" in a subcategorization frame (i.e. necessary or simply expected), while the adjuncts are totally free. Some of the subrelations of the relation *Compl*, "Complement", are shown: *Origine*, "Origin", *Termine*, "Indirect Object", *Fine*, "Goal", *Mezzo*, "Instrument", *S_in_Luogo*, "Static Location", ... [5].

2. the range I of the number of the possible instantiations of the grammatical relations can be reduced. If $I = [0, inf]$, the corresponding relation can be instantiated an indefinite number of times, including none: in this case I corresponds to Kleene's star. $I' = [0, 1]$ restricts I: in this case the relation can be optionally instantiated just once. $I'' = [1, 1]$ restricts both I' and I, and forces the relation to be necessarily instantiated only once.

3. the set S can be restricted to one of its proper subsets. Usually, they are names of top classes (syntactic categories), but sometimes they can also be names of subclasses (as we will see in the example in figure 4).

3 An example

To test the suitability of the formalism to represent the syntactic knowledge of an actual natural language, we have carried out an experiment on the hierarchy of verbal frame classes. The restriction of investigation to verbs does not affect the generality of the model, since verbs present the most varied subcategorization frames. The material presented in the appendix (and partially here below) is a part of the empirical investigation. We have classified 105 verbal frames by analyzing a corpus of 500,000 words. The corpus includes short news reports, daily newspapers articles, novels, scientific dissertations and young students compositions. The methodology of investigation has been the following: we have started with the verbal frames proposed in [13] (and further ones selected from [11]), and we have organized them in a hierarchy, according to the formalism described above. Note that a verb can have several verbal frames, and that a verbal frame is usually common to many verbs. Then, we have automatically extracted from the corpus all the sentences that contained these verbs, and we have manually checked whether their use was accounted for by the classes already defined, and whether we needed some refinements and further classes. In this phase we have discovered some less common assignments of verbal frames to the verbs already classified: this type of information is usually neglected in the textbooks of linguistics. We have classified 105 verbal frames in 40 classes; we show 80 frames (in 23 classes) in the appendix. The result is a promising starting point for a project that aims at developing a large scale dependency grammar for Italian. Note that,

---

[5] Note that we use Italian terms to label grammatical relations. Since subcategorization frames are language-dependent, we prefer to avoid confusions due to different terminology across languages. For example, the relation *Termine* actually corresponds to the indirect object in English. However *I-Obj* undergoes the double accusative transformation into *Obj*, while *Termine* doesn't.

in our approach, developing a large scale grammar is not an extra effort with respect to developing the lexicon. However, once the lexicon is developed, the definitive test will be the application of the parsing algorithm outlined in the next section to unrestricted texts, and the evaluation of the results in terms of the number of structures explored.

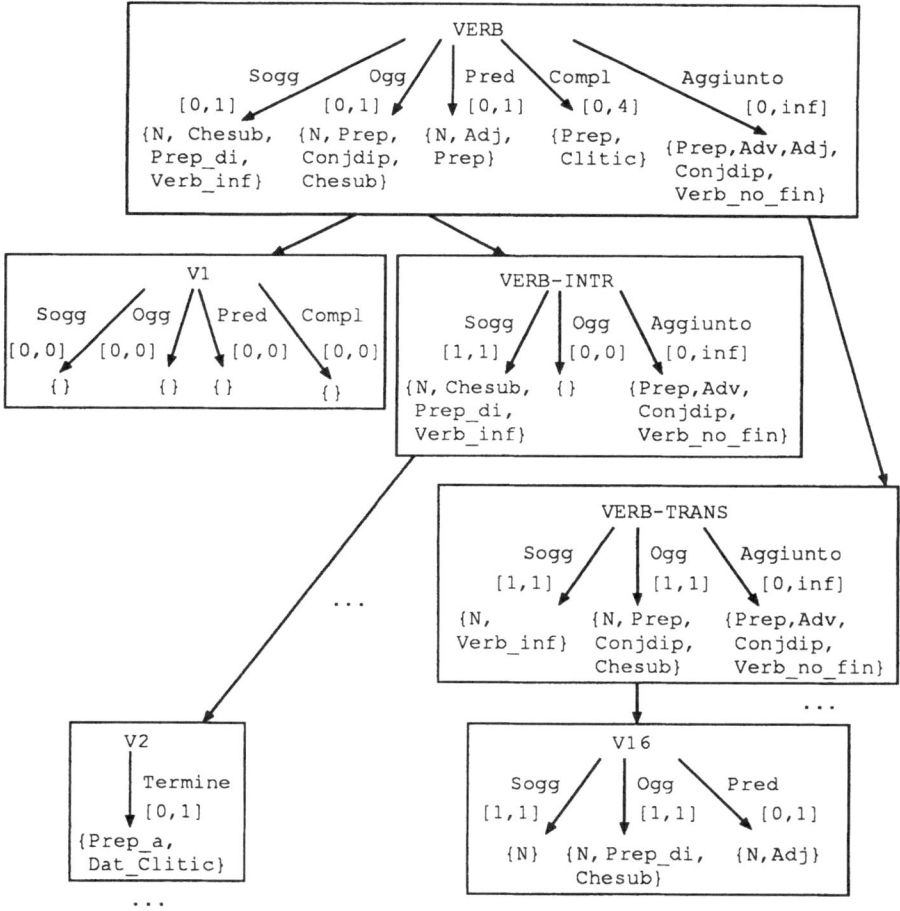

Fig. 4. Sketch of subcategorization hierarchy for Italian verbs

The hierarchy in figure 4 is a simplified sketch of the upper level of the hierarchy, for explanation purposes. Frame classes can be abstract or concrete: abstract classes (named VERB, VERB-INTR and VERB-TRANS) do not contain any actual verbal frame but are intermediate nodes in the hierarchy and serve computational purposes; concrete classes (named VI) contain actual verbal frames (see the appendix for some examples). The top class (VERB) represents the general loose constraints for Italian verbs. Even if such constraints may not seem so natural to the reader, s/he may consider that they have been automatically abstracted from the constraints at the lower levels. A generic verb can subcategorize for 5 types of dependents: an optional subject (*Sogg*, [0,1]), realized by a nominal group (that has a nominal element, *N*, as head) or an embedded clause (headed by a complementizer, *Chesub*, by a preposition *di*, *Prep_di*, or by an infinitive verb, *Verb_inf*); an optional object (*Ogg*, [0,1]), realized by one of nouns, prepositions, conjunctions, complementizers; an optional predicative complement; at most 4 complements, including none, realized by prepositional groups or pronouns; finally, an indefinite number of adjuncts. The subclasses inherit and restrict the constraints at the top of the hierarchy. The top class has three daughters. V1 is the class of impersonal verbs, that can only have adjuncts as dependents (the restriction is on the range, [0, 0], of the other relations). For example, we can say *Piove sui tetti della città*, "It rains on the roofs of the town". The abstract classes VERB-INTR and VERB-TRANS corresponds to intransitive and transitive verbs, respectively. VERB-INTR requires an obligatory subject ([1, 1]) and it cannot have a direct object ([0, 0]). VERB-TRANS requires an obligatory subject ([1, 1]), that can just be headed by a nominal element or by an infinitive verb, and an obligatory object ([1, 1]). A subclass of VERB-INTR, V2, is shown: its only restriction is on the relation *Compl*, which is specialized on the subrelation *Termine*, having a range [0, 1], and having *Prep_a* (preposition *a*, "to") and *Dat_Clitic* (dative clitic) as associated categories (these last ones are subcategories of *Prep* and *Clitic*, respectively). For example, the verb *sembrare*, "seem", belongs to this class (we can say *A Luigi Maria sembra bellissima*, "Maria seems to Luigi as a very nice girl"). V16, a subclass of VERB-TRANS, makes some restrictions on the set of categories associated to the relations *Sogg*, *Ogg*, *Pred*.

4 Discussion and Parsing Issues

There exist other lexicalized approaches that make use of hierarchies to organize the information. Hudson [7], for example, adopts a dependency approach and uses hierarchies to organize all kinds of information (morphological, syntactic, semantic). However, he does not go deep in the subcategorization problem; more important, the computational aspects are not examined.

HPSG theory [12] proposes a hierarchical organization of lexical information. As concerns subcategorization in HPSG, two problems arise: the first one is the interaction between rule schemata and subcategorization information ([3]), the second one is the formal treatment of a hierarchical organization of subcategorization restrictions. With this second point we mean that there is an intrinsic difficulty to represent subsumption of subcategorization frames, because of the limitations of the data structure used in HPSG to represent subcategorization frames, namely lists. In the dependency approach described above these problems do not arise: first, as the grammatical constraints are expressed in the hierarchy itself, the information about the dependents subcategorized for by a lexical item is sufficient to define the structure rooted by that item; second, the parameters used to define classes have well-defined restrictions in terms of the hierarchy of grammatical relations, interval inclusion, and set inclusion, respectively.

Another important lexicalized approach is given by LTAG [8]. In this formalism, the lexical items are associated with the syntactic structures in which they can appear (lexicalized elementary trees). Hierarchical representations of LTAG have been proposed (e.g. [4]), defining tree families: a tree family contains the different possible trees for a given canonical subcategorization (or predicate-argument structure). The computational properties of LTAG have also been studied: Joshi and Schabes [8] developed, for extremely lexicalized TAG (not the hierarchical form), a bottom-up parser that uses top-down information in order to have the valid prefix property. Even in this case, empirical results are needed to evaluate the suitability of the approach for practical parsing.

In terms of our formalism, we need a parser which is able to navigate the class hierarchies [6]. Then we sketch an Earley-type parser [7].

Initially, the parser guesses the presence of a node of a root category in the dependency tree. Then, in general, given a node N of class D and a word w in the input sentence (from left to right), we can apply three phases:

- PREDICTOR: Predictor guesses the presence of the left dependents of N (according to the constraints of its class D) and, after the Scanner scans the head word, of its right dependents.

- SCANNER: Scanner scans w, head word of N, after all the left dependents. The class of w must be a subclass (proper or not) of the current class D of N. Incompatibility of classes causes the analysis path to be abandoned.

- COMPLETER: When all the right dependents of N have been analyzed, Completer returns the control to the node N', the father of N. The successful completion of a dependent of N' allows to descend the class hierarchy towards more specific classes (and more restrictive constraints). In general, the following rule holds (necessary and sufficient conditions). Let's suppose that D' is the current class of N', $Daughters = \{D'_1, \ldots, D'_p\}$ is the set of the classes that are daughters of D' in the hierarchy, the node N of category D is linked to N' via a relation rel. The set $Daughters$, associated with N', can be reduced by eliminating the classes D'_i in which rel is restricted with a range $I = [0,0]$ or in which D does not belong to the set of categories S specified for rel in D'_i. If just one class D'_j remains in the $Daughters$ set, it is possible to descend directly in this class, i.e. the class D' is replaced by D'_j in N'. Reducing the set of the daughters classes allows to cut off hypotheses that in any case will turn out to be wrong.

---

[6] For practical parsing, transformation rules are also needed, from the "deep" frames to the "superficial" frames as passives, null-subject sentences, ... We do not treat them in this paper.

[7] The description in Earley's terms is not compelling (one of the authors has already implemented an Earley-type parser for a non-lexicalized dependency grammar [10]): any parsing schema with a predictive component can suffice (e.g. a chart parser).

Let's consider two intuitive examples, on the hierarchy of figure 4. If, starting from the top, we read in input a noun (N) and we consider it as the subject, we can rule out the class of impersonal verbs ($V1$), as the latter does not admit a subject. Let's suppose, on the contrary, that, starting from the top, a direct object is read (of any one of the possible categories): in this case, we can directly descend in the class of the transitive verbs (*Verb-trans*), as the other classes at the same level do not admit a direct object. The same mechanism is valid on the subsequent levels of the hierarchy, for other modifiers.

5 Conclusion

This paper has illustrated a hierarchical dependency grammar, based on the abstraction of subcategorization frames. We have described the grammar formalism, and sketched a parsing algorithm that exhibits the valid prefix property, by employing a predictive component. We have applied the formalism to classify 105 Italian verbal frames.

The next step of the work will be to develop a large scale lexicon in a semiautomatic way, and then to test the coverage of the classification and the improvements given by the predictive component (number of alternative hypotheses for a sentence, computation time) in the analysis of Italian texts.

References

1. G. Ravera Aira, R. Maurizzi, and F. Piazzi. *Grammatica italiana*. Paccagnella Editore, 1980.
2. C. Barbero. *Subcategorization in Dependency Grammar and Parsing*. Doctoral Dissertation, Centro di Scienza Cognitiva, Università di Torino, forthcoming, 1997.
3. R. Borsley. Subjects and complements in HPSG. *Report CSLI, Stanford, CA: Center for the Study of Language and Information*, pages 87–107, 1987.
4. M.H. Candito. A principle-based hierarchical representation of LTAGs. In *Proceedings of COLING'96*, 1996.
5. G. Gazdar, E. Klein, G.K. Pullum, and I.A. Sag. *Generalized Phrase Structure Grammars*. Blackwell Publishing, Oxford, 1985.
6. XTAG Group. A Lexicalized Tree-Adjoining Grammar of English. *Techical Report, IRCS, University of Pennsylvania*, 1995.
7. R. Hudson. *English Word Grammar*. Basil Blackwell, 1990.
8. A. Joshi and Y. Schabes. Tree-Adjoining Grammars. In A. Salomaa and G. Rozenberg, editors, *Handbook of Formal Languages and Automata*. Springer-Verlag, Berlin, 1996.
9. R. Kaplan and J. Bresnan. Lexical-Functional Grammar: a Formal System for Grammatical Representation. In J. Bresnan, editor, *The Mental Representation of Grammatical Relations*, pages 173–281. MIT Press, Cambridge, Mass., 1983.
10. V. Lombardo and L. Lesmo. An Earley-type recognizer for Dependency Grammar. In *Proceedings of COLING'96*, 1996.
11. F. Palazzi and G. Folena. *Dizionario della lingua italiana*. Loescher, 1992.
12. C. Pollard and I. Sag. *Head-Driven Phrase Structure Grammar*. The University of Chicago Press, Chicago, IL, 1994.

13. L. Renzi. *Grande grammatica italiana di consultazione*. Il Mulino, 1988.
14. Y. Schabes. *Mathematical and Computational Aspects of Lexicalized Grammars*. PhD thesis, University of Pennsylvania, 1990.
15. H.L. Somers. *Valency and Case in Computational Linguistics*. Edinburgh University Press, 1987.
16. M. Steedman. Combinatory Grammars and parasitic gaps. *Natural Language and Linguistic Theory*, 5:403–439, 1987.
17. O. Stock. Parsing with flexibility, dynamic strategies, and idioms in mind. *Computational Linguistics*, 15:1–18, 1989.
18. M. Tomita. *Efficient Parsing for Natural Language*. Kluwer Academic Publishers, 1985.
19. D.H. Younger. Recognition and parsing of Context-Free languages in time n^3. *Information and Control*, 10/2:189–208, 1967.

A   Appendix: classification of 80 Italian verbal frames

We show here the classification that we have individuated for 80 Italian verbal frames, by examining the corpus above described. For each class, we indicate the name of the class, the list of its subclasses, the verbs that came out to belong to that class from the analysis of the corpus, and the grammatical relations that characterize the class (with specification of the range and the set of categories associated to the relations). For each class, the whole set of its relations is indicated (by means of the inheritance mechanism on the hierarchy).

- VERB (subclasses [V1,VERB-INTR,VERB-TRANS]).
- VERB-INTR (subclasses [V2,V7,V10,V11]).
- VERB-TRANS (subclasses [V12,V16,V17,V19,V22]).
- V1 (subclasses []): NEVICARE-1 ("snow"), PIOVERE-1 ("rain"), TUONARE-1 ("thunder"), DILUVIARE-1 ("pour"), GRANDINARE-1 ("hail"), LAMPEGGIARE-1 ("lighten"), PIOVIGGINARE-1 ("drizzle").
  $< Aggiunto, [0, inf], \{Prep, Adv, Adj, Conjdip, Verb\_no\_fin\} >$
- V2 (subclasses [V3,V6]): SEMBRARE ("seem"), PARERE ("appear").
  $< Sogg, [1, 1], \{N, Chesub, Verb\_inf, Prep\_di\} >$
  $< Pred, [0, 1], \{N, Adj, Prep\} > < Termine, [0, 1], \{Prep\_a, Dat\_Clitic\} >$
  $< Aggiunto, [0, inf], \{Prep, Adv, Conjdip, Verb\_no\_fin\} >$
- V3 (subclasses [V4]): ESSERE-1 ("be").
  $< Sogg, [1, 1], \{N, Chesub, Verb\_inf\} > < Pred, [0, 1], \{N, Adj, Prep\} >$
  $< Aggiunto, [0, inf], \{Prep, Adv, Conjdip, Verb\_no\_fin\} >$
- V4 (subclasses [V5]): DIVENTARE ("become").
  $< Sogg, [1, 1], \{N, Verb\_inf\} > < Pred, [0, 1], \{N, Adj, Prep\_come, Prep\_di\} >$
  $< Aggiunto, [0, inf], \{Prep, Adv, Conjdip, Verb\_no\_fin\} >$
- V5 (subclasses []): PRANZARE ("dine"), TOSSIRE ("cough"), NEVICARE-2 ("snow"), PIOVERE-2 ("rain"), TUONARE-2 ("thunder"), GRANDINARE-2 ("hail"), LAMPEGGIARE-2 ("lighten"), DILUVIARE-2 ("pour"), PIOVIGGINARE-2 ("drizzle").
  $< Sogg, [1, 1], \{N\} > < Pred, [0, 1], \{Adj\} >$
  $< Aggiunto, [0, inf], \{Prep, Adv, Conjdip, Verb\_no\_fin\} >$
- V6 (subclasses []): CONVENIRE-1 ("suit"), PIACERE ("like"), OCCORRERE-1 ("need").
  $< Sogg, [1, 1], \{N, Chesub, Verb\_inf\} > < Pred, [0, 1], \{Adj\} >$

$< Termine, \; [0,1], \; \{Prep\_a, Dat\_Clitic\} >$
$< Aggiunto, \; [0,inf], \; \{Prep, Adv, Conjdip, Verb\_no\_fin\} >$
- V7 (subclasses [V8,V9]): SERVIRE-1 ("serve").
  $< Sogg, \; [1,1], \; \{N, Chesub, Verb\_inf\} >$
  $< Pred, \; [0,1], \; \{Adj, Prep\_da, Prep\_come\} >$
  $< Fine, \; [0,1], \; \{Prep\_a, Prep\_per\} > \; < Termine, \; [0,1], \; \{Prep\_a, Dat\_Clitic\} >$
  $< Aggiunto, \; [0,inf], \; \{Prep, Adv, Conjdip, Verb\_no\_fin\} >$
- V8 (subclasses []): CORRERE-2 ("run").
  $< Sogg, \; [1,1], \; \{N\} > \; < Pred, \; [0,1], \; \{Adj\} > \; < Fine, \; [1,1], \; \{Prep\_a\_inf\} >$
  $< Aggiunto, \; [0,inf], \; \{Prep, Adv, Conjdip, Verb\_no\_fin\} >$
- V9 (subclasses []): BASTARE ("be enough").
  $< Sogg, \; [1,1], \; \{N, Chesub, Verb\_inf\} > \; < Fine, \; [0,1], \; \{Prep\_a, Prep\_per\} >$
  $< Termine, \; [0,1], \; \{Prep\_a, Dat\_Clitic\} >$
  $< Aggiunto, \; [0,inf], \; \{Prep, Adv, Conjdip, Verb\_no\_fin\} >$
- V10 (subclasses []): SALIRE-2 ("go up"), SCENDERE-2 ("go down").
  $< Sogg, \; [1,1], \; \{N\} > \; < Pred, \; [0,1], \; \{Adj\} > \; < Estensione, \; [1,1], \; \{Prep\_di\} >$
  $< Aggiunto, \; [0,inf], \; \{Prep, Adv, Conjdip, Verb\_no\_fin\} >$
- V11 (subclasses []): SALIRE-1 ("get on"), CORRERE-1 ("run"), SCAPPARE-1 ("escape"), SALTARE-1 ("jump").
  $< Sogg, \; [1,1], \; \{N\} > \; < Pred, \; [0,1], \; \{Adj\} >$
  $< Moto\_da\_luogo, \; [0,1], \; \{Prep\_da\} >$
  $< Moto\_a\_luogo, \; [0,1], \; \{Prep\_a, Prep\_su, Prep\_in, Prep\_sopra, Prep\_verso\} >$
  $< Moto\_per\_luogo, \; [0,1], \; \{Prep\_per, Prep\_attraverso\} >$
  $< Aggiunto, \; [0,inf], \; \{Prep, Adv, Conjdip, Verb\_no\_fin\} >$
- V12 (subclasses [V13]): SCRIVERE-1 ("write").
  $< Sogg, \; [1,1], \; \{N\} > \; < Locativo, \; [0,1], \; \{Prep\_in, Prep\_su\} >$
  $< Pred, \; [0,1], \; \{Adj\} > \; < Ogg, \; [1,1], \; \{N, Chesub, Prep\_di\} >$
  $< Termine, \; [0,1], \; \{Prep\_a, Dat\_Clitic\} >$
  $< Aggiunto, \; [0,inf], \; \{Prep, Adv, Conjdip, Verb\_no\_fin\} >$
- V13 (subclasses [V14]): LEGGERE-1 ("read").
  $< Sogg, \; [1,1], \; \{N\} > \; < Locativo, \; [0,1], \; \{Prep\_in, Prep\_su\} >$
  $< Pred, \; [0,1], \; \{Adj\} > \; < Ogg, \; [1,1], \; \{N, Chesub\} >$
  $< Termine, \; [0,1], \; \{Prep\_a, Dat\_Clitic\} >$
  $< Aggiunto, \; [0,inf], \; \{Prep, Adv, Conjdip, Verb\_no\_fin\} >$
- V14 (subclasses [V15]): DISEGNARE-1 ("draw"), CANTARE-1 ("sing"), DIPINGERE-1 ("paint"), CUCINARE-1 ("cook"), SUONARE-1 ("play").
  $< Sogg, \; [1,1], \; \{N\} > \; < Pred, \; [0,1], \; \{Adj\} >$
  $< Ogg, \; [1,1], \; \{N\} > \; < Termine, \; [0,1], \; \{Prep\_a, Dat\_Clitic\} >$
  $< Aggiunto, \; [0,inf], \; \{Prep, Adv, Conjdip, Verb\_no\_fin\} >$
- V15 (subclasses []): MANGIARE-1 ("eat"), BERE-1 ("drink"), STUDIARE-1 ("study"), ALLATTARE-1 ("suckle").
  $< Sogg, \; [1,1], \; \{N\} > \; < Ogg, \; [1,1], \; \{N\} > \; < Pred, \; [0,1], \; \{Adj\} >$
  $< Aggiunto, \; [0,inf], \; \{Prep, Adv, Conjdip, Verb\_no\_fin\} >$
- V16 (subclasses []): CREDERE-1 ("believe"), PENSARE-1 ("think"), SUPPORRE ("suppose"), GIUDICARE ("judge"), PRESUMERE ("presume").
  $< Sogg, \; [1,1], \; \{N\} > \; < Pred, \; [0,1], \; \{N, Adj, Prep\} >$
  $< Ogg, \; [1,1], \; \{N, Chesub, Prep\_di\} >$
  $< Aggiunto, \; [0,inf], \; \{Prep, Adv, Conjdip, Verb\_no\_fin\} >$
- V17 (subclasses [V18]): DICHIARARE ("declare"), ANNUNCIARE ("announce"), RIVELARE ("reveal"), CONFESSARE ("confess"), PROVARE ("prove"),

PROMETTERE ("promise").

$< Sogg, [1,1], \{N\} > < Termine, [0,1], \{Prep\_a, Dat\_Clitic\} >$
$< Pred, [0,1], \{Adj\} > < Ogg, [1,1], \{N, Chesub, Prep\_di\} >$
$< Aggiunto, [0,inf], \{Prep, Adv, Conjdip, Verb\_no\_fin\} >$

- V18 (subclasses []): SOSTENERE ("maintain"), CONSTATARE ("ascertain"), ASSUMERE ("assume").

$< Sogg, [1,1], \{N\} > < Pred, [0,1], \{Adj\} >$
$< Ogg, [1,1], \{N, Chesub, Prep\_di\} >$
$< Aggiunto, [0,inf], \{Prep, Adv, Conjdip, Verb\_no\_fin\} >$

- V19 (subclasses [V20]): PROPORRE ("propose").

$< Sogg, [1,1], \{N\} > < Termine, [0,1], \{Prep\_a, Dat\_Clitic\} >$
$< Pred, [0,1], \{Adj, Prep\_come\} > < Ogg, [1,1], \{N, Chesub, Prep\_di\} >$
$< Aggiunto, [0,inf], \{Prep, Adv, Conjdip, Verb\_no\_fin\} >$

- V20 (subclasses [V21]): BACIARE ("kiss"), GRAFFIARE ("scratch"), PALPARE ("touch"), AFFERRARE ("seize"), PIZZICARE ("pinch"), AFFITTARE ("rent"), CEDERE ("give"), PAGARE-1 ("pay"), COMPORRE ("compose"), COSTRUIRE ("build").

$< Sogg, [1,1], \{N\} > < Ogg, [1,1], \{N\} > < Pred, [0,1], \{Adj\} >$
$< Termine, [0,1], \{Prep\_a, Dat\_Clitic\} >$
$< Aggiunto, [0,inf], \{Prep, Adv, Conjdip, Verb\_no\_fin\} >$

- V21 (subclasses []): COLLEZIONARE ("collect"), AMMASSARE ("heap"), FORGIARE ("forge"), SEMINARE ("sow"), ACCUMULARE ("accumulate"), RACCOGLIERE ("gather"), GUIDARE ("drive").

$< Sogg, [1,1], \{N\} > < Ogg, [1,1], \{N\} > < Pred, [0,1], \{Adj\} >$
$< Aggiunto, [0,inf], \{Prep, Adv, Conjdip, Verb\_no\_fin\} >$

- V22 (subclasses [V23]): DARE ("give"), REGALARE ("make a present").

$< Sogg, [1,1], \{N, Verb\_inf\} > < Pred, [0,1], \{Adj\} >$
$< Ogg, [1,1], \{N\} > < Termine, [0,1], \{Prep\_a, Dat\_Clitic\} >$
$< Aggiunto, [0,inf], \{Prep, Adv, Conjdip, Verb\_no\_fin\} >$

- V23 (subclasses []): AVVICINARE ("approach"), CONDURRE ("lead").

$< Sogg, [1,1], \{N, Verb\_inf\} > < Pred, [0,1], \{Adj\} >$
$< Ogg, [1,1], \{N\} > < Termine, [0,1], \{Prep\_a\} >$
$< Aggiunto, [0,inf], \{Prep, Adv, Conjdip, Verb\_no\_fin\} >$

Flexible Response Choice Using Problem-Solving Plans and Rhetorical Relations

Paolo Barboni and Dario Sestero

Dipartimento di Informatica
Università degli Studi di Torino
Corso Svizzera n. 185 - 10149 Torino - Italy
e-mail: barboni.paolo@educ.di.unito.it
dario@di.unito.it

Abstract. In this paper we present an architecture for choosing a flexible response in a natural language system involved in information-seeking tasks. Our work considers the crucial issue of choosing what information to provide and how to structure it, considering from the generation perspective a model of dialogue that was previously developed to study the recognition activity of an agent. In such a model the underlying reasoning activity of an agent is represented by means of problem-solving plans, that manage domain and linguistic actions. The correct choice of the information to provide depends on the ability to select the action that best suits the domain situation and an answer that conveys the information in a way appropriate to the user. For this reason we provide heuristic evaluation criteria that consider both participants' goals and some other context-related factors impacting on the evaluation of the action to allow the problem-solving plans to make a choice among the available alternatives. Furthermore, we discuss how to convey the raw material in a suitable and understandable way by using different rhetorical relations. A detailed example illustrates how our approach models in a flexible way aspects of the interaction overlooked by previous systems.

1 Introduction

In building a system capable of natural language interaction with a human being, a key issue is how the context (dialogic and pragmatic) constrains the structure of the ongoing dialogue[1]. In fact, the context provides the basis both for the recognition of an agent's goals and plans and for the construction of an answer that "makes sense".

In the analysis of linguistic context, previous research has identified several kinds of relationships between sentences; these relationships can be understood in terms of different kinds of knowledge: *domain* (e.g. in (1) A refers to a domain plan, C to a constraint on it, and D to an alternative plan for a related[2] goal); *rhetorical* (in (1) C is clearly intended as a justification for B, and E as an enablement allowing the user to perform D; furthermore, BC and DE stand in a relation of contrast, while A and the complex BCDE constitute a question-answer pair); and *problem-solving* (in (1) the user is asking A because there is a problem-solving plan saying that in order to reach a goal, an action having the goal among its effects can be selected; for what concerns

---

[1] At present time we are considering two-participants dialogues.

[2] We consider as related two goals having a common subgoal; in the example meeting professor Verdi and sending him an e-mail are related because both include the more generic goal of communicating with him.

the goal of obtaining an exchange with professor Verdi, meeting him is such an action. On the other hand, the system is suggesting D as an alternative action because it has the goal "minimize the time spent by the professor talking with students outside his office hours" and is performing a problem-solving plan that tries to balance this goal with the user's one).

(1)   A: May I meet professor Verdi?
        B: No, you cannot,
        C: because he does not receive now;
        D: but you can send him an e-mail
        E: at verdi@di.unito.it.

As can be seen from the previous example, the structure and content of the system answer are made out of the interaction of various layers of knowledge. Previous research in generation focused on the relationship between discourse and domain knowledge ([1], [17], [20], [10]) or on the rhetorical and pragmatic goals of the explainer ([16], [12], [19]). On the recognition side, some attention has been devoted to the problem-solving activity of an information-seeking agent and the way he moves when considering possible future courses of actions ([21], [7]). Although these studies gave important insights about an agent's plans and goals, we argue that none of them provides an explicit account of the relationship between the domain goals of the interactants and their response behavior. For example, in dialogue (1) these approaches cannot explain why the system chooses to provide professor Verdi's e-mail address rather than his office hours.

Our goal is to develop the content-selection component of a consultation system on a restricted domain[3]; the system should decide what to say by keeping into account both the user's and the system's goals. In particular, given some general goals of the system (like "maintain a good face"[4]), and some specific ones related to the domain of interest (like the above-mentioned one regarding professor-time scheduling), a *main content* selection phase considers how possible alternative courses of action realize to a lesser or greater extent the system's goals and the other agent's expectations. A subsequent *structuring* phase decides which rhetorical strategies are best suited to convey the previously selected material, what additional material is needed, and the structure to impose over it. The same mechanism is used to plan the system's behavior in both phases: a problem-solving plan layer represents explicitly the reasoning activity of a rational agent interacting through natural language with another agent in a restricted domain and the process of selecting a reasonable act.

Our problem-solving layer is designed to be used in generation as well as in recognition; in this paper we will focus on the analysis of the possible courses of action and on their scoring according to a number of context-related factors, including user's and system's goals, complexity of the candidate action, its applicability in the current situation, and user's knowledge of it. In such a way it is possible to obtain a

---

[3]The system should provide consultation about the services offered by a Computer Science department.

[4]In pragmatics the concept of face was introduced by Brown and Levinson [6] to characterize some wants that every participant to a dialogue normally has about freedom of action and self-image. They use this notion to explain why the interlocutors tend to smoothe the interaction by exploiting indirect forms of communications.

broad range of behaviors, resulting in the production of flexible responses. The approach we adopt accounts for the relationship between clarification subdialogues and the agents' goals in information-seeking dialogues, i.e. for the need of an agent to know enough to choose among different alternatives. Furthermore, such an approach enforces an agent model that can be used to define a notion of coherence in a dialogue.

2 Related Work

Recently, various models have been proposed to deal with plan recognition and sentence planning in dialogue.

Carberry and her collaborators [9] structured a cycle of actions for modeling collaborative activities adopting a tripartite dialogue model that deals with intentions at three levels: domain, problem solving and discourse. The first one contains the domain plan being constructed for later execution; the problem-solving level registers agents' intentions about how to construct the *domain* plan, and the discourse level contains the communicative plan initiated to further their mutual problem-solving intentions. These authors focus on the detection and resolution of the conflicts arising between two agents involved in building a shared plan. On the other hand, we are more concerned with a cooperative system, able to adopt goals and choose linguistic or domain actions in order to achieve them. Furthermore, using their framework for generation purposes requires to apply some planner to each of the three layers, while our problem-solving layer, representing the knowledge that an agent exploits in building a plan, *is* the planner. This means that we encoded in a declarative form all the knowledge responsible for rational, goal-oriented behavior of an agent interacting with another one, so that we have it available both for recognition and generation purposes. In particular, in generation, we need only an interpreter of the problem-solving plan representation language to build the partially instantiated plans that constitute the output of the system.

In our approach linguistic plans include speech acts and rhetorical relations where the latter express coherent ways to link speech acts in a discourse [16]. Hovy [13] showed how rhetorical relations can be operationalized by means of a plan library but he conflated intentional and rhetorical structure (see the discussion in [18]).
In [8] it is claimed that rhetorical relations, though necessary, are not sufficient. So we use rhetorical relations in the content structuring phase for choosing how to best combine the material coming from the content selection phase. In this way the inadequate treatment of intentions doesn't affect the content selection, confining them on linking the contents in a coherent way, appropriate to the user level of expertise and to the dialog context.

Moore [19] works out the conflate of intentional and rhetorical structure by allowing a many to many mapping of intentions on rhetorical relations. Her system PEA, designed to aid users in enhancing LISP programs by suggesting transformations that improve their readability and maintainability, is concerned with explanatory dialogues. It doesn't possess natural language understanding capabilities: the user can react by pointing to the portion of text not understood or typing predefined sequences of words in order to have extra information. On the contrary we are concerned with dialogues: in our system the input is interpreted, a user model dynamically updated, and goals not explicit in the text are inferred.

Furthermore, on the basis of this input, the system can perform an action in the domain or provide information about the action execution. This information may be either about the action itself (in which case it is communicated to enable the user to succesfully perform the plan), or it may concern the problem-solving process (in which case it is communicated to keep the synchronization between the agents). For such a task, having a set of communicative strategies that consider all possible things to say would be redundant, and this is one of the reasons for adopting a two-phases process where the main content is selected on the basis of the current system's goals and general rhetorical strategies are subsequently used to structure the content and make it understandable.

To provide a flexible explanation, when the first reply is not satisfactory, PEA uses a set of selection heuristics to choose the best plan. These heuristics refer either to the user acquaintance with the concepts involved, giving high scores to plans that avoid making assumptions on user's knowledge or mental state, or to features of the communicative plans, like their coherence with the previous dialogue, specificity and verbosity. We have adopted scoring criteria resembling Moore's ones in our *Explore* problem-solving plan with some important differences. First, we added some heuristics to take into account the current situation (by considering the truth value of the preconditions) and the action complexity (in terms of its decomposition). Second, while Moore's heuristics implicitly encode the linguistic behavior of the system, we made explicit all the system's goals. In particular, the system has some basic goals (like *be-cooperative*, *mantain-good-face*, or *preserve-resource-integrity*) and is able to derive new ones, related to the current situation, from these and the ones recognized from the user's utterance by means of some intention-acquisition heuristics. In this way the same mechanism can be used to derive both domain and linguistic goals. After the selection of the goal to be pursued, scoring criteria are used to evaluate the candidate actions that reach it. For these reasons our scoring criteria take into account also the impact of the action on the user's and system's goals.
Furthermore, in our system, the scoring criteria affect the evaluation of every action planned by the system, since they are used every time actions are planned, and not only in case the first system output was unsatisfactory.

Cawsey [10] takes into account the crucial aspect of interactivity in human explanatory dialogue. Her system EDGE plans tutorial explanations on structure and behavior of electric circuits and covers aspects like conversation management (e.g. handling user interruptions), topic shift and generation of meta-comments (e.g. "We'll be getting to this argument in a moment").
Though Cawsey uses discourse plans to model different interactions between system and user, she doesn't have a general mechanism to make the discourse dependent on the available content and the participants' goals. On the other hand we achieve a more flexible result by making the problem-solving plans direct the system behavior, entrusting the rhetorical strategies with the task of including all the information relevant and structuring it in order to make an understandable contribution to the dialog.

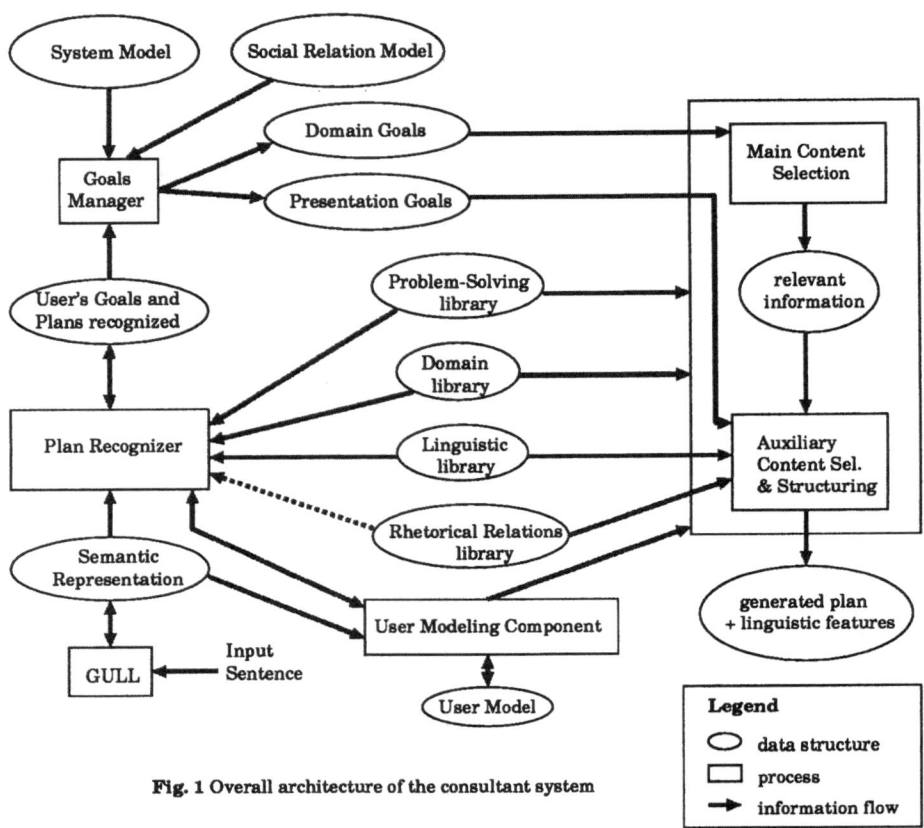

Fig. 1 Overall architecture of the consultant system

3 Overall Architecture

The overall architecture of our dialogue system is shown in fig. 1; on the left side are visible the main recognition components and on the right side the content selection and structuring components on which we focus in this paper. We adopt a library of problem-solving meta-plans manipulating domain and linguistic (including indirect and rhetorical) plans. Fig. 1 also shows that the same libraries serve both the recognition and the generation phases; in this way the relevant knowledge can be expressed only once in a declarative way, and the procedures used in the two phases are simpler. Furthermore, exploiting common knowledge for both processes seems reasonable from a cognitive point of view .

Input sentences from the user are first syntactically and semantically analyzed by the GULL natural language interpreter [15].
The semantic representation is given in input to the plan recognizer that extracts the user's goals and plans [1], [2]. After each input sentence the user model is updated on the basis of the meaning of the input and the goals recognized [4]. After the pragmatic analysis is completed, the goal manager decides which goal to adopt by means of some heuristics that consider the balance between user's and computer's goals. Currently the goal manager is not fully developed and it simply adopts all the user's domain goals that doesn't explicitly conflict with computer's ones. Furthermore, the

manager activates some presentational goals related to the way in which the selected material should be conveyed to the particular user.

Domain goals are used to choose the actions that satisfy them and the information needed to an agent to carry them out. Presentational goals allows to choose suitable linguistic forms, which can then suggest the inclusion of further domain-related material.

The output consists of an instantiated three-fold plan containing problem-solving, domain and linguistic actions. In particular, the linguistic part could be the input for a subsequent surface generator module that would use also the linguistic features associated to the adopted rhetorical relation to relate different text spans.

The system makes use of four action libraries that contain, respectively, the knowledge about the problem-solving plans, the actions of the domain, the speech-acts and the rhetorical relations. These libraries are written using a common formalism derived from Kautz [14]. It employs generalization and decomposition hierarchies to relate the actions and provides standard means for specifying constraints, preconditions, effects, and optional steps.

While the decomposition hierarchy specifies the steps needed to perform an action, the generalization hierarchy allows to represent alternative ways to perform each of them, inheriting common parts (e.g. the *Exchange-info* action may be specialized in *Talk* and *Send-e-mail)*.

The problem-solving library describes the reasoning activity of an agent building a plan to reach a goal and trying to perform it. In particular, our library models the interactions between agents produced by this activity. According to the principles of rational interaction [11] two agents acting in a common environment interact to notify to each other some conditions related to the planning process (e.g. unfeasibility of an action, satisfaction of wanted goal) and some aspects of the actions they consider relevant in order to successfully perform them (e.g. constraints, preconditions).

The main action in the problem-solving library is the $Satisfy(a,s,g)$ action, representing how an agent behaves when he wants to satisfy a goal, possibly interacting with another agent. It has three arguments specifying the agent that acts (a, for actor), the agent that made the request (s, for source), and the goal g. *Satisfy* chooses a feasible action among those having the goal in their effects list, makes true the preconditions not yet satisfied, and performs the actions in its decomposition, possibly interacting with the other agent according to the above-mentioned principles of rational interaction.

Standard epistemic operators like *Know-recipe*, *Know-if*, *Know-ref*, and *Goal* are used to deal with user and system beliefs. An agent know-recipe an action if he knows its constraints, preconditions, effects and decomposition. He know-if a condition if he knows its truth value. *Know-ref* denotes the agent knowing which values of a variable satisfy a condition. Finally, *Goal* registers states of the world desired by the agents.

4 Choosing a Response by Evaluating Alternative Actions

A crucial part of the *Satisfy* problem-solving plan is the choice of the best action to perform among those having the goal in their effect list.

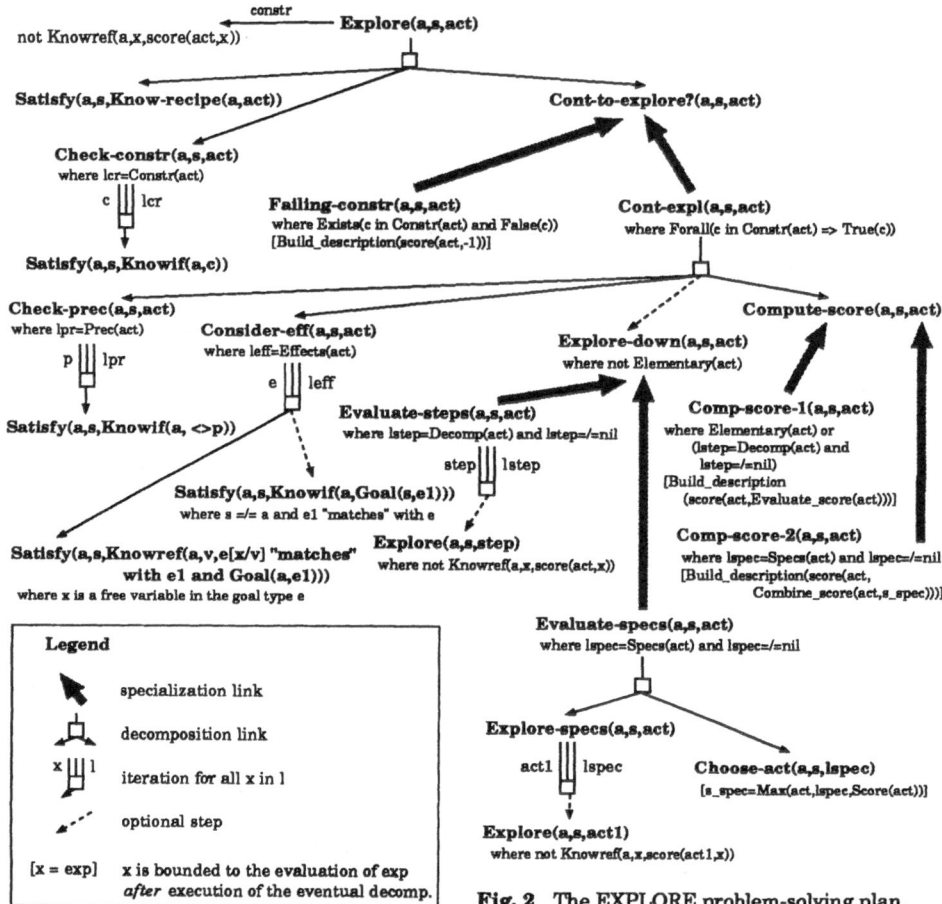

Fig. 2 The EXPLORE problem-solving plan.

This choice is performed by the *Explore* plan (see fig. 2) that evaluates the goodness of every candidate action by testing several of its features, like constraints, preconditions, steps, preferred effects for the system or the user. The evaluation proceeds in a hierarchic way: first the class of general actions reaching the given goal are considered, then each of them is refined by recursively evaluating its alternative specializations and choosing one of them. In this way if an action has any specializations, the exploration phase is interleaved with the evaluation of the alternatives. The function *Evaluate-score* implements some heuristic criteria that score the action on the basis of the above-mentioned features, while the function *Combine-score* merges the score associated to the chosen specialization with that coming from the information available at the current level of the hierarchy. The idea is that the information inherited through the generalization hierarchy, hence common to all the specializations of an action, is not relevant to choose among them, though it affects the score of the selected action. When there are no more specializations, either the action is an elementary one, or it has a decomposition; in the latter case, the *Explore* is applied recursively to evaluate each single step. Note that the evaluation process is simplified if the system already knows the action score. In fig. 2 the "where" conditions, representing applicability restrictions for the action, are evaluated when an action is considered for execution. They are exploited either to establish bindings for the variables used to define the action (e.g. lcr = Constr(act) binds lcr to the list of constraints of act), or to determine if the action itself is appropriate to the current situation (allowing the interpreter of the problem-solving meta-plans to choose among alternative specializations, or to decide if an optional step has to be performed).

The evaluation of an action begins by ascertaining that the agent knows its relevant features, i.e. its constraints, preconditions, effects, and decompositions. Then all the features are considered with respect to their number, truth-value and relationship with the agents' goals. Constraints are checked; if just one of them is not satisfied, a negative score is associated to the action. This fact prevents from selecting the action because it is generally difficult or impossible to satisfy a constraint. The need for the agent to know these pieces of information in order to decide which action best further his goals is expressed by invoking the *Satisfy* action with the needed knowledge-related goal as argument; this accounts for the posting of new subgoals, that can lead the agent to initiate a clarification subdialogue.

Clarification subdialogues can start for knowing the various features of the action (first step of *Explore* in fig. 2[5]), the truth value of its constraints and preconditions (second and third steps), and to understand how the action effects impact on the agents' goals (see the *Consider-eff* step). In particular, the first step of the *Consider-eff* action states that a clarification subdialogue can start when the actor has a goal involving a value, if he doesn't know whether it can fit in the considered action; in fact he needs this information to know if the action achieves something that he wants or not[6]. The second step states that if the considered action originated from a request made by some other agent, then it is important to know what are his attitudes toward the various effects.

The scoring criteria assign higher values to actions that better suit the current situation:

- *preconditions*: the score is negatively affected by the number of preconditions not yet satisfied.
- *effects*: they are evaluated according to how they match with the agents' goals, taking into account both user and system perspectives (as they are represented, respectively, in the user and system model). The general idea is that only effects for which the agents got a (positive or negative) preference should affect the action score.
- *steps*: they are taken into account by combining the score of each of them so that simpler actions could gain a higher score.
- *user's knowledge of the action*: if he knows the action, things are simpler because

---

[5] Since in our application the system plays the role of the domain expert, this step is specially important to recognize user's intentions underlying his questions during the recognition phase. In general, however, an agent may be willing to reach a goal and perform the action himself but he may lack the knowledge about how to do it.

[6] E.g. one may have the goal: $at(agt,dest,t)$ where $t \in (now,now+30')$, i.e. *agt* wants to be at *dest* in less than 30 ' from now. In this case he is interested in knowing what value takes t in the action *go-by-bus* in order to evaluate it with respect to *go-by-car*.

this prevents the system from planning a new explanation and the user hasn't to learn a new action; so, a known action is scored higher.

All these factors are combined in a weighted sum to obtain a value that is indicative of the action worth. Changing the weights it is possible to model different choice principles of the system: e.g. by weighting the effects more than the steps, it is possible to obtain a high score for an action preferred by both interlocutors even if its execution is complex. Another situation could be giving more importance to the system's goals with respect to the user's ones in case the system should fit a more prominent role with respect to the user. So the choice of the weights influences the degree of cooperativity of the system.
Our scoring criteria, described in detail in [5], though simple, proved useful to study how different factors affect the choice process.

5 RST Library

The RST (Rhetorical Structure Theory) library can be seen as an extension of the basic speech act library in that, as the latter provides different ways (locutionary acts) to express a particular illocutionary act, the former supports more complex discourses by relating sequences of locutionary acts according to their rhetorical achievements. For each basic illocutionary speech act (we consider inform, obtain-info, request, and promise) the RST library provides different rhetorical means to realize them, exploiting additional information directly related to the content expressed by the illocutionary act. E.g. an action can be justified by providing information about its constraints or preconditions. In (3) below two alternative ways are shown for asking a question adopting different realizations of the basic *obtain-info* illocutionary act.

(3) U: I want to send an e-mail to professor Red.
     S1: Do you have an account?[7]
     S2: For sending an e-mail an account is required. Do you have it?

The system adopts for the response S1 an *obtain-info-direct* plan, while in S2 adopts an *obtain-info-background*. S2 appears to be a more appropriate response because it gives more material and prevents a user clarification dialogue. But if a preference of the hearer was for simple discourse, S1 would be chosen.

Rhetoric plans are represented using the same formalism of domain and problem-solving plans. In particular, the problem-solving plans use all the above mentioned scoring criteria for choosing a rhetorical action among the ones available for conveying the previously selected material. The effects of a rhetorical action are matched against the system presentational goals, while its constraints are used to specify the relationships occurring among the main content (nucleus in RST terms) and some additional material of the domain action (satellites, in RST terms; e.g. its preconditions) that has to be mentioned in order to achieve the presentational goal. The decomposition field specifies how to link the whole material collected including the linguistic feature that connects the spans of text produced by the single statements.

---

[7] Although the system understands input in natural language, at the moment the generation component doesn't provide surface realization, but simply outputs instantiated plans. We write system output in natural language only for clarity purposes.

Here is a portion of the rhetorical plan *Inform-motivation*:

```
(setq Inform-motivation (make-action
    :type 'RST-plan
    :arguments '((SPKR a1) (HEAR a2) (ACTION act))
    :var-types '((autonomous-agent a1) (autonomous-agent a2)
              (relat-node cond) (action-node act))
    :constr '(AND (NOT (Goal a2 (Perform a2 act)))
              (Goal a2 cond))
    :wh-restrictions '(member cond (effect (act)))
    :effect '(increase-desire a1 a2 act)
    :ling-feat '(in_this_way  so)
    :more-general '(inform)
    :decomposition '((var nil)
      (block (Statement (SPKR a1) (HEAR a2) (PROP-CONTENT act))
              (ling-feat)
              (Statement (SPKR a1) (HEAR a2) (PROP-CONTENT cond))))))
```

6 Example

The structures described above can be used in producing responses like the system's one in (4):

(4) U: I'm a computer science student. I would like to talk with professor Red[8].
    S: You could send him an e-mail. In this way he will answer as soon as possible.

The interpretation of the first part of the user utterance in (4) lets the system activate the 'computer-science-student' stereotype in the user model; from the stereotype it is possible to know that *need-soon-answer* is one of the goals of the user.

The interpretation of the other part of the user utterance allows the system to identify the goal:

$$Goal(U, Perform(U, Talk(U, Red)))$$

Let's suppose that the *Talk* action has the following effects:

$$complete\text{-}response(professor, person),$$
$$NOT\ soon\text{-}answer(professor, person),$$
$$[shortened\text{-}research\text{-}time(professor)$$
$$where\ NOT\ office\text{-}hours(professor, t)]$$

representing the fact that by talking face to face one can get an extended response, but he will normally have to fix a date far in advance; furthermore, the professor will have less time left for research if this happens outside his office hours (note that it is not a "constraint" of the *Talk* action, so that in other situations, e.g. when the 'graduating student' stereotype is active, the *Talk* action could be preferred over other actions). Since the latter effect conflicts with the system goal:

$$Goal(S, NOT\ shortened\text{-}research\text{-}time(professor))$$

---

[8] We suppose that present time is not professor Red's office hours. At the moment we do not consider the temporal evolution of the state of the world: we suppose that the world remains as it is when the system makes the plan. Furthermore, we suppose that some actions are to be performed immediately after the interaction (e.g. meeting a professor), while others could be planned for the future (e.g. giving an exam).

the goal manager adopts a related goal, i.e. the most generic user's goal that doesn't conflict with the system's ones; this leads the *Explore* to evaluate the more generic action *Exchange-info*. The Explore is then recursively applied to its alternative specializations, *Talk* and *Send-e-mail*; the latter having the following effects:

$$\text{complete-response(professor, person)},$$
$$\text{soon-answer(professor, person)},$$

that are both desired by the user. Furthermore, a person needs an account to send an e-mail, so this is represented as a precondition of the action, possibly not true in the present situation. Skipping various details for simplicity of exposition, the *Explore* problem-solving plan balances the mentioned aspects of the current situation according to the chosen weights and eventually selects the *Send-e-mail* action, although it has a precondition that needs to be checked.

Since the system selected an action different from the one requested by the user, the goal manager activates the system presentational goal:

$$\text{Goal}(S, \text{increase-desire}(S, U, \text{Send-e-mail}))$$

Hence in the structuring phase the *Explore* selects from the RST library the *Inform-motivation* plan. This plan links in its decomposition the selected act (*Send-e-mail*) with its further effect matching with the user's goal *need-soon answer*.

7 Conclusions and Further Work

In this paper we have been concerned with the production of a natural and cooperative response. Starting with a model of the dialogue previously used for recognition purposes, we considered it from the generation perspective, providing new insights on the two related problems of content selection and structuring of the text in information-seeking settings.

In our model the same plan libraries are shared knowledge between the recognition and generation processes. Furthermore, our system provides an output that seems acceptable for both agents involved in the dialogue.

The system is implemented in Common Lisp on Sun workstations. However, the goal manager has to be completed with a more sophisticate intention acquisition module. We are also considering how it is possible to introduce some defaults in the mechanism of actions choice, in order to avoid producing too many clarification dialogues.

References

[1] Appelt, D.E. 1985. *Planning English Sentences*. Cambridge University Press, Cambridge, England.
[2] Ardissono L., Lombardo A., and Sestero D. 1993. A flexible approach to cooperative response generation in information-seeking dialogues. In *Proceedings of the 31st Annual Meeting of the ACL*. 274-276. Columbus, OH.
[3] Ardissono L, Boella G., and Sestero D. 1996. Uso di piani di problem-solving nel riconoscimento di piani e obiettivi. *Interfacce Intelligenti*. AI*IA Notizie.

Periodico dell'Associazione Italiana per l'Intelligenza Artificiale. Supplemento Anno IX-3

[4] Ardissono L., and Sestero D. 1996. Using dynamic user models in the recognition of the plans of the user. *User Modeling and User-Adapted Interaction*, 5(2):157-190

[5] Barboni P., and Sestero D. 1997. Scoring alternative actions for producing flexible responses. *Internal report of the Natural Language Group* at Dipartimento di Informatica, Università degli Studi di Torino.

[6] Brown P., and Levinson S. C. 1987. *Politeness: some universals on language usage*. Cambridge University Press, Cambridge.

[7] Carberry S, Kazi Z., and.Lambert L. 1992. Modeling discourse, problem-solving, and domain goals incrementally in task-oriented dialogue. *Proceedings 3rd Int. Workshop on User Modeling*. 192-201. Wadern.

[8] Carberry S., Chu-Carrol J., Green N., and Lambert L. 1993. Rhetorical Structure Theory: Necessary but not sufficient. *Proceedings of the ACL Workshop on Intentionality and Structure in Discourse Relations*.

[9] Carberry S., and Chu-Carrol J. Response Generation in Collaborative Negotiation. *In Proceedings of the 33rd Annual Meeting of the Association for Computational Linguistics,* State University of New York, Buffalo, 136-143. Association for Computational Linguistics, Arlington, Va.

[10] Cawsey A. 1993. *Explanation and Interaction: The Computer Generation of Explanatory Dialogues*. MIT Press, Cambridge, Mass.

[11] Cohen P.R. and Levesque H.J. 1990. Rational interaction as the basis for communication. In Cohen, Morgan, and Pollack, editors, *Intentions in communications*, 221-255. MIT Press.

[12] Hovy E.H. 1988a. *Generating Natural Language under Pragmatic Constraints*. Lawrence Erlbaum, Hillsdale, N.J.

[13] Hovy E.H. 1991. Approaches to the planning of coherent text. In Cécile L. Paris, William R. Swartout, and William C. Mann, eds., *Natural Language Generation in Artificial Intelligence and Computational Linguistics*, 83-102. Kluwer, Boston.

[14] Kautz H. 1990. A Circumscriptive Theory of Plan Recognition. In P.R. Cohen, J. Morgan, and M.E. Pollack, eds., *Intentions in Communication*, 105-133. MIT Press.

[15] Lesmo L., and Lombardo V. 1993. Un approccio computazionale all'interpretazione del linguaggio. *Epistemologia*. Fascicolo speciale su Linguaggi e Macchine. 165-190.

[16] Mann W.C., and Thompson S.A. 1988. Rhetorical Structure Theory: Towards a functions theory of text organization. *TEXT* 8(3):243-81.

[17] McKeown K.R. 1985. *Text Generation: Using Discourse Strategies and Focus Constraints to Generate Natural Language Text*. Cambridge University Press, Cambridge, England

[18] Moore J.D., and Pollack M.E. 1992. A problem for RST: The need for multi-level discourse analysis. *Computational Linguistics* 18(4):537-44

[19] Moore J.D. 1995. *Participating in Explanatory Dialogues. Interpreting and Responding to Questions in Context*. MIT Press, Cambridge, Mass.

[20] Paris C.L. 1988. Tailoring Object Descriptions to a User's Level of Expertise. *Computational Linguistics* 14(3),64-78

[21] Ramshaw L.A. 1989. A metaplan for problem-solving discourse. In *Proceedings of the 29th Annual Meeting of ACL*, 39-46, Berkeley, CA, 1991.

A Variant of Earley Parsing

Mark-Jan Nederhof[1]* and Giorgio Satta[2]

[1] Faculty of Arts
University of Groningen
P.O. Box 716
NL-9700 AS Groningen
The Netherlands
markjan@let.rug.nl
[2] Dipartimento di Elettronica ed Informatica
Università di Padova
via Gradenigo, 6/A
I-35131 Padova
Italy
satta@dei.unipd.it

Abstract. The Earley algorithm is a widely used parsing method in natural language processing applications. We introduce a variant of Earley parsing that is based on a "delayed" recognition of constituents. This allows us to start the recognition of a constituent only in cases in which all of its subconstituents have been found within the input string. This is particularly advantageous in several cases in which partial analysis of a constituent cannot be completed and in general in all cases of productions sharing some suffix of their right-hand sides (even for different left-hand side nonterminals). Although the two algorithms result in the same asymptotic time and space complexity, from a practical perspective our algorithm improves the time and space requirements of the original method, as shown by reported experimental results.

1 Introduction

Earley parsing is one of the most commonly used methods for the (automatic) syntactic analysis of natural language sentences, given a context-free grammar model. This method does not use backtracking, resulting in time and space efficiency, and is quite flexible, in that it does not require the input grammar to be cast in any particular form. Earley parsing was first defined in [6], in the context of formal language parsing. This method has later been rediscovered in [10, 11] from the perspective of application to natural language processing, where it was called *active chart parsing*. Active chart parsing makes also use of a data structure, called *agenda*, which allows a more flexible control of competing analyses.

---

* Research by the first author is carried out within the framework of the Priority Programme Language and Speech Technology (TST). The TST-Programme is sponsored by NWO (Dutch Organization for Scientific Research).

A considerable number of results and applications regarding Earley parsing have been published in the literature. From a theoretical perspective, improvements of the Earley algorithm have been reported in [9], [15] and [16]. Several reformulations of Earley parsing have also been presented. Most remarkably, in [3] Earley parsing is related to the deterministic simulation of a particular kind of nondeterministic pushdown automaton, and a recursive reformulation of Earley parsing has been proposed in [14].

From the perspective of natural language parsing, the Earley method has been adapted to work with context-free grammars enriched with feature structures in [22], [26] and [7], and to cope with on-line semantic interpretation in [27]. Comparison of Earley parsing with other parsing strategies has been experimentally carried out and reported in [30] and [24].

In this paper we focus on a drawback of the Earley algorithm: the recognition of a production within the input is started by looking for the constituents in its right-hand side, proceeding from left to right. In this process, the algorithm keeps track of the position within the input at which the recognition has started. Since this information is needed only if the whole recognition can be carried to an end, the algorithm behaves in a rather inefficient way in several cases in which production recognition cannot be successfully completed. We propose a variant of the original method, in which the problem is solved by delaying some of the computation until the involved productions have been fully recognized. This is achieved using an idea first presented in [13] in the context of left-corner parsing, as it will be discussed at length in the final section. When applied in the framework of active chart parsing, our technique results in the "inversion" of the fundamental rule [10, 11] that combines a left active edge with a right inactive edge. Although our proposal does not result in an asymptotic improvement of the time and space complexity of the Earley algorithm, reported experimental results provide evidence that in practical cases our method achieves an increase in time and space efficiency.

The remainder of this paper is organized as follows. In Section 2 some preliminaries are discussed. We review the Earley parsing method in Section 3, and then introduce our variant in Section 4. Some empirical results are given in Section 5, and related work is discussed in Section 6.

2 Preliminaries

We introduce the formal notation that will be used throughout the paper.

A string w is a finite sequence of symbols over some alphabet. We denote as $|w|$ the length of w, and as ε the (unique) string of length zero. The set of all strings over some alphabet Σ, ε included, is denoted Σ^*. A context-free grammar (CFG) is a rewriting system $G = (V_T, V_N, P, S)$, where V_T and V_N are two finite, disjoint sets of terminal and nonterminal symbols, respectively, $S \in V_N$ is the start symbol, and P is a finite set of productions. Each production has the form $A \to \alpha$ with $A \in V_N$ and $\alpha \in (V_N \cup V_T)^*$. The size of G, written $|G|$, is defined as $\sum_{(A \to \alpha) \in P} |A\alpha|$.

We generally use symbols $A, B, C, \ldots$ to range over V_{N}, symbols $a, b, c, \ldots$ to range over V_{T}, symbols X, Y to range over $V_{\mathrm{N}} \cup V_{\mathrm{T}}$, symbols $\alpha, \beta, \gamma, \ldots$ to range over $(V_{\mathrm{N}} \cup V_{\mathrm{T}})^*$, and symbols $v, w, x, \ldots$ to range over V_{T}^*. For a fixed grammar, the binary relation $\Rightarrow$ is defined over $(V_{\mathrm{N}} \cup V_{\mathrm{T}})^*$ such that $\gamma A \delta \Rightarrow \gamma \alpha \delta$ whenever $A \rightarrow \alpha$ belongs to P. We will mainly use the reflexive and transitive closure of $\Rightarrow$, denoted $\overset{*}{\Rightarrow}$.

3 Earley Parsing

We briefly present here the Earley algorithm, before introducing the variant of this method in the next section.

Let $G = (V_{\mathrm{T}}, V_{\mathrm{N}}, P, S)$ be a CFG. We associate with G a set of symbols, called *dotted items*, specified as:

$$I_{\mathrm{E}} = \{[A \rightarrow \alpha \cdot \beta] \mid (A \rightarrow \alpha\beta) \in P\}. \tag{1}$$

Dotted items are used below to represent intermediate steps in the process of recognition of a production of the grammar, where the sequence of symbols in between the arrow and the dot indicates the sequence of constituents recognized so far at consecutive positions within the input string. More precisely, given a production $p : (A \rightarrow X_1 X_2 \cdots X_r)$, $r \geq 0$, the process of recognition of the right-hand side of p is carried out in several steps. We start from item $A \rightarrow \cdot X_1 X_2 \cdots X_r$, attesting that the empty sequence of constituents has been collected so far. This item represents a prediction for p. We then proceed with item $A \rightarrow X_1 \cdot X_2 \cdots X_r$ after the recognition of a constituent X_1, and so on. Production p has been fully recognized only if we reach item $A \rightarrow X_1 X_2 \cdots X_r \cdot$, attesting therefore the complete recognition of a constituent A. In active chart parsing, items in I_{E} with the dot not at the rightmost position of the right-hand side are used to label the so called *active edges*.

Given a string $w = a_1 a_2 \cdots a_n$, with $n \geq 0$ and each a_i a terminal symbol, we call *position* within w any integer i such that $0 \leq i \leq n$. In what follows, E is a square matrix whose entries are subsets of I_{E} and are addressed by indices that are positions within the input string. Entries are denoted as $E_{i,j}$. The insertion by the algorithm of item $[A \rightarrow \alpha \cdot \beta]$ in $E_{i,j}$, $i \leq j$, attests the fact that the sequence of constituents in α exactly spans the substring $a_{i+1} \cdots a_j$ of the input. (See below for a more precise characterization of the algorithm.) Control flow is not specified in the method below, since it is usually regulated by means of a data structure called *agenda*, which directs the incremental construction of the table by means of an iteration: starting from an empty table, items are added as long as needed, and with the desired priority.

Algorithm 1 (Earley) Let $G = (V_{\mathrm{T}}, V_{\mathrm{N}}, P, S)$ be a CFG. Let $w = a_1 a_2 \cdots a_n$ be an input string, $n \geq 0$, and $a_i \in V_{\mathrm{T}}$ for $1 \leq i \leq n$. Compute the least $(n + 1) \times (n + 1)$ table E such that $[S \rightarrow \cdot \alpha] \in E_{0,0}$ for each $(S \rightarrow \alpha) \in P$, and

1. $[A \rightarrow \cdot \gamma] \in E_{j,j}$ if $[B \rightarrow \alpha \cdot A\beta] \in E_{i,j}$, $(A \rightarrow \gamma) \in P$;
2. $[A \rightarrow \alpha a_j \cdot \beta] \in E_{i,j}$ if $[A \rightarrow \alpha \cdot a_j \beta] \in E_{i,j-1}$;
3. $[A \rightarrow \alpha B \cdot \beta] \in E_{i,j}$ if $[A \rightarrow \alpha \cdot B\beta] \in E_{i,k}$, $[B \rightarrow \gamma \cdot] \in E_{k,j}$.

The string w is accepted if and only if $[S \to \alpha \bullet] \in E_{0,n}$ for some $(S \to \alpha) \in P$.

The correctness of the algorithm immediately follows from the property below, whose proof can be found in [6] and [8].

Proposition 1. *In Algorithm 1, an item $[A \to \alpha \bullet \beta]$ is inserted in $E_{i,j}$ if and only if the following conditions hold:*

A1. $S \overset{*}{\Rightarrow} a_1 \cdots a_i A \gamma$, *some γ; and*
A2. $\alpha \overset{*}{\Rightarrow} a_{i+1} \cdots a_j$.

For methods cruder than the Earley algorithm, membership of an item in some entry may merely be subject to condition *A2*, which is sufficient for determining the correctness of the input. However, Earley's algorithm is more selective, as is apparent from condition *A1*, which characterizes the so called top-down filtering capability of the method. Condition *A1* guarantees that only those constituents are predicted that are compatible with the portion of the input that has been read so far.

Assuming the working grammar as fixed, a simple analysis reveals that Algorithm 1 runs in time $\mathcal{O}(n^3)$.[3] This will be more carefully discussed in the next section.

4 A Variant of Earley Parsing

In this section we introduce a variant of Earley parsing that can be obtained by reconsidering the way in which the results of the intermediate steps are stored in the process of production recognition.

Let us focus on the dependence of the running time of Algorithm 1 on the length of the input string. From this perspective, the most expensive step is Step 3. Intuitively, this is the case because there might be $\mathcal{O}(n^2)$ items that are inserted at this step in some entry of E, and each item can in turn be the result of $\mathcal{O}(n)$ different combinations of pairs of items already in E. In practice, the total number of different combinations of dotted items attempted by Step 3 when processing an input string dominates the running time of Algorithm 1. The change to the new method consists in a decomposition of Step 3 that results, in some cases, in a reduction of this number. We introduce the basic idea through an example.

Consider a production $p : (A \to A_1 A_2 \cdots A_r)$, $r \geq 3$. Let D be a set containing $d > 2$ positions within the input string. Assume that the dotted item $[A \to A_1 \bullet A_2 \cdots A_r]$ has been inserted in the entry E_{i,j_1}, for each $i \in D$ and for some fixed j_1. This corresponds to d constituents A_1 recognized within the input. Assume also that, for each t with $2 \leq t \leq r - 1$, a constituent A_t has been recognized in entry E_{j_{t-1},j_t}. Finally, assume that no constituent A_r is found

---

[3] When both the input string and the grammar are taken as input parameters, Algorithm 1 runs in time $\mathcal{O}(|G|^2 n^3)$. An improvement of Algorithm 1 has been presented in [9], running in time $\mathcal{O}(|G| n^3)$.

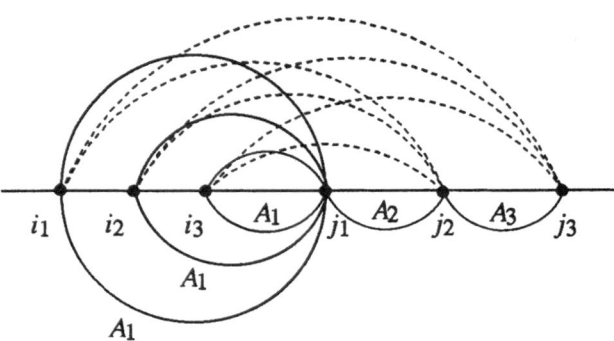

Fig. 1. We depict the case of $d = 3$, $r = 4$, and assume $D = \{i_1, i_2, i_3\}$. We represent the input string by means of an horizontal line and each dotted item in E by means of an arc; only the relevant positions within the input string are depicted. In the attempt to recognize production $A \rightarrow A_1 \cdots A_4$, the algorithm has created 3 dotted items $[A \rightarrow A_1 \bullet A_2 A_3 A_4]$, one for each position in D, depicted by solid arcs above the horizontal line. Since each of these items has a different left position, the Earley algorithm is forced to instantiate 3 independent processes for the recognition of $A \rightarrow A_1 \cdots A_4$. These processes will create the dotted items depicted by the dashed arcs. Note that in collecting the remaining constituents A_2, A_3, A_4 the method duplicates the needed effort.

starting at position j_{r-1} (see Figure 1). Under these assumptions, Step 3 will be executed $d(r - 2)$ more times, carrying out d independent recognition processes for p, to find out at the end that none of these processes can be successfully completed, because of the lack of constituent A_r. The fact that the above recognition processes are independent one of the other is due to the fact that in Step 3 we record the position within the input where each process started (the positions in D).

We observe that the left position of p in the input string is needed only if the recognition process of p can be successfully completed, in order to locate the constituent corresponding to the left-hand side of p for use in the remaining analysis of the input. On this basis, we reformulate Step 3 by splitting it up into two substeps. The first substep performs the recognition of p in a forward manner, without maintaining any record of the left position. This is done using an array U in whose entries we store only the suffixes of p's right-hand side that must still be recognized. If the recognition can be successfully completed, we apply the second substep and compute the left positions of p in a backward manner, starting from the rightmost constituent in p's right-hand side and proceeding toward the left, storing the intermediate results in table T.

The proposed technique thus delays part of the computation from the former Step 3 until we are granted that p can be successfully recognized. In this way we avoid the computational inefficiency revealed by our example. In fact, whenever p's recognition cannot be completed, no backward computation is performed by our method, resulting in some time and space savings. More precisely, the same computation performed by the $d(r-2)$ executions of Step 3 in Algorithm 1 will be performed by $r-2$ executions of the forward substep, and 0 executions of the backward substep. In addition we observe that, even in the presence of a constituent A_r with left position j_{r-1} in the input string, the proposed technique performs more efficiently than the original formulation of Step 3. In fact, since the backward substep proceeds from right to left, constituents $A_r, A_{r-1}, \ldots$ will be visited only once in the attempt to find all possible left positions for p.

We observe that for the technique described above to work in its full generality, also Step 2 from Algorithm 1 should be split into two substeps. This allows correct treatment of productions containing terminal symbols in their right-hand sides. Finally, it is not difficult to see that the problem described above can be generalized to productions sharing some suffix of their right-hand sides, that is productions of the form $A \to \alpha\gamma$ and $B \to \beta\gamma$, in cases that γ is, at some position, predicted independently for both productions.

We are now in a position to give a precise specification of the proposed parsing algorithm. Let $G = (V_T, V_N, P, S)$ be a CFG. We associate with G a set of symbols, called *suffix items*, specified as:

$$I_V = \{[\beta] \mid (A \to \alpha\beta) \in P\}. \tag{2}$$

Suffix items serve two different purposes. First, the insertion of suffix item $[\alpha]$ in entry U_j, where U is a one-dimensional array, means that the process of forward recognition of a production $A \to \alpha\beta$, for some A and α, has been successfully carried out, up to position j and up to the constituents in the sequence α. In other words, there exists at least one i, $i \leq j$, such that some dotted item $[A \to \alpha \bullet \beta]$ would have been inserted in $E_{i,j}$ by Algorithm 1. Second, the insertion of suffix item $[\beta]$ in $T_{i,j}$ means that at least one production $A \to \alpha\beta$, for some A and α, has been completely recognized and the constituents in the sequence β have been collected backwards so far, spanning the substring $a_{i+1} \cdots a_j$.

Algorithm 2 (Variant of Earley) Let $G = (V_T, V_N, P, S)$ be a CFG. Let $w = a_1 a_2 \cdots a_n$ be an input string, $n \geq 0$, and $a_i \in V_T$ for $1 \leq i \leq n$. Compute the least $(n+1) \times (n+1)$ table T and the least $(n+1)$ array U such that $[\alpha] \in U_0$ for each $(S \to \alpha) \in P$, and

1. $[\gamma] \in U_j$ if $[A\beta] \in U_j$, $(A \to \gamma) \in P$;
2. $[\beta] \in U_j$ if $[a_j\beta] \in U_{j-1}$;
3. $[\beta] \in U_j$ if $[B\beta] \in U_k$, $(B \to \gamma) \in P$, $[\gamma] \in T_{k,j}$;
4. $[\varepsilon] \in T_{m,m}$ if $[\varepsilon] \in U_m$;
5. $[a_j\beta] \in T_{j-1,m}$ if $[a_j\beta] \in U_{j-1}$, $[\beta] \in T_{j,m}$;
6. $[B\beta] \in T_{k,m}$ if $[B\beta] \in U_k$, $(B \to \gamma) \in P$, $[\gamma] \in T_{k,j}$, $[\beta] \in T_{j,m}$.

The string w is accepted if and only if $[\alpha] \in T_{0,n}$ for some $(S \to \alpha) \in P$.

Step 1 of Algorithm 1 exactly corresponds to Step 1 of Algorithm 2. Step 2 of Algorithm 1 has now been split into Steps 2 and 5 of Algorithm 2, which act as forward and backward substeps, respectively. Similarly, Step 3 of Algorithm 1 has been split into Steps 3 and 6 of Algorithm 2. Step 4 of Algorithm 2 is needed to initiate the backward process of recognizing a production, after the forward process has completed recognition of the right-hand side.

The correctness of the method directly follows from the property stated below, which characterizes the presence of suffix items in entries of U and T.

Proposition 2. *In Algorithm 2, an item $[\beta]$ is inserted in U_j if and only if the following conditions hold:*

A1. $S \overset{*}{\Rightarrow} a_1 \cdots a_i A\gamma$, some i, A and γ;
A2. $(A \to \alpha\beta) \in P$, some α; and
A3. $\alpha \overset{*}{\Rightarrow} a_{i+1} \cdots a_j$,

and an item $[\beta]$ is inserted in $T_{j,k}$ if and only if the following conditions hold:

B1. the conditions A1, A2 and A3 hold; and
B2. $\beta \overset{*}{\Rightarrow} a_{j+1} \cdots a_k$.

The proof of the above statement is similar to that of Proposition 1.

It is not difficult to see that Algorithm 2 has running time $\mathcal{O}(n^3)$ (again, we assume the working grammar is fixed). Therefore Algorithms 1 and 2 present the same asymptotic time complexity. For the purpose of more carefully comparing the two algorithms, we give below an alternative to Proposition 2, which characterizes the entries in U and T in terms of the entries in E.

Proposition 3. *In Algorithm 2, an item $[\beta]$ is inserted in U_j if and only if the following condition holds:*

A1. at least one item $[A \to \alpha \bullet \beta]$ is inserted in $E_{i,j}$ by Algorithm 1, for some A, α and i,

and an item $[\beta]$ is inserted in $T_{j,k}$ if and only if the following conditions hold:

B1. the condition A1 holds; and
B2. $\beta \overset{*}{\Rightarrow} a_{j+1} \cdots a_k$.

This proposition clearly shows that the number of items in U is always smaller than the number of items in E: several items $[A \to \alpha \bullet \beta]$ in $E_{i,j}$ for fixed j but differing A, α and i correspond to one single item $[\beta]$ in U_j.

On the other hand, the number of items in T may be larger than the number of items in E since for each $[A \to \alpha \bullet \beta]$ in $E_{i,j}$ we may have $[\beta]$ in several $T_{j,k}$ for distinct values of k. Since there may be up to n such k in the worst case, the number of items in T may be up to n times larger than the number of items in E.

One example of a CFG were this phenomenon is apparent is the following.

$$S \to AB \qquad A \to C \qquad B \to C \qquad C \to aC \qquad C \to \varepsilon$$

For input a^n, some n, Algorithm 1 computes $n+1$ items of the form $[S \to A \bullet B] \in E_{0,i}$, $0 \leq i \leq n$, and $n+1$ items of the form $[S \to AB \bullet] \in E_{0,j}$, $0 \leq j \leq n$. On the other hand, Algorithm 2 computes $\frac{n^2+n}{2}$ items of the form $[B] \in T_{i,j}$, $0 \leq i \leq j \leq n$.

We define $|E| = \Sigma_{i,j}|E_{i,j}|$, $|U| = \Sigma_i|U_i|$, $|T| = \Sigma_{i,j}|T_{i,j}|$, and summarize the above as follows.

Proposition 4. *For a fixed CFG and input of length n, let E be constructed by Algorithm 1 and U and T by Algorithm 2. Then:*

1. $|U| \leq |E|$*; and*
2. $|T| \leq n \cdot |E|$*.*

The second part of this proposition seems to suggest that the table size may be much larger for the variant. The empirical data presented by the next section however show that such worst-case behaviour does not seem to occur for the practical grammars at hand.

Based on the number of items that are stored in the respective tables, we can investigate the number of steps that are performed by the two algorithms. We count the number of elementary parsing steps consisting in the derivation of one item in a table from one or more objects, such as productions, input symbols, or other items in a table. For example, in the case of Algorithm 2 every combination of four objects of the form $[B\beta] \in U_k$, $(B \to \gamma) \in P$, $[\gamma] \in T_{k,j}$, and $[\beta] \in T_{j,m}$ is counted as one elementary parsing step according to Step 6. For a certain CFG and input, let us denote the number of applications of Steps 1, 2 and 3 of the Earley algorithm by $\mathcal{E}_1$, $\mathcal{E}_2$ and $\mathcal{E}_3$. Similarly, we introduce the notation $\mathcal{V}_1, \ldots, \mathcal{V}_6$ for the six steps of the variant. We further define $\mathcal{E} = \mathcal{E}_1 + \mathcal{E}_2 + \mathcal{E}_3 + |\{\alpha \mid (S \to \alpha) \in P\}|$, and $\mathcal{V} = \mathcal{V}_1 + \mathcal{V}_2 + \cdots + \mathcal{V}_6 + |\{\alpha \mid (S \to \alpha) \in P\}|$.

Based on condition *A1* in Proposition 3, we may conclude that $\mathcal{V}_1 \leq \mathcal{E}_1$, $\mathcal{V}_2 \leq \mathcal{E}_2$ and $\mathcal{V}_3 \leq \mathcal{E}_3$. The number of applications of Step 4 is bounded by the number of items $[\varepsilon] \in U_j$, which is bounded by the number of items $[A \to \gamma\bullet] \in E_{i,j}$. This in turn is bounded by the number of items $[A \to \bullet\gamma] \in E_{i,i}$ times the number of j such that $\gamma \overset{*}{\Rightarrow} a_{i+1} \cdots a_j$. The number of such j is bounded by $n+1$, and the number of $[A \to \bullet\gamma] \in E_{i,i}$ is bounded by $\mathcal{E}_1$ plus $|\{\alpha \mid (S \to \alpha) \in P\}|$. Therefore we have $\mathcal{V}_4 \leq (n + 1) \cdot (\mathcal{E}_1 + |\{\alpha \mid (S \to \alpha) \in P\}|)$

Steps 5 and 6 cannot be applied more than once for each application of Steps 2 and 3 and $[\beta] \in T_{j,m}$, for at most $n + 1$ different values of m. Therefore we have $\mathcal{V}_5 \leq (n + 1) \cdot \mathcal{V}_2 \leq (n + 1) \cdot \mathcal{E}_2$ and $\mathcal{V}_6 \leq (n + 1) \cdot \mathcal{V}_3 \leq (n + 1) \cdot \mathcal{E}_3$.

Combining the above, we obtain:

Proposition 5. *For fixed CFG and input of length n, we have $\mathcal{V} \leq (n + 2) \cdot \mathcal{E}$.*

In the worst case, the number of steps for the variant may thus be greater than the number of steps for the original Earley algorithm by a factor which is $\mathcal{O}(n)$. Again, the data presented by the next section suggest that this consideration has little bearing on practical cases.

5   Empirical Results

We have performed some experiments with Algorithms 1 and 2 for four practical context-free grammars.

The first grammar generates a subset of the programming language ALGOL 68 [28]. The second and third grammars generate fragments of Dutch,

$G = (V_T, V_N, P, S)$	$\|G\|$	$\|V_N\|$	$\|P\|$	$\|w\|$	Parses
ALGOL 68	783	167	330	13.7	$2.6 * 10^0$
CORRie	1141	203	424	12.3	$2.3 * 10^{14}$
Deltra	1929	281	703	10.8	$1.1 * 10^{73}$
Alvey	5072	265	1484	10.7	$3.2 * 10^4$

Table 1. The test material: the four grammars and some of their dimensions, the average length of the test sentences (20 sentences of various lengths for each grammar), and the average number of parses per sentence (excluding parses containing cycles, i.e. subderivations of the form $A \xrightarrow{+} A$).

	Earley		Variant				τ_2 + Earley	
G	$\mathcal{E}$	$\|E\|$	$\mathcal{V}$	$\|U\|$	$\|T\|$	$\|U\|+\|T\|$	$\mathcal{E}$	$\|E\|$
ALGOL 68	2,062	1,437	2,054	1,302	119	1,421	2,107	1,483
CORRie	19,164	8,361	15,492	3,498	2,746	6,244	17,450	8,751
Deltra	60,849	12,694	34,238	4,759	4,071	8,830	57,582	15,114
Alvey	47,562	6,304	27,786	5,398	180	5,578	47,552	6,314

Table 2. Dynamic requirements: average time and space per sentence.

and are referred to as the CORRie grammar [29] and the Deltra grammar [23], respectively. These grammars were stripped of their arguments in order to convert them into context-free grammars. The fourth grammar, referred to as the Alvey grammar [4], generates a fragment of English and was automatically generated from a unification-based grammar.

The test sentences have been obtained by automatic generation from the grammars, using a random generator to select productions, as explained in [19]; therefore these sentences do not necessarily represent input typical of the applications for which the grammars were written. Table 1 summarizes the test material.

Our implementation is merely a prototype, which means that absolute duration of the parsing process is little indicative of the actual efficiency of more sophisticated implementations. Therefore, our measurements have been restricted to implementation-independent quantities, viz. the number of elements stored in the parse table and the number of elementary steps performed by the algorithm. In a practical implementation, such quantities will strongly influence the space and time complexity, although they do not represent the only determining factors. Furthermore, all optimizations of the time and space efficiency have been left out of consideration.

In our experiments we have also considered an alternative way of introducing suffix items $[\beta]$ (albeit only those with $|\beta| \geq 2$) into the parsing process, namely by first applying a grammar transformation τ_2, and then executing Algorithm 1 as usual. This was motivated by the literature on *covers* [21, 12], which shows that some complicated parsing algorithms can be simulated by means of grammar transformations and simpler parsing algorithms. We have not found any way to completely simulate Algorithm 2 in this manner, but the following transformation captures some of its behaviour.[4] For an arbitrary grammar $G = (V_T, V_N, P, S)$, we define $\tau_2(G) = (V_T, V_N \cup I_V, P', S)$, where P' contains the following productions:

$A \rightarrow X[\alpha]$ for all $(A \rightarrow X\alpha) \in P$ with $|\alpha| > 1$;

$A \rightarrow \alpha$ for all $(A \rightarrow \alpha) \in P$ with $|\alpha| \leq 2$;

$[X\alpha] \rightarrow X[\alpha]$ for all $[X\alpha] \in I_V$ with $|\alpha| > 1$;

$[XY] \rightarrow XY$ for all $[XY] \in I_V$.

Note that the transformed grammar is in *two normal form*, which means that the length of right-hand sides of productions is at most 2.

Table 2 presents the costs of parsing the test sentences. These data show that there is a significant gain in space and time efficiency in moving from Algorithm 1 to Algorithm 2. The biggest improvement in the number of parsing steps is observed in the case of the Alvey grammar, where it amounts to a decrease by over 41%. The biggest improvement in the total number of items stored in the tables occurs for de Delta grammar, where it amounts to a decrease by over 30%. Only for *individual* sentences for ALGOL 68 was there an increase in time and space, by at most 1.2% and 0.2%, respectively.

In the case of ALGOL 68 and Alvey, it is striking that T is so much smaller than U and E. This may be explained by the relatively low level of ambiguity, as compared to the other two grammars (see Figure 1). Both the Earley algorithm and its variant predict many productions in the form of items in U and E, but only a limited number of these productions will be recognized in their entirety, resulting in items in T. Although less striking in these cases, we see that also for CORRie and Delta T is smaller than U. This suggests that the potential undesirable behaviour of the variant with regard to the original Earley algorithm, as discussed in the previous section, does not occur in practice.

The approach using the grammar transformation is not competitive with the other two approaches. Although the number of steps is sometimes slightly smaller than in the case of Algorithm 1, the space requirements are larger in all cases.

6   Concluding Remarks

We have presented a variant of the Earley algorithm and have discussed cases in which it achieves space and time savings with respect to the original algorithm. Our variant is based on the following two main ideas. First, we do not compute left positions of productions until we are granted that production recognition can be completed within the input. Second, we only use suffix items as defined in (2).

---

[4] Algorithm 2 avoids any use of items of the form $[A \rightarrow X \bullet Y]$. The same cannot be achieved by means of a grammar transformation and Algorithm 1. An alternative would be to apply some other kind of tabular algorithm to the transformed grammar. See e.g. [20].

The idea of dropping left positions of productions has first been proposed by [13], where a functional realization of left-corner parsing is presented. This idea was rediscovered by [5] and expressed in a more direct way, using a table similar to our table U.

The idea of using suffix items has also been proposed in [13]. It has later been rediscovered by [5]. It was also applied to LR parsing in [20]. In the literature on chart parsing, e.g. in [2], one sometimes also finds a weaker form of this idea, where the set of items used in labeling edges is $I_{\mathrm{C}} = \{[A \to \beta] \mid (A \to \alpha\beta) \in P\}$. One observes that, with respect to items $[A \to \alpha \cdot \beta]$ from I_{E}, the α is omitted as in the case of I_{V}, yet the left-hand side A is retained. If this idea is not combined with the idea of dropping left positions, then the benefit of this is limited to grammars containing many pairs of productions of the form $A \to \alpha\beta$ and $A \to \gamma\beta$, with $\alpha \neq \gamma$. The idea of using suffix items is related to the difference between two kinds of Earley parsing for the ID/LP formalism: in [25] the items are of the form $[A \to \alpha \cdot \beta]$, where α is a string of constituents and β is a set of constituent, whereas in [1], both α and β are sets. This allows representation of several items according to [25] by a single item according to [1], as has been argued in [17, Section 9.2].

The ideas above rely on productions or items having some suffix in common. Alternatively, one can investigate optimizations that rely on productions that have *prefixes* in common [18].

References

1. G. E. Barton, Jr. On the complexity of ID/LP parsing. *Computational Linguistics*, 11(4):205–218, 1985.
2. J. Bear. A breadth-first parsing model. In *Proc. of the Eighth International Joint Conference on Artificial Intelligence*, volume 2, pages 696–698, Karlsruhe, West Germany, August 1983.
3. S. Billot and B. Lang. The structure of shared forests in ambiguous parsing. In *Proc. of the 27th ACL*, pages 143–151, Vancouver, British Columbia, Canada, 1989.
4. J. A. Carroll. Practical unification-based parsing of natural language. Technical Report No. 314, University of Cambridge, Computer Laboratory, England, 1993. PhD thesis.
5. J. Dowding, R. Moore, F. Andry, and D. Moran. Interleaving syntax and semantics in an efficient bottom-up parser. In *Proc. of the 32nd ACL*, pages 110–116, Las Cruces, New Mexico, 1994.
6. J. Earley. An efficient context-free parsing algorithm. *Communications of the Association for Computing Machinery*, 13(2):94–102, 1970.
7. D. Gardemann. Using restriction to optimize unification parsing. In *International Workshop on Parsing Technologies*, pages 8–17, Pittsburgh, 1989.
8. S. L. Graham and M. A. Harrison. Parsing of general context free languages. In *Advances in Computers*, volume 14, pages 77–185. Academic Press, New York, NY, 1976.
9. S. L. Graham, M. A. Harrison, and W. L. Ruzzo. An improved context-free recognizer. *ACM Transactions on Programming Languages and Systems*, 2(3):415–462, 1980.

10. R. Kaplan. A general syntactic processor. In E. Rustin, editor, *Natural Language Processing*. Prentice-Hall, Englewood Cliffs, NJ, 1973.

11. M. Kay. Algorithm schemata and data structures in syntactic processing. Technical report CSL-80, Xerox Palo Alto Research Center, Palo Alto, CA, 1980. Also in: B. J. Grosz, K. Sparck Jones and B. L. Webber, editors, *Natural Language Processing*, pages 35-70, Kaufmann, Los Altos, CA, 1986.

12. R. Leermakers. How to cover a grammar. In *Proc. of the 27th ACL*, pages 135-142, Vancouver, British Columbia, Canada, 1989.

13. R. Leermakers. A recursive ascent Earley parser. *Information Processing Letters*, 41(2):87-91, February 1992.

14. R. Leermakers. Recursive ascent parsing: from Earley to Marcus. *Theoretical Computer Science*, 104:299-312, 1992.

15. H. Leiss. On Kilbury's modification of Earley's algorithm. *ACM Transactions on Programming Languages and Systems*, 12(4):610-640, 1990.

16. J. M. I. M. Leo. A general context-free parsing algorithm running in linear time on every $LR(k)$ grammar without using lookahead. *Theoretical Computer Science*, 82:165-176, 1991.

17. S. Naumann and H. Langer. *Parsing*. B.G. Teubner, Stuttgart, 1994.

18. M. J. Nederhof. An optimal tabular parsing algorithm. In *Proc. of the 32nd ACL*, pages 117-124, Las Cruces, New Mexico, 1994.

19. M. J. Nederhof. Efficient generation of random sentences. *Natural Language Engineering*, 2(1):1-13, 1996.

20. M. J. Nederhof and G. Satta. Efficient tabular LR parsing. In *Proc. of the 34th ACL*, pages 239-246, Santa Cruz, CA, 1996.

21. A. Nijholt. *Context-Free Grammars: Covers, Normal Forms, and Parsing*, volume 93. Springer-Verlag, Berlin, Germany, 1980.

22. F. C. N. Pereira and D. H. D. Warren. Parsing as deduction. In *Proc. of the 21st ACL*, pages 137-144, Cambridge, MA, 1983.

23. J. J. Schoorl and S. Belder. Computational linguistics at Delft: A status report. Report WTM/TT 90-09, Delft University of Technology, Applied Linguistics Unit, 1990.

24. P. Shann. Experiments with GLR and chart parsing. In M. Tomita, editor, *Generalized LR Parsing*. Kluwer Academic Publishers, 1991.

25. S. M. Shieber. Direct parsing of ID/LP grammars. *Linguistics and Philosophy*, 7:135-154, 1984.

26. S. M. Shieber. Using restriction to extend parsing algorithms for complex-feature-based formalisms. In *Proc. of the 23rd ACL*, pages 145-152, Chicago, IL, 1985.

27. O. Stock. Parsing with flexibility, dynamic strategies, and idioms in mind. *Computational Linguistics*, 15(1):1-18, 1989.

28. A. van Wijngaarden et al. Revised report on the algorithmic language ALGOL 68. *Acta Informatica*, 5:1-236, 1975.

29. T. G. Vosse. *The Word Connection*. PhD thesis, University of Leiden, 1994.

30. M. Wiren. A comparison of rule-invocation strategies in parsing. In *Proc. of the 3rd EACL*, pages 226-233, Copenhagen, Denmark, 1987.

Autonomous Robot Navigation Using a Reactive Agent

Maurizio Piaggio, Antonio Sgorbissa, Gianni Vercelli[†], and Renato Zaccaria

DIST - University of Genova, Via Opera Pia 13, Genova, Italy
[†]DEEI- University of Trieste, Via A. Valerio 10, Trieste, Italy

Abstract

The paper discusses the architecture of a Reactive Agent, capable of carrying out autonomous navigation. The agent extends the artificial potential field approach, used for trajectory formation, to environment exploration and symbolic feature detection. The agent's capabilities range from obstacle avoidance to maze navigation, carried out autonomously or under the supervision of higher cognitive levels.

1 Introduction

The reference scenario of this paper is that of a *service robot*, capable of moving among people in *civil environments*, for carrying out *assistive tasks*. Examples are night surveillance tasks in large buildings like museums, exhibitions, banks, warehouses; transportation of things (food, drugs, blankets ...) on demand and/or on schedule in hospitals and communities; guiding people in departments and exhibitions. The robot must be highly autonomous and capable of carrying out safe navigation in presence of unpredictable obstacles, humans or unforeseen situations.

The paper discusses the architecture of a Reactive Agent, capable of carrying out autonomous navigation. The agent extends the artificial potential field approach, used for trajectory formation, to environment exploration and symbolic feature detection. The agent's capabilities range from obstacle avoidance to maze navigation, carried out autonomously or in a multi-level cognitive framework schematised in figure 1, in which three levels are present, related to the different kinds of knowledge needed. The upper box is responsible for the high level reasoning, including reasoning about plans and actions, and plan generation. The intermediate box typically is the depository of actual plans which are selected and adapted. The lower box is the reactive level, in which reasoning is performed on-line, exclusively basing on sensing signals.

The overall cognitive architecture joins two different approaches known in literature as functional (symbolic) and reactive. The presence of the two components, other than for plausibility reasons, well fits the two different approaches to robot intelligence, based on explicit knowledge and on *emerging intelligent behaviour*. In our approach, the former is responsible for classifying plans, situations, goals and tasks, and for providing supervisor/user interaction; the latter, for fast, adaptable and situated planning. The two activities have, of course, different time constraints, spanning over at least one order of magnitude in computational speed requirements. The integration of these two aspects results in rich, autonomous and self-adapting behaviour basing on a rather simple structure of small and fast algorithms. The mobile robot can be connected through a communication infrastructure (using intelligent building technologies commercially available) to the higher levels of knowledge and reasoning.

However, sometimes the connection may get lost or noisy; or the remote description of the operating environment may be wrong or not available: in these cases, the robot must be able to navigate in any case in total autonomy.

The Autonomous Agent presented in this paper is able to act as the *reactive level* of the multi-level architecture, in the restricted domain of robot navigation and with the following special characteristics:

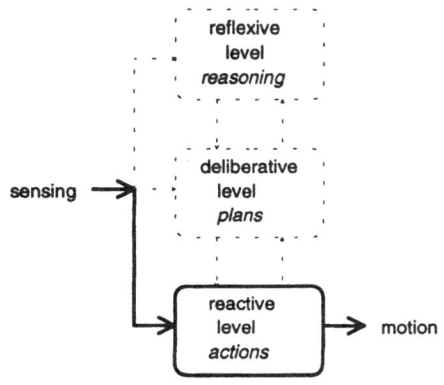

Figure 1 The general cognitive architecture

a) it has a minimal internal structure, in terms of memory and computation,

b) it acts basing on limited sensor data, mostly local,

c) it solves trajectory formation with tunable personality (by a higher level),

d) it explores the environment generating lists of relevant sites ("*landmarks*") that a higher level can use for recognition, reasoning, planning and so on,

e) it can travel in complex environments under the supervision of a higher level by tuning few "*behavioral parameters*" (similar to *navigation templates* [1]),

f) if left without supervision, is in any case capable (although in inefficient way) of solving the navigation problem, and gives the higher level the list of "*discoveries*" found during wandering,

g) it has a robust autonomous behavior, suitable for a real implementation on a very simple machine.

2 The Formal Model of the Agent

The structure of the agent A is shown in figure 2. Globally, it is a finite-memory machine able to generate, at any instant τ, a value for A's vector velocity $v(\tau)$, basing on the actual, local perception (position $p(\tau)$, time τ, obstacles) and its *internal state*, which is, in turn, changed by rules for classifying the different situations encountered inside a limited set of cases defined *a priori*. The most of A's memory is used for managing state history; this memory, as shown in the following, is in any case very limited. The agent is hence purely reactive. A's inputs are *sensing* data and *behavior parameters* from a higher level planner; its outputs are *control signals* and aggregate information about the environment (*discoveries*) toward the higher level planner. The agent A is composed by 4 main internal units:

1. a *Global Perceptor*, a memory-less machine, whose task is *positioning*; it computes the values of the position $p(\tau)$ and the direction towards the goal g;

2. a *Local Perceptor*, a "small memory" machine, whose task is proximity sensing, which: computes the actual value of a potential field $U(p)$ (used to model obstacles

as repulsive forces as in Khatib [2]); computes the local repulsive force **f** by local differentiation of $U(\mathbf{p})$ and the best local tangent **t**;

3. a *Reactive Motion Generator*, a memory-less machine, which: at any **p** computes a value for $\mathbf{v}(\tau)$ which depends on a weighted sum of directions (**t,g, f**) tuned by the navigation planner;

4. a *Navigation Planner*, a finite state machine, whose task is on-line computation of trajectory formation and free navigation, which, basing on actual localization (**p, g**), field values (U, **f**, **t**), and an internal *state* (list of *landmarks*, V_{ref}, U_L) generates the actual pilot values for the reactive motion generator;

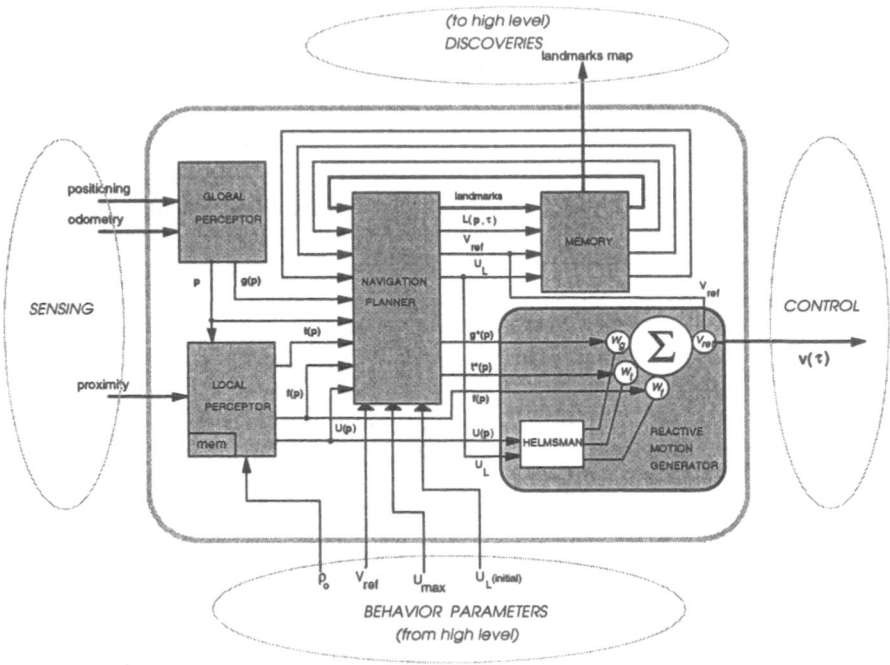

Figure 2 The Agent's structure

2.1 The Reactive Motion Generator

The reactive motion generator is a purely algebraic device, responsible for the generation of a smooth law of motion. Its output is a velocity value **v** obtained with a dynamically weighted composition of **g**, **t** and **f** modulated by the current value of U and a reference scalar velocity V_{REF} :

$$\mathbf{v}(\mathbf{p}) = \left[W_g(U, U_L) \cdot \mathbf{g}^*(\mathbf{p}) + W_t(U, U_L) \cdot \mathbf{t}^*(\mathbf{p}) + W_f(U, U_L) \cdot \mathbf{f}(\mathbf{p}) \right] \cdot V_{ref}$$

The instantaneous velocity vector is the weighted composition of three directions: the first aims to the goal, the second follows the current equipotential line, the third keeps

A, in a very small range, far from a given equipotential line U_L. The two weights W_g and W_t are the "main drivers" of A, since W_f becomes relevant only when A is very close to some obstacle boundary. When A is far from obstacles it moves towards the goal following **g**; when A is "deep inside" the field generated by an obstacle, it moves along an equipotential line at constant U. At intermediates levels of potential, the formula above generates an intermediate weighted direction. Moreover, if $U{\approx}U_L$, the third weight W_f makes the **f** component relevant so that A is strongly repulsed, down along the field's gradient, ensuring collision avoidance despite of measurement uncertainties and model accuracy.

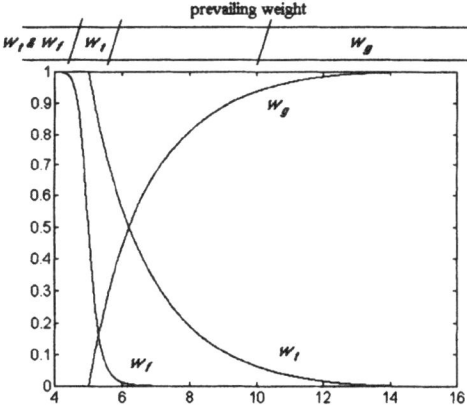

Figure 3 A typical plot of W_g, W_t and W_f

Smoothness and stability of the trajectory in presence of obstacles depend largely on the compositional law of the three components; we defined three non linear laws which exhibit a smooth and robust dynamic behaviour also in presence of realistic disturbances. In figure 3 W_g, W_t and W_f are plotted versus the distance ρ from an obstacle and given some typical values for other parameters; The motion generator's formulae define the *smart reflexive behaviour* on which the whole navigation method is founded. They solve the problem of switching smoothly and fluently the agent's tactics between "go towards the target" and "go around the obstacle". Smoothness is a key point, and is achieved by the non linearity of the weights in the figure.

2.2 The Navigation Planner

As shown in figure 2, the navigation planner works on-line, on the basis of actual perceptual data (**g**, **t**, **f**, U, **p**) and its internal state (landmark list, potential parameter U_L, reference velocity V_{REF}), and computes two kinds of outputs: (a) "tuning" values for the motion generator (U_L, **g***, **t***); (b) updated values for its internal state.

The navigation planner is defined by a series of heuristic *asynchronous rules* (some of them can be fired independently and concurrently). They are divided in three groups:

1. first two rules define the repulsive abstract potential field as in [2];
2. two other rules defines the *navigation vectors* **g*** and **t*** (used by the Reactive Motion Generator), switching between possible alternatives for **g** and **t** vectors, and basing on the actual motion **v**;

3. remaining rules define the *landmark management* for exploring cluttered environments and escaping from concavities and mazes: in particular, two rules are dedicated to the *landmark generation* process, whereas other rules express the *landmark list revision* process.

The concept of *landmark* is slightly different here from the classical meaning of natural/artificial reference point during navigation. We could define it as a *"region of space* relevant to the navigation planner which is procedurally generated, updated and labeled by the agent A during its motion". It is a region with a *basin of recognition* as the agent moves in a continuous abstract space (the potential field); A landmark is typed normally by the agent as:

- T-Point (*turn point*), when the agent, heading towards an obstacle, encounters an obstacle, and start an avoidance maneuver deciding whether to turn left or right (using the most promising tangent with respect to the actual equipotential line of the repulsive field);
- L-Point (*leave point*), when the agent abandons the followed obstacle (the chosen equipotential line) to head towards the target.

The *landmark generation* procedure marks the current position of the agent A as a new L-point or T-point, storing the relevant information for future passages. The *landmark list revision* procedure normally updates the information stored in landmarks revisited during navigation, except when the agent reaches the maximum allowed potential (equal to the minimal safe distance from obstacles) U_{max}: in case of L-point the agent marks the landmark as *follow*, which means that from the current passage on the leaving of the obstacle is no more convenient; in case or T-point the agent clears the landmark, which means that the turning direction becomes indifferent.

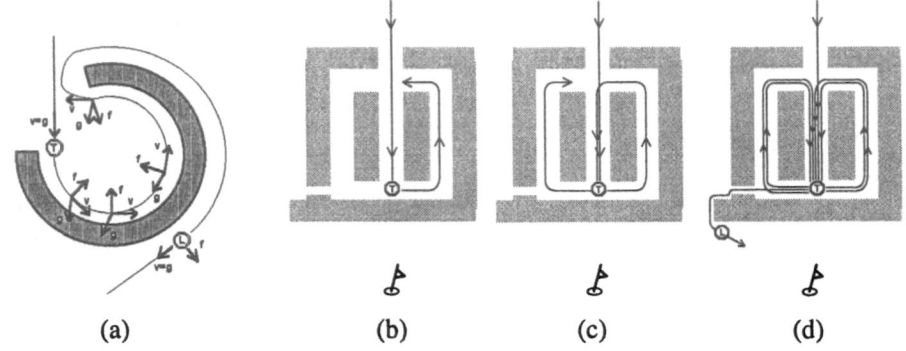

(a)   (b)   (c)   (d)

Figure 4 Applying landmarks rules

The basic concept which allows the extension from trajectory formation to environment exploration (hence to symbolic navigation) is the *heuristic classification* of the relationship among **f**, **g**, **v** versors during motion. In the example of figure 4a, the rules generate T-Point (when **f** exceeds a given threshold), L-Point (when **v** is once more equal to **g** and orthogonal to **f**) and inside the concavity **g*** is set to zero. This gives the agent more powerful capabilities than hill-climbing in traditional artificial potential field-based approaches.

Figure 4(b,c,d) shows how the landmark generation and updating rules for T-points work together with the rules defined for navigation vectors. When the agent A detects an obstacle in the **g** direction, as when entering the door of the depicted scenario, it crosses straightforward the door (climbing the potential field until the saddle is found); then it goes on through the corridor until it detects the wall at the end: as the potential grows up to the limit U_L, a T-point landmark is generated, and the best tangent **t** is computed (in case of bare symmetry, the direction is chosen randomly).

The agent A starts to follow the concavity, and if it encounters again the previously generated landmark (which means that the taken direction was not correct) it update the T-point landmark taking the other tangent direction. It is important to remind that the agent moves itself inside the potential field, which is a continuum: so far each landmark has a *basin of attraction* (tunable by the high level), and the looping inside the concavity could be iterated several times. The second time the landmark is encountered (as depicted in the picture on the right), the turning direction is inverted once again, but the U_L is augmented of a fixed step, in order to facilitate the hill climbing with a spiral motion inside the concavity. From then onwards landmark rules are alternatively applied, until the U_{max} is reached. Finally, in the right figure the agent finds the little door on the left wall after two passages.

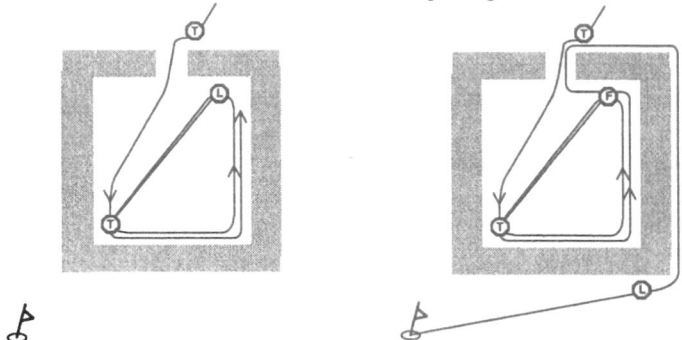

Figure 5 Applying landmark rules for L-points

L-Points are useful, in general, to avoid large circumnavigation (like in BUG algorithms [3]). A problem could arise when generating an L-point inside a narrow concavity (a local minimum, as the loop in figure 5): the agent starts a spiral motion by augmenting its U_L and, when it reaches U_{max}, the landmark is marked as "follow", so that the agent could escape from the concavity.

3 Solving Navigation Problems

Different classes of navigation problems of increasing complexity could be solved starting from the Abstract Potential Field (APF) model: reactive navigation (obstacle avoidance), escaping from local minima (hill climbing and saddle crossing, looping inside a concavity), knowledge-based navigation and navigation in mazes.

The agent has been implemented on real robot, a TRC Labmate, with an on board computer, two proximity sensors rings (8 sensors each) and a novel positioning system based on active beacons (DLPS© [4]). An analogous version which operated in a simulated environment has also been developed to facilitate the testing of new implementations (the example figures in the previous sections were obtained in this way). In simulation we took into account both positioning, control and sensor data errors to obtain comparable results with real world navigation. The perceptive rate of ultrasonic sensor rings was fixed at a frequency of 20 Hz, a value which experimentally gave us the best trade-off between average map quality and the time for a complete scan. The sensors were placed in order to privilege perception on the front of the robot for navigational purposes. In addition, different sensor orientations allow a better the detection of obstacle borders.

3.1 Reactive navigation (Obstacle avoidance)

The Agent has good capabilities in forming smooth trajectories for avoiding obstacles in a reactive manner; its behavior depends basically on the choice of U_L and ρ_0 parameters, that can be tuned during motion to cope with local problems. The higher U_L (up to U_{max}), the greater is the effect of the compass **g** with respect to APF. At the same time, the lower ρ_0 is, the greater are the capabilities of moving close to obstacles (tactile navigation), hence to allow more difficult maneuvers in between obstacles. On the other side the higher ρ_0 is, the greater are the capabilities of perceiving the APF, hence to start earlier the avoidance maneuver.

3.2 Escaping from local minima

During navigation inside APF the Agent must face the well-known problem of local minima, without using a complex global modeling of the APF itself (for avoiding the formation of local minima in the field) nor considering only convex shapes or convex hulls. In order to escape from cul-de-sac the Agent uses two simple strategies: *(i)* hill climbing up to U_L to cross possible saddles in the field, and *(ii)* looping inside a concavity upgrading U_L (up to U_{max}) when a cycle is discovered.

Hill climbing requires a suitable backtracking mechanism in the traditional Potential Field approach; in our model the climbing capability is naturally excited when using high values of U_L, which corresponds to a greater weight of the compass direction with respect to the tangential direction due to the limit equipotential curve of the APF. In this sense U_L is in relation with the capability of crossing saddle points in the field, which corresponds in the real case to narrow passages between obstacles: doors, corridors, dead-ends, etc.

Local minima generated by a concavity cannot be avoided by simply examining the local APF. The strategy used to escape from a concavity is to generate a smooth climbing of the APF (a sort of *spiral motion* depicted in figure 5) using previously generated landmarks as "loop markers". A limit cycle could be generated in a concavity (where the Agent could start to wander indefinitely) due to a bad choice of

U_L. It is simple to demonstrate that, if obstacles are separated and of finite shape, a saddle is formed, and a sufficiently high value of U_L will allow the Agent to climb on top of the saddle and leave the depression in which it had fallen.

3.3 Knowledge-based Navigation

The lower-level behaviors of the Agent so far described assume no prior knowledge of the environment in which the navigation takes place: the landmark map is initially empty and the U_L parameter set to an initial low value. It is during the agent's navigation that landmarks are created (and updated) and the U_L value is increased in order to cross narrow passages. It can be noted however that the agent is also well suited for navigating in a partially known environment. This prior knowledge can be of different types; we consider the possibility of using (i) a map of prior landmarks or (ii) a map of U_L regions.

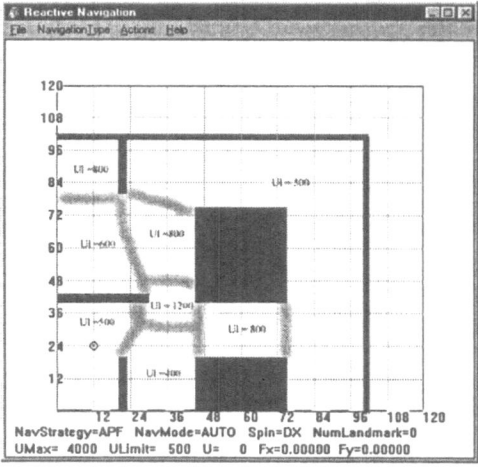

Figure 6 Map of U$_L$ regions

The map of prior landmarks consists in a set of landmarks associated to a region of space and to an potential value U_L. The only difference is the additional possibility of having "fixed" prior landmarks: a fixed landmark will not be modified by the landmark rules. This feature allows the usage of landmarks to force a pre-defined behavior in the associated region of space: the agent can be forced to turn left when it meets a given obstacle, to leave the equipotential line to head towards the target, to follow the equipotential line instead of leaving it and to increase its limit energy value U_L. In this way landmarks are used as *navigation templates* [1]. Thus if the agent needs to carry out a particular mission, an agent responsible of high level activities might generate a prior map to facilitate the navigation.

The map of U_L regions (figure 6) can be used alternatively or together with the map of prior landmarks. It is a map divided into different regions, each associated to a portion of space in the environment. Every region captures information about the part of the world it refers to by indicating the limit energy value U_L the agent should have when moving within its boundaries. The knowledge of these values is useful to perform better paths in critical regions: an high value of U_L when crossing narrow passages (saddles of U), or a low value in free space. An example could be a cluttered environment where there are several regions with a low value of U_L in large empty parts of a room, a medium value in corridors, and higher values near the doors (figure 6). The choice of different U_L also affects the law of motion of the agent: speed and curvature radii are inverse proportional to U_L. It is important to note that such map of U_L-regions can be obtained from the map generated automatically during the normal missions, as a secondary result of obstacle avoidance. An interesting class of problems, as finding maze's solutions, could exploit efficiently this "local tuning" property of the Agent.

3.4 Maze Problems

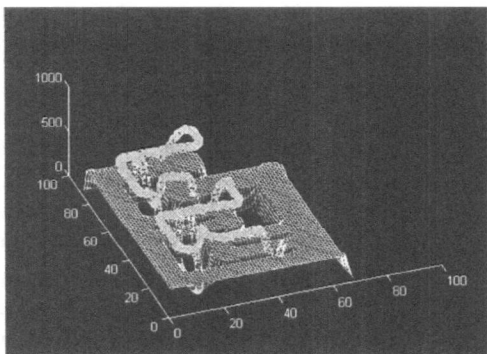

Figure 7 Navigating into a maze

Finding the path to exit a maze has been widely studied in the literature, as well as path optimality criteria and minimum path planning. The agent we propose here has not been particularly designed for maze problems, but, as a consequence of tactile navigation plus landmark map management, it could be usefully applied to discover the way out of a mazes. Figure 7 shows a simulation result of a navigation inside a maze problem inspired from [3] in a 3-dimensional space (x, y, U). It is worth noting how the agent is able to freely climb and descend the field while finding a way out. With respect to BUG1/BUG2 our agent has shown even better results, but the most interesting feature is that it uses a continuous representation of the world (APF), which leads to a real implementation of a physical robot.

4 Conclusions

It is well known that the navigation problem is a difficult task for on-line systems based on local perception. In particular methods that use the potential field metaphor suffer from local minima and limit cycles. Arkin [5] uses Motor Schemas within AuRA as a collection of individual motor behaviors which are composed into complex navigation task executions. Payton [6] proposed a winner-take-all mechanism to select the dominant behaviour among a collection of reflexive motor responses. On the contrary, the agent we propose in this paper is based on a single motor behavior, thus simplifying the system architecture. However, it is still capable of solving a variety of navigation problems of different complexity and, in particular, even path finding in a maze. It is our conjecture, although not proved yet, that these capabilities hold from a theoretical point of view. The potential field used by the agent is constructed in real-time from sensor data, leading to a working implementation in a physical robot . The system has proved to be very robust even in crowded environments, very narrow passages (such as doors) or in the sudden presence of an obstacle. A different approach with similar results is the Task Control Architecture (TCA) of the Xavier robot developed at CMU [7].

Finally, a remarkable feature of our agent is the easier integration with higher level components. The landmarks it produces can be used both during a single task and for subsequent off-line planning or environment reconstruction. In particular they can be regarded as symbolic information which can be dealt with concurrently by a higher architectural level. Current work is focused on the implementation of a cognitive hybrid architecture capable of dealing with high level tasks and robot-human interaction.

References

[1]   Miller D., and Slack D., (1993), Navigation templates: mediating qualitative guidance and quantitative control in mobile robots, *IEEE Transactions on Systems, Man, and Cybernetics*, 23 (2).

[2]   Khatib O. (1986), Real time obstacle avoidance for manipulators and mobile robots, *Int. J. Robotics Res.*, 5 (1), 90-99.

[3]   Lumelsky V. (1987), Algorithmic and Complexity Issues of Robot Motion in an Uncertain Environment, *Journal of Complexity*, 3, 146-182.

[4]   Giuffrida F., Morasso P., Vercelli G., Zaccaria R. (1996), Active localization techniques for mobile robots in the real world, Proc. IROS'96, Osaka, Japan.

[5]   R. Arkin (1991), Integrating Behavioural, Perceptual, and World Knowledge in Reactive Navigation, *Designing Autonomous Agents*, MIT/Elsevier.

[6]   D. Payton (1991), Internalized Plans: A Representation for Action Resources, *Designing Autonomous Agents*, MIT/Elsevier.

[7]   R. Simmons, R. Goodwin, K. Zita Haigh, S. Koenig, J. O'Sullivan (1997), A Modular Architecture for Office Delivery Robots, *Autonomous Agents*, ACM.

[8]   Brooks R.A. (1990), Elephants don't play chess, in *Designing Autonomous Agents*, (P. Maes Ed.), MIT Press, Cambridge (Ma).

[9]   Ferguson I. (1995), Integrating Models and Behaviours in Autonomous Agents: Some Lessons Learned on Action Control, AAAI Spring Symposium on Lessons Learned from Implemented Software Architecture for Physical Agents, Stanford, CA, AAAI Press, Menlo Park, CA.

[10] M.Frixione, M.Piaggio, G.Vercelli, and R.Zaccaria (1995), A cognitive hybrid model for autonomous navigation, Proc. 4th Congress of the Italian Association for Artificial Intelligence, AIIA 1995, Florence, Italy.

A Hybrid Architecture for Autonomous Agents

Antonio Chella, Salvatore Gaglio, Giuseppe Sajeva, and Fausto Torterolo

Dipartimento di Ingegneria Elettrica, Università di Palermo, Viale delle Scienze, 90128 Palermo, Italy

Abstract. A new *hybrid* approach for autonomous agents is described. The approach integrates in a principled way the functional and the behavioral approaches of agent design. The integration is based on the introduction of a *conceptual space* representation that links the subsymbolic level, which is a repository of reactive modules, with the symbolic level, in which rich symbolic descriptions of the agent environment take place. Results are reported obtained by an experimental implementation of the agent.

1 Introduction

The main architectural approaches adopted in the autonomous robots design may be subdivided in two big categories: the *functional* approach and the *behavioral* approach [13].

The functional approach, at the basis of the classic *Strip-Planex* [10] system, is based on the idea that the architecture of an autonomous agent may be decomposed in a hierarchy of functional layers. The bottom layers are related to the processing of data flowing by sensors and actuators; their main task is the execution of the plan generated by the top layers. The top layers process the information coming out from the bottom layers in order to find a strategy to satisfy the goals of the agent. These layers then feed back the commands to the bottom layers.

The main interest in this architecture is posed on the top layers that build deliberate plans controlling the agent behavior. This approach allows for the adoption of the symbolic AI methodologies of knowledge representation and planning, thus aiming for a rich and complete descriptions of the agent environment, its goals and its actions. But some limitations have been found in real-world situations. This architecture does not take into account the fact that the world changes in unpredictable manner, and a complex plan may be continuously rebuilt by adapting itself to the new situations. The link with the external world simply refers to some form of procedural attachments of the symbols of the planning system, without taking into account the complexity of the interactions of the agent with its environment (Agre [2])

Instead, the behavioral approach to the design of autonomous agents is based on the idea that the control architecture of an agent may be well decomposed as a set of *behavior modules* arranged in parallel. Each module receives a sensory input and produces a control signal responsible for a specific behavior of the robot (see Maes [15]). The data processing occurring in a single behavior module is generally very simple as it is essentially based on a list of *condition-action* rules. The main claim of this approach is that the complex tasks of the agent are not explicitly programmed in some sort of "central control module" as the top layer of the functional approach, but they emerge from the interactions of these simpler modules. Representative works are the *subsumption* architecture proposed by Brooks [6], the *Pengi* system proposed by Agre and Chapman [3] and the *situated automata* framework proposed by Kaelbling and Rosenschein [18].

According to these approaches, it is necessary to precisely define, at the time of agent design, its interaction with the working environment. The description of the goals of the agent and its control strategy to arbitrate among the behavior modules is in fact "hard-wired" in the architecture description, as in the *subsumption* architecture and in the *Pengi* system, or it is defined by a high-level language as in the *situated automata* framework. It is therefore required that the designer should be able to define the best behavior in all the possible situations of interaction with the environment, as pointed out by Maes [15].

Only a few proposals have been pointed in the direction to link the functional with the behavioral approaches. Brady and Hu [13] propose a robot architecture based on the *LICA* (Locally Intelligent Control Agent) module. The module is able to act reactively, as in the behavioral approach, but it has some high level reasoning capabilities. Several modules may then be organized in a functional hierarchy as in the functional approach. Malcom and Smithers [16] propose the *Somass* system, a hybrid architecture for an autonomous agent subdivided as in the *Strips-Planex* system; the high level is a Prolog assembly planner, while the low level is a plan execution agent build up by behavioral modules which defines the symbol grounding for the planner. Arkin [4] proposes a behavioral architecture, named *AuRA*, for an autonomous agent in which a distinction is made between the "a priori" and the "dynamic" knowledge of the robot. The first one is a sort of long term memory of the agent. In Arkin's work, in particular, it is a cartographic knowledge of the agent environment; the second one is acquired during the robot operations and it represents a sort of environmental context in which the robot operates.

We propose an architecture for the design of autonomous agents which links together in a principled way the two different research traditions of the functional and behavioral approaches of robot architectures. We agree with the behavioral approach that simple modules better implement the reactive behaviors which should be described by immediate associations between percepts and actions. But we maintain that, in order to have an intelligent behavior of the robot, a rich and concrete knowledge representation of the agent environment and an intelligent planning of the actions of the agent are needed.

The proposed architecture extends to the autonomous agents design the previously proposed cognitive architecture for artificial vision [8]. Our proposal is based on a cognitive decomposition of the agent architecture in three main layers:

- **The subconceptual level** which is a repository of behavior modules in the sense of the behavioral approach.

- **The conceptual level** where the information is characterized in terms of a metric space defined by a number of *cognitive* dimensions, independent of any specific language. This level aims at generating the essential representation of the agent's external environment and at providing a precise interpretation of the subsequent high level (see Gärdenfors [11]).
- **The linguistic level** in which information is expressed by a symbolic language. This level should be considered as a first level that is nevertheless sufficient to ground successively higher symbolic reasoning activities, as knowledge representation, spatial reasoning and planning.

A correlated cognitive topic of our architecture is the role of the *expectation* generation processes to detect the relevant aspects in the working environment of the agent. The linguistic level in fact processes the information acquired through the conceptual space to create expectations and to form contexts in which hypotheses can be verified and, if necessary, adjusted. These expectations are then sent to the subconceptual level to drive the overall behavior of the robot.

The needs for a "central engagement module" that controls the whole behavior of the agent, as our linguistic level, has been summarized, among others, by Balkenius [5]. He notes that the behavior modules of an agent may not be executed all at the same time, and the arbitration between them may not be always local. The behavior modules may be activated instead on the basis of the *internal drives*, i.e. the goals of the agent; the *external incentives*, which are strictly related to the perceived situations, and *internal incentives* that are related to the previous knowledge of the agent. The robot behavior is in fact driven by expectations generated at the linguistic level, thus aiming at the generation of contexts controlling the robot actions, as proposed by Roth and Jain [19].

Our architecture proposal is in the line of the functional decomposition approach, as it is a hierarchy of three levels of representation; but the subconceptual level is made up by behaviors modules as in the *subsumption* architecture. These modules are more similar to the *LICA* modules [13], as they may have some form of reasoning, as the module performing wandering with obstacle avoidance. They allow for a reactive behavior for the agent in unpredictable situations, without the needs of the linguistic level processing. The linguistic level is similar to the top level of the functional decomposition as in allows for planning and knowledge representation, thus allowing for a central decision module. The linguistic level may contain a structured description of the agent environment and it is not constrained to simple cartographic information as in the *AuRA* architecture [4]. The symbols at the proposed linguistic level are precisely defined by the conceptual space, thus avoiding the symbol grounding problem for the agent. The conceptual space may be, we believe, a rich and structured interpretation domain, more richer than the simple collection of behavior modules as in the *Somass* architecture [16]. It should be noted in fact the main role of the conceptual space: it is built by data processing acting at the subconceptual level by the behavior modules and it allows for a precise interpretation level for the symbols at the linguistic level.

The architecture has been implemented on a *Real World Interface* RWI-B12 autonomous robot equipped with an Ethernet radio link and a vision head with a CCD video camera on a pan-tilt. Fig. 1 shows the robot in its working environment. The experimented task of the robot is the exploration of its environment. It starts by wandering; when it find an obstacle or a wall it is able to avoid it and continue its wandering. When it finds an "interesting" object, it self-localizes, and it describes the 3D characteristics of the object and its position by a high level language. Furthermore, interesting objects generate contexts in which the robot operates: when the robot finds, for instance, a hammer in a certain position, it assumes to be in an hardware context and it tries to find screws and nails. All the other objects that do not belong to the activated contexts are then ignored.

In the following, Sect. 2 presents the overall proposed architecture of the autonomous agent while Sect. 3 describes in details the subconceptual level of the architecture. Sect. 4 presents some experimental results of the implemented architecture.

2 The Architecture of the Autonomous Agent

The cognitive assumptions presented above provide the guidelines for the design and implementation of the proposed architecture for autonomous agents. Fig. 2 shows the overall architecture in which the previously described three levels of representation are pointed out.

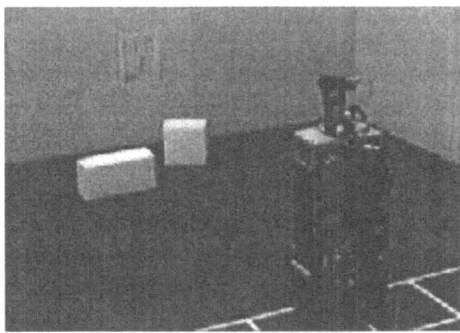

Fig. 1. The autonomous robot in the working environment.

Block A receives the input from the camera on the head of the robot; this input is sent to the behavior modules belonging to the subconceptual level. The modules are displaced in parallel and each module receives the same input. Some modules are tightly connected with the robot actuators, e.g. the localization module and the obstacle detection module. The modules send an output to the conceptual space.

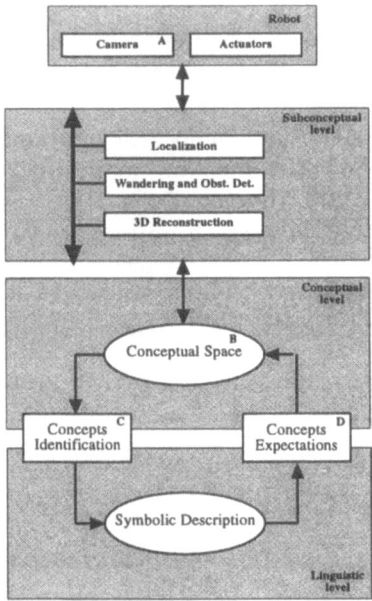

Fig. 2. The proposed architecture in which the three levels of representation are pointed out.

Block B is the conceptual space of the architecture; it receives inputs from the behaviors modules of the subconceptual level and it acts as the interpretation level for the linguistic level. According to Gärdenfors, a conceptual space is a metric space defined by a certain number of cognitive dimensions, independent from any specific language [11]. Examples of such dimensions would be color, pitch, mass, spatial coordinates, and so on. The dimensions are "cognitive" in that they correspond to qualities of the represented environment, without reference to any linguistic descriptions. In this sense, a conceptual space is prior to any symbolic characterization of cognitive phenomena; this level generates the very internal representation of the agent's external environment. We call *knoxel* a generic point in a conceptual space; accordingly, each knoxel is related to measurements, obtained via the agent sensors, of the parameters describing the percepts of the agent [8].

In our agent design we have adopted a very simple conceptual space in which a knoxel corresponds to the set of parameters of suitable 3D geometric primitives, i.e. the *superquadrics* [17]. Their boolean composition allows for the representation of a great variety of familiar shapes, particularly those corresponding to human artifacts. They offer an acceptable compromise between the compression of information in the scene and the necessary computational costs [20].

Block C implements the mapping between this conceptual level and the linguistic level; this block aims at recognizing the objects and the situations. The input to block C is a structure at the conceptual level, i.e. a set of superquadrics;

its output is sent to the linguistic level to produce a sentential description of the scene. This link is performed by a particular kind of Hopfield neural network with delayed connections (see [8] for details). The *symbolic knowledge base* is the kernel of the linguistic level. The aim of this block is twofold: it describes in a high-level language the objects and situations perceived by the agent by interpreting the input coming from block C, and it generates, by means of its inference capabilities, the *expectations* that drive the robot actions. Block D is responsible for the the expectation generation mechanism. It receives as input the instances of concepts from the knowledge base and it suitably generates the robot actions to seek for the corresponding expected objects in the scene.

3   The Subconceptual Level

As previously stated, the subconceptual level is a repository for the behaviors modules. These modules are responsible for the reactive operation of the agent. Some of these modules are also directly connected to the actuators of the agent, i.e. the mobile base and the pan tilt in our implementation. The modules process data coming from the sensors, i.e. the camera and the odometer, and feeds the conceptual space. We have implemented several behaviors modules, as the self-localization module, the wandering and obstacle detection module, the time-to-impact estimation module, the 3D reconstruction module and the occluding contour module. The behaviors modules useful to our discussion are briefly described below.

3.1   The Self-Localization Module

The main task of the self-localization module is to define the absolute coordinate system of the agent moving in a room environment, by knowing also approximately the dimensions of the room. The module is based on the application of the Hough Transform [9] to find the corners of the room representing the robot environment. The candidate corners are localized by finding all the intersection points of two approximately horizontal edge lines with one vertical edge line on a large image acquired by the robot camera at low definition. Each candidate corner is verified by applying the same procedure on a new acquired image centered at the the candidate corner point. The new image is very small but with a high definition. After the localization of three corners the robot estimates, by simple trigonometric calculations, its position in the room. To ensure consistency of the found position, the robot estimates and verifies the position of the fourth corner of the room. If the error is low, the robot concludes its self-localization and send the information to the conceptual space.

This method is very simple and efficient and it does not require artificial landmark (Adorni et at. [1]), color or light intensities information (Cassinis et al. [7]), because the only reference points considered are the corners of the room. Fig. 3 shows the intersection of two approximately horizontal edge lines with a vertical edge line and the localization of an upper corner of the room.

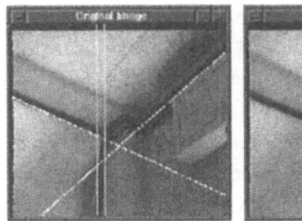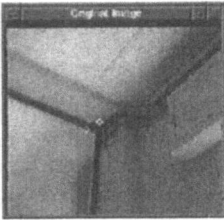

Fig. 3. Localization of a corner of the robot environment by the Hough Transform and results of the self-localization operation

3.2 The Wandering and Obstacle Detection Module

The wandering and obstacle detection module is able to estimate if there is an obstacle or free space in front of the robot, by analyzing the images acquired by the robot camera. The recognition of the situation in front of the robot is based on a SOM (Self Organizing Map) neural network [14] trained by examples of typical obstacles and free floor situations in the robot environment. This network processes a low definition image acquired by the camera and it classify the image as "obstacle", "wall" or "free_space" The output of the neural network activates a simple motor action, as "base_right" in order to avoid the obstacle, if possible, or to stop the robot in waiting of a new command.

The method is in the line of the *Core Visual Routines* proposed by Horswill [12] but the approximate distances in our method are estimated by the SOM neural network, thus allowing for an adaptation of the robot to the working environment.

Fig. 4 shows the operations of the robot when it encounter an obstacle: it recognized the obstacle, it turns to the right to find a free path, it moves to the right and it turns to left to restore its original orientation. Fig. 5 shows an example of procedures, written in Prolog, linking the neural network outputs previously described to the corresponding simple motor actions.

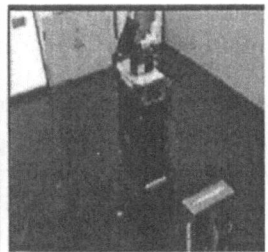

Fig. 4. The operation of the robot when it encounters an obstacle.

```
action(X,Y):-X=free_space,Y=base_forward.
action(X,Y):-X=wall,Y=base_halt.
action(X,Y):-X=obstacle,Y=base_right_100.
action(X,Y):-X=obstacle,Y=base_right;Y=base_left;write(I can't move),wait.
```

Fig. 5. Procedures linking the neural network outputs to motor actions.

3.3 The 3D Reconstruction Module

The 3D reconstruction module acquires the image from the vision head of the robot and estimated the superquadric parameters described in the scene. This module is described in details in a previous paper [8]; here we briefly resume its operation.

Starting from the acquired image, the module computes the segmentation map by means of a region growing algorithm, while the relative depth map is computed by applying a shape from shading algorithm. Both the depth map and the information about the segmented regions are used to obtain the volumetric representation of the input depth map by *voxels*, i.e., in terms of primitive volume elements. Each part of the scene is then approximated by means of the best fitting superquadric. Fig. 6 shows a scene acquired by the robot representing a hammer, along with results of the recovery of the superquadrics.

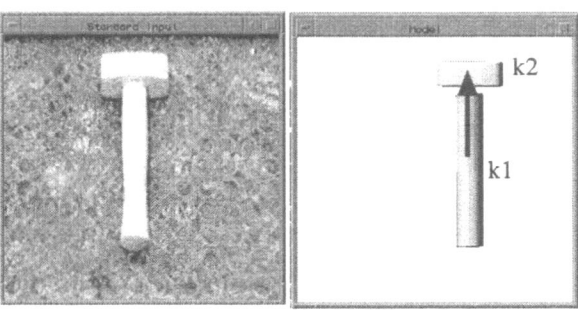

Fig. 6. A scene acquired by the robot camera and its superquadric reconstruction.

4 Experimental Results

As described in Sect. 1, the proposed architecture has been implemented on a *Real World Interface* RWI-B12 autonomous robot equipped with an Ethernet radio link and a vision head composed of a pan-tilt in which a CCD video camera is mounted. The task of the robot is to explore its room environment and to describe the "interesting" objects that it finds during its exploration. In this section we sketch the operation of the robot performing the task.

The robot starts by calling the self-localization module (see Sect. 3.1) to calibrate its position, as in fig. 3. Then it starts wandering by calling the the wandering and obstacle detection module (see Sect. 3.2). When the space in front of the robot is not free, as in fig. 4, the robot recognizes the obstacle by means of the SOM neural networks and it avoids collision by turning around the obstacle if it is possible. If the robot is in front of a wall it simply turns back. During its wandering in the room environment, when it encounter a little object, it supposes it should be an interesting thing. Then it activates the 3D reconstruction module in order to estimate the superquadric parameters of the object, as described in Sect. 3.3. In order to find the absolute position of the object, the self-localization module is again called.

The 3D module fills the conceptual level with the superquadric parameters of the object, activating the process of recognition and expectation generation (see fig. 2) as described in [8]. Then, when the robot recognizes a hammer, as in fig. 6, it expects to find nails since in the linguistic level the hammers are associated with nails and screws, by using simple rules as in fig. 7.

```
expectation(X,Y):-X=hammer,Y=nail.
expectation(X,Y):-X=hammer,Y=screw.
```

Fig. 7. Procedures describing the expectation generation process at the linguistic level.

The robot then assumes to be in an hardware context and it tries to find screws and nails. All the other objects that do not belong to the activated contexts are then ignored.

5 Conclusions

The proposed architecture is a step toward the effective integration between the functional and behavioral approaches to autonomous agents. The integration is based on cognitive consideration and it maintains the main advantages of both approaches.

Acknowledgments

Authors would like to thank Marcello Frixione for interesting discussions about the proposed architecture. Fulvio Ornato, Nunzio Ingraffia, Ignazio Infantino and Salvatore Vitabile contributed to the software implementation of the behavior modules. This work has been partially supported by Progetto Coordinato SARI of the CNR (Consiglio Nazionale delle Ricerche).

References

1. G. Adorni, G. Destri, M. Mardonini, and F. Zanichelli. Robot Self-Localization by means of vision. In IEEE Computer Society Press, editor, *Proc. of the First EUROMICRO Workshop on Advanced Mobile Robots*, pages 160–165, Los Alamitos, CA, 1996.
2. P.E. Agre. Computational research on interaction and agency. *Artif. Intell.*, 72:1–52, 1995.
3. P.E. Agre and D. Chapman. What are plans for? *Robotics and Autonom. Systems*, 6:17–34, 1990.
4. R.C. Arkin. Integrating behavioral, perceptual, and world knowledge in reactive navigation. *Robotics and Autonom. Systems*, 6:105–122, 1990.
5. C. Balkenius. *Natural Intelligence in Artificial Creatures*. PhD thesis, Lund University Cognitive Studies, Lund, Sweden, 1995.
6. R.A. Brooks. A robust layered control system for a mobile robot. *IEEE J. Robotics and Automation*, 2:14–23, 1986.
7. R. Cassinis, D. Grana, and A. Rizzi. Using colour information in an omnidirectional perception system for autonomous robot localization. In IEEE Computer Society Press, editor, *Proc. of the First EUROMICRO Workshop on Advanced Mobile Robots*, pages 172–176, Los Alamitos, CA, 1996.
8. A. Chella, M. Frixione, and S. Gaglio. A cognitive architecture for artificial vision. *Artif. Intell.*, 89:73–111, 1997.
9. R.O. Duda and P.E. Hart. Use of the Hough transform to detect lines and curves in pictures. *Commun. ACM*, 15:11–15, 1972.
10. R.E. Fikes, P.E. Hart, and N.J. Nilsson. Learning and exectuing generalized robot plans. *Artif. Intell.*, 3:251–288, 1972.
11. P. Gärdenfors. Three levels of inductive inference. In D. Prawitz, B. Skyrms, and D. Westsrståhl, editors, *Logic, Methodology, and Philosophy of Science IX*. Elsevier Science, Amsterdam, The Netherlands, 1994.
12. I. Horswill. Analysis of adaptation and environment. *Artif. Intell.*, 73:1–30, 1995.
13. H. Hu and M. Brady. A parallel processing architecture for sensor-based control of intelligent mobile robots. *Robotics and Autonomous Systems*, 17:235–257, 1996.
14. T. Kohonen. *Self-Organizing Maps*. Springer-Verlag, Berlin, 1995.
15. P. Maes. Designing autonomous agents. *Robotics and Autonom. Systems*, 6:1–2, 1990.
16. C. Malcom and Smithers T. Symbol grounding via a hybrid architecture in an autonomous assembly system. *Robotics and Autonom. Systems*, 6:123–144, 1990.
17. A.P. Pentland. Perceptual organization and the representation of natural form. *Artif. Intell.*, 28:293–331, 1986.
18. S.J. Rosenschein and L.P. Kaelbling. A situated view of representation and control. *Artif. Intell.*, 73:149–173, 1995.
19. Y. Roth and R. Jain. Knowledge caching for sensor-based systems. *Artif. Intell.*, pages 257–280, 1994.
20. F. Solina and R. Bajcsy. Recovery of parametric models from range images: The case for superquadrics with global deformations. *IEEE Trans. Patt. Anal. Mach. Intell.*, 12(2):131–146, 1990.

3-D Facets Construction for Stereovision

Ezzeddine ZAGROUBA

Faculty of Sciences of Monastir - Departement of Computer Science. LARIMA
Faculty of Sciences of Monastir - Departement of Computer Science - Route de Kairouan,
5019 Monastir - TUNISIA

Abstract : in this paper, we describe a 3-D facets construction system which relies on the simultanueous analysis of regions and contours of stereo-images in order to reconstruct 3-D indoor scenes. Firstly, a Split-And-Merge algorithm cooperating with an edge extractor is used to compute an initial region segmentation which is improved by using a rule-based system. Then, the system matches relevant regions in both images. After this, the contours detected by an edge extractor are used to replace irrelevant region boundaries after which the algorithm yields homologous subsets of contour segments. By comparing the results in each image, pairs of 2-D facets are extracted from the homologous subsets. Next, three-dimensional triangulation data are approximated by planes. Finally, planar 3-D facets are computed by an iterative algorithm to improve the initial estimation of the facets. These 3-D facets define the 3-D model of the observed scene.

1. INTRODUCTION

To derive structural 3-D information from stereo-images, it is necessary to extract precise 2-D information and to group the 2-D information from the same 3-D surface. Two methodologies are available. The most commonly used methods rely on use of low level primitives such as characteristic points or segments [1,5,8,11,16]. The 3-D objects can be reconstructed by means of triangulation [7]. Unfortunately, edge extractors produce unsatisfactory results : segments are split into several parts and some junctions are lost [21]. The quality of the resulting 3-D maps is often too poor to reconstruct the 3-D scene accurately and the scene interpretation relying on these maps is a difficult process, often generating wrong results [14,18,19].

The methods belonging to the other methodology are based on region analysis [11,12,18,20]. In previous reviews of stereopsis, we can find a survey [9] of the more well known methods and the most common constraints used to resolve the correspondance problem in its general components. But, no general framework has emerged to survey the more well known methods for the 3-D reconstruction. Four classes of region-based methods are distinguished depending on the information they rely on for the 3-D reconstruction. The class one and two methods use particular points of the region [4], or certain geometric attributes of the region [13], respectively, whereas class three makes use of all the points of the region [2,3,10,17], and class four takes all the points of the region boundaries into account [6,21]. As there exists no clear strategy for segmentation of images into regions, the results of the reconstruction are often unreliable. We propose to exploit the complementarity of region and contour information to produce 3-D models representing object surfaces. The aim of this work is to develop a global cooperative method to process indoor scenes in which, most of the time, the object surfaces are convex and can be approximated by planar surfaces, called "3-D facets". We suppose also that the two cameras are located closely together so that the two images are quite similar.

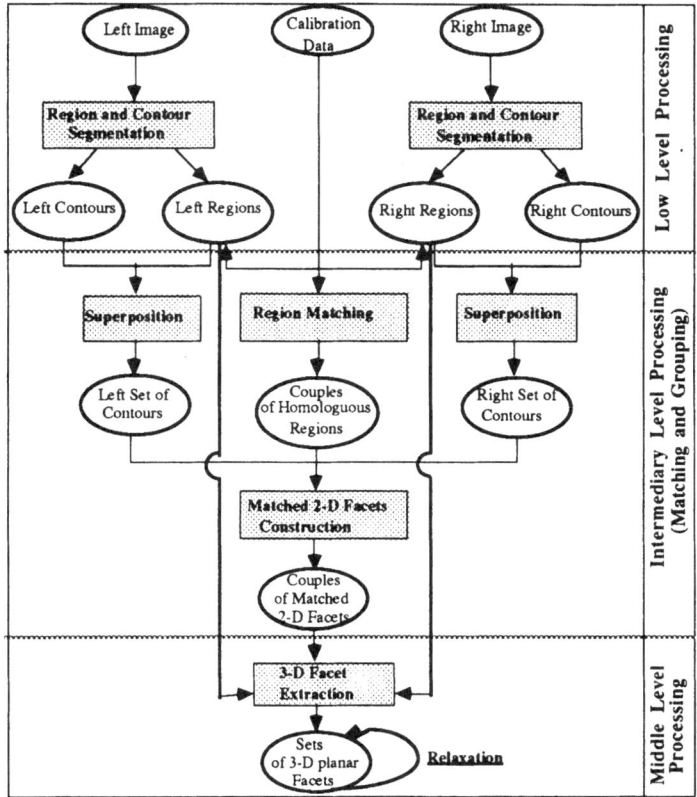

Figure 1 : Global Cooperative Stereo System Architecture

2. REGION AND CONTOUR SEGMENTATION

Our algorithm takes into account the edges which are supposed to be detected more precisely and more reliably than the region boudaries. As chown in the following schema (see fig. 2), the method is carried out in several steps. The principal goals of image segmentation are to extract the main features of the images and to decrease the data necessary for the image description. But, it is usually admitted that it does not exist a universal method for image segmentation and this is the reason why the algorithms are only adapted to a domain or even to an application. So, the aim of this method is to improve the region segmentation of images by considering each image seperately and taking into account the results of the matching process.

The contour segmentation consists on *three subprocesses*, the first one is a median filter [5] in order to eliminate the noise on the images. Then, after having computed the gradient image with a Prewitt Operator, an edge extractor provides the edge segmentation. The last two subprocesses are detailed in [5,21]. The region segmentation algorithm has *two subprocesses* and is based on the Split-and-Merge algorithm : the first one splits the image until obtaining a partition P such as all the regions satisfy a homogeneity criterion ; the second one cooperates with the edge extractor in order to merge adjacent regions by considering the contour segmentation and a new homogeneity criterion. Then, the small regions located near each significant boundary are eliminated and a curve approximation process is done to

118

describe the boundaries of the regions. The segmentation algorithm creates many horizontal or vertical boudaries without physical meaning. Therefore we defined a rule-based system dealing with this type of boundaries where the gradient mean of each boundary is used in order to decide if the boudary has a physical reality [21].

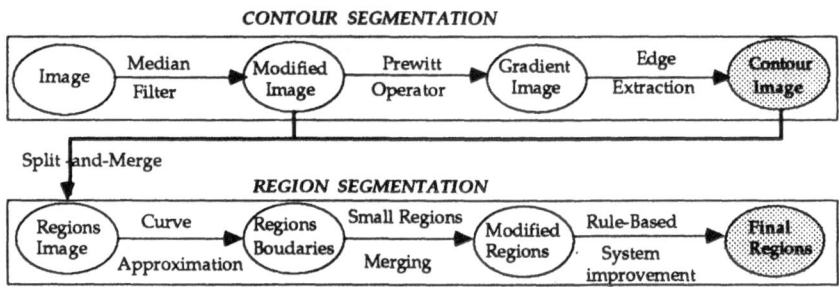

Figure 2 : Contour and Region Segmentation method

3. REGION MATCHING

The radiometric properties of the regions are very sensitive to camera location and two regions representing the same face of object in a pair of stereoscopic images can be very different from a radiometric point of view. More, the region growing process which gathers pixels as long as some radiometric characteristics remain unchanged (such as similarity, for instance), yields most of the time different boundaries for two homologous regions. Hence, we can say that : if two regions have been matched and if they are quite similar from a radiometric and geometric point of view, they are very likely to represent the same face of object. The method selects couples of regions which are very similar from a radiometric and geometric point of view, and attempts to match them if they satisfy the epipolar constraint. These couples of matched regions are referred to as "basic couples". Then the matching process is extended to the neighboring regions of the "basic couples" by using a property of adjacency : the adjacent regions are considered first and matched if possible. Then, the process is gradually extended to all the regions of the image. Finally, the regions that cannot be matched are the regions which have not been detected correctly by the region growing process. Nevertheless, a last process tries to deal with these regions by merging them into other regions. This algorithm has been tested on images taken by the robot of INRIA (cf table 1). The basic couples detection selects about 1/4 of the total number of regions ; it is noticeable that the basic couples correspond to the well-segmented regions representing real objects faces. The propagation increases the rate of matched regions up to 60 % representing 80 % of the image surface. Finally, the single region merging process improves the segmentation and adds 2 % to 10 % of matched surface depending on the initial segmentation as chown on the figures 3, 4 and 5.

Images	Number of Left Regions	Number of Right Regions	Basic Couples	Matched by Propa gation	Merged Regions	% of Matched Surface Left	Right
1st example	101	106	28	30	38	84	81
2nd example	101	115	28	29	34	82	85

Table 1 : Statistic results of the region matching process

This method reduces the combinatory complexity of the problem by using the adjacency constraint. The results are very satisfying since the most reliable matching is done first and then extended to the other regions by exploiting the previous results.

4. SELECTION OF CONTOUR SEGMENTS BY SUPERPOSITION

Most of the homologous-region boundaries are not similar on the two images because the region growing process behaved differently or failed to find the real boundary. For this reason, these irrelevant boundary segments are replaced by contour segments detected by an edge extractor and localized in the neighborhood of the boundary. In order to reduce the combinatorial complexity, the algorithm superposes the contours and the regions. Then, the contour segments in the neighborhood of a matched region are selected by means of three filters : Neighborhood, Colinearity and Length criteria. For each matched region, the three filters select contour segments which are likely to represent the region boundary. Hence, to each couple of homologous regions (R_l, R_r), the algorithm associates a couple of contour subsets (Σ_l, Σ_r) and we suppose that the homologous of any segment of a subset belongs to the associated subset.

5. CONTOUR MATCHING

A 2-D facet is a set of 2-D segments describing the boundary of a 3-D region. The aim of this process is to extract homologous 2-D facets representing the projection on each image of the same 3-D region. The homologous 2-D facets are extracted from the subsets (Σ_l, Σ_r) previously associated to the homologous regions by the superposition process. The first step of the 2-D facet extraction consists in matching the segments of (Σ_l, Σ_r).

Given a couple of regions (R_l, R_r) and the associated couple of subsets (Σ_l, Σ_r) :

$$\Sigma_l = (S_l^1, S_l^2, ...,S_l^i, ...,S_l^q) \quad \text{and} \quad \Sigma_r = (S_r^1, S_r^2, ...,S_r^j, ...,S_r^p).$$

The algorithm produces couples of homologous segments extracted from (Σ_l, Σ_r). The left (respectively right) facet, F_l (respectively F_r) is defined by all the left (respectively right) segments of the couples generated by the matching algorithm. For each segment of Σ_l, all the possible homologous segments are searched in Σ_r by means of four constraints (length, orientation and relative position); each selected segment of Σ_r generates a matching hypothesis and finally all the hypothesis are ordered by an evaluation function.

For a couple (S_l, S_r) of possible homologous segments, the similarity between the two segments according to an attribute A is measured by the function : $Sim_A[A(S_l),$ $A(S_r)] = \dfrac{Min[A(S_l), A(S_r)]}{Max[A(S_l), A(S_r)]}$. Then, we define the quality Q of a matching hypothesis (S_l, S_r) by the function :

$$Q(S_l, S_r) = \frac{1}{cardinal(A)} \sum_{A \in A} Sim_A(A(S_l), A(S_r)), \text{ with } A = \{Length, Orientation,$$

Relative Position}. Finally, the matching hypothesis are ordered according to decreasing values of the function Q and an ordered list of matching hypothesis is associated to each segment. Unfortunately, the lists of segments produced by the filters contain more than one segment, but the number of selected segments is low (average number = 3) and the filters have eliminated the spurious segments while keeping the real homologous one in about 98% of the cases. In 70% of the cases, the real homologous segment is in the first position in the ordered list.

6. 2-D FACET EXTRACTION

The 2-D facet extraction is based on the ordered lists of matching hypothesis. Couples of matched segments are generated by considering first the hypothesis with the highest quality value. New couples are created as long as the global consistency of the matching is valid. Finally, the homologous 2-D facets are made of all the couples of matched segments which have been validated.

6.1. The consistency checking algorithm

. Couples of segments are generated by grouping each segment with the first element of its associated list. The consistency checking algorithm compares all the matching hypothesis and ensufes that the uniqueness assumption is fulfilled. Given two left segments S_l^i and S_l^j and their associated lists $L_l^i = (s_r^{1,i}, s_r^{2,i}, ..., s_r^{ni,i})$ and $L_l^j = (s_r^{1,j}, s_r^{2,j}, ..., s_r^{nj,j})$. If the first segments of the two lists are identical ($s_r^{1,i} = s_r^{1,j}$), according to the uniqueness assumption of matching, S_l^i and S_l^j cannot be matched to s_r^i and s_r^j : the two segments are in conflict. To solve this conflict, we cancel one matching hypothesis, and if possible generate a new matching hypothesis, while maximizing the quality of the matching or the number of matched segments. We distinguish 3 cases :

1) card(L_l^i) = 1 and card(L_l^j) = 1 : in this case, no other matching hypothesis can be generated and we keep the matching with the highest quality value.

2) card(L_l^i) = 1 and card(L_l^j) > 1 : the couple ($S_l^i, s_r^{1,i}$) is validated and a new matching hypothesis is generated with the next element of L_l^j.

3) card(L_l^i) > 1 and card(L_l^j) > 1 : let Q_1^i and Q_2^i (resp. Q_1^j and Q_2^j) the quality of the matching hypothesis ($S_l^i, s_r^{1,i}$) and ($S_l^i, s_r^{2,i}$) (resp. ($S_l^j, s_r^{1,j}$) and ($S_l^j, s_r^{2,j}$)). We choose the couple with the maximum sum of qualities values ;
IF ($Q_1^i+Q_2^j$) ≥ ($Q_2^i+Q_1^j$) THEN we validate the couples ($S_l^i, s_r^{1,i}$) and ($S_l^j, s_r^{2,j}$)
OTHERWISE   we validate the couples ($S_l^i, s_r^{2,i}$) and ($S_l^j, s_r^{1,j}$).
This checking algorithm is iterated until all the conflicts have disappeared.

6.2. 2-D facet construction

For each segment S_i of the boundary of a region R, the oriented angle α_i which defines its relative position is computed. Then, every 2-D facet F_R is characterised by a sequence of increasing angles, called the "F_R-signature" and noted $S[F_R]$. If $F_R = (S_1, S_2, ..., S_i, ..., S_n)$ is a 2-D facet then $S[F_R]$ is defined by : $S[F_R] = (\alpha_1, \alpha_2, ..., \alpha_i, ..., \alpha_n)$ such as $\alpha_1 \leq \alpha_2 \leq ... \leq \alpha_i \leq ... \leq \alpha_n$.

A couple of homologous 2-D facets (F_{R_l}, F_{R_r}) is extracted from the couple of subsets (Σ_l, Σ_r) by comparing the order of each segment and its homologous. First, F_{R_l} (resp. F_{R_r}) is initialized to Σ_l (resp. Σ_r). Then, their signature is computed and the segments of each facet are ordered according to the facet signature. If the segment S_l^i and its homologous S_r^i are not ranked at the same place in the segment sequence, they are eliminated from the facets F_{R_l} and F_{R_r} (see fig. 6). S_l^3 and S_r^3 are eliminated.

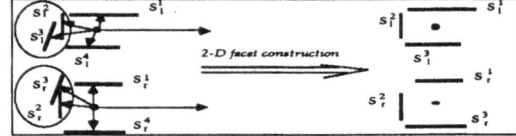

Figure 6 : Example of 2-D facet extraction

6.3. Experiments and results

The algorithm brings good results concerning the 2-D facet extraction and the matching of the segments of each couple of homologous 2-D facets (see figure 7). The percentage of segment matching is about 88% of the segments under consideration and the matching error is less than 2%. It must be noted that the method does not consider the connection property of the segments to perform grouping and matching operations. Instead of the segment connections, it considers the relative position to the region barycenter. The usual process of segment joining in order to increase the number of junctions is no longer necessary. The matching algorithm is fast since the number of matching possibilities for each couple of regions is low (see figures 7, 8 and 9).

7. 3-D FACET CONSTRUCTION

The construction of 3-D facets is achieved in three steps. First, from each couple of homologous segments, the algorithm extracts homologous points and computes 3-D points. Then, the 3-D points are approximated by a plane by means of an iterative algorithm. Finally, 3-D facet boundaries are computed from the projections of the corresponding 2-D facet boundaries.

Each swarm of 3-D points is approximated by a plane. The initial equation of the 3-D plane is computed by the Principal Axis Method. Then, the initial estimation of the plane is adjusted by an iterative process eliminating the wrong points of the swarm and updating the equation of the 3-D plane. The wrong points are the points whose suppression from the swarm results in a noticeable change in the plane orientation. When a new 3-D plane equation is obtained, the swarm points are projected onto this plane. The resulting 3-D points are then projected onto each image ; if the projections are close enough from the 2-D points at the previous step, the iterative process is stopped.

To compute the 3-D facet boundaries, the extremity points of the homologous 2-D facets boundary are projected onto the 3-D plane. Usually the projections of two homologous boundary points generate two different points on the 3-D plane. The middle of these two points is computed and all the middle points define the 3-D facet boundary.

8. RESULTS AND CONCLUSION

The method has been tested on the same indoor scenes as other methods : [1] and [5]. Table 2 summarizes the results obtained by the three methods. We can notice that the depth intervals of the main surfaces are quite similar. However, our method generates more couples of matched segments than the other methods and consequently, the number of reconstructed 3-D facets is larger. In particular, we can easily recognize the walls. Finally, the plane orientation is known within 10 degrees.

	Ayache's Method [2]	Buvry's Method [6]	Our Method
Left Wall and Windows	[+140, +448]	[177, +430]	[+150, +451]
Right Wall and Cupboards	[+282, +448]	[+299, +430]	[+299, +451]
Table	[-89, +30]	[-86, +40]	[-90, +35]

Table 2 : Depth results of the three methods (in cm).

Segment matching based on region matching gives good results since the ambiguities of the segment matching process are partially solved by the region matching outcomes. Particularly, segment matching is possible even if the segments and junctions are detected inaccurately. Nevertheless, the final results depend strongly on the initial region segmentation : only if a correct region segmentation is made, can the regions be matched successfully.

The 3-D reconstruction produces results better than those obtained by methods based on segment matching [1,5]. In our global method, the projections of the 2-D facets generate an uncertainty zone which is exploited in a subsequent optimization. In it, a dedicated algorithm [21] moves the 3-D facet boundaries inside the uncertainty zone until a cost function, based on the planarity property of regions, reaches a minimal value. We have presented a global cooperative stereo system wich integrate the low, the intermediary and the middle levels processing in order to make easier the improvement of the reconstructed 3-D model of the observed scene. The use of the complementarity of region and contour information have made possible the improvement of the results at every step of the treatement. In fact, the global cooperative stereo system presented brings interesting results and it should facilitate both the positionning of the robot and the interpretation of the observed scene. The following figures (10,11,12) show the results obtained for an other pair of stereoscopic images.

ACKNOWLEDGMENT

The author is grateful to Mrs Alain Ayache and Charlie Krey for their helpful comments on supervising this research work. I would also like to thank the ENSEEIHT - INPT (Toulouse-France) for their technical and financial support during my stay at Toulouse (France).

Figure 3 : Step 1 : the basic couples of region.

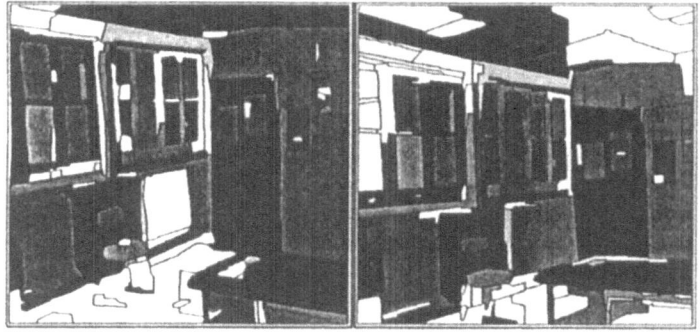

Figure 4 : Step 2 : propagation of the matching process.

Figure 5 : Step 3 : final matching.

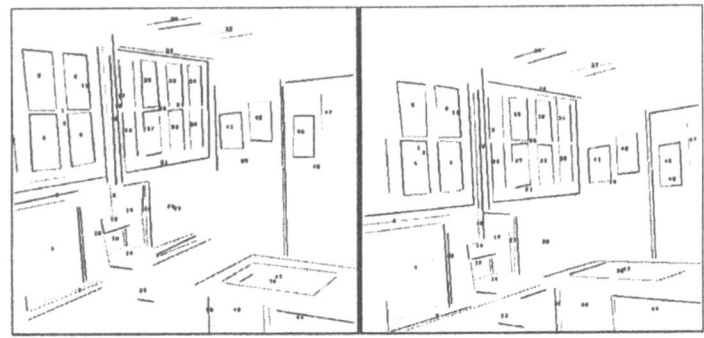

Figure 7 : Couples of homologous 2-D facets

Figure 8 : 3-D Description by 3D segments

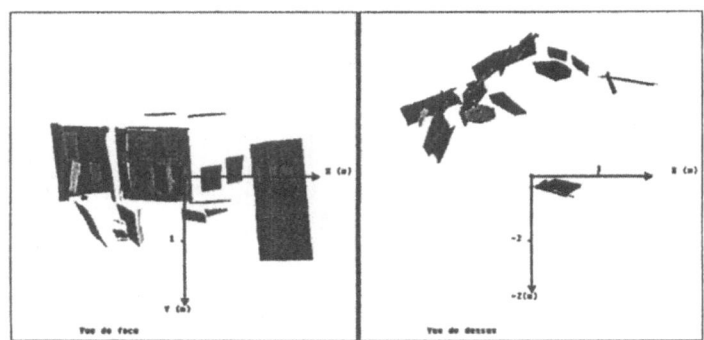

Figure 9 : 3-D Description by Planar 3-D facets

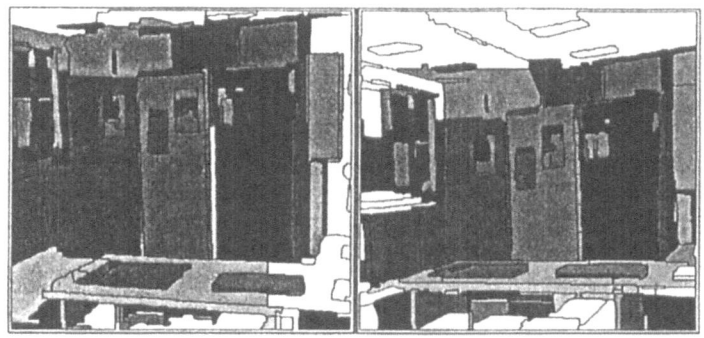

Figure 10 : Couples of homologous regions

Figure 11 : Couples of homologous 2-D facets

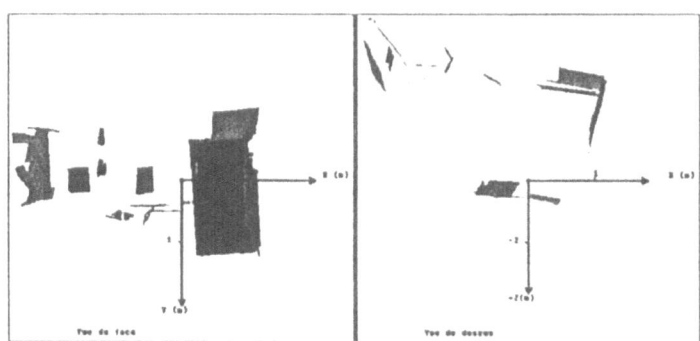

Figure 12 : 3-D Description by Planar 3-D facets

REFERENCES
[1]   Ayache N. "Construction et fusion de Représentations Visuelles 3D - Applications à la robotique Mobile". PhD Universite de Paris Sud, Centre d'Orsay, France, May 1988.
[2]   Barrow G. - J. M. Tenenbaum "Interpreting line drawings as 3D surfaces". Computer Vision by JM Brady, pp. 75-116, 1981.
[3]   Blake A., Zisserman A. "Visual Reconstruction", MIT Press, 1987.
[4]   Bonnin P. "Méthode Systématique de Conception et de Réalisation d'Applications en Vision par Ordinateur", PhD thesis, Université Paris VII, 12- 1991.
[5]   Buvry M. "Un Système de Vision Stéréoscopique : Segmentation-Appariement de Composantes Connexes-Description Surfacique", PhD INP-ENSEEIHT, France, October 1993.
[6]   Chabbi H. "Construction de Facettes 3D par Stéréovision Intégrant des Principes de Géométrie Projective", PhD INP Lorraine, Febrary 1993.
[7]   Faugeras O.D. and Toscani G. "The Callibration Problem for stereo". In Proc. Computer Vision and Pattern Recognition, pp 15 - 20, Miami Beach, Florida, USA, June 1986.
[8]   Fornland P., G.A. Jones, G. Matas, J. Kittler "Stereo Correspondance from Junctions", 8th Proc. SCIA'93, IAPR, Vol 1, pp. 449-455, Mai 1993.
[9]   Graeme A. Jones "Constraint, Optimization, and hierarchy : Reviewing stereoscopic correspondance of complex feature", Journal of Computer Vision and Image Understanding, Vol. 65-1, pp. 57-78, January 1997.
[10] Grimson W.E.L. "Computational Experiments with a Feature Based Stereo Algorithm", IEEE PAMI-7-1, pp 17-34, Jannuary 1985.
[11] Horaud R. and Skordas T. "Stereo correspondance through Feature Grouping and Maximal Cliques". PAMI Vol 11, Num 11, pp. 1168-1180 November 1989.
[12] Kristensen S. and Nielsen H.M. and Christensen H.I. "Cooperative Depth Extraction". In Proc. of 8th SCIA, IAPR, pp. 321-328, Tromso, Norway, Mai 1993.
[13] Lutton E. , J.M. Vezien, A. Gagalowicz "Model-based stereo reconstruction by energy minimization", 2nd International Conference Dedicated to Image Communication (Image'Com 93), pp 367-372, Bordaux, France, March 1993.
[14] Macapane S.B. and Trivedi M.M. " Multi-Primitive Hierarchical (MPH) Stereo Analysis ". PAMI, Vol.1b, n°3, pp. 227-240, March 1994.
[15] Marr D. : "Vision A Computational investigation into human representation and processing of visual information". W.H. Freeman and all. San Francisco, 1982.
[16] Mohan G. - R. Nevatia "Using perceptual organization to extract 3-D structures". IEEE PAMI-11-11, pp 1121-1139, November 1989.
[17] Olsen S.I. "Stereo Correspondance by Surface Reconstruction", IEEE PAMI-12-3, pp 309-315, March 1990.
[18] Sander P.T. - Vinet L. - Cohen L. and Gagalowitz A. "Hierarchical Region Based Stereo Matching". In Proc. of the SCIA'6, pp.71-78, Ouslu, Finland, 6-1989.
[19] Terzopoulos D. "Multilevel Computational Processes for Visible Surface Reconstruction", CVGIP-24, pp. 52-96, 1983.
[20] Zagrouba E. and Krey C. "Region Matching by Adjacency Propagation in Stereovision". In Proc. ICARCV'92, Vol.1, pp. cv-8.5.1, cv8-5..5. Singapore, September 1992.
[21] Zagrouba E., Buvry M., Krey C. "A rule-based system for region segmentation improvement in stereovision". IS&T-SPIE, Image and Video-Processing II, Vol. 21-82, pp. 357-367, Californie-USA, February. 1994.

Extraction of Discriminant Features from Image Fractal Encoding

Matteo Baldoni, Cristina Baroglio,
Davide Cavagnino, Giuseppe Lo Bello

Dipartimento di Informatica — Università degli Studi di Torino
Corso Svizzera, 185 — I-10149 Torino (Italy)
Tel. +39 11 74 29 111, Fax +39 11 75 16 03

E-mail: {baldoni,baroglio,davide,lobello}@di.unito.it
URL: http://www.di.unito.it/~baldoni/fractals/

Abstract. In this paper we face the problem of finding characteristic information about images of different objects, showing that the fractal encoding based on *Iterated Function Systems*, besides allowing very high compression rates, can be successfully applied *also* for capturing discriminatory features that can be exploited for *non-fractal* image classification. An original feature extraction algorithm was developed and applied to encode the hand-written digits data set. Then, different learning algorithms were applied and their performances were compared both to those obtained using a general purpose fractal encoder (*enc* by Fisher) and to the work done in the StatLog project on the same data set.

Keywords: Machine learning, feature extraction, fractal encoding.

1 Introduction

In this paper we tackle the problem of classifying visual representations of objects w.r.t. a set of classes given a priori: a central problem in many artificial vision tasks, e.g., optical character recognition [13], face recognition [24] for security systems, and object recognition for assembly. The approach we present is divided in three main steps: (1) finding a way that allows to *extract*, in an automatic way, a small set of *features* characterizing the instances of the target classes; (2) learning a *classifier* that maps the extracted features on the target classes; (3) using the obtained classifier for recognition purposes. Differently than what can be found in the literature, this approach does not use any model of the objects at issue (as, instead, [6, 9, 14]) nor it needs a set of templates to be defined in advance (as, instead, [22, 2]). On the contrary, it simply exploits the values of a set of *descriptive features* which characterize the *visual representations* of the objects. The ideal features we would like to identify are easy to extract, robust, and well suited to a fast and reliable interpretation. Moreover, since we deal with image recognition, they should be *invariant* w.r.t. the distance, keeping a high *discriminatory power*, i.e., be different for different classes.

In particular, in this work we investigated the use a new type of feature derived from a *fractal* description that is obtained by means of an *Iterated Function*

System (IFS). The motivation for studying fractal features is that they are *already* used for image transmission purposes; reconstructed images are impressive for their fidelity and greatly reduce the computational cost of encoding, allowing compression rates as high as $2,000 : 1$. Nevertheless, the focus of our attention was not to use IFSs to *reproduce* images but to see if they can be used to *extract discriminant information* about images. The question was: given that IFSs are a powerful encoding tool, do they also contain enough information to distinguish images belonging to different classes? This topic was already addressed in [8] but only in the case of (1) images with an intrinsic *fractal* structure where (2) feature extraction was hand-made. Here, instead, we have investigated the use of IFSs to capture discriminant information about *non-fractal* objects, on one hand, by developing an original *application-oriented* algorithm that allows to extract fractal discriminant features in an automatic way; on the other, we applied a well-known, general purpose fractal encoder (*enc* see [10]). This algorithm was applied to StatLog hand-written digits and the encoded samples were used to train different learning algorithms (heading to different approaches to learning, i.e., Genetic Algorithms, Neural Networks, and Symbolic Induction), whose performances are reported at the end of this paper.

The paper is organized as follows. In Section 2 the basic notions on IFSs are provided. Section 3 describes how to use IFSs to extract meaningful features. Experiment descriptions and results are reported in Section 4 together with a description of the algorithms used. Conclusions are drawn in Section 5.

2 IFSs theoretical background

This section is a summary of a few concepts about fractal theory that are particularly relevant to this work. More details can be found in [3, 4].

The basic idea underlying fractal generation is that a fractal contains, at any scale, smaller copies of itself, i.e., it is *self-similar*. One way of generating fractal images in the plane is to *iterate* simple geometrical transformations starting from a predefined shape. For instance, from a geometrical point of view, the *rule* that allows the curve of Figure 1(d) to be built consists in repeatedly *mapping* the initial segment AB (Figure 1(a)) to each of the segments AC, CE, ED and DB, respectively (Figure 1(b)) [11]. Each mapping (or *transformation*) consists of a *rotation* and a *contraction*[1] (the length of the segment reducing to one third of the original).

A particular kind of transformation is the *affine contractive transformation*, which, in words, allows to reproduce a smaller copy of an initial pattern, keeping its original shape. More formally, let us consider the n-dimensional space $\mathbb{R}^n$ and let $\mathbf{z}$ be a point in $\mathbb{R}^n$: a mapping $M : \mathbb{R}^n \to \mathbb{R}^n$ is an *affine transformation* if it has the form $M(\mathbf{z}) = T(\mathbf{z}) + \mathbf{w}$, where T is a linear transformation on $\mathbb{R}^n$ and $\mathbf{w}$ is a vector in $\mathbb{R}^n$. In other words, an *affine transformation* is a combination

---

[1] Given a closed subset E of $\mathbb{R}^n$, a mapping $M : E \to E$ is a *contraction* on E if there is a number c, with $0 < c < 1$, such that $|M(x) - M(y)| \leq c|x - y|$ for all $x, y \in E$. We will consider the modulo norm in E, i.e. the Euclidean distance.

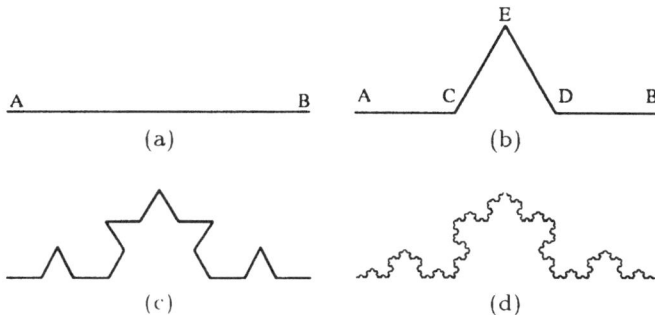

Fig. 1. Successive stages in the construction of the von Koch curve [11]. At each step, the middle third of each existing segment is removed and replaced by the two sides of an equilateral triangle. (a) Initial segment. (b) Basic transformation. (c) Curve after 2 steps. (d) The von Koch curve.

of *rotations*, *scalings* and *translations* of the coordinates. For instance, a two dimensional affine transformation has the general matrix form

$$M\left(\begin{bmatrix} x \\ y \end{bmatrix}\right) = \begin{bmatrix} a & b \\ c & d \end{bmatrix}\begin{bmatrix} x \\ y \end{bmatrix} + \begin{bmatrix} e \\ f \end{bmatrix} = \begin{bmatrix} r\cos\theta & -s\sin\phi \\ r\sin\theta & s\cos\phi \end{bmatrix}\begin{bmatrix} x \\ y \end{bmatrix} + \begin{bmatrix} e \\ f \end{bmatrix} \tag{1}$$

where θ and φ are rotations and r and s are scalings on the x and y components, respectively; an example is shown in Figure 2.

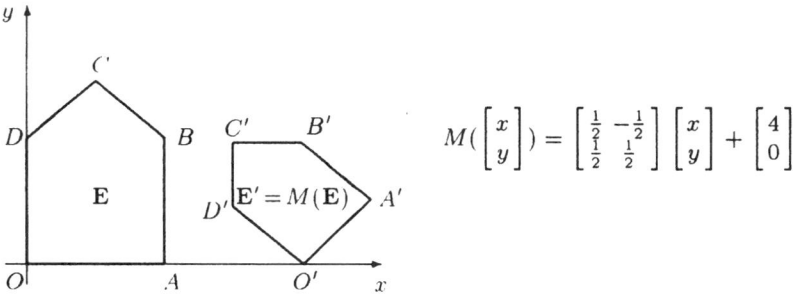

$$M\left(\begin{bmatrix} x \\ y \end{bmatrix}\right) = \begin{bmatrix} \frac{1}{2} & -\frac{1}{2} \\ \frac{1}{2} & \frac{1}{2} \end{bmatrix}\begin{bmatrix} x \\ y \end{bmatrix} + \begin{bmatrix} 4 \\ 0 \end{bmatrix}$$

Fig. 2. Example of affine transformation: figure **E** is mapped on **E′** by means of M.

An affine transformation for which the *contractive* property holds is said to be *contractive*. Affine contractive transformations are fundamental in this work; in fact, although, in general, an IFS is *any* collection of contractions, here we focus on collections of affine contractive transformations $\{M_1, \ldots, M_m\}$.

For every IFS in $\mathbb{R}^n$ there exists a set F such that $F = \bigcup_{i=1}^m M_i(F)$. F is called *invariant set*; it is *unique* and *non-empty* and can be a *fractal*. Moreover, due to the *Collage Theorem* [3, 11], given any subset E of $\mathbb{R}^n$ and an arbitrary precision of approximation, it is always possible to find an IFS, whose invariant set approximates E as finely as desired. In the plane the Collage Theorem helps in reconstructing an image by giving a method for doing it, ensuring at the same time the accuracy of the reconstruction. In particular, an image can be reconstructed by covering it with a set of contracted affine copies of itself (see Figure 3). Other characteristics of the IFS are that it is *robust* and *stable*, i.e., small changes in the transformations produce small changes in its invariant set; hence, varying the coefficients in a continuous way, the shape of the invariant set also changes in a continuous manner.

In the literature, many methods for automatically finding an IFS that encodes a given image, such as [5], can be found. One of them, derived from the works by Jacquin and Fisher (see [16] and [10]), was used in some of the experiments.

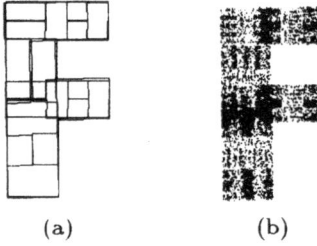

	a	b	c	d	e	f
	-0.03	-0.37	-0.52	0.02	0.17	-0.50
	-0.03	-0.37	-0.52	0.02	0.39	4.38
	0.50	-0.06	0.00	-0.80	1.23	-2.48
	-0.50	-0.02	0.01	-0.80	1.69	-2.56
	0.01	-0.37	0.52	-0.02	0.15	-0.99
	0.01	-0.37	0.52	-0.02	0.38	3.93

(a) (b) (c)

Fig. 3. (a) It is possible to cover a capital "F" with copies of itself in many ways. One possibility is shown here (from [20]): the "F" is covered with six contracted copies of itself, each "bar" being covered with two contracted copies placed side by side. (b) The corresponding invariant set. (c) Its IFS code.

3   IFSs as Descriptive Features

In this work, the Collage Theorem was applied to extract the meaningful aspects of an object, which are, then, encoded by an IFS. More precisely, given an image ξ in 256 grey levels, let $M(\xi) = \{M_i | 1 \leq i \leq r\}$ be the set of affine transformations which cover the image according to the Collage Theorem. The *idea* is to use this set of transformations as a set of *descriptive features*. This is done by associating to ξ the vector $\mathbf{x} = \langle x_1, x_2, \ldots, x_n \rangle$ of the parameters of the r transformations. The number of features n necessary to characterize an object will, then, be equal to the number of parameters defining each transformation (e.g., in (1), they are the six coefficients a, b, c, d, e, and f) times the number r of transformations used (see Figure 3(c)). Since the image is not to be reconstructed but only *distinguished* from others, the number of transformations needed is by far lower than that required to reproduce an image with high fidelity.

One way of using descriptive features is to define a set of prototypes for each target class, using a distance measure to find which of them are the most similar to the instances to be classified. However, defining such prototypes is not trivial. In this work we solved the problem by applying different learning algorithms, whose performances are reported in the following section.

4 Experimental results

All experiments were done on the *ten digits* test-bed, also used in StatLog [18]. Briefly, this data set is a collection of hand-written samples of the ten digits (collected by the German Federal Post), acquired with a resolution of 16×16 pixels with 256 grey levels (some examples are reported in Figure 6(a)). In some experiments the samples were binarized, i.e., all pixels whose value was higher than a certain threshold were considered as elements of the digit otherwise they were considered as background.

First of all, we tried to understand, in a short time, if IFSs capture characteristic information about (non-fractal) images; to this purpose, the samples were hand-coded in the following way: given the binarized image of a digit, we extracted the fractal features by covering it by means of four self-affine transformations, mapping the whole digit to parts of itself (see Figure 4). Due to the

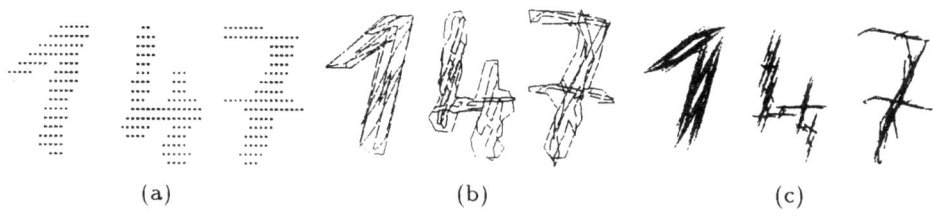

(a)	(b)	(c)

Fig. 4. (a) Binarized instances of the digits "1", "4" and "7". (b) Digit covering with four self-affine transformations. (c) Digit fractal reconstruction.

long time required by sample hand-coding, only digits "1", "4", and "7" were taken into account because of their similarity in hand-writing. A three-layered Multi Layer Perceptron (MLP) with 24 input units (4 transformations × 6 parameters each, see Section 2), 80 hidden neurons and 3 output neurons was used. The learning set was made of 30 examples (10 per class). The test set consisted of 120 examples (40 per class). Results show a 100 % recognition rate both on the learning and on the test sets.

Afterwards, an original algorithm was developed so to make the above hand-made encoding *automatic*. This algorithm is application-oriented, i.e. it was developed to find IFS encodings for non-fractal, linear images. Finally, a *general-purpose* algorithm for fractal image compression, *enc*, was applied to the same data for comparing the performances.

The learner was implemented in many different ways for comparison purposes. In particular, we have used feed-forward neural networks (classical multilayer perceptron, a Conjugate Gradient method, SCG [23], and cascade correlation networks), CART [7], and genetic algorithms [12]. When not specified otherwise, the learning sets were made of 300 samples (30 samples per class) while the test sets were made of 700 samples (70 per class), all different than those shown during training. Cross-validation was used to check the independence of the results from the particular learning and test sets used: each experiment was repeated on three different learning/test set pairs; the percentages reported in Table 1 are the averages of the performances obtained in the various trials.

Table 1. Recognition rates obtained using: (a) CART; (b) GAs; (c) NNs (SCG); (d) NNs (Cascade-correlation); (e) NNs on features extracted by *enc*.

	(a) CART	(b) GA	(c) SCG-NN	(d) CC-NN	(e) NN/*enc*
"0"	75.7 %	85.7 %	85.0 %	85.7 %	79.6 %
"1"	92.9 %	90.0 %	96.7 %	95.7 %	78.0 %
"2"	84.3 %	75.7 %	91.9 %	94.3 %	71.6 %
"3"	54.3 %	74.3 %	84.2 %	75.7 %	60.8 %
"4"	70.0 %	44.3 %	81.4 %	72.9 %	65.6 %
"5"	75.7 %	77.1 %	86.7 %	75.7 %	81.6 %
"6"	68.6 %	77.1 %	90.2 %	82.9 %	72.4 %
"7"	82.9 %	84.3 %	92.4 %	90.0 %	69.2 %
"8"	60.0 %	41.4 %	62.4 %	45.7 %	26.0 %
"9"	60.0 %	58.6 %	79.0 %	75.7 %	47.2 %
avg.	72.4 %	70.9 %	85.0 %	79.4 %	65.2 %

Experiments with an automatic covering. The algorithm we developed is based on the following two observations. The first is that since we are looking for some discriminant features, we do not need to perfectly cover a given image: an approximation of it will be sufficient. The second is that, differently than what done in the first experiment, we cover an image by means of a set of auto-affine copies of a shape that is *different* (and simpler) than the one of the digit to cover. This can be done because, in the line of the first observation, this approach is sufficient to extract an information that is *intrinsic* to the covered digit and does *not* depend on the particular objects used for covering. Moreover, using predefined simple shapes has also the advantage of simplifying the covering operation.

In particular, our algorithm is based on covering the *binarized* image of a digit by means of a *fixed* number of affine contractions of the *square box* containing it. In order to reduce the complexity of the computation, only a *limited number* of geometric transformations is allowed. With reference to equation (1), all rotations belong to the set $\{0°, 45°, 90°, 135°\}$, the scaling is fixed a priori and depends on the experiment, while the translations are not bounded. Consequently, we were able to use a more *compact* IFS representation; each transformation is encoded by means of only three numbers: the translations (e and f) plus a number t, between 0 and 3, which encodes the geometric transformation.

This procedure was implemented in a Constraint Logic Programming (CLP) language with constraints on finite domains [1]; it iteratively tries to cover a yet uncovered part of the digit with a contracted box; among all the possible transformations, it chooses the one that covers the greatest number of pixels belonging to the digit (Figure 5). CLP was used because it allows a fast prototyping and also because it allows to cut the search space in a very simple way.

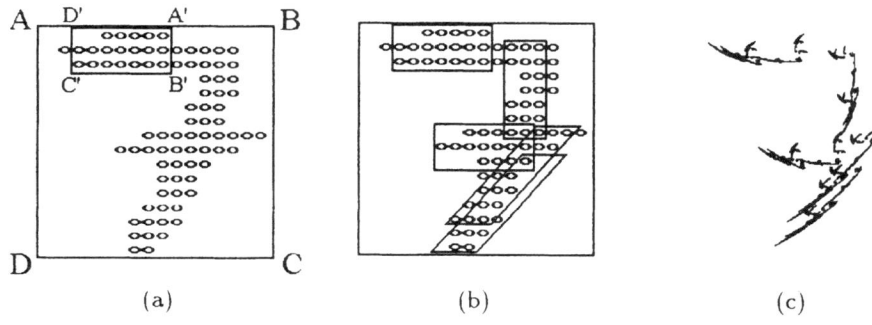

(a) (b) (c)

Fig. 5. (a) Sample digit inside its square box $ABCD$ ("o"s represent black pixels): application of the first affine contraction resulting in $A'B'C'D'$; (b) Final coverage using 5 contractions; (c) Fractal reconstruction: note how the digit structure is captured.

Different experiments were carried on: on one hand, we used different parameter values in order to find the encoding that gave the best results, while on the other we have applied different learning algorithms to compare their performances. In particular, the best results were obtained (alternatively) covering the data set by means of: 5 transformations where the 16×16 pixel frame square box is scaled to a 7×3 pixel rectangle; 6 transformations with a scaling to a 5×3 pixel rectangle; 6 transformations with a scaling to a 5×3 pixel rectangle, the difference with the previous case being that now the data were not binarized any more, i.e., the 256 grey levels were maintained and the search for the best matching transformations took into account also the intensity level of the pixels.

The best results of this series of experiments are reported in Table 1. They were obtained using 6 transformations with a scaling to a 5 × 3 pixel rectangle. Columns (a), (b), (c), and (d) contain the average recognition rates obtained on the test sets digit per digit. Column (a) reports the results obtained using CART. Two different experiments were carried on: in the first, we used *symbolic* features only (this could be done because positions are discrete and vary in between 0 and 15 and the transformations allowed are only four), whereas in the second, the positions were considered *numerical* values. The best results were obtained in the second case.

Column (b) contains the results obtained by the Genetic Algorithms (here, all features are *symbolic*). They were obtained by means of system REGAL [19].

The greatest performances were obtained by neural networks (see columns (c) and (d)). Different network models were tried. Column (d) reports the results obtained by using Cascade-correlation; however, the model that gave the best and more stable (w.r.t. the parameters used during encoding) performances is the SCG network [23]. This network is full-connected and is characterized by a learning rule that exploits the second derivatives and converges faster than classical gradient descent methods. The nets we used always had 500 hidden neurons and 10 output neurons and were run for about 500 epochs.

Experiments with a general purpose encoder. At last, we tried a general purpose fractal image compression program for generalizing the method in order to apply it to *any* kind of image: *enc* by Fisher [10]. This algorithm exploits the Collage Theorem for *local IFSs* (see [5]): instead of covering the whole image with contracted affine copies of itself, it covers the image with contracted affine copies of *parts* of itself. A transformation can be specified by only *five numbers*:

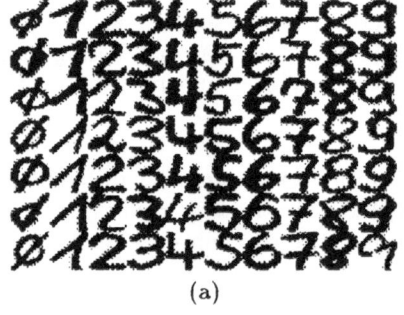
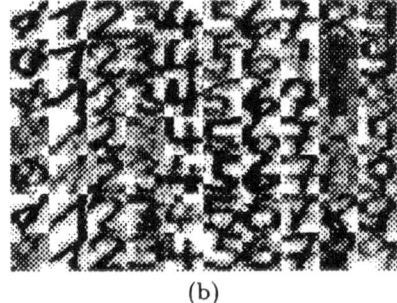

| (a) | (b) |

Fig. 6. (a) Some images we have used in our experiments. (b) Their reconstruction with 16 transformations.

a number t between 0 and 7 that codes the selected geometrical transformation (only the identity, 90°, 180° and 270° anticlockwise rotations, the reflection in the two axes — x and y — and in the two diagonals are allowed), two numbers, e and f, for the translation, and two real numbers, s and o, indicating the luminance transformation (these two numbers are necessary to compression because enc works on grey scale images, see for more details [16]).

In these experiments each digit was approximated by 16 transformations (each R_i being a 4×4 square), making 80 features in all (16 transformations $\times 5$ parameters). For instance, Figure 6(b) contains the reconstructions of the images of Figure 6(a). Due to the dimension of the input space, and also to the results obtained in the previous experiments, the learner was implemented by means of neural networks only. Three NNs had to be used: the first, having 250 hidden neurons (as well as the third one), was trained to recognize digits from "0" through "3" using as counterexamples also all digits from "4" through "9". The second had only 200 hidden neurons and was trained to classify digits "4", "5," and "6". The third learned to classify the remaining digits. The learning set was made of 500 digits (50 per class) while the test set was made of 2500 samples (250 per class). Results are reported in column (e) of Table 1.

5 Conclusions

Since Mandelbrot [17] defined them, fractals have been widely addressed in the literature and, in strict connection with them, IFSs have been developed and used in various domains [21]. In this paper we tackled the problem of using *IFS encodings* for classifying images of objects which do *not* have a self-affine nature by, first, showing that such features *capture* discriminant information and, then, presenting an *algorithm* that allows to extract them in an *automatic way* for the specific application of the ten digits. Experiments show that the IFSs can, actually, be used for classification tasks, achieving, in the best case, an average 85% recognition rate. Even using an automatic fractal encoder that was designed for image compression and *not* for recognition purposes, a recognition rate greater than 70% was achieved for five classes out of ten.

The digits application was chosen because, on one hand, it is a *real-world* (non-fractal) image recognition problem and, on the other, it was used in the StatLog project, it is well-understood and was tackled by means of many different learning algorithms. Nonetheless, those experimental settings and results have been an important reference point and lead to the following conclusions. First, the use of IFSs allows to work on a *very small* input space by reducing both the number of space dimensions and the set of possible values for each input feature. Consequently, the learning time diminishes. For instance, let's consider the input space of column (b) in Table 1: each of the 6 transformations is determined by 3 parameters, two of them (the translations e and f) range between 0 and 15 (the image side size), and one, t, ranges between 0 and 3. The original images, instead, are represented by 256 pixels, each of which has a value in between 0 and 255 (the grey level).

Another appealing characteristic is that the number of features used for encoding is *independent* from the size of the image, being related to its intrinsic complexity only. These characteristics are extremely important because, as explained in [18], many learning algorithms cannot deal with applications having hundreds of dimensions, while those that can take a too long time before converging.

However, if we compare the *recognition rates* obtained in the experiments carried on during StatLog to ours we see that a lot of work is yet to be done: some of the methods used in this project achieve a 90–95% average recognition performance. Taking into account these percentages only, those methods seem better than ours. In order to better understand the meaningfulness of fractal features, we have, then, applied the neural network model that gave the best results on fractal features (the SCG model) to the 300 learning samples, now encoded as in StatLog. In the average, the net could recognize about 80% of the the 700 test samples. This difference of performance between the results obtained during StatLog and those obtained in this last experiment is due to the different number of learning examples used: in StatLog the classifiers were trained on 9,000 images while our classifiers are trained on 300 images only. Taking into account this result and also the fact that the encoder we developed is quite rough, we can reasonably suppose that finding more sophisticate encoding algorithms fractal features will allow to obtain (or even outperform) recognition rates that are very close to those obtained with different pre-processing methods, using less examples and training the classifiers in a shorter time.

Some interesting conclusion can be drawn also by comparing the performances of the different learning methods we applied. As can be observed, *numerical* methods (i.e. neural networks) gave the best results. Depending on the parameters of the encoding algorithm, SCG networks achieved a recognition rate in between 82% and 85%. Cascade-correlation networks (as an example of a different network model) achieved 79%. Symbolic methods, instead, achieved a maximum 72%. We believe that the reason for which neural nets (and, in particular, full-connected neural nets) perform better is that they can capture the structure of a sample, leaving out the particular order of the transformations in it. In different words, since digits are hand-written and binarized (i.e. they are affected by noise) and since the encoding algorithm selects first those transformations that cover more bits on the sample, if we take two samples of a same digit, say two "4", we cannot expect that the order of the transformations used to cover the two samples is the same. Let's suppose, for instance, that in the first "4" the vertical bar is strongly marked while in the second, the oblique line is strongly marked. Then, it is very likely that the first transformations generated to encode the first "4" cover the vertical line whereas those created to cover the second "4" cover the oblique line. This means that the two samples will be encoded by two sequences $T_{11}, ..., T_{1n}$ and $T_{21}, ..., T_{2n}$ where, for example, T_{11} covers the vertical bar in the first sample while T_{21} and T_{23} cover respectively the oblique and the vertical lines in the second sample. Note that the information contained in the two sequences will be the same, the only difference is the *order* of the transformations. Now, our algorithm imposes a simple ordering of the transformations which is based on the position of the baricentre of the contractions; however, due to the non-regularity of hand-writing, the above mentioned problem can still arise (it is easy to imagine examples of instances of a same digit where such an ordering rule produces different sequentializations). Unfortunately, the symbolic methods we used are not able to generalize over different attributes, i.e., over information placed at different points in the sequences, e.g. T_{11} and T_{23} in the example. To overcome this limit, we mean to try *First Order* learning tools. Two alternatives are either to search for more sophisticate ordering rules that, for instance, take into account the relationships between the transformations, or to produce reacher learning sets that take into account any possible ordering of the transformations for any given sample.

A second and more challenging future research will consist in studying a fractal feature extraction method that is *domain-independent* and allows to characterize *any* kind of image. Actually, the experiment with *enc* was a first step towards this goal. *Enc*, was chosen because it *is* domain-independent; the problem is that it is too *application-dependent*, where the application, in this case, is compression. An idea we would like to explore is to try to change the range and domain shapes using a segmentation algorithm to drive the selection. Another possibility is to try to exploit the Hausdorff distance [15], used in fractal geometry to evaluate the distance between sets of points.

Acknowledgments. The authors are indebted to prof. Lorenza Saitta for the helpful discussions and suggestions and thank prof. Charles Taylor for all the information about the StatLog project.

References

1. *ECL' PS^e 3.5 Extensions User Manual.* ECRC GmbH, 1995.
2. R. Anand, K. Mehrotra, C. K. Mohan, and S. Ranka. Analyzing images containing multiple sparse pattern with neural networks. In *Proc. of IJCAI-91*, Sidney, Australia, 1991.
3. M. Barnsley. *Fractals Everywhere.* Academic Press, San Diego, 1988.
4. M. Barnsley and S. Demko. Iterated function systems and the global construction of fractals. In *The Proceedings of the Royal Society of London*, volume A399, pages 243–275, 1985.
5. M. Barnsley and L. P. Hurd. *Fractal Image Compression.* AK Peters, Ltd., Wellesley, Massachusetts, 1993.
6. P. Besl and R. Jain. Three dimensional object recognition. *ACM Computing Surveys*, (17):75–154, 1985.
7. L. Breiman, J. Friedman, J. Ohlsen, and C. Stone. *Classification and Regression Trees.* Wadsworth & Brooks, Pacific Grove, CA, 1984.
8. G. Le Chiara and L. Saitta. Using fractals to learn image descriptions by means of artificial neural networks. In *IEEE International Conference on Neural Networks*, Orlando, USA, 1994.

9. R. Chin and C. Dyer. Model-based recognition in robot vision. *ACM Computing Surveys*, (18):67–108, 1986.
10. Y. Fisher (Ed.). *Fractal Compression: Theory and Application to Digital Images*. Springer Verlag, New York, 1994.
11. K. Falconer. *Fractal Geometry, Mathematical Foundations and Applications*. John Wiley & Sons Ltd., Chichester, UK, 1990.
12. D.E. Goldberg. *Genetic Algorithms*. Addison-Wesley, Readings, MA, 1989.
13. V. K. Govindan and A. P. Shivaprasad. Character recogniton - A review. *Pattern Recognition*, 23(7):671–683, 1990.
14. W. Grimson, Lozano-Pérez, and D. Huttenlocher. *Recognition by Computer: The Role of Geometric Constraints*. The MIT Press, Cambridge, MA, 1990.
15. D. Huttenlocher, G. Klanderman, and W. Rucklidge. Comparing images using the Hausdorff distance. *IEEE Trans. Pattern Analysis and Machine Intelligence*, (PAMI-15):850–863, 1993.
16. A. Jacquin. Image coding based on fractal theory of iterated contractive image transforms. In *Proc. of SPIE, Visual Communications and and Image Processing '90*, volume 1360, 1990.
17. B. Mandelbrot. *The Fractal Geometry of Nature*. Freeman & Co., San Francisco, CA, 1982.
18. D. Michie, D. J. Spiegelhalter, and C. C. Taylor. *Machine learning, neural and statistical classification*. Ellis Horwood series in artificial intelligence. Prentice Hall, 1994.
19. F. Neri and A. Giordana. A distributed genetic algorithm for concept learning. In *Int. Conf. on Genetic Algorithms*, pages 436–443, Pittsburgh, PA, 1995. Morgan Kaufmann.
20. D. Oliver. *Fractal Vision, Put Fractals to Work for You*. Sams Publishing, Indiana, USA, 1992.
21. A. P. Pentland. Fractal-Based Description of Natural Scenes. *IEEE Transactions on Pattern Analysis and Machine Intelligence*, PAMI-6(6):661–674, 1984.
22. A. Rosenfeld and A. Kak. *Digital Picture Processing*. Academic Press, New York, NY, 1982.
23. P. D. Wasserman. *Neural computing*. 1995.
24. C. J. Wu and J. S. Huang. Human face profile recognition by computer. *Pattern Recognition*, 23(3/4):255–259, 1990.

Learning Relational Concepts
at Different Levels of Granularity

G. Armano and G. Fumera
DIEE, Dept. of Electrical and Electronic Engineering,
Piazza d'Armi, 09123, Cagliari, e-mail: {armano, fumera}@diee.unica.it

Summary

In this paper, an alternative approach to the induction of relational concepts is presented. The underlying framework relies on the concept of *exception*, an exception being a counterexample left within the scope of a description devoted to classifying examples of the given target concept. While trying to characterize the target concept, first an initial description is searched for. Such a solution must be complete, although not necessarily consistent. This means that some counterexamples are allowed to be misclassified. As counterexamples (i.e., exceptions) must be taken into account in order to properly classify them, the corresponding learning process is performed in several steps, each step devoted to coping with exceptions generated during the previous one. Eventually, the process comes to an end, usually leading to a description that uses a kind of Vere's counterfactuals to refine, at different levels of granularity, the underlying concept.

Introduction

Learning concepts from examples is aimed at finding a description able to represent a given concept starting from positive examples and (possibly) negative examples. Such a description must be able to properly classify all examples given as a training set, as well as to make an accurate prediction on the instances submitted to the corresponding classifier.

There are basically two classes of such problems being currently investigated. The former refers to a zero-order (i.e., propositional) logic, and is able to represent any given instance as a fixed-length t-uple of values (each value being conceptually related to a given feature). Within such a framework a concept can be represented by using decision trees or production rules. The latter refers to a first-order predicate logic, and its goal is to find an intensional description of a target concept, being given as a set of t-uples of ground terms (negative ground terms can be either explicitly asserted or generated by using a closed-world assumption), together with some background relations that might be intensionally or extensionally defined. The target concept has to be described in terms of some of the background relations and possibly in terms of the target concept itself (provided that the learner is able to cope with recursive concepts).

Basically, algorithms that deal with such relational concepts can be classified into two main groups, according to the way training examples are considered.

The first group of algorithms is based on the successive revision method, in which the description of the target concept is built incrementally, modifying it when a t-uple of ground terms (representing a new positive or negative example) is given that does not match the current concept description.

The second group of algorithms uses a separate-and-conquer strategy introduced by Michalski [Mic80]: first a consistent definition is built, then all positive examples covered are deleted from the training set. The procedure iterates such steps until a complete and consistent description of the target concept is found. Within such a group of algorithms, a further distinction can be made, according to the way they try to reach a solution. Top-down algorithms (e.g., FOIL [Cam93], [Qui95]), and FOCL [Paz91]) start from a general description that contains the target relation only and try to specialize it by adding background relations (i.e., introducing further constraints) until no negative examples are covered. On the other hand, bottom-up algorithms (e.g., GOLEM [Mug92]) start from a most specific generalization of a (small) subset of positive examples, generalizing it as far as it remains consistent.

In this paper a top-down algorithm for learning relational concepts is presented, able to find an initial (complete, but not necessarily consistent) description of a concept and to iteratively refine it until all inconsistencies are removed. At each step, the current concept is refined by adding, where necessary, suitable background relations (see the definition of counterfactual in [Ver80] and censor in [Win86]) that prevent exceptions being misclassified.

Exceptions-Based Concept Learning

Before introducing the basic mechanism exploited by an exceptions-based learner, let us first recall how top-down learners tackle the problem of inducing a relational concept.

Algorithms that belong to the top-down separate-and-conquer family start with a target-relation clause characterized by an empty body. Background relations are iteratively added until the current description is consistent. After that, all positive examples covered by the current description are removed from the training set, and then the whole process is iterated until the covering is complete.

The alternative approach presented here relies on the concept of *exception*, an exception being a counterexample left within the scope of a description devoted to classifying examples that satisfy the given target relation. While trying to characterize the target relation, first an initial description is searched for. Such a solution must be complete, although not necessarily consistent (i.e., some counterexamples could be misclassified). As counterexamples (i.e., exceptions) must be taken into account in order to properly classify them, the learning process is performed in several steps, each step devoted to coping with exceptions generated during the previous one. Eventually, the process comes to an end, usually leading to a description that uses a kind of Vere's counterfactuals to refine, at different levels of granularity, the underlying concept.

From a conceptual point of view, learners able to induce relational concepts characterize the target concept through a set of Horn clauses having the target relation as a head (e.g., FOIL, FOCL, GOLEM), or through some "enriched" first-order logic notation (e.g., INDUCE [Mic83], RIGEL [Gem91]).

In particular, while characterizing target concepts by means of Horn clauses, each ground term is usually typed, whereas negation can be dealt with by using the operator *not(.)*, to be interpreted as "negation-by-failure".

Let us now define the operator "~" (*unless* operator) whose semantics is the following: $A \sim B$ is *true* **iff** A is *true* and B is *false*. Disregarding any problem related to a fixed-point semantics (no recursion is allowed, yet), such an operator can be used to specify unless conditions within a Horn clause, which is another way of dealing with the negation-by-failure.

To this end, extended Horn clauses (say *xHorn clauses*) have been defined as follows:

<xHorn-clause> ::= <head> ← <body> [~ <xbody>].
<xbody> ::= <body> [~ <xbody>].
<head> ::= <relation>(<args>)
<body> ::= (background-relation(<args>) {, background-relation(<args>) })*
<relation> ::= target-relation | background-relation
<args> ::= <arg> {,<arg> }*
<arg> ::= variable | constant

An *xHorn clause* can be recursively evaluated as follows: first an attempt to match <body> is performed. If such an attempt fails, the whole evaluation fails, otherwise an attempt to match <xbody> (if any) is performed. If such an attempt fails, then the evaluation of <body> succeeds and vice-versa. Note that the evaluation of an <xbody> is given in a recursive way.

As an example, let us consider the following one that refers to the well-known trains problem:

```
eastbound(A) ← (part-of(B,A),load-shape(B, circle)) ~
               (_COUNTERF_0(B)).

  _COUNTERF_0(B) ←double(B, true).
  _COUNTERF_0(B) ←n-loads(B,3).
  _COUNTERF_0(B) ←position(B,1).
```

The semantics of the xHorn clauses above is the following: a train A can be classified as *eastbound* if:

"a wagon exists whose load-shape is circular, unless such a wagon is double-sided, or contains three loads, or it is in the first position of the train".

Note that the counterfactual _COUNTERF_0 has been automatically generated to cope with disjunctions without explicitly representing them. In fact, the clause containing the newly generated counterfactual could also be represented -in a more compact form- as follows:

```
eastbound(A) ← ( part-of(B,A) ∧ has-shape(B, circle) ) ~
               ( double(B, true) ∨ n-loads(B,3) ∨ position(B,1) ).
```

The process of learning a relational concept by means of an exception-based mechanism consists of learning a complete and consistent set of xHorn clauses. In other words, first of all an exceptions-based relational learner (EXCRL) tries to find a complete and consistent description of the target concept as a set of Horn clauses.

The subgoal of finding a background relation to be added to the current clause under construction is tackled by using a branch-and-bound search driven by a cost-function that basically takes into account (i) the number of positive examples covered by the current clause, (ii) the number of negative examples, and (iii) its length.

When the best clause found is consistent, it is labelled as "*consistent*" and stored as a candidate, whereas all positive examples it covers are removed from the training set. The proposed approach differs from the above top-down algorithms in that the search is interrupted when all available memory has been used or the complexity in time has reached a given threshold. When the search has been interrupted, the most promising set of non-consistent clauses (according to the given cost-function) is extracted from the current search-tree, each clause being labelled as "*to-be-refined*", and stored as a candidate.

After selecting a set of non-redundant clauses from the current set of candidates, the algorithm proceeds as follows (i) if all selected clauses are *consistent*, then the whole process ends, (ii) otherwise a suitable counterfactual must be appended to the <body> of any *to be refined* clause. To this end, while searching for counterfactuals, the same mechanism described for finding a description of the target concept is used.

It is worth noting, though, that the positive and negative examples of the target relation "toggle" each time a counterfactual is to be added to the current description (i.e., positive examples "become" negative, and vice-versa). In other words, considering the process of finding an initial description as the zero-th step, at the first step a counterfactual is searched for by considering as counterexamples the positive examples covered by the current clause and vice-versa. At the second step, the former positive and negative "revert" to their initial meaning. In general, an odd step will by characterized by reversing the assumptions about "positive" and "negative" examples, whereas even steps leave them unchanged.

Of course, the whole process ends when no further exceptions are generated, i.e., when all clauses found during the current step are consistent. It is worth noting that, at each step, a complete description is always found; in other words, the process of finding a concept description by iteratively adding counterfactuals allows to find a hierarchical description that is complete at any level of granularity.

Experimental Results

The EXCRL has been implemented in MCL (on a PowerMac 6100/66) for the sake of rapid prototyping. The proposed algorithm has been tested out on some well-known problems taken from the GMD ML Repository.

First of all let us describe the results obtained in a test taken from a paper describing the RIGEL system [Gem91]. The task is to classify, in a geometric domain, fifteen objects belonging to three classes. The descriptions found by RIGEL and by our algorithm (EXCRL), respectively, are the following:

RIGEL:

```
class C1 :: (∃.(x y) [ SHAPE(x) = square][ SIZE(x) = small]
                      [ SHAPE(y) = circle][ TEXTURE(y) = shaded] )

class C2 :: (∃.(y)(IN(1..2))  [ SIZE(y) = small ∨ medium]
                              [ TEXTURE(y) = clear]
                              [ SHAPE(y) = rectangle] )

class C3 :: (∃.(x y) [ ONTOP(x y)]
                     [ SHAPE(y) = triangle ∨ rectangle]
                     (∃.(z)(=2)[ SIZE(z) = large] ))
```

EXCRL:

```
C1(A) ←  part-of(B,A), size(B,small), shape(B,square),
         part-of(C,A), shape(C,circle), texture(B,shaded).

C2(A) ←  ( part-of(B,A), shape(B,rectangle),
           texture(B,clear) ) ~ ( COUNTERF_0(A,B) ).

   _COUNTERF_0(A,B) ← size(B,large).
   _COUNTERF_0(A,B) ← ontop(B,C), ontop(B,D).

C3(A) ←  part-of(B,A), size(B,large), shape(B,polygon),
         part-of(C,A), size(C,large), ontop(C,B).
```

Note that the variables introduced by EXCRL in the body of clauses defining C1(A), C2(A), and C3(A) are bounded to different constants (i.e., to different objects).

A second test, described in [Qui89], is the family relationship learning task, in which two families of twelve members each are given. The target relation is *mother(person,person)*, and the background relations are *father(person,person)*, *wife(person,person)*, *son(person,person)* and *daughter(person,person)*. The definition found by EXCRL does not contain any counterfactual and is the same obtained by running FOIL:

```
mother(A,B) ←  father(C,B), wife(A,C).
```

After that, Michalski's trains [Mic80] have been classified. On a basis of 20 trains [Tur95] divided into two groups of 10 trains each, the following description of the target relation *eastbound(train)* has been found:

```
eastbound(A) ← part-of(B,A), load-shape(B, triangle),
               position(B,3).

eastbound(A) ← (part-of(B,A),
                load-shape(B, circle))~(_COUNTERF_0(B)).

   _COUNTERF_0(B) ←double(B, true).
   _COUNTERF_0(B) ←n-loads(B,3).
   _COUNTERF_0(B) ←position(B,1).
```

Target Relation	FOIL errors	FOIL error %	EXCRL errors	EXCRL error %
sender	3	0.8%	3	0.8%
receiver	7	1.9%	5	1.4%
logo	0	-	0	-
reference	3	0.8%	7	1.9%
date	23	6.5%	8	2.2%

Table 1. Finding rules for identifying sender, receiver, logo, reference, and date within a sample of businnes letters (document identification task).

A fourth test is aimed at finding rules for classifying documents [Esp93], namely finding rules for identifying sender, receiver, logo, reference, and date within a sample of businnes letters. Thirty documents have been considered, each of them containing a variable number of the above components, together with some other component considered not relevant within the test. A leave-one-out cross-validation test has been performed, whose results, compared to the ones obtained by running FOIL, are shown in Table 1. EXCRL performed better than FOIL in almost all subtasks (its error rate is worse than the one obtained by using FOIL only when considering the target relation *reference*).

Moves	Positions	FOIL Clauses	F. P.	F. N.	EXCRL Clauses	F. P.	F. N.
zero	27	3	-	-	6	-	-
one	78	4	-	-	15	-	-
two	246	8	-	3	28	-	-
three	81	11	-	7	44	-	-
four	198	26	-	11	90	-	-
five	471	44	-	38	165	-	-
six	592	53	-	44	253	-	-
seven	683	77	-	69	333	-	-
eight	1433	112	-	77	482	-	1
nine	1712	168	-	72	768	-	1
ten	1985	189	1	93	856	-	1
eleven	2854	237	1	80	1051	-	-
twelve	3597	226	1	141	1039	-	-
thirteen	4194	197	1	157	961	-	-
fourteen	4553	146	1	58	867	-	-
fifteen	2166	54	-	14	314	-	-
sixteen	390	6	-	-	12	-	-
drawn	2796						

Tab. 2. Results on chess endgame.

The fifth test is concerned with the simplest chess endgame, King and Rock versus King. Let us assume that a database of all positions in wich the Rock's side wins in 0 through 16 moves, together with draw positions, is given. For each number of moves to win, say k, a theory is learned that discriminates positions won in k moves from drawn positions and from positions won in more than k moves. The results obtained by EXCRL and FOIL are shown in Table 2: for each number of moves, the number of positive examples, the number of clauses, and the number of misclassified positive and negative examples (False Positive and False Negative) are reported. Note that the definitions found by FOIL, although more compact, often do not cover all positive examples.

Conclusions and Future Work

In this paper, an alternative approach for dealing with the problem of learning relational concepts from examples has been presented. Such an approach is characterized by the way counterexamples (exceptions) are dealt with while searching for the target concept. The process of finding the description of a concept by using an exceptions-based approach consists of finding an initial description and of refining it by applying suitable counterfactuals, at different levels of granularity. As far as future work is concerned, we are currently dealing with the problem of finding recursive definitions of a concept, thus obtaining a system able to deal with most of the classical ILP problems.

References

[Cam93]   Cameron-Jones, R.M., and Quinlan, J.R., "Efficient top-down induction of logic programs," SIGART, 5, 33-42, 1993.

[Esp93]   Esposito, F., Malerba, D., Semeraro, G., and Pazzani M.J., "A Machine Learning Approach to Document Understanding," *Proc. 2nd Int. workshop on Machine Learning*, Harpers Ferry, WV, pp. 276-292, May 1993.

[Gem91]   Gemello, R., Mana, F., and Saitta, L., "Rigel: An Inductive Learning System," *Machine Learning*, Vol. 6, pp. 7-35, 1991.

[Mic80]   Michalski, R.S., "Pattern Recognition as Rule-Guided Inductive Inference," *IEEE Trans. on Pattern Analysis and Machine Intelligence*, Vol. 2, pp. 349-361, 1980.

[Mic83]   Michalski, R.S., "A Theory and Methodology of Inductive Learning," *Artificial Intelligence*, Vol. 20, pp. 111-161, 1983.

[Mug92]   Muggleton, S., and feng, C., "Efficient Induction of Logic Programs," in S. Muggleton (Ed.), *Inductive Logic Programming*, pp. 281-298, London, Academic Press, 1992.

[Paz91]   Pazzani, M.J., Brunk, C.A., and Silverstein, G., "A Knowledge Intensive Approach to Learning Relational Concepts," *Proc. 8th International Workshop on Machine Learning*, Evanston, Illinois, pp. 432-436, 1991.

[Qui89]   Quinlan, R., "Learning relations: Comparison of a symbolic and a connectionist approach," *Technical Report 346,* Basser Dept. Comp. Science, University of Sydney, Sydney, Australia, 1989.

[Qui95]   Quinlan J.R., and Cameron-Jones, R.M., "Induction of Logic Programs: FOIL and Related Systems," *New Generation Computing,* Vol. 13, pp. 287-312, 1995.

[Tur95]   Turney, P., "Low Size-Complexity Inductive Logic Programming: The East-West Challenge Considered as a Problem in Cost-Sensitive Classification," *Proc. of the Fifth International Inductive Logic Programming Workshop, ILP-95,* pp. 247-263, 1995.

[Ver80]   Vere, S.A., "Multilevel Counterfactuals for Generalizations of Relational Concepts and Productions," *Artificial Intelligence,* Vol. 14, pp. 139-164, 1980.

[Win86]   Winston, P.H., "Learning by Augmenting Rules and Accumulating Censors," in Michalski, Carbonell, Mitchell (eds.), *Machine Learning: An AI Approach,* Vol. 2, 1986.

Inferring Minimal Rule Covers from Relations

Claudio Carpineto and Giovanni Romano
Fondazione Ugo Bordoni
Via Baldassarre Castiglione 59, 00142, Rome, Italy
{carpinet, romano}@fub.it

Abstract

An implication rule Q→R is roughly a statement of the form "for all objects in the database, if an object has Q then it has also R". We introduce a definition of minimal cover for the set of implication rules that hold in a relation, by analogy with earlier work on functional dependencies, and present an approach to computing it. The core of the proposed approach is an algorithm for inferring a reduced cover containing only maximally general rules, i.e., such that no attribute-value pair on any left side is redundant. We study the computational complexity of the proposed approach and present an experimental comparison with another method that confirms its validity, especially when the number of attributes in the database is limited.

1. Introduction

Recent research across a number of fields including databases, machine learning, and knowledge discovery has addressed the problem of automatic extraction of data dependencies from relational databases. Several types of dependencies have been investigated, ranging from classical functional dependencies (Schlimmer 1993; Mannila and Räihä 1994) to several types of attribute-oriented rules (Piatetsky-Shapiro 1991; Agrawal and Srikant 1994; Godin and Missaoui 1994, Ziarko and Shan 1996), and a number of systems for their extraction have been presented. While differing in many respects, most of this work has two main common features. The first is the goal of finding *all* possible rules of a given type that can be extracted from data, as opposed to other methods for inducing rules from data, such as those developed in machine learning, which are primarily biased towards producing minimum subsets of classification rules (Michalski 1983, Quinlan 1986, Cai *et al.* 1991). As a general consequence, specific methods must be devised for exhaustively searching a large hypothesis space and producing a virtually unbiased set of rules; by contrast, the use of classical machine learning algorithms, such as decision trees, would typically result in the omission of many possible, and equally plausible, rules (Carpineto and Romano 1993), while a straightforward adaptation of such methods, although possible, would suffer from serious inefficiency as well as redundancy problems (Schlimmer 1993). The second common objective of rule discovery systems is the ability to deal with compact representations of the set of rules generated. As such sets may grow very large, thus making the presentation, comprehension and utilization of the rules themselves very difficult, it is necessary to focus only on the interesting rules, discarding the irrelevant ones. Of the many optimality and pruning criteria that have been presented (Piatetsky-Shapiro 1991; Shan *et al.* 1995, Toivonen *et al.* 1995), the notion of *cover*, as developed in the database theory (Maier 1983; Ullman 1988), is probably one of the best well-founded and understood, for which there exists a large body of concepts and methods. While the use of this notion has been traditionally confined to functional dependencies, it can also be applied to attribute-oriented dependencies.

In this paper we deal with the problem of finding a minimal cover for a class of data dependencies called implication rules, useful for discovering hidden patterns in data (Godin and Missaoui 1994, Ziarko and Shan 1996). An implication rule Q→R is roughly a statement of the form "for all objects in the database, if an object has Q then it has also R". We provide a definition of minimal cover for the set of implication rules that hold in a relation, based on an analogous definition provided by Ullman (1988) for functional dependencies, and present a method for computing it. The main component of our method is an algorithm that finds a cover containing only maximally general rules; this reduced, although not minimal, cover is subsequently processed by a procedure that removes the remaining redundant rules from it. A study of the computational complexity of the algorithm, along with an experimental comparison with an alternative clustering-based approach, suggests that the proposed approach performs favourably, especially in those situations where the number of attributes is limited.

The rest of the paper has the following structure. In the next section, we introduce implication rules and characterize their minimal covers. In section 3, we describe the algorithm for computing a reduced cover for the set of implication rules that hold in a relation; then we discuss how to remove redundancy from the reduced cover to obtain a minimal cover. Section 4 deals with the complexity of inferring implication rules and analyses the complexity of the algorithm for finding maximally general rules. Section 5 contains an experimental comparison between the approach described in this paper and that based on lattice conceptual clustering, which was first proposed by Godin and Missaoui (1994) and has been later improved by Carpineto and Romano (submitted). Section 6 concludes the paper with a summary and some directions for future work.

2. Minimal covers for implication rules

Following the attribute-value representation model widely used in machine learning, knowledge discovery, and databases, we assume that the data are represented by a relation. More precisely, given a set of objects (O), a set of attributes (A), and a set of attribute values (V), a relation is a quadruple (O, A, V, I) where I is a ternary relation between O, A, and V (i.e., $I \subseteq O \times A \times V$) such that $(o,a,v_1) \in I$ and $(o,a,v_2) \in I$ imply $v_1 = v_2$. Note that $(o,a,v) \in I$ reads: the object o has the value v for the attribute a; instead of writing $(o,a,v) \in I$ we can write a(o) = v. Implication rules are defined in the following way.

Definition 1. An implication rule (IR) between two sets of attribute-value pairs is an expression $[(r_1, s_1), (r_2, s_2),....(r_h, s_h)] \rightarrow [(t_1, u_1), (t_2, u_2),.... (t_k, u_k)]$ where $(r_x, s_x), (t_x, u_x) \subseteq (A \times V)$. A relation (O, A, V, I) satisfies the IR $[(r_1, s_1), (r_2, s_2),....(r_h, s_h)] \rightarrow [(t_1, u_1), (t_2, u_2),.... (t_k, u_k)]$ if $\forall o \in O$, $\forall i \in [1,h]$, $\forall j \in [1,k]$, $r_i(o) = s_i \implies t_j(o) = u_j$.

In other terms, an implication rule between two subsets of attribute-value pairs Q and R means that if a set of objects satisfies the attribute-value pairs contained in Q then it necessarily satisfies the attribute-value pairs contained in R. For the sake of conciseness, in the following we often refer to an IR between two subsets of attribute-value pairs as $Q \rightarrow R$.

Although it is always theoretically possible to find all the IRs that a context satisfies, such an approach would be impractical. Fortunately, knowing some members of a set of IRs S, it is often possible to infer other members of S. In fact, owing to the nature of IRs, the inference system developed in database theory for functional dependencies (Maier 1983) holds also for IRs. This contrasts with other types of attribute oriented rules, such as association rules (Agrawal and Srikant 1994), that cannot support reasoning.[1] The following definitions are useful to find succint representations of the complete set of IRs that hold in a context.

Given a set S of IRs, the closure S^+ is the set of rules implied by S by application of Armstrong's inference axioms. Two sets S and S' are equivalent if they have the same closure. If S and S' are equivalent, then S' is a *cover* for S. By analogy with Ullman (1988), we propose the following definition for minimal cover.

Definition 2. A cover S' is minimal if:
a) Every right side of an implication rule in S' is a single attribute-value pair.
b) For no $Q \rightarrow R$ in S' is the set $S' - \{ Q \rightarrow R \}$ equivalent to S'.
c) For no $Q \rightarrow R$ in S' and proper subset S of Q is $S' - \{ Q \rightarrow R \} \cup \{ S \rightarrow R \}$ equivalent to S'.

Intuitively, condition (b) guarantees that no rule is redundant, while condition (c) guarantees that no attribute-value pair on any left side is redundant (i.e., left sides are maximally general). Condition (a) and (c) may help the user focus on relevant rules; condition (b) allows well-founded more-succint representations of the set of rules. In the next section we describe a procedure for computing a minimal set of implication rules according to definition 2.

3. Inferring a minimal cover for implication rules

The core of our method is an algorithm, described in section 3.1, for finding a reduced cover that satisfies property a) and c) of Definition 2, while property b) is handled by an additional procedure, described in section 3.2, that applies to the reduced cover.

3.1 Finding maximally general rules

For each attribute-value pair (a,v) present in the relation, we want to find the set LHS (left-hand side) containing all possible maximally general rules of the form $Q \rightarrow$ (a,v). Since all rules $Q \rightarrow R$ can be derived from rules with a single attribute-value

---

[1] A thorough discussion of the differences between implication rules and association rules, as well as of the relation between implication rules and functional dependencies, is contained in Carpineto and Romano (submitted).

pair on the right-hand side, the total set of rules generated this way is a cover for the relation.

A simple method to infer the set LHS is the following. Since each object o will typically support some rules (among those whose right side is equal to a subset of the attribute-value pairs present in o) as well as prevent some other rules (among those whose right side is *not* equal to any of the attribute-value pairs present in o), we could maintain a set containing all possible *lhs* candidates and update it by examining one object at a time. Candidates contradicted by the object should be removed from the candidate set, candidates confirmed should be marked. After all objects have been examined, the set of marked rules is a cover (although not maximally general). This approach, however, would require to examine p^m candidates for each object, where p is the number of values per attribute and m is the number of attributes.

The algorithm we present is based on partitioning the set of objects in the relation in two classes, i.e, the set of "positive" objects such that a(o) = v, and the set of "negative" objects such that a(o) $\neq$ v. The main loop of the algorithm iterates on the positive objects. The algorithm keeps and updates for each positive object the set of rules that can be theoretically generated from it; i.e., all the possible 2^{m-1} subsets of the attribute-value pairs present in the object, except for (a,v). On an abstract level, the algorithm must first remove the rules that are contradicted by some negative objects, then it must check that any rule is not equal to any other rules produced by the other positive examples, and finally it must collect only the most general rules of the remaining ones. These are three computationally difficult problems.

The key idea of the algorithm is to use an ordered structure for representing the candidate rule space, over which the three operation can be performed efficiently and in an integrated manner. Consider an ordered set $\{ \mathcal{P}(o); \geq \}$, formed by the power set of the attribute-value pairs present in the object, except for (a,v), and by the standard set inclusion relation (i.e., x $\geq$ y if x$\subseteq$y). This ordered set is well formed with respect to the task at hand. In particular, if an element is ruled out by some negative object then all its greater ($\geq$) elements are also ruled out; conversely, if an element is the *lhs* of a valid rule then all its smaller elements are also valid rules. Using $\{ \mathcal{P}(o); \geq \}$ allows us to handle pruning due to negative objects in a straightforward manner. For each negative object the algorithm finds the intersection between the negative object and the current positive object and prunes all the elements that are greater than or equal to the intersection from $\{ \mathcal{P}(o); \geq \}$. Dealing with the rule duplication issue due to the other positive objects is also easy. If we lexicographically order the set of positive objects, we can ignore in the current candidate space all those rules that will be considered when examining subsequent positive objects. The "deferred" candidates are those elements that are greater than or equal to the intersection between the current positive object and any subsequent positive object. This way we can avoid generating rules more than once. The final operation involved in each iteration is the collection of the most general rules, performed through a specific-to-general breadth-first search through the elements of $\{ \mathcal{P}(o); \geq \}$ that have neither been pruned nor deferred.

A complete description of the algorithm is given in Table 1.

Table 1. The algorithm for inferring a rule cover

Find-LHS

<u>Input</u>: a relation (O, A, V, I), an attribute-value pair (a, v) such that
  (o, a, v) ∈ I for some o∈ O.

<u>Output</u>: the set LHS relative to (a, v)

  LHS := ∅

  O^+ := { o ∈ O | a(o) = v}   ; *set of positive objects*

  O^- := { o ∈ O | a(o) ≠ v}   ; *set of negative objects*

  Loop for i ∈ [1, || O^+||] **do**

   Loop for o^- ∈ O^- **do**   ; *pruning*

     int^- := O_i^+ ∧ o^-

     Loop for c ∈ {$\mathcal{P}$(O_i^+ - {a,v}); ≥} such that c ≥ int^- **do**
       label (c) = "del"

   Loop for j ∈ [i+1, || O^+||] **do**   ; *deferment*

     int^+ := O_i^+ ∧ O_j^+

     Loop for c ∈ {$\mathcal{P}$(O_i^+ - {a,v}); ≥} such that c ≥ int^+ **and** label (c) ≠ "del"
       do
        label (c) = "def"

   Loop for c ∈ {$\mathcal{P}$(O_i^+ - {a,v}); ≥} such that label (c) ≠ "del"   ; *collection*
                  and label (c) ≠ "def"
     when for all parents of c label (parent (c)) = "del" **do**

      LHS := LHS ∪ {c}

We have to emphasize that from a practical point of view it is convenient to implement { $\mathcal{P}$(o); ≥} using a vector with two specialised access funtion. More precisely, we coded each element of $\mathcal{P}$ (o) by a bit vector, where position i is equal to 1 or 0 depending on whether the attribute-value pair i is present or not in the element. These bit vectors are used as indices to a fixed-length 2^{m-1} cell vector that contains the information about the elements of $\mathcal{P}$(o). The address of the parents (according to ≥) can be easily computed from the address of the element itself through bit masking. Thus, this implementation allows direct acces to each element of $\mathcal{P}$(o) and to its parents.

To illustrate the working of the algorithm, we refer to a simple database consisting of four objects described by four attributes (see Table 2). Let d_1 be the current *rhs* and consider the step relative to the first positive object ($a_1b_1c_1d_1$). For the sake of clarity, we represent the set ($\mathcal{P}(a_1b_1c_1d_1); \geq$) as a graph rather than as a vector (see Figure 1). Examinaton of the first negative object ($a_1b_1c_2d_2$) causes pruning of a_1b_1 (intersection between $a_1b_1c_2d_2$ and the current positive object) and of its ancestors (a_1 and b_1) from the graph. Object $a_2b_2c_1d_2$ causes pruning of element c_1. Finally, the effect of the positive example $a_1b_2c_1d_1$ is deferment of element a_1c_1. In Figure 1, pruned elements are encircled, while deferred elements are boxed. Once all three objects have been examined the unlabeled elements in the graph are visited ($a_1b_1c_1$ and b_1c_1) and the most general of them are collected. The result is the rule $b_1c_1 \rightarrow d_1$.

Table 2: An example database.

a_1	b_1	c_1	d_1
a_1	b_1	c_2	d_2
a_2	b_2	c_1	d_2
a_1	b_2	c_1	d_1

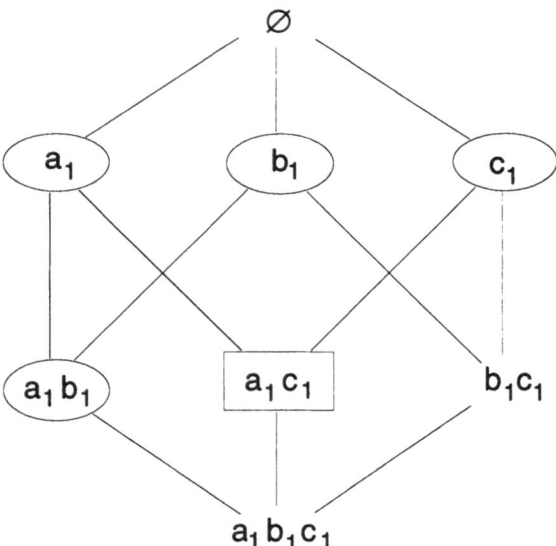

Figure 1. The ordered set of the candidate *lhs* rules associated with the first object of the database shown in Table 2. Encircled elements are pruned by negative objects, boxed elements are deferred by positive objects.

The cover returned by the algorithm described in Table 1 satisfies condition (a) and (c) of Definition 2, but it will not, in general, satisfy condition (b) because whenever the cover contains the rules $Q \rightarrow R$ and $R \rightarrow S$ it will also contain the rule $Q \rightarrow S$.

3.2 Removing cover redundancy

In order to generate a nonredundant cover for a set S of implication, we must delete from S each $Q \rightarrow R$ such that $Q \rightarrow R$ is "member" of S - $\{Q \rightarrow R\}$. To determine if the rule $Q \rightarrow R$ can be derived from the set S - $\{Q \rightarrow R\}$, it is sufficient to compute the closure of Q under S - $\{Q \rightarrow R\}$, denoted Q^+, and then check whether $R \subseteq Q^+$. Maier (1983) describes an efficient algorithm for computing Q^+ for functional dependencies that can be easily adapted to implication rules. The algorithm has $O(k)$ time complexity, where k is the cardinality of S. Therefore the time complexity of the procedure for removing redundant rules from S is $O(k^2)$, which may be exceedingly hard for many real problems. We will see in section 5 that when the input (redundant) cover is large the procedure for removing redundancies may easily run into computational barriers. In the next section we discuss the computational complexity of IR inference and analyse the complexity of the algorithm for finding maximally general rules.

4. Complexity of IR inference

We first consider how the growth of the two main problem parameters, i.e., the number of objects *n* and the number of attributes *m*, affects the size of the set of IRs that hold in a relation.

As the number of objects grows, the number of IRs may decrease or it may increase. To explain this, consider that the introduction of a new object may result in new IRs between combinations of attribute-value pairs that had not been seen before; but it may also disconfirm IRs that held previously. Furthermore, things are made slightly more complicated by the fact that when some formerly-valid rule in the cover becomes invalid as a consequence of the introduction of a new object, it may be replaced by more rules (e.g., $P \rightarrow Q$ may be replaced by $PR \rightarrow Q$ and $PS \rightarrow Q$); thus, the size of the cover may increase even while the set of IRs that hold in a relation decreases. In fact, we have observed that an increase in the number of objects *n* usually results in a noticeable increase in the cover size, at least for small values of *n*.

The number of IRs that hold in a relation grows monotonically with respect to the number of attributes in the relation. Mannila and Räihä (1994) have shown that for some relations over *m* attributes all the covers of *functional dependency* sets are of exponential size in *m*. Thus, the covers of the *IR* sets of those relations are - *a fortiori* - of exponential size in *m*. On the other hand, experience with real data sets confirms that covers of IR sets may indeed be exponential in the number of attributes (see Table 3). In many situations, however, this problem may not become very serious, because in real domains it is often the case that the number of attributes in a relation is relatively small. Furthermore, the growth of the number of IRs may be dramatically reduced by allowing for statistical significance of the holding rules, as mentioned in the last section.

We now analyse the complexity of the *Find-LHS* algorithm described in Table 1. For each positive object we must check all other objects and update the candidate-rule space. Since each update, including the final collection, requires visiting distinct nodes and testing their parents, the time complexity involved is bounded by the maximum branching factor times the cardinality of the candidate-rule space. In fact, we experimentally checked that for each positive object the number of nodes visited is constant: $(m/2)2^{m-1}$, where $m/2$ is just the average branching factor of the elements in ($\mathcal{P}(o); \geq$). Thus, the time complexity for each positive object cannot exceed $O(n+(m/4)2^m)$, and the time complexity of the Find-LHS algorithm is therefore $< O(n_p(n+m2^m))$, where n_p is the number of positive objects. In practice, $n << m2^m$; furthermore, n_p is usually a small fraction of the number of objects. As a consequence, in many practical applications, the complexity is nearly $O(m2^m)$.

5. Related work

IRs, sometimes called implications (Guiges and Duquenne 1986) or simply rules (Ziarko and Shan 1996), have not been deeply investigated until recently.

Ziarko and Shan (1996) have presented an IR-finding method based on the computation of prime implicants of Boolean expressions. Similar to our approach, the cover output by Ziarko and Shan's contains only maximally general rules. However, the complexity of the method, as also noted by the authors, seems to be prohibitively high even for databases of limited size; in fact, no evidence is reported in the paper that in some real domains such an approach would be feasible.

The only other IR-finding method that we are aware of has been presented by Godin and Missaoui 1994, and later improved by Carpineto and Romano (submitted). This method is based on a particular representation of the input relation called concept lattice, from which the rules are then extracted. The found rules are not maximally general; the cover satisfies a weaker property than condition (b) of Definition 2, explained in Carpineto and Romano (submitted). For the scope of this paper, suffice it to say that the cover returned by the concept lattice method is a superset of the cover returned by Ziarko and Shan's method or by the algorithm described in this paper.

We now compare the Find-LHS algorithm with the concept lattice method, in particular with Carpineto and Romano (submitted)'s version. A theoretical comparison is difficult because the complexity of the concept lattice method cannot be directly expressed in terms of the main problem parameters; it would also require an in-depth analysis of the concept lattice method which is outside the scope of this paper. Our goal is rather to get some indications about the behaviour of the Find-LHS algorithm; therefore we compare the performance of the two algorithms on some real domains.[2]

---

[2] All the programs tested in this paper are written in Common Lisp. For the experiments we used a SUN Ultra 2 equipped with 248 Mbytes of RAM.

For the experiment, we used five machine learning benchmarks available from the repository at University of California at Irvine, whose main features are described in Table 3. Numeric values were discretized into ten equal-length intervals.[3] For the missing values, we used the overall modal (most frequent) value for nominal attributes and Boolean features and used the overall mean for numeric attributes. We ran the concept lattice method and the Find-LHS algorithm on each data set, computing the following variables: (a) CPU time necessary to find the cover, (b) size of the cover,.

The results are shown in Table 3. "CPU time" columns labeled "ET" indicate that the algorithm exceeded a time limit of 1000 seconds, while "NA" in the "cover size" column indicates that the procedure ran into computational barriers, and therefore the datum was not available.

Table 3. Experimental evaluation of the Find-LHS algorithm versus the concept lattice method.

Dataset				Concept Lattice Method		Find-LHS	
Name	#objects	#attributes	missing values	CPU time	Number of rules	CPU time	Number of rules
Bridges 2	108	12	Y	23	28399	74	7151
Breast Cancer	286	10	Y	76	38678	48	14739
Liver Disorders	345	7	N	29	7775	11	5326
Breast Cancer W.	699	11	Y	174	110391	259	55394
Tic Tac Toe	958	10	N	ET	NA	290	27491

The results of the experiments show that the cover returned by the Find-LHS algorithm are significantly smaller than those produced by the concept lattice method. As for time performance, Find-LHS beat the concept lattice method on three of the five benchmarks, and lost on the remaining two. The results show that as the number of objects increase, the number of attributes staying stable, the performance of Find-LHS tends to improve over that of the concept lattice method. This may suggest that the number of objects may be a less critical factor for the Find-LHS algorithm's complexity than for the concept lattice method's complexity. This indication, however, is partially contradicted by the behaviour of the Breast-cancer-Winsconsin data set. In fact, an increase in the number of objects may sometimes be more harmful for Find-LHS than for the concept lattice method. This happens when the objects in the relation have very few similarities (i.e., their attributes values are

---

[3] In another series of experiments numeric attributes were treated as if they were nominal. The results were different but consistent with those reported below.

different). In this case, while the intermediate representation used by the concept lattice method is small and easy to compute, the Find-LHS algorithm must be invoked many times because there are plenty of values taken on by each attribute.

We have also to emphasize that all data sets used in the experiment have a limited number of attributes. While the number of attributes represents an inherent limitation for the performance of the Find-LHS algorithm, the concept lattice method may work with data sets described by tens of attributes (Carpineto and Romano; submitted). On the other hand, the comparison between the CPU time of the two algorithms can only be taken as indicative because the returned covers have different characteristics. In particular, the time necessary to remove the rules that are not maximally general from the cover returned by the concept lattice method may significantly worsen its performance.

In order to obtain a better estimate of the relative performance of the two algorithms, in Table 4 we show the CPU times normalised with respect to the time necessary to find a minimal cover. The results show a marked superiority of the Find-LHS algorithm and give some insights into the cover reduction due to redundancy removal.

Table 4. Experimental comparison of time performance normalised with respect to redundancy removal.

Dataset	Concept Lattice Method			Find-LHS		
Name	Size of redundant cover	CPU time for minimal cover	Size of minimal cover	Size of redundant cover	CPU time for minimal cover	Size of minimal cover
Bridges 2	28399	275	1240	7151	146	1236
Breast Cancer	38678	ET	NA	14739	489	3462
Liver Disorders	7775	76	2011	5326	57	2062
Breast Cancer W.	110391	ET	NA	55394	ET	NA
Tic Tac Toe	NA	ET	NA	27491	ET	NA

6. Conclusion

In this paper we considered the problem of finding a minimal cover for the set of implication rules that hold in a relation. We presented an algorithm for finding a cover containing only maximally general rules, from which a minimal cover can then be extracted. We analysed the complexity of the proposed approach and compared it with another IR-finding algorithm. Our approach performed favourably, especially for data sets with a limited number of attributes.

Work on analysis, computation and application of implication rules is still in its infancy. Among several issues that need be investigated, extraction of significant subsets of the set of rules inferred is important for practical applications. Following Definition 1, an IR holds even if there is only one object that satisfies the rule; consequently, we may discover many irrelevant or spurious rules. One way to cope with this problem is to restrict the set of valid rules to those rules that are supported by a given percentage of the objects. The introduction of such a parameter does not adversely affect reasoning in that inference axioms hold also for statistically-supported IRs; furthermore, it dramatically reduces the number of valid rules in a data set (Carpineto and Romano; submitted).

A further anticipated difficulty for the application of our approach to real-life problems is the presence of noise in the data. Noisy data may cause two main problems. The first is the discovery of meaningless rules due to the presence of erroneus attribute values in some objects, although the use of the support threshold mentioned above may greatly help reduce this inconvenience. The second problem is that the system may fail to produce interesting rules, because it does not permit exceptions (i.e., the rules must hold for all the objects in the relation). To deal with this issue it is necessary to allow for some form of nondeterministic or approximate dependencies, with the goal of handling noise while keeping reasoning capabilities. This is an avenue for future research.

Acknowledgments

This work has been carried out within the framework of the agreement between the Italian PT Administration and the Fondazione Ugo Bordoni.

References

AGRAWAL, R., and R. SRIKANT. 1994. Fast algorithms for mining association rules. *In* Proc. of the 20th VLDB Conference, Santiago, Chile, 487-499.

CAI Y., N. CERCONE, and J., HAN. 1991. Learning in relational databases: an attribute-oriented approach. Computational Intelligence, **7**: 119-132.

CARPINETO C., and G. ROMANO. 1993. GALOIS: An order-theoretic approach to conceptual clustering. *In* Proc. of the Tenth International Conference on Machine Learning, Amherst, MA: Morgan Kauffmann, pp. 33-40.

CARPINETO C., G. ROMANO, and P. d'ADAMO (submitted). Inferring dependencies from relations: a conceptual clustering approach. Submitted for publication.

GODIN, R., and R. MISSAOUI. 1994. An incremental concept formation approach for learning from databases, Theoretical Computer Science: Special Issue on Formal Methods in Databases and Software Engineering, **133**:387-419.

GUIGES, J. L., and V. DUQUENNE. 1986. Famille nonredundantes d'implications informatives résultant d'un tableau de données binaires. Mathématique and Sciences Humaines, **95**:5-18.

MAIER, D. 1983. The theory of relational databases. Computer Science Press, Rockville, MD.

MANNILA, H., and K. RÄHIÄ. 1994. Algorithms for inferring functional dependencies from relations. Data & Knowledge Engineering, 12(1):83-99.

MICHALSKI, R. 1983. A theory and methodology of inductive learning. Artificial Intelligence, 20:111-161.

PIATETSKY-SHAPIRO, J. 1991. Discovery, analysis and presentation of strong rules. *In* Knowledge Discovery in Databases. *Edited by* G. Piatetsky-Shapiro and W. Frawley. AAAI Press, 1991, pp. 229-248.

QUINLAN, R. 1993. C4.5: programs for machine learning. Morgan Kaufmann, San Mateo, CA.

SCHLIMMER, J. 1993. Efficiently inducing determinations: A complete and systematic search algorithm that uses optimal pruning. *In* Proc. of the.10th International Machine Learnig Conference, Amherst, MA, Morgan Kaufmann, pp.284-290.

SHAN, N., W. ZIARKO, H. HAMILTON, and N. CERCONE. 1995. Using rough sets as tools for knowledge discovery. *In* Proc. of the First International Conference on Knowledge Discovery and Data Mining, Montreal, Canada, AAAI Press, pp. 263-268.

TOIVONEN, H., M. KLEMETTINEN, P. RONKAINEN, K. HAETOENEN, and H. MANNILA. 1995. Pruning and grouping of discovered association rules. *In* Working Notes of the MLnet Workshop on Statistics, Machine Learning and Knowledge Discovery in Databases. Crete, Greece.

ULLMAN, J. 1988. Principles of database and knowledge-base systems, Vol. I, Computer Science Press.

ZIARKO, W., and N. SHAN. 1996. A method for computing all maximally general rules in attribute-value systems. Computational Intelligence, 12(2):223-234.

Corpus-Driven Unsupervised Learning of Verb Subcategorization Frames

Roberto Basili, Maria Teresa Pazienza, Michele Vindigni

Department of Computer Science, System and Production
University of Roma, *Tor Vergata*
Via Della Ricerca Scientifica s.n.c., 00133, Roma, ITALY
e-mail: {basili,pazienza,vindigni}@info.utovrm.it

Abstract. The behavior of verbs in sublanguages is highly specific and does not follow general principles of lexical decomposition. NLP applications require specific lexicons for tasks like surface parsing and shallow semantic interpretation. The reduced set of verbal senses specific to a given domain is more appropriate for efficient processing in real world tasks (e.g. information extraction and retrieval). In this paper a method for learning verb subcategorization patterns from corpora is proposed. Conceptual clustering techniques are applied to the results of surface parsing in order to extract relevant domain typical senses and automatically build a lexicon of subcategorization frames. The aim is to learn a core of lexico-grammatical knowledge suitable to support more sophisticated parsing strategies to be applied in a target NLP application. Results derived for the Italian language from several corpora are presented.

1   Problem Definition

Verb argument structures are crucial components of most parsing theories. They are widely used both as grammatical models in linguistic theories (Pollard e Sag, 1987, 1992) and as control rules in parsing systems (e.g. (XTAG,1995)). Verb argument structures provide either formal constraints to the notion of grammatical well-formedness and systematic principles to recognize (or build) sentences in an argument oriented fashion (from less oblique to maximally oblique arguments).

The notion of verb argument structures, early introduced by (Chomsky,1965), refers to subcategories of the syntactic class of verbs in a generative grammar. Each subcategory describes the specific sets of syntactic constituents (e.g. prepositional modifiers, infinitival subsentences) allowed to be used with its member verbs. The set of the legal constituents is also referred to as *verb subcategorization frame*: it includes all the legal modifiers required to fully express the meaning of the event denoted by the verb. In GPSG (Gazdar et al.,1985) and HPSG (Pollard and Sag,1987,1993) the role of the lexicon is even stronger and the lexical knowledge is organized in hierarchies of feature structures expressing subcategorization information. If for example a simple sentence like

$$...gli \quad enti \quad danno \quad la \quad notizia \quad a \quad tutti \quad gli \quad uffici \quad ... \qquad (1)$$
$$...(the \quad organizations \quad give \quad advice \quad to \quad the \quad offices)...$$

is to be parsed, a useful source of information is the subcategorization frame

Table 1. A Lexicalized subcategorization scheme for the verb *to give*

to give: V[Subcat < NP[*nom*] NP[*acc*] PP[*to*]>]

reported in Table 1, where information about the verb subject and the two objects (the receiver and the given object, respectively) are described. The result is a sharp separation between a general mechanism of grammatical formation (i.e. argument consumption[1]) and a large number of rules that guide parsing and interpretation in terms of composition of lexical items.

Real NLP system requires huge lexicons and availability of them is questionable: (1) large scale resources are missing or hard to reuse when application domains (and sublanguages) change; (2) sublanguages exhibit several idiosyncratic phenomena, that are often independent from general principles of the underlying languages (Basili et al., 1992, 1993).; (3) verbal lexicons are also more difficult to build and maintain as verbs are a particularly complex category (i.e. they exhibit a wider polisemy and their use is crucial during parsing and semantic interpretation). Measures based on English dictionaries (Grimshaw,1977) suggest that building a verbal entry in a full English lexicon takes a time of about an hour. Problems with polisemy and relatively free word order suggest that the required time is even longer for a language like Italian. For these reasons several inductive approaches to the development of verbal lexicons (specifically devoted to the automatic derivation of verb subcategorization frames) have been designed. Several methods make use of large corpora to extract verb use examples and build sets of verb subcategorization frames appropriate in the sublanguage. In (Brent,1992) a large database of syntactic information (i.e. annotated trees in the Penn TreeBank) has been used to derive verb subcategorization frames. The method uses conditioned probabilities to guess the sets of arguments. The probability estimation is more accurate but the effort required to hand validate source data may be prohibitive in languages other than English. Furthermore, when the underlying sublanguage changes (according to some new applications) the validity of the observed subcategorization frames is questionable in the new language. In the rest of the paper a method that automatically derives verb subcategorization frames from a source corpus is described. It does not require manually validated data, as the corpus is first processed by using a robust parser, and a conceptual clustering algorithm is then applied to the resulting instances. True argument structures are derived as clusters of surface patterns that are judged

---

[1] see the IDP principle in (Pollard and Sag,1987)

on a statistical and linguistic basis. The linguistic bias is applied to tune the clustering process to the particular (and noisy) syntactic information at hand. The inheritance relationships resulting from the learning activity are useful for the manual validation and for the suitable organisation of the lexical knowledge. In section 3, experimental evaluation carried out against hand-coded resources is reported. Encouraging results suggest that the method is useful either to build from scratch an early verbal lexicon or to tune a general lexicon to a given domain.

2 Inducing a subcategorization lexicon from a corpus

The derivation of a lexicon of subcategorization frames from a corpus requires the following three main phases:

1. *Corpus Pre-Processing*, in which syntactic data on verb behavior are extracted from raw texts;
2. *Clustering verb phrases* to induce argumental information (i.e. knowledge about systematic phenomena in the verb contexts)
3. *Selection of subcategorization schemata* and compilation of the target lexicon

Step 1 is based on the linguistic processing implemented in the ARIOSTO system (Basili et al,1992,1996). The following linguistic processors are used:

- a *tokenizer*, aiming to format the source text, recognize the word boundaries and carry out other utility functions;
- a *lemmatizer*, that recognizes sentential phrases, locutions, numbers and dates. In this phase the source lemma is recognized together with morphological features, like gender, number as well as tense and mode for verbs;
- a *robust parser*, aiming to derive all the (potentially ambiguous) legal syntactic relations among words in sentences

Step 2 and 3 are based on a conceptual clustering method fed with information expressing the syntactic structure of each verbal context, as it has been derived by the robust parser over the source examples of verb occurrences.

2.1 Corpus Pre-Processing

The problem of deriving in an unsupervised fashion syntactic information from a corpus is crucially dependent on methods of incomplete parsing. As an exhaustive grammatical model of the underlying language is still absent in the early acquisition phases an approximate approach is required. Furthermore most inductive methods require very large samples so that time complexity is also an important issue. The robust syntactic analyzer (SSA) used in ARIOSTO (Basili et al,1992,1994) builds the set of legal syntactic relations among words in a source sentence according to a discontinuous grammar (Dahl,1989). The typical structures derived by the robust parsing from the corpus are elementary syntactic links (*esl*) expressing relations like

$$esl(h, mod(p, w))$$

where h is the head of an X-bar like constituent (Chomsky, 1981) and $mod(p, w)$ generally expresses a syntactic modifier (Basili et al., 1992b): p denotes the syntactic relation (i.e. a preposition for indirect objects, or nil for direct objects or subjects) and w is the modifier head. For istance if sentence 2 is processed, due to syntactic ambiguity undesired constituents may be produced (e.g. the noun phrase $(notizia - a - ufficio)_{NP}$ (*advice-to-offices)). A graded grammaticality score (called *plausibility* (see (Basili et al,1994)) is assigned by SSA to esl to weight locally ambiguous links. The elementary syntactic links and the corresponding plausibility scores (pl) obtained for the sentence 2 are the following

```
i)    esl( dare, subj(nil,ente))     pl=1.0    %organization-to_give
ii)   esl( dare, obj(nil,notizia))   pl=1.0    %to_give-advice
iii)  esl( dare, pp(a,ufficio))      pl=0.5    %to_give-to-offices
iv)   esl( notizia, pp(a,ufficio))   pl=0.5    %advice-to-offices
```

Note that conflicting sentence readings are implied by the two last *esl* so that their overall plausibility is simply 0.5. Technical details about assignment of plausibility values are described in (Basili et al.,1994). The ambiguous syntactic graphs of each sentence are initially collected, then sets of potential arguments are extracted: specific components have been designed to compile linear representations from (possibly complex) surface grammatical structures (e.g. ambiguity, passive constructions, subject ellipsis). The kind of subcategorization frame derived from the sentence 2 with such an approach is thus

$$[dare \ [SUBCAT \ < \ NP[nom] \ NP[acc] \ PP[a] \ >] \ ]$$

Note that noisy arguments can be extracted from wrong attachments detected in ambiguous prepositional phrases. In recent studies (Basili et al.,1996), the number of ambiguous prepositional modifiers (i.e. confliting sentence readings due to PP_attachment resolution) has been evaluated on two corpora: 10,433 were found in the ENEA corpus (about 300,000 words) and 30,130 in a legal corpus (about 500,000 words). The average number of conflicting prepositional attachments per phrase was about 4 in both corpora. This noise highly affects subcategorisation frame discovery.

2.2   Learning Verb Arguments by Galois Lattices

Methods of clustering are widely adopted within the machine learning community to example-driven learning tasks (Gennari and Fisher,1989). They are generally based on incremental search within concept (or class) spaces, in order to select the most useful classification for the underlying task. In our case a separate search space must be used for each verb. The following steps are applied:

1. All the verbal phrases of a given verb are collected from the corpus.
2. Clusters of similar verb behaviours are organized into a hierarchical structure (e.g. a lattice)
3. Finally, a set of valid subcategorization rules corresponding to some derived classes are selected: clusters, in fact, suggest separate verbal senses and their corresponding grammatical constraints.

The clustering techniques based on conceptual lattices (Carpineto and Romano,1993) derive classes as conjunctive concepts according to a boolean feature-value language. Each derived concept is a couple (S, F) where S is a subset of instances, called *extent*, and F is the set of features of the cluster, called *intent*. Each couple is complete, that is F is the set of those features shared by all the instances of S, and dually, S is exactly the set of instances that in fact share the features in F (Carpineto and Romano,1993). The set of couples can be ordered according to the standard set inclusion of the extents S. The (partially) ordered set turns out to be a lattice. According to the completeness requirement the resulting lattice includes only a small number of the potential subsets S, precisely those necessary to describe all the shared features. The Galois based clustering technique has some interesting properties that favor its application to our inductive task. First, it is well suited to deal with symbolic information. Propositional formulas are used to express features F, as F is the conjunction of the attributes shared by instances in S. Such a language expresses the presence (or absence) of grammatical relations that we would like to find in a subcategorization scheme. Second, it is exhaustive according to the completeness criteria. In fact, each feature shared by distinct instances appears in the intention of the cluster including those instances. Overlapping features represent recurrent syntactic relations in corpus data and are in fact markers of argumental information. Third, it is incremental. New instances are added to an existing lattice in a time linear in the number of nodes (i.e. extracted classes). This has beneficial effects on the time complexity of the resulting lexical acquisition system.

We adopted the following representation: grammatical relations observed in a sentence are attributes of the corresponding instance. Subject, Object and indirect (or prepositional) objects are the corresponding atomic values. Prepositions are used to denote the indirect objects. A set of linguistic processes are applied to source syntactic data. A *syntactic graph generator* collects elementary syntactic links into a graph structure. A *feature vector compiler* is then used to rewrite the non-linear graph structure into one or more attribute-value vectors [2]

Table 2. Example of feature matrix for the verb *dare (to give)*

dare	DO	a	con	Feature Vectors
...danno un aiuto agli altri... (... they give help to someone)	•	•		[DO a]
...dando manforte... (... giving help ...)	•			[DO]
La penna data a Marco...(The pen given to Marco)	•	•		[DO a]
Dare a prestito (Give (as) a loan, (to lend))		•		[a]
dava acqua per mezzo di (con) un mestolo (he gave water by a spoon)	•		•	[DO con]

After all the contexts of a given verb have been preprocessed a feature matrix is built. As an example,5 sentences for the verb *dare (to give)* are reported in Table 2. Here DO denotes the syntactic object relation.

---

[2] typically some locutionary forms are here rewritten into simple prepositions

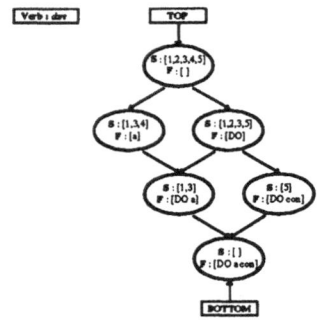

Fig. 1. Galois lattice of the feature matrix of Table 1

An example of the derived Galois lattice for the feature matrix in Table 2 is reported as an Hasse diagram in Figure 1. Higher nodes in the lattice subsume their descendents: inheritance of grammatical information is relevant to the activity of parsing as well as to the human driven validation of the induced lexical knowledge. This information is absent in other pure probabilstic approaches while here it is a natural consequence of the adopted representation and learning mechanism.

The coverage of a given concept varies according to the size of S. The higher is the number of elements in S, the more relevant is the corresponding set of features F. Simple statistical operators (e.g. relative frequencies) may be adopted to weight the relevance of a concept in the sample space (i.e. the set of contexts of a given verb). The simplest measure of the coverage of a couple $C = (S, F)$ in a lattice L is given by $c(C) = \frac{n_C}{n_L}$ where n_C is the cardinality of the set S, and n_L is the cardinality of the set of instances on which L has been built. As a result c is a non decreasing monotonic function along the set inclusion order in the lattice, taking its values in the range [0,1]. The coverage criteria is thus unsatisfactory for the purpose of selecting valid subcategorization frames, as it is unable to capture the linguistic relevance of the information stored in the intent F. The coverage criteria is thus unsatisfactory for the purpose of selecting valid subcategorization frames, as it is unable to capture the linguistic relevance of the information stored in the intent F.

2.3 Argument Selection from Context Lattices

The last step in the acquisition of verb subcategorization frames is the selection of suitable concepts in the Galois lattice. This inference depends on the whole lattice structure and from the intent F of that node. The structure says if a node is truly representative of its members (i.e. the contexts of the extent S). We will call a measure of this property the *selectivity* of a node C, $s(C)$. The set of arguments proposed by F is also a relevant source of information. We will call *linguistic preference* of a node C, $l(C)$, the measure of the utility of its intent F as a valid subcategorization frame. The overall preference is thus a combination of two functions: selectivity (s) and linguistic preference (l).

Selectivity of a Concept in the lattice The selectivity of a node C is the strength by which C represents the set of its contexts. The contexts of a node $C = (S, F)$, that have more attributes than those described by F, are also members of some cluster, son of C in the lattice (these are possibly singleton clusters). The higher is the number of sons where some contexts of C are found, the lower is the relevance of C: its information in fact, is also carried out by more specific nodes. Let $C = (S, F)$ be a concept in the lattice L. Let $Sons(C)$ denote the set of concepts that are sons of C in L. Let t denote generic contexts of some node. For any node $C = (S, F)$ in the lattice the *selectivity* of C, $s(C)$, is defined by:

$$s(C) = \sum_{t \in S} \frac{w(t, C)}{n_L} \qquad (2)$$

where

$$w(t, C) = \prod_{C' \in Sons(C)} 1 - s(C')\delta(t, C') \qquad (3)$$

and $\forall t, \quad C = (S, F) \qquad \delta(t, C) = 1$ iff $t \in S$ and 0 otherwise.

The function s may be recursively evaluated in a bottom-up fashion by imposing $s(BOTTOM) = 0$.

In general $0 \leq s(C) \leq 1$ but s is not a monotonic function along the set inclusion order. s is higher in the intermediate levels of the lattice, where the trade-off between generality and representativity is optimum. As an example for the lattice in Fig. 1 we have:

s(((1,3,4),[a]))=0.44   s(((1,2,3,5),[DO]))=0.6   s(((1,3),[DO a]))=0.4
while s(TOP) is only 0.28.

Linguistic Evaluation of a Concept in the Lattice During the conceptual clustering each feature in the context vector has the same relevance for the target induction. However, the selection of subcategorization frame is not just a matter of structural analysis of the lattice, or coverage optimization. First, data are inerently affected by noise. Second, the target phenomenon is not so underspecified. Although we have no information on the suitable argument structures that are valid in the underlying sublanguage, we surely know what is a subcategorization frame, and what is the general behavior of verbs in the source natural language. For example, several temporal and spatial specifications may in principle modify the events related to any verb: they are thus usually accidental (i.e. not argumental), though frequently observed with some verb. Simple probabilistic models may be used to evaluate the attitude of prepositions to denote verb arguments according to the variance of their distributions throughout domains and sublanguages. In a probabilistic framework to each preposition p (or more generally to each grammatical relation suitable to be used as an argument) can be assigned a weight $w(p)$ such that[3]

---

[3] For our purpose we started from conditioned probabilities of verb-preposition bigrams and adjusted them to fit the suitable preferences

$$\sum_p w(p) = 1$$

Let ARG be the set of grammatical relations (e.g. direct object, or any preposition) appearing in at least one context used to build a lattice L. As an example the lattice of Fig 1 has ARG={DO,a,con}. Given any node $C = (S, F)$ in the lattice L, the linguistic preference $l(C)$ assigned to the node is:

$$l(C) = \prod_{p \in ARG} w(p, C) \tag{4}$$

where $w(p, C) = w(p)$ iff $p \in F$ and $w(p, C) = 1 - w(p)$ otherwise.

The global evaluation $pref(C)$ of a node C depends on the selectivity $s(C)$ and on the linguistic preference $l(C)$ of the node. The former expresses distributional properties of grammatical relations (e.g. prepositional modifiers). The latter constraints the resulting intent F to be meaningful as a possible subcategorization pattern. The trade-off between the two objective functions l and s is expressed by the following utility function, *preference*:

$$pref(C) = s(C)l(C) \tag{5}$$

Given a experimentally set threshold σ, the intent F of a node $C = (S, F)$ is a valid subcategorization frame iff:

$$pref(C) > \sigma \tag{6}$$

Table 3. Preprocessing of the legal corpus: main results

	500 verb set	(%)	40 verb set	(%)
Syntactic Graph	24,000		3,400	
Esl	74,512		10,012	3.1±3.4 esl/ctxt
Prepositional esl (V_P_N)	54,078	75%	7,478	74.7%
Noun-verb esl (N_V)	5,352	7%	752	7.4%
Verb-noun esl (V_N)	14,722	18%	1,824	18.02%
Entries in the Subcategorization lexicon	1,850		105	

3 Experimental Evaluation.

The learning system has been applied to two different corpora in Italian. Two separate subcategorization lexicons have been derived. The first corpus is a collection of legal texts (of about 500,000 words). A lexicon of about 500 verbs has been derived from a set of 24,000 contexts. The second is a collection of short abstract on environmental pollution and its size is 350,000 words. A lexicon of about 800 words has been extracted from a set of 65,000 contexts. The extensive evaluation discussed here refers only to the legal corpus, for sake of synthesis. Main results of the legal corpus preprocessing are reported in Table 3. Some differences among the different syntactic relations can be observed: subject relations (i.e. N_V links) are less numerous as extracting them is more problematic partly due to the relatively free word order of Italian. Moreover, data on verb subjects are statistically weaker due to the subject ellipsis phenomenon. For this reason we decided to observe other subcategorization phenomena (direct objects and prepositional modifiers) for which more stable data have been obtained. Table 3 also reports the available data on a subset of the corpus related to 40 more frequent (> 50) verbs on which performance measures have been applied. As a reference information a number of hand-validated sources have been selected:

1. the LIFUV lexicon (LI), currently used within the GETA semantic analyzer (Del Monte and Dolci,1989). The lexicon is based on a lexical functional grammar (Kaplan and Bresnan,1982) and describes grammatical functions, subcategorization frames and thematic roles for a set of about 5,000 verbal entries
2. a dictionary (D) (Zingarelli,1970) with no subcategorization information. To obviate to this problem the set of verb use examples have been extracted by hand and compiled into subcategorization frames
3. a subcategorization lexicon for the 40 test verbs, manually compiled by a computational linguist (LL) in the legal domain

The first two sources (LIFUV and the dictionary) express a general linguistic knowledge while the linguist was very expert of the legal domain and the results of its work are much more domain specific. As an example, Table 4 reports the information related to the verb *versare* (*to pour, to pay, to spill*), as it is described in the three lexicons and as it has been derived automatically. This verb is particularly polisemic in Italian as the number of proposed subcategorization frames suggests.

Table 4. Subcategorization frames for the verb *versare*(to fill,to pay,...)

Versare (to pour, to pay, ...)	Subcategorization Frames
GALOIS (0.05< σ <0.3)	[DO] [a] [DO a]
LI	[DO] [in] [da] [su] [DO da] [DO su]
D	DO a
LL	DO in a

Note that the sense:

versare liquido su... [DO su]   *to pour < some liquid > < on something >*

has not been acquired: in fact, it is totally absent from the legal corpus where *versare* is generally referred to as a **money trasfer** activity (*to pay, to pay some money into the bank, ...*). This last specific sense is in fact captured by the system. The method has been evaluated by means of the classical measures of *recall* (r) and *precision* (p). Given a set H of subcategorization frames described in a reference source and the set S generated by the inductive system, precision (p) and recall (r) are defined as follows:

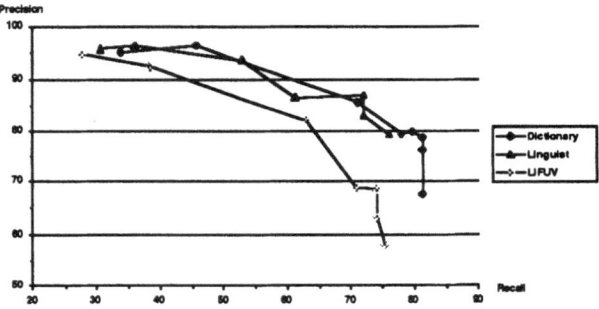

Fig. 2. Recall vs. Precision over the three reference lexicons

$$r = \frac{card(H \cap S)}{card(H)} \qquad p = \frac{card(H \cap S)}{card(S)}$$

Performance evaluation has thus been carried out by: (i) fixing a threshold σ for the preference function of the Galois lattice; (ii) building the set S according to (6), (iii) measuring Precision and Recall over S using the three sources as H. The three different results are plotted in Fig. 2. As Fig. 2 shows, results are good. The significant values of recall and precision suggest that the method is directly usable, especially as a support tool for the lexicon engineering. In Fig. 2 the comparison with the LL lexicon (compiled by the linguist) is less penalizing for the automatically derived lexicon. The other two lexicons in fact are much more general and include less information than necessary in the underlying sub-language. On the contrary the LL lexicon includes many phenomena that are (i) very frequent in the corpus but (ii) not argumental. Note that non argumental information is absent from the LIFUV. However, a strict separation between arguments and adjuncts tends to disappear within a given corpus. In both cases in fact the kind of information on frequent verb modifiers can be effectively used as control knowledge in a parsing system. In this view, the inductive method works slightly better than the measured 74% precision measured against the LIFUV: non argumental structures (those absent from LIFUV) are in fact very useful to increase the precision and the speed of parsers within the underlying sublanguage. When no counterpart is found for an automatically induced sense (i.e. subcategorization frame), two alternatives are possible:

- the new sense is missing from the LIFUV as it is built from a set of adjuncts that are particularly relevant for the domain; they can be used as parsing heuristics. In this case the new sense is a specialization of some of the LIFUV senses. The pattern [DO a] as a specialization of the LIFUV subcategorization [DO] is an example in Table 4;
- the new sense is a truly wrong guess of the system, as it has been generated because of some (systematic) parsing errors.

These observations should help to better read the gap of about 20% in precision that characterizes the evaluation against the LIFUV. A sense missing from the LIFUV is not always a wrong guess.

Finally, it is worth noticing that the dictionary (i.e. a general source of knowledge for the language) does not contain the *pouring* sense of *versare*. An overall recall of 77% has been measured for the D lexicon against the LIFUV. The inductive system seems to work with a performance similar to the dictionary, even if it is not yet fully satisfactory. However, its results are much more domain specific: infact the recall of the D lexicon against the legal domain expert (LL lexicon) is only 68%, while the system has a recall of 76% (precision is 83% instead)(see Fig. 2).

4 Conclusions

In this paper a method for automatic acquisition of verb subcategorization frames in domain specific sublanguages has been presented. A number of work hypothesis have been used: distributional properties of verb arguments are different from other accidental grammatical modifiers; sentence surface parsing is applied to derive atomic instances of argumental information; a global analysis of corpus derived data is applied to build patterns of syntactic relations as potential verb subcategorization frames; induction of conjiunctive concepts is used as a learning device; a combination of corpus driven and language oriented criteria is used to select the target lexical information.

The main results (about 75%-80% of precision and recall, against hand validated sources) are more than promising, even if compared with other supervised approaches (Brent,1992). The methodology has been widely applied to data from different corpora: differently from other probabilistic models it is not crucially dependent on the size of the training set and it is not very sensitive to noisy data. The compiled lexicon has a coverage similar to that of a dictionary, while being very sensible to the domain sublanguage. The applications of the proposed method involve not only the derivation of a full lexicon (from scratch) but also the tuning of a general source (e.g. a syntactic lexicon, that can be redundant and overgeneral for a given domain). The structured information resulting from the system learning is a valuable information either for unification based approaches to parsing (e.g. grammatical type hierachies, as in HPSG)) or for human corpus analysis and lexical knowledge design. Incrementality of the learning method is also a crucial adaptation capability for dealing with the highly dynamic nature of the language.

Open problems are the systematic definition of linguistic weights by which the syntactic relations used as features in the derived concepts are evaluated. Also better combinations of selectivity and linguistic preference should be experimented in order to improve the method robustness against source noise (i.e syntactic errors). From the point of view of representation a more complex set of syntactic relations (including sential complements, or infinitival, for example) should be used to deal with a wider class of syntactic phenomena (and verbal senses).

5 References

(Basili 1992) Basili R., M.T. Pazienza, P. Velardi, A shallow syntactic analyser to extract word associations from corpora, Literary and Linguistic Computing, 1992, vol.7, n. 2, 114- 124.

(Basili 1993) Basili R., M.T. Pazienza, P. Velardi, What can be learned from raw texts?, Journal of Machine Translation, 8: 147- 173, 1993.

(Basili 1994) Basili R., A. Marziali, M.T. Pazienza, Modelling Syntactic Uncertainty in Lexical Acquisition from Texts, Journal of Quantitative Linguistics, 1,1: 62- 81,1994.

(Basili et al.,1996) Basili R., Marziali A., Pazienza M.T., and Velardi P, Unsupervised learning of syntactic knowledge: Methods and measures,in Proceedings of the International Conference on Empirical Methods in Natural Language Processing, Philadelfia, Pennsylvania, 1996.

(Basili 1997) Basili R., M.T. Pazienza, P. Velardi, Integrating General Purpose and Corpus-based Verb Classifications, to appear in Computationa Linguistics 1997.

(Brent 1992) Brent M. R. Automatic Acquisition of Subcategorisation Frames from Unrestricted English, PhD Thesis, 1989.

(Carpineto 1993) Carpineto C., Romano G. GALOIS: An order-theoretic approach to conceptual clustering, Fondazione Ugo Bordoni, 1993.

(Chomsky 1965) Chomsky N., Aspects of the Theory of Syntax, MIT Press, Cambridge, MA, 1965.

(Chomsky 1981) Chomsky N., Lectures on Government and Binding, Foris Publications, Dordrecht, 1981.

(Del Monte, Dolci,1989), Del Monte, R. and Dolci, R. " Parsing Italian with a Context-free recogniser" Annali di Ca' Foscari XXVIII,1-2, 1989.

(Gennari 1989) Gennari J. H. & Langley P. & Fisher D. H. Models of incremental concept formation, Artificial Intelligence, 40, 11-61, 1989.

(Gazdar 1985) Gazdar G. Klein E., Pullum K. Sag I. Developments in GPSG theory Indiana University Linguistics, 38- 68, 1985

(Grimshaw 1977) Grimshaw J. Complement selection and the Lexicon. Linguistic Inquiry 10 (2):279- 326, 1977.

(Kaplan and Bresnan 1982) Kaplan R., Bresnan J. Lexical-Functional Grammar: A Formal System for Grammatical Representation, in J. Bresnan Ed., The Mental Representation of Grammatical Relations, MIT Press, Cambridge, MA, 1982.

(Pollard 1987) Pollard C. & Sag I. Information-Based Syntax and Semantics, CSLI Lecture Note Series, Chicago, 1987

(Pollard 1994) Pollard C. & Sag I. Head-Driven Phrase Structure Grammar, CSLI Lecture Note Series, Chicago, 1994

(XTAG,1995), XTAG Research Group. A Lexicalized Tree Adjoining Grammar for English, Technical Report IRCS 95-03, University of Pennsylvania, 1995.

(Zingarelli 1970), N. Zingarelli, Vocabolario della lingua italiana, 1970

Learning the Syntax and Semantic Rules of an ECG Grammar

Gabriella Kókai[1], János Csirik[2] and Tibor Gyimóthy[3]

[1] Institute of Informatics, József Attila University
Árpád tér 2, H-6720 Szeged, Hungary
Phone: (36) +(62) 311184, Fax: (36) +(62) 312292
e-mail: kokai@inf.u-szeged.hu

[2] Department of Computer Science József Attila University
Árpád tér 2, H-6720 Szeged Hungary
Phone: (36) +(62) 311184, Fax: (36) +(62) 312292
e-mail: csirik@inf.u-szeged.hu

[3] Research Group on Artificial Intelligence
Hungarian Academy of Sciences,
Aradi vértanuk tere 1, H-6720 Szeged, Hungary
Phone: (36) +(62) 454139, Fax: (36) +(62) 312508
e-mail: gyimi@inf.u-szeged.hu.

Abstract. In this paper a learning system is presented that is able to learn both the syntax (from an over-generalized grammar) and semantic rules (containing threshold values and relations) of an ECG grammar. These rules are used to direct the classification of QRS complexes and to distinquish between QRS and non-QRS patterns. The system demonstrates how a theory revision method can be used to refine large Prolog programs. [1]
Keywords: syntactic pattern recognition, ECG, inductive logic programming

1 Introduction

In this paper a learning system is presented that is able to learn the syntax and some semantic rules of an ECG classifier program (these rules are used to direct the classification of QRS complexes and to distinquish between QRS and non-QRS patterns). The system helps the user to correct the classifier program if it cannot recognize the given input waveforms.

The system presented in [4] and [5] integrates an electrocardiogram (ECG) waveform classifier called PECG with an interactive learner called IMPUT. In both papers it was shown how this integrated tool can improve the syntax of the classifier program starting from an *over-generalized* grammar. However, the

---
[1] This work was supported by the grants ESPRIT 20237 ILP2 and the project PHARE TDQM 9305-02/1022 ("ILP2/HUN").

PECG program contains user-defined numeric threshold values and decision rules for the classification of QRS complexes and for deciding about the QRS and non-QRS parts, as well. In this paper we will show that the extended PECG system is able to infer these threshold values and rules by using positive and negative examples and the IMPUT learning procedure.

The basic idea behind the original PECG system was to integrate the classifier program (implemented in Prolog) with an Interactive Diagnosis, Testing and Slicing (IDTS) module [9] and a graphic viewer. This integrated tool could then recognize whether any modification in the classifier program was needed. If the system could not properly analyze the input data then the built-in IDTS debugger module was used to find the false clause.

The learning part of the PECG was based on an Inductive Logic Programming (ILP) [2], [7] method called IMPUT introduced in [1]. The IMPUT system combined the interactive debugging technique IDTS with an specialization algorithm SPECTRE presented in [3].

The new method we have devised integrates of PECG with the IMPUT interactive learning system. With the help of it not only can the precise place of the error be located in the program but in many cases starting from a *buggy* Prolog program we can infer a *correct* program using an unfolding transformation and the IDTS debugger. So applying the IMPUT method, the extended PECG system is quite capable of suggesting a correct solution to the user and of replacing the buggy clause recognized during the debugging process.

From the users point of view the most difficult task is to produce a correct grammar that will recognize ECG waveforms and give threshold values and rules to classify different partitions of it. The main contribution of this paper is a solution to all this and demonstration that the new PECG system can effectively assist the user overcoming such difficulties. As the ECG classifier program is over than 2000 lines long in Prolog, our approach shows that a *theory-revision learning method can effectively be applied to large programs*.

In the remainder of this paper a brief overview of PECG, the IMPUT method and the overall integrated system will first be given in Section 2. Section 3 contains the syntax learning part. While in Section 4 an explanation of the learning of threshold values and decision rules is given. Finally in Section 5 we present a summary and one or two comments on future work .

2 The extended PECG system

In this section we provide a short overview of the PECG, and IMPUT systems, a more detailed description of these being found in reference [1] & [4].

2.1 The PECG system

The original PECG system contained three main parts: the ECG processing part, the IDTS part, and graphic viewer module. It was based on an attribute grammar approach to ECG waveform analysis published by Skordalakis [12].

The ECG processing module was essentially composed of four submodules. In the *primitive pattern selection* part an ECG waveform could be considered as a composite pattern which could be decomposed into primitive patterns. The main task of the *primitive pattern extraction* was to select the peaks, while in the *linguistic representation* part the result of the last two steps were represented as a string of symbols from an alphabet. The *ECG classifier* module recognizes the ECG waveforms from their linguistic representations.

The IDTS partion uses a method based on an algorithmic program debugging technique introduced by Shapiro [11]. This method can isolate any erroneous procedure given a program and an input on which it behaves incorrectly. A major drawback of this debugging technique is the great number of queries which must be made to the user about the correctness of intermediate results of procedure calls. An improvement in the bug localization process was achieved in IDTS by combining the *category partition testing method* [8] with the *slicing method* [9] and then adding it to the algorithm introduced in [11]. The main idea is basically the following. If the program has already been tested the test results for the program procedures can be applied directly in the debugging process without consulting the user.

In the PECG system the algorithmic debugger IDTS was extended with a graphic viewer. This graphic module shows the ECG waveform currently being analyzed, which obviously aids the user in answering questions invoked by the debugger (see Figure 1).

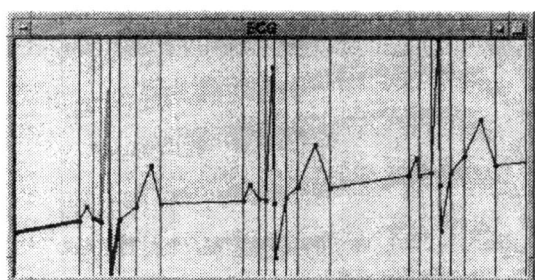

Fig. 1. Graphical representation of a recognized QRS segment

2.2 The IMPUT system

The IMPUT system consists of two main parts. The specialization algorithm part comes from the SPECTRE system while the interactive debugger part was imported from IDTS. The original specialization algorithm had to be extended in order to be able to revise multiple recursive predicates simultaneously and to handle DCG rules.

The algorithm SPECTRE [3] specializes logic programs with respect to positive and negative examples by applying the transformation rule *unfolding* [13] together with clause removal. The choice of which literal to apply an unfolding upon is controlled by a computation rule, which is is entered as input data to the system. A detailed description of SPECTRE can be found in [3].

The IMPUT system is really an integration of the SPECTRE and IDTS methods, that is a hybrid of two. The main idea behind IMPUT is that the identification of the next clause to be unfolded has a crucial importance on the effectiveness of the specialization process. The specialization steps are invoked by the negative examples covered by the target predicate. It is assumed that when a negative example is covered by the current version of the program there is at least one clause which is responsible for this incorrect covering. IMPUT then uses the IDTS debugging algorithm to track down a buggy clause of the program. A clause located in this process will then be unfolded in the next step of the specialization algorithm.

2.3 The structure of the extended system

The extended PECG system involves an integration of PECG with the IM-PUT interactive learning system. As mentioned earlier with the help of this not only can the precise place of the error be located in the program but in many cases starting from a *buggy* Prolog program we can infer a *correct* program using an unfolding transformation and the IDTS debugger. Applying the IMPUT method, the extended PECG system suggests a correct solution to the user and can replace the buggy clause recognized during the debugging process with its resolvents. The general system structure is conveniently displayed in Figure 2.

3 Learning the syntax of the grammar

In the following we explain how the integrated system refines an initial DCG representation of a waveform. As an example a cardiac cycle description is selected from the whole ECG waveform record. Every cardiac complex contains one or more cardiac waves, but the most important phase in the heart action is the QRS complex. This part was chosen here to demonstrate the syntax learning process. In the correct description a QRS complex can be built up from one to seven peaks in a special sequence (each positive peak being followed by negative one) and it is these peaks which making up the QRS pattern. In the learning process we started from a very general initial grammar which could recognize any sequence of peaks as a QRS complex (see Appendix 6.1) Then we tried to refine the original DCG program so as to get it to recognize the correct series of peaks in the QRS complex. The input description contained the *over-generalized* grammar for cardiac cycles, background knowledge and positive and negative examples (see Appendix 6.1). The task of our integrated system was to find the correct program which could recognize only the positive examples.

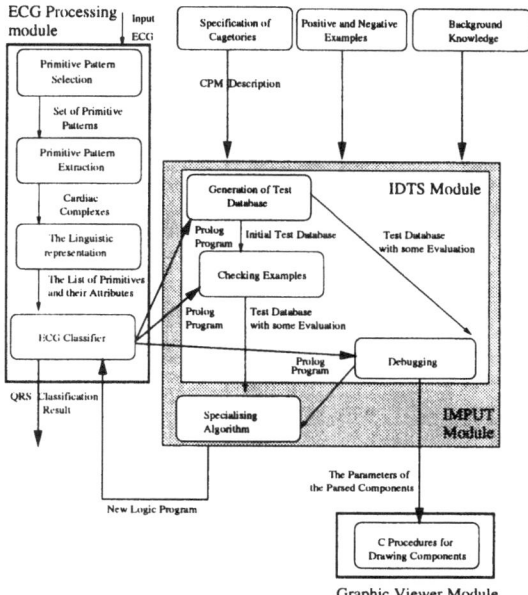

Fig. 2. The structure of the extended PECG system

During the learning process all clauses read were numbered. The clauses obtained by unfolding were numbered by pairs of numbers i-j where the first number the parent, the second denotes the substituted clause.

In the first step PECG checked for negative examples. If the system found a negative example covered by the initial program then the learning phase was invoked, otherwise the system was deemed to have obtained the correct program. Only the negative examples covered were displayed.

The next step of the learning was to find the clause to be unfolded by means of the debugger. The questions asked by the system could be answered with *yes* or *no*. The answer *no* meaning that the debugger had found the false clause. In this case the debugging process finished and the unfolding process could be started. In the opposite case the debugging were on to the next predicate. In our example the last question was

```
Is it ok [qrs([p_peak,p_peak])] (y/n) n
```

The answer was *no* because in a correct pattern a positive peak had to be followed by negative peak.

The most complicated step of the system was the unfolding part. As mentioned befor, it was supposed that if a negative example was covered by the current version of the initial program, there had to be at least one clause which is responsible for this incorrect covering. We found that the clause
$peaks(A, B) - - > peak(A, C), peaks(C, B)$ was incorrect. However this clause could

not be removed from the initial program because the derivation of a positive example contained this clause.

```
Unfolding at the clause instance:
   3: qrs-->peak([p_peak,p_peak,line,...],[p_peak,line,p_peak,...]),
          peaks([p_peak,line,p_peak,...],[line,p_peak,par,...])

   - trying resolvent(s): [3-1] actual minimum is: 12.5101.
   - trying resolvent(s): [3-2] actual minimum is: 0.

The result of the unfolding is:

0: cardiac_cycles-->cardiac_cycle(A,C),cardiac_cycles(C,B)
1: cardiac_cycles-->B=A
2: cardiac_cycle-->qrs(A,C),non_qrs(C,B)
3-4: qrs(A,B):-peak(A,C),peak(C,D),peaks(D,B)
3-5: qrs(A,B):-peak(A,C),B=C
...
```

The new program did not cover the first 3 negative examples but covered the other ones. By repeatedly using the debugger we found further erroneous clauses.

The learning process terminated when the program had finished covering all positive examples and had failed on all the negative ones. The refinement result is listed in Appendix 6.2.

4 Learning the threshold rules of an ECG grammar

In the previous Section we showed that the extended PECG system was readily able to assist the user in preparing a correct syntax for an ECG grammar. By using this grammar the morphologies of QRS complexes could then be determined. However, to decide whether a given sequence of peaks belongs to a class of QRS complexes we had to use the numeric features of these peaks as well. It meant, that the ECG grammar had to contain rules which checked these numeric values (energies, angles of the peaks) as well as some threshold values for decisions (we call these rules *threshold rules*).

In this section we will demonstrate how the extended PECG can be applied so as to infer these threshold values and rules. This problem could be solved using an attribute value learner but we chose to use a consistent ILP learning method to infer both the syntactic and semantic parts of the ECG grammar.

4.1 The threshold values in the ECG grammar

The question of whether a sequence of peaks belongs to a QRS class or not, can be decided with the aid of threshold values ε_1, ε_2, ε_5. But the following conditions must be obeyed:

(1) the energy of at least one peak is greater than ε_1.

(2) the angle between the right arm of peak i and left arm of peak $i+1$ is less than ε_2

(3) the angle of each peak is less than ε_5

P or T complexes can only be found between two QRS complexes. It means that complexes are not detected before the first QRS complex or after the last QRS complex. P or T complexes consist of one or two consecutive peaks which they are discriminated from other peaks with the help of semantic routines that examine the peak energies. The peaks are recognized as a P or T complex when the height and the duration of each arm for each peak are greater than ε_3 and ε_4, respectively.

4.2 The learning process

In the learning process described below it was supposed that the user did not know the exact threshold values and rules mentioned in the previous section, that he/she can only define general rules and broad intervals for threshold values.

Let us suppose that we are examining a QRS pattern which contains only two peaks. The other different types of the QRS can be defined in similar manner, so what we are doing is really quite general. We would like to learn the following clause:

```
decide_flag(TeR,TeS,AngR,AngS,Angle) :-
    possible_threshold(Eps1,Eps2,Eps5),
    define_flag1(TeR,TeS,Eps1),
    define_flag2(AngR,AngS,Eps5),
    define_flag1(Angle,Eps2).
```

where the values of arguments *TeR, TeS* mean the energy of the peaks, *AngR, AngS* define the angle between the left and the right arm of the peak respectively, *Angle* denoting the angle between the right arm of peak i and left arm of peak $i+1$. We will assume here that these values have already been computed.

There are two different tasks to the learning process. They are:

- Learning the relationship between the particular components
- Learning the values of Eps1, Eps2, Eps5

At the outset we began with a very general program, a portion of which is listed below.

```
possible_threshold(Eps1,Eps2,Eps5) :-
  threshold1(Eps1),
  threshold2(Eps2),
  threshold5(Eps5).

threshold1(Eps1) :- Eps1 is 10000.
threshold1(Eps1) :- Eps1 is 20000.
...
```

```
threshold1(Eps1) :- Eps1 is 180000.

threshold2(Eps2) :- Eps2 is 20.
...
threshold2(Eps2) :- Eps2 is 50.

threshold5(Eps5) :- Eps5 is 10.
...
threshold5(Eps5) :- Eps5 is 120.

flag1(TeR,Tes,Eps1) :- TeR > Eps1 ; TeS > Eps1.
flag1(TeR,Tes,Eps1) :- TeR < Eps1 ; TeS < Eps1.
flag1(TeR,Tes,Eps1) :- TeR > Eps1 , TeS > Eps1.
flag1(TeR,Tes,Eps1) :- TeR < Eps1 , TeS < Eps1.

flag2(AngR,Angs,Eps5) :- AngR > Eps5 ; AngS > Eps5.
flag2(AngR,Angs,Eps5) :- AngR < Eps5 ; AngS < Eps5.
flag2(AngR,Angs,Eps5) :- AngR > Eps5 , AngS > Eps5.
flag2(AngR,Angs,Eps5) :- AngR < Eps5 , AngS < Eps5.

flag3(Angle,Eps2) :- Angle >Eps2.
flag3(Angle,Eps2) :- Angle <Eps2.

positive decide_flag(158466,34405,11.1,27.7,36.8).
positive decide_flag(162693,44257,11,29.4,34.3).
positive decide_flag(177737,35542,10.4,28.2,35.1).
positive decide_flag(35672,23211,11,29.2,36.8).
...
negative decide_flag(1939,0,113.8,0,0).
negative decide_flag(5860,42508,79.9,29.2,31.2).
negative decide_flag(21600,32811,10.2,11,23.2).
negative decide_flag(6280,5413,32.5,45.3,28.2).
...
```

This program accepts many relationships and threshold values. The effects of this over-generalization is that many negative examples are recognized as QRS complexes. However using the IMPUT ILP method this program can radily be transformed into a correct one. We do not really want to elaborate on this as the process is very similar to that described for the learning of the syntax structure of the cardiac cycles. But we noted that if the unfolding transformation cannot be executed the clause is removed and at the end of the learning sessions all redundant threshold values are deleted. The transformed program obtained here is listed below.

```
decide_flag(TeR,TeS,AngR,AngS,Angle) :-
    possible_threshold(30000,30,30),
    define_flag1(TeR,TeS,30000),
    define_flag2(AngR,AngS,30),
    define_flag1(Angle,30).
```

```
possible_threshold(30000,30,30) :-
  threshold1(30000),
  threshold2(30),
  threshold5(30).
```

```
threshold1(30000).
threshold2(30).
threshold5(30).
```

```
flag1(TeR,Tes,Eps1)     :- TeR > Eps1 ; TeS > Eps1.
flag2(AngR,Angs,Eps5)   :- AngR < Eps5 , AngS < Eps5.
flag3(Angle,Eps2)       :- Angle <Eps2.
```

5 Conclusion, Further Work

In this paper it was shown that the integrated PECG tool can improve both the syntax and semantic parts of an ECG classifier program.

The learning process starts from an *over-generalized* grammar and afterwards tries to find the correct syntax of the QRS complex. The PECG program contains user-defined numeric threshold values and decision rules for the classification of QRS complexes and for deciding about the QRS and non-QRS parts as well. So the second step of the learning is the refinement of the semantic rules and determination of the threshold values.

The current version of the PECG system is about 3500 lines in Prolog,[2] while 500 lines written in C is required for the implementation of the graphic viewer. The IDTS module itself is about 1400 Prolog lines and contains 150 predicates, while the classifier program is more than 2000 lines in Prolog. The IMPUT system itself is made up more than 800 lines without the IDTS module.

Our approach has shown that theory-revision methods can be effectively used to refine large Prolog programs.

In the near future we are going to extend our system in the following ways after realising that, the PECG system was not able to make any diagnostic decisions. Firstly we plan to integrate a diagnostic modul into the system to make our tool more applicable to clinical situation where it is important to recognize particular types of heart abnormality. Afterwards we also plan to apply more ILP methods to the learning part of PECG system.

References

1. Alexin, Z., Gyimóthy, T., Boström, H.: *Integrating Algorithmic Debugging and Unfolding Transformations in an Interactive Learner* In: Proceedings of the 12th European Conference on Artificial Intelligence ECAI-96 ed. Wolfgang Wahlster, Budapest, Hungary (1996) 403–407 John Wiley & Son's Ltd. 1996.

---

[2] The implemented language is currently the SICStus Prolog Version 3.0 #3 or Quintus Prolog Version 3.2 runn on a SUN SPARCStation

2. Bergadano, F. Gunetti, D.: *Inductive Logic Programming Form Machine Learning to Software Engineering* The MIT Press (1996)
3. Boström, H., Idestam-Almquist, P.: *Specialization of Logic Programs by Pruning SLD-trees* In: Proc. of the Fourth International Workshop on Inductive Logic Programming (ILP-94) Bad Honnef/Bonn Germany September 12-14. (1994) 31–47
4. Kókai, G., Alexin, Z.,Gyimóthy, T.: *Analyzing and learning ECG Waveforms.* In Proc. of the Sixth International Workshop on Inductive Logic Programming (ILP'96) 28-30 August, 1996 Stockholm, Sweden, 152-171
5. Kókai, G., Alexin, Z., Gyimóthy, T.: *Application of Inductive Logic Programming for Learning ECG Waveform.* In Proc. of AIME'97 The 6th Conference on Artificial Intelligence in Medical Europa, 23rd - 26th March 1997 Grenoble, France 126-130
6. Moratis, C., Papakonstantinou, G., Skordalakis, E. *A Syntactic Model for Pattern Generation* Proceedings Int. AMSF. Conf. "Modelling & Simulation" Athens, June 27-29, 1984, Vol. 1.2, p. 1-8
7. Muggleton, S., De Raedt, L.: *Inductive Logic Programming: Theory and methods* Journal of Logic Programming 19 (20) (1994) 629–679
8. Ostrand, T. J., Balker, M. J.: *The Category-Partition Method for Specifying and Generating* In: Functional Tests CACM 31:6 June (1988) 676–686
9. Paakki, J., Gyimóthy, T., Horváth T.,: *Effective Algorithmic Debugging for Inductive Logic Programming.* In Proc. of the Fourth International Workshop on Inductive Logic Programming (ILP-94) Bad Honnef/Bonn Germany September 12-14. (1994) 175–194
10. Pereira, F. C. N., Warren, D. H. D.: *Definite clause grammars for language analysis - a survey of the formalism and a comparison with augmented transition networks.* In Artificial Intelligence 13: 231-278, (1980)
11. Shapiro, E. Y.: *Algorithmic Program Debugging* MIT Press (1983)
12. Skordalakis, E.: *ECG Analysis in Syntactic and Structural Pattern Recognition* Theory and Applications ed. Bunke, H. and Sanfeliu, A. World Scientific (1990) 499–533
13. Tamaki, H., Sato, T.: *Unfold/Fold Transformations of Logic Programs.* In Proceedings of the Second International Logic Programming Conference, Uppsala University, Uppsala, Sweden (1984) 127–138

6 Appendix

6.1 The input for the extended PECG

```
0: cardiac_cycles --> cardiac_cycle, cardiac_cycles.
1: cardiac_cycles --> {true}.

2: cardiac_cycle  --> qrs, non_qrs.

%%%%%%%%%%%%%%%%%%%%%%%%%%%%%%%%%%%%%%%%%%%%%%
%% the over-generalized part of the grammar %%
%%%%%%%%%%%%%%%%%%%%%%%%%%%%%%%%%%%%%%%%%%%%%%
3: qrs      --> peak,peaks.
4: peaks    --> peak,peaks.
5: peaks    --> {true}.
%%%%%%%%%%%%%%%%%%%%%%%%%%%%%%%%%%%%%%%%%%%%%%
```

```
6: non_qrs --> sr.
7: non_qrs --> interwave_segment, t, interwave_segment .
8: non_qrs --> interwave_segment, p, interwave_segment .
9: non_qrs --> interwave_segment, t, interwave_segment, p,
              interwave_segment.


10: sr  --> segment, interwave_segment.
11: sr  --> peak, interwave_segment.

12: interwave_segment --> segment, interwave_segment.
13: interwave_segment --> {true}.
14: interwave_segment --> peak, interwave_segment .

15: t  --> t_or_p.
16: p  --> t_or_p.

17: background (t_or_p  --> [p_peak], [n_peak]).
18: background (t_or_p  --> [n_peak], [p_peak]).
19: background (t_or_p  --> [p_peak]).
20: background (t_or_p  --> [n_peak]).
21: background (peak    --> [p_peak]).
22: background (peak    --> [n_peak]).
23: background (segment --> [line]).
24: background (segment --> [par]).

25: positive cardiac_cycles([p_peak,n_peak,line,...],[]).
26: positive cardiac_cycles([n_peak,p_peak,line,...],[]).
27: positive cardiac_cycles([n_peak,p_peak,n_peak,...],[]).
28: positive cardiac_cycles([p_peak,n_peak,p_peak,...],[]).
...
37: negative cardiac_cycles([p_peak,p_peak,line,...],[]).
38: negative cardiac_cycles([n_peak,n_peak,line,p_peak,...],[]).
39: negative cardiac_cycles([p_peak,p_peak,n_peak,...],[]).
40: negative cardiac_cycles([n_peak,n_peak,p_peak,...],[]).
...
```

6.2 The output of the extended PECG by learning the syntax part

```
0: cardiac_cycles --> cardiac_cycle,cardiac_cycles
1: cardiac_cycles --> {true}
2: cardiac_cycle  --> qrs,non_qrs
3-4-4-21-21-4-4-22-4-22-4-21: qrs -->
  [p_peak],[n_peak],[p_peak],[n_peak],[p_peak],[n_peak],[p_peak],peaks

3-4-4-21-21-4-4-22-4-22-5: qrs -->
  [p_peak],[n_peak],[p_peak],[n_peak],[p_peak],[n_peak]

3-4-4-21-21-4-4-22-5-21: qrs -->
  [p_peak],[n_peak],[p_peak],[n_peak],[p_peak]
```

```
3-4-4-21-21-4-5-22: qrs -->
  [p_peak],[n_peak],[p_peak],[n_peak]

3-4-4-21-21-5: qrs --> [p_peak],[n_peak],[p_peak]

3-4-4-22-22-4-21-4-21-4-22-21-4-22: qrs -->
  [n_peak],[p_peak],[n_peak],[p_peak],[n_peak],[p_peak],[n_peak],peaks

3-4-4-22-22-4-21-4-21-4-22-21-5: qrs -->
  [n_peak],[p_peak],[n_peak],[p_peak],[n_peak],[p_peak]

3-4-4-22-22-4-21-4-21-5-22: qrs -->
  [n_peak],[p_peak],[n_peak],[p_peak],[n_peak]

3-4-4-22-22-4-21-5: qrs -->
  [n_peak],[p_peak],[n_peak],[p_peak]

3-4-4-22-22-5: qrs --> [n_peak],[p_peak],[n_peak]
3-4-5-21-22: qrs --> [n_peak],[p_peak]
3-4-5-22-21: qrs --> [p_peak],[n_peak]
3-5: qrs --> peak
5: peaks --> {true}
6: non_qrs --> sr
7: non_qrs --> interwave_segment, t, interwave_segment
8: non_qrs --> interwave_segment, p, interwave_segment
9: non_qrs --> interwave_segment, t, interwave_segment, p,
                interwave_segment
10: sr  --> segment, interwave_segment.
11: sr  --> peak, interwave_segment
12: interwave_segment --> segment, interwave_segment
13: interwave_segment --> {true}
14: interwave_segment --> peak, interwave_segment
15: t  --> t_or_p
16: p  --> t_or_p
```

Introducing Abduction into (Extensional) Inductive Logic Programming Systems

E. Lamma[1], P. Mello[2], M. Milano[1], F.Riguzzi[1]

[1] DEIS, Università di Bologna
Viale Risorgimento 2, 40136 Bologna, Italy
{elamma,mmilano,friguzzi}@deis.unibo.it
Tel.+39 51 6443086, Fax. +39 51 6443073
[2] Istituto di Ingegneria, Università di Ferrara
Via Saragat, 41100 Ferrara, Italy
pmello@ing.unife.it

Abstract. We propose an approach for the integration of abduction and induction in Logic Programming. In particular, we show how it is possible to learn an abductive logic program starting from an abductive background knowledge and a set of examples. By integrating Inductive Logic Programming with Abductive Logic Programming we can learn in presence of incomplete knowledge. Incomplete knowledge is handled by designating some pieces of information as abducibles, that is, possible hypotheses which can be assumed, provided that they are consistent with the current knowledge base. We then specialize the framework for FOIL, an ILP system adopting extensional coverage. In particular, we propose an extension of the FOIL algorithm that is able to learn from incomplete data.

Content Areas: Machine Learning, Nonmonotonic reasoning

1 Introduction

Both abduction and induction have been recognized as powerful mechanisms for hypothetical reasoning in the presence of incomplete knowledge [9, 12, 13]. Abduction is generally understood as reasoning from effects to causes or explanations, and captures also other important issues such as reasoning in presence of incomplete information and reasoning with defaults and beliefs (see for instance [14]). Incomplete knowledge is handled by designating some pieces of information as abducibles, that is possible hypotheses which can be assumed, provided that they are consistent with the current knowledge base.

Integrating induction and abduction makes it possible to learn in the presence of incomplete information on the background or target predicates. Incompleteness of information is a common problem of real learning systems because the knowledge acquisition process in practice rarely produces complete information. Target predicates are usually incompletely specified because we are given only a sample of them in the training set. If the number of examples is small, the learning process can be difficult. The system FOIL-I [8] is able to learn from incomplete samples of target predicates. A more difficult problem is the one of incompleteness of background predicates: some predicates may be not completely defined and there may be integrity constraints between them.

The main contributions of the paper are the following:

- to present a unifying framework for the integration of Inductive Logic Programming (ILP [3]) and Abductive Logic Programming (ALP [9]). In particular, we present a general approach where it is possible to learn an abductive logic program starting from an abductive background knowledge.
- to specialize the framework for an extensional ILP system, FOIL [15]. In particular, we present an *Extensional Abductive Proof Procedure* for checking the coverage of positive and negative examples.

The following simplified example shows how we would like to learn a program for performing fault diagnosis from a set of (incomplete) bicycle faults.

Example 1. Let us consider the case of a background knowledge containing the following clauses, where the last one represents a constraint:

$flat\_tyre(bike_1) \leftarrow .$
$tyre\_holds\_air(bike_3) \leftarrow .$
$tyre\_holds\_air(bike_4) \leftarrow .$
$\leftarrow flat\_tyre(X), tyre\_holds\_air(X).$

and let the set of abducible predicates be $\{flat\_tyre, broken\_spokes\}$. We would like to learn the definition of *wobbly_wheel*, when the training set is constituted by:

$E^+ = \{wobbly\_wheel(bike_1), wobbly\_wheel(bike_2), wobbly\_wheel(bike_3)\}$
$E^- = \{wobbly\_wheel(bike_4)\}$

By integrating abduction and induction, we would like to produce the clauses:

$wobbly\_wheel(X) \leftarrow flat\_tyre(X).$
$wobbly\_wheel(X) \leftarrow broken\_spokes(X).$

This theory entails all the positive and none of the negative examples provided that we make certain assumptions. $wobbly\_wheel(bike_2)$ is covered by assuming $flat\_tyre(bike_2)$ or $broken\_spokes(bike_2)$, $wobbly\_wheel(bike_3)$ is covered only by assuming $broken\_spokes(bike_3)$ because $flat\_tyre(bike_3)$ is incompatible with the integrity constraint. The negative example $wobbly\_wheel(bike_4)$ is not covered if we assume both $not\_flat\_tyre(bike_4)$ and $not\_broken\_spokes(bike_4)$.

A standard ILP system would be able to learn the clauses above only when the user also specifies the abduced hypotheses in the background knowledge. Nonetheless, in many cases one can not define a complete background knowledge, namely all the information about predicates *flat_tyre* and *broken_spokes*, but he only gives some hints about them (e.g. their relationships with other predicates through constraints).

In the paper, we first extend a basic top-down ILP algorithm with abduction in order to obtain the behavior informally explained through the example above. We then specialize this framework for FOIL, an ILP system adopting the notion of extensional coverage.

2 Preliminaries about Abduction and Induction

In the following, we use the basic concepts and terminology of logic programming. We limit the language to have no function symbol in order to have a finite Herbrand Universe.

2.1 Abductive Logic Programming

We recall now the basic concepts of Abductive Logic Programming. For a more detailed presentation the reader is referred to the survey [9].

Definition 1 Abductive Logic Program. An *abductive logic program AT* is a triple $\langle P, A, IC \rangle$ where

- P is a normal logic program, i.e., a set of clauses of the form
  $A_0 \leftarrow A_1, \ldots, A_m, not\ A_{m+1}, \ldots, not\ A_{m+n}$
  where $m, n \geq 0$ and each A_i $(i = 0, \ldots, m + n)$ is an atom;
- A is a set of *abducible predicates*;
- IC is a set of first order closed formulae called *integrity constraints*.

For simplicity, we will consider as integrity constraints only denials of the form
$\leftarrow A_1, \ldots, A_m, not\ A_{m+1}, \ldots, not\ A_{m+n}$
Negation as Failure is replaced, in ALP, by Negation by Default [6] and is obtained in this way: for each predicate symbol p, a new predicate symbol not_p is added to the set A and the integrity constraint $\leftarrow p(\mathbf{X}), not\_p(\mathbf{X})$ is added to IC, where $\mathbf{X}$ is a tuple of variables. Now, all the Negation as Failure literals $not\ p(\mathbf{X})$ are substituted by Negation by Default literals $not\_p(\mathbf{X})$.

Given an abductive theory $T = \langle P, A, IC \rangle$ and a formula G, the goal of abduction is to find a set of ground atoms Δ (*abductive explanation*) on the set of predicates in A which together with P entails G, i.e. $P \cup \Delta \models G$. It is also required that the program $P \cup \Delta$ is consistent with respect to IC, i.e. $P \cup \Delta \models IC$. When there exists an abductive explanation for e from T we say that T *abductively entails* e and we write $T \models_A e$.

In the following, we adopt the three-valued semantics for abductive logic programs defined in [4]. The semantics $\mathcal{M}_{AT}$ of a program AT is defined in terms of three sets:

- $\mathcal{M}_{AT}^+$, the set of ground atoms *true* for AT,
- $\mathcal{M}_{AT}^-$, the set of ground atoms *false* for AT,
- $\mathcal{M}_{AT}^u = \overline{\mathcal{M}_{AT}^+ \cup \mathcal{M}_{AT}^-}$, the set of ground atoms *undefined* for AT.

The semantics $\mathcal{M}_{AT}$ is the set of ground *literals* true for AT and is given by $\mathcal{M}_{AT} = \mathcal{M}_{AT}^+ \cup \neg \mathcal{M}_{AT}^-$ where $\neg \mathcal{M}_{AT}^- = \{\neg a | a \in \mathcal{M}_{AT}^-\}$

Operationally, we rely on the proof procedure defined by Kakas and Mancarella [10]. The proof procedure uses the notion of *abductive* and *consistency derivation*. Intuitively, an abductive derivation is the usual logic programming derivation suitably extended in order to consider abducibles. As soon as an abducible atom δ is encountered, it is added to the current set of hypotheses, and it must be proved that any integrity constraint containing δ fails via a consistency derivation. During this latter procedure, when an abducible is encountered, in order to prove its failure, an abductive derivation for its complement is attempted.

2.2 Inductive Logic Programming

The ILP problem can be defined as [3]:

Given:
    a set $\mathcal{P}$ of possible programs
    a set E^+ of positive examples
    a set E^- of negative examples
    a consistent logic program B (*background knowledge*)
Find:
    a logic program $P \in \mathcal{P}$ such that
    $\forall e^+ \in E^+, B \cup P \models e^+$ (P *covers* e^+)
    $\forall e^- \in E^-, B \cup P \not\models e^-$ (P *does not cover* e^-).

In order to integrate abduction and induction, we consider a modified version of the ILP problem where both the background knowledge and the learned program are abductive logic programs. Moreover, coverage of examples through entailment is replaced by coverage through abductive entailment:
$\forall e^+ \in E^+, B \cup P \models_A e^+$ (P *covers* e^+)
$\forall e^- \in E^-, B \cup P \models_A not\_e^-$ (P *does not cover* e^-).
The training sets, E^+ and E^-, define possibly partial information for the learning process, and both positive and negative examples can be enlarged by the addition of some positive or negative abducible atoms provided that they are consistent with the background knowledge, and integrity constraints in particular.

The basic top-down inductive algorithm [3] (figure 1) learns programs by generating clauses one after the other, and generates clauses by means of specialization.

2.3 Overview of FOIL

FOIL [15] is an *extensional* ILP system: the coverage of examples is performed by using a notion of coverage, called *extensional coverage* [3], that differs from the one seen in section 2.2, called *intensional coverage*.

Definition 2 Extensional Coverage. Let P be the program defining the target predicate, let E^+ be the set of positive examples of the target predicate, let $\mathcal{M}_{BK}$ be a two-valued model of the background knowledge, and let $e = p(\mathbf{t})$ be an example. $\mathcal{P}$ *extensionally covers* the example e (and the tuple $\mathbf{t}$) if there exists a clause of P, $l \leftarrow l_1, \ldots, l_n$ such that l unifies with e with substitution θ and for all i, $[l_i]\theta \in (E^+ \cup \mathcal{M}_{BK})$.

```
T := ∅ /* T is the target theory */
while some positive examples in E⁺ are not covered by a clause in T do
    Generate one clause C
    Remove from E⁺ positive examples covered by C
    Add C to T

Generate one Clause C:
Select a predicate P that must be learned
Set clause C to be p(X) ← .
while C covers some negative example do
    Select a literal L from the language bias
    Add L to the antecedent of C
    if C does not cover any positive example
        then backtrack to different choices for L
return C (or fail if backtracking exhausts all choices for L)
```

Fig. 1. Basic ILP algorithm

With extensional coverage, a newly generated clause is tested for coverage of examples using only the background knowledge and the training set, while with intensional coverage it is tested using the background knowledge together with already learned clauses.

Extensional coverage has been introduced in order to learn effectively recursive and multiple predicates program. In these cases, the coverage of examples of a clause depends also on previously learned clauses and learning them independently one after the other, as it is done in the top-down algorithm, may lead to the impossibility of finding a solution even if there is one. The top-down algorithm searches the space of possible clauses while it should search the space of possible programs, i.e. all possible combinations of clauses. By adopting extensional coverage, the testing of clauses is independent from other clauses, therefore the top-down algorithm is guaranteed to find a solution if it exist and the worst case complexity is linear in the size of the space of possible clauses. However, the price to pay for containing the complexity is the fact that the solutions found with extensional coverage may not be complete and/or consistent according to the ILP problem definition.

In FOIL, both target and background relations are described extensionally by the sets of *tuples* that belong (*positive* tuples) or do not belong *negative* tuples) to the relation. In the following we will refer to such tuples as ⊕ and ⊖ respectively. The learned definition is a logic program that *covers* all the ⊕ tuples and none of the ⊖ tuples of the target relation(s).

FOIL's algorithm differs from the basic top-down ILP algorithm shown in figure 1 only in the way the clause is specialized (procedure "Generate one clause", figure 2). During clause specialization, FOIL keeps a set of labelled tuples (called *bindings*) specifying the values of all variables for an instantiation of the current clause. At the beginning, the set of bindings contains only the positive tuples for the target predicate, labelled ⊕, and the negative tuples, labelled ⊖. Each time a literal is added to the clause, each binding is tested to see if the correspondent example is covered by the clause. If it is, the binding is extended with the values for the eventual new variables introduced by the literal and the extended binding is added to the new set, otherwise it is discarded. Clause specialization ends when there are no more bindings in the set labelled $\ominus$.

```
Generate one clause C:
Select a predicate p that must be learned
Set clause C to be p(X) ← .
T₁ = training set tuples labeled with ⊕ or ⊖
i = 1
While (Tᵢ contains one or more tuples labeled ⊖)
        /* Add a literal */
        Select a literal Lᵢ₊₁ (using heuristics)
        Add it to the current partial clause
        Tᵢ₊₁ = ∅
(1)     For each binding b ∈ Tᵢ
                Find all the tuples t of Lᵢ₊₁ matching b
                        on instantiated variables of Lᵢ₊₁
                For each t, add to Tᵢ₊₁ b
                        extended with t
        i = i + 1
```

Fig. 2. FOIL: clause specialization algorithm

3 Integrating Abduction and Induction

In this section we first discuss how the basic top-down learning algorithm has to be modified in order to learn abductive logic programs. Then we discuss the special case of extending the FOIL system.

The basic inductive algorithm has to modified in the following respects:

- First, the literal L that is added to the body of rules, can be an abducible literal, in analogy with the framework in [5, 7].
- Second, in order to determine the positive examples covered by the generated clause C, and to be removed, an *abductive* derivation is started for each of them. As well, in order to check that no negative example is covered by the generated clause C, an *abductive* derivation is started for the negation of each negative example. In both cases, this is achieved by exploiting the abductive proof procedure defined in [10] or by extending it with the notion of extensional coverage, as presented in section 3.1, for the extensional ILP systems. During the abductive procedure, some abducibles can be assumed true or false. Note that literals abduced during the abductive derivation have to be recorded to avoid inconsistent future assumptions.

3.1 Extending FOIL with Abduction

Each relation is described by a set of $\oplus$ tuples and a set of $\ominus$ tuples. We assume all the tuples not specified by the user as $\oplus$ or $\ominus$ to be unknown ($\odot$ in the following). We would like FOIL to make assumptions about $\odot$ tuples in order to cover positive examples or exclude negative ones. By using abduction, we ensure that the assumptions made are consistent. The $\odot$ tuples for each relation determine the set of abducible ground atoms. We need to give as input to FOIL as well a set of integrity constraints.

In addition, we have to modify the notion of extensional coverage for coping with abductive logic programs.

Definition 3 Extensional Abductive Coverage. Let BK be the abductive program defining the background knowledge, P be the abductive program defining the target predicates. Let E^+ and E^- be the set of positive and negative examples of the target predicates, and $e = p(\mathbf{t})$ be an example. P *extensionally covers* the example e (and the tuple $\mathbf{t}$) if there exists a model $\mathcal{M}_{BK}$ under the three valued abductive semantics, a clause of P, $l \leftarrow l_1, \ldots, l_m, not\_l_{m+1} \ldots not\_l_n$ and a set Δ of abducibles atoms, consistent with $IC \cup \mathcal{M}_{BK}$, such that l unifies with e with substitution θ and $[l_i]\theta \in (E^+ \cup \Delta^+ \cup \mathcal{M}_{BK}^+)$ for $1 \le i \le m$ and $[l_i]\theta \in (E^- \cup \Delta^- \cup \mathcal{M}_{BK}^-)$ for $m < i \le n$, where $\Delta^+ = \{a | a \in \Delta\}$ and $\Delta^- = \{a | not\_a \in \Delta\}$.

When FOIL adds a new literal to a clause, it tests if the tuples covered by the previous clause are covered as well by the new clause. If, for a certain tuple, the new literal is unknown and the corresponding predicate is abducible, we try to abduce it. We use an abductive derivation modified to deal with extensional coverage. If the abductive derivation succeeds, the literal can be assumed true and has to be recorded because future abductive derivations should not derive anything that is inconsistent with them. Therefore, the corresponding tuples are added to the set of $\oplus$ or $\ominus$ tuples for the relations.

More in detail, FOIL algorithm must be modified in point (1) (in figure 2). At that point, the set of bindings T_i is tested. For each binding b in T_i, if it matches with one or more $\oplus$ (resp. $\ominus$ if L_{i+1} is negative) tuples of L_{i+1}, the original tuple for the target relation is covered and b is extended and added to T_{i+1}. If b matches with a $\ominus$ (resp. $\oplus$ if L_{i+1} is negative) it is discarded. Otherwise (b does not match neither with a $\oplus$ nor with a $\ominus$ tuple), b matches with at least an $\odot$ tuple. Therefore, if b is labelled $\oplus$, we try to cover it by means of abduction. In particular, we pick up one of the matching $\odot$ tuples u of L_{i+1}, we assume it true (resp. false if L_{i+1} is negative), and we verify that this is consistent with integrity constraints and with other abduced literals. This is done by starting an *extensional abductive derivation* for L_{i+1}. In order to assume it true, u is temporarily added to the set of $\oplus$ tuples of L_{i+1} (or to the $\ominus$ if the literal is negative). If the abductive derivation succeeds, the tuple is retained, otherwise it is discarded and a different undefined tuple for L_{i+1} is tested. When a consistent u tuple is found, the binding b is extended with the (eventual) new variables in u and it is added to T_{i+1}.

If b is labelled $\ominus$, we have to do the opposite: u has to be assumed false if L_{i+1} is positive (true if L_{i+1} is negative). Therefore, an abductive derivation is started for $\overline{L_{i+1}}$[3]

If L_{i+1} is a target predicate, we may have already learned a definition for it. In this case we need to check the rules learned against the new tuples eventually added to the extensional definition of L_{i+1} and, possibly, revise the theory. If a learned rule extensionally covers one of the new negative tuples, the rule must be further specialized. We must run the specialization algorithm for each of the learned rules, each time starting with a training set containing only the new positive and negative tuples. The positive tuples that are covered, are not included in the initial training set for the successive rules, while the negative tuples are kept for all the rules.

This increases the average complexity of standard extensional top-down algorithms because when a clause is added to the theory, each learned clause must be reconsidered to see if it is consistent with the new negative examples, and eventually specialized. However, it does not increase the worst case complexity, that is $\mathcal{O}(n)$ where n is the size of the space of possible clauses. In fact, the search space explored before has not to be re-explored because a previous inconsistent clause can not become consistent, since the number of negative examples has increased.

If some of the new positive tuples are not covered by any rule, then new rules must be learned to cover these tuples.

The algorithm for extensional consistency derivation is a modification of the one for standard consistency derivation defined by Kakas and Mancarella [10]. Let L be a ground literal to be derived, with $L = R(\mathbf{t})$ or $L = not\_R(\mathbf{t})$. We say that L is *true* if $\mathbf{t}$ is among the $\oplus$ tuples of R ($\ominus$ if L is negative). We say that L is *false* if the opposite is true. We say that it is *unknown* if $\mathbf{t}$ is neither among $\oplus$ nor $\ominus$ tuples of R.

Extensional abductive derivation

$\mathbf{t}$ is temporarily added to the $\oplus$ tuples of R ($\ominus$ if L is negative) and an *extensional consistency derivation* from L to $\{\}$ is attempted.

Extensional consistency derivation

An extensional consistency derivation from a literal L to F_n is a sequence $L, F_1, F_2, \ldots, F_n$ where:

(Ci) F_1 is the union of all goals of the form $\leftarrow L_1, \ldots, L_k$ obtained by resolving L with the denials in IC, with no such goal being empty, $\leftarrow$.

(Cii) for each $i > 1$, F_i has the form $\{\leftarrow L_1, \ldots, L_k\} \cup F_i'$ and for some $j = 1 \ldots k$, F_{i+1} is obtained according to one of the following rules:

---

[3]

$$\overline{L_{i+1}} = \begin{cases} not\_p(\mathbf{X}) & \text{if } L_{i+1} = p(\mathbf{X}) \\ p(\mathbf{X}) & \text{if } L_{i+1} = not\_p(\mathbf{X}) \end{cases}$$

(C1) if L_j is true, then $F_{i+1} = \{\leftarrow L_1, \ldots, L_{j-1}, L_{j+1}, \ldots, L_k\} \cup F_i'$ (the literal is removed);

(C2) if L_j is false, $F_{i+1} = F_i'$ (the denial is removed because it is verified);

(C3) if L_j is unknown, an extensional abductive derivation is started for $\overline{L_j}$. If it succeeds, $F_{i+1} = F_i'$.

The extensional consistency derivation fails if at least one F_i contains an empty goal $\leftarrow$, and succeeds if $F_n = \{\}$. In the case it fails, all the tuples added to the extensional definition of predicates must be removed.

Let us consider the example presented in the introduction. The set of $\odot$ tuples for the relation $flat\_tyre$ is $\{\langle bike_2 \rangle, \langle bike_3 \rangle, \langle bike_4 \rangle\}$, and for the relation $broken\_spokes$ is $\{\langle bike_1 \rangle, \langle bike_2 \rangle, \langle bike_3 \rangle, \langle bike_4 \rangle\}$. The first generated clause is:

$wobbly\_wheel(X) \leftarrow flat\_tyre(X)$

This clause covers $wobbly\_wheel(bike_1)$ because $flat\_tyre(bike_1)$ is specified in the background knowledge. In order to cover $wobbly\_wheel(bike_2)$, the system starts an abductive derivation for $flat\_tyre(bike_2)$. The tuple $\langle bike_2 \rangle$ is added to the set of $\oplus$ tuples for $flat\_tyre$ and a consistency derivation is started. The literal is resolved with

$\leftarrow flat\_tyre(X), tyre\_holds\_air(X).$

giving the goal $\leftarrow tyre\_holds\_air(bike_2)$ (step (Ci)). Since $\langle bike_2 \rangle$ is among the $\ominus$ tuples for $tyre\_holds\_air$ (that is a complete predicate), the consistency derivation succeeds.

The example $wobbly\_wheel(bike_3)$, however, cannot be covered: in fact, we cannot assume $flat\_tyre(bike_3)$ since it is inconsistent with the integrity constraint and $tyre\_holds\_air(bike_3)$. The negative example $wobbly\_wheel(bike_4)$ is tested by starting an extensional abductive derivation that succeeds by abducing $not\_flat\_tyre(bike_4)$ (and therefore adding $\langle bike_2 \rangle$ to the $\ominus$ tuples for $flat\_tyre$). In order to cover $wobbly\_wheel(bike_3)$, the system generates the clause:

$wobbly\_wheel(X) \leftarrow broken\_spokes(X)$

which covers the example by abducing $broken\_spokes(bike_3)$. Similarly to the previous case, the negative example is ruled out by assuming

$not\_broken\_spokes(bike_4).$

By introducing abduction in FOIL, however, we do not solve the main problem of extensionality, namely the fact that the learned program can be inconsistent and/or incomplete. However, extensional system usually need a complete or nearly complete training set for learning recursive predicates, because in order to cover an example, the precedent example in the recursive chain must be present. By using abduction, we are able to learn from an incomplete training set, completing it with the examples that are missing, as it is shown in the next example.

Example 2. Suppose we want to learn the predicate *member* from

$B = \{components([H|T], H, T) \leftarrow\}$ (for brevity, we give the intensional description)

$E^+ = \{member(1, [1]), member(2, [1, 2])\}$

$E^- = \{member(1, []), member(1, [3]), member(1, [2, 3])\}$

The system first generates the clause

$member(A, B) \leftarrow components(B, C, D), member(A, D)$

Then the clause is tested. The example $member(1, [1])$ is not covered because $member(1, [])$ is among the negative examples. When trying to cover the example $member(2, [1, 2])$, the system starts an extensional abductive derivation for $member(2, [2])$ that succeeds and the $\oplus$ tuple $\langle 2, [2] \rangle$ is added to the training set. Negative example $member(1, [])$ is not covered because no tuple for $components(B, C, D)$ matches with $\langle [], \_, \_ \rangle$. Negative examples $member(1, [3])$ and $member(1, [2, 3])$ are not covered because $member(1, [])$ and $member(1, [3])$ are among negative examples.

The clause is consistent and therefore it is added to the theory. The training set now is:

$E^+ = \{member(1, [1]), member(2, [2])\}$

$E^- = \{member(1, []), member(1, [3]), member(1, [2, 3])\}$

Then the system generates the clause

$member(A, B) \leftarrow components(B, A, D)$

that covers all the remaining positive examples and no negative one without abducing anything. The clause is added to the hypothesis and the algorithm terminates.

4 Related Works

The relationship between abduction and learning has been studied recently by several authors. In general, the question of how abduction and induction could be integrated and how they would cooperate, complement and affect each other is emerging as an important problem.

This paper continues the work started in [7], where we proposed a first approach for the integration of induction and abduction and we specialized it for intensional ILP systems. The algorithm proposed in that paper has been here refined and specialized for the case of extensional system.

In [11] the authors propose an intensional algorithm for learning abductive logic programs and present some non-toy experiments of learning from incomplete information. Moreover, they suggest a way in which it can be integrated with existing learning systems in order to learn integrity constraints in their general form.

As concerns the integration of abduction and induction, a notable work is that by Dimopoulos and Kakas [5] where they present the framework of Abductive Concept Learning, to which our extended learning problem is inspired.

In [2], the authors propose an algorithm for learning normal logic programs obtained by the substitution of abduction with induction in an abductive proof procedure, namely SLDNFA. In our framework, the two techniques are mixed in order to learn not only normal but also abductive logic programs.

Another related work is reported in [1], where the authors present a system, called RUTH, for theory revision based on ILP. RUTH is able to cope with definite, functor-free clauses, and integrates intensional database updating with incremental concept-learning. Apart from adding and deleting clauses and facts, in [1] the authors also employ an abductive operator which allows RUTH to introduce missing factual knowledge into the knowledge base. As [1], we do not rely on any oracle, but rather on abductive proof procedure for determining the proof of an atom. Furthermore, both RUTH and our framework can treat as abducibles *some* of the program predicates. Differently from [1], we avoid clause retraction.

5 Conclusions and Future Work

In this paper, we propose a framework where abduction and induction are combined, thus solving the problems of learning in presence of incomplete knowledge. In the devised framework, the user can partially specify background and target predicates. We rely on a three-valued logic in which an atom can be *true, false* or *unknown*. Unspecified information are considered unknown and possibly abduced (as true or false) during the learning process in order to cover positive examples and rule out negative ones. In this way, not only we enlarge the content of the background knowledge, but also improve the learning process.

We propose an extension of FOIL, an extensional top-down ILP system, by means of an abductive proof procedure. We have shown, by means of examples, that the extended system can cope with missing knowledge.

A number of issues are subject for future work. First, we have to further investigate new heuristics for the selection of abductive literals. Unknown tuples should be given a smaller weight with respect to defined ones. Second, we will extend FOIL in order to learn also integrity constraints, as proposed, for instance, in [11].

References

1. H. Adé and M. Denecker. RUTH: An ILP theory revision system. In *Proceedings of the 8th International Symposium on Methodologies for Intelligent Systems*, 1994.
2. H. Adé and M. Denecker. AILP: Abductive inductive logic programming. In *Proceedings of the 14th International Joint Conference on Artificial Intelligence*, 1995.
3. F. Bergadano and D. Gunetti. *Inductive Logic Programming.* MIT press, 1996.
4. A. Brogi, E. Lamma, P. Mancarella, and P. Mello. An Abductive Framework for Extended Logic Programming. In *Proceedings 3rd Int. Workshop on Logic Programming and Non Monotonic Reasoning*, 1995.
5. Y. Dimopoulos and A. Kakas. Abduction and learning. In *Advances in Inductive Logic Programming.* IOS Press, 1996.
6. K. Eshghi and R.A. Kowalski. Abduction compared with Negation by Failure. In *Proceedings of ICLP89*, 1989.
7. F. Esposito, E. Lamma, D. Malerba, P. Mello, M. Milano, F. Riguzzi, and G. Semeraro. Learning abductive logic programs. In M. Denecker, L. De Raedt, P. Flach, and A. Kakas, editors, *Proceedings of the ECAI96 Workshop on Abductive and Inductive Reasoning.* Catholic University of Leuven, 1996.

8. N. Inuzuka, M. Kamo, N. Ishii, H. Seki, and H. Itoh. Top-down induction of logic programs from incomplete samples. In S. Muggleton, editor, *Proceedings of the 6th International Workshop on Inductive Logic Programming*, pages 119–136. Stockholm University, Royal Institute of Technology, 1996.

9. A.C. Kakas, R.A. Kowalski, and F. Toni. Abductive logic programming. *Journal of Logic and Computation*, 2:719–770, 1993.

10. A.C. Kakas and P. Mancarella. On the relation between truth maintenance and abduction. In *Proceedings of the 2nd Pacific Rim International Conference on Artificial Intelligence*, 1990.

11. A.C. Kakas and F. Riguzzi. Learning with abduction. Technical Report TR-96-15, University of Cyprus, Computer Science Department, 1996.

12. R. Michalski, J.G. Carbonell, and T.M. Mitchell (eds). *Machine Learning - An Artificial Intelligence Approach*. Springer Verlag, 1984.

13. R. Michalski, J.G. Carbonell, and T.M. Mitchell (eds). *Machine Learning - An Artificial Intelligence Approach Vol. II*. Morgan Kaufmann, 1986.

14. D.L. Poole. A logical framework for default reasoning. *Artificial Intelligence*, 32, 1988.

15. J. R. Quinlan and R.M. Cameron-Jones. Induction of Logic Programs: FOIL and Related Systems. *New Generation Computing*, 13:287–312, 1995.

An Efficient Algorithm for Temporal Abduction

Vittorio Brusoni, Luce Console, Paolo Terenziani, Daniele Theseider Dupré

Dipartimento di Informatica, Università di Torino
Corso Svizzera 185, 10149 Torino, Italy
Phone: +39 11 7429111 — Fax: +39 11 751603
E-mail: {brusoni,lconsole,terenz,dtd}@di.unito.it

Abstract. In this paper, we consider the following form of temporal abduction: given a domain theory where each explanatory formula is augmented with a set of temporal constraints on the atoms occurring in the formula, and given a set of observed atoms, with associated temporal constraints, the goal is the generation of a temporally consistent abductive explanation of the observations.

Temporal abduction is the basis of many problem solving activities such as temporal diagnosis or reasoning about actions and events. This paper presents an efficient nondeterministic algorithm for temporal abduction which exploits the STP framework [8] in order to represent temporal information. In particular, we exploited some properties of STP, proved in [3], which allow us to efficiently prune temporally inconsistent candidate explanations as soon as possible. The pruning is achieved by interleaving abductive steps with temporal reasoning localized to the constraints on the formula used at each abductive step. The paper discusses the properties of the algorithm, providing both analytical and experimental evaluations of its performance.

1   Introduction

Abduction is the process of generating explanations for an observation O, starting from a domain theory T [12].

Several approaches, after [10, 9], recognized that time is an essential dimension in explanation, since, e.g., observations occur in time and explanatory relations involve temporal constraints (e.g., delays between causes and effects). Dealing with temporal explanations is essential in many problem solving activities, such as temporal diagnosis and reasoning about actions and events. Thus, one has:

1) to extend the classical notion of abduction in order to consider the temporal dimension both in the observations and in the theory;
2) to devise new reasoning algorithms to compute *temporal* explanations.

While item 1 is briefly addressed in section 2, and in more detailed and formal way in [4, 5], in the rest of the paper we address item 2.

Temporal explanations could be computed using first an abductive reasoner as a generator of candidates and then a temporal reasoner for checking the consistency of each candidate. However, pruning temporally inconsistent candidate explanations as soon as possible during the generation process provides great focusing and computational advantages. One way to achieve such a goal is to perform, at each abductive step, temporal constraint propagation on all the variables in the candidate being built, as it is done, e.g., in [11] in an algorithm for temporal diagnosis. This approach will be denoted as the *global propagation* one.

In this paper we present an algorithm which achieves the same pruning results of the global propagation approach, but that operates more efficiently, exploiting some properties about local propagation of STP constraints.

2 Temporal explanation

We assume that the domain theory T is a set of explanatory formulae:

$$a_1, \ldots, a_n \ explains \ b_1, \ldots, b_m \ \{C(t_{a_1}, \ldots, t_{a_n}, t_{b_1}, \ldots, t_{b_m})\} \tag{1}$$

where a_i, b_j are atoms and t_a denotes a time interval in which a is true (an **episode** of a); a **maximal episode** for a is a maximal (wrt set inclusion) interval in which a is true. The formula (1) means that the conjunction of a maximal episode for each one of $a_1, \ldots, a_n$ is a direct explanation of an episode of each b_i, where the set of temporal constraints $C(t_{a_1}, \ldots, t_{a_n}, t_{b_1}, \ldots, t_{b_m})$ is imposed on the intervals corresponding to the episodes. We do not impose maximality of episodes of each b_i since overlapping intervals due to different formulae where b_i occurs in the consequent may give rise to a single maximal episode for b_i. However, we assume that C relates a maximal episode for each one of $a_1, \ldots, a_n$ and a *virtually maximal* episode for b_i, that is an episode that would be maximal in the absence of any other reason for having b_i (i.e., in case there are no episodes of other atoms implying b_i). In other words, such episodes can be seen as maximal by default.

In the following we assume that there is at most one maximal episode of each atom a (we shall comment later on this). We also require that T is acyclic. The atoms that occur only in antecedents will be considered as **abducible**, i.e., those in terms of which explanations have to be provided.

An observation O to be explained has the form:

$$o_1, \ldots, o_k \ \{C(t_{o_1}, \ldots, t_{o_k})\} \tag{2}$$

where each o_i is an atom and $C(t_{o_1}, \ldots, t_{o_k})$ is a set of temporal constraints on the observations.

Given a model T and an observation O, we define a **temporal explanation** as a set E of abducibles such that:

- the observed atoms in O are explained by E through chains of explanatory formulae in T (E is an abductive explanation in the usual sense [12]);
- the set TE of temporal constraints formed by the constraints on the observation O and the constraints associated with the explanatory formulae involved in the explanation is consistent.

TE can provide constraints on the temporal extents of the assumptions in E; these constraints can be considered as part of the explanation.

3   Locality properties in STP

In our approach, the temporal constraints associated with the theory and the observations are expressed in terms of conjunctions of bounds on differences constraints between variables representing the starting/ending points of atoms (called STP constraints in [8] and in the following). A bound on difference is an inequality over $\mathcal{R}$ of the form $d_1 \leq X - Y \leq d_2$, meaning that the temporal distance between the time points (endpoints of episodes in our case) X and Y is between d_1 and d_2. Different types of qualitative (as in Allen's algebra [1]) and quantitative (e.g., dates, durations, delays) temporal constraints can be represented using the STP framework (see e.g., [2]), which is expressive enough for most applications, as noticed, e.g., in [13] as regards qualitative temporal constraints.

A set of STP constraints on a set K of variables can be represented in terms of a graph called **temporal constraint network** (TCN_K in the following). The consistency of TCN_K can be checked (using a constraint propagation algorithm) in time cubic in the number of variables in K. This computation also produces the **minimal network** TCN'_K, which is a compact representation of all the solutions to the set of constraints, consisting of the *strictest constraints* between all pairs of variables in the TCN_K [8]. In the paper, we use two properties of

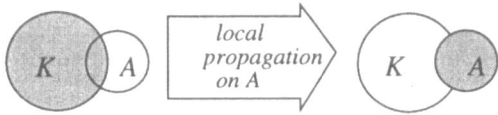

Fig. 1. Locality properties: grey areas represent the networks that are minimal (i.e. strictest), before and after applying local propagation on A.

STP (called **locality properties** in the following) that have been proved in [3]:

(1) Given a minimal network TCN_K on a set K of variables, checking whether a set of constraints on a set A of variables (represented by TCN_A) is consistent with TCN_K can be done in time cubic in the number of variables in A, regardless of the number of variables in K; this can be done by propagating on the variables in A the constraints in TCN_K concerning only the variables in A, plus the constraints in TCN_A (**local propagation** on A).

(2) After the local propagation on A, which produces a modified TCN'_A, the constraints on the variables in A are the same (the strictest ones) that would be obtained by a **global propagation** of the constraints in $TCN_K \cup TCN_A$ on all the variables in $K \cup A$. This means that TCN'_A is a *minimal constraint network* for the variables in A (see figure 1).

4   Reasoning issues

4.1   Locality properties in explanation

Given a model T and an observation O, we compute an explanation by means of a depth-first backward nondeterministic search: the abducible atoms forming the explanation are searched starting from the atoms in O and applying the formulae in T backwards. Temporal consistency is checked whenever a new formula is selected.

In the following we demonstrate how, due to the locality properties, local temporal propagation can achieve the same pruning results as the global propagation approach in case of both singly connected[1] and non-singly connected explanation graphs.

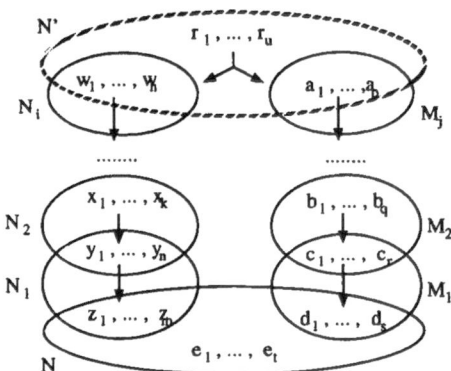

Fig. 2. Two chains of explanatory formulae. For example, N_1 corresponds to the formula: $F_1 : y_1, \ldots, y_n$ *explains* $z_1, \ldots z_m$ $\{C_1\}$. The graph is non-singly connected if and only if the formula $F' : r_1, \ldots r_u$ *explains* $w_1, \ldots w_h$, $a_1, \ldots a_p$ $\{C'\}$, corresponding to the dashed N', is included.

Case (a). Consider the case where different observations (or different atoms in the antecedent of a formula) are explained with independent assumptions, so that the formulae used in the explanation form a singly connected graph (as in Figure 2, without the dashed N', where $w_1 \ldots w_h$ and $a_1 \ldots a_p$ are abducible).

Let us first consider the chain of explanatory formulae $N, N_1, \ldots, N_i$. Suppose that the minimal network for N containing (besides the others) the atoms $z_1 \ldots z_m$ has been computed, and F_1 is selected in order to explain some of the atoms in $z_1, \ldots, z_m$. The current explanation graph and temporal constraint network have to be extended using F_1 and its constraints C_1.

The locality properties guarantee that (local) propagation to N_1 produces a minimal network for the variables in N_1 only, such that the constraints in it are

---

[1] A graph is singly connected if there is at most one path connecting any pair of nodes.

the same that would be obtained by (global) propagation to $N \cup N_1$. This allows us to localize constraint propagation to the atoms in a formula F when using F in an explanation step. This principle can be iteratively applied to the chain $N_1, \ldots, N_i$ in figure 2: given the minimal network for N_1 (produced by local propagation), the minimal network for N_2 can be computed with local propagation to the atoms in N_2, and so on. When the abducible atoms $w_1 \ldots w_h$ are reached, such a set of local propagations guarantees that the temporal constraints on such atoms are the same (strictest) ones that would be obtained with global propagation. Thus, we have that inconsistencies are detected by local propagation when they would be detected with global propagation.

Since now N is no longer a minimal network (only the constraints between $w_1, \ldots, w_h$ are now minimal), before moving to explaining $d_1, \ldots, d_s$, the minimal constraints between them must be computed. We can thus proceed as follows:

1. backward visit from N_1 to N_i with local propagation to each N_k;

2. forward visit from N_i to N_1 with local propagation to each N_k;

3. local propagation to N, which ensures (after steps 1 and 2) that the strictest constraints on $d_1, \ldots, d_s$, given the information on $N_1, \ldots, N_i$ are computed;

4. backward visit of $M_1, \ldots, M_j$, as in step 1.

5. forward visit of $M_j, \ldots, M_1$, as in step 2.

Thus, in general, if the explanation graph is singly connected, a backward visit followed by a forward visit of each branch is sufficient to detect temporal inconsistencies, if any, as they would be detected with global propagation to all the visited atoms.

Case (b). Let us consider now the case of a non-singly connected explanation, as in Figure 2, including the dashed N', corresponding to:

$$F' : r_1, \ldots r_u \ explains \ w_1, \ldots w_h, \ a_1, \ldots a_p \ \{C'\}$$

In order to apply the locality properties to F' at the end of step 4 of the strategy of case (a), we need to have the strictest constraints for $w_1, \ldots w_h$, $a_1, \ldots a_p$ before propagating C' to the atoms in F'. Unfortunately, this is not necessarily the case since the strategy for case (a) would only provide the strictest constraints for $a_1, \ldots a_p$ (given $N_i, \ldots N, \ldots M_j$), but not those for $w_1, \ldots w_h$, because the constraints collected during the backward visit of $M_1, \ldots, M_j$ have not been propagated to $w_1, \ldots, w_h$. It is possible to compute such strictest constraints if all the local propagations performed during the forward visit of $N_i, \ldots, N$ and the backward visit of $M_1, \ldots, M_j$ also involve the atoms which "join" the two chains (e.g., $w_1, \ldots w_h$, $a_1, \ldots a_p$); these atoms (called **junction atoms**) must be taken into account for the local propagations until $r_1, \ldots, r_u$ can be reached again, after which they can be disregarded. In the following, this procedure is implemented by maintaining a set of visited junction atoms (not necessarily all the visited ones) to be considered in the local propagations.

4.2 Explanation algorithm

In Figure 4, we present a nondeterministic algorithm for temporal abduction which implements the strategies for local temporal propagation discussed in the previous subsection. Given an explanatory formula F, $Ant(F)$ is the set of antecedents, $Cons(F)$ is the set of consequents, $Atoms(F)$ is $Ant(F) \cup Cons(F)$ and $TC(F)$ is the set of temporal constraints.

Given a theory T and an observation $o_1, \ldots, o_k$ $\{C(t_{o_1}, \ldots, t_{o_k})\}$, the algorithm finds a temporal explanation in terms of a set E of abducible atoms and a constraint network TCN_{VTE} on the variables VTE involved in the set of constraints TE (those on the observation and the ones associated with the explanatory formulae involved in the explanation). For the sake of simplicity, the observation is given in terms of a formula defined as follows:

$$F_{dummy} : o_1, \ldots o_k \text{ explains } a_{dummy} \{C(t_{o_1}, \ldots, t_{o_k})\}$$

The global variables J (the set of junction atoms), E (the explanation being built), and TCN_{VTE} (the temporal constraint network of the set of constraints TE being built) are initialized to the empty set, and the algorithm starts invoking $Explain(a_{dummy})$. For the sake of simplicity in the formulation of the algorithm, we assume that the theory T is transformed as follows:

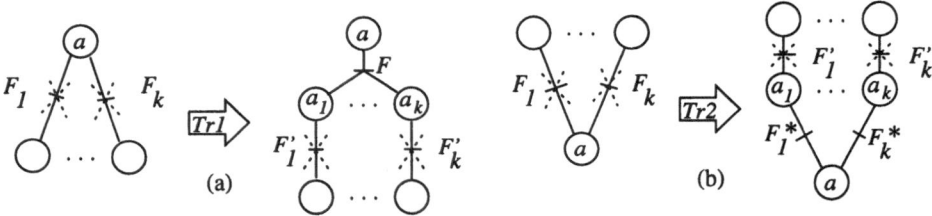

Fig. 3. Transformations Tr1 and Tr2 (see text).

Tr1. If a occurs in the antecedent of k formulae $\{F_1, \ldots, F_k\}$, then each F_i is replaced with F_i' and the formula F is added (see Figure 3a):

$F_i' = F_i[a/a_i]$, for $i = 1, \ldots, k$ (a is replaced by a_i in F_i)

$F = a$ explains $a_1, \ldots, a_k \{t_a \text{ equal } t_{a_1}, \ldots, t_a \text{ equal } t_{a_k}\}$

Tr2. If a occurs in the consequent of $k > 1$ formulae $\{F_1, \ldots, F_k\}$, then each F_i is replaced with F_i' and F_i^* (see Figure 3b):

$F_i' = F_i[a/a_i]$ $i = 1, \ldots, k$

$F_i^* = a_i$ explains a $\{t_{a_i} \text{ nsduring } t_a\}$ $i = 1, \ldots, k$

where t_1 *nsduring* t_2 (*non-strictly during*) means that t_1 is properly or improperly included in t_2. The temporal extent of a_i corresponds to the part of the extent of a due to F_i. Since this transformation does not preserve the semantics of the formulae, the algorithm deals with the formulae F_i^* in a special way in the nondeterministic step, as described below.

function *Explain(a)*
if *a* is abducible **then** add *a* to the explanation *E* being built; **return(true)**;
step 1: selection of the formula F for explaining a
   if there is only one formula F' such that $a \in \text{Cons}(F')$ **then** $F = F'$;
   if *a* occurs in the consequent of *k* formulae $F_1^* \ldots F_k^*$ (generated by
     transformation Tr2) **then**
      choose nondeterministically a subset $F_{i_1}^* \ldots F_{i_m}^*$;
      replace $F_{i_1}^* \ldots F_{i_m}^*$ with $F = a_1', \ldots, a_m'$ *explains a* $\{t_a$ *equal* $t_{a_1'} \cup \ldots \cup t_{a_m'}\}$;
step 2: use F to explain a
   if *F* is visited for the first time **then** add to TCN_{VTE} the constraints of TC(*F*);
   propagate TCN_{VTE} locally to Atoms(*F*) $\cup$ *J*;
   if a temporal inconsistency is detected **then return(false)**;
   if *F* is visited for the first time **then**
     for each atom a_i in Ant(*F*) **do**
      if not *Explain(a_i)* **then return(false)**;
      propagate TCN_{VTE} locally to Atoms(*F*) $\cup$ *J*;
     end for;
step 3: update the junction atoms set J
   add to *J* the atoms in Cons(*F*); **return(true)**;

Fig. 4. Function *Explain* computes an explanation of an atom *a*.

The function *Explain* is nondeterministic and visits the theory using a depth-first strategy, moving backward from observations to abducible atoms and propagating backward and forward the temporal constraints using local propagation to the formulae and to the set *J* of junction atoms as discussed above. Given an atom *a*, *Explain* returns true if a temporally consistent explanation of *a* can be found, false otherwise.

In case an atom *a* to be explained is abducible, *Explain* returns true and adds the atom to the explanation being built. Otherwise, *Explain* performs the following three steps.

Step 1. It first selects nondeterministically which formula(e) have to be used to explain *a*. If there is only one formula *F* having *a* as a consequent, it is selected. Otherwise, if *a* is the consequent of more than one formula $F_1^*, \ldots, F_k^*$, (produced by transformation Tr2; notice that by construction these formulae have only one atom in the antecedent and *a* in the consequent) a nondeterministic choice is needed in order to select the subset of such formulae to be used for explaining *a*, attributing part of the episode of *a* to each of the selected formulae. When the subset $\{F_{i_1}^*, \ldots, F_{i_m}^*\} \subseteq \{F_1^*, \ldots, F_k^*\}$ is selected, with antecedents $a_1', \ldots, a_m'$ (i.e., $F_{i_j}^* : a_j'$ *explains a*), all such atoms must be explained and the constraint t_a *equal* $t_{a_1'} \cup \ldots \cup t_{a_m'}$ must be imposed. For such a reason, $F = a_1', \ldots, a_m'$ *explains a* $\{t_a$ *equal* $t_{a_1'} \cup \ldots \cup t_{a_m'}\}$ replaces the formulae $\{F_{i_1}^*, \ldots, F_{i_m}^*\}$.

Step 2. The atom *a* is explained using the formula *F* provided by step 1. Consistency of TC(*F*) is checked by propagating the constraints in TCN_{VTE} locally to Atoms(F) $\cup$ J (when the formula F is visited for the first time, TCN_{VTE} must be updated in order to include also the temporal constraints of F). If a temporal inconsistency is detected, the function returns "false" and the algorithm backtracks on the last nondeterministic selection due to step 1; in this case a new F (if there exists) can be considered at step 1. Otherwise, if the formula F is visited for the first time, each one of its antecedents must be explained. After each antecedent has been explained, local propagation of TCN_{VTE} is performed in order to propagate the temporal constraints forwards.

Step 3. After all the antecedents of F have been explained, its consequences are added to J and the function returns. In this way the atoms in Cons(F) will be involved in the propagations that will be performed after the call $Explain(a)$ returns, i.e., when other atoms which are explained using F are considered.

If $Explain(a_{dummy})$ returns true, an explanation has been found: E is the set of abducibles corresponding to the explanation and TCN_{VTE} is the constraint network of the temporal constraints TE between the atoms involved in the formulae visited during the explanation process.

An easy optimization (called OPT_1 in the following) about the management of the set J of junction states is possible. Instead of adding all the atoms in Cons(F) to J, one could only add those atoms that have a consequence yet to be explained. This can be easily decided, given precompiled information specifying which are the possible consequences of atoms. Moreover, when an observation has been explained, all the atoms in J having no consequences yet to be explained can be removed.

Several techniques can be used to control the nondeterminism; for example, subsets of formulae directly explaining an atom a should be explored in order of increasing cardinality, starting from the set of formulae whose antecedent has already been visited. If choosing a subset S leads to a solution, choosing a superset of S can be avoided since it may be considered a redundant solution, in a similar way as in abductive reasoning minimal abductive explanations are preferred; this is particularly significant if a singleton subset succeeds, since it does not require a constraint involving union (see section 5.3). Finally, focusing techniques similar to those discussed in [7] can be adopted.

After the application of the algorithm in figure 4, a *prediction algorithm* should be performed in order to compute other observable consequences of the assumptions, that could be used for discriminating between alternative explanations. Local propagation can also be exploited for prediction.

5   Evaluation of the algorithm

We showed that if local propagation follows the strategy discussed in section 4.1, the ability to detect inconsistencies is the same that would be obtained with global propagation. Thus, we proved Property 1 by showing that the algorithm Explain follows such a strategy.

Property 1 *A propagation of TC(F) in the algorithm in figure 4 detects an inconsistency if and only if an inconsistency is detected propagating TC(F) to all the atoms in the (possibly partial) candidate explanation being built.*

We now analyze the overhead on the computation of one explanation[2] due to temporal constraint propagation in the global propagation case and the local propagation case (also considering the optimization OPT_1). We consider the case where a solution is found without search, i.e., without backtracking on the nondeterministic choices. In case of search, we have similar advantages also on the failed branches.

5.1 Analytical evaluation

The analytical evaluation is based on the number of elementary operations on the temporal knowledge base. For each propagation the number of operations (and thus the time complexity of the overhead) is cubic in the number of atoms involved in the propagation. We show that although the asymptotic complexity of the global and local propagation approaches is the same, in practice we have a significant improvement while for the singly connected case there is also an improvement in the asymptotic complexity. In the following, N_{FE} denotes the number of formulae involved in an explanation, N_{AF} denotes the average number of atoms in each formula; for the sake of simplicity we suppose that in each formula, $N_{AF}/2$ atoms are antecedents and $N_{AF}/2$ consequents.

In the global propagation approach, the total number of operations is given by the sum of the number of operations performed each time a new formula is selected; since, on the average, each formula introduces $N_{AF}/2$ new atoms (those in its antecedent), the complexity of the overhead is quartic in N_{FE}:

$$\text{global}(N_{FE}, N_{AF}) = \sum_{i=1}^{N_{FE}} (\frac{N_{AF}}{2} * (i+1))^3 \qquad (3)$$

In our algorithm, whenever an explanatory formula is visited, local propagation is performed on the atoms in the formula (i.e., N_{AF}) plus the atoms in J (in the following, N_J denotes the average number of junction atoms in J). Each selected formula is visited once when it is selected to explain an atom and then $N_{AF}/2$ times (once for each antecedent of the formula), so that our algorithm performs $N_{FE} * (1 + \frac{N_{AF}}{2})$ local propagations to the formulae. The overall complexity is:

$$\text{local}(N_{FE}, N_{AF}, N_J) = N_{FE} * (1 + \frac{N_{AF}}{2}) * (N_{AF} + N_J)^3 \qquad (4)$$

where $N_J = K_{AF} * K_{AT} * N_{AF} * N_{FE}$, $(0 \leq K_{AF}, K_{AT} \leq 1)$. K_{AF} represents the average fraction of atoms in a formula that are inserted in J when the formula is

---

[2] For the sake of simplicity, the evaluations are made in the case where each atom is explained using a single formula. We shall return later on the case where multiple formulae are selected.

visited. K_{AT} represents the average fraction of computation time in which each junction atom is contained in J (i.e., the fraction of local propagations for which a junction atom remains in J).

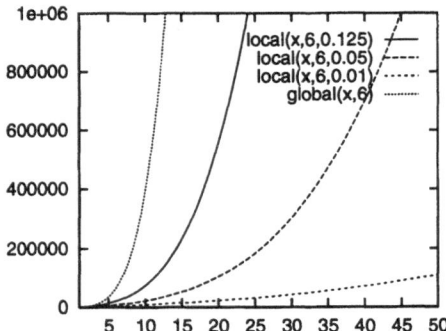

Fig. 5. Complexity of the global propagation approach and of our approach (local), for $N_{AF} = 6$ and for different values of K (0.01, 0.05 and 0.125). The x axis corresponds to N_{FE}; the y axes to the number of operations.

In the worst case N_J is $O(N_{FE})$ and then the complexity is quartic as in the global propagation case. See however figure 5 which compares the complexity of the overheads (3) and (4) for the global and local algorithms, when $N_{AF} = 6$. For our algorithm, we consider three values of $K = K_{AF} * K_{AT}$. For instance, $K = 0.125$ may correspond to the unfavourable case where half of the formulae contain junction atoms, half of the atoms in the consequents of such formulae are junction atoms ($K_{AF} = 0.25$ since only the consequents of a formula may be junction atoms) and each junction atom stays in the set J for half of the computation ($K_{AT} = 0.5$). Even in such a case, our approach is advantageous.

Such an overhead tends to be negligible as K gets closer to 0; if $K = 0$, it reduces to $N_{FE} * (1 + \frac{N_{AF}}{2}) * N_{AF}^3$. Assuming that N_{AF} does not depend on N_{FE}, the overhead is thus $O(N_{FE})$. Notice that $K = 0$ if, possibly using the optimization, no atom is ever put in J. In particular, this holds if the theory plus the dummy formula for the observations form a singly connected graph. The fact that in this case the overhead is negligible is a further advantage of our approach wrt the global propagation one which is not sensitive to the topology.

5.2 Experimental evaluation

We now discuss some experimental results which compare three cases:

- The algorithm based on global propagation that checks the temporal consistency by means of global propagation whenever a new formula is selected, as, e.g., in [11] (ALG$_{global}$ in the following). In particular, in order to make the comparison more significant, we implemented ALG$_{global}$ using depth-first backward search, as our approach in Figure 4.

- The algorithm in Figure 4, which uses local propagation ($\text{ALG}_{\text{local}}$);
- An extended version of the algorithm in Figure 4, which exploits the optimization OPT_1 discussed at the end of Section 4.2 (ALG_{opt}).

The algorithms have been implemented in C and Prolog and uses LaTeR [2], an efficient manager of temporal information capable of exploiting the locality properties of STP mentioned in Section 3.

Figure 6 reports the ratio between the computation time for the three algorithms, as a function of the number of atoms in the explanation, in case of highly multiply connected explanations. Notice that the optimized algorithm has a significant advantage over the non-optimized local propagation algorithm.

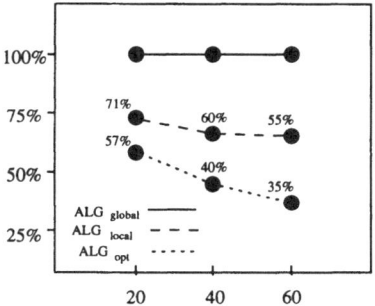

Fig. 6. Ratio between computation time of $\text{ALG}_{\text{local}}$ and ALG_{opt} with respect to $\text{ALG}_{\text{global}}$ for multiply connected explanation graphs.

5.3   Branching factor

It is now interesting to discuss about the number of candidates to be explored, i.e., whether or not the presence of time increases the branching factor in the search for explanations, which, in general, is an NP-complete problem [6]. The branching factor is the same if only single formulae are selected at each nondeterministic step (step 1 in the algorithm). If more than one formula is selected, both the global and the local approach have to deal with the union of temporal extents, thus increasing the branching factor with respect to the atemporal case. For example, in order to deal with a union $I = I_1 \cup I_2$ of two intervals, in general four cases must be considered, corresponding to the fact that the start (end) of I corresponds to the start (end) of I_1 or I_2. However, additional information about I_1 or I_2 (e.g., the fact I_1 overlaps I_2) may allow the disambiguation or reduction of such cases.

Similar issues arise for the relaxation of the restriction to single episodes of atoms. If multiple episodes are allowed, any time two potentially different maximal episodes I_1 and I_2 are hypothesized for an atom, three alternatives should be considered: they are the same interval, I_1 is before I_2 or I_1 is after I_2 (in the sense of Allen's algebra [1]). Also in this case the alternatives could be disambiguated given other information on I_1 and I_2, or at least the "same interval" case could be explored before the other cases.

Notice that, in general, all the propagations that, as the ones above, have exponential complexity in the worst case, will benefit from the local propagation approach, since the exponential propagation will only be applied to a small constraint network rather than to the whole explanation.

We have shown in section 5.1 that in some cases (which may be typical in some domains) in our algorithm temporal reasoning adds a constant factor overhead on explanation. In other cases, it adds a polynomial overhead. In worst cases, the presence of temporal knowledge worsens the nondeterminism inherent in abductive reasoning. It must be observed that temporal knowledge might be necessary to avoid finding incorrect explanations, and, if temporally inconsistent candidates are pruned as soon as possible in an efficient way (as in our approach), temporal knowledge may also contribute to *reducing* the nondeterminism.

References

1. J. Allen. Maintaining knowledge about temporal intervals. *Communications of the ACM*, 26:832–843, 1983.
2. V. Brusoni, L. Console, B. Pernici, and P. Terenziani. LaTeR: a general purpose manager of temporal information. In *Methodologies for Intelligent Systems 8*, pages 255–264. Lecture Notes in Computer Science 869, Springer Verlag, 1994.
3. V. Brusoni, L. Console, and P. Terenziani. On the computational complexity of querying bounds on differences constraints. *Artificial Intelligence*, 74(2):367–379, 1995.
4. V. Brusoni, L. Console, P. Terenziani, and D. Theseider Dupré. Characterizing temporal abductive diagnosis. In *Proc. DX 95, Sixth Int. Workshop on Principles of Diagnosis*, Goslar, 1995.
5. V. Brusoni, L. Console, P. Terenziani, and D. Theseider Dupré. A spectrum of definitions for temporal model-based diagnosis. Technical report, Dip. di Informatica, Università di Torino, 1997.
6. T. Bylander, D. Allemang, M. Tanner, and J. Josephson. The computational complexity of abduction. *Artificial Intelligence*, 49(1-3):25–60, 1991.
7. L. Console, L. Portinale, and D. Theseider Dupré. Using compiled knowledge to guide and focus abductive diagnosis. *IEEE Transactions on Knowledge and Data Engineering*, 8(5):690–706, 1996.
8. R. Dechter, I. Meiri, and J. Pearl. Temporal constraint networks. *Artificial Intelligence*, 49:61–95, 1991.
9. W. Hamscher and R. Davis. Diagnosing circuit with state: an inherently underconstrained problem. In *Proc. AAAI 84*, pages 142–147, 1984.
10. W. Long. Reasoning about state from causation and time in a medical domain. In *Proc AAAI 83*, pages 251–254, Washington, 1983.
11. W. Nejdl and J. Gamper. Harnessing the power of temporal abstractions in model-based diagnosis of dynamic systems. In *Proc. 11th ECAI*, pages 667–671, 1994.
12. D. Poole. Explanation and prediction: An architecture for default and abductive reasoning. *Computational Intelligence*, 5(2):97–110, 1989.
13. P. VanBeek. Temporal query processing with indefinite information. *Artificial Intelligence in Medicine*, 3:325–339, 1991.

Experimental Analysis of the Computational Cost of Evaluating Quantified Boolean Formulae

Marco Cadoli and Andrea Giovanardi and Marco Schaerf

Dipartimento di Informatica e Sistemistica,
Università di Roma "La Sapienza",
Via Salaria 113, I-00198 Roma, Italy
email: (cadoli|giovanardi|schaerf)@dis.uniroma1.it

Abstract. Although Knowledge Representation is full of reasoning problems that have been formally proved to be both NP-hard and coNP-hard, the experimental analysis has largely focused on problems belonging to either NP or coNP. We still do not know, for example, whether well-studied phenomena such as "phase transition", which show up for many NP-complete problems (e.g., SAT) happen for Σ_2^p-complete problems, and whether they are related to an "easy-hard-easy" pattern or not. The goal of this paper is to show some results of an ongoing experimental analysis that aims to provide reasonable answers to such questions. We analyze the problem of evaluating Quantified Boolean Formulae, which is the prototypical complete problem for all levels of the Polynomial Hierarchy, the computationally simplest hierarchy of complexity classes above NP of great interest to KR.

1 Introduction

In recent years, the AI community witnessed a growing interest in rigorous analysis of computational aspects of reasoning. On one hand, studies in complexity of formalisms such as non-monotonic logics, temporal logics, planning, etc. were concerned both with showing a detailed picture of the "tractability threshold" between polynomiality and NP-hardness, and with measuring in a precise way "how much intractable" is, in general, a reasoning problem. On the other hand, experimental studies in performance of algorithms showed that there are reasoning problems (e.g., satisfiability testing of propositional formulae) which admit a parameter such that the hardest instances appear to be located in a particular range of its values.

Main motivation behind experimental study is to know exactly "where the really hard instances are" [CKT91], and what are the most effective techniques for attacking them. Such a knowledge should help us in the overall goal of designing fast, reliable systems that are able to handle large quantities of knowledge.

The motivation of this paper is the following: although Knowledge Representation is full of reasoning problems that have been formally proved to be both NP-hard and coNP-hard, the experimental analysis has largely focused on problems belonging to either NP or coNP [HHe96] (an exception being [GS96]). We still do not know, for example, whether well-studied phenomena such as "phase transition", which show up for many NP-complete problems (e.g., SAT) happen for credulous reasoning in default logic –a Σ_2^p-complete problem [Got92]–, and whether they are related to an "easy-hard-easy" pattern or not. Moreover we do not have a precise idea of "how much harder" is in practice default reasoning wrt classical propositional reasoning.

The goal of this paper is to show some results of an ongoing experimental analysis that aims –eventually– to provide reasonable answers to such questions. Two important methodological choices we made are the following. We did not want to commit, at this stage, to a specific reasoning formalism such as autoepistemic logic or STRIPS. Therefore we looked for formalism-independent problems. Moreover, in order to allow comparison of results, we did not want to consider problems "too much harder", e.g., PSPACE-complete, than those already analyzed by others. Such choices lead us to analyze *Quantified Boolean Formulae* (QBF), which have several interesting features. Evaluation of a QBF is the prototypical complete problem for all levels of the *Polynomial Hierarchy* [GJ79], the computationally simplest hierarchy of complexity classes above NP of great interest to Knowledge Representation (KR). As a consequence, all instances of reasoning problems which are complete for a level of the polynomial hierarchy, e.g., credulous default reasoning, can be translated into evaluation of a QBF. Moreover a QBF has a simple syntactic form which resembles that of a propositional formula. This facilitates comparison of our results to the existing ones on 3SAT, because we can still use parameters such as the famous "#clauses/#variables ratio" [MSL92].

Choosing QBFs as the objective of our investigation has of course advantages as well as disadvantages. On the negative side, no KR problem can be directly modeled as QBF evaluation, and polynomial-time transformations might introduce some noise (as an example, there is no guarantee that the reduction preserves hardness or easiness of the instances). As a consequence, our results are still not sufficient to reach any conclusion on credulous default reasoning or other KR problems. Nevertheless we believe that such shortcomings are balanced by the simple structure of QBFs, their similarity with propositional formulae, and the property of their crucial parameters being immediately identifiable. As a consequence experiments on evaluation of QBFs can be compared with the large body of literature on SAT. Our ultimate goal is to experiment on KR formalisms on both randomly generated and "real-world" instances.

We present the results of the experimental analysis starting from the simplest cases, and moving towards the complex ones. We investigated the effects of increasing the number of quantifiers alternations of a QBF, increasing the length of the clauses in its matrix, unbalancing existential and universal variables, and introducing variable-length clauses. We reached a number of interesting conclusions, and collected several starting points for future investigation.

2 Quantified Boolean Formulae

A QBF has the form

$$Q_1 x_1 \cdots Q_n x_n E(x_1, \ldots, x_n) \tag{1}$$

where E is a propositional formula involving the propositional variables $x_1, \ldots, x_n$ and every Q_i ($1 \le i \le n$) is either an existential quantifier $\exists$ or a universal one $\forall$. The expression $\exists x_i \phi$ is an abbreviation for "there exists a truth assignment to x_i such that ϕ is true". Analogously, $\forall x_i \phi$ is an abbreviation for "for each truth assignment to x_i, ϕ is true". As an example,

$$\forall x_1 \exists x_2 \ (x_1 \lor x_2) \land (\neg x_1 \lor \neg x_2) \tag{2}$$

means "for each truth assignment to x_1 there exists a truth assignment to x_2 such that $(x_1 \lor x_2) \land (\neg x_1 \lor \neg x_2)$ is true". QBF (2) is indeed true: if $x_1 = \mathsf{T}$ then x_2 can be assigned to F; if $x_1 = \mathsf{F}$ then x_2 can be assigned to T; in both cases $(x_1 \lor x_2) \land (\neg x_1 \lor \neg x_2)$ is true. The *evaluation problem* for a QBF is to decide whether a given QBF is true or not. Inverting quantifiers in a QBF may change its truth value. As an example, inverting quantifiers in (2) yields $\exists x_1 \forall x_2 \ (x_1 \lor x_2) \land (\neg x_1 \lor \neg x_2)$, which is indeed false.

Given a generic QBF, we can group in the same set all consecutive variables having the same quantifier. For example, the following QBF:

$$\forall x_1 \exists x_2 \exists x_3 \forall x_4 \forall x_5 (x_1 \lor \neg x_2 \lor x_5) \land (x_3 \lor \neg x_5) \land (\neg x_4)$$

can be rewritten as:

$$\forall\{x_1\}\exists\{x_2, x_3\}\forall\{x_4, x_5\}(x_1 \lor \neg x_2 \lor x_5) \land (x_3 \lor \neg x_5) \land (\neg x_4).$$

In such a formula, each quantifier is applied to a set of variables rather than to a single propositional variable. Moreover, the sequence of quantifiers alternates: an existential quantifier follows a universal quantifier and vice-versa.

A *kQBF* (with k constant integer) is a QBF in which the quantifiers are applied to k disjoint sets of variables and the sequence of quantifiers alternates; sometimes we will add a subscript denoting the type of the most external quantifier in the formula. For example, if X_1, X_2, and X_3 are mutually disjoint sets of propositional variables, then the formula $\exists X_1 \forall X_2 \exists X_3 \ E(X_1, X_2, X_3)$ is a 3QBF$_\exists$. The well-known SAT problem coincides with the evaluation problem for 1QBF$_\exists$.

From a theoretical point of view, the study of QBFs is important since they characterize complexity classes [GJ79]. The evaluation problem for a QBF is PSPACE-complete, and plays the role of prototypical problem for such a class. The problem of evaluating a kQBF$_\exists$ is Σ_k^p-complete, whereas the problem of evaluating a kQBF$_\forall$ is Π_k^p-complete, Σ_k^p and Π_k^p being the classes at the k-th level of the Polynomial Hierarchy.

In the rest of this paper we refer to QBFs in *Conjunctive Normal Form* (CNF), i.e., QBFs of the form (1) in which the boolean formula E is a conjunction of *clauses*, each one being a disjunction of *literals* —a negated or non-negated variable. In this case E is called *matrix* of the formula. A QBF is said to be in *hCNF* if every clause contains exactly h literals.

Considering QBF in CNF is not a restriction, since the problem of evaluating such formulae is still PSPACE-complete. With respect to kQBFs, the evaluation problem of kQBFs in 3CNF is complete for the same complexity class of the general case if the most internal quantifier is an existential [Sto76]. As a consequence, in the following we will consider kQBFs of the form

$$Q_1 X_1 Q_2 X_2 \cdots \exists X_k \ E(X_1, \ldots, X_k) \tag{3}$$

in which $E(X_1, \ldots, X_n)$ is in CNF, the most internal quantifier is existential and the sequence of quantifiers, as usual, alternates. Fixing the type of the most internal quantifier makes the use of subscripts in, e.g., kQBF$_\exists$ useless. As an example, a 2QBF has the form $\forall X_1 \exists X_2 \ E(X_1, X_2)$, while a 3QBF has the form $\exists X_1 \forall X_2 \exists X_3 \ E(X_1, X_2, X_3)$.

QBFs and propositional formulae have similar syntax. Nevertheless evaluating a QBF is inherently more difficult than deciding satisfiability of a propositional formula. Intuitively, in SAT we just need to find a truth assignment for each variable that satisfies the formula; instead proving that a 2QBF is true requires to solve an exponential number of SAT instances (one for each assignment to the universally quantified variables), proving that a 3QBF is true requires to evaluate an exponential number of 2QBFs, and so on.

In order to perform our experimental investigation, we designed and implemented in C++ an algorithm to evaluate QBFs. This algorithm, called **Evaluate**, is a recursive generalization of the Davis-Putnam algorithm (i.e., branching + unit resolution) to the more general setting of QBFs. Variables bound by the external quantifier are dealt with before others. Moreover several special rules for QBFs are used (e.g., if a QBF has a non-tautologous clause in which all literals are universally quantified, then it is false). The complete algorithm, including all special rules, optimized data structures, and some heuristics for the choice of the literal to branch upon, is non-trivial, and has been presented in [CGG+96]. Two important parameters that characterize a run of **Evaluate** are: the number of recursions, and the total number of truth value assignments (tries); the latter is conceptually similar to the number of nodes of the search space visited by an algorithm that solves an NP-complete problem such as SAT.

3 Experimental results

In this section we present the most important experimental results obtained applying our evaluation algorithm on randomly generated kQBF instances. In our tests we have mainly generated kQBF instances according to the *Fixed Clause Length* (FCL) model (cf. e.g., [MSL92]).

The FCL model for QBFs has the following parameters:

- the number k of distinct sets of propositional variables in formula (3),
- the cardinality $|X_1|, \ldots, |X_k|$ of each set,

- the number m of clauses in E,
- the number h of literals per clause.

In this model each formula is generated so that all m clauses contain exactly h literals. If V is the set $X_1 \cup X_2 \cup \cdots \cup X_k$, then a clause is produced by randomly choosing h distinct variables in V and negating each one with probability 0.5. In our tests we ensured that all the m clauses were different from one another and that none of them included both a literal and its complement. Moreover, to avoid generating trivially false kQBF instances, we disallowed a clause to contain only universally quantified variables.

For all the considered parameters settings we ran 500 experiments; for each one we recorded several data like: the truth value of the randomly generated QBF, the running time, the number of recursions, and the number of tries. Such data were successively processed to obtain the mean and the median values. Moreover, we split these results considering separately data for the true and false instances. We performed our tests on a SPARC 10 SUN workstation, equipped with a 75MHz processor and 32 MB of RAM.

Our analysis aims to understand whether certain computational phenomena observed in the experimental analysis of several NP-complete problems also arise in the context of QBF evaluation. Among these phenomena, the most important ones are "phase transition" and "easy-hard-easy" patterns. A phase transition is an abrupt change of a global value due to a small local change. In SAT it has been observed that there exists a crucial parameter, the #clauses/#variables ratio, whose small changes can cause a large change in the probability that a formula is satisfiable. This phenomenon only occurs when the value of the parameter is close to the "crossover point", that is the point where the probability of a formula being satisfiable is 50%. In SAT, it has also been observed that the phase transition is related to the computational resources needed to solve the problem. In fact, instances that are far away from the phase transition appear to be computationally simple (on average), while instances close to the phase transition are computationally very demanding. This pattern is known as easy-hard-easy.

2QBF-3CNF results. The instances of formulae $\forall X_1 \exists X_2 \ E(X_1, X_2)$ were generated according to the FCL model; moreover, we chose the same cardinality for the two different sets of variables (that is $|X_1| = |X_2|$). The tests were executed varying the number of variables *per set* from 10 to 500, with a step of 10 variables. Note that, as an example, a 2QBF with 500 variables per set contains 1,000 variables. For every number of variables per set, we varied the #clauses/#variables per set ratio from 0.05 to 1, with a step of 0.05.

Fig. 1 (left) reports the percentage of true 2QBF-3CNF instances as a function of the #clauses/#variables per set ratio, for 100, 200, 300, 400, and 500 variables per set respectively. The curves show that phase transition occurs. Moreover, as in the 1QBF case, the phase transition becomes steeper and steeper as the number of variables is increased; in the meanwhile, the crossover point

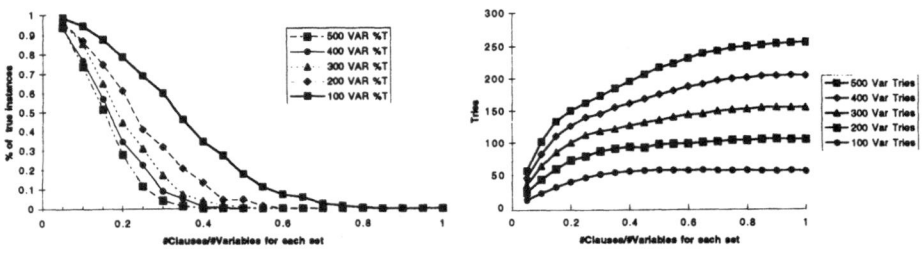

Fig. 1. % of true instances (left) and number of tries (right) for 2QBF-3CNF

moves to the left. The curves in Fig. 1 (left) do not intersect, whereas in the 1QBF case they do (cf. [LT93]).

Fig. 1 (right) shows the median number of tries needed, as a function of the #clauses/#variables per set ratio. The curves do not follow an easy-hard-easy pattern: the number of tries initially increases as the ratio is increased, but successively settles on almost constant values. Moreover, we did not notice any correlation between the hardness of evaluating 2QBF-3CNF instances and the crossover point.

As a matter of fact, the Evaluate algorithm performed the evaluation of this kind of formulae quite easily, as Fig. 1 (right) displays. For example, in the most difficult test cases, Evaluate needed on average 250 tries for evaluating a 2QBF-3CNF with 500 variables per set —that is, it was necessary to instantiate only one variable out of four. As for the CPU time, a 2QBF-3CNF with 500 variables per set and 500 clauses was evaluated in about 0.7 seconds on average. For comparison, Evaluate needs about 11,000 tries, 900 recursions and 27 seconds on average for 1QBFs with 100 variables at the crossover point, i.e., about 430 clauses.

2QBF-4CNF and 3QBF-3CNF results. The results we obtained for both 2QBF-4CNF and 3QBF-3CNF are very similar to the 2QBF-3CNF ones. In particular, we could verify in both cases the existence of phase transition, which becomes steeper and steeper as the number of variables is increased. Moreover, there is no easy-hard-easy pattern, and the computational effort for evaluating instances is quite modest: even for 500 variables per set, the average number of recursions was never greater than 2, whereas the average CPU time was about 1 second for both 2QBF-4CNF and 3QBF-3CNF. The crossover point for 2QBF-4CNF is about at 0.25 clauses per variable per set, thus close to the analogous parameter for 2QBF-3CNF.

An interesting result we obtained is concerned with the relation between the number of clauses at the crossover point and the number of variables per set. For each of the three types of formulae considered so far we determined the value of the crossover point and the number of clauses in it. For each of the three cases, the best interpolation function is:

$$c = av^b \qquad (4)$$

rather than a linear function as in the 1QBF case ($c = 4.24v + 6.21$, cf. [CA93]). In (4) c is the number of clauses at the crossover point, v is the number of variables per set (in our experiments: from 10 to 500 with a step of 10), a and b are constants depending on the type of formula considered. The values of a and b for each case are listed in Table 1.

Formula type	a	b	correlation
2QBF-3CNF	3.41	0.495	0.9984
2QBF-4CNF	5.63	0.48	0.9966
3QBF-3CNF	7.40	0.52	0.9988

Table 1. Constants a and b and correlation coefficients

Note that the values of b are always very close to 0.5: this suggests that the number of clauses at the crossover point is proportional to the square root of the number of variables per set.

2QBF-5CNF results. The hardness of evaluating 2QBF increases sharply considering 5CNF rather than 4CNF. As a matter of fact, for 2QBF-5CNF we could not consider a wide range for the number of variables per set, as we did, instead, for the type of formulae previously seen. As an example, the evaluation process of 2QBF-5CNF instances with 20 variables per set needed, on average, about 16,500 tries and about 45 seconds; since we run, as usual, 500 different tests, this means that the collection of the data for 2QBF-5CNF with 20 variables per set required more than 15 days.

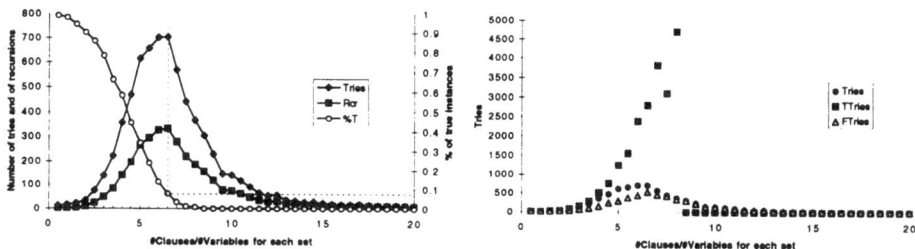

Fig. 2. Results for 2QBF-5CNF (10 vars per set)

In our experiments, we considered both 10 and 20 variables per set. For each fixed number of variables per set, we varied the #clauses/#variables per set ratio from 0.5 to 20, incrementing by 0.5. Fig. 2 (left) shows the results we obtained for 10 variables per set (the results for 20 variables are quite similar). For convenience, three different curves are drawn: the percentage of true instances, the average number of tries, and the average number of recursions, all as a function of the #clauses/#variables per set ratio. As usual there is phase transition, but this time we can also observe an easy-hard-easy pattern for the number of tries and for the number of recursions. The peak of the tries curve is located in correspondence to a #clauses/#variables per set ratio of 6.5 and a percentage of true instance of about 10% –thus not in the crossover point. The value of the crossover point, instead, is about 4.2, much higher than the previous ones.

The number of tries needed for evaluating this kind of formulae is remarkably higher wrt the formulae considered before: as an example, Evaluate needed on average less than 280 tries for evaluating 2QBF-4CNF with 500 variables per set, whereas it needed more than 700 tries, in the peak point, for evaluating 2QBF-5CNF with only 10 variables per set. Apparently, going from 4 to 5 literals per clause causes a drastic reduction of "forced" assignments in the Evaluate algorithm.

In Fig. 2 (right) the number of tries needed for evaluating 2QBF-5CNF with 10 variables per set is split considering the false and true instances separately. It can be seen that the hardness of the true instances increases as the #clauses/#variables ratio is increased, whereas the difficulty of the false instances remains modest for every value of the ratio.

We believe that the easy-hard-easy pattern for the number of tries in 2QBF-5CNF is mostly due to the true instances: for a #clauses/#variables per set ratio of about 6.5, they are already so hard and still so many to influence the average values of tries. Instead, the absence of an easy-hard-easy pattern for the number of tries in 2QBF-3CNF and 2QBF-4CNF could be due to the fact that their phase transitions are sharper than the 2QBF-5CNF ones: increasing the number of clauses, the true instances become rare, and cannot influence significantly the average number of tries.

Unbalancing existential and universal variables. In order to understand whether the proportion between the number of universally-quantified variables (∀-variables) and the existentially-quantified ones (∃-variables) has an impact on our results, we ran two different groups of tests; in the first group, we considered 2QBF-5CNF with 14 ∀-variables and 7 ∃-variables. We call this kind of formulae 2QBF-5CNF 14-7 vars. We also considered 2QBF-5CNF 7-14 vars. Since both kinds of formulae contain a total number of 21 variables, the corresponding results can be compared with the 2QBF-5CNF 10 variables per set ones.

Figs. 3 (left and right) show the percentage of true instances and the average number of tries we obtained respectively for 2QBF-5CNF 14-7 vars and 2QBF-5CNF 7-14 vars. In both figures, the x-axis represents the ratio between the number of clauses and the *average number of variables per set*—a value that in this case is $(14 + 7)/2 = 10.5$.

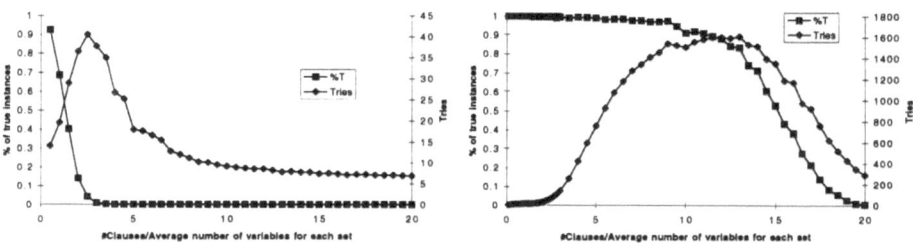

Fig. 3. Results for 2QBF-5CNF 14-7 vars (left) and 7-14 vars (right)

Comparing Figs. 2 (left) and 3 (left), we can notice that evaluating 2QBF-5CNF 14-7 vars formulae is much easier than evaluating formulae with 10 variables for each set: though in both cases we can observe an easy-hard-easy pattern, in the former case the highest number of tries needed is 40, whereas in the latter case is over 700. We believe that such a drastic reduction in the number of tries can be explained as follows: an increase of the number of $\forall$-variables with respect to the number of $\exists$-variables causes a reduction of the number of true instances; in fact, the phase transition is steeper for 14-7 vars than in 10 variables per set. Since the true instances are the hardest ones (cf. Fig. 2 (right)), their decrease causes a reduction of the average number of tries.

Fig. 3 (right) shows an opposite phenomenon for formulae of the type 2QBF-5CNF 7-14 vars: they are harder than those with 10 variables per set. In fact, in the former case the number of tries in the peak point is about 1600, whereas in the latter case is 700. This fact can be explained in the same way as before: increasing the number of $\exists$-variables and decreasing the number of $\forall$-variables causes an increase of the number of true instances; this, in turn, causes an increase of the average number of tries, together with a decrease in the slope of the phase transition.

2QBF-6CNF results. Evaluating random 2QBF-6CNF is even harder than 2QBF-5CNF. We ran tests for 10 variables per set only, varying the #clauses/ #variables per set ratio from 0.1 to 20, with a step of 0.1.

The number of tries follows an easy-hard-easy pattern, but this time the peak occurs where about 50% of the instances are true—that is, at the crossover point. The number of tries at the peak point is about 4,400, a very high value (700 tries are needed at the peak point for 2QBF-5CNF, cf. Fig. 2 (left)). Indeed, the evaluation process of 2QBF-6CNF instances with 10 variables per set at the peak point, i.e., 110 clauses, required on average about 20 seconds.

Moreover, we could verify that, as in the 2QBF-5CNF case, the hardest instances were the true ones; rare true instances occurring at a #clauses/#variables per set ratio of 18 required more than 9,500 tries for being solved.

2QBF-Average 6CNF results. In the experiments discussed so far, the instances were generated according to the FCL model. We made this choice since it has been verified that, for 1QBF, instances generated by means of the *Constant Probability* (CP) model (i.e., fixing the average length of a clause) turned out to be easily evaluated (cf. [MSL92]). With the aim of verifying if this is also the case for kQBF with $k > 1$, we ran the Evaluate algorithm on 2QBF randomly generated instances with 10 variables per set and an average of 6 literals per clause; the tests were executed varying the number of clauses from 10 to 200, with a step of 1.

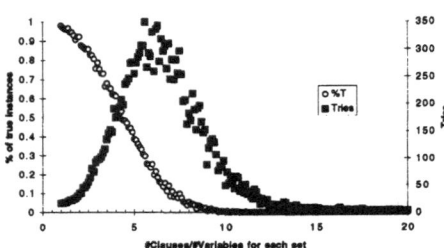

Fig. 4. Results for 2QBF-Average 6CNF (10 vars per set)

Fig. 4 reports the percentage of true instances and the number of tries as a function of the #clauses/#variables per set ratio. The curve of the number of tries shows an easy-hard-easy pattern, with the peak point being associated to the crossover point. Comparing 2QBF-6CNF results and Fig. 4, we can notice a remarkable difference between the number of tries in the peak points: 4,400 tries for 2QBF-6CNF and 350 tries for 2QBF-Average 6CNF. Thus, these results seem to confirm that, also for kQBF with $k > 1$, the instances generated with the FCL model are, on an average, much harder than the instances generated by means of the CP model. Apparently, in the latter model, short clauses allow simplifications in the evaluation process that are predominant with respect to complications due to long clauses.

3QBF-6CNF results. In the last group of experiments we considered 3QBF-6CNF with 10 variables per set. For this kind of formulae, we varied the number of clauses from 10 to 300, with a step of 10 clauses.

Fig. 5 (left) reports the percentage of true instances, the average number of tries and the average number of recursions as a function of the #clauses/#variables per set ratio. The curves regarding the number of tries and the number of recursions show, also in this case, an easy-hard-easy pattern, with the hardest instances being associated with the crossover point. The number of tries in the peak point is about 5,000; thus, formulae of this kind are even harder than 2QBF-6CNF (the number of variables per set being equal).

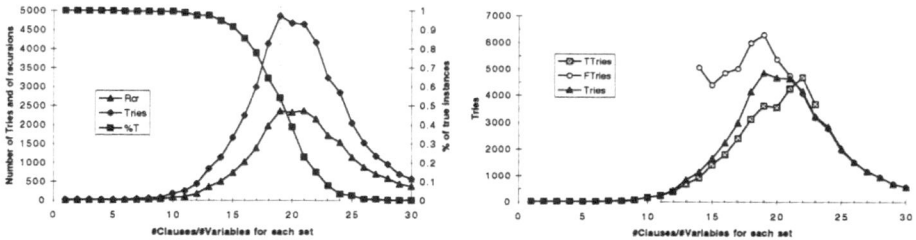

Fig. 5. Results for 3QBF-6CNF (10 vars per set)

In Fig. 5 (right) we have split the number of tries considering true and false instances separately. It is interesting to notice that, in this case, the hardest instances are the false ones (the same result was obtained for 1QBF, cf. [MSL92]). Instead, for all the kind of 2QBF considered before, the hardest instances were the true ones. This phenomenon can be explained as follows: for kQBF with k even, the most external quantifier is universal, and so **Evaluate** can stop running as soon as it finds an assignment to the variables of the most external set that makes the formula false. Thus, for kQBF with k even the easiest instances are the false ones. On the contrary, for kQBF with k odd the most external quantifier is existential; in this case, the easiest instances are the true ones, since **Evaluate** can stop running as soon as it finds an assignment to the variables of the most external set that makes the formula true.

4 Conclusions and future work

The experimental results we obtained can be summarized as follows:

- Evaluation of 3QBF is more difficult than 2QBF.
- Phase transition phenomena exist in all the investigated cases of QBF.
- An easy-hard-easy pattern has been observed in the following cases: 2QBF-5/6CNF and 3QBF-6CNF. The easy-hard-easy pattern, instead, has not been observed in all the other cases.
- The number of clauses in the crossover point is not a linear function of the number of variables (as it is for 1QBF); in all the cases in which we could examine a wide range for the number of variables per set (2QBF-3CNF, 2QBF-4CNF and 3QBF-3CNF), the number of clauses at the crossover point is proportional to the square root of the number of variables per set.
- As in the 1QBF case, instances generated according to the CP model are, on an average, much easier than those generated by means of the FCL model.
- In all the considered cases, for kQBF with k odd the true instances are easier, whereas for k even the false ones are easier.

- Unbalancing the number of existentially-quantified and universally-quantified variables has remarkable effects on the difficulty of 2QBF instances. If ∃-variables are increased, the instances become much harder. An opposite phenomenon occurs when ∀-variables are increased.

For the future, we plan to investigate on kQBF with k higher than 3, and eventually not bounded by a constant (i.e., on PSPACE-complete problems). Moreover, we want to verify the conjecture on the crossover point (cf. eqn. (4)) for kQBF-hCNF with other values of k and h. Finally, we plan to experiment on KR formalisms such as circumscription and default logic.

Acknowledgments

This work has been supported by ASI (Italian Space Agency), MURST (Italian Ministry for University and Scientific and Technological Research) and CNR (Italian Research Council) under the SARI project.

References

[CA93]   J. M. Crawford and L. D. Auton. Experimental results on the crossover point in satisfiability problems. In *Proceedings of the Eleventh National Conference on Artificial Intelligence (AAAI-93)*, pages 21–27, 1993.

[CGG⁺96] M. Cadoli, A. Giovanardi, E. Giunchiglia, F. Giunchiglia, M. Schaerf, and R. Sebastiani. Experimental analysis of the computational cost of satisfiability checking in logics for commonsense reasoning. Technical Report MRG/DIST 96-0040, Dipartimento di Informatica, Sistemistica e Telematica, Università di Genova, July 1996.

[CKT91]   P. Cheeseman, B. Kanefski, and W. M. Taylor. Where the really hard problem are. In *Proceedings of the Twelfth International Joint Conference on Artificial Intelligence (IJCAI-91)*, pages 163–169, 1991.

[GJ79]   M. R. Garey and D. S. Johnson. *Computers and Intractability, A Guide to the Theory of NP-Completeness*. W.H. Freeman and Company, San Francisco, Ca, 1979.

[Got92]   G. Gottlob. Complexity results for nonmonotonic logics. *Journal of Logic and Computation*, 2:397–425, 1992.

[GS96]   F. Giunchiglia and R. Sebastiani. A SAT-based decision procedure for $\mathcal{ALC}$. In *Proceedings of the Fifth International Conference on the Principles of Knowledge Representation and Reasoning (KR-96)*, pages 304–314, 1996.

[HHe96]   T. Hogg, B. A. Hubermann, and C. P. Williams (eds.). Special volume on frontiers of problem solving: Phase transitions and complexity. *Artificial Intelligence Journal*, 81, 1996.

[LT93]   T. Larrabee and Y. Tsuji. Evidence threshold for random 3CNF formulas. In *Proceedings of the Eleventh National Conference on Artificial Intelligence (AAAI-93)*, pages 112–118, 1993.

[MSL92]   D. Mitchell, B. Selman, and H. Levesque. Hard and easy distributions for SAT problems. In *Proceedings of the Tenth National Conference on Artificial Intelligence (AAAI-92)*, pages 459–465, 1992.

[Sto76]   L. J. Stockmeyer. The polynomial-time hierarchy. *Theoretical Computer Science*, 3:1–22, 1976.

A Proof Theory for Tractable Approximations of Propositional Reasoning

Fabio Massacci

Dipartimento di Informatica e Sistemistica
via Salaria 113, I-00198 Roma, Italy
e-mail: massacci@dis.uniroma1.it

Abstract. This paper proposes an uniform framework for the proof theory of tractable approximations of propositional reasoning. The key idea is the introduction of *approximate proofs*. This makes possible the development of an approximating sequent calculus for propositional deduction where proofs can be sound, complete or multi-directional approximations of classical logic. We show how this calculus subsumes existing approaches to approximation such as the $BCP - k$ family of anytime reasoners by Dalal and $S - 1, S - 3$ entailments by Cadoli and Schaerf.

1 Introduction

The use of logic for modeling and reasoning is widespread in Computer Science and Artificial Intelligence. It ranges from logics for knowledge and belief to action, time, processes, classical or multi-valued logics (e.g. [9–11]).

Yet the practical use of logical deduction is hindered by its computational complexity: propositional deduction is co-NP complete and more expressive logics range from PSPACE to EXPTIME [13,11,18]. A computational barrier that one can smooth with proof tactics, heuristics or even passing from theorem proving to model checking [12] but never really overcome.

To overcome this barrier, approximating algorithms for satisfiability have been proposed from the very beginning [13] and are now an established field (see [2] for an overview). On the contrary, much less research has been carried out for its dual, deduction. As noted by Wang in [26]:

> If we compare calculating with proving... we do not have a clear conception of approximate methods in theorem proving. We possess efficient calculating procedures while with proofs... even in a decidable theory, the decision method is not practically feasible. [...] The concept of approximate proofs, though undeniably of a kind other than approximations in numerical calculations, is not incapable of more exact formulation in term of ... gradual improvements towards a correct proof.

Notice that we should distinguish between logics or deduction for approximate reasoning, such as fuzzy or multi-valued logics [1,10,27] from *approximating deduction*. Those logics aim at modeling uncertainty and imprecise concepts, and are NP-complete too [18]. The idea of approximating deduction stems from an engineering perspective: if finding an exact proof of a classical theorem is too hard, why not looking for an approximate one?

To fill this gap, a number of approximation methods for logical consequence have been developed in AI: knowledge compilation [22], semantical approximations [4,15,16,21] and syntactic anytime reasoners [7,6,8].

Knowledge compilation or "vivification" [7,22] is a preprocessing step to transform a theory into another one for which deduction is faster: Horn theories in [22] and boolean constraints propagation in [7]. So it doesn't exactly match the intuition of approximation as an incremental process. Syntactic approximation [7,6,8] is incremental but its essential use of cut (for the incremental steps of the construction) forces to use knowledge compilation for a constructive formulation. These techniques change the formulae of the theory, and lead to an exponential blow up of the approximating theories [4,7,22].

Logical approximation, developed by [4,21] from the initial work of [15,16], is based on semantical approximation of classical logic by multiple valued logic. It is incremental and can be used for both sound or complete approximations. Although algorithms for incremental entailment exist [21] they are based on model enumeration and do not yield a notion of proof (besides making difficult to re-use past computations).

Beyond the restriction to clausal normal form of these approaches, we still miss the notion of *approximate proof* advocated by Wang.

To provide an answer in this direction a comparison with approximating satisfiability is useful. Satisfiability requires a *witness* which satisfies all constraints. An approximate witness only satisfies part of them. Deduction has the dual notion of *proof* e.g. a proof that a counterexample witness does not exists (with refutational theorem proving).

This paper advocates the introduction of approximate proofs which satisfy only some of the constraints a classical proof must have, thus generating the proof space of Fig. 1. This requires an *approximating calculus* where proofs converge to classical proofs, with increasing precision. Since proof are expected to be sound and complete, this also implies the development of a corresponding *superficial semantics*. The idea of approximate proofs has also been useful for proving properties of Frege systems [3] by using unsound steps in a Frege proof.

We sketch some (desirable) requirements for an approximating calculus:

multi-directional: sound, complete or multi-directional approximations (partly sound and partly complete) must be possible as in Fig 1;

incremental: old approximate proofs can be re-used to get better results and eventually converge to a classical proof;

flexible: the user can set the degree of approximation;

direct: the (sub)formulae of the original theory should be used;

almost classical: each proof should "look-like" a classical proof with the exception of approximating steps;

semantically grounded: there should be a superficial semantics so that each step of approximation is sound and complete with respect to such semantics and the semantics itself should converge to a classical one;

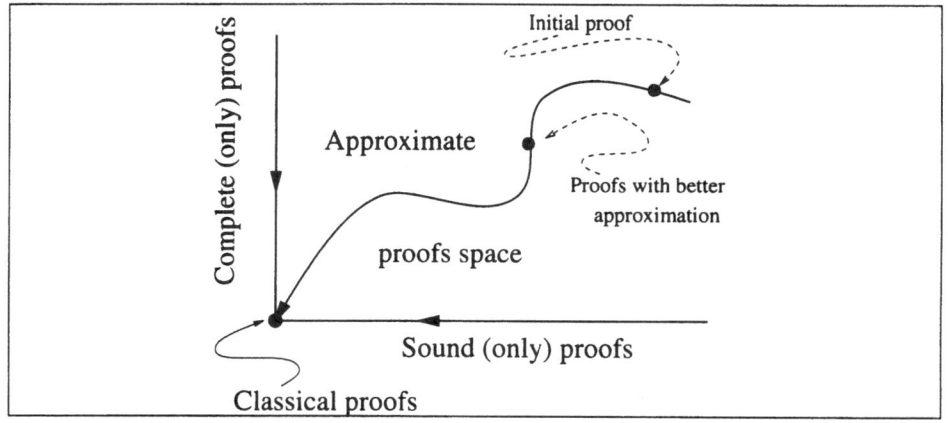

Fig. 1. A Multi-directional Approximate Proofs Space

computationally appealing: approximation should be *more tractable* and it must be possible to use it for an anytime algorithm [20].

The approximating sequent calculus proposed here makes it possible to define multi-directional approximations and can be used to generate a sequence of approximate proof (classical-like) which converge to a classical proof with the performance guarantee required by anytime algorithms[20]. The main idea is to progressively increase the "interesting" (non approximable) elements of a proof.

In what follows, we explain some of the underlying intuitions (§2), introduce some preliminaries (§3) and a sequent calculus for approximate proofs (§4), with a superficial semantics (§5). We show the construction of an anytime deduction procedure (§6) and how other approaches are subsumed (§7).

2 Intuitions

The intuition underlying the sequent calculus we propose is that *not all propositional variables are equal at a first approximation*, developing the ideas and intuition of [4,21] in a proof theoretic setting.

Some atoms describe *interesting* properties and deserve a classical interpretation. They appear in the formulae of an "interesting" (yet approximate) proof or in the truth conditions of a model. Other variables represent *trivial* properties and so are the formula composed with them. They cannot be used for "interesting proofs". Dually other atoms corresponds to *weird* or meaningless properties. They cannot give "interesting models".

For instance suppose that we have a knowledge base representing a circuit [5] where propositional variables of level i are equivalent to a certain formula composed by variables of level $i-1$. We may want to prove a property (a formula) of level i without getting bogged down in the implementation details of level $i-2$, $i-3$, ... 0. Thus, at a first approximation, we may consider the propositional variables of level lower than $i - 1$ as expressing some trivial properties (and so would be the formulae composed only by them) and disregarding them in the search for an approximate proof.

Dually, suppose that we have coded a planning problem into propositional logic and we are looking for a satifiable assignment representing a plan [14]. Again, at a first approximation, we may consider that some properties (and the formulae composed by them) are useless for an interesting plan and therefore regard them as weird: we disregard any model which may require to consider them (i.e. require to give them a truth value).

3 Preliminaries

Propositional formulae, denoted by φ and ψ, are constructed from a set of propositional variables $p \in \mathcal{P}$ with the connectives $\neg$ and $\wedge$. Other connectives are abbreviations e.g. $\varphi \supset \psi \doteq \neg(\varphi \wedge \neg\psi)$. Γ and Δ are sets of formulae. In the sequel by $\mathbf{vars}(\varphi)$ we indicate the set of propositional variables occuring in φ.

Classical logical consequence [23] is denoted by $\Gamma \models \varphi$ and derivability by $\Gamma \vdash \varphi$, while indices represent approximating versions.

Definition 1. A relation $\Gamma \vdash_a \varphi$ is a *sound (complete) approximation* of $\Gamma \models \varphi$ iff for every Γ and φ it is $\Gamma \vdash_a \varphi \Rightarrow \Gamma \models \varphi$ (resp. $\Gamma \nvdash_a \varphi \Rightarrow \Gamma \nmodels \varphi$). It is a *multidirectional* one if the above properties depends[1] on Γ and φ.

The intuition is that sound approximations are reliable for yes answers (theorems) whereas complete approximations for no answers (non-theorems).

We are not interested in simply once-off approximation but rather in an *approximating sequence* (of increasing precision). For instance for sound approximations we expect a sequence of $\vdash_a^k$ such that for some n:

$$\Gamma \vdash_a^0 \varphi \Rightarrow \ldots \Gamma \vdash_a^k \varphi \Rightarrow \Gamma \vdash_a^{k+1} \varphi \ldots \Rightarrow \ldots \Gamma \vdash_a^n \varphi \Leftrightarrow \Gamma \models \varphi$$

Approximating sequences should provide performance guarantee so that any-time deduction algorithms can be constructed [20]: each $\vdash_a^k$ should require at most time $t_k = O(2^{ck})$ for some c. So, if an answer (possibly approximate) is desired in time t, then one could choose a k such that $t_k \leq t < t_{k+1}$.

4 An Approximating Sequent Calculus

We define an *approximating partition* (AP for short) of the propositional variables $\mathcal{P}$ into three disjoint sets I, T and W with the intuitive meaning described in §2. By changing the partition we can change the nature and the precision of our approximation. In the sequel a formula φ_T (resp. φ_W) is *completely trivial (weird)* with respect to an approximating partition iff it is composed only by trivial (weird) variables i.e. $\mathbf{vars}(\varphi_T) \subseteq T$ (resp. $\mathbf{vars}(\varphi_W) \subseteq W$).

---

[1] For multidirectional approximation it is desirable a closure w.r.t. composition with connectives [6] e.g. if it is sound for φ and φ' it should be sound for $\varphi \wedge \varphi'$ or $\neg\varphi$ etc.

$$A_L : \Gamma, \varphi_I, \neg\varphi_I \Longrightarrow \Delta \qquad A_R : \Gamma \Longrightarrow \Delta, \varphi_I, \neg\varphi_I \qquad A_M : \Gamma, \varphi_I \Longrightarrow \Delta, \varphi_I$$

Axioms for interesting formulae $\mathbf{vars}(\varphi_I) \subseteq I$

Connectives elimination rules

$$\neg_L : \frac{\Gamma, \varphi \Longrightarrow \Delta}{\Gamma, \neg\neg\varphi \Longrightarrow \Delta} \qquad\qquad \neg_R : \frac{\Gamma \Longrightarrow \Delta, \varphi}{\Gamma \Longrightarrow \Delta, \neg\neg\varphi}$$

$$\wedge_L : \frac{\Gamma, \varphi, \psi \Longrightarrow \Delta}{\Gamma, \varphi \wedge \psi \Longrightarrow \Delta} \qquad\qquad \wedge_R : \frac{\Gamma \Longrightarrow \Delta, \varphi \qquad \Gamma \Longrightarrow \Delta, \psi}{\Gamma \Longrightarrow \Delta, \varphi \wedge \psi}$$

$$\vee_L : \frac{\Gamma, \neg\varphi \Longrightarrow \Delta \qquad \Gamma, \neg\psi \Longrightarrow \Delta}{\Gamma, \neg(\varphi \wedge \psi) \Longrightarrow \Delta} \qquad \vee_R : \frac{\Gamma \Longrightarrow \Delta, \neg\varphi, \neg\psi}{\Gamma \Longrightarrow \Delta, \neg(\varphi \wedge \psi)}$$

Axiom and deletion for trivial formulae $\mathbf{vars}(\varphi_T) \subseteq T$

$$T_L : \frac{\Gamma \Longrightarrow \Delta}{\Gamma, \varphi_T \Longrightarrow \Delta} \qquad\qquad T_R : \Gamma \Longrightarrow \Delta, \varphi_T$$

Axiom and deletion for weird formulae $\mathbf{vars}(\varphi_W) \subseteq W$

$$W_L : \Gamma, \varphi_W \Longrightarrow \Delta \qquad\qquad W_R : \frac{\Gamma \Longrightarrow \Delta}{\Gamma \Longrightarrow \Delta, \varphi_W}$$

Fig. 2. Approximating Sequence Rules

The sequent calculus for approximating deduction is close, except for the approximation steps, to an *analytic symmetric Gentzen system* [23,24].

Thus, given an *AP*, a *sequent* is a pair $\Gamma \Longrightarrow_{AP} \Delta$ where Γ and Δ are sets of propositional formulae (we may drop *AP* for simplicity), called respectively the antecedent and the succedent. As usual we abbreviate $\Gamma \cup \{\varphi\}$ with Γ, φ.

A *sequent tree* Π is a binary tree where each node is labelled with a sequent and whenever a parent node is labelled with a sequent, its children must be labelled with the sequents resulting from the application of one rule from Fig. 2. The root will be labelled with the goal sequent we are trying to prove. We say that rule A is applied before rule B when the former labels a node closer to the goal sequent i.e. the root of the tree[2].

We do not use structural rules (such as exchange, contraction or weakening) since they are incorporated directly into the set-oriented formalism.

Notice how rules have been substantially divided into three categories:

- axioms for interesting formulae which matches the classical symmetric rules in Gentzen systems [23];
- rules for the elimination of connectives which can be applied irrespectively of the composition of the formulae and which are also classical;
- rules for deleting formulae or extra axioms which involve only completely trivial or weird formulae.

---

[2] In this way the terminology itself mirrors closely the process of proof search where we start from the goal and apply rules until we find a proof or a countermodel.

An *approximate proof* is a sequent tree where each leaf is labelled by an axiom sequent. An *open leaf* is labelled by a non axiom sequent to which no rule can be applied. For instance $\phi_T \Longrightarrow$ is not an open leaf because deletion can still be applied. We refer to open leaves as *approximate counter models* for the root sequent. A *branch* is path from the root to a leaf which we call open if the leaf is open and closed if it is labelled by an axiom.

The extra rules for deleting formulae or the extra axioms are indeed the approximations steps of our proofs. For instance using an "extra" axiom corresponds to an complete-only approximate step: we close a branch even if couldn't close it yet by interesting formulae and thus we may get closer to a "proof".

Notice also that *deletion rules* W_R and T_L are not equivalent to thinning, which is just an unrestricted version of the deletion rules [24,23]. Indeed, if thinning is always applied first during the proof search in classical logic, one may not get a proof (we may delete a formula necessary for the proof) whereas this doesn't happen for W_R and T_L (we state this formally in §6,Thm.6).

The interesting features of the calculus come out with formulae with variables of different nature. As an example consider $\Gamma = \{a, a \supset b, b \supset c, c \supset d\}$ and fix $W = \emptyset$, $I = \{a, b, d\}$ and $T = \{c\}$. Then $\Gamma \Longrightarrow_{AP} b$ and $\Gamma \Longrightarrow_{AP} c \wedge \neg c$, yet $\Gamma \not\Longrightarrow_{AP} d$. Modus ponens does not propagate through trivial formulae: at the stage of approximation defined by the AP, they are not interesting for a proof.

It is important to notice that the choice of a symmetric sequent calculus is not simply a matter of taste. The key observation is that formulae never change side of the sequent during a proof. Many of the following results would not hold without this property and the only way to use rules which allow formulae to change side (e.g. for negation) is to restrict them to interesting formulae.

However, the property of "keeping the sign" is also necessary for intuitionistic or nonmonotonic logics. Thus the system proposed here is robust since it is easily adapted e.g. to circumscription [19].

5   A Superficial Semantics

We modify and extend the various propositional semantics proposed in [7,16,21].

Definition 2. Let $W \cdot I \cdot T$ be an AP, a *superficial interpretation* for $W \cdot I \cdot T$ is any function $\mathcal{I}$ from literals to $\{\top, \bot\}$ such that:

1. $\mathcal{I}(p) \neq \mathcal{I}(\neg p)$ iff $p \in I$;
2. $\mathcal{I}(p) = \mathcal{I}(\neg p) = \top$ iff $p \in T$;
3. $\mathcal{I}(p) = \mathcal{I}(\neg p) = \bot$ iff $p \in W$;

This is *not a multi-valued* logic although it looks like Belnap's 4-valued logic [1] with the extra values "unknown" and "over-constrained", or the multi-valued assignment for non-S variables of the $S - 3$ entailment in [21]. In Belnap, and in any other multi-valued logic, every variable $p \in P$ can assume every value of the domain: $\{\top, \bot, u, o\}$. Here variables in I can only assume values $\top$ or $\bot$; all variables in T are bound to over constrained and cannot assume other values while W variables are fixed as undefined.

We can extend this interpretation to formulae as follows:

$$\mathcal{I}\Vdash l \qquad iff\ \mathcal{I}(l) = \top \text{ for all literals } l = p \text{ or } l = \neg p$$
$$\mathcal{I}\Vdash \neg\neg\varphi \qquad iff\ \mathcal{I}\Vdash\varphi$$
$$\mathcal{I}\Vdash\varphi\wedge\psi \qquad iff\ \mathcal{I}\Vdash\varphi \text{ and } \mathcal{I}\Vdash\psi$$
$$\mathcal{I}\Vdash\neg(\varphi\wedge\psi)\ iff\ \mathcal{I}\Vdash\neg\varphi \text{ or } \mathcal{I}\Vdash\neg\psi$$

If $W = T = \emptyset$ then $\mathcal{I}$ is a classical interpretation and for any φ_I s.t. $\mathbf{vars}(\varphi_I) \subseteq I$ a superficial interpretation is indistinguishable from a classical one. Logical consequence and satisfiability are introduced in the usual way:

Definition 3. Let $W \cdot I \cdot T$ be an AP, a formula φ is *satisfiable* for $W \cdot I \cdot T$ if there is a superficial interpretation $\mathcal{I}$ such that $\mathcal{I}\Vdash\varphi$. It is a *logical consequence* of a set of formulae Γ, i.e. $\Gamma \models_{AP} \varphi$, iff for every superficial interpretation $\mathcal{I}$ if $\mathcal{I}\Vdash\bigwedge\Gamma$ then $\mathcal{I}\Vdash\varphi$.

The model theoretic interpretation of sequents is also standard: a superficial interpretation $\mathcal{I}$ satisfies a sequent $\Gamma \Longrightarrow \Delta$ iff whenever $\mathcal{I}\Vdash\bigwedge\Gamma$ then $\mathcal{I}\Vdash\bigvee\Delta$.

The following properties have a particular role in the definition of the approximate sequent calculus as they are the semantics analogue of the corresponding axioms and deletion properties:

Proposition 4. *Let $W \cdot I \cdot T$ be an AP, then for any interpretation $\mathcal{I}$ and any completely trivial φ_T, weird φ_W, and interesting φ_I it is:*

- $\mathcal{I}\Vdash\varphi_T$ *and* $\mathcal{I}\Vdash\neg\varphi_T$
- $\mathcal{I}\not\Vdash\varphi_W$ *and* $\mathcal{I}\not\Vdash\neg\varphi_W$
- $\mathcal{I}\Vdash\neg\varphi_I$ *iff* $\mathcal{I}\not\Vdash\varphi_I$.

The soundness and completeness of the calculus with respect to the approximate semantics can be easily established by using proposition 4:

Theorem 5. *Let $W \cdot I \cdot T$ be an AP, then $\Gamma \Longrightarrow_{AP} \varphi$ is provable iff $\Gamma \models_{AP} \varphi$.*

A counter model for the root sequent can be built from an open leaf by setting all literals in Γ to $\top$ and those in Δ to $\bot$.

6 Anytime (Approximate) Deduction

It is well known that the time and size complexity of a sequent proof is worst case exponential in the size of the root sequent [25]. So we can gain from this machinery only if we can

1. discard more formulae than classical proof search will do;
2. anticipate the finding of "classical" proof (or countermodel);
3. arrange the above two steps into an anytime algorithm.

The first property, which also shows that deletion is different from thinning is guaranteed by the following theorem:

Theorem 6. *If $\Gamma \Longrightarrow_{AP} \Delta$ has an approximate proof then it has an approximate proof where deletion rules are the only rules used to reduce weird and trivial formulae. other rules.*

In alternative to deletion we may simply postpone the reduction of the main connective of the corresponding weird or trivial formula and consider as open leaves those where the only unreduced formulae are either weird (in the succedent) or trivial (in the antecedent).

To "anticipate" classical proofs we use the following properties:

Proposition 7. *If $\Gamma \Longrightarrow_{AP} \Delta$ has an approximate sequent proof Π where all leaves are labelled by axioms for interesting formulae then Π is a classical proof.*

Proposition 8. *If $\Gamma \Longrightarrow_{AP} \Delta$ has an approximate sequent tree Π with a path from the root to an open leaf without application of deletion rules then the leaf is a classical counter model.*

Hence, if a branch is closed by an axiom for interesting formulae we can discard it. It is valid for classical proofs and it is of no use for classical counter models. So the *active frontier* of the approximate proof (the part we must store and eventually revise for better approximations) is only made by closures due to axioms for non interesting formulae (rules W_L, T_R) or, for open branches, by the application of deletion (rules W_R, T_L).

We have now the formal machinery to construct an approximating sequence of proofs of increasing precision as in Fig. 1. To decide whether $\Gamma \vdash \varphi$

1. start with an AP choosing W_0, I_0, T_0 so that the set of interesting variables I_0 is small (e.g. logarithmic in the size of Γ and φ);
2. derive an approximate sequent proof Π_k (or counter model) exploiting the trivial/weird axioms and rules to close as many branches as possible or discard as many formulae as possible;
3. if the approximate proof (counter model) is also a classical one then stop;
4. else (if we still have time) change the AP and enlarge I_k to I_{k+1}, visit only the part of Π_k where trivial/weird axioms and rules have been applied since they may no longer be "valid rules", and go to (2) for a new Π_{k+1};

If we time out after Π_k, we have available either an approximate proof (all branches of Π_k are closed) or an approximate counter model (an open leaf of Π_k). On the contrary, with sufficient resources we can always arrive at $I = \mathcal{P}$ and thus derive exactly a classical sequent tree.

Notice that we always re-use older proofs since after (4) we still have an "almost everywhere" correct labeling: the search must continue only where $W_{L,R}$ or $T_{L,R}$ rules have been applied.

From the viewpoint of the computational complexity we can check in polynomial time if a formula is completely weird, trivial or interesting and do *not need branching* for $\wedge, \vee$ of trivial or weird formulae: rather we use deletion rules to delete them (Thm. 6) or the corresponding axioms to close the branch.

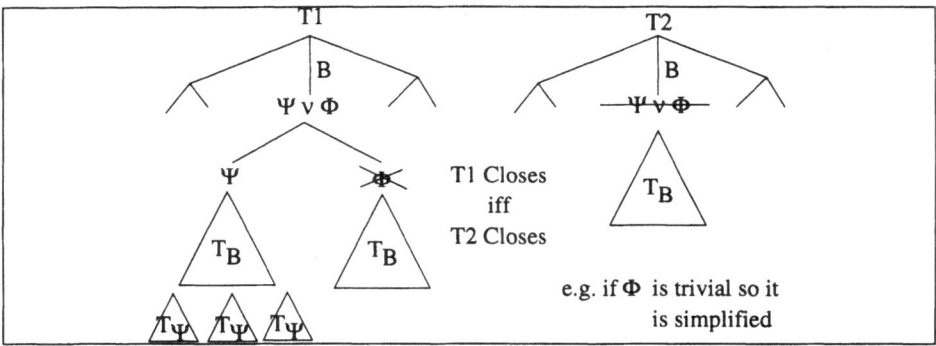

Fig. 3. Cutting the Search Space

A further gain is obtained by *look ahead branch subsumption* as sketched in Fig. 3, where Φ is deleted due to some weird/trivial deletion rule.

Thus one can prove that for an AP *the proof search is (worst case) exponential only in the size*[3] *of interesting formulae*. This means that the cost of finding Π_k is exponential in size the interesting part (according I_k) of $\Gamma \Longrightarrow_{AP_k} \varphi$ while Π_{k+1} is exponential in the size of the I_{k+1} part. If I_0 is logarithmic in the size of the sequent, the first steps will be polynomial and afterwards we have the desired anytime approximating algorithm.

For theoremhood, $\Longrightarrow \varphi$, an approximating sequence of only sound (only complete) proofs is given by setting $T \doteq \emptyset$ (resp. $W \doteq \emptyset$) and progressively increasing I and decreasing W (resp. T).

For logical consequence (usually $|\Gamma| \gg |\varphi|$), an approximating sequence of sound (complete) proofs is built by initializing $\mathbf{vars}(\varphi) \subseteq I$ and $W \doteq \emptyset$ (resp. $T \doteq \emptyset$). Subsequently we can increase I and decrease T (resp. W).

7 Incorporating Other Systems

For the comparison with other systems we restrict our general framework to the clausal normal form (CNF) used in [21,7,6]. Therefore in the sequel we assume that Γ is a set of clauses and $\Delta = \{\varphi\}$ where φ is a clause.

In [21] two approximate entailments are defined, $\models_S^3$ and $\models_S^1$, where S is a set of "interesting" variables. The first corresponds to a sound approximation whereas the second is a complete one. $S - 1$ entailment corresponds to our superficial entailment when all variables not in S are weird. To define $S - 3$ entailment we need to change the definition of interpretation so that not interesting variables are interpreted with Levesque's 3-valued logic [15] which is close to Belnap's relevance logic [1]. Thus an $S - 3$ interpretation $\mathcal{I}_S^3$ maps all interesting literals as a classical interpretation whereas for not interesting literals p, $\neg p$ we

---

[3] Note that in tree-like analytic sequent calculi as the one designed here we must count each occurrence as a distinct formula [25].

have simply the constraints that at least one of $\mathcal{I}_S^3(p) \neq \perp$ or $\mathcal{I}_S^3(\neg p) \neq \perp$ (see [21] for details). In a nutshell, with $S - 3$ entailment not interesting variables can either have a classical interpretation or the same interpretation of trivial variables in a superficial interpretation.

The equivalence with our system is described by the following properties:

Theorem 9. *For every Γ, φ in CNF and set $S \subseteq \mathcal{P}$, the AP_1 with $T \doteq \emptyset$ and $I \doteq S$ is such that $\Gamma \models_S^1 \varphi$. iff $\Gamma \Longrightarrow_{AP_1} \varphi$ is provable.*

Theorem 10. *For every Γ, φ in CNF and set $S \subseteq \mathcal{P}$, the AP_3 with $W \doteq \emptyset$ and $I \doteq S \cup \mathbf{vars}(\varphi)$ is such that $\Gamma \models_S^3 \varphi$ iff $\Gamma \Longrightarrow_{AP_3} \varphi$ is provable.*

To prove this theorem we use a result in [21, Lemma 5.2], i.e. $\Gamma \models_S^3 \varphi$ if and only if $\Gamma \models_{S'}^3 \varphi$ where $S' = \mathbf{vars}(\varphi) \cup S$, and then prove the equivalence between AP_3 and the new $\models_{S'}^3$.

Notice the asymmetry between $S-1$ and $S-3$ entailment. Indeed Theorem 10 does not hold if φ is an arbitrary formula (but then $S - 3$ entailment is not tractable anymore [21]).

The family $\Gamma \vdash_{BCP}^k \varphi$ of sound approximate reasoners [7] applies boolean constraints propagation (BCP), a variant of unit resolution, as a basic tractable inference and subsequently uses cut on clauses of increasing size $k = 1, 2 \ldots$ [6,7]. So if φ_k is a clause with *at most* k literals we have the following rules:

$$BCP : \frac{\Gamma \vdash_{BCP} \varphi}{\Gamma \vdash_{BCP}^k \varphi} \qquad k - cut : \frac{\Gamma \vdash_{BCP}^k \varphi_k \qquad \Gamma, \varphi_k \vdash_{BCP}^k \psi}{\Gamma \vdash_{BCP}^k \psi}$$

Since unit resolution is easily translated into an analytic sequent proof, the transformation of a $\vdash_{BCP}^k$ derivation into an approximate proof is simply an application of cut-elimination [24,23]. The AP is then chosen by setting $W \doteq \emptyset$ and I as the set of variables such that the relative literals occurs along the branches corresponding to unit resolution. Dually, for non valid formulae, take for I the literals occurring in the equivalents classes defined by $\vdash_{BCP}^k$ in [7].

Beside this easy equivalence, it is also possible a more interesting construction which (i) is independent from the particular $\vdash_{BCP}^k$ derivation of φ from Γ and, especially, (ii) gives us an example of a possible construction of the I_k sets in the anytime algorithm described in §6.

$$I_k^{(0)} = \mathbf{vars}(\varphi)$$
$$I_k^{(n+1)} = I_k^{(n)} \cup \{\mathbf{vars}(\psi) \mid \psi \in \Gamma \text{ and } |\mathbf{vars}(\psi) \setminus I_k^{(n)}| \leq k + 1\}$$
$$I_k = \cup_n I_k^{(n)}$$

Once I_k is computed we do not need to restart from scratch and can simply put $I_{k+1}^{(0)} = I_k$. The preliminary computation of I_k is polynomial in $|\Gamma \cup \{\varphi\}|$.

Theorem 11. *For every Γ, φ in CNF and integer k, the AP_k with $W \doteq \emptyset$ and $I \doteq I_k$ is such that $\Gamma \vdash_{BCP}^k \varphi$ implies $\Gamma \Longrightarrow_{AP_k} \varphi$ is provable.*

8 Conclusions

This paper proposes a logical calculus and a semantics for approximating classical deduction by faster and semantically grounded approximations. It based on the idea of developing a sequence of approximate proofs which converge to a classical proof with the performance of anytime algorithms.

It provides sound, complete or multidirectional approximations and subsumes previous families of approximate reasoners [7,21]. It can be also used as an interactive system for computationally sound proofs [17]: the verifier chooses the "interesting variables" and asks the prover for an approximate proof.

This approach can be directly extended to tableaux for circumscription [19] or modal and first order logic (the extension of weird predicates, and their negation, is empty while trivial ones hold for the whole universe). An different approximation is possible where objects can be impossible or interesting.

However the key question is whether we should accept the idea of trading accuracy for speed in the case of proofs. This could be the case for deductive planning in reactive systems and also for formal verification, where approximate but quick proof can be useful for the design and prototyping phase.

Acknowledgements

I would like to thank L. Carlucci Aiello, F. Pirri and M. Schaerf and an anonymous referee for many useful suggestions. Part of this work has been done while the author was visiting the Computer Laboratory at the University of Cambridge (UK). This work has been partly supported by ASI, CNR and MURST grants.

References

1. A. Anderson and N. Belnap. *Entailment: the Logic of Relevance and Necessity.* Princeton University Press, Princeton, NJ, 1975.
2. G. Ausiello, P. Crescenzi, and M. Protasi. Approximate solution of NP optimization problems. *Theor. Comp. Sci.*, 150(1):1–55, 1995.
3. S. Bellantoni, T. Pitassi, and A. Urquhart. Approximation and small-depth frege proofs. *SIAM J. of Computing*, 21(6):1161–1179, 1992.
4. M. Cadoli. *Tractable Reasoning in Artificial Intelligence*, volume 941 of *Lecture Notes in Artificial Intelligence*. Springer-Verlag, 1995.
5. L. J. Claesen, editor. *Formal VLSI Correctness Verification: VLSI Design Methods*, volume II. Elsevier Sci. Publishers (North-Holland), Amsterdam, 1990.
6. M. Dalal. Anytime families of tractable propositional reasoners. In *International Symposium on Artificial Intelligence and Mathematics AI/MATH-96*, pages 42–45, 1996. Extended version submitted to Annals of Mathematics and Artificial Intelligence.
7. M. Dalal. Semantics of an anytime family of reasoners. In *Proc. of the 12th Eur. Conf. on Artificial Intelligence (ECAI-96)*, pages 360–364. John Wiley & Sons, 1996.

8. M. Dalal and D. W. Etherington. Tractable approximate deduction using limited vocabularies. In *Proceeding of the 9th Canadian Conference on Artificial Intelligence (AI-92)*, pages 206–221, 1992.

9. N. J. Fisher and R. E. Ladner. Propositional dynamic logic of regular programs. *J. of Comp. and System Sci.*, 18:194–211, 1979.

10. R. Hähnle. *Automated Deduction in Multiple-Valued Logics*, volume 10 of *International Series of Monographs on Computer Science*. Oxford University Press, 1994.

11. J. Y. Halpern and Y. Moses. A guide to completeness and complexity for modal logics of knowledge and belief. *Artificial Intelligence*, 54:319–379, 1992.

12. J. Y. Halpern and M. Y. Vardi. Model checking vs. theorem proving: A manifesto. In J. Allen, R. Fikes, and E. Sandewall, editors, *Proc. of the 2nd Int. Conf. on the Principles of Knowledge Representation and Reasoning (KR-91)*, 1991.

13. D. S. Johnson and M. R. Garey. *Computers and Inctractability: A Guide to the Theory of NP-Completeness*. Freeman, S. Francisco, 1979.

14. H. Kautz and B. Selman. Planning as satisfiability. In *Proc. of the 10th Eur. Conf. on Artificial Intelligence (ECAI-92)*, pages 359–363. John Wiley & Sons, 1992.

15. H. J. Levesque. A logic of implicit and explicit belief. In *Proc. of the 4th Nat. Conf. on Artificial Intelligence (AAAI-84)*, pages 198–202, 1984.

16. H. J. Levesque. Logic and the complexity of reasoning. *J. of Philosophical Logic*, 17:355–389, 1988.

17. S. Micali. CS proofs (extended abstract). In *Proc. of the 35th Annual Symp. on the Found. of Comp. Sci. (FOCS-94)*, pages 436–453. IEEE Comp. Society Press, 1994.

18. D. Mundici. Satisfiability in many-valued sentential logic is NP-complete. *Theor. Comp. Sci.*, 52(1-2):145–153, 1987.

19. N. Olivetti. Tableaux and sequent calculus for minimal entailment. *J. of Automated Reasoning*, 9:99–139, 1992.

20. S. Russel and S. Zilberstein. Composing real-time systems. In *Proc. of the 12th Int. Joint Conf. on Artificial Intelligence (IJCAI-91)*, pages 212–217, 1991.

21. M. Schaerf and M. Cadoli. Tractable reasoning via approximation. *Artificial Intelligence*, 74:1–62, 1995.

22. B. Selman and H. Kautz. Knowlege compilation and theory approximation. *J. of the ACM*, 43(2):193–224, 1996.

23. R. M. Smullyan. *First Order Logic*. Springer-Verlag, 1968. Republished by Dover, New York, in 1995.

24. M. Szabo, editor. *The collected papers of G. Gentzen*. North-Holland Publ. Co., Amsterdam, Amsterdam, 1969.

25. A. Urquhart. The complexity of propositional proofs. *The Bulletin of Symbolic Logic*, 1(4):425–467, Dec 1995.

26. H. Wang. Towards mechanical mathematics. *IBM Journal for Research and Development*, 4:2–22, 1960.

27. M. Ying. A logic for approximate reasoning. *J. of Symbolic Logic*, 59(3):830–837, 1994.

Embedding Minimal Knowledge
into Autoepistemic Logic

Riccardo Rosati

Dipartimento di Informatica e Sistemistica
Università di Roma "La Sapienza"
Via Salaria 113, 00198 Roma, Italy
rosati@dis.uniroma1.it

Abstract. We investigate the epistemological properties of *MKNF*, Lifschitz's logic of minimal knowledge and negation as failure. In particular, we show that the expressive power of *MKNF* is equivalent to Moore's autoepistemic logic (*AEL*), by defining an embedding of *MKNF* into *AEL* and vice versa. We also prove that the negation as failure modality *not* of *MKNF* exactly corresponds to the negative introspection operator in *AEL*. The two previous results imply that *MKNF*'s minimal knowledge modality *K* can be represented by means of negation as failure *not*, i.e. *MKNF* theories admit an equivalent representation in terms of unimodal theories using the *not* operator only. This in turn implies that negation as failure is "more expressive" than minimal knowledge.

1 Introduction

Research in the formalization of commonsense reasoning has pointed out the need of formalizing agents able to reason introspectively about their own knowledge and ignorance (see e.g. [Moore, 1985]). Modal epistemic logics have thus been proposed, in which the modalities are interpreted in terms of knowledge/belief. Generally speaking, the conclusions an introspective agent is able to draw depend on both what she knows and what she *does not* know. Hence, any such conclusion may be retracted when new facts are added to the agent's knowledge, i.e. when the agent's ignorance decreases. For this reason, many *nonmonotonic* modal formalisms have been proposed in order to characterize the reasoning abilities of an introspective agent.

Among the nonmonotonic modal logics proposed in the literature, Lifschitz's logic of minimal knowledge and negation as failure (*MKNF*) [Lifschitz, 1991, Lifschitz, 1994] is one of the most studied formalisms [Chen, 1994, Bochman, 1995, Beringer & Schaub, 1993]. *MKNF* is a bimodal logic, with a "minimal knowledge" operator *K* and a "negation as failure" (or "negation by default") operator *not*. In particular, the modality *K* coincides with the epistemic operator of the modal logic defined by Halpern and Moses in [Halpern & Moses, 1985] (also known as ground nonmonotonic modal logic $S5_G$ [Donini, Nardi, & Rosati, 1997b]), which modifies modal logic S5 through a very intuitive preference semantics [Shoham, 1987]: consider only the models of the knowledge base (i.e.

the epistemic states of the agent modeled) in which the knowledge on the objective facts is minimal (i.e. the ignorance of the agent is maximal). The operator *not* can be considered as a generalization of the negation as failure operator in logic programs interpreted under the stable model semantics (see e.g. [Inoue & Sakama, 1994]).

The logic *MKNF* is generally considered a unifying framework for nonmonotonic reasoning, due to its ability of isomorphically containing all the most studied nonmonotonic formalisms, such as default logic, autoepistemic logic, circumscription, and (disjunctive) logic programs with negation as failure. For this reason it is also considered a very expressive formalism.

Recently, *MKNF* has also been regarded as a suitable knowledge representation formalism, since the combined usage of its modalities allows for the formalization of several nonmonotonic features of frame-based systems [Donini, Nardi, & Rosati, 1997b]. As a consequence, the computational properties of *MKNF* have been investigated. It has been proven [Rosati, 1997] that reasoning in propositional *MKNF* is harder than reasoning in all the best known propositional nonmonotonic logics. In particular, it has been shown that such an higher degree of complexity is due to the presence of the minimal knowledge operator K, which adds more complexity to the deduction problem than the modality *not*. Hence, minimal knowledge in *MKNF* is computationally harder than negation as failure.

In this paper we investigate the relative expressive power of the modalities K and *not* of *MKNF*. First, we prove that the negation as failure modality *not* of *MKNF* exactly corresponds to negative introspection in Moore's autoepistemic logic *AEL*, which allows for a straightforward embedding of *AEL* into *MKNF*. Then, we show that the expressive power of *MKNF* is equivalent to that of *AEL*, by defining an embedding of *MKNF* into *AEL*. This result can also be viewed as a generalization of previous results concerning the problem of expressing default theories in autoepistemic logic [Gottlob, 1995, Schwarz, 1996].

The two above results imply that the minimal knowledge modality K can be represented in terms of negation as failure *not*, since *MKNF* theories can be expressed in terms of unimodal theories using the *not* operator only. Notably, the converse does not hold, i.e. theories with occurrences of *not* cannot in general be represented by theories using the modality K only: hence, negation as failure is "more expressive" than minimal knowledge. This result appears in contrast with the computational properties mentioned above: however, the higher degree of complexity of the minimal knowledge operator is due to its ability of expressing information in "compact" form, as shown in [Rosati, 1996].

In the following, we first briefly recall the logic *MKNF*. In Section 3 we study the problem of embedding autoepistemic logic into *MKNF*, showing that the negation as failure operator *not* of *MKNF* exactly corresponds to the negated modality of autoepistemic logic. Then, in Section 4 we study the problem of embedding *MKNF* theories into autoepistemic logic. We finally draw some concluding remarks in Section 5.

2 Preliminaries

In this section we briefly recall the logic *MKNF* [Lifschitz, 1994] and Moore's autoepistemic logic [Moore, 1985]. We assume that the reader is familiar with the basics of modal logic [Hughes & Cresswell, 1968].

We use $\mathcal{L}$ to denote a fixed propositional language built in the usual way from an alphabet $\mathcal{A}$ of propositional symbols (atoms) and the propositional connectives $\vee, \wedge, \neg, \supset$. We denote with $\mathcal{L}_M$ the modal extension of $\mathcal{L}$ with the modalities K and *not*. Moreover, we denote with $\mathcal{L}_M^1$ the set of *flat MKNF* formulas, that is the set of formulas from $\mathcal{L}_M$ in which each propositional symbol appears in the scope of exactly one modality, with $\mathcal{L}_K$ the set of formulas from $\mathcal{L}_M$ in which the modality *not* does not occur (called *positive* formulas), and with $\mathcal{L}_N$ the set of formulas from $\mathcal{L}_M$ in which K does not occur (called *negative* formulas).

We now recall the notion of *MKNF* model. An *interpretation* is a set of propositional symbols. Satisfiability of a formula in a structure (I, M_k, M_n), where I is an interpretation and M_k, M_n are sets of interpretations (worlds), is defined inductively as follows:

1. if φ is an atom, φ is true in (I, M_k, M_n) iff $\varphi \in I$;

2. $\neg\varphi$ is true in (I, M_k, M_n) iff φ is not true in (I, M_k, M_n);

3. $\varphi_1 \wedge \varphi_2$ is true in (I, M_k, M_n) iff φ_1 is true in (I, M_k, M_n) and φ_2 is true in (I, M_k, M_n);

4. $K\varphi$ is true in (I, M_k, M_n) iff, for every $J \in M_k$, φ is true in (J, M_k, M_n);

5. *not* φ is true in (I, M_k, M_n) iff there exists $J \in M_n$ such that φ is not true in (J, M_k, M_n).

Given a pair (M_k, M_n) of sets of interpretations, and a formula $\varphi \in \mathcal{L}_M$, we write $(M_k, M_n) \models \varphi$ iff for each $I \in M_k$, φ is true in (I, M_k, M_n).

Definition 1. A set of interpretations M, where $M \neq \emptyset$, is an *MKNF model* of a theory $\Sigma \subseteq \mathcal{L}_M$ iff each formula φ from Σ is such that $(M, M) \models \varphi$ and, for each set of interpretations M', if $M' \supset M$ then at least one formula from Σ is such that $(M', M) \not\models \varphi$.

We say that a formula φ is entailed by Σ in *MKNF* (and write $\Sigma \models_{MKNF} \varphi$) iff φ is true in every *MKNF* model of Σ.

E.g., let $\Sigma = \{Kp\}$. The only *MKNF* model for Σ is $M = \{J : J \models p\}$. Hence, $\Sigma \models_{MKNF} Kp$, and $\Sigma \models_{MKNF} \neg K\varphi$ for each $\varphi \in \mathcal{L}$ such that $\not\models p \supset \varphi$. Therefore, the agent modeled by Σ has minimal knowledge, in the sense that she only knows p and the objective facts logically implied by p. Also, let $\Sigma = \{notp \supset q\}$. It is easy to see that the only *MKNF* model for Σ is $M = \{J : J \models q\}$, since $\neg p$ can be "assumed by default" by the agent modeled by Σ, which is then able to conclude q.

We finally briefly recall Moore's autoepistemic logic (*AEL*). In order to keep notation to a minimum, we change the language of *AEL*, using the modality K instead of L. Thus, in the following a formula of *AEL* is a formula from $\mathcal{L}_K$.

Definition 2. A consistent set of formulae T from $\mathcal{L}_K$ is a *stable expansion* for a set of initial knowledge $\Sigma \subseteq \mathcal{L}_K$ if T satisfies the following equation:

$$T = Cn_{\mathsf{KD45}}(\Sigma \cup \{\neg K\varphi \mid \varphi \notin T\})$$

where Cn_{KD45} is the logical consequence operator of modal logic **KD45**.

Given a theory $\Sigma \subseteq \mathcal{L}_K$ and a formula $\varphi \in \mathcal{L}_K$, $\Sigma \models_{AEL} \varphi$ iff φ belongs to all the stable expansions of Σ.

Notably, each stable expansion T is a *stable set*, i.e. (i) T is closed under propositional consequence; (ii) if $\varphi \in T$ then $K\varphi \in T$; (iii) if $\varphi \notin T$ then $\neg K\varphi \in T$. We recall that each stable set S corresponds to a *maximal* universal S5 model $\mathcal{M}_S$ such that S is the set of formulas satisfied by $\mathcal{M}_S$ (see e.g. [Marek & Truszczyński, 1993]).

With the term *AEL model* for Σ we will refer to an S5 model whose set of theorems corresponds to a stable expansion for Σ in *AEL*: without loss of generality, we will identify such a model with the set of interpretations it contains. We will also denote with $\langle J, M \rangle$ a KD45 model whose initial world is associated with the interpretation J and whose final S5 cluster contains the interpretations in M.

Finally, notice that, as in e.g. [Marek & Truszczyński, 1993], we have adopted the notion of *consistent* autoepistemic logic, i.e. we do not allow the inconsistent theory consisting of all modal formulas to be a (possible) stable expansion. The results we present can be easily extended to this case (corresponding to Moore's original proposal): however, this requires to change the semantics of *MKNF*, allowing the empty set of interpretatons to be a possible model in *MKNF*.

3 Embedding autoepistemic logic into *MKNF*

In this section we study the problem of embedding *AEL* into *MKNF*. In the following, we use the term *embedding* (or translation) to indicate a transformation function for modal theories. Following [Gottlob, 1995, Schwarz, 1996], we are interested in finding *faithful* embeddings, in the following sense. Let S_1, S_2 be modal logics among *MKNF*, *AEL*. Then, τ is a faithful embedding of S_1 into S_2 if, for each modal theory Σ and for each model $\mathcal{M}$, $\mathcal{M}$ is an S_1 model for Σ iff $\mathcal{M}$ is an S_2 model for $\tau(\Sigma)$.

It is already known that *AEL* theories can be embedded into *MKNF* theories. In particular, it has been proven [Lin & Shoham, 1992, Schwarz & Truszczyński, 1994] that *AEL* theories with no nested occurrences of K (called *flat* theories) can be embedded into *MKNF*. And since in *AEL* any theory can be transformed into an equivalent flat theory (which has in general size exponential in the size of the initial theory), it follows that any *AEL* theory can be embedded into *MKNF*.

However, in the following we prove a much stronger result: negation as failure in *MKNF* *exactly* corresponds to negative introspection in *AEL*, i.e. *AEL*'s modality $\neg K$ and *MKNF*'s modality *not* are semantically equivalent. Hence, such a correspondence is not only limited to modal theories without nested modalities, and induces a polynomial-time embedding of *any* *AEL* theory into *MKNF*.

We first define the translation $\tau_M(\cdot)$ of modal theories from *AEL* to *MKNF* theories.

Definition 3. Let $\varphi \in \mathcal{L}_K$. Then, $\tau_M(\varphi)$ is the *MKNF* formula obtained from φ by substituting each occurrence of K with $\neg not$. Moreover, if $\Sigma \subseteq \mathcal{L}_K$, then $\tau_M(\Sigma)$ denotes the *MKNF* theory $\{\tau_M(\varphi) | \varphi \in \Sigma\}$.

We now show that the translation $\tau_M(\cdot)$ embeds *AEL* theories into *MKNF*.

To this aim, we exploit the semantic characterization of *AEL* defined in [Schwarz, 1992]. Roughly speaking, according to such a possible-world semantics, an *AEL* model for Σ is an **S5** model M satisfying Σ such that, for any interpretation J not contained in M, the **KD45** model obtained by "concatenating" J with M (i.e., each world in M is accessible from J while J is not accessible from any world in M) does not satisfy Σ. Formally:

Lemma 4. Let $\Sigma \subseteq \mathcal{L}_K$. Then, M is an AEL model for Σ iff $M \models \Sigma$ and, for each interpretation $J \notin M$, the **KD45** model $\langle J, M \rangle$ is such that $\langle J, M \rangle \not\models \Sigma$.

Based on the previous property, we prove the following theorem.

Theorem 5. Let $\Sigma \subseteq \mathcal{L}_K$. Then, M is an AEL model for Σ iff M is an MKNF model of $\tau_M(\Sigma)$.

Sketch of the proof. We first prove that, in the case of negative theories, the possible-world semantics for *MKNF* (defined in Section 2) is equivalent to a semantics which restricts the first set of interpretations M_k (in which the modality K is interpreted) to a *single* interpretation, since the only formulas interpreted in M_k in the evaluation of Σ are the propositional subformulas from Σ which are not within the scope of a *not*: hence, in the case of negative theories, there exists a set $M' \supset M$ such that $(M', M) \models \Sigma$ iff there exists a single interpretation $J \notin M$ such that $(\{J\}, M) \models \Sigma$.

Then, it is easy to see that the above property together with Lemma 4 imply the exact correspondence between the semantic characterizations of *MKNF* and *AEL*, which in turn implies the theorem. □

The previous theorem implies that the modality *not* has in *MKNF* the *same interpretation* of the modal operator of autoepistemic logic. This property extends previous results relating *MKNF* with *AEL* [Lin & Shoham, 1992, Lifschitz & Schwarz, 1993, Chen, 1994], and has several consequences both in the logic programming framework and in nonmonotonic reasoning. In particular, since *MKNF* generalizes the stable model semantics for logic programs [Gelfond & Lifschitz, 1988], the above result strengthens the idea that *AEL* is the *true* logic of negation as failure (as interpreted according to the stable model semantics). Moreover, positive theories have the same interpretation both in *MKNF* and in Halpern and Moses's logic of minimal knowledge [Halpern & Moses, 1985], also known as ground nonmonotonic modal logic $S5_G$ [Donini, Nardi, & Rosati, 1997b]; consequently, the logic *MKNF* can be interpreted as the exact composition of two nonmonotonic modal formalisms: Halpern and Moses's $S5_G$ and Moore's *AEL*.

4   Embedding *MKNF* into autoepistemic logic

We start by recalling the *MKNF-normal form* $\mathcal{NF}_{MBNF}(\varphi)$ of a formula $\varphi \in \mathcal{L}_M$, which is a formula from $\mathcal{L}_M^1$ in conjunctive normal form. Such a formula is obtained from $K\varphi$ by exhaustively eliminating nested occurrences of the modalities, which is based (i) on the following equivalences in *MKNF*:

$$KK\varphi \equiv K\varphi \quad not\, K\varphi \equiv \neg K\varphi$$
$$K\neg K\varphi \equiv \neg K\varphi \quad not\, \neg K\varphi \equiv K\varphi$$
$$K\, not\, \varphi \equiv not\, \varphi \quad not\, not\, \varphi \equiv \neg not\, \varphi$$
$$K\neg not\, \varphi \equiv \neg not\, \varphi \quad not\, \neg not\, \varphi \equiv not\, \varphi$$

and (ii) on the fact that both modalities can always be distributed inside a formula in which there is at least one occurrence of a modality. We do not report the detailed transformation: to our purposes, it suffices to recall that for each $\varphi \in \mathcal{L}_M$ the formula $\mathcal{NF}_{MBNF}(\varphi) \in \mathcal{L}_M^1$ has the following form [Chen, 1994]:

$$\mathcal{NF}_{MBNF}(\varphi) = \bigwedge_{j=1}^{l} C_j$$

where

$$C_j = \neg K\psi_0^j \vee not\, \psi_1^j \vee \neg not\, \xi_1^j \vee \ldots \vee \neg not\, \xi_{m_j}^j \vee K\varphi_1^j \vee \ldots \vee K\varphi_{n_j}^j$$

in which all φ_i^j's, ψ_i^j's, and ξ_i^j's are formulas from $\mathcal{L}$.

Notice that in general $\mathcal{NF}_{MBNF}(\varphi)$ has size exponential wrt the size of φ, which is informally due to the fact that, in order to transform a modal formula of the form $K\varphi$, it is in general necessary to put φ in a conjunctive normal form. The formulas φ and $\mathcal{NF}_{MBNF}(\varphi)$ are equivalent, in the sense that the set of *MKNF* models of φ coincides with the set of *MKNF* models of $\mathcal{NF}_{MBNF}(\varphi)$.

In the rest of the section we deal with finite *MKNF* theories, hence we restrict our attention to single *MKNF* formulas (and interpret a finite theory as the formula corresponding to the conjunction of all the formulas belonging to the theory).

We now define a translation function which transforms an *MKNF* formula φ into an *AEL* formula. In the following, we assume that the finite set of propositional variables appearing in φ is $p_1, \ldots, p_m$. We also denote with $\varphi(p^i)$ the result of the substitution of the new variables $p_1^i, \ldots, p_m^i$ for the variables $p_1, \ldots, p_m$ in φ.

Definition 6. Let

$$C_j = \neg K\psi_0^j \vee not\ \psi_1^j \vee \neg not\ \xi_1^j \vee \ldots \vee \neg not\ \xi_{m_j}^j \vee K\varphi_1^j \vee \ldots \vee K\varphi_{n_j}^j$$

in which all φ_i^j's, ψ_i^j's, and ξ_i^j's are formulas from $\mathcal{L}$. Then,

$$\tau'(C_j) = \neg(K\psi_0^j \wedge \psi_0^j) \vee \neg K\psi_1^j \vee K\xi_1^j \vee \ldots \vee K\xi_{m_j}^j \vee$$
$$(K\varphi_1^j \wedge \varphi_1^j) \vee \ldots \vee (K\varphi_{n_j}^j \wedge \varphi_{n_j}^j)$$

Definition 7. Let $\varphi \in \mathcal{L}_M$, and let $\mathcal{NF}_{MBNF}(\varphi) = \bigwedge_{j=1}^{l} C_j$, where

$$C_j = \neg K\psi_0^j \vee not\ \psi_1^j \vee \neg not\ \xi_1^j \vee \ldots \vee \neg not\ \xi_{m_j}^j \vee K\varphi_1^j \vee \ldots \vee K\varphi_{n_j}^j$$

Then, $\tau_{AEL}(\varphi) = \bigwedge_{i=1}^{l} \tau_{AEL}(C_j)$, where

$$\tau_{AEL}(C_j) = \neg(K\psi_0^j \wedge \psi_0^j \wedge (\bigwedge_{i=1}^{l} \psi_0^j(p^i))) \vee \neg K\psi_1^j \vee K\xi_1^j \vee \ldots \vee K\xi_{m_j}^j \vee$$
$$(K\varphi_1^j \wedge \varphi_1^j \wedge (\bigwedge_{i=1}^{l} \varphi_1^j(p^i))) \vee \ldots \vee (K\varphi_{n_j}^j \wedge \varphi_{n_j}^j \wedge (\bigwedge_{i=1}^{l} \varphi_{n_j}^j(p^i)))$$
$$\vee \tau'(C_j)$$

The translation $\tau_{AEL}(\cdot)$ is a generalization of Schwarz's embedding of default logic into AEL [Schwarz, 1996]. The ideas underlying such a translation can be roughly explained as follows:

- as shown in the previous section, it is easy to translate the modality *not* in AEL, hence the disjuncts *not* ψ_1^j, *not* ξ_i^j are translated by simply converting each *not* into $\neg K$;

- the modality K is interpreted as knowledge in *MKNF*, whereas it is interpreted as belief in AEL: in particular, the modal axiom schema T (i.e., $K\varphi \supset \varphi$) is not valid in AEL. This implies e.g. in the translation of a conjunct $K\varphi_i^j$, that the objective formula φ_i^j must be explicitly added in conjunction with $K\varphi_i^j$. However, as discussed in [Schwarz, 1996], in general this is not enough to guarantee a faithful embedding, and it is necessary to use a set of new, auxiliary variables

$$\bigcup_{i=1,\ldots,l} \bigcup_{j=1,\ldots,m} p_j^i,$$

i.e. we create one copy of the set of the initial variables $p_1, \ldots, p_m$ for each conjunct C_j appearing in the normal form of the initial formula φ;

– the disjunct $\tau'(C_j)$ is added in order to obtain a "strictly faithful" embedding, i.e. an embedding in which the knowledge on all the auxiliary variables p_i's is empty.

Theorem 8. *Let $\varphi \in \mathcal{L}_M$. Then, M is an MKNF model for φ iff M is an AEL model for $\tau_{AEL}(\varphi)$.*

Sketch of the proof. The proof exploits Schwarz's proof of the embedding of default logic into AEL, since it can be shown that there exists a correspondence between an *MKNF* formula of the form of a conjunct C_j, and default rules. However, the conjunct C_j generalizes the notion of default rule in two different ways:

1. besides standard justifications (corresponding to the $\neg \xi_i^j$'s) there exists an *autoepistemic* justification ψ_1^j, which semantically corresponds to the notion of *positive occurrence of negation as failure* studied in logic programming (see e.g. [Inoue & Sakama, 1994, Lifschitz & Woo, 1992]);

2. the conclusion is an epistemic disjunction ($K\varphi_1 \vee K\varphi_{n_j}$) instead of a propositional formula, which creates a correspondence between C_j and the notion of *disjunctive default* [Gelfond et al., 1991].

By extending Schwarz's proof, it can be shown that both such generalizations can be formalized (in the way specified by the translation $\tau_{AEL}(\cdot)$) inside AEL.
□

Hence, *MKNF* and *AEL* have the same "expressive power", in the sense that each finite *MKNF* theory Σ can be translated in a finite *AEL* theory $\tau_{AEL}(\Sigma)$ (whose size is in general exponential in the size of Σ) which expresses the same set of models of Σ.

Notice that, as shown in the previous section, *AEL* theories exactly correspond to negative *MKNF* theories, by substituting each instance of K with $\neg not$. Hence, previous theorem implies the following property.

Corollary 9. *Let $\Sigma \subset \mathcal{L}_M$ be a finite theory. Then, the finite theory*

$$\Sigma' = \tau_{AEL}(\tau_M(\Sigma)) \subset \mathcal{L}_N$$

is such that the set of MKNF models of Σ and Σ' coincide.

Therefore, for each finite *MKNF* theory there exists an equivalent finite negative *MKNF* theory. It is known (see e.g. [Gottlob, 1995]) that the dual property does not hold, i.e. theories with occurrences of *not* cannot in general be faithfully represented by theories using the modality K only. This is shown by the following example: suppose $\varphi = not\, p \vee p$. Then, φ has two models, M_1 and M_2, which correspond respectively to the set of all interpretations, and the set of all interpretations satisfying p. Hence, M_1 contains M_2. Now, it is easy to see that it is impossible to find a positive formula having both M_1 and M_2 as models, since for positive formulas minimality of models must hold, i.e. each model cannot be contained into another model of the same formula. Therefore, in general the modality *not* cannot be expressed in terms of the modality K.

These results imply that the modality *not* is "more expressive" than the modality K.

5 Conclusions

In this work we have investigated the relative expressive power of the modalities K and *not* of *MKNF*. Our results can be summarized as follows:

1. the negation as failure modality *not* of *MKNF* exactly corresponds to negative introspection in *AEL*. This implies that the logic *MKNF* can be viewed as the exact composition of two different nonmonotonic modal logics: Halpern and Moses's logic of minimal knowledge $S5_G$ and Moore's *AEL*;

2. the minimal knowledge modality K can be represented in terms of negation as failure *not*, since *MKNF* theories can be expressed in terms of unimodal theories using the *not* operator only. This implies that *AEL* and *MKNF* have the same expressive power, which is a surprising result, since *MKNF* is generally considered as a very expressive formalism;

3. however, notice that the embedding of *MKNF* into *AEL* (as well as Gottlob's and Schwarz's embeddings of default logic into *AEL*) only holds for finite theories. It would be interesting to investigate whether it is possible to embed infinite *MKNF* theories into *AEL*;

4. the embedding of *MKNF* into *AEL* that we have presented generalizes Schwarz's embedding of Reiter's default logic into *AEL*, and points out an alternative interpretation of *MKNF* theories (in normal form) as "generalized" disjunctive defaults. The implications of such an observation are the goal of our current research;

5. the modality *not* is "more expressive" than K, i.e. negation as failure can represent minimal knowledge, whereas the opposite does not hold. This result is particularly interesting when compared with the computational properties of such modalities: since reasoning with minimal knowledge is harder than reasoning with negation as failure, the higher degree of complexity of K does not appear to correspond to a higher expressive power. However (as shown in [Rosati, 1996]), it turns out that minimal knowledge allows for a more "compact" representation of information, which makes reasoning harder than using the notion of negation as failure only.

Acknowledgments

This research has been partially supported by MURST, "Tecniche di Ragionamento Non Monotono", and by EC Esprit LTR Project "Foundations of Data Warehouse Quality". The author is thankful to three anonymous referees for their useful comments.

References

[Beringer & Schaub, 1993] A. Beringer and T. Schaub, 1993. Minimal belief and negation as failure: a feasible approach. In *Proc. of AAAI-93*, 400–405.

[Bochman, 1995] A. Bochman, 1995. On bimodal nonmonotonic modal logics and their unimodal and nonmodal equivalents. In *Proc. of IJCAI-95*, 1518–1524.

[Chen, 1994] Y. Chen, 1994. The logic of only knowing as a unified framework for non-monotonic reasoning. *Fundamenta Informaticae*, 21, 205–220.

[Donini, Nardi, & Rosati, 1997] F. M. Donini, D. Nardi, and R. Rosati, 1997. Ground nonmonotonic modal logics. *Journal of Logic and Computation*, 7(4). To appear.

[Donini, Nardi, & Rosati, 1997b] F. M. Donini, D. Nardi, and R. Rosati, 1997b. Autoepistemic description logics. To appear in *Proc. of IJCAI-97*.

[Gelfond & Lifschitz, 1988] M. Gelfond and V. Lifschitz. The stable model semantics for logic programming. In *Logic Programming: Proc. of the fifth International Conference and Symposium*, 1070–1080, 1988.

[Gelfond et al., 1991] M. Gelfond, V. Lifschitz, H. Przymusinska, and M. Truszczyński, 1991. Disjunctive defaults. In *Proc. of KR-91*, 230–237.

[Gottlob, 1995] G. Gottlob. Translating default logic into standard autoepistemic logic. *Journal of ACM*, 42:4:711–740, 1995.

[Halpern & Moses, 1985] J. Y. Halpern and Y. Moses. Towards a theory of knowledge and ignorance: Preliminary report. Technical Report CD-TR 92/34, IBM, 1985.

[Hughes & Cresswell, 1968] G. E. Hughes and M. J. Cresswell. An introduction to modal logic. Methuen, London, 1968.

[Inoue & Sakama, 1994] K. Inoue and C. Sakama. On positive occurrences of negation as failure. In *Proc. of KR-94*, pages 293–304. Morgan Kaufmann, Los Altos, 1994.

[Lifschitz, 1991] V. Lifschitz, 1991. Nonmonotonic databases and epistemic queries. In *Proc. of IJCAI-91*, 381–386, Sydney.

[Lifschitz, 1994] V. Lifschitz, 1994. Minimal belief and negation as failure. *AI Journal*, 70:53–72.

[Lifschitz & Schwarz, 1993] V. Lifschitz and G. Schwarz, 1993. Extended logic programs as autoepistemic theories. In *Proc. of LPNMR-93*, 101–114, MIT Press.

[Lifschitz & Woo, 1992] V. Lifschitz and T. Woo, 1992. Answer sets in general nonmonotonic reasoning (preliminary report). In *Proc. of KR-92*, 603–614, Morgan Kaufmann.

[Lin & Shoham, 1992] F. Lin and Y. Shoham, 1992. Epistemic semantics for fixedpoint non-monotonic logics. *AI Journal*, 57:271–289.

[Marek & Truszczyński, 1993] W. Marek and M. Truszczyński, 1993. *Nonmonotonic Logic – Context-Dependent Reasoning*. Springer-Verlag.

[Moore, 1985] R. C. Moore, 1985. Semantical considerations on nonmonotonic logic. *AI Journal*, 25:75–94.

[Rosati, 1996] R. Rosati, 1996. Minimal knowledge states in nonmonotonic modal logics. *Proceedings of the Second Conference on Advances in Modal Logic (AiML-96)*, CSLI, Stanford, USA.

[Rosati, 1997] R. Rosati, 1997. Reasoning with minimal belief and negation as failure: algorithms and complexity. To appear in *Proceedings of AAAI-97*.

[Schwarz, 1992] G. Schwarz, 1992. Minimal model semantics for nonmonotonic modal logics. In *Proceedings of the Seventh International Conference of Logic in Computer Science (LICS-92)*, pages 34–43. IEEE Computer Society Press, 1992.

[Schwarz & Truszczyński, 1994] G. Schwarz and M. Truszczyński, 1994. Minimal knowledge problem: a new approach. *AI Journal*, 67:113–141.

[Schwarz, 1996] G. Schwarz. On embedding default logic into Moore's Autoepistemic Logic. *AI Journal*, 80:349:359, 1996.

[Shoham, 1987] Y. Shoham. Nonmonotonic logics: Meaning and utility. In *Proc. of IJCAI-87*, pp. 388–392, 1987.

User Model-Based Information Filtering

Fabio A. Asnicar, Massimo Di Fant, and Carlo Tasso

Department of Mathematics and Computer Science – University of Udine
Via delle Scienze, 206 – 33100 UDINE (Italy)
e-mail: tasso@dimi.uniud.it

Abstract The IFT (Information Filtering Tool) project has the goal of developing new approaches to information filtering which are based on user modeling techniques for building and managing the representation of the user information preferences. In this paper we describe three prototypes which have been developed and evaluated within the project. All of them are dealing with textual semistructured documents and exploit a semantic network representation of user preferences: the first two prototypes (IFTool and PIFT) are characterized by two different matching algorithms utilized for assessing the relevance of an incoming document against the user model, whereas the third (ifWeb) concerns an application of IFTool to the navigation and filtering of documents in the INTERNET. The three prototypes have been evaluated in order to compare their performance with similar systems presented in the literature. The results achieved show that information filtering can positively profit from user modeling techniques, and point out interesting challenges for future investigations.

1 Introduction

The recent development of communication networks and multimedia systems provide potential users with the availability of a huge amount of information, making worse and worse the problem of information overload ([12]). This situation has favoured the development of systems capable of automatically identifying the subset of the available information, which is potentially relevant to the user information needs. More specifically, filtering systems have been proposed ([3]), which interface the information source to the user, and are aimed at automatically evaluating the potential relevance of incoming information on the basis of an explicit description of the user information interests (user profile). However, while the need for these systems has been widely recognized ([10], [14], [4]) and adequate techniques for their implementation have emerged — we mainly refer to the intelligent agent technology ([17]) — two basic problems still remain open and need further investigation: (i) the mechanisms for learning, representing and updating the user's information preferences, and (ii) the processing algorithms to be adopted to extract the information content of the incoming documents and the matching algorithms to be exploited to assess their potential relevance.

The *IFT (Information Filtering Tool)* project has the goal of developing and evaluating new approaches to information filtering, where the potential relevance of incoming information is computed by comparison with an explicit and dynamic user model, which represents user information needs and preferences. More specifically, we have investigated new representation and matching paradigms for classifying incoming documents and evaluating their potential relevance. Another major point of investigation has been the development of suitable tools capable of learning and tracking over time the information preferences of the user. The proposed approaches have been experimented in two main applications, namely SDI services and information gathering on the WWW.

The goal of this paper is to illustrate two specific prototype systems, where (i) the user model includes an explicit representation of the co-occurrence relationship ([7]) between pairs of terms appearing simultaneously in the documents, and (ii) two specific mechanisms (relevance feedback and rent) are exploited in order to manage the temporal evolution of the content of the user model.

In section 2, we present the *IFTool* (*Information Filtering Tool*) prototype, which is based on a matching algorithm specifically designed for taking advantage of the co-occurrence relationship. In section 3 we introduce the *PIFT* (*Probabilistic Information Filtering Tool*) prototype, characterized by a probabilistic approach to filtering. For both prototypes we show also the results of a systematic evaluation activity, which support the claim that a specific user modeling component improves the performance with respect to other filtering system reported in the literature. In section 4 we illustrate the *ifWeb* (*Information Filtering Web*) prototype, which extends the proposed approach to the navigation and filtering within the WWW, providing also an account of its evaluation and a comparision with commercial search engines. Section 5 concludes the paper.

2 IFTool

IFTool ([11]) is a prototype of an information filtering system devoted to semistructured textual documents, which exploits the *UMT* (*User Modeling Tool*) ([5]) shell for building and managing the user model devoted to represent the user information preferences.

2.1 The User Model

The model includes information which represents both the interests and the 'not interests' of the user. More precisely, it is constituted by a weighted semantic network whose nodes correspond to terms (concepts) found in documents and where arcs link together terms which co-occurred in some document. Each node has an associated weight, which is positive (negative) if the corresponding term has been extracted from a document which has been judged "interesting" ("not interesting") by the user. Each arc is characterized by a weight which represents the frequency of co-occurrence of the two terms in the previously analyzed documents. The specific method described above has been proposed to overcome the polisemy problem ([9]) which stems from the use of keywords for representing the information preferences of the user: the co-occurrence relationships allows to associate to each term a 'pragmatic context' which helps in the disambiguation of the meaning of the term.

The content of the user model is acquired and managed by the Feedback Handler Module (see next section). In this way the main technique available to the user for providing information about his/her preferences is constituted by relevance feedback ([18]). Direct inspection and modification of the user model by the user is also possible through a specialized interface.

2.2 The Architecture

The main modules of IFTool (cfr Figure 1(a)) are illustrated in the following.

The *Document Representation Module* analyses the incoming documents and produces an internal representation, containing information about their content. In particular, this is constituted by a weighted vector of terms which is obtained trough standard techniques (such as segmentation, stop list deletion, stemming and weighting) and a specific algorithm which is devoted to identify the best terms that represent the content of a document (compression).

The *Document Classifier Module* receives in input the internal representation of a document and the current user model, and produces in output a classification of the document with respect to its potential relevance for the user. The algorithm exploited includes two phases: the comparison of the internal representation of the document with the user model and, later, the classification of the document on the basis of the results of the previous phase. The comparison phase produces two numerical values representing the similarity between the current document and (a) the information preferences and (b) the 'not interests' of the user. More specifically, the comparison phase exploits in an original way the co-occurrence relationship. In standard keyword matching, a simple count is performed of the terms which are simultaneously present in the document representation and in the user model. IFTool, on the other hand, considers also a contribution obtained by the pairs of terms included in the document which have already co-occurred in previous documents (information represented by arcs in the semantic network): this allows to add more evidence to the classification process. The classification of the document is then performed by means of a suitable criteria which considers the two matching values produced by the comparison phase and results in the final classification ("interesting", "not interesting" or "indifferent").

The *Feedback Handler Module* receives in input the relevance judgements possibly provided by the user and the internal representation of the corresponding document and updates the user model accordingly. Updates are constituted by (i) insertions of new nodes with corresponding weights in the semantic network included in the user model and/or (ii) changes in the weights associated to nodes and arcs of the semantic network, taking into account the frequency of occurrence of terms and of co-occurrence of pair of terms in the considered document. The Feedback Handler Module allows IFTool to better follow the temporal evolution of the user information preferences and this is obtained by means of an increase (decrease) of the weights associated to nodes and arcs. The module is also used to initialize the content of a new user model.

The *Rent Handler Module* is devoted to delete from the user model the terms which have been inserted accidentally in it through the feedback operation. This allow to highlight the terms that better represent the user preferences. The module is activated periodically on the user model and it identifies the changes which have to be performed on the model: these are constituted by a decrease of the weight associated to the nodes, so as to results as the payment of a rent ([1]). After the rent has been paid, all the terms which have a weight lower than a given threshold are deleted from the model.

The *User Modeling Subsystem* has been obtained by extending the original representational capabilities of the UMT shell (basically attribute-value pairs and frame-based stereotypes) with semantic networks.

The *User Interface* is devoted to manage the interaction with the user.

Finally, the *Document Data Base* stores the original version of the documents and their internal representation.

2.3 Experiments and Evaluation

The goal of the experimental activity performed on IFTool has been the evaluation of the performance of the prototype. Several experiments have been performed. The most significant one has been concerned with the filtering operation of 2000 abstracts of technical report on the basis of the information preferences of four subjects. We have simulated the following situation: IFTool receives 20 documents per day (globally 100 sessions) which are classified according to the user model and then are shown to the user. Every day the Rent Handler Module is activated. For each set of 20 documents, each subject provides a relevance ranking which is then utilized for computing normalized precision and recall ([18]) for both "interesting" and "not interesting" classifications. In Figure 1(b) the evolution of the normalized precision of the interesting documents is reported. At the beginning of the 100 session sequence, the user model, initially empty, is incrementally acquired through relevance feedback. The performance increases until a saturation value is reached (94% for precision, 93% for recall). The dotted line refers to a simple keyword matching algorithm, whereas the continuous line refers to the new algorithm exploited in IFTool: the obtained results show an average improvement of the precision of 18% and an average improvement of the recall of 30%. The performance of IFTool have also shown better values than those reported in [9].

A specific experiment has been performed to evaluate the behaviour of IFTool when the user preferences drastically change. The results obtained show that, after an initial strong decrease of the performance, the prototype can learn and adapt quickly to the new information preferences of the user.

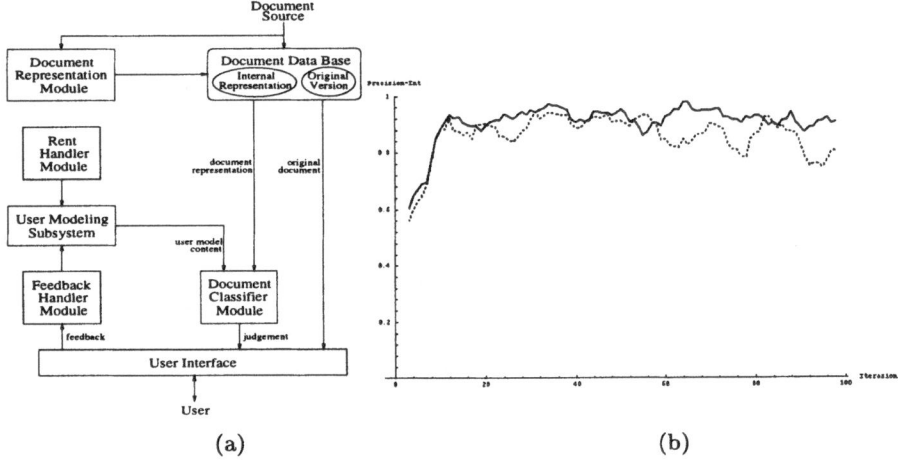

Figure1. *(a) The architecture of the IFTool prototype. (b) Normalized precision of interesting documents over 100 sessions.*

3 PIFT

PIFT is a prototype of a filtering system for semistructured documents, where their potential relevance is computed by means of two bayesian networks ([16]). These are built through statistical analysis of the terms which occurred in the documents judged as "interesting" and, respectively, "not interesting" by the user.

Several similarities characterize PIFT and the InRoute ([6]) system, essentially due to the same approach based on bayesian networks. However, PIFT is characterized by an explicit and dynamic user modeling activity which is absent in InRoute.

3.1 The Architecture

PIFT has basically the same architecture of IFTool. However, for supporting the statistical analysis of the documents, a specific data base (*Term Dictionary*) has been introduced, together with a corresponding *Term Dictionary*

Handler Module. Moreover, the User Modeling Subsystem is not based on the UMT shell, but a new reduced version of it has been ad hoc developed. Another difference between the two prototypes concerns the co-occurrence relationship, that in the PIFT prototype is not computed by exploiting the entire document, but only a part of it.

The two main modules of PIFT are described in the following.

The *User Modeling Subsystem* is devoted to represent the information preferences of the user. Analogously to IFTool, the user information preferences are represented by means of two semantic networks, one for the interests and one for the 'not interests'. The co-occurrence between words is verified within a *contextual window* of size m: two words are considered to co-occur if they appear together in the same document and the number of words between them is not greater than m. The exploitation of contextual windows is aimed at reducing inconsistencies in the model, since in long documents the co-occurrence relationship between a term at the beginning and a term at the end of the document may mean nothing ([20]). Each node of the semantic network is associated to a weight which is computed by means of tf.idf weighting ([18]), where tf represents the sum of values proportional to the absolute frequency of occurrence of the term, and idf represent the reciprocal of the number of documents where the term has appeared. Analogously, each arc of the semantic network is associated to a numerical value which is a function of the frequency of co-occurrence of the linked terms.

The *Document Classifier Module* builds two bayesian networks on the basis of the internal representation of the current document, of the information stored in the Term Dictionary, and of the content of the user model. The first network is devoted to compute the probability that the current document satisfies the user interests, and the second one is devoted to the user 'not interests'. The networks are constituted by $n+2$ nodes $S, T_1, \ldots, T_n, Q_I$, where n is the number of terms present in the semantic network describing the interests (or not interests) of the user. Each node is associated with a proposition: S is associated with the proposition "the document is present in input to the system", each T_i with the proposition "the term t_i is present in the representation of the user interests (not interests)" and Q_I (Q_{NI}) with the proposition "the interests (not interests) of the user are satisfied". There are $2 \cdot n$ arcs $S \rightarrow T_i$ and $T_i \rightarrow Q_I$ ($T_i \rightarrow Q_{NI}$): the first n arcs link S with each of the T_i nodes and the second n arcs link each T_i with the proposition Q_I (Q_{NI}). Each arc is associated with a numerical value which represents the relevance of the term respectively in the representation of the document and in the representation of the user interests (not interests) and it is expressed by means of a generalised tf.idf weighting ([19], [6]). The networks are simplified by means of the conditioning method ([16]) and are evaluated by means of the noisy OR-gate model ([16]). This results in two probability values (one for the interests and one for the 'not interests'), which are exploited in order to compute a final relevance classification for the document.

3.2 Experiments and Comparision with IFTool

We have performed on the PIFT prototype the same experimental evaluation which has been performed on the IFTool prototype. The diagram reported in Figure 2(a) show that the performance of PIFT is only slightly worse than IFTool.

Moreover, in order to better understand which is the optimum size of the contextual window for computing co-occurrence, we have measured the percentage of the documents which PIFT has correctly classified as interesting (not interesting), with a different size of the contextual window. Figure 2(b) reports a diagram which shows the different percentage after the analysis of 2000 documents with a different size of the contextual window. The diagram shows that the performance increases until the size of the contextual window is near 20 and decreases for higher values.

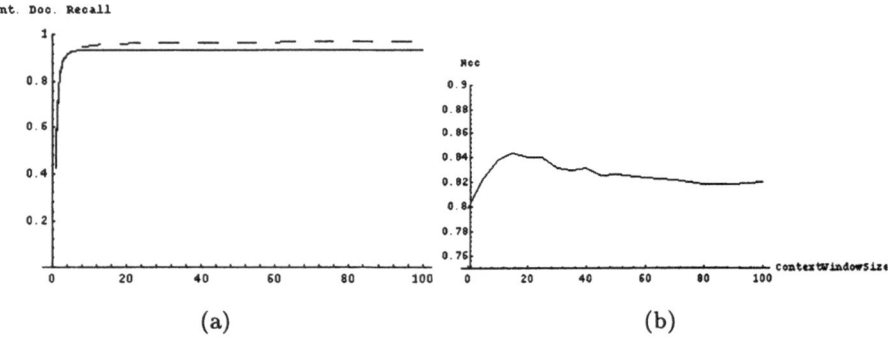

Int. Doc. Recall

(a) (b)

Figure2. *(a) The normalized recall (polynomial interpolation) of the interesting documents in the PIFT prototype (continuous line) and in the IFTool prototype (dotted line). (b) The percentage of the documents correctly classified by PIFT (N_{CC}) with respect to a different size of the contextual window (ContextWindowSize).*

4 ifWeb

ifWeb is a prototype of user model-based intelligent agent capable of supporting the user in the navigation of the WWW, the retrieval and the filtering of documents. Following [3], the filtering process can also be viewed as the process of accessing and retrieving information from remote data bases: in such case the incoming data (document source) is the result of the WWW navigation.

Several tools have been proposed in the literature which are aimed at gathering information from the WWW on the basis of a user profile ([15], [8],

[13], [2]). All of them, however, share some basic limitations: the technique used to represent knowledge in the user profile is based on simple lists of keywords; the types of the considered knowledge are very limited, usually restricted to single words, or to (some) structural characteristic; the learning capabilities are usually very poor, if any; and the navigation strategies, if any, are usually based on very heuristic and limited criteria. ifWeb is aimed at overcoming the above limitations by exploiting the possibilities of the information filtering approach proposed in the IFT project.

ifWeb is characterized by two modes of operation. The first one is called *navigation support*: from a specific WWW document pointed out by the user, ifWeb starts an autonomous navigation, it collects WWW documents, it analyses and classifies them and, as a result, it shows graphically to the user the structure of the hypertextual links present in the documents which have been accessed. The second mode of operation is called *document search*: from a specific WWW document pointed out by the user, the system autonomously performs an extended navigation in the WWW, retrieves and classifies documents. As a result, the system shows to the user the set of the documents which have been classified as most relevant, ordered downward from the most interesting one.

4.1   The Architecture

Figure 3(a) shows the functional architecture of ifWeb which includes the following modules: the *ifWeb Interface Agency* which manages all the interaction with the user; the *ifWeb Agency* which performs the specific function of navigation support and document search; the *IFTool Agency* based on the IFTool prototype, which is devoted to classify incoming documents on the basis of the content of the user model.

The overall operation is the following. The ifWeb Agency requires from the Network through an URL the retrieval of a specific document; when the document is retrieved, information about its content is extracted and is then exploited in order to build the document internal representation.

ifWeb considers only HTML documents. The analysis of these documents is performed by a syntax direct parser for the HTML (Data Type Definition) format and, moreover, it includes some basic processing (segmentation, stop list deletion, stemming, contextual weighting, and compression). The document internal representation produced is then sent to the IFTool Agency for comparison with the user model. The result of the comparison allows the classification of the document in one of the three categories "interesting", "not interesting" or "indifferent". Then, the ifWeb Agency manages the choice about accessing or not the documents mentioned in the links (URLs) specified in the currently analyzed document. In case of a positive decision it forwards the request for access, and the operation continues in an analogous way.

The strategies for the autonomous navigation performed by ifWeb are based on the evaluation of how much a link (URL) is considered *promising* for accessing other documents which can be relevant to the user interests. The computation of the *degree of promise* of a link is executed by means of two parameters: the first one is called *expectation rate*, and it is a function of the values obtained from the comparison carried out with the user model and the consequent classification performed on the currently analyzed document (i.e., the document containing the URLs whose potential is considered for further navigation). The second parameter, called *confidence rate*, is a function of the values of the degree of promise of the documents previously accessed on the path which concludes with the currently analyzed document. In navigation support mode, all the promising link are considered, whereas in document search mode an hybrid best/breadth-first search is adopted. Figure 3(b) shows the user interface: it includes a normal browser window

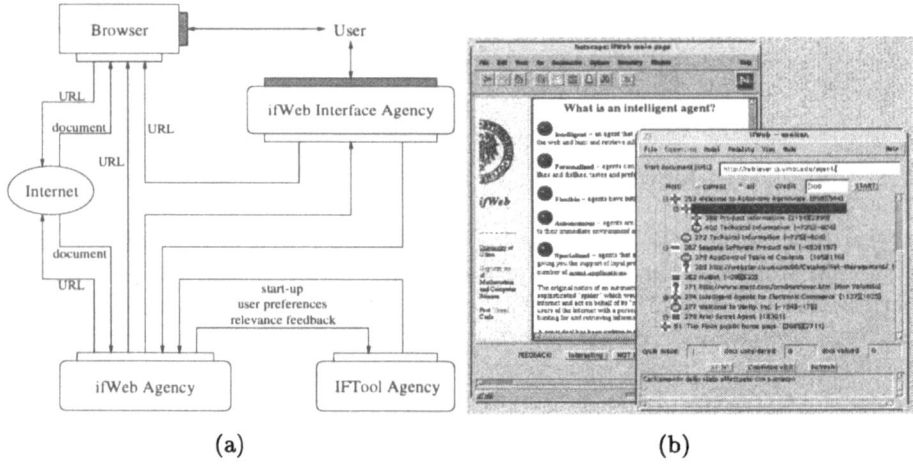

(a) (b)

Figure3. *(a) Functional architecture of ifWeb. (b) User interface of ifWeb.*

and a specific window managed by the ifWeb Interface Agency. This window is used for showing to the user the intermediate status and the results of the various analyses and for allowing the user to modify some system parameter.

The documents are displayed in a tree-like structure, where the arcs correspond to hypertextual links. The various icons represent the result of the classification performed on the documents: '+' means "interesting", '=' means "indifferent", '-' means "not interesting", '?' means 'analysis not performed' (i.e. document not available), 'STOP' means that the ifWeb Agency has decided not to continue the analysis from that document. The user can easily modify the order of analysis, request the access to links which where considered not promising by ifWeb, exclude some document from navigation, and ask for display (through the browser) of a specific document in its original form. In the browser window, two specific buttons allow the user to provide relevance feedback on a document.

4.2 Experiments and Evaluation

A specific evaluation activity has been carried out on ifWeb. The main goals of the evaluation were: (i) assessing the quality of the learning capability and the quality of the results of the classification performed on the documents and (ii) comparing ifWeb with some traditional search engines.

The evaluation activity has been performed through real-time access to INTERNET: four subjects where using ifWeb having in mind a specific field of interest (usually their specific field of expertise). Each subject was carrying out 9 sessions with ifWeb. ifWeb was started with a user model obtained through (positive and negative) relevance feedback on a limited set of 4–6 documents. The model was later incrementally refined by ifWeb, thank to further relevance feedback provided by the user. During each session ifWeb was working autonomously and, at the end of the session, it displayed the results to the subject. The subject was then requested to provide relevance feedback, and to order the results according to his/her relevance judgement. The data collected at the end of each session were then used for computing two performance figures: ndpm ([21]) (a measure of the capability to order correctly the documents from interesting to not interesting) and standard precision ([18]).

Figure 4(a) shows the results of this experimentation. After the initial session where ifWeb has a too limited knowledge of user preferences, both the computed figures show that the system progressively improves its performance through the user feedback, both in terms of overall precision of classification (upper continuous line) and of the capability to order correctly the documents according to their potential interest for the user (lower dotted line). Comparisons with similar tools found in the literature are difficult, because those systems have been scarcely evaluated and cannot be well compared one to the other.

Moreover, we have performed a comparision with the standard search engines AltaVista and ExCite. More specifically, the most relevant keywords included in the user model of ifWeb at the end of the 9 session experiment described above, were submitted to the two search engines as query. On the outcome, ndpm and precision were computed, according to the relevance ranking provided by the subjects.

Figure 4(b) illustrates the results: they show that ifWeb provides more precise results and better ordering.

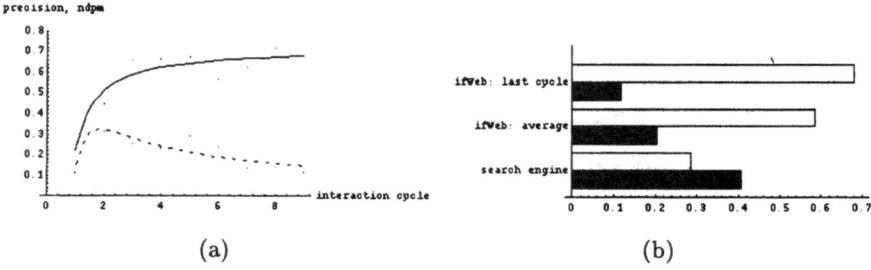

Figure4. *(a) Precision (continuous line) and ndpm (dotted line) over the 9 sessions (polynomial interpolation). (b) ifWeb vs. standard search engines (precision in grey, ndpm in black).*

5 Conclusions

In this paper we have described the IFTool, PIFT, and ifWeb prototypes, three user model-based information filtering systems developed and evaluated within the IFT project. All of them deal with textual semistructured documents: the first two prototypes are characterized by two different matching algorithms utilized for assessing the relevance of the documents, whereas the third prototype concerns an application of the IFTool prototype to the navigation and filtering of documents in the INTERNET.

The evaluation activity carried out on the three prototypes allows to support the claim that the use of sophisticated user modeling techniques can improve the performance of intelligent agents for information filtering. Specific results in this direction have been produced in the IFT project and are reported in this paper.

A basic problem whose importance has emerged from our research and which needs further effort, is constituted by the methodologies which are exploited for the evaluation of these systems. The availabilty of such methodologies — frequently not reported in the literature — is strongly needed in order to compare the various approaches. The performance measures and the experimental procedures adopted in the IFT project can be considered a first step towards this goal.

References

1. P. E. Baclace. Competitive Agents for Information Filtering. *CACM* 35(12), p. 50, Dec. 1992.
2. M. Balabanovic. An Adaptive Web Page Recommendation Service. In *Proc. of the 1st Int.l Conf. on Autonomous Agents*, Marina del Rey CA, Feb. 1997.
3. N. J. Belkin, W. B. Croft. Information Filtering and Information Retrieval: Two Sides of the Same Coin? *CACM* 35(12), pp. 29–38, Dec. 1992.

4. T. A. Bell, A. Moffat. The Design of a High Performance Information Filtering System. In *Proc. of the 19th Int.l ACM SIGIR Conf. on Research and Development in Information Retrieval*, pp. 12–20, Zurich, CH, Aug. 1996.

5. G. Brajnik, C. Tasso. A shell for developing non-monotonic user modeling systems. *Int. J. of Human-Computer Studies* 40, pp. 31–62, 1994.

6. J. Callan. Document Filtering with Inference Networks. In *Proc. of the 19th Int.l ACM SIGIR Conf. on Research and Development in Information Retrieval*, pp. 262–269, Zurich, CH, Aug. 1996.

7. W. B. Croft. Effective Text Retrieval Based on Combining Evidence from the Corpus and Users. *IEEE Expert*, pp. 59–63, Dec. 1995.

8. P. Edwards, D. Bayer, C. L. Green, T. R. Payne. Experience with Learning Agents which Manage Internet-Based Information. In *Proc. of the AAAI Spring Symposium on Machine Learning in Information Access*, Stanford, Mar. 1996.

9. P. W. Foltz. Using Latent Semantic Indexing for Information Filtering. In *Proc. of the ACM SIGOS Conf. on Office Information Systems*, pp. 40–47, Boston, MA, 1990.

10. M. Höfferer, B. Knaus, W. Winiwarter. An Evolutionary Approach to Cognitive Information Filtering. In *Proc. of the 18th Int.l ACM SIGIR Conf. on Research and Development in Information Retrieval*, pp. 1–15, Seattle, WA, July 1995.

11. M. Minio, C. Tasso. IFT: un'interfaccia intelligente per il filtraggio di informazioni basato su modellizzazione di utente. *AI*IA Notizie* IX(3), pp. 21–25, Sep. 1996.

12. M. Morita, Y. Shinoda. Information Filtering Based on User Behavior: Analysis and Best Match Text Retrieval. In *Proc. of the 17th Int.l ACM SIGIR Conf. on Research and Development in Information Retrieval*, pp. 272–281, Dublin, IR, June 1994.

13. A. Moukas. Amalthaea: Information Discovery and Filtering using a Multiagent Evolving Ecosystem. In *Proc. PAAM96, The Practical Application of Intelligent Agents and Multi-Agent Technology*, London, UK, Apr. 1996.

14. S. Mukhopadhyay, J. Mostafa, M. Palakal, W. Lam, L. Xue, A. Hudli. An Adaptive Multi-level Information Filtering System. In *Proc. of the 5th Int.l Conf. on User Modeling*, pp. 21–28, Kailua-Kona, Hawaii, Jan. 1996.

15. M. Pazzani, J. Muramatsu, D. Billsus. Syskill & Webert: Identifying interesting web sites. In *Proc. of the 13th National Conf. on Artificial Intelligence*, pp. 54–61, Portland, OR, Aug. 1996.

16. J. Pearl. *Probabilistic Reasoning in Intelligent Systems: Networks of Plausible Inference*. Morgan-Kauffman, 1988.

17. C. J. Petrie. Agent-Based Engineering, the Web, and Intelligence. *IEEE Expert*, pp. 24–29, Dec. 1996.

18. G. Salton, M. J. McGill. *Introduction to Modern Information Retrieval*. McGraw-Hill, New York, NY, 1983.

19. H. R. Turtle, W. B. Croft. Evaluation of an Inference Network-Based Retrieval Model. *ACM TIS* 9(3), pp. 188–222, July 1991.

20. J. Xu, W. B. Croft. Query Expansion Using Local and Global Document Analysis. In *Proc. of the 19th Int.l ACM SIGIR Conf. on Research and Development in Information Retrieval*, pp. 4–11, Zurich, CH, Aug. 1996.

21. Y. Y. Yao. Measuring Retrieval Effectiveness Based on User Preference of Documents. *Journal of the American Society for Information Science* 46(2), pp. 133–145, 1995.

A Comparative Analysis of Horn Models and Bayesian Networks for Diagnosis*

Luigi Portinale, Pietro Torasso

Dipartimento di Informatica - Universita' di Torino
C.so Svizzera 185 - 10149 Torino (Italy)
e-mail: {portinal,torasso}@di.unito.it

Abstract. The aim of the paper is to formally relate logical Horn models and Bayesian Networks (BNs) in the framework of diagnostic reasoning. This is pursued by pointing out similarities between the two formalisms at the modeling level and by introducing into BNs a suitable notion of derivation. We also discuss modeling issues underlying the choice of Horn-based models vs BNs, by making explicit the "completion semantics" underlying a BN. This correspondence between "completed " Horn theories and BNs allows us to formally justify classical diagnostic schemata adopted for BNs.

1 Introduction

In recent years increasing attention has been paid to analyzing the relationships between the representation formalisms (and associated reasoning mechanisms) and the tasks. Even if most of the work has been done at the *knowledge level* [19], interesting results have been obtained also at the *representation level*. In a seminal work [10], Pearl has pointed out some erroneous inferences obtained in rule-based systems and advocated the adoption of Bayesian Networks (BN) as a primary representation formalism for a variety of tasks (mainly classification and diagnosis). In the reasoning under uncertainty community BNs have become the most important formalism not only because of the algorithms for computing probabilities, but also because the graphical structure underlying them plays a major role in representing significant features of the domain to be modeled. Such a structure is used for representing in a simple and natural way conditional independence and therefore the need of expressing conditional probabilities among all the entities of the domain is strongly reduced. In this way one of the main obstacles in adopting probabilistic methods for real-world applications has been removed [17]. Despite the use of BNs for solving diagnostic problems, most of the recent theories of diagnosis [5, 6, 1] have been developed for logical formalisms. In fact, in Model-Based Reasoning significant efforts have been made for developing formalisms which are able to model in a principled way the system to be diagnosed. In particular, behavioral models and causal models have been developed and formalized in terms of logics and a number of methods with a clear semantics have been developed for solving diagnostic problems.

Bayesian methods and logical models have often been viewed as alternative approaches to diagnostic problem solving and so far little attention has been paid to

---

* The work has been partially supported by CNR project SCI*SIA.

compare the two approaches in terms of modeling issues. Such an analysis is much needed since there is a consensus that the real problem in the diagnostic task (as well as in many other tasks) is modeling. In this paper we aim at analyzing and comparing Bayesian network and logical approaches to diagnosis in a number of aspects, in order to single out not only differences in the two approaches but also important aspects that deserve attention from a modeling point of view. In particular, we analyze the role of structure (the graph of dependencies among entities) that can be considered an important contribution provided by the BN formalism. The second aspect we analyze is the notion of explanation for a diagnostic problem. In logical approaches to Model-Based Diagnosis (MBD), the notion of explanation is critical for the definition of diagnostic solution; a major contribution of the present paper is to discuss to what extent such a notion can be extended to BNs. In particular, we focus our attention on models represented as Horn theories since these are the most frequent formalism adopted in logical approaches. The third aspect concerns the requirement of completeness of the model, a very critical point for any significant application; correspondence between completed Horn theories and BNs is formally proved, justifying the purely abductive characterization of diagnosis usually adopted in the BN formalism.

2 Model Comparison: the Role of Structure

In the MBD community a large variety of models has been developed: this can be explained both in terms of granularity (models describing systemic faults vs models describing the behavior of single components and the connection among components) and in terms of the perspective (behavioral models vs structure plus function models vs causal models). Despite that, all these models can be translated into a logical formalism [13] and in most cases at least the core of the model can be approximated as a Horn theory (more specifically as a set of *definite clauses* [8])[2]. It is worth noting that Horn theories can be viewed as an approximation since there could be aspects of the model that are not fully captured in a Horn clause (for example, in a causal model the fact that the effect is not necessarily observed even if the cause is observed). Given a set M of definite clauses, the *Predicate Dependency Graph* (PDG) of M is a graph such that nodes correspond to predicates of M and there is a directed arc from node p to node q iff there is a clause in M having p in the body and q in the head. In case the PDG is a DAG, M is called *hierarchical* [2]. It is worth noting that in most cases, models abstract from time both because of the nature of the modeled system (e.g. combinatorial digital circuits) or because of the decomposition of the dynamic problem into two components: one static and one devoted to temporal aspects [3]. This decomposition is not only useful for reducing computational time, but has a relevant consequence on the model: there is no recursion in the Horn theory representing the model and its PDG is just a DAG[3].

---

[2] Constraints on mutual disjunction between faults or behavioral modes cannot be captured via Horn clauses, however these constraints are not directly used in finding diagnoses, but to rule out inconsistent diagnoses.

[3] Notice that in case of input-output models a first-order formalism is often used and the absence of recursion is usually assumed at the ground level, however when the set

The idea of explicitly considering the structure of influences via the PDG has not been emphasized in the MBD literature, even if it is sometimes exploited in focusing diagnostic algorithms.

On the other hand, probabilistic frameworks based on BNs use such a kind of structure as a primary source of modeling. A (discrete) Bayesian Network is a pair $N = \langle \langle V, E \rangle, P \rangle$ where $\langle V, E \rangle$ is a DAG representing through edges E conditional dependences among random variables V and P is a probabilistic distribution over V such that

$$P[X_1, X_2 \dots X_n] = \prod_{i=1}^{n} P[X_i | Parent(X_i)] \qquad (1)$$

In a BN we can then identify a qualitative part (the structure represented by the DAG) and a quantitative part (the set of conditional probabilities). In particular, the quantitative part is specified by considering the probability of each value of a variable conditioned by every possible instantiation of its parents; variables having no parents are called "root variables" and prior probabilities are associated with them. An example of a BN is shown in figure 1; the net is intended to represent some causal

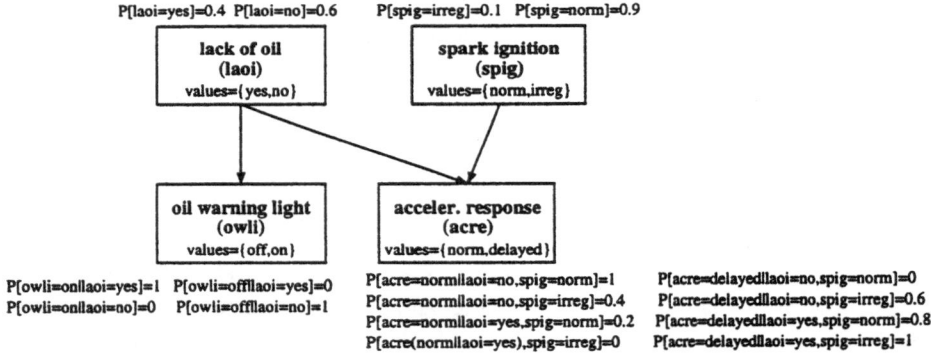

Fig. 1. Example of Bayesian Network

relations concerning the behavior of a car engine and variable names are acronyms for particular conditions (as shown in the figure). From the above definitions, it turns out that a first similarity between BNs and definite clause models can be identified. In fact, a BN can be represented by means of a set of formulae syntactically viewed as *definite clauses* annotated with conditional probability values.

Definition 1. A conditional probabilistic clause (or simply cp-clause) is a labeled formula of the type

$$Q_1(q_1) \wedge Q_2(q_2) \wedge \dots \wedge Q_k(q_k) \rightarrow Q(q) : p \quad (k \geq 0)$$

---

of possible instantiations is finite the model can always be reformulated in terms of hierarchical set of clauses (i.e. with acyclicity at the predicate level).

where $Q(q)$ and each $Q_i(q_i)$ are ground atoms, $p = P[Q(q)|Q_1(q_1), \ldots Q_k(q_k)]$ and $p > 0$.

Given a Bayesian network N we can translate it into $\mathcal{L}_N$, the *clausal form* of N, by representing each entry of the conditional probability tables $p = P[Y = y|X_1 = x_1, X_2 = x_2, \ldots X_n = x_n]$ by means of a cp-clause where there is a one-to-one correspondence between the random variables of N and the predicates occurring in the cp-clauses. Obviously, since "pure " definite clause models do not allow the expression of probability values, we start by considering BNs with *extreme probabilities* i.e. probability values in the set $\{0, 1\}$. In this case, we can notice that cp-clauses annotated with $p = 1$ directly correspond to definite clauses, since it can be easily proved that if $P[\alpha] \neq 0$ then $P[\beta|\alpha] = 1 \Leftrightarrow P[\neg\alpha \vee \beta] = 1$. A BN with $\{0, 1\}$ probabilities is then equivalent to a hierarchical set of definite clauses corresponding to cp-clauses with annotated value equal to 1. Notice that, especially for diagnostic purposes, one is often interested in considering only probability values of N which are not prior probabilities (i.e. cp-clauses with non empty body); in case non-prior probabilities of N are all equal to 0 or 1, the corresponding set of definite clauses will be indicated as $\mathcal{D}_N$.

On the other hand, a hierarchical set of definite clauses M can be in general considered as an *underspecified* BN with $\{0, 1\}$ probabilities. Indeed, being the PDG of M a DAG, it can be considered as the structure of a BN; the underspecification may arise since in writing the model there is no explicit commitment (as in BNs) to model the influence of every instantiation of parents (wrt to the PDG) on a given predicate.

Example 1. Consider the following set of definite clauses:
$T_1 = \{\text{laoi(yes)} \rightarrow \text{owli(on)}; \text{laoi(yes)} \rightarrow \text{acre(delayed)}; \text{spig(irreg)} \rightarrow \text{acre(delayed)}\}$

The PDG corresponds to the structure of the BN in figure 1; however, the set of definite clauses T_1 has a basic difference with respect to the BN: it only shows influences among abnormal values (i.e. the model is a *fault model*). The fact that acre(delayed) can be caused by either laoi(yes) or spig(irreg) implicitly represents the following situation:

$S_1 = \{\text{laoi(yes)} \wedge \text{spig(norm)} \rightarrow \text{acre(delayed)}; \text{spig(irreg)} \wedge \text{laoi(no)} \rightarrow \text{acre(delayed)};$
laoi(yes) $\wedge$ spig(irreg) $\rightarrow$ acre(delayed)$\}$

The model S_1 is underspecified because, for instance, nothing is said about the consequences of having "laoi(no) $\wedge$ spig(norm)$"$; on the contrary, this piece of information has to be provided when using the formalism of Bayesian Networks. Indeed, let figure 2 be a set of extreme conditional probabilities for non-root nodes of the BN N of figure 1: the corresponding set of definite clauses is composed by

$\mathcal{D}_N = S_1 \cup \{\text{laoi(no)} \wedge \text{spig(norm)} \rightarrow \text{acre(norm)}; \text{laoi(no)} \rightarrow \text{owli(off)}; \text{laoi(yes)} \rightarrow$
owli(on)$\}$

Notice that explicitly considering the structure induced by the influences of the modeled entities (variables in BNs and predicates in Horn models) allows one to conceptually separate the modeling and the reasoning tasks. As recognized by researchers in both logical [15] and probabilistic area [10], thinking about direct influences among entities in constructing the model allows all basic patterns of plausible reasoning (prediction, explanation and explaining away) to be naturally performed.

$$\begin{array}{ll} P[owli = on|laoi = yes] = 1 & P[acre = delayed|laoi = no, spig = irreg] = 1 \\ P[owli = off|laoi = no] = 1 & P[acre = delayed|laoi = yes, spig = norm] = 1 \\ & P[acre = delayed|laoi = yes, spig = irreg] = 1 \\ & P[acre = norm|laoi = no, spig = norm] = 1 \end{array}$$

Fig. 2. A set of extreme probabilities

In the following, we will concentrate on the notion of explanation and its role in characterizing diagnostic solutions; this allows us to compare Horn models and BNs, by taking into account one of the major area of attention of both formalisms (and of AI in general).

3 Characterizing Diagnostic Problems

3.1 Logic-Based Characterization

A very general characterization of diagnostic problems, using Horn theories, has been proposed in [5] as a form of abduction with consistency constraints.

Definition 2. A diagnostic problem is a 3-tuple[4] $DP = \langle\langle S, H\rangle, \Psi^+, \Psi^-\rangle$ where:

- S is a *hierarchical* set of definite clauses representing the model of the behavior of the system and H is a set of predicates called *abducible predicates* used to express diagnostic hypotheses;
- Ψ^+ is the set of observable parameters to be covered (i.e. accounted for) in the problem;
- Ψ^- is the set of observable parameters conflicting with the set of observations.

OBS denotes the whole set of observations of the current problem; since we abstract from temporal aspects, we assume that every value of a parameter different than the observed one is conflicting with OBS, i.e. $\Psi^- = \{Q(x)|Q(y) \in OBS, x \neq y\}$.

Definition 3. Given a diagnostic problem $DP = \langle\langle S, H\rangle, \Psi^+, \Psi^-\rangle$, an *ap-assignment* is a set $W = \{Q(a)|Q \in H\}$; it is said *consistent* iff $Q(a) \in W \to Q(b) \notin W$ for $b \neq a$; it is said *total* iff $\forall Q \in H$ Q is mentioned in W (otherwise is said to be *partial*).

Definition 4. Given a diagnostic problem $DP = \langle\langle S, H\rangle, \Psi^+, \Psi^-\rangle$, a *diagnosis* is a consistent total ap-assignment W such that

$$\forall m(a) \in \Psi^+ \ S \cup W \vdash m(a); \quad \forall m(b) \in \Psi^- \ S \cup W \nvdash m(b)$$

This general characterization can be specialized by making explicit the relation between Ψ^+ and OBS and by identifying the kind of entities which can be considered as diagnostic hypotheses [18]. As shown in [5], this definition captures in the same

---

[4] In the original characterization of [5] contextual information is also taken into account, however for the sake of simplicity we do not consider it here.

framework the classical definitions of *consistency-based diagnosis* and *abductive diagnosis* in case $\Psi^+ = \emptyset$ or $\Psi^+ = OBS$ respectively. In general $\Psi^+ \subseteq OBS$ and the choice of Ψ^+ has a big impact on what we finally get as solutions to the diagnostic problem. In the above definition, a diagnosis is committed to mention all possible abducible predicates; one can accept a partial ap-assignment W as a diagnosis if and only if every total consistent extension of W is still a diagnosis following definition 4 (see the notion of kernel diagnosis introduced in [6]). Moreover, definition 4 also implies that the set of possible values for abducibles is known in advance; one can relax this requirement by considering W to be a set of ground literals constructed from H; the abducible term $\neg Q(a)$ can then be used to state that the value of abducible Q must not be a, without making additional assumptions on the actual value of Q.

Concerning the choice of abducible predicates, a common assumption is to consider as abducibles the predicates not appearing in the head of any clause. For instance, in *component oriented diagnosis* abducible predicates are identified with behavioral modes of the components [7] which are assumed to be primitive entities and to be mutually independent. In some other cases, the real evolution followed by the system has to be determined and abducibles are identified with predicates appearing in the derivational trace from primary causes to ultimate observable consequences.

It is worth noting that, in the above characterization, i alot of emphasis is given to the notion of derivation. Such a notion is crucial in order to determine the actual definition of diagnostic problems that one wants to choose from the "spectrum" of definition 2. Since the main goal of the paper is to extract commonalities between Horn models and BNs when used for diagnostic reasoning, the introduction of a notion similar to that of logical derivation into BNs becomes very important. In the following we will discuss how this can be done by exploiting the cp-clause representation for BNs.

3.2 A Formal Notion of Derivation for Bayesian Networks

Let N be a Bayesian network and $M = \mathcal{L}_N$ be its clausal form, we denote as B_M the set of ground atoms of M (the corresponding of the Herbrand base of M thought as a set of unannotated clauses). If $\alpha \subseteq B_M$, we denote as $Pred(\alpha)$ the set of predicates mentioned in α. Given a BN N, if Λ is a set of ground atoms in $M = \mathcal{L}_N$, we indicate with $\mathcal{V}_\Lambda$ the corresponding variable assignment in N. We call Λ a *predicate instantiation*; Λ is *consistent* iff $Q(a) \in \Lambda \to Q(b) \notin \Lambda$; Λ is *total* iff $Pred(\Lambda) \equiv Pred(B_M)$ (otherwise is *partial*). Consider the clausal form $\mathcal{L}_N$ of a BN N and let
$\Omega = \{W | W \subseteq B_M \text{ and } W \text{ be a consistent total predicate instantiation.}\}$ and
$\forall W \in \Omega \ P'(W) = P(\mathcal{V}_W)$ with P given by equation (1). It is well-known [9] that $(\Omega, 2^\Omega, \pi)$ is a probability space where $\forall \beta \in 2^\Omega$

$$\pi(\beta) = \sum_{W \in \Omega \wedge \beta \in W} P'(W)$$

This result can be interpreted as a form of derivation and in particular, if $p = \pi(\beta)$, we will say that $\mathcal{L}_N$ **derives** β **at probability** p and we write $\mathcal{L}_N \vdash \beta : p$. The fact that the above notion can be interpreted as a form of derivation follows from the fact that $\pi(\beta)$ can be actually obtained by means of a bottom-up application of the set of cp-clauses of $\mathcal{L}_N$. Because of the length limitation of the paper no further detail is provided here; however, in an extended version [14] it is formally shown how the value $\pi(\beta)$ could be characterized in terms of the fixpoint of a transformation operator on the set of cp-clauses, i.e. using the same machinery adopted in Horn models for characterizing the notion of bottom-up derivation[5].

Example 2. Let us consider again the simple BN of figure 1; the corresponding set M of cp-clauses is shown in figure 3. We obtain for instance that

```
laoi(yes) : 0.4          spig(irreg) : 0.1
laoi(no) : 0.6           spig(norm) : 0.9

laoi(yes) → owli(on) : 1   laoi(no) ∧ spig(norm) → acre(norm) : 1
laoi(no) → owli(off) : 1   laoi(no) ∧ spig(irreg) → acre(delayed) : 0.6
                           laoi(no) ∧ spig(irreg) → acre(norm) : 0.4
                           laoi(yes) ∧ spig(norm) → acre(norm) : 0.2
                           laoi(yes) ∧ spig(norm) → acre(delayed) : 0.8
                           laoi(yes) ∧ spig(irreg) → acre(delayed) : 1
```

Fig. 3. Set of cp-clauses for the example net

$M \vdash$ acre(norm):0.636. Indeed there are three sequences of cp-clauses leading to acre(norm):
⟨laoi(no):0.6, spig(norm):0.9, laoi(no) ∧ spig(norm) → acre(norm):1⟩ at probability 0.54,
⟨laoi(yes):0.4, spig(norm):0.9, laoi(yes) ∧ spig(norm) → acre(norm):0.2⟩ at probability 0.072
⟨laoi(no):0.6, spig(irreg):0.1, laoi(no) ∧ spig(irreg) → acre(norm):0.4⟩ at probability 0.024,
resulting in a total probability value of 0.636.

The above notion of derivation can be exploited to characterize probabilistic schemata of diagnosis in a way very similar to the logical one. In the BN framework classical schemata for characterizing explanations of a given set of observations (i.e. diagnoses) can be identified as follows[6]:

- *most probable root nodes assignment*: the explanation is the most probable assignment to root variables;
- *most probable explanation* (MPE) also called *maximum a-posteriori model* (MAP): the explanation is the total variable assignment (excluded evidence variables) having highest probability value given the observations.

The first scheme is the closest to abductive logical characterizations. However, both such schemata can be redundant if no further restriction is imposed on the set of

---

[5] Actually, also classical model-theoretic and resolution-based semantics can be adapted to cp-clauses.

[6] A further scheme called *node posterior probability model* is often used, but as shown in [10], it is not really adequate so we will not consider it.

assigned variables. Two basic approaches can be devised; the first considers assignments restricted to variables (root variables in the first scheme) that are "causally related" to observations [10]. Such variables are usually called *evidentially supported*; for example in figure 1 "laoi" is evidentially supported by "owli", while "spig" is not. The second approach considers the so called *independence-based* (IB) *assignments* having highest probability (IB-MAP) (i.e. variable assignment $\mathcal{V}$ where unassigned ancestors of each variable X assigned in $\mathcal{V}$ remain unassigned if they cannot affect the value of X [16]). In the following we will show how the notion of probabilistic derivation allows us to define a uniform declarative framework, in such a way to extend the logical proposal to diagnosis characterization, in order to capture the probabilistic ones. This also suggests some considerations concerning important modeling issues arising in both Horn models and BNs, with particular attention to aspects concerning the completion of the model.

3.3 Relating Notions of Diagnosis

Let us now show how the explanation schemata for BNs previously discussed can be uniformly captured in a single framework naturally extending the logical characterization.

Definition 5. A **probabilistic diagnostic problem** DP is a triple $DP = \langle M, OBS, h \rangle$, where:

- M is the clausal form of a BN representing the model of the system to be diagnosed;
- OBS is a set of ground atoms denoting the set of the observations of the problem;
- $h : 2^{B_M} \to 2^{B_M}$ is a *diagnostic hypothesis function* specifying the set of predicates representing the diagnostic hypotheses, depending in general on the set of observations.

The formalization of different characterization of diagnosis can then be captured through h as follows:

- *Most Probable Root Assignment:* $h^{\mathcal{R}}(OBS) = \{Q | Q$ is a root$\}$
- *MPE Assignment:* $h^{MPE}(OBS) = Pred(B_M) - Pred(OBS)$
- *Evidentially Supported Assignments:* $h^{\epsilon}(OBS) = \{Q | Q$ is ev. supp. by $OBS\}$
- *Evidentially Supported Root Assignments:* $h^{\epsilon\mathcal{R}}(OBS) = \{Q | Q$ is a root ev. supp. by $OBS\}$

Definition 6. Given a probabilistic diagnostic problem $DP = \langle M, OBS, h \rangle$, a predicate instantiation Λ of M s.t. $Pred(\Lambda) = h(OBS)$ is a **probabilistic diagnosis** for DP if and only if

$$M \vdash (\Lambda \wedge OBS) : p_\Lambda \text{ with } p_\Lambda > 0$$

Notice that $p_\Lambda = \pi(\Lambda \wedge OBS) = P[\mathcal{V}_{\Lambda \wedge OBS}]$ and the posterior probability $\pi(\Lambda | OBS)$ can be computed from such a value after having computed the complete set of diagnoses for DP. Knowing the exact posterior probability value is just a matter of normalization and one is often interested only in the ranking of solutions. The ranking provided by posterior probabilities is the same provided by p_A; moreover, bounds on the posterior probability can be computed even if only some of the diagnoses have been singled out. The MPE model chooses the instantiation A s.t. $Pred(A) = h^{MPE}(OBS)$ having highest p_A and similarly other schemata of explanation[7].

Consider for instance the example of figure 3 with $OBS_2 = \{\text{owli(on)},\text{acre(delayed)}\}$; we have that $h^R(OBS_2) = h^{MPE}(OBS_2) = h^{\epsilon}(OBS_2) = h^{\epsilon R}(OBS_2) = \{\text{laoi},\text{spig}\}$. According to definition 5 there are two diagnoses $A_1 = \{\text{laoi(yes)},\text{spig(norm)}\}$ and $A_2 = \{\text{laoi(yes)},\text{spig(irreg)}\}$ such that $p_{A_1} = 0.288$ and $p_{A_2} = 0.04$; they can be obtained by searching the net starting from OBS_2 as shown in figure 4.

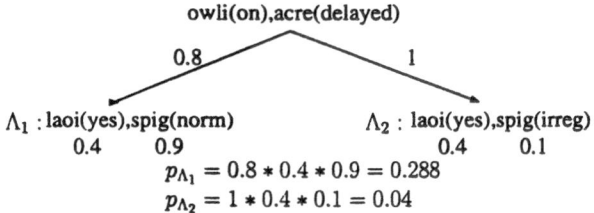

Fig. 4. Example of diagnosis computation

Posterior probabilities can then be computed as
$$\pi(A_i|OBS_2) = \frac{p_{A_i}}{\sum_{i=1}^{2} p_{A_i}} \quad \text{(i.e. } \pi(A_1|OBS_2) = 0.878 \text{ and } \pi(A_2|OBS_2) = 0.122\text{)}.$$

We have now to show how the above characterization is related to the one of section 3. While both frameworks are defined in terms of a notion of derivation, there are at least two apparent differences: the first is that in the logical framework the set of diagnostic hypotheses is on the left-hand side of the derivation symbols; the second (and more important) is that the above characterization is "purely abductive", i.e. there is no counterpart for the two sets Ψ^+ and Ψ^- induced by OBS. The first point is only a technical detail concerning the fact that in the probabilistic setting "facts" are considered part of the model (because they have associated a prior probability), while in the logical framework this is not the case. The second point concerns modeling issues and will be discussed in the next section.

4 Modeling Issues and Completion

As already discussed, an important modeling requirement of a BN concerns the fact that each value of a variable must be considered explicitly. This requirement of "completeness" seems very demanding, but it is worth noting that probabilities can be used to summarize exceptions to modeled processes. In logical models for diagnosis

---

[7] In case of diagnoses as IB-assignments, the above definition must be refined by restricting predicate instantiations A to be corresponding to variable assignments V_A which are IB-assignments.

there is no constraint on the explicit modeling of all values of the entities represented, but such a form of incompleteness and the difficulty in capturing exceptions and uncertainty require the introduction of specialized mechanisms. In definition 2, the right choice of Ψ^+ from OBS cannot be done without taking into consideration the degree of incompleteness of the logical model that consequently influences the combination of consistency and explicit covering in the definition of diagnosis. In order to illustrate the point and to single out some subtleties, let us consider the following logical model T_3 based on a modification of model T_1.

$T_3 = \{$laoi(severe) $\rightarrow$ owli(on); laoi(moderate) $\rightarrow$ owli(on);
laoi(severe) $\rightarrow$ acre(delayed); spig(irreg) $\rightarrow$ acre(delayed)$\}$

The set of abducibles is $H = \{$laoi,spig$\}$, the possible values of "owli" are $\{$on,off$\}$ and the ones of "acre" are $\{$norm,delayed$\}$. The above model is clearly incomplete (for instance nothing is said about the effect of laoi(moderate) on "acre" and there is no need for explicitly representing the combined effect of "laoi" and "spig" on "acre"). Despite this incompleteness, diagnostic solutions can be obtained by properly combining abduction with consistency. Let us suppose that $OBS_3 = \{$owli(off),acre(delayed)$\}$; if we require that $\Psi^+ = OBS_3$ there is no solution to the problem since we require covering of manifestations that have normal value and the model is incomplete as regards this aspect. On the contrary, if we put $\Psi^+ = \{$acre(delayed)$\}$ (and consequently we have $\Psi^- = \{$acre(norm),owli(on)$\}$), according to definition 4 and by considering diagnoses as literals, we obtain the diagnosis $W = \{\neg$laoi(severe), $\neg$laoi(moderate),spig(irreg)$\}$.

In [5] it is shown that a "strong" abductive approach to diagnosis (where the set of parameters to be explicitly covered by an explanation is very close to the whole set of observations) makes sense only if the model is reasonably complete or if incompleteness has been explicitly singled-out (for instance through special assumption symbols). This intuition is formally supported by results concerning abductive reasoning on "completed theories"; in particular, by considering Clark's predicate completion $\mathbf{comp}(T)$ [8] of non abducible predicates of a definite clause theory T, abduction can be regarded as deduction on $\mathbf{comp}(T)$ [4]. This shows that an abductive approach to diagnosis requires some form of complete knowledge, either explicitly provided by the designer of the model or implicitly assumed through a completion semantics of the model itself. Some form of completeness is required not only for the theory T but also for observable entities; in particular, according to definition 2 the construction of Ψ^- requires that for the observable entities the set of possible values is known a priori and is exhaustive. More formally, we assume that for each predicate symbol m corresponding to an observable parameter, $m(a_i) \wedge m(a_j) \rightarrow$ false if $a_i \neq a_j$ and $m(a_1) \vee \ldots \vee m(a_n)$ where a_i are the possible values of m.

It is worth pointing out that this is essentially the same assumption we have in BNs, where it is extended to every modeled entity (and not only to observable ones). In particular, this corresponds to assuming the axiom $NA : \neg Q(y) \equiv \bigvee_{x \neq y} Q(x)$ for each predicate Q corresponding to a variable of the BN. This models the BN requirement of having an exhaustive set of values for each modeled entity. Beside this correspondence between completeness assumptions on values of modeled entities, another important relationship can be established between completed logical theories and BNs. In particular, the following result provides a kind of "completion semantics" for BNs.

Theorem 1. *Given a discrete BN N with non-prior extreme conditional probabilities and the set of definite clauses $\mathcal{D}_N$ corresponding to them, $\mathcal{D}_N \cup NA \equiv \text{comp}(\mathcal{D}_N)$ (Clark's completion of non root predicates of $\mathcal{D}_N$).*

Proof (sketch) Consider a given node B of N having nodes $A_1 \ldots A_k$ as its parents. Let β be a generic variable assignments to B and $\overline{\alpha}_1 \ldots \overline{\alpha}_n$ be the possible combinations of variable assignments to parent variables $A_1 \ldots A_k$ ($n = \prod_{i=1}^{k} |A_i|$); let now r be the number of parent instantiations leading to a generic assignment β on B

$$P[\beta|\overline{\alpha}_1] = P[\beta|\overline{\alpha}_2] \ldots = P[\beta|\overline{\alpha}_r] = 1$$

This implies that

$$P[\neg\beta|\overline{\alpha}_{r+1}] = P[\neg\beta|\overline{\alpha}_{r+2}] = \ldots = P[\neg\beta|\overline{\alpha}_n] = 1$$

with $\neg\beta$ interpreted following axiom NA. It follows that

$\overline{\alpha}_1 \rightarrow \beta; \ \overline{\alpha}_2 \rightarrow \beta; \ \ldots \overline{\alpha}_r \rightarrow \beta$ and
$\overline{\alpha}_{r+1} \rightarrow \neg\beta; \ \overline{\alpha}_{r+2} \rightarrow \neg\beta; \ x \ldots \overline{\alpha}_n \rightarrow \neg\beta$.

Now, since $\overline{\alpha}_1 \vee \ldots \overline{\alpha}_r \equiv \neg\overline{\alpha}_{r+1} \wedge \ldots \neg\overline{\alpha}_n$ we obtain that $\beta \leftrightarrow \overline{\alpha}_1 \vee \ldots \overline{\alpha}_r$, from which the theorem follows. $\square$

The above theorem shows that the a BN can be interpreted in terms of a completion semantics; in particular this means that completion is essentially encoded in the formalism, rather than assumed as happens in logical formalisms where the model is usually incomplete. Therefore, when the system to be diagnosed is modeled through a BN, diagnostic problem solving relies then on some form of "complete" knowledge and a strong notion of explanation based on "pure" covering of observations is fully justified. In this way, there is no need of deciding which subset of OBS has to be explicitly covered, so the distinction between Ψ^+ and Ψ^- becomes irrelevant.

5 Conclusions

In the present paper, a formal comparison has been proposed at the modeling level between Horn models and Bayesian networks, with particular attention to diagnostic reasoning. Commonalities between such models have been pointed out, especially when a "completion semantics" is assumed for Horn models. Therefore, the two approaches are less different than usually believed: the benefits of the structure typical of BN formalism can be easily exploited in the logical one; on the other hand important results (such as precise definition of diagnostic solutions) developed in the MBD approach can be extended to the probabilistic one.

An important contribution in relating logical abduction and probabilistic reasoning is represented by Poole's *Probabilistic Horn Abduction* (PHA) [12]; however the emphasis of PHA is in using abductive explanations to compute probabilities of atoms and PHA introduces the definition of a logical language with probability to express conditional dependences, while our approach exploits the use of a direct Horn-like form of a BN. Our approach and PHA are then complementary. Beside the capture of the formal relation between notions of diagnosis in Horn-based models and BNs, an interesting side effect of the declarative representation we introduced in section 2 concerns the possibility of exploiting the algorithmic style of logical abduction (i.e. backward chaining on the set of clauses). As also showed by Poole within the PHA framework [11], this can lead to the definition of a goal-directed best-first search approach for diagnostic reasoning on BNs, having *anytime* features. The search algorithm can compute diagnoses by constraining their posterior probabilities within intervals that become tighter as more computation is allowed. Experiments have been extensively performed on different domains; they have shown that a direct abductive search on the cp-clause formalism can be a promising (and advantageous with respect to PHA) approach to anytime diagnostic inference on Bayesian nets.

References

1. C. Böttcher and O. Dressler. A framework for controlling model-based diagnosis with multiple actions. *Annals of Mathematics and Artificial Intelligence*, 11:241–262, 1994.
2. K. Clark. Negation as failure. In H. Gallaire and J. Minker, editors, *Logic and Data Bases*, pages 293–322. Plenum Press, 1978.
3. L. Console, L. Portinale, D. Theseider Dupré, and P. Torasso. Diagnosing time-varying misbehavior: an approach based on model decomposition. *Annals of Mathematics and Artificial Intelligence*, 11(1-4), 1994.
4. L. Console, D. Theseider Dupré, and P. Torasso. On the relationship between abduction and deduction. *Journal of Logic and Computation*, 1(5):661–690, 1991.
5. L. Console and P. Torasso. A spectrum of logical definitions of model-based diagnosis. *Computational Intelligence*, 7(3):133–141, 1991.
6. J. de Kleer, A. Mackworth, and R. Reiter. Characterizing diagnoses and systems. *Artificial Intelligence*, 56(2-3):197–222, 1992.
7. J. de Kleer and B.C. Williams. Diagnosis with behavioral modes. In *Proc. 11th IJCAI*, pages 1324–1330, Detroit, 1989.
8. J.W. Lloyd. *Foundations of Logic Programming*. Springer-Verlag, 1987.
9. R.E. Neapolitan. *Probabilistic Reasoning in Expert Systems*. J. Wiley, 1990.
10. J. Pearl. *Probabilistic Reasoning in Intelligent Systems*. Morgan Kaufmann, 1989.
11. D. Poole. Logic programming, abduction and probability. *New Generation Computing*, 11:377–400, 1993.
12. D. Poole. Probabilistic horn abduction and bayesian networks. *Artificial Intelligence*, 64(1):81–129, 1994.
13. D. Poole. Representing diagnosis knowledge. *Annals of Mathematics and Artificial Intelligence*, 11:33–50, 1994.
14. L. Portinale and P. Torasso. Diagnostic problem solving: Relating logical and probabilistic characterizations. Technical Report RT 40/97, Dip. Informatica, Universita' di Torino, 1997. ftp://ftp.di.unito.it/pub/portinal/tr40-97.ps.
15. M. Shanahan. Prediction is deduction but explanation is abduction. In *Proc. 11th IJCAI*, pages 1055–1060, Detroit, 1989.
16. S.E. Shimony. The role of relevance in explanation I. *Int. Journal of Approximate Reasoning*, 8:281–324, 1993.
17. P. Szolovits and S.G. Pauker. Categorical and probabilistic reasoning in medicine revisited. *Artificial Intelligence*, 59:167–180, 1993.
18. A. ten Teije and F. van Harmelen. An extended spectrum of logical definitions for diagnostic systems. In *Proc. DX 94*, New Paltz, 1994.
19. B. Wielinga, W Van de Velde, G. Schreiber, and H. Akkermans. Towards a unification of knowledge modelling approaches. In J-M. David, J-P Krivine, and R. Simmons, editors, *Second Generation Expert Systems*, pages 199–335. Springer Verlag, 1993.

Multi-agent Negotiation and Planning Through Knowledge Contextualization

Enver Sangineto

Dipartimento di Informatica e Sistemistica
Università di Roma La Sapienza
via Salaria 113, 00189 Roma
e-mail: sanginet@dis.uniroma1.it

Abstract. Behaviour protocols are often used to coordinate the action of a group of two or more agents by limiting the nature of the agents' goals and the possibility of backtracking in the negotiation.

The solution presented in this paper achieves the maximum flexibility because the negotiation itself is object of the planning activity. We extend the reasoning mechanism with the introduction of the concept of "knowledge contextualization": each context is a set of constraints to the agent action used to describe both plans and agreement offers.

A working example is presented to illustrate these ideas. It shows the simulation of a player of "Diplomacy", a complete (and difficult) game of strategy and diplomacy.

Finally, we propose a backtracking mechanism to solve the contradictions between the constraints of different contexts. This mechanism is compared with the Dependency Directed Backtracking (DDB) of the TMSs and it is shown that, in our case, it is complete while, DDB is not.

1 Introduction

Distributed Artificial Intelligence is interested in groups of autonomous agents, each of them with own goals, possibly in contrast with those of the others. If there is no contrast, we speak of "cooperative domain" otherwise of "non-cooperative domain". Agents can communicate among them and possibly decide a coordination of their actions. The problem of negotiation is how the agents can divide their tasks, help each other, solve conflicts and reach agreements.

There are several proposals, all based on particular behaviour protocols, that keep the rule of negotiation separate from that of planning.

For example, Rosenschein (see [12]) treats only cooperative domains in which the agents can divide a set of tasks among themselves. This is done in a series of steps in the following way.

At each step each agent offers a deal. It can repeat the offer of the previous step or it can make a new less demanding one. In this way, the process is monotonic and it either converges to a deal (when there is a step where the offer of some agent is more advantageous to the others then their requests), or it fails in conflict (no deal) if none wants to concede anything.

This protocol completely separates negotiation and planning. Once the negotiation phase is over and each agent knows the tasks it has to reach, it performs its planning activity independently of the other agents and completely ignores their presence. This is possible thank to the hypothesis that the set of tasks can be divided and each task must be executed only by an agent. Hence, the behaviour of the typical agent consists in trying to take for itself a number of tasks of minimum total cost, even though, at negotiation time, it does not know how to solve them. A typical example is the "Postmen Problem", where the agents must deliver some letters and, before the start, they can exchange letters to minimise the path of each postman.

Ephrati instead presents a proposal, in [4], where the domains can also be non-cooperative. He uses the example of the "Slotted Blocks World", in which there are some blocks and some numbered slots and each agent has a final configuration of the blocks in the slots to achieve. If these configurations are incompatible, a compromise configuration is an acceptable solution.

Ephrati uses a special protocol based on a voting mechanism. The plan is a group plan incrementally built by all the agents with an alternation of proposals and votings. At each step all the agents make their own proposal about the next joint action in the group plan to reach the next desired state. Later on, each agent gives a vote to all the proposals as a weight that takes into account its own goal function. The winning proposal is the one that gets the maximum weight. Of course an agent may cheat and give a proposal a weight that does not correspond to its goal function with the purpose of biasing the result of the vote. Cheating is discouraged by the presence of a centralised mechanism that taxes the agents whose votes were too different from the winning alternative.

This is not a real negotiation, because the agents plan their actions autonomously and the interaction among them is simply decided by the outcome of the voting. They could be not conscious at all of the existence of the other agents, while there is an unnatural centralised unit that decides for them and taxes with penalty scores the liars.

Both in Ephrati and in Rosenschein protocols it is not possible to backtrack: this ensures convergence, but forbids to withdraw mistaken decisions.

Contributions about the problem of negotiation come also from Game Theory [11]. The typical example is the "Prisoner problem". Each player must decide whether to confess, thus deceiving the companion, or remain faithful to him, hoping that he does the same. In the "multiple shot" games there is a series of turns in which this decision is iterated. Game Theory has formulated a series of strategies that are "statistically winning". These strategies have a coarse grain, because they have a binary output: to be loyal or to deceive. In more real situations of decision making, it is instead important to take into account the aspects contingent to the actual state (objective costs and benefits of a particular choice) and to have a more articulate output, i.e. a detailed agreement and not just a binary output.

The solution presented in this paper is more flexible than the previous ones, because the negotiation itself is object of the planning activity. The process of planning make each single agent must first of all be conscious of what it needs and what it can give to the others. Afterwards, it can deal with the others, conceding something or demanding something for itself.

2 Knowledge in contexts

2.1 Agent-contexts

In order for the planning mechanism to take into account the behaviour of the other agents, it is necessary to contextualise knowledge. Namely, the reasoning of each agent must depend on the supposed reasoning of the other ones. An agent must explicitly handle "knowledge about knowledge" using some kind of epistemic logic (see, for instance, [2, 3, 10]). We will not enter into details but we limit ourselves to observe that, with epistemic logics, we can split the reasoning into different, possibly conflicting, contexts [1, 6, 7].

Imagine we want to describe the planning process of one of the agents, say A, and the way in which it organises its knowledge. In the sequel we will leave A implicit whenever it is clear from the context.

First of all there is a context for each agent: context c_A, c_B, c_C, and so on, that are A's representations of "the mind" of, respectively, A itself, B, C,... In general we have the following:

Definition 1. An *agent–context* c_X contains all the private knowledge attributed to the agent X.

In the above definition and in the following we use as meta-variables, X, Y and Z to range over names of agents.

In c_X we can find, for example, the offer of agreement made by X to A (or by A to X). Note that this knowledge is only shared by A and X, without being known to all the group.

All the contexts have the same (first order) language (this is not necessarily always true: see, for example, [7]). Besides, the agent–contexts share a Common Knowledge (CK) describing the rules of the world in which the agents act.

By switching from c_X to c_Y, it is possible to simulate a change of point of view. For this reason in the language there exists a constant I denoting "self" with an interpretation depending on the agent–context. In each agent– context c_X, in fact, a private axiom asserts that: $I = X$. In this way c_X "knows who is" and it can applies the common knowledge to its point of view.

2.2 Plans

The contextualization of knowledge is also present in the agent–contexts, to describe different situations.

Definition 2. A *situation P* describes a possible evolution of the scenario with respect to a particular goal G and depending on particular assumptions on the behaviour of the agents.

Definition 3. For each P and each agent–context c_X, a *plan* c_{XP} is the context in which c_X tries to deduce a series of actions that allows X to achieve G.

Each plan can be seen as a *set of constraints*. Each hypothesis on the actions of an agent is, in fact, a constraint on its behaviour and a plan is a collection of actions that uniquely determines the agent behaviour.

We have more than one situation both because for the same goal G there may be several situations depending on different assumptions, and because we suppose that an agent can execute more actions simultaneously, so as to achieve more goals. This is a generalisation of the classical planning problem in which a serialisation of the agents' tasks is not imposed.

The situation P is then incrementally analysed by switching from the context c_{XP} to the context $c_{YP'}$, ... starting from some hypotheses about $X, Y,...$ and continuing by deducing the plausible consequences. If, for some reason, we think that some of the hypotheses on which c_{XP} (for some X) is based are no longer founded, it is necessary to re-analyse P, namely create c_{XP}, and, consequently, c_{YP}, c_{ZP}.... This means that X has now different ideas about P, its behaviour is supposed to be different from the previous one, then, also Y, Z,... will behave differently to suitably answer to X.

In this way a series of situations is created, and each situation describes how things will go if all agents behave according to its hypotheses. By changing the hypotheses all the possible situations are covered. In other words, it is the process of planning that makes each agent conscious of the tools and the goals and subgoals it has (and the others have...). Then, only by integrating negotiation with planning, it is possible for the agent to correctly valuate requests and offers that it receives and that it must ask.

Definition 4. Given an agent context c_X, two plans c_{XP} and $c_{XP'}$ are mutually *(globally) inconsistent* when there is at least an action $a1$ in c_{XP} and an action $a2$ in $c_{XP'}$ such that $a1 \wedge a2 \wedge CK$ is inconsistent.

This means that c_{XP} and $c_{XP'}$ contain actions that the Common Knowledge about the world forbids to execute together. For instance in the Blocks World two plans will be inconsistent if they move the same block to two different places.

When this holds, the planning mechanism explicitly signals it by adding the pair $\langle c_{XP}, c_{XP'} \rangle$ to a special *Inconsistency* relation among plans. In Section 7 we will see how planning tries to solve this inconsistency re–planning c_{XP} or $c_{XP'}$ (i.e. re–analysing P or P'). At the end of the planning, if not all the inconsistencies are solved, it is necessary to do a choice of actions executable which maximises the gain of A. The strategy that says to A what to do is constituted by the maximal consistent set of plans:

Definition 5. A set of plans M is *maximal consistent* when, $\forall c_{AP}, c_{AP'} \in M$, the pair $\langle c_{AP}, c_{AP'} \rangle \notin$ *Inconsistency* and does not exist $M' \supset M$ with the same property.

3 Agreements as sets of duties

Returning to the concept of plan as a set of constraints, it is possible to generalise and to see an agreement as a plan. In fact, an agreement is (first of all) a set of duties, i.e. constraints to the action of the agents that want to respect it.

Definition 6. For each offer of agreement made by X to Y, a *Partially Specified plan* (PS) P_{XY} contains the description of the actions not to be done in order to respect the agreement. P_{XY} belongs both to the agent–context c_X and to the agent–context c_Y.

Thus a normal plan is a collection of actions that can be executed, while a PS plan contains a list of negations and can not be executed. PS plans are treated like normal plans, thinking of them as contexts based on some constraining assumptions. For example, suppose that in the plan c_P, A does not respect the engagements taken with B. c_P is then inconsistent with the PS plan P_{BA} (there is an action a s. t. a is in c_P and P_{BA} implies $\neg a$). Consequently, the planning mechanism adds the pair $\langle c_P, P_{BA} \rangle$ to the Inconsistency relation. At this point a new situation P' is analysed, by changing the hypotheses on A's behaviour, which in this case is fair, and the process continues normally. At the end of the planning process, if the plan $c_{P'}$ was successful (i.e. it was possible to create a plan $c_{P'}$ in which A achieves the same goal G as in c_P, but with the hypothesis of fairness with respect to B), then there exists a strategy that allows A to achieve G and to accept the offer of B. Otherwise, A must choose between c_P and P_{BA}, i.e. A knows that it can achieve G with the plan c_P or it can be faithful to B, but not both.

4 Do ut des

Nevertheless, an agreement is not only a set of duties, i.e. a set of things that the contracting parties must not do. In some cases, in fact, it can also contain an accord of reciprocal help among different agents (do ut des). Namely, it is possible that the agent A, in order to achieve a goal, asks another agent B to do some actions in its place. Thus, a plan c_{AP} could be constituted of actions made by A and other actions made by B. The execution of these last ones is not under A's control, because they are constraints on the behaviour of another agent (B). So, A must include them in the requests that it will issue to B in the final offer of agreement.

The plan c_{AP} must thus contain actions made by B together with actions made by A. So, during the planning of c_{AP}, A can also use "operators" of other agents, marking these actions as "not own". Of course this does not ensure that B will really execute the requests. This situation can be as usual described by creating a new plan $c_{AP'}$ in which A is bound to use only own operators (c_{AP} and $c_{AP'}$ together obviously inconsistent).

The next sections show a complex and complete example fully worked out and implemented to better explain all the previous ideas. The example is a procedure that simulates a player of a social game called Diplomacy. This game has been chosen because it contains all the elements of a real negotiation: devising tasks, reciprocal help, and also the possibility to deceive the agreements made.

5 Diplomacy: A complete example of negotiation

Diplomacy is a social game based on strategy and diplomacy. There are several players (from two to seven) and there is only a winner. This means that at some point players must conflict. Nevertheless, during the game it is important (essential) to form alliances with someone to join forces against the others.

Let us now give a short description of the game.

There is a geographic map of Europe as it was at the time World War I, divided into "Lands", and among those, the "Centres" give a score to their owners. Each Land can be occupied by at most one army. In each turn a player can move as many of its armies as he wants, but each army can receive at most one order (i.e. do at most one move) in each turn. This is a case in which an agent can execute more than an action at one time, as we saw in Section 2.

There are three main types of moves: stop (i.e. no action, which can be assimilated to defence), *movement* (i.e. attack), *support* (which increases the power of a defence or of an attack). If an army attacks another one that defends itself, the army wins that has received more supports. Finally, the order to an army A to support another one B is nullified if an enemy army, say C, attacks A during the same turn.

Diplomacy is a multiple shot game with no random elements and an "imperfect" information. In fact each player at each move does not know the intentions of the others. An important peculiarity of this game is in fact that, differently from Chess (a game with perfect information) where black and white alternate, here all the players play simultaneously: at each turn all the players write their moves on a piece of paper; later on all of them read their moves and the ones which do not create a deadlock are executed.

Another important characteristic of Diplomacy is that at the beginning of each turn, each couple of players can negotiate secret agreements of every kind. These agreements are not constraining, i.e., during the second part of the turn (when writing the moves), they can be deceived.

We have chosen Diplomacy because it is a game where the negotiation problem is present in its most general form: agreements can be of any nature and each player is uncertain about the fairness of the others, due to the synchronism of the action. Moreover, Diplomacy, as all expert players know, is an "intelligent" game of the same difficulty level as Chess.

6 An implementation of Diplomacy

We developed [13] a working program called MD that simulates a player of Diplomacy which competes with other two (human) players. Of course, MD is easily extendible to play against n human players.

MD is written in GETFOL [8], a proof editor derived from the system FOL developed by Weyhrauch [14]. GETFOL is based on a first order language with self reference capabilities, in which contexts can be defined in the form of first order theories, by defining a set of symbols (the theory language) and a set of facts (the nonlogical axioms and the derived theorems). Another peculiarity of GETFOL is the possibility of mixing a double computational approach: a declarative (logical) description and a procedural (Lisp like) one. For the purpose of the present work, GETFOL has been extended to be used as an automated theorem prover, by the addition of a Prolog like resolution facility [13].

6.1 Axiomatisation

In MD there are four static contexts and a variable number of dynamic (run time) ones. The static contexts are: c_M, c_A and c_B, that contain the private knowledge attributed by MD (the machine) to MD itself, A and B (the two human players). Besides, there is a fourth context called Meta that is the supervisor of the three former ones.

The axioms belonging to the CK describe the topology of the map, the position of the armies on it and a list of rules representing at the same time the rules of the game and the "know how", i.e. the heuristics that MD uses to guess what kind of move an army may do in each particular situation. All the axioms have an Horn clause form. Examples of axioms are:

$$Next(la1, la2)$$
$$OwnsArmy(B, la)$$
$$Attacks(g, supports(x, moves(y, g))) \Leftarrow Moves(y, g) \land OwnsArmy(I, y) \land$$
$$Next(x, g) \land OwnsArmy(I, x) \land$$
$$\neg Busy(x)$$

where la, $la1$ and $la2$ are constants that stand for Lands, B is a constant that stands for the name of the player B; I is the constant denoting "self", and x, y and g are variables ranging over Lands.

The first axiom states that lands $la1$ and $la2$ share a border; the second one states that (in the current turn of the game) in la there is an army of the player B. The last axiom states that a player (say X) can strengthen its attack to the Land g (not necessarily a Centre) with the move $supports(x, moves(y, g))$ (which reads the army in x supports the army in y that moves into g) if:

1. there is an army y just moving in g (i.e. the actual plan for g just contains the action: $moves(y, g)$));
2. X owns y (remember that in c_X holds $I = X$);
3. the Land g is next to the Land x;
4. X has got an army in x;
5. the army in x is not busy in some other move.

Note that the last condition forces x and y to be two distinct armies. Note also that "Moves" is a predicate and "moves" is a function. This distinction is essentially due to the restriction of first order languages that forbids the presence of predicates as arguments to other predicates.

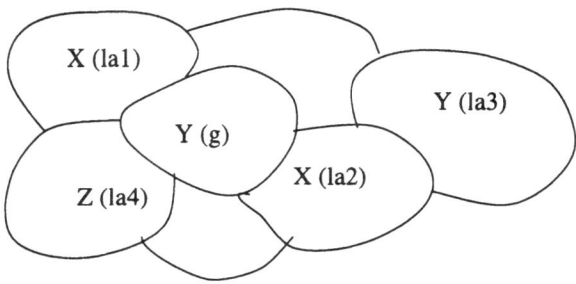

Fig. 1. The scenario of a conflict

6.2 Planning

Plans to conquer (or to defend) the Centres are built incrementally by collecting, for each of them, a series of moves deduced by the procedure below. Looking at Figure 1, we suppose that X (i.e. one among MD, A or B) owns armies in $la1$ and $la2$, Y in g (a Centre) and $la3$, and Z in $la4$. We also suppose that there is no alliance among the players. We show the steps of the procedure in an informal way, intermixed with some comments:

1. For all the Centres g:
2. create the contexts: c_{Mg}, c_{Ag} and c_{Bg};
3. starting from some context c_X, a move $m1$ is deduced.

When we say "deduced" we mean automatically inferred by a Prolog like resolution theorem prover. The goal clause is of the form: $Attacks(g, m)$, where g is a constant and m is a variable that the resolver tries to instance by looking for a possible move. If the resolution successes the system asserts $m1$ in c_{Xg}. In our example $m1$ is $m = moves(la1, g)) \Rightarrow Attacks(g, m)$.

4. $m1$ is suitably treated in the context Meta. Here, among other things, some functions of the solution are transformed into predicates (for example, the formula "$m = moves(la1, g) \Rightarrow Attacks(g, m)$", is transformed into: "$Moves(la, g))$". This is possible thank to the fact that in Meta formulas of the other contexts are reified to become terms of its language;
5. $m1$ is assumed in c_{Yg} and c_{Zg};
6. a switch into c_{Yg} is performed.

The meaning of 4. and 5. is: X changes its point of view and –for a moment– it thinks as if it were Y, and Y were aware of $m1$.

7. In c_{Yg} a counter-move $m2$ is deduced (example: the army in g stops);
8. $m2$ is assumed in c_{Xg} and in c_{Zg};
9. a switch into c_{Zg} is performed;
10. $m3$ is deduced in c_{Zg} (example: $la4$ moves in g);

11. if at least two among $m1$, $m2$ and $m3$ are not the null move, then go to 3;

The process continues by switching again into c_{Xg}, where X tries to deduce a counter–counter–move $m4$ (example: the army in $la2$ supports the army in $la1$); then MD looks, in c_{Yg}, for a counter–move $m5$ (such as, for instance, $la3$ moves in $la2$ to nullify $la2$ support...) and so on.

12. otherwise the "winner" is the last agent that has performed a counter–move;
13. go to 1 to analyse the next Centre.

At Step 11 the process terminates when only one player still has counter–moves to perform. Suppose that Y is such a winner: c_{Yg} now contains a series of moves that allow Y to defend g against X and Z. This plan can, obviously, be performed in the case that X, Y and Z behave as assumed in c_{Yg} (i.e. in the situation g). For the moment there are no good reasons to suppose the contrary, namely, it is natural to suppose that X, Y and Z will use all the armies available to them in the best way to conquer (or to defend) g. In the coming section we see that this assumption is not necessarily true.

The planning method proposed so far resembles the Situation Calculus in its use of first order logic and in the presence of action precondition axioms. We now point out some differences between them. The Situation Calculus [9] uses a special function do(a,S), in which a is a sequence of actions and S is the initial situation. The resolution has to instantiate a that becomes a term of the form: $do(action1, do(action2, do(...)))$, that describes the plan. In our procedure, instead, the resolver is called in more than one step, each time looking for a single move m instead of a sequence. This simplifies the axioms a lot. Besides, the possibility to manage directly actions rather then having atomic sequences of actions facilitates Meta to discover inconsistencies among plans (see Definition4).

7 An efficient algorithm to choose the strategy

7.1 Meta–backtracking among plans

In the example above, X Y and Z use all the armies in the conflict for the Centre g. In a more realistic situation the same army could be useful in more then one conflict for different Centres. It is a partition resource problem and it is the main difficulty of this game.

Every time MD (in the context c_X) plans a plan (c_{XP}), it looks for the availability of armies not just assigned to some other plans. This knowledge is given by the relation Busy, inherited by c_X. Vice–versa, when c_{XP} used an army a in some move, the assumption Busy(a) is lifted in c_X .

Suppose that MD has just examined the Centres $g_1, ..., g_n$, finding, for each of them, the plans $P_1, ..., P_n$ (for simplicity we consider only one agent, so P stands for c_{XP}).

Suppose now that MD examines g_{n+1} and there are no more free armies for it. Then MD allows P_{n+1} to use all the armies it wants, without any constraint.

At this point we have a situation globally inconsistent because P_{n+1} uses armies that CK asserts to be Busy (see Definition4). Thus MD has to do a "meta" backtracking on plans, looking for a better partition of the armies used.

An easy but expensive way to backtrack in the set $T = (P_1, ..., P_{n+1})$ is: nullify P_{n+1}, come back to P_n (here change the assumptions on the armies' availability) create P'_n, and, possibly, repeat the procedure until P_1 is chosen. Nevertheless the armies used in P_{n+1} interest only some of the $P_1, ..., P_n$ (we suppose P_i): the other plans are independent of the change of assumptions.

So, the algorithm we are going to describe ("meta" from now on) behaves like in TMSs [5]: it tries to change only the necessary, leaving the rest unaltered. It does not follow the chronological order of the choices but accurately selects what it needs. The fundamental idea is that the backtracking queue is not T, but it starts with $Q = (P_{n+1})$ and takes what it needs out of T.

At this point, meta changes the assumptions in the context-agent (say c_X) father of P_{n+1}, assigning to P_{n+1} the armies it uses. Then it increases Q with P_i and tries to plan a new solution P'_i for the centre g_i (with the new assumptions in c_X, P'_i can not use the armies of P_{n+1}).

If P'_i, in its turn, uses some other busy armies (for instance, of P_j), then Q becomes: (P_{n+1}, P'_i, P_j) and meta tries with P'_j. If P'_i does not use just busy armies, then meta succeeds, otherwise, if it does not find armies at all, if fails: in both cases Q decreases (otherwise it continues to increase...). If Q returns to P'_i with a failure, then meta tries with P''_i, else P'_i is popped from Q.

Finally, each time two plans P_1 and P_2 are inconsistent, meta adds the pair $\langle P_1, P_2 \rangle$ to the already mentioned Inconsistency relation (in the previous example, $Inconsistency(P_{n+1}, P'_i)$ holds).

7.2 Dependency Directed versus meta backtracking

The difference between meta and the Dependency Directed Backtracking (DDB) used in TMSs is worth pointing out.

Both algorithms, when they come to a failure, try to modify as little as possible, leaving unaltered the deductions not involved in the failure. Besides, both use a relation of dependency among the elements of the domain (meta uses Busy). Nevertheless the similarities end here.

Suppose that DDB fails when its choice set is $T = (A_1, ..., A_n)$. Then it starts from A_n and, following the (possible) logical dependencies among elements of T, it jumps to (for instance) A_i, thus cutting the portion of the search tree between A_n and A_i. Meta, instead, is based on the assumption that the sequence of elements in T is "random", namely, if A_j precedes A_{j+1}, this does not mean that the choice of A_j influences the choice of A_{j+1}. So, simply, the search tree of the algorithm is not represented by T, but T is only a place where to take the components of the backtracking queue. Starting from A_n, and assuming, as above, that there is a dependency between A_n and A_i, the queue representing the search tree is given by: $Q = (A_n, A_i)$. In this way nothing is cut.

Each time Q increases, meta controls that the new elements are not present in order to avoid loops. From this it derives that in the worst case Q increases to cover T, and then the complexity equals that of the classical chronological backtracking (but, of course, also DDB in the worst case behaves in the same way). In the average case, instead, the gain is very big, as it is shown by the implementation of Diplomacy, which, otherwise, would be intractable. In fact, with about 30 Centres in the map, T would have 15 elements in average, which, with chronological backtracking, gives 15 as the average depth of the search tree, while the branching factor is approximately 5 (the average number of Lands that share a boarder only with a Land)...

On the contrary, meta re-examines all and only the Lands actually interested in that area, ignoring the others, thank to the property of locality of the conflicts.

Note that we can not use a DDB because we do not want to jump from A_n to A_i cutting $(A_{i+1}, ..., A_{n-1})$. In fact, A_i could be inconsistent with some A_k, with $i + 1 \leq k \leq n - 1$, hence the algorithm should jump to A_k. Jumping to A_i and forgetting the rest means loosing completeness of the search.

7.3 The diplomatic case

Meta becomes particularly powerful when it deals with inconsistency between plans and agreements. The latter, as we previously said, are PS plans, so, when a normal plan P violates the constraints described by the PS plan P_{XY}, meta creates $Q = (P_{XY}, P)$ and starts by looking for P', as described above.

MD computes the possibility to ask someone to execute some specific moves that can help it by creating plans in which MD uses both its armies and its ally's armies. As usual, meta computes the opposite situation in which MD uses only own forces by using other plans inconsistent with the former ones.

Once MD has examined all the Centres of the map, it selects the set W of all the plans in which it is the winner (see Section 6). In W there can be, of course, pairs of elements belonging to Inconsistency. MD now has to choose its diplomatic strategy so it computes all the possible diplomatic scenarios. An example of diplomatic scenario is: MD accepts A's agreement offer and refuses B's one. Thus, by W it derives S_1 deleting both those plans inconsistent with P_{AM} and the ones which use B's armies. MD then calculates the maximal consistent set (M_1) of plans belonging to S_1 and repeats the operation with S_2, and so on. Finally, the diplomatic strategy together with the final set of moves is chosen by taking the maximum M_i.

8 Conclusions

The reasoning mechanism of an agent has to be conscious of the presence of the other agents. In this way it can plan together its action and its agreements, taking into account the dependencies between them.

Integration between planning and negotiation is smartly achieved using only a general frame for plans and for agreements, both viewed as constraints sets.

This concept, together with a special mechanism of meta backtracking among contexts, allows us to examine in a very efficient and complete manner all the possible evolutions of the scenario and decide the best negotiation strategy.

In this paper we have shown a working implementation of these ideas in the solution of a diplomacy and strategy game that contains the negotiation problems in their most general form.

Finally, the meta backtracking mechanism proposed has been compared with the Dependency Directed backtracking and with the chronological backtracking, showing that it has the completeness of the latter (applied to our problem) and the efficiency of the former.

Acknowledgements

This paper presents some results taken from my tesi di laurea [13], completed in December 1995 at the University of Pisa, under the supervision of G. Prini and M. Simi. Thank to F. Giunchiglia for his suggestions and stimulating discussions, and to L. Carlucci Aiello for helping with the presentation.

References

1. L. Carlucci Aiello, D. Nardi, M. Schaerf; Reasoning about reasoning in a meta-level architecture, *Journal of Applied Intelligence* 1, 55-67,1991.
2. L. Carlucci Aiello, D. Nardi, M. Schaerf; Reasoning about knowledge: the meta-level approach, *S.C.A.I.*, 4-18, 1991.
3. G. Attardi, M. Simi; A formalization of viewpoints; *Fundamenta informaticae* **23**, n. 2,3,4 June-August 1995, 149-173.
4. E. Ephrati, J. S. Rosenschein; *Multi-agent planning as a dynamic search for social consensus*, Proceedings of IJCAI-93, 423-429, n. 1, 1993.
5. K. D. Forbus, J. de Kleer; *Building problem solvers*, The MIT Press, 1993.
6. F. Giunchiglia, L. Serafini; *Multilanguage first order theories of propositional attitudes*, IRST-Technical Report number 9001-02, 1990.
7. F. Giunchiglia, L. Serafini; Multilanguage hierarchical logics, *Artificial Intelligence* **65**, 29-70, 1994.
8. F. Giunchiglia; *GETFOL Manual*, DIST Technical Report number 92-0010, University of Genoa, 1994.
9. J. McCarthy, P. Hayes; Some philosophical problems from the standpoint of AI.; in *Machine Intelligence*, 4, 463-502, Edinburgh University Press, 1969.
10. D.Perlis; Languages with self-reference II: knowledge, belief, and modality, *Artificial Intelligence* **34**, 179-212, 1988.
11. R. Ragionieri; Notes on game theory, unpublished manuscript distributed as course at University of Pisa, March 1995.
12. J. S. Rosenschein, G. Zlotkin; A domain theory for task oriented negotiation, *Proceedings of IJCAI-93*, 1, 416-422, 1993.
13. E. Sangineto; *Diplomacy in FOL: il meta-ragionamento applicato alla diplomazia*, tesi di laurea, University of Pisa, December 1995.
14. R. W. Weyhrauch; Prolegomena to a Theory of Mechanized formal reasoning, *Artificial Intelligence* **13**, 133-170, 1980.

From Task Delegation to Role Delegation

Cristiano Castelfranchi and Rino Falcone

IP - CNR National Research Council

Group of "Artificial Intelligence, Cognitive Modelling and Interaction"

Viale Marx, 15 - 00137 ROMA - Italy
E-mail: {cris, falcone}@pscs2.irmkant.rm.cnr.it

Abstract. Roles may be analyzed in many ways: as "abstract agents"; as power positions; as sets of obligations; etc. For sure one of the main facets of roles is their Delegation-Adoption nature. This is exactly the perspective we assume here: it is a partial view of roles, but a fundamental one.
In this paper we try to analyze a role just as a special kind of task-delegation, or contract. We recapitulate the various *levels* of delegation and adoption (help), characterizing their basic principles and representations on the basis of a theory of plans, actions and agents. Then we show how *delegation creates roles as well as delegation creates tasks*. However, once roles exist they constraint also task delegation among agents. We examine also this dialectics between role and task delegation.

Introduction

The huge majority of DAI and MA, CSCW and negotiation systems, communication protocols, cooperative software agents, etc. are based on the idea that *cooperation works through the allocation of some task (or sub-task) by a given agent (individual or complex) to another agent*, via some "request" (offer, proposal, announcement, etc.) meeting some "commitment" (bid, help, contract, adoption, etc.). This core constituent of any interactive, negotial, cooperative system is not so clear, well founded and systematically studied as it might seem. Our claim is that *any support system for cooperation and any theory of cooperation require an analytic theory of delegation and adoption. Our contribute to this theory is a plan-based analysis of delegation.*

Moreover, the theories of the organization and of the social structure are centred on the notion of "role". There are many apparent analogies and relations between "roles" and "tasks", like the commitment and the responsibility of the agent "in charge of", like the fact that the role player has to carry out some tasks, etc.. Computational analyses of organization and AI privileged the "commitment" relation [1,2,3,16]. We claim that this is not in contrast with a role-based theory of organization. In fact, roles may be analyzed in many ways: as "abstract agents" [4]; as power positions; as sets of obligations [5]; etc. However, for sure one of the main facets of roles is their Delegation-Adoption nature. This is exactly the perspective we assume in this paper: this is a partial view of roles, but a fundamental one.

In this paper we try to analyze a role just as a special kind of task-delegation, or contract. We recapitulate the various *levels* of delegation and adoption (help), characterizing their basic principles and representations on the basis of a theory of plans, actions and agents. Then we show how *delegation creates roles as well as delegation creates tasks*. However, once roles exist they constraint also task delegation among agents. We examine also this dialectics between role and task delegation.

1 A plan-based theory of Delegation/Adoption

1.1 Definitions

Informally, *in delegation an agent A needs or likes an action of another agent B and includes it in its own plan*. In other words, *A is trying to achieve some of its goals through B's actions; thus A has the goal that B performs a given action*. A is constructing a Multi-Agent (MA) plan [6, 7] and B has a "part", a share in this plan: B's task (either a state-goal or an action-goal).
In adoption an agent B has a goal since and until it is the goal of another agent A, i.e. B has the goal of performing an action since this action is included in the plan of A.
So, also in this case B plays a part in A's plan.
Both delegation and adoption may be unilateral: B may ignore A's delegation while A may ignore B's adoption. In both cases A and B are, in fact, performing a MA plan (in these cases we have Weak Delegation and Weak Adoption respectively [8]).
In the following we present a plan-based formal analysis of delegation/adoption.
We assume that, *to delegate an action necessarily implies to delegate some results of that action*. Conversely, *to delegate a goal state always implies the delegation of at least one action (possibly unknown by A) that produces such a goal state as result*.
Thus, we consider the couple action/goal $\tau=(\alpha,g)$ as the real object of the delegation, and we will call it *task*. Then by τ, we will refer to the action (α), to its resulting world state (g), or to both. The action (α) may be either elementary or complex (i.e. a plan).

1.2 Plan Ontology

In this section we will introduce a more formal representation of agents, actions, plans [9] and action results. For a more detailed description of these concepts see [10, 8].
Let Act=$\{\alpha_1, ..., \alpha_n\}$ be a finite set of *actions*, let Agt=$\{A_1, .., A_n, B, C, ...\}$ a finite set of *agents*. Each agent has an action repertoire, a plan library, resources, goals (in general we intend with "goal" term a partial situation (a subset) of the "world state"), beliefs, interests [11].
The *general plan library* is $\Pi = \Pi^a \cup \Pi^d$, where Π^a is the abstraction hierarchy rule set and Π^d is the decomposition hierarchy rule set. As usual for each action there are: body, preconditions, constraints, results (Notice that we do not call, as usual, "body" the decomposition rule of a plan but only the procedural attachment of the elementary actions and their procedural composition in case of complex actions).
We will call α a *composed action* (plan) in Π if there is in Π^d at least one rule: $\alpha \rightarrow \alpha_1,..,\alpha_n$. (The actions $\alpha_1, ..., \alpha_n$ are called component actions of α).
We will call α an *abstract action* (plan) in Π if there is in Π^a at least one rule:

$\alpha \dashrightarrow \alpha_1$. ($\alpha_1$ is called a specialized action of α).

An action $\alpha' \in$ Act is called *elementary action* in Π if it does not exist a rule r in Π such that α' is the left part of r.

We will call BAct (*Basic Actions*), the set of elementary actions in Π and CAct (*Complex Actions*) the remaining actions in Act: BAct$\subseteq$Act, CAct = Act - BAct.

Given α_1, α_2 and Π^a, we will say that α_1 *dominates* α_2 (or α_2 *is dominated by* α_1) if there is a set of rules $(r_1, .., r_m)$ in Π^a, such that: $(\alpha_1 = Lr_1) \wedge (\alpha_2 \in Rr_m) \wedge (Lr_i \in Rr_{i-1})$ where: Lr_j and Rr_j are, respectively, the left part and the right part of the rule r_j and $2 \le i \le m$. We will say that α_1 *dominates at level k* α_2 if the set $(r_1, .., r_m)$ includes k rules. In the same way it is possible to define the dominance relation between two actions in the decomposition hierarchy rule set. Hereafter, we will consider the dominance relation in the decomposition hierarchy rule set, Π^d.

We will call Act_A, the set of actions known by the agent A. $Act_A \subseteq Act$. Called Π_A the A's plan library, the set of the irreducible actions (through decomposition or specification rules) included in it is composed of two subsets: the set of actions that A believes to be elementary ($BAct_A$) and the set of actions that A believes to be complex but has not reduction rules for ($NRAct_A$: *Non Reduced actions*).

Then $BAct_A \subset Act$ and it might be that $BAct_A \not\subseteq BAct$.

In fact, given an elementary action, an agent knows (or does not) the body of that action. We will call *skill set* of an agent A, S_A, the actions in $BAct_A$ whose body is known by A (action repertoire of A). $S_A \subseteq BAct_A$. US_{A_i} (on all $A_i \in$ Agt) $\subseteq BAct$.[1]

In sum, an agent A has his own plan library, Π_A, in which some actions ($CAct_A$ and $NRAct_A$) are complex actions (and he knows the reduction rules of $CAct_A$) while some other actions ($BAct_A$) are elementary actions (and he knows the body of a subset - S_A - of them).

A has a *complete executable know-how* of α if either $\alpha \in S_A$ or in Π_A there are a set of rules $(r_1, .., r_m)$ able to transform α in $(\alpha_1, .., \alpha_k)$ and for each $1 \le i \le k$, $\alpha_i \in S_A$. We can define an operator CEK(A,α) that returns α if $\alpha \in S_A$ and $((\alpha_1, .., \alpha_k))$if there are the rules able to transform α as above said. Then CEK(A,α)$\neq \theta$ (θ is the empty set) when A has at least a complete executable know-how of α.

In fact, CEK(A, α) characterizes the executive autonomy of the agent A relative to α.

From the previous assertions it follows that an action α might be an elementary action for the agent A while it might be a plan for another agent B. Again, the same plan α could have, for different agents, different reduction rules.

---

[1] Notice that we do not call, as usual, "body" the decomposition rule of a plan but only the procedural attachment of the elementary actions and their procedural composition in case of complex actions.

$R_A(\alpha)$ returns the results that A believes α will produce when executed. $R_A(\alpha)$ might (or not) correspond with $R(\alpha)$, however when an action has been executed each agent in Agt has the same perception of its results: exactly $R(\alpha)$.

We will call *relevant results* of an action for a goal, the subpart of the results of that action which correspond with the goal; more formally, given α and g, we define the operator Rr such that:
$Rr(\alpha,g)=\{g_i \mid g_i \in g\}$ if $g \subseteq R(\alpha)$, $=\theta$ otherwise.
Then, *the same action used for different goals has different relevant results.*

Let us suppose that α is a component (or specialized) action of α' and $Rr(\alpha',g)\neq\theta$; we define *pertinent results* of α in α' for g, $Pr(\alpha,\alpha',g)$, the results of α useful for that plan α' aimed at the goal g; they correspond with a subset of $R(\alpha)$ such that:
1) if α is a component action of α':
$Pr(\alpha,\alpha',g) = \{q_i \in R(\alpha)) \mid (q_i \in Rr(\alpha',g)) \lor ((q_i=P(\alpha_1))\wedge(\text{dominate-level-1 } \alpha'$
$\alpha_1)\wedge(\alpha\neq\alpha_1))\}$; where $P(\alpha_1)$ returns the preconditions of α_1.
in other terms, an action α is in a plan α' (aimed at a goal g) either because some of its results are relevant results of α' (aimed at g) or because some of its results produce the preconditions of another action α_1 in that plan.
2) if α is a specialized action of α':
$Pr(\alpha,\alpha',g) = \{q_i \mid (q_i \in R(\alpha)) \wedge (\exists q_j \mid (q_j \in Rr(\alpha',g)) \wedge (q_i \text{ is a specialization of } q_j)\}$.
The pertinent results of an action α in α' represent the real reason for which that action α is in that plan α'.

2 Delegation

In the following we will consider only strict delegation and adoption (the delegate knows that the delegee is relying on him and accepts the task, on the other hand the helped agent knows about the adoption and accepts it) based on implicit or explicit request/offer.

Delegation is a "social action" [11,10], and also a meta-action, since its object is an action. We define the Delegation action with 4 parameters: Delegates (A B τ d), where $A,B \in$ Agt, $\tau=(\alpha,g)$, d=deadline. This means that A delegates to B the task τ with the deadline d. In the following we will put aside both the deadline of τ, and the fact that in delegating τ, A could *implicitly delegate also the realization of α preconditions* (that normally implies some problem-solving and/or planning).

One can distinguish among at least the following kinds of delegation:
- *pure executive delegation Vs open delegation;*
- *delegation Vs non delegation of the monitoring of the action;*
- *domain task delegation Vs planning task delegation (meta-actions);*
- *delegation to perform Vs delegation to delegate.*
We describe here, just the kinds of delegation in relation to the task. For an accurate analysis of the other dimensions of the delegation see [8].

2.1 Task-based kinds of delegation

The object of delegation (τ) can be minimally specified (*open delegation*), completely specified (*close delegation*) or specified at any intermediate level.

Let us consider two main cases from A's point of view:

- *Pure Executive (Close) Delegation*: when either $\alpha \in S_A$ or $\alpha \in BAct_A$, or g is the relevant result of α (and $\alpha \in S_A$ or $\alpha \in BAct_A$). In other words, the delegating agent believes to delegate a completely specified task.

- *Open Delegation*: either $\alpha \in CAct_A$, or $\alpha \in NRAct_A$; and also when g is the relevant result of α (and $\alpha \in CAct_A$ or $\alpha \in NRAct_A$). In other words, agent A believes to delegate an incompletely specified task: either A is delegating a complex or abstract action, or he is delegating just a result (state of the world). The agent B can (or must) realize the delegated task in an autonomous way.

Implicit aspects of the delegation produce various possible *misunderstandings* among the agents. A's perspective can be in contrast with B's point of view: τ can be considered at different levels of complexity from the two interacting agents.

It is worth to understand the great importance of *open delegation* in collaboration theory.

On the one hand, we would like to stress that *open delegation* is not only due to A's preference (utility) or practical ignorance or limited ability (know how). Of course, when A is delegating to B τ, he is always *depending on* B as for τ [12]: he needs B's action for some of his goals (either some domain goals or goals like saving time, effort, resources, etc.). However, *open delegation* is fundamental because it is also due to A's ignorance about the world and its dynamics. In fact, frequently enough *it is neither possible nor convenient to fully specify* τ because some local and updated knowledge is needed in order for that part of the plan to be successfully executed. *Open delegation* is one of the basis of the *flexibility* of distributed and MA plans. To be radical, delegating actions to an autonomous agent always requires some level of "openness": the agent cannot *avoid monitoring and adapting* its own actions.

On the other hand, we would like to show how the distributed character of the MA plans derives from the *open delegation*.

As we saw, A can delegate to B either an entire plan or some part of it (*partial delegation*). The combination of the *partial delegation* (where B might ignore the other parts of the plan) and of the *open delegation* (where A might ignore the sub-plan chosen and developed by B) creates the possibility that A and B (or B and C, both delegated by A) collaborate in a plan that they do not share and that *nobody* entirely knows: that is a *distributed plan* [13, 11]. However, for each part of the plan there will be at least one agent that knows it.

3 Adoption (Help)

Since *Adoption* can be unilateral and spontaneous, or can be "critical", it *can go beyond the request and the delegation* of the client. In other words, B can adopt some of A's goals independently of A's delegation or request. This creates an interesting problem: *what kind (or level) of goals can B adopt beyond the request-delegation of A?*

This problem is well known in conversation theory [14,15]. Exactly the same problem can be found in any kind of "cooperation" or help (goal adoption): *when A ask B for a practical action, B can "over-answer"* . Going beyond the request opens different possibilities (depending on what kind of goal B is adopting): a theory is needed about these levels of adoption that characterize different kinds of "over-answering" and different helping relation and roles among agents [11].

3.1 Levels of adoption relative to the delegated task

In analogy with the delegation we introduce the corresponding operator for the adoption: Adopts (B A τ). We identify several levels of help of B, starting from the general condition: Delegates (A B $\tau=(\alpha,g)$) with α' dominating α, where A delegates τ within $\tau'=(\alpha',g')$.

Conservative Help

- Literal help: Adopts (B A τ) - In other words, B adopts exactly what has been delegated by A (elementary or complex action, etc.).

- Sub help: Adopts (B A τ_1) $\wedge$ (dominates α α_1); in other words, B does not satisfy the delegated task. Example: A asks B to prepare "fettucini-pesto" and B prepare "pesto-sauce".

- Over help: Adopts (B A τ_1) $\wedge$ (dominates α_1 α) $\wedge$ (dominates-or-equal α' α_1). In other words, B goes beyond what has been delegated by A without changing A's plan.

Example in conversation: A: "What time is it?", B: "Be calm, is 5pm and our meeting is at 6pm, we are in time". Both, the delegated action (to inform about time) and the higher, non-delegated results (plan) (to know whether we are late or not; to not be anxious) are adopted by the contractor.

Critical help

Adopts (B A τ_x) $\wedge$ ($\tau_x=(\alpha_x,g)$). In fact, what happens is that B adopts g, that is to say it is sufficient for B to find in Act$_s$ an action α_x whatever, such that $g\subseteq R_s(\alpha_x)$. In other words, B satisfies the relevant results of the requested plan/action, but modifies that plan/action.

Critical help holds in the following alternative cases:

a) $(CEK(B,\alpha)=\theta)\vee(g\not\subseteq R_B(\alpha))\vee(P(\alpha)=\text{false})$; that is to say, B either is not able to execute α or on the basis of his knowledge on action results, guesses that g is not among the results of α or the preconditions of α are not true (and he is unable to realize them). Correspondingly he must guess that there is an action α_x such as: $(CEK(B,\alpha_x)\neq\theta)\wedge(g\subseteq R_B(\alpha_x))\wedge(P(\alpha_x)=\text{true})$; in other words B finds another way to realize g, using another action α_x such that: B is able to realize it, the new action contains g among its results and the conditions of α_x are satisfied.

b) B thinks that the other results of α (beyond g) are in conflict with other goals - in plan or off plan - or interests of the client. Moreover, he thinks that there is an action

α_x with: $(CEK(B,\alpha_x)\neq\theta)\wedge(g\subseteq R_B(\alpha_x))\wedge(P(\alpha_x)=true)$ and the results of α_x are not in conflict with other goals or interests of the client.

c) There is again the case of optimization, where the conditions in (a) are all false but there is an action α_x such that g is reached in a more profitable way (relative to any criterion).

OverCritical help

where B realizes an Overhelp and in addition modifies/changes that plan/action. It is a mixed case in which there are *Over help* and *Critical help* at the same time.

If Adopts $(B\ A\ \tau_x)\wedge(\tau_x=(\alpha_x,g'))$ then we have OverCritical help. It holds in the following alternative cases:

i) $Pr(\alpha,\alpha',g')=\theta$ and in addition $(\exists\ \alpha_x\in Act_B\ |\ Pr(\alpha_x,\alpha',g')\neq\theta\wedge CEK(B,\alpha_x)\neq\theta\wedge P(\alpha_x)=true)$. In other words, there are not pertinent results of α in α'; but there exists at least an action α_x which is pertinent in α' towards g. This means that α is <u>useless</u> for τ'. It is even possible that it is noxious: i.e. that $R(\alpha)$ produces results that contradict those intended with τ'. A is delegating to B a plan that in B's view is wrong or self-defeating.

ii) $Pr(\alpha,\alpha',g')\neq\theta\wedge CEK(B,\alpha)\neq\theta\wedge P(\alpha)=true$ and in addition $(\exists\ \alpha_x\in Act_B\ |\ CEK(B,\alpha_x)\neq\theta\wedge P(\alpha_x)=true\wedge Pr(\alpha_x,\alpha',g')\neq\theta)$, moreover

ii1) $R(\alpha_x)$ achieves the *goals internal to the plan* (i.e. g') *in a better way (maximization)*.

Example: A asks B "to buy second class train tickets for Naples" (action α) for her plan "to go to Naples by train cheaply" (action α'). B adopts A's goal "to be in Naples and spend little money" (goal g') replacing the whole plan (α_x) with another plan: "go with Paul by car".

ii2) $R(\alpha_x)$ achieves not only the goals of the plan (i.e. g') but also *other goals of A* external to that plan (ex. g''): $(g'\subset R(\alpha_x))\wedge(g''\subset R(\alpha_x))$.

Example: A asks B "to buy second class train tickets for Naples" (action α) for her plan "to go to Naples by train cheaply" (action α'). B adopts A's goal "to be in Naples and spend little money" (goal g') replacing the whole plan (α') with another plan (α_x) "to go with Paul by car" that satisfies also another goal of A - that she did not consider or satisfy in her plan - but B knows: "to travel with friends".

ii3) $R(\alpha_x)$ achieves not only the goals of the plan but also *some interests (i) of A*: $(g'\subset R(\alpha_x))\wedge(i\subset R(\alpha_x))$.

Example: A asks B "to buy second class train tickets for Naples" (action α) for her plan "to go to Naples by train cheaply" (action α'). B adopts A's goal "to be in Naples and spend little money" (goal g') replacing the whole plan (α') with another plan (α_x) "to go to Naples by bus" that satisfies an interest of A of "not risking to meet Paul that she ignores to be on the same train".

HyperCritical help

where B adopts goals or interests of A that A itself did not take into account: by doing so, B neither performs the action/plan nor satisfies the results that were delegated.

In fact, Adopts $(B\ A\ g_i)$ where g_i is an interest (or an off-plan goal) of A more important than g' (we leave here this notion just intuitive). Since there is a conflict between the result $R(\alpha)$ (and/or the result $R(\alpha')$) and some g_i of A, to adopt g_i would imply to not obtain $R(\alpha)$ (or $R(\alpha')$).

In sum, the contractor's criticism of the delegation can be aimed at safeguarding various goods of the client (we are just considering the fully cooperative cases: the contractor changes or refuses the task just for the wellbeing of the client):

a) the expected result of the requested action;

b) some higher goal of that action in that plan;

c) some other active goal of the client;

d) some goal of the client, the client itself did not consider;

e) a client's interest;

f) a goal of the role the client is holding;

g) a goal/interest of a third agent the client is representing;

h) some goal of the organization the client is acting in/for.

4 Delegation and Role theory

Agents delegate roles as they delegate tasks [16]. In a broad sense *any task delegation is the creation of a role*: in fact, given an occasional execution of any plan through the execution of its component actions by more than one agent, one might say that these agents have a given "role" in that plan and group. This is a "transitory" or occasional role. However, we decide to use (as usual) the term "role" only for more long term and stable organizations; and to use just the term "task" for occasional delegation.

4.1 Definition of Role: delegation-adoption of *generic tasks*

As we saw, we can consider the couple action/result $\tau=(\alpha,g)$ as the delegation-adoption object. We can specialize the defined contract relation in two subtypes: the *task-contract* and the *role-contract*. The task-contract concerns an occasional delegation.

Let us define as Role contract or relation (ρ), the triple $\rho=\{A, B, T\}$; where A is the *Role Client class*, B is the *Role Contractor class* and T is the Role Task class. In fact, $\rho=\{A, B, T\}$ implicates Delegates (A, B, T) that means that for each $A \in A$, $B \in B$, $\tau \in T$ we have Delegates (A, B, τ). More precisely:

- T is the "Role domain" or "Role competence": it is a set of types of tasks $\{\tau_1, \tau_2, ..., \tau_n\}$, where each τ_i ($1 \le i \le n$) represents either a type of domain task or a type of meta-domain one. In fact, T is the set of the services the role can provide.

Usually, there are some constraints among the τ_i in each T_j. Not only obvious constraints of non-contradictoriness but also other constraints depending on the kind of organization and the kind of roles: for example the task τ_1 and the task τ_2 of monitoring the performance of τ_1 cannot be part of the same T_j.

- A and B are the classes of the contractor agents and of the client agents respectively and there is a relation of Delegation-Adoption between these two types of agents about the Role Task (Generic Task).

Then, for each task $\tau \in T$ if $B_i \in B$, τ is a potential task of B_i, that is to say there exists at least an agent $A_i \in A$ such that the agent B_i is delegated by A_i to bring it about. Analogously, for each task $\tau \in T$ if $A_i \in A$, τ is its potential task to delegate to B_i with $B_i \in B$.

4.2 Role as a social relation

Since a role relation concerns a task (or better a set of types of tasks), and a task is something (action or result) delegated-adopted, then *a Role is in fact always a social relation* between contractor(s) and client(s).

The role-relation is an asymmetrical and focused relation: there is a main agent (or agent class) that is the contractor; the contractor is the *role-player*: the role is *her* role, the role-task is *her* task. The role client is a subordinate role: we will call it the *co-role* in the relation.

One should not mix up the co-role (client) of a role relation with a possible sub-client (or beneficiary) of the role, or with complementary and reciprocal roles.

- *sub-client*

Suppose to have: Delegates (**A B T**) with $\tau_i \in T$ and τ_i=Adopts (**B C T'**). Then the role relation ρ=(**A, B, T**) permits to define, through **T**, a new role relation ρ'=(**C, B, T'**). So we can say that the role relation ρ' is *directly dependent* on the role relation ρ: for example **C** is the client class (*sub-client class*) of **B** in ρ' only because **A** is the client class of **B** in ρ; this means that it is impossible to break the role relation ρ' without breaking also the role relation ρ (in some cases it is not viceversa true). The baby-sitter role, or the shopman role are typical examples of such a kind of composition of roles.

- *reciprocal and symmetrical roles*

We will define ρ' and ρ *reciprocal roles* when:

ρ'=(**A, B, T'**) and ρ''=(**B, A, T''**) where the role relation ρ' exists iff at the same time exists ρ''. The wife-husband, doctor-patient role relations are typical examples.

We will say that ρ' and ρ'' are *symmetrical roles* when **T'**=**T''**=**T**: **A** is the client of **B** for **T** and viceversa (ex.: friendship).

4.3 Role in/for/of a plan, a group, an organization

Given our plan-based analysis of delegation and our delegation-based view of the Roles, we claim that:

1) *A role is a role in a plan* [7] *and relative to that plan*. In fact a role concerns a task and a task is a piece of a delegated plan. We will say that both actions (tasks) and agents are complementary when they are in the same plan, they contribute to the same pertinent results: two roles are *complementary roles* when they are roles in at least one and the same plan.

More formally, given ρ=(**A, B, T**), ρ'=(**A', B', T'**), ρ''=(**A'', B'', T''**), we can say that **B'** and **B''** are complementary roles when are contemporaneously true:

a) $\exists\ \tau, \tau', \tau''$ (with τ=(α,g)$\in$ **T**, τ'=(α',g')$\in$ **T'**, τ''=(α'',g'')$\in$ **T''**) | (Pr(α',α,g)$\neq\theta$) $\wedge$ (Pr(α'',α,g)$\neq\theta$) $\wedge$ (Pr(α',α,g)$\neq$Pr(α'',α,g)); b) (**A'** $\cup$ **A''** $\subseteq$ **A**); c) (**B'** $\cup$ **B''** $\subseteq$ **B**). In other words, τ' and τ'' contribute to the same task τ (in terms of plans: α' and α'' are component actions of α).

In the *exactly complementary roles*:

(g $\subseteq$ (Pr(α',α,g) $\cup$ Pr(α'',α,g))) $\wedge$ (**A'** $\cup$ **A''**=**A**) $\wedge$ (**B'** $\cup$ **B''**=**B**).

Then, we can define in a preliminary way an *organization* as an abstract agent with goals and plans for those goals, more precisely, an organization determines:

a set of goals (**G**), a set of relative plans (**P**) and a set of role relations $\Sigma=\{\rho_1, ...,\rho_m\}$. Where the tasks for each ρ in Σ is included in **P**.

A *necessary condition* to individuate the agents belonging to an organization is to say that these agents must have directly (or indirectly through a given class of agents) a role (as a role player) in at least a role relation of Σ. Unfortunately, this condition is not sufficient because it includes also some agents that does not belong to the organization.

2) *A role is a role in/for a group, an organization*: the group of the cooperating agents in that multi-agent plan. Then, *roles in an organization are always complementary roles at some level*.

Normally, the client is the intere organization or group that creates such a role relation, and in/for which the role relation is used. *The role player "belongs to" such a group or organization.*

4.4 Kinds of task, plan hierarchies and role hierarchy

Complementary roles could be in a hierarchical relationship because of the plan-relation between the corresponding role-tasks.

A) Role hierarchy mirrors two hierarchical plan principles: the *hierarchy of abstraction* and the *hierarchy of composition*: Given ρ', ρ'' as above defined, we can say that **B'** is an higher role respect to **B''** when are contemporaneously true:

i) ($\exists\ \tau'=(\alpha',g')\in$ **T'**, $\tau''=(\alpha'',g'')\in$ **T''** | (dominates $\alpha'\ \alpha''$)) and

ii) for each couple τ', τ'' it is never satisfied the relation (dominates $\alpha''\ \alpha'$).

In an organization the roles "in charge of" the highest goals and motivations of the organization itself, are hierarchically superior.

B) Another hierarchical ordering of roles derives from the distinction between *domain-task delegation* and *meta-task delegation*: if τ' is a meta-task (planning action) relative to a domain where τ'' is a domain task, then **B'** will be higher than **B''**.

C) A third criterion is related to monitoring delegation: if the monitoring-action α' relative to an action α has been delegated to a role ρ', and the execution of α has been delegated to a role ρ, ρ' will hierarchically dominate ρ in the organizational role structure.

It is possible to envisage other criteria (ex. the more important the **T** the more important the role); all these criteria are partially independent on each other.

5 Two levels of Delegation, two levels of negotiation

On the basis of this delegation-based analysis of Role, we can predict/explain why there are two levels of delegation and negotiations, and they relationships. Given the agents A_1, B_1, a task τ, and a contract Delegates/Adopts ($A_1\ B_1\ \tau$) we can consider two possible cases:

i) the interaction is independent from any other structural relation between the agents (mere task-relation);

ii) the interaction is in a well definite role relation ρ: that is to say exists $\rho=($**A**, **B**, **T**$)$ with $A_1\in$ **A**, $B_1\in$ **B** and $\tau\in$ **T**.

The existence or not of a role-relation between A_1 and B_1, completely changes the delegation-adoption process and the negotiation process between A_1 and B_1. In the case (ii) there are two levels of negotiation and two levels of contract: the role-contract and role-negotiation vs the contract and negotiation about a specific task. The two levels are not independent. There should be a *coherence between role-contract and task-contract*.

a) *The Role-contract constrains task delegation and negotiation.*

Since there is an agreement about a set of classes of task **T** [16], the agent class **B** commits herself by the agent class **A** to do (under given circumstances), this agreement will constrain the specific agreement that will occur between A_1 and B_1 on the same domain. The role contract specifies the validity conditions of requests, adoptions, negotiations, refusals of case by case delegations. A_1 should delegate to B_1 only tasks τ that are the *instanciation* of one of the classes of the Role Task **T**, in the appropriate circumstances.

b) *Task-negotiation or agreement can invalidate the Role-contract* and can induce the Role-contract revision (Role (re)negotiation).

Many kinds of *conflicts* are predictable between the role contract and the delegation-adoption of a specific task.

Let us notice that this double level of negotiation which characterizes the organizations is not taken into account by current negotiation protocols or CSCW systems. We think that the negotiation protocols should distinguish between the role and the task contract that would be very simplified. One of the advantages of role is in fact that of avoiding or pruning local and occasional negotiation.

6 Conclusions

Let us just recapitulate what we attempted to show:

i) There are several levels of cooperation - more or less "deep" and helpful - and several levels of task delegation.

ii) These levels are related to the hierarchical structure of plans or tasks.

iii) There is a fundamental distinction between the delegation/adoption of a domain task (practical action) or of a planning or problem solving or monitoring action;

iv) There are different kinds of role corresponding to different levels of tasks, implying different levels of autonomy (*executive* vs *open*; *domain* vs *metalevel*; *simple* vs *over-help* or *critical*).

v) There exists a hierarchical structure of roles which is related to the kind of task and to the plan structure.

vi) Once established a role (role-contract) this creates constraints for task-delegation.

vii) There could rise conflicts between task-delegation and role-contract, and the negotiation about specific tasks can re-discuss the related role-contract.

In conclusion, we claim that a fundamental aspect of role theory is the analysis of roles in terms of delegation and that a plan based analysis of delegation is needed. One should also study the analogy between role-assignment criterion and task-assignment criterion [10], and the reasons for goal delegation and adoption [11].

Many of this notions are current, and many of this issues are well known, but we claim that a principled systematisation is still lacking. We tried to contribute to this aim.

References

[1] Winograd,T.A. 1987. Language/Action perspective on the Design of Cooperative Work,. In HCI 3, 1: 3-30.

[2] Fikes, R. E. 1982. A commitment-based framework for describing informal cooperative work. *Cognitive Science*, 6: 331-347.

[3] Bond, A.H., Commitments, Some DAI insigths from Symbolic Interactionist Sociology. In *Proceedings of the 9^ International AAAI Workshop on Distributed Artificial Intelligence*, .239-261. Menlo Park, 1989.

[4] Werner, E., Cooperating agents: A unified theory of communication and social structure. In L.Gasser and M.N.Huhns, editors, *Distribuited Artificial Intelligence*: Volume II. Morgan Kaufmann Publishers, 1990.

[5] Jones, A. & Sergot, M., Institutionalized power: a formal characterization. In MEDLAR II, special issue of *Journal of IGPL*, 1995.

[6] Castelfranchi, C., Falcone, R., Towards a theory of single-agent into multi-agent plan transformation. *The 3rd Pacific Rim International Conference on Artificial Intelligence*, Beijing, China, 16-18 agosto 1994.

[7] D.Kinny, M. Ljungberg, A.Rao, E.Sonenberg, G.Tidhar and E.Werner, Planned Team Activity, in C. Castelfranchi and E. Werner (Eds.) *Artificial Social Systems* (MAAMAW'92), Springer-Verlag, LNAI-830, 1994.

[8] Castelfranchi, C., Falcone, R. (1997), Delegation Conflicts, in M. Boman & W. Van de Velde (eds.) Multi-Agent Rationality, Lecture Notes in Artificial Intelligence, 1237. Springer-Verlag pg.234-254, 1997.

[9] Pollack, M., Plans as complex mental attitudes in Cohen, P.R., Morgan, J. and Pollack, M.E. (eds), *Intentions in Communication*, MIT press, USA, pp 77-103, 1990.

[10] Castelfranchi, C. & Falcone, R., Levels of help, levels of delegation and agent modeling. *AAAI-96 Agent Modeling Workshop*, 4 august1996.

[11] Conte,R. & Castelfranchi, C. *Cognitive and Social Action*, UCL Press, London, 1995

[12] Sichman, J, R. Conte, C. Castelfranchi, Y. Demazeau. A social reasoning mechanism based on dependence networks. In *Proceedings of the 11th ECAI*, 1994.

[13] Grosz B., Kraus S., Collaborative plans for complex group action, *Artificial Intelligence* 86, pp. 269-357, 1996.

[14] Pollack, M., *Plans as complex mental attitudes* in Cohen, P.R., Morgan, J. and Pollack, M.E. (eds), Intentions in Communication, MIT press, USA, pp 77-103, 1990.

[15] Chu-Carroll J. & Carberry, S., *A Plan-Based Model for Response Generation in Collaborative Task-Oriented Dialogues* in Proceeedings of AAAI-94. 1994.

[16] Castelfranchi, C., Commitment: from intentions to groups and organizations. In *Proceedings of ICMAS'96*, S.Francisco, June 1996, AAAI-MIT Press.

Automated Reasoning On-Board
Autonomous Spacecraft

N.D.Monekosso[1] and P.Remagnino[2]

[1]Surrey Satellite Technology Ltd., Centre for Satellite Engineering
Research, University of Surrey, GU2 5XH, UK
[2]The University of Reading, Whiteknights, PO Box 225, Reading,
Berkshire, RG6 6AY, UK

Abstract. Traditionally spacecraft operations are automated by increasing the levels of automation in the ground segment. Certain missions, however, are only possible with high levels of on-board automation and autonomy with respect to the ground. These include missions to distant planets and bodies for which the light or radio signal travel time is too long to accommodate real time control and where the spacecraft spends long periods of time out of sight of ground stations. This paper reports on work done within the scope of the spacecraft autonomy research project[1] which has as one objective to investigate architecture for on-board autonomy. The paper describes the autonomous spacecraft architecture and focuses on the on-board decision making mechanism. A highly decentralised and distributed architecture was adopted. The autonomous spacecraft is modelled as a collection of intelligent sub-systems that must co-operate to achieve goals. The decentralised nature of the system implies a heavy reliance on communication for the co-ordination of actions, a mechanism for continued co-ordination in the event of failure resulting in incomplete and uncertain spacecraft status information is described.

1 Introduction

Spacecraft autonomy with respect to ground control is expected to bring significant advantages to space missions. The benefits include improving the management of resources (electrical power, propulsion fuel, communications bandwidth) and simplifying the operation of complex and demanding payloads. Furthermore, reliability can be increased by making the spacecraft autonomously fault tolerant. Traditionally spacecraft operations are automated by increasing the levels of automation in the ground segment.

This research project focuses on a class of space missions for which on-board autonomy is mandatory. These are missions to distant planets and bodies where the light or radio signal travel time is too long to permit real time control from the ground or where the spacecraft spends long periods of time out of sight of ground stations.

A definition of spacecraft autonomy that goes beyond the traditional definition states that the spacecraft must react to unplanned events not just by executing pre-planned command sequences or event-driven rules, but by having inference capabilities

---

1. The research is supported by Surrey Satellite Technology Ltd., and undertaken at the Centre for Satellite Engineering Research, University of Surrey, UK.

on-board to generate the commands necessary to respond to whatever unplanned events are encountered [3]. One objective of the project is to investigate architectures for such autonomous spacecraft. An architecture that provides the spacecraft with a capability for on-board decision making was defined. It is highly decentralised and distributed. The choice of such architecture resulted from a decision to build upon the architecture of our current satellites which has evolved over the years to become increasingly distributed and modular. The second motive for selecting the architecture is to investigate the applicability of DAI paradigm to spacecraft.

In the architecture definition, the spacecraft is modelled as a collection of intelligent systems that must co-operate to accomplish the mission goals. The decentralised nature of the system implies a heavy reliance on inter-module communication for the co-ordination of actions. The focus of this paper is agent co-ordination. The layout of the paper is as follows. Section 2 introduces the problem domain and provides background information. In Section 3, the autonomous spacecraft architecture is described. Section 4 describes the proposed mechanism for automated reasoning. Finally in Section 5 other fundamental issues are addressed and future work discussed.

2 Spacecraft control

The work described here is concerned with high level control but focuses on a primary spacecraft function, navigation and guidance. The problem is that the spacecraft *must autonomously control its trajectory* for the *autonomy period*. This is defined as the time during which the spacecraft must operate autonomously (within given autonomous functions). The duration can last from a few hours to a few months [11].

The spacecraft sub-system primarily responsible for trajectory control is the navigation and guidance sub-system. The propulsion, the attitude control and the power sub-systems also have a major role to play in trajectory control. The propulsion system produces the thrusts to maintain the spacecraft on course. The attitude control sub-system must point the thrusters in the required direction prior to thruster firing. And the power sub-system produces the electrical power.

Returning to the navigation and guidance system, navigation refers to orbit determination (spacecraft position, velocity or orbital elements). Guidance or orbit control means adjusting the orbit to meet some pre-determined state [7]. Guidance requires first determination of the spacecraft current orbital parameters from sensor data and then computation of the required spacecraft velocity change to achieve the desired orbit. The navigation and guidance system generates and oversees the execution of the orbit control commands. The elements of a navigation system are usually shared between the ground and the space segment. Typical elements include sensors, orbit estimator, orbit propagator, manoeuvre command planning, and actuators. The aim of the project is to reduce elements in the ground segment.

2.1 Orbit Determination and Propagation

Orbital parameters are determined from the sensor data. The computation of orbital parameters in a manual system is carried out entirely in the ground segment while in an autonomous system it must be performed on-board. The sensors are either on-board or shared between the ground and space segment as is the case with tracking systems.

Propagation is an element of a navigation system closely related to orbit determination. This function allows orbital parameters to be propagated to determine the spacecraft position at a time in the future. The accuracy of the propagated orbital parameters or orbit estimates degrades with time.

2.2   Orbit Control

The current orbital parameters are compared to the desired (or reference) parameters. If the error is outside predefined limits, orbit adjustments are made to reduce the error. The change in spacecraft velocity that is required to correct the orbit is computed. Based on the required velocity change a sequence of commands is generated to control the propulsion engine firing and the engine nozzle or thruster orientation. The sequence of events described is referred to as a manoeuvre, and the sequence of commands the manoeuvre plan. During the manoeuvre, the engine nozzle must be pointing in the correct direction. If the thrusters are mounted on gimbals, these must be commanded to point as required. In the case of thrusters mounted fixed to the spacecraft body, the thrusters' direction is controlled by the spacecraft attitude (orientation).

The elements of an autonomous navigation system are shown in Figure 1(a) [17]. The trajectory is continuously monitored as described next. First sensor data are collected and validated. Using the data the orbital parameters are determined. Current parameters can be propagated into the future in the propagator. Propagation allows advance planning. Next the estimated and propagated parameters are compared to the reference (desired) orbit. If a correction is deemed necessary, a manoeuvre to correct the spacecraft trajectory is planned and executed. All elements of the system are carried out by human operators at the ground station. However on-board orbit determination and propagation have been done in space. The diagram in Figure 1(b) shows the control loop model.

2.3   Automating the navigation and guidance sub-system

The navigation and guidance sub-system is composed of basic irreducible functions inspired by the reactive control architectures [2] and behavioural architecture[9][10]. The functions are orbit determination, orbit propagation, and manoeuvre planning and are used as building blocks to achieve goals which are the complex operation's activity normally performed on the ground by human operators.

Goals are generated either internally or externally. An autonomous navigation system will determine that a manoeuvre correction is needed, produce and execute a plan. This is an internally generated goal. Externally generated goals, as the name suggests, come from outside the agent. Another agent including the human operator can request an action. The action constitutes an external goal. The reference orbit is stored on-board for comparison. Knowledge of the spacecraft capabilities and limitations is also needed on-board to plan the manoeuvre, and respond to contingencies such as failures within the spacecraft.

The navigation and guidance sub-system described in this section is but one of many sub-systems that make up the spacecraft. The architecture for an autonomous spacecraft is described in the next section.

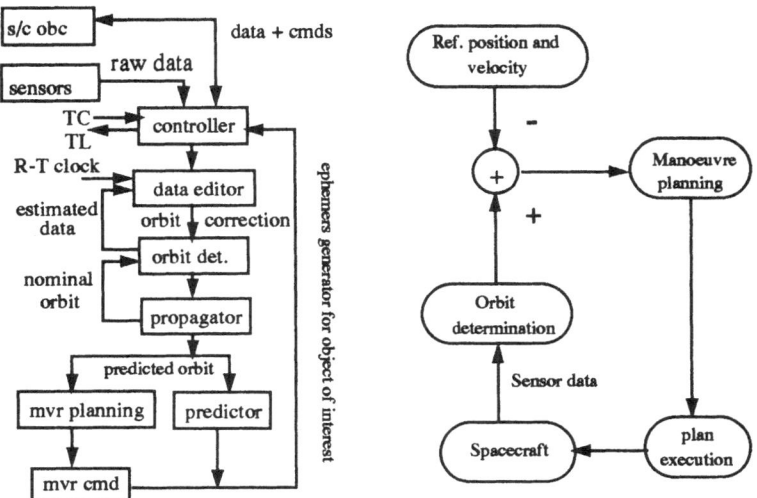

Fig. 1.(a) Elements of Guidance, (b) Autonomous system control.

3   A Multi-Agent System Approach to spacecraft control

In the multi-agent system (MAS) approach, the spacecraft is modelled as a collection of autonomous controllers or agents. The agents have a common internal structure with a different functional speciality. They do have a common top level goal and must co-operate in planning and executing actions to achieve this goal. An example of top level or mission goal is to reach a distant planet. Each agent has responsibility for a special-isation. The guidance control agent assumes responsibility for trajectory control, while the attitude control agent oversees the spacecraft pointing. This paper focuses on the guidance control agent. The control requirements are dynamic over the course of the mission. In the architecture definition, the ground segment is modelled as another au-tonomous agent, whose roles are to generate top level goals, to take over the role of one or more on-board agents if necessary, and ultimately has override capability. A diagram of the generic spacecraft agent is shown in Figure 2 (a), and is described in the next sub-section.

3.1   The generic intelligent module

Referring to Figure 2(a), the specialist unit differs from agent to agent, and provides the specialist functions. In the case of the navigation and guidance sub-system, these func-tions are orbit determination and propagation, and manoeuvre planning. The communi-cation unit (CX) is identical in all. Fault detection, isolation and recovery (FDIR) unit, as its name suggests, provides fault management. The status unit generates telemetry (status information) and information for the audit trail. The latter keeps a log of deci-sions, actions, and outcome of actions.

The generic agent has the basic input, compute, output structure. The three structures are akin to the H, M, and G modules of NASREM [1] with a single level of hierarchical task decomposition. Not unlike TCA [16] task decomposition is based on functionality. The operation is based on discrete time cycles.

3.2 Action control

The space mission is divided into phases, each phase has specific requirements and thus goals to pursue. The control sequence is based on these mission phases. At the start of a phase, the appropriate goals are selected. Actions must take place to realise a goal, this is achieved through the activation of tasks in a manner similar to the subsumption architecture [2]. Two navigation and guidance agent goals are *monitor trajectory* and *monitor fault status*. The goals are concurrent and referred to as background.

The sequence controller

The control sequence of a typical phase can be described as follows. Following identification of the current phase, the goals are selected and tasks activated. Once the 'monitor trajectory' is entered, it remains in this state until the end of current phase. In the 'monitor trajectory' state, the sensors are read, validated, and orbital parameters computed. A comparison is made against a model to determine if a correction manoeuvre is needed. If a correction manoeuvre is required, a 'manoeuvre goal' is generated. The im-

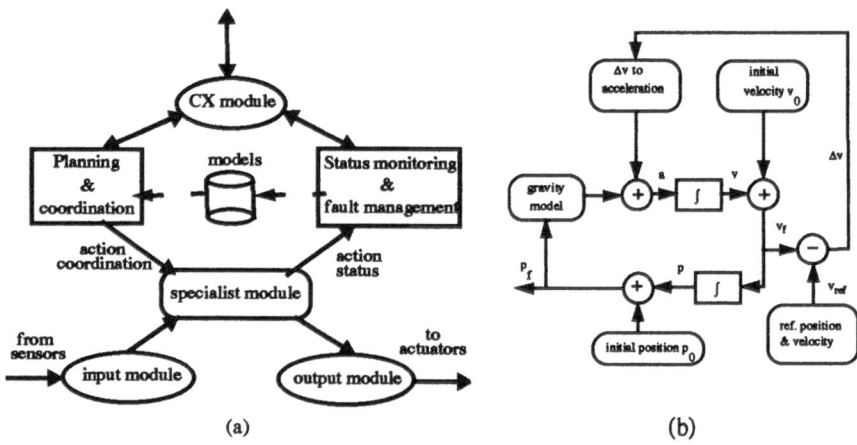

(a)   (b)

Fig. 2.(a) Generic agent, (b) Trajectory control model

plementation of the goal 'monitor trajectory' is shown in Figure 2 (b).

Agents Services and Tasks

The agents provide services. Co-operation between agents means providing a service requested by an agent (co-agent). For a given autonomous function, one agent is in charge while the co-agents co-operate. Within the generic agent, the specialist functions constitute the services. Each agent provides a number of services, the service set. Depending on the functional status, the service may be available or not. At a lower level, tasks control the physical system (sensors and actuators). A service is provided by tasks, each service is composed of one or more tasks.

Agent Co-operation

The agents achieve local goals (provide a service) by activating locally controlled tasks. However high level goal execution requires agent co-operation and action co-ordination. The co-ordination mechanism is message based. There are two basic types of messages, *request* and *inform*. A request message is either a request to perform an action, or a request for status information. An inform message is used to broadcast status information.

The architecture relies heavily on agent co-operation for action co-ordination. A breakdown in one agent must not prevent the continuation of action in others. Section 4 reports on the method used.

3.3 Knowledge on-board spacecraft

Automated decision making requires that knowledge is available on-board the spacecraft. Each agent will maintain information pertaining to what it knows about itself e.g. status information, and what it knows about other co-operating agents (co-agents), as well as other information relating to the specialist functions. The agents provide services and therefore contained within the knowledge base is a list of services it can provide and the availability status of these services i.e. operational or not, active or not. Each agent also has knowledge of services (of interest to it for co-operation) provided by its co-agents and the status of these services.

Knowledge structure and content

The knowledge is encoded as 'knowledge structures'. The generic knowledge structure is based on frames. A frame is a collection of attributes and associated values that describe an entity [15]. Six kinds of knowledge structure have been defined for the spacecraft control architecture. The first type is the *agent* knowledge structure, which contains information pertaining to the agent's service set, applicable constraints, and lists the co-operators (co-agents). The second type is the *service* knowledge structure which provides information on the availability and operating status of each service. An example of a navigation and guidance service is the 'orbit position determination'. The third type is the *task* knowledge structure. Every service has a set of tasks that must be activated to enable the service. The task knowledge structure provides information on the availability and operating status of each task. The fourth type is the *fault* knowledge structure. This information relates to fault management activities, and links a fault to a set of tasks i.e. which tasks are affected by the fault. As part of the fault management activities, the FDIR unit will determine which task(s) is affected by a fault and update the task availability status. The FDIR maintains a model of system/task interactions from which it can determine which tasks are affected. There is a domino effect such that services using the affected task also have their availability status updated. The fifth type is the *co-agent* structure which is a sub-set of the first type (agent), with information on the service they provide and the availability of the services. Finally, the sixth type is the *constraint* knowledge structure describing the constraints applicable to an agent. A constraint limits (partially or completely) the agent's capability to provide a service. The tasks can query the status of pertinent constraints when running.

Our implementation follows an object oriented approach. The agents, the services, the tasks, and the fault knowledge structures are inter-connected hierarchy of objects. Agents have services, services are made up of tasks. Associated with each tasks are faults that can disable it.

4 Automated reasoning with uncertain information

Two methods were investigated for co-ordination in the event of breakdown. The remainder of this paper reports on one of them. It implements a method for reasoning with uncertain knowledge caused by a system failure. A simplified but realistic scenario is used as an the example.

4.1 Description of scenario

The scenario described is a situation where a failure results in *uncertain* status information. During a manoeuvre a failure occurs in the propulsion system. The propulsion system fault management module should diagnose the fault but depending on the extent of failure may not update its status in the knowledge base. The sequence of events is described as follows. While monitoring the manoeuvre, the navigation and guidance agent detects that it is not proceeding according to plan. It checks the propulsion system availability status, and decide on the next course of action depending on whether

(a) the propulsion system status was updated and indicates a failure,

(b) the propulsion system has not reported fault, its availability status is not updated

In (a), the navigation and guidance agent re-plans based on knowledge of fault in the propulsion system. There is a contradiction in (b), the guidance control agent can only re-plan after assessing the situation to identify which of its services and co-agent services are unavailable.

4.2 Solution to scenario problem

Given that the trajectory is detected as 'not OK' and given a set of locally available status information, the navigation and guidance agent must decide where the problem lies. It has access to local information regarding the availability of the services provided by the attitude control agent (ADC), and the propulsion control agent (PCS), and can query for the spacecraft attitude (pointing) state.

The guidance control agent (NGC) will perform tests. First of all the NGC will request locally maintained information (check NGC 'manoeuvre-planning', ADC 'manoeuvre-pointing', and PCS 'manoeuvre-execution' service status). Then NGC will request non-local information (check attitude information, engine and communication link status) to confirm the information obtained in the previous tests.

The plan of action will be dependent on the test results. Assume for a moment that only the test on the engine status returns a *not OK*. The most probable source of the problem is a propulsion system breakdown, and the recovery plan would be based on this assumption. If alternatively it was the communication link status to be *not OK*, then the problem to be assumed would be a communication problem, and the propulsion system might then make use of a default plan.

4.3 Modelling the scenario

An Influence Diagram (ID) is used to model the scenario. IDs are probabilistic models represented by directed acyclic graphs. The topology of such graphs - that is the way nodes and links between nodes are laid out - embodies the qualitative nature of the underlying problem; the probabilities associated to the nodes and links embody its quantitative nature. Usually an ID has three different types of nodes to represent the different objects: a decision node (pictorially represented by a square), a chance node (represented by a circle), and a utility or value node (represented by a diamond). A chance node encodes the belief of the underlying object in terms of a random variable which can take on a set of possible values. A decision node represents the set of choices available to the decision making agent. A utility node represents the objective to be maximised. Arcs between nodes indicate their causal influences, and the strength of the influences is quantified by conditional probabilities. IDs are commonly dealt with as augmented Bayesian networks [14], where actions are decided based on the probability derived in the decision nodes. Such probabilities are inferred by means of a probabilistic message passing as described in [5]. For further information on Bayesian networks and Influence Diagrams, the reader is referred to [4][14][5].

Influence Diagram to identify the cause of a failure

The network for the scenario is shown in Figure 3.

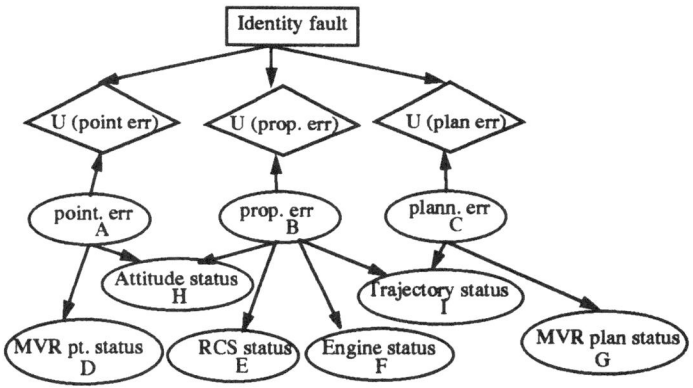

Fig. 3.Influence Diagram for scenario

The decision node (identify fault) represents the choice between three possible causes of the failure, namely attitude error, propulsion error, and manoeuvre planning error. In the case of the decision node, the arcs show that the decision has an impact on the utility nodes alone. The nodes A, B and C are the variables we wish to determine i.e. whether there is an error or not. The nodes D, E, F, G, H, and I are 'sensor' nodes, meaning that their value represents states of the controllers. Node D represents the operational status of the attitude control system, is the system in working order or not. Node G represents the operational status of the trajectory control system. Similarly, nodes E and F represent the operational status of the reaction control (RCS) thrusters used for pointing control and the main propulsion engine respectively. The spacecraft attitude and trajectory states (i.e. whether in or out of predefined limits) are also sensed and represented by the nodes H and I respectively.

Referring to Figure 3, a failure in the attitude (pointing) control system is indicated by the operational status of the attitude control system and by the attitude state. Therefore there are links from node A to nodes D and H. A failure in the manoeuvre planning system is indicated by the operational status of the trajectory control system and by the trajectory state. This causal influence is indicated by the links from node C to nodes I and G. A failure in the propulsion system shows in either the RCS thrusters or main engine operational status or both, and also shows in the attitude state or the trajectory state. Thus we have links from node B to nodes H, E, F, and I.

Certain simplifying assumptions were made in the design network. During a manoeuvre, the attitude state has an influence on the final trajectory state, however these two variables are assumed independent.

Spacecraft status information, referred to as *evidence,* are injected into the 'sensor' nodes, in the form of probabilities (likelihoods). After propagating this evidence throughout the network, the highest utility value indicates to the decision made by the network.

Utility values and Conditional probabilities

A simple scale was used with equal measures for each decision, a value of zero is assigned for an incorrect decision and maximum for a correct decision. Prior probabilities are assigned to root nodes (i.e. nodes without parents) and conditional probabilities assigned to the causal arcs. Conditional probabilities are based on frequency measurements drawn from spacecraft dynamics modelling e.g. trajectory state modelling, power status modelling. Prior probabilities are based on reliability figures for spacecraft components and systems.

4.4   Results of propagating evidence in the network

In this section, the results of propagating probabilities after injecting evidence, in the form of spacecraft status, are described. Four cases representing different failure conditions are shown and a decision made based on the largest utility result.

The probability value given to the injected evidence can reflect the belief in the sensor information, for example that the exactness of information obtained from local sensor is deemed better than information from remote sensors, particularly in cases of failure. Furthermore status information of co-agents obtained prior to the occurrence of the problem is considered less exact and if possible co-agents must be queried for confirmation. In the above example this is achieved by querying directly for attitude state (H) information to confirm (D). Sensors can give contradictory evidence but the effects of this are eliminated.

Case 1 Planning error

In this case, a fault in the guidance control agent affecting the manoeuvre planning function is the cause of the non nominal trajectory. We start by injecting evidence into node I, indicating that the trajectory state is unsatisfactory, and the probabilities are propagated. Further evidence is injected successively into the sensor nodes G, F, E, D, and H, at each step the probabilities are propagated. The results are shown in Table 1(a). At the first step, the only evidence injected is that the trajectory state is unsatisfactory, however er this information alone is insufficient for the network to make a decision. With more information, the ID identified the problem as originating in the navigation and guidance. In the final row H*, the decision is further strengthened by the attitude state sensor indicating a unwanted state.

Table 1: (a) Manoeuvre planning error, (b) Propulsion engine error

Nd	evidence ~OK, OK	point, prop., plan error	fault location	Nd	evidence ~OK, OK	point, prop., plan error	fault location
I	0.9, 0.1	0.50, 0.50, 0.50	unkn.	I	0.9, 0.1	0.50, 0.50, 0.50	unkn.
G	0.9, 0.1	0.50, 0.72, 0.83	mvr	G	0.1, 0.9	0.50, 0.25, 0.12	point.
F	0.1, 0.9	0.50, 0.59, 0.77	mvr	F	0.9, 0.1	0.50, 0.60, 0.25	engine
E	0.1, 0.9	0.50, 0.45, 0.71	mvr	E	0.1, 0.9	0.50, 0.46, 0.19	point.
D	0.1, 0.9	0.12, 0.45, 0.71	mvr	D	0.1, 0.9	0.12, 0.46, 0.19	engine
H	0.1, 0.9	0.03, 0.15, 0.57	mvr	H	0.1, 0.9	0.03, 0.15, 0.08	engine
H*	0.9, 0.1	0.21, 0.78, 0.86	mvr				

Case 2 Propulsion Engine error

In this case, a fault in propulsion engine affecting the pointing, causes the trajectory to deviate from the reference. Again we start by injecting evidence indicating that the trajectory state is unsatisfactory, into node I, and the probabilities propagated. Further evidence is injected successively into the sensor nodes G, F, E, D, and H, at each step the probabilities are propagated. The results are shown in Table 1(b). As with the previous case, at the first step, the only evidence injected is that the trajectory state is unsatisfactory, this information alone is insufficient for the network to make a decision. After injecting evidence into G and E, the network wrongly identifies the fault. However this incorrect decision does not affect the overall or final performance. After injecting all evidence, the correct decision was made, namely that the fault is in the propulsion engine.

Case 3 Propulsion RCS error

There is a failure in the propulsion system reaction control thrusters causing the non nominal trajectory. we start by injecting evidence indicating that the trajectory state is unsatisfactory, into node I, and the probabilities propagated. Further evidence is injected successively into the sensor nodes G, F, E, D, and H, at each step the probabilities are propagated. The results are shown in Table 2(a). The network finally determines that the problem is with the attitude control system thrusters after all the evidence is injected. In the last step H*, the network's decision is correct despite the fact that contradictory information is fed into the network.

Case 4 Pointing error

There is a failure in the attitude control agent causing the trajectory to deviate from the reference. we start by injecting evidence indicating that the trajectory state is unsatisfactory, into node I, and the probabilities propagated. Further evidence is injected successively into the sensor nodes G, F, E, D, and H, at each step the probabilities are propagated. The results are shown in Table 2(b). The network indicates that the problem is in the attitude control system. In the last step H*, the network's decision is correct despite the fact that contradictory information is fed into the network.

Table 2: (a) Propulsion RCS error, (b) Pointing error

Nd	evidence ~OK, OK	point, prop., plan error	fault location	Nd	evidence ~OK, OK	point, prop., plan error	fault location
I	0.9, 0.1	0.50, 0.50, 0.50	unkn.	I	0.9, 0.1	0.50, 0.50, 0.50	unkn.
G	0.1, 0.9	0.50, 0.25, 0.12	point.	G	0.1, 0.9	0.50, 0.25, 0.12	point.
F	0.1, 0.9	0.50, 0.15, 0.08	point.	F	0.1, 0.9	0.50, 0.15, 0.08	point.
E	0.9, 0.1	0.50, 0.46, 0.19	point.	E	0.1, 0.9	0.50, 0.09, 0.06	point.
D	0.1, 0.9	0.12, 0.46, 0.19	RCS	D	0.9, 0.1	0.83, 0.09, 0.06	point.
H	0.9, 0.1	0.21, 0.79, 0.32	RCS	H	0.9, 0.1	0.96, 0.11, 0.07	point.
H*	0.1, 0.9	0.03, 0.15, 0.08	RCS	H*	0.1, 0.9	0.51, 0.04, 0.04	point.

5   Future work

In the scenario described, a single goal (monitoring trajectory) was pursued. The attitude control agent may be pursuing other concurrent goals such as Sun tracking to provide spacecraft power. Sun tracking is a high priority task since the manoeuvre cannot take place if there is insufficient power. In the event of multiple and possibly mutually exclusive (due to constraints) goals, some form of goal arbitration is required. The role of the goal arbitrator would be to receive requests for services, prioritise the requests, and generate goals from requests. Goal arbitration was implemented using Influence Diagrams, the results are described in [13].

In the example reported in this paper, events taking place were considered in isolation and a single scenario was modelled. In practice many more events must be taken into account. The next step is to build on the spacecraft model, covering a wide range of concurrent activities. As the model grows both the size in terms of memory requirements and the complexity grow. The complexity will impact both the reactivity of the model and the reliability. It is planned to investigate these issues in the next stage of the project.

6 Conclusion

The architecture for an autonomous unmanned spacecraft was described. It is based on a decentralised intelligence concept with a distributed decision-making capability. It was shown how Influence Diagrams can be used for automating decision making by describing the results of a specific scenario modelled with an influence diagram. The results show that the ID was successful in identifying the cause of faults for the purpose of re-planning. The context is not fault diagnosis as such but action control so that the depth of the model is minimal. It is envisaged that several such small model will be used.

References

1. Albus, J.S.: NASA / NBS Standard Reference Model for Tele-robot Control System Architecture (NASREM) NIST Technical Note 1235, 1989
2. Brooks, R.: A Robust Layered Control System for a Mobile Robot IEEE J. Robotics & Automation volRA2 03/1986
3. Carraway, J.B., Squibb, G.: Spacecraft autonomy metrics second IAA Conference. Low cost planetary missions JHU/APL Apr. 1996
4. Charniak, E.: Bayesian networks without tears, 1991, AI Magazine Winter 91 vol12 4
5. Jensen, F.A.: Bayesian Networks, 1996 UCL press
6. Gat, E.: News from the trenches : An overview of unmanned Spacecraft for AI researchers,1996 AAAI spring Symposium. on planning with incomplete information. for robot problems
7. Larson, W.J., and Wertz, J.R.: Space Mission Analysis and Design, 2nd Edition 1992, Microcosm Inc. & Kluwer Academic Pub.
8. Lindley,: An Autonomous Spacecraft Architecture integrating Deliberative Reasoning and Behavioural, 1993 Goddard Space Flight Centre Conference
9. Lindley, C.A.: On-Board Emergent Scheduling of Autonomous Spacecraft Payload Operations, 1994 Goddard Space Flight Centre Conference
10. Lindley, C.A.: Behavioural system for autonomous spacecraft power distribution and control, 1994 Workshop on AI and KBS ESA/ESTEC, Nordwijk, Holland
11. Marshall,: Goals for Air Force Autonomous Spacecraft 1881 USAF Report st-tr-81-72 JPL Report 7030-1- Issue 1
12. Monekosso, N. D.: 10Th ASA/USU Annual Small Satellite Conference Logan, Utah, Sept 1996
13. Monekosso, N. D.: Goal Arbitration for Autonomous Spacecraft, to be published
14. Pearl, J.: Probabilistic reasoning in intelligent systems, Morgan Kaufmann 1988
15. Rich, E, Knight, K.: Artificial Intelligence McGraw Hill 1993
16. Simmons,R.G.: Structured Control for Autonomous Robots IEEE Trans.Robot.&Autom.v10 no1 Feb. 1994
17. Turner, P.R.: Autonomous spacecraft design and validation methodology handbook, JPL-7030-4 SD-TR-82-58 NAS7-100

A Weakly Backjumping Strategy to Solve Hard Scheduling Problems

Angelo Oddi

IP-CNR, National Research Council of Italy
Viale Marx 15, I-00137 Rome, Italy
oddi@pscs2.irmkant.rm.cnr.it

Abstract. In this paper, we propose and evaluate the use of an incomplete backtracking strategy for solving job shop scheduling problems with non-relaxable deadlines and complex metric constraints. Previous research in constraint satisfaction scheduling [4] has developed highly effective, heuristics for this class of problems based on simple measures of temporal sequencing flexibility. However, they are not infallible, and the possibility of search failure raises in the so called *phase transition* region, where a problem changes to being soluble to insoluble and where it is reasonable to conjecture [3, 5, 12, 13] there are the hardest problems. Chronological backtracking is one possibility to find a solution to this type of problems, but such systematicity generally implies high computational cost. We instead design an incomplete backtracking procedure based on the intuition that it is more productive to deviate from the sistematic chronological backtracking search in cases where the heuristic is more knowledgeable, and likewise better to follow the sistematic search when heuristic is less informed. Experimental results on job shop scheduling CSPs of increasing size demonstrate comparative advantage over complete chronological backtracking.

1 Introduction

Recent research on the solution of many famous combinatorial problems has demonstrated the existence of a *phase transition* behavior [3, 5, 12, 13], where for critical values of constraints tighness, a problem changes from being soluble to insoluble and the computational effort to solve it is orders of magnitude then elsewhere.

For example, it has been shown that graph colouring problems exhibit a phase transition, where problems change from being colourable to un-colourable [3] and this occours at a critical value of the graph connectivity. Problems that occour below the critical value are easy to colour, and problems above the critical value are obviously un-colourable. It is only around the critical value of connectivity that it is hard to decide if a problem can be coloured. In [12] the author also shows that the binary Constraint Satisfaction Problem (CSP) has a phase transition behavior. He carried out a set of experiments by utilizing a backtracking algorithm on randomly generated problems.

The study shows that for the binary CSP there is a critical value for the tighness of the constraints where the probability that a problem is soluble goes rapidly from one to zero and the search effort becomes orders of magnitude harder than elsewhere.

An interesting question is if also complex scheduling problems has a phase transition behavior and how we can create a strategy to solve them in the phase transition region. In this papers we propose a study on a problem which is a variant of the famous *Job Shop Scheduling Problem* (JSSP) [7] called Job Shop Deadline Scheduling Problem (JSDSP) where all the temporal constraints are metric. The problem was considered in [4] where the authors developed highly effective, greedy heuristics for this class of problems based on simple measures of temporal sequencing flexibility, and in [11] where a set of stochastic procedures were proposed which are a randomized counterpart of the deterministic ones tested in [4].

Here we consider the same scheduling problem and an analogous random methods to generate instances of JSDSP problem, but with the particular target to generate instances of the problem in the *phase transition* region. The general idea to build difficult problems is to create instances where the number of solutions in very low, an extreme situation is when the number of solution is one. In [13] B. Smith conjectures that given a Constraint Satisfaction Problem, the hardest instances occur when the expected number of solutions is only one.

An interesting alternative to chronological backtracking for solving hard problems is to explore the search space in incomplete way on the base of heuristic information. Where, at each step of backtracking search process, it is possible to select two alternatives: to try the other possible choices or to escape to a previous level.

A related approach to solve a discrete Constraint Satisfaction Problem (CSP) can be found in [9], where two interesting variants of the backtracking procedure are explained: *backjumping* and *dynamic backtracking*. In both techniques, each time a new value is assigned to a CSP's variable, the effects are propagated to the other variables' domains by the deletion of some domains' elements. In addition, for each element deleted in a variable's domain, a set of eliminating explanations have to be memorized. So, the overload in memory occupation is in the worst case $O(i^2v)$, where i is the number of variables and v is the maximum cardinality of the domains' variables.

In this paper we propose an incomplete backtracking procedure based on a high-performance, deterministic constraint satisfaction scheduling procedure called SP-PCP [4]. This procedure does not need to memorize eliminating explanations, but it can be effective in the case there is a strong heuristic to decide in each search node if the search process has to follow the classical chronological backtracking or jumps back on more interesting search nodes.

The paper is organized as follows. Section 2 introduces the scheduling problem. Section 3 illustrates the basic idea to explore the search space in incomplete way. Section 4 proposes some experiments which show the usefulness of the search strategy introduced. Finally, in Section 5, we give some conclusions.

2 Problem Definition

The extended Job Shop Deadline Scheduling Problem (JSDSP) considered in [4] involves synchronizing the use of a set of resources $R = \{r_1 \ldots r_m\}$ to perform a set of jobs $J = \{j_1 \ldots j_n\}$ over time. The processing of a job j_i requires the execution of a sequence of n_i activities $\{a_{i1} \ldots a_{in_i}\}$, and the execution of each activity a_{ij} is subject to the following constraints:

- *resource availability* - each a_{ij} requires exclusive use of a single resource $r_{a_{ij}}$ for its entire duration.
- *processing time constraints* - each a_{ij} has a minimum and maximum processing time, $proc_{ij}^{min}$ and $proc_{ij}^{max}$, such that $proc_{ij}^{min} \leq e_{ij} - s_{ij} \leq proc_{ij}^{max}$, where the variables s_{ij} and e_{ij} represent the start and end times respectively of a_{ij}.
- *separation constraints* - for each pair of successive activities a_{ij} and $a_{i(j+1)}$, $j = 1 \ldots (n_i - 1)$, in job j_i, there is a minimum and maximum separation time, sep_{ik}^{min} and sep_{ik}^{max}, such that $\{sep_{ik}^{min} \leq s_{i(k+1)} - e_{ik} \leq sep_{ik}^{max} : k = 1 \ldots (n_i - 1)\}$.
- *job release and due dates* - Every job j_i has a release date rd_i, which specifies the earliest time that any a_{ij} can be started, and a due date dd_i, which designates the time by which all a_{ij} must be completed.

The problem is to determine whether there is an assignment of start and end times to all activities of all jobs which satisfies all constraints. It is well known that this problem is strongly NP-hard [8].

There are different ways to formulate this problem as a Constraint Satisfaction Problem (CSP). In [4], the problem is treated as one of establishing precedence constraints between pairs of activities that require the same resource, so as to eliminate all possible conflicts in resource use. In CSP terms, a decision variable O_{ijr} is defined for each pair of activities a_i and a_j requiring resource r, which can take on one of two values: $a_j\{before\}a_i$ or $a_i\{before\}a_j$.

To support the search for a consistent assignment to this set of decision variables, we can define for any JSDSP a directed graph $G_d(V, E)$, where the set of nodes V represents time points (i.e., the origin point and the start and end time points, s_{a_i} and e_{a_i}, of each activity a_i) and the set of edges E represents temporal distance constraints between couple of time points. That is, processing time constraints of activities, separation constraints and precedence constraints between couple of activities. Every previous constraint has the general form $a \leq tp_j - tp_i \leq b$ and can be represented in the graph $G_d(V, E)$ with two weighted edges. The first one is directed from tp_i to tp_j with weight b and the second one is directed from tp_j to tp_i with weight $-a$. The graph $G_d(V, E)$ corresponds to a *Simple Temporal Problem* (STP) [6] and its consistency can be efficiently determined via shortest path computations [1, 2, 10]. Thus, a search for a solution to JSDSP can proceed by repeatedly adding new precedence constraints into $G_d(V, E)$ and recomputing shortest path lengths to confirm that $G_d(V, E)$ remains consistent (i.e., no negative weight cycles). Let $d(tp_i, tp_j)$ designate the shortest path length in graph $G_d(V, E)$ from node tp_i to node tp_j.

3   Incomplete Exploration of the Search Space

The SP-PCP scheduling procedure (Shortest Path-based Precedence Constraint Posting) [4] utilizes shortest path information in $G_d(V, E)$ in two ways to enhance the basic search process sketched above.

First, it is possible to define *dominance conditions* [4, 10, 11], which identify unconditional decisions and promote early pruning of alternatives. For any pair of activities a_i and a_j that are competing for the same resource, four possible cases of conflict are defined:

1. $d(e_{a_i}, s_{a_j}) < 0 \ \wedge \ d(e_{a_j}, s_{a_i}) < 0$
2. $d(e_{a_i}, s_{a_j}) < 0 \ \wedge \ d(e_{a_j}, s_{a_i}) \geq 0 \ \wedge \ d(s_{a_i}, e_{a_j}) > 0$
3. $d(e_{a_j}, s_{a_i}) < 0 \ \wedge \ d(e_{a_i}, s_{a_j}) \geq 0 \ \wedge \ d(s_{a_j}, e_{a_i}) > 0$
4. $d(e_{a_i}, s_{a_j}) \geq 0 \ \wedge \ d(e_{a_j}, s_{a_i}) \geq 0$

Condition 1 represents an *unresolvable conflict*. There is no way to sort a_i and a_j without inducing a negative cycle in graph $G_d(V, E)$, and the search has reached an inconsistent state. Conditions 2, and 3, alternatively, distinguish *uniquely resolvable conflicts*. Here, there is only one feasible ordering of a_i and a_j and the decision of which constraint to post is thus unconditional. In the case of Condition 2, only $a_j\{before\}a_i$ leaves $G_d(V, E)$ consistent and similarly, only $a_i\{before\}a_j$ is feasible in the case of Condition 3. Condition 4 designates a final class of *resolvable conflicts*. In this case, both orderings of a_i and a_j remain feasible and it is necessary to make a choice.

The second way in which shortest path information is exploited within SP-PCP is in the definition of *variable* and *value ordering* heuristics for selecting and resolving conflicts in the set characterized by Condition 4. In this context, $d(e_{a_i}, s_{a_j})$ and $d(e_{a_j}, s_{a_i})$ provide measures of the degree of sequencing flexibility that remains with respect to a_i and a_j. The SP-PCP variable ordering heuristic attempts to focus first on the conflict with the least amount of sequencing flexibility (i.e., the ordering decision that is closest to being forced). More precisely, the conflict (a_i, a_j) with the overall minimum value of $VarEval(a_i, a_j) = min\{bd_{ij}, bd_{ji}\}$ is always selected for resolution, where:

$$bd_{ij} = \frac{d(e_{a_i}, s_{a_j})}{\sqrt{S}}, \quad bd_{ji} = \frac{d(e_{a_j}, s_{a_i})}{\sqrt{S}}$$

and

$$S = \frac{min\{d(e_{a_i}, s_{a_j}), d(e_{a_j}, s_{a_i})\}}{max\{d(e_{a_i}, s_{a_j}), d(e_{a_j}, s_{a_i})\}}$$

The $\sqrt{S}$ bias is introduced to hedge when the conflict with the overall value $min\{d(e_{a_i}, s_{a_j}), d(e_{a_j}, s_{a_i})\}$ has a very large $max\{d(e_{a_i}, s_{a_j}), d(e_{a_j}, s_{a_i})\}$, and a second conflict has two shortest path values just slightly larger than this overall minimum. In such situations, it is not clear which conflict has the least sequencing flexibility.

The value ordering heuristic used within SP-PCP to resolve a selected conflict (a_i, a_j) simply chooses the precedence constraint that retains the most

ND-SP-PCP($Jsdsp,S_0$)
1. **if** Unresolvable-Conflict($Jsdsp$)
2.   **then return**(NIL)
3.   **else**
4.   **if** Uniquely-Resolvable-Conflicts($Jsdsp$)
5.   **then** Post-Unconditional-Constraints($Jsdsp$)
6.   **else begin**
7. $Conflict$::=Select-Resolvable-Conflict($Jsdsp$)
8.   **if** ($Conflict = NIL$)
9.   **then return**(Solution)
10.   **else if** ($S(Conflict) > S_0$)
11.   **then choose**(Prec-Constraints($Jsdsp, Conflict$))
12.   **else begin**
13. $Const$::=Select-Prec-Constraint($Jsdsp, Conflict$)
14.   Post-Constraint($Jsdsp,Const$)
15.   **end**
16.   **end**
17. **ND-SP-PCP**($Jsdsp,S_0$)

Fig. 1. Non Deterministic SP-PCP Algorithm

sequencing flexibility. Specifically, $a_i\{before\}a_j$ is selected if $bd_{ij} > bd_{ji}$ and $a_j\{before\}a_i$ otherwise.

Figure 1 gives a non deterministic and recursive version of the incomplete backtracking procedure proposed, which takes as an input an instance of the problem ($Jsdsp$) and a threshold S_0 (the meaning of S_0 will be explained below). The procedure interleaves the application of dominance conditions (Steps 1 and 4) with variable and value ordering heuristic (Steps 7 and 13 respectively) and incremental updating of the solution graph $G_d(V, E)$ (Steps 5,11 and 14) to conduct a single pass through the search tree.

The real difference wrt a chronological backtracking procedure is in Steps 10-15, where on the basis of the test $S(Conflict) > S_0$ the algorithm decides when to branch the computation (**choose**(Prec-Constraints($Jsdsp, Conflict$))), and start two different search paths (one for the decision $a_i\{before\}a_j$ and another one for $a_j\{before\}a_i$). It is clear that in terms of chronological backtracking this means to make the second ordering choice instead of jumping to a previous level. In order to take this decision, we use the information given from the parameter S. By the definition of S given above, it is simple to see that when Condition 4 holds, S represents a measure of the "similarity" in the in the lost of temporal flexibility in the current solution wrt the two possible ordering choices: $a_i\{before\}a_j$ and $a_j\{before\}a_i$. As is possible to verify $S \in [0, 1]$. Values of S close to 1, indicates a simmetry in the lost of flexibility in the current solution rispect the two possible ordering choices. On the other hand, values close to 0 indicate a great difference in the lost of temporal flexibility.

The complete backtracking search version of SP-PCP is obtained by putting the threshold $S_0 = 0$, instead it is possible to explore in partial way the search space by setting the threshold S_0 to a value contained in the interval $(0, 1]$. In particular, with $S_0 = 1$ backtracking is completely avoided and the procedure explores a single path in the search tree.

The idea below this search strategy is founded on the meaning of the parameter S, that is, a measure of the similarity in the lost of temporal flexibility when a conflict is resolved wrt the two possible ordering choices. So, we propose this idea: during the backtracking search, given a conflict which can be resolved in two ways (Condition 4), after the first attempt, it might be convenient to avoid to do the second ordering choice, when the lost of temporal flexibility is great wrt the previous one.

In the next section we try to demonstrate the previous thesis in experimental way, by showing a set of experiments where we compare the search procedure with two different values of S_0.

4 Experimental Evaluation

In this section, we evaluate the incomplete backtracking procedure on a set of randomly generated job shop deadline scheduling problems. Following the same experimental design used in [4], we considered scheduling problems of size $N \times M$, where the structure of each problem instance is as follows. There are N jobs to be scheduled. Each job requires operations to be performed on each of M different resources, and the order in which each job must visit each resource is random. Using precisely the same problem generation scheme and parameters for specifying release dates, due dates, processing times and separation constraints as used in [4], we generated problem sets of 30 instances at each of three different sizes: 8×5, 10×5 and 12×5.

The evaluated procedure was implemented in *Allegro Common Lisp*. The 8×5 and 10×5 experiments were run on a SUN Sparc 10 workstation, instead 12×5 experiments on a SUN Sparc 20. We use two values of the threshold for the similarity S, $S_0 = 0$ and $S = 0.67$ (2/3). In all cases limit on the maximum number of search nodes was imposed as an upper bound on the amount of backtracking allowed in solving any one problem instance. Precisely, for 8×5 problems a limit of 1000 nodes was imposed, instead for 10×5 and 12×5 problems we imposed a limit of 2000 nodes. Performance was measured in terms of number of problems solved and average solution time (over all instances).

In Table 1, Table 2 and Table 3 are shown the results obtained for both performance measures (*Cpu-time* and *Nbr. Solved*) where it is possible to compare the performances for the complete chronological backtracking ($S_0 = 0$) and for the incomplete backtracking ($S_0 = 0.67$). In order "to move" the procedure in the phase transition region and try to solve hard scheduling problems, we decrement a parameter called *Slack*, which controls the amplitude of the allocation windows of the jobs (see Section 2) $[rd_i, dd_i]$. The idea is rather simple: the lesser

Table 1. Performance on 8 × 5 problem set

Slack	Cpu-time (seconds)		Nbr. Solved	
	$S_0 = 0$	$S_0 = 0.67$	$S_0 = 0$	$S_0 = 0.67$
1	8	7	30	30
0.9	69	36	26	26
0.85	128	36	23	21
0.8	192	36	15	15

is the space to allocate activities, the harder are the problems to be solved. In practice, the real windows for a job j_i is $[Slack * rd_i, Slack * dd_i]$. We use four values for the parameter $Slack$:1, 0.9, 0.85 and 0.8 .

Table 2. Performance on 10 × 5 problem set

Slack	Cpu-time (seconds)		Nbr. Solved	
	$S_0 = 0$	$S_0 = 0.67$	$S_0 = 0$	$S_0 = 0.67$
1	14	16	30	30
0.9	266	145	26	28
0.85	785	388	14	20
0.8	1166	497	5	6

Comments on the results of Table 1, Table 2 and Table 3 are quite similar, the incomplete backtracking procedure in some cases gets more solutions than chronological backtracking and only in two cases the number is slightly less. However, there is always an improvement of the *cpu-time*, where in same cases the incomplete procedure significantly outperforms the complete procedure.

5 Conclusions

In this paper, we have investigated the use of an incomplete backtracking search procedure as a means of improve the performance to solve scheduling problems with non-relaxable deadlines and complex metric constraints in the phase transition region, where we can conjecture [3, 5, 12, 13] there are the hardest problems.

Table 3. Performance on 12×5 problem set

Slack	Cpu-time (seconds)		Nbr. Solved	
	$S_0 = 0$	$S_0 = 0.67$	$S_0 = 0$	$S_0 = 0.67$
1	9	9	30	30
0.9	237	154	18	22
0.85	429	295	9	14
0.8	500	372	3	1

Building from prior research [4] which has developed strong variable and value ordering heuristics for this class of constraint satisfaction scheduling problems, we have focused on the design of backtracking procedure which implement a weakly form of backjumping based only on the heuristic information. The key idea underlying our approach is to use heuristic information to escape from a search node during the backtracking procedure or to continue chronological sistematic search. In an experimental study on randomly generated scheduling problems of increasing scale, the incomplete procedure was found in most cases to significantly outperform its complete backtracking-search counterpart.

Acknowledgements

Angelo Oddi's work was supported by Italian Space Agency, CNR Committee 12 on Information Technology (Project SCI*SIA), CNR Committee 04 on Biology and Medicine, and Italian Ministry of Scientific Research. He is currently supported by a scholarship from CNR Committee 12 on Information Technology. Part of this work was devoleped when the author was visiting student at the Robotics Institute (Carnegie Mellon University, Pittsburgh) and during his Ph.D. program at the Department of Computer and System Science of the University of Rome "La Sapienza". The author would like to thank Amedeo Cesta and Stephen F. Smith for the useful comments on this work. The author is of course the only responsible for any mistake still in the paper.

References

1. Ausiello G., Italiano G.F., Marchetti Spaccamela A., Nanni U., Incremental Algorithm for Minimal Length Paths, Journal of Algorithms 12, 1991, 615-638.
2. Cesta A. and Oddi A., Gaining Efficency and Flexibility in the Simple Temporal Problem, Proceedings of the Third International Conference on Temporal Representation and Reasoning (TIME-96) 45-50, IEEE Computer Society Press, Los Alamitos, California, 1996.

3. Cheeseman P., Kanefsky B. and Taylor W.M., Where the *really* hard problems are. Proc. IJCAI-91. 331-337, 1991.
4. Cheng C. and Smith S.F., Generating Feasible Schedules under Complex Metric Constraints, Proceedings 12th National Conference on AI (AAAI-94), Seattle, WA, August 1994.
5. Crawford J.M. and Auton L.D., Experimental Results on the Crossover Point in Satisfability Problems. Proceedings 11th National Conference on AI (AAAI-93), 21-27.
6. Dechter R., Meiri I. and Pearl J., Temporal Constraint Networks. Artificial Intelligence, 49, 1991, 61-95.
7. French S., Sequencing and Scheduling: an Introduction to the Mathematics of the Job-Shop. Hellis Horwood Lim., 1982.
8. Garey M.R. and Johnson D.S., Computers and Intractability, a Guide to the Theory of NP-Completeness, W.H. Freeman Company 1979.
9. Ginsberg M.L., Dynamic Backtracking, Journal of Artificial Intelligence Research 1 (1993) 25-46.
10. Oddi A., Metodi di Sequenziamento ed Algoritmi di Ragionamento Temporale Applicati alla Gestione di Risorse Mediche. Tesi Dottorato di Ricerca in Informatica Medica, Dipartimento di Informatica e Sistemistica, Università di Roma "La Sapienza", Febbraio 1997.
11. Oddi A. and Smith S.F., Stochastic Procedures for Generating Feasible Schedules, to appear in: Proceedings Fourteenth National Conference on Artificial Intelligence (AAAI-97), Providence, Rhode Island, July 27-31, 1997.
12. Prosser P., Binary Constraint Satisfaction Problems: Some are Harder than Others, Proc. ECAI-94, ed. A.G.Cohn, Wiley 1994.
13. Smith B.M., Phase Transition and the Mushy Region in Constraint Satisfaction Problems, Proc. ECAI-94, ed. A.G.Cohn, Wiley 1994.

Compiling Task Networks into Partial Order Planning Domains

M. Baioletti, S. Marcugini, A. Milani

Dipartimento di Matematica
Università degli Studi di Perugia
Via Vanvitelli
06100 Perugia - Italy

Abstract. This paper presents theoretical results and techniques for representing and managing task network goals in the framework of partial order planning. Task oriented formalisms are more expressive than partial order based formalism for problem goals in dynamical and changing domains, but they are not more powerful. We prove that it is always possible to express a task network problem in terms of an equivalent problem stated in partial order planning formalism. The task network model has been extended to describe external events (EETN), a feature not present in many planning models. The equivalence between this new model and PO formalism is also proved.

These results allow to reuse existing partial order planners as tools in order to solve task network goals. We introduce a linear cost technique of domain transformation which compiles a given task domain in an equivalent operator based domain which is then submitted to a nonlinear planner. This technique has been successfully demonstrated by the implementation of a EETN planner based on domain tranformations for UCPOP.

1 Introduction

The success of Hierarchical Task Network (HTN) approach to planning have raised a great interest and an increasing literature ([14],[6],[4], [7],[5]), which confirms the effectivity of the approach both from the expressivity and computational sides.

The works of Yang [14], Erol et al.[4] [6] and Kambhampati [9] have extensively investigated semantics and complexity of this approach. They show that HTN is strictly more powerful than ordinary (STRIPS-like) planning. This result basically derives from the fact that the set of solution plans of an ordinary planning problem is a regular language, while the set of solution plans of HTN planning problems is a higher level language, (i.e. the solutions space can be expressed as intersection of some context free languages).

HTN planning allows the user to define problems in terms of a task network, in which each task can be replaced itself by a task network. While the possibility of defining recursive plans clearly has a great effect in the expressivity, there are other features of HTN planning that have no equivalent in PO planning.

Typical examples of problems which cannot be directly modeled in STRIPS-like planners are problems in which the activity is more significant than the goal state, like problems with identical initial and final state (i.e. "making a round trip from Rome to Florence", "using the computer in the lab but leaving it in the same state it was found "); or problems requiring that some particular actions are to be executed in some specific order ("knock the door, then ring the bell, then knock the door again, then open"); or some specific intermediate states are to be achieved ("be in Florence, then be in Venice"). The main reason is the lack of an explicit notion of time in partial order (PO) planners, in which a problem goal is described in term of reaching a final state from some initial condition, without any regards about what happens in the middle. The results of HTN shows that managing explicit time (and the associated computational overhead) is not strictly necessary to model this class of problems.

Therefore we restrict our study to a significant subset of HTN planning, that we call Task Network planning (TN), showing that problems in this formalism can be solved, by a appropriate domain transformation, within the partial order planning (PO) model. The same equivalence result is obtained when TN planning is extended to cope with external events. This formalism, that we call Task network with external events (EETN), is not usually included in most HTN planners on the literature. The EETN framework allows to specify external events which are known to happen in some intermediate instants, in this case the planner is required to generate a solution plan which reaches the goals taking into account the external events.

The paper is organized as following: in paragraph 2 and 3 the Task Nework model is introduced, in 4 the External Events Task Network model is introduced, in 5 transformation techniques are defined, in 6 the equivalence theorems for both TN and EETN are stated and 7 some implementation issues are described.

2   PO Planning

PO planning is relevant because it is a well established planning model whose theoretical features are well known (see for instance [3], [13], [11]). Also many implementations of PO planners are available.

A simple widely accepted Partial Order planning model (PO) is used as reference in the following.

A planning problem is a tuple $(\mathcal{I}, \mathcal{A}, \mathcal{G})$, where $\mathcal{I}$ is an initial state, $\mathcal{G}$ a set of conjunctive user goals, and $\mathcal{A}$ is the set of available action schemata. Each action a of $\mathcal{A}$ is described by a triple (v, p, e), where v, p, e respectively represent its variables, preconditions and effects. Conversely we will denote by vars(a), precond(a) and effect(a), the variables, preconditions and effects of an action a.

A plan P is a triple $(\mathcal{S}, \mathcal{C}, \mathcal{O})$ where elements of $\mathcal{S}$, the plan steps, are instances of actions in $\mathcal{A}$, $\mathcal{C}$ is a set of constraints (binding and auxiliary) and $\mathcal{O}$ is a partial order relation on $\mathcal{S}$. P is a solution plan if it reaches the final goal $\mathcal{G}$ when executed in the initial state $\mathcal{I}$.

Our PO model assumes the classical semantics of PO planning model as that of UCPOP [13].

3 Task Network Planning

While usual PO planning only allows to define initial states and final goals, a Task Network planning model allows in addition to describe: intermediate goals, execution goals and goals ordering.

Intermediate goals

Intermediate goals, $G_p = (p_1, \ldots, p_n)$, represent "partial" goals which are required to be achieved in some intermediate state of the solution plan. They represent a generalization of the concept of final goals.

A partial order relation $\preceq$ is defined on G_p and it states in which order the partial goals must be verified, i.e., $p_1 \preceq p_2$ iff p_1 must be true in an instant preceding the instant in which p_2 must be true.

Note that the final goal is a particular case of intermediate goals: the last one.

A typical case in which intermediate or "partial" goals are useful is when the user final goal is equal to the initial state, but it is also required a different intermediate state. In the round trip example of the introduction, the initial and final state are the same, (i.e. be_in(Florence)) while the intermediate state is different (i.e. be_in(Rome)). Let us point out that a classical PO planner would trivially (and unlikely) solve any given problem where $\mathcal{I}$ and $\mathcal{G}$ coincide by generating an empty plan.

Another application of intermediate goals is when the user wants to obtain contradictory results but in different times, for example pick up an object (in order to observe it) and then put it down. In this case the two goals taken(object) and ¬taken(object) would be in contradiction if expressed as a unique final goal.

Execution goals

Execution goals, $G_e = (e_1, \ldots, e_n)$, represent the fact that some specific actions have to be executed in some specific instants, in order to solve the task problem. In other words, it is required that any final solution plan contains the specific actions instantiation in G_e. Also for execution goals it is possible to specify a partial order relation $\preceq$ which holds on G_e. A typical example of task problem with intermediate actions is the buy_a_house problem [9]. This problem requires that the solution space should be constrained to all those plans which reach the final goal (have(house)) using a specific intermediate action (buy(house)), thus avoiding to use other actions (like build(house)). It is worth noting, as it is already shown in [9], that we cannot trivially exclude the build operator from the operators domain, because it could be used in other problems, or possibly in the same solution plan.

Task planning problem

Our notation in the following will be similar to that one of [4], [6] and [9].

A task planning problem is a tuple $(\mathcal{I}, \mathcal{A}, \mathcal{T}, \mathcal{O})$ where $\mathcal{I}$ and $\mathcal{A}$ are defined as in PO, and the pair $(\mathcal{T}, \mathcal{O})$ is a task network, where $\mathcal{T} = (T_1, \ldots, T_n)$ is a set of tasks, and $\mathcal{O}$ is a set of temporal constraints on tasks of $\mathcal{T}$.
There exist two types of tasks:

- $\text{do}(\alpha)$, which requires to execute an action α, that can be a possibly instantiated action belonging to $\mathcal{A}$; they correspond to execution goals;
- $\text{achieve}(p)$, which requires to achieve a condition p; they correspond to intermediate goals.

Task Planning Solution Plan

A plan is a solution for task planning problem only if it achieves the intermediate goals and performs the activity goals in the specified ordering.

The Task Network (TN) model incorporates the possibility of specifying partial intermediate goals, execution goals and orderings. It is clearly a subset of HTN therefore semantics of TN can easily derived from that one of HTN.

4 External Event and Task Network Planning

A natural extension of TN planning is to allow to manage external events, in addition to intermediate goals and actions. While intermediate goals are generalization of final goals, i.e. intermediate states which the planner has to obtain, external events are generalization of initial states, i.e. intermediate states which the planner has to take into account in order to find a solution plan.

The main application for external events is to model, in dynamical domain, some expected events whose effects cannot be modified by the planner actions. These intermediate partial states are generated by external events which are assumed, at planning time, unavoidable and fully expected, even if the istant in which the events will take place is not known, or it is only *qualitatively* known by means of a temporal partial order relation. Consider, for instance, to have to take into account of astronomical events as day and night cicle, or events like "banks are closed", or even simpler events like "John will be at home".

External Event and Task Network Problem

An External Event and Task Network (EETN) problem is defined by a tuple $(\mathcal{I}, \mathcal{A}, \mathcal{T}, \mathcal{O})$ where $\mathcal{A}$ and $\mathcal{T}$ are defined as in TN planning, but $\mathcal{I} = (I_1, \ldots, I_m)$ is a set of intermediate state (or external events) and O is a partial order relation defined over $\mathcal{I} \cup \mathcal{T}$.

The semantics of EETN is similar to that one of TN: a plan P is a solution for an EETN problem if any execution of P includes $\mathcal{T}$ and verifies constraints in $\mathcal{O}$, and any action a_i can be executed in a state which take into account of each I_i which belong to $\mathcal{I}$ and possibly preceeds a_i. The main difference between a partial plans in TN and EETN planning is that in the latter the ordering of the plan steps is also defined with respect to the intermediate states.

5 TN/EETN Planning into PO Planning

In this section we will show how the constraints embedded in a TN/EETN planning problem can be expressed in a PO domain. A PO problem P encapsulates a TN/EETN constraint c if each solution plan verifies c.

The basic idea is to add to the PO knowledge $(\mathcal{I}, \mathcal{A}, \mathcal{G})$ some dummy actions, facts and goals which induce the required constraints. It is worth noting that the use of dummy actions is not new to planning: dummy initial and final actions are used by most planners to represent respectively initial and goal states of the problem. The differences are that the we do not restrict to initial and final states and we add dummy objects to the domain, instead of adding them to the plan under development.

We now describe some techniques for coding different kinds of constraints which will be used in compiling TN problems: action existence, intermediate goal, use-once and ordering contraints.

In the following a given TN problem $(\mathcal{I}, \mathcal{A}, \mathcal{T}, \mathcal{O})$ is assumed and a corresponding PO problem $(\mathcal{I}', \mathcal{A}', \mathcal{G}')$ is incrementally generated, starting with $\mathcal{I}' = \mathcal{I}$, $\mathcal{A}' = \mathcal{A}$ and $\mathcal{G}' = \emptyset$.

Action existence constraints

If an action a_i, instance of operator op_a, is required to be in each solution plan, then a new operator op_{a_i} is added to the set $\mathcal{A}$ of action operators. op_{a_i} is obtained from a_i by adding a dummy unique fact, say occur_a_i, to its effects, which represents the occurrence of action instance. The dummy goal occur_a_i, is also added to the set of goals $\mathcal{G}$ to represent the fact that action existence is required. If some parameters of a_i are bound to constants then the corresponding codesignation constraint on op_{a_i} operator description is added. Every solution of the modified planning problem will reach the goal occur_a_i and therefore must contain op_{a_i}.

Intermediate goals constraints

If the solution plan in the task network is required to contain an intermediate goal g_i, then a dummy operator op_{g_i} is added to the set $\mathcal{A}$. op_{g_i} has preconditions g_i and a single dummy unique effect (occur_g_i). The goal occur_g_i is also added to the set of goals $\mathcal{G}$.

Note this dummy operator does not correspond to real actions and has not to be executed by the execution monitoring system.

Every solution of the modified planning problem will reach the goal occur_g_i, the solution must contain op_{g_i} and then must achieve op_{g_i} preconditions, i.e.

g_i. This transformation is always used togheter with a use-once constraint (see below) on the dummy action.

Use-once constraints

If it is required that a given action instance or intermediate goal t_i occurs at most once in every solution plan, then the dummy fact **use-once_t_i** is added to the initial state $\mathcal{I}$, and the operator op_{t_i} is modified by adding the same dummy fact to the preconditions and its negation ¬**use-once_t_i** to the effects. no PO plan solutions exists in which op_{t_i} is used more than once, because the effects of op_{t_i} negates the preconditions of any other instance of op_{t_i}, and the uniqueness of the dummy **use-once_t_i** guarantees that no other action instance can re-establish it again.

Precedence Constraints between Actions and States

If a precedence constraint between two action instances or intermediate goals, say $t_i \preceq t_j$, is required then the operators op_{t_i} and op_{t_j} are modified as following: a unique dummy fact (**before_t_i_t_j**) is added to the effects of op_{t_i} and to the preconditions of op_{t_j}. The PO establishment rule will guarantee that in every solution plan op_{t_i} preceeds op_{t_j} in order to reach precondition **before_t_i_t_j** .

Compacting the dummy items

Given a task network N with a set of execution goals and/or intermediate and final goals t_i a solution plan P for N requires that each op_{t_i} has to exist in the final plan and to be used only once and any precedence constraint stated in the goal network must be verified in the solution plan.

A direct application of the preceeding transformation rules will lead to a proliferation of dummy items (actions and facts), which could increase the PO planner overhead (see fig.1a). It is possible to reduce the number of dummy actions, goals and facts by exploiting the fact that these constraints are needed at the same time. It is easy to see that the dummy facts (**occur_t_i**), not (**use-once_t_i**), (**before_t_i_t_j**) can be merged in a unique dummy fact, say u_{t_i}, as shown in the example in the figure 1b. Note that: the postcondition u_{t1} of $t1$ is the only one which reaches the final goal u_{t1} (it guarantees the existence of action $t1$); the precondition $not(u_{t1})$ of $t1$ is reached only by initial fact $not(u_{t1})$ and negated after $t1$ execution (it guarantees that $t1$ is used only once); finally precondition u_{t1} of $t2$ is reached only by $t1$ (it guarantees that $t1$ must precede $t2$ in every solution plan).

Intermediate states

Using a similar technique it is also possible to express an intermediate state of EETN model within a PO planning domain.

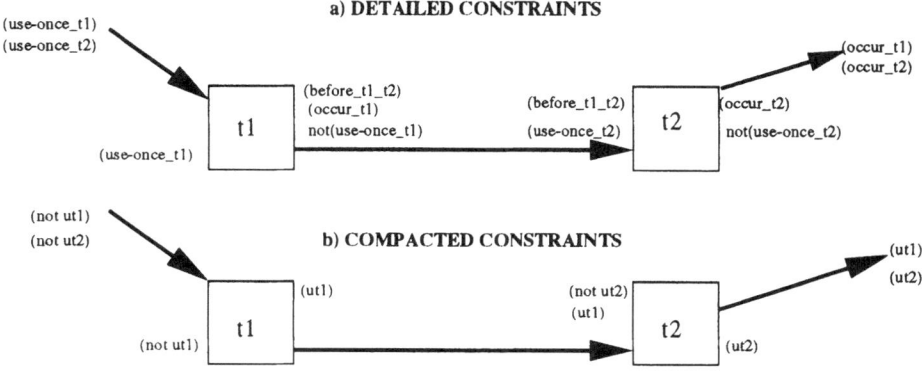

Fig. 1. Compacting dummy items

An intermediate external event I_i is modeled in a PO problem by a dummy action op_{I_i}, representing the event that it is required to exist in any final plan of PO problem. The dummy action will have as effects the conditions that will be true in the intermediate state and empty preconditions.

Some dummy facts are added, in a completely similar way, to preconditions and effects of op_{I_i} in order to guarantee its existence, its uniqueness and its temporal relations with the other events and tasks.

By iterating the application of domain transformations described in the former paragraphs it is possible to generate a PO domain such that all the solution the constraints are satisfied. This leads to the theorems described in the next section.

6 Theoretical results

In this section we will investigate the relationships between TN and PO planning and between EETN and PO planning, using the following definition of problem equivalence.

Definition

Two planning problems P and P', not necessarily belonging to same planning models, are equivalent modulo a plan transformation function ψ (in symbols $P \sim_\psi P'$) if s is a solution of P if and only if there exists a solution s' of P' such that $s = \psi(s')$.

Theoretical results for TN planning

Theorem

TN planning is not more powerful than PO planning, in that for each TN planning problem $P = (\mathcal{I}, \mathcal{A}, \mathcal{T}, \mathcal{O})$ there exists a PO planning problem $P' = \phi(P) = (\mathcal{I}', \mathcal{A}', \mathcal{G}')$ which is equivalent to P modulo ψ. ψ is the plan transformation function which eliminates from a solution s' of P' the dummy actions op_{p_i}

associated to each intermediate goal p_i and renames the dummy actions op_{a_i} associated to execution goal with the original name a_i.

Proof

A constructive proof is given by building up the function ϕ according to the following algorithm which computes the equivalent PO problem of a given TN problem:

begin
    $\mathcal{I}' := \mathcal{I}; \mathcal{A}' := \mathcal{A}; \mathcal{G}' := \emptyset;$
    for $g \in \mathcal{T}$ **do**
        if $g =$achieve(p) **then**
          $u_g :=$new_cond$()$;
          $op_g :=$new_op$(\mathrm{vars}(p), \neg u_g \wedge p, u_g)$;
        else if $g =$do(α) **then**
          $u_g :=$new_cond$()$;
          $op_g :=$new_op$(\mathrm{vars}(\alpha), \neg u_g \wedge \mathrm{precond}(\alpha), u_g \wedge \mathrm{effects}(\alpha))$;
        end if
        $\mathcal{A}' := \mathcal{A}' \cup \{op_g\}$
        $\mathcal{G}' := \mathcal{G}' \wedge u_g$
        $\mathcal{I}' := \mathcal{I}' \wedge \neg u_g$
    end for
    for $(g1, g2) \in \mathcal{O}$ **do**
        $\mathrm{precond}(op_{g2}) :=\mathrm{precond}(op_{g2}) \wedge u_{g1}$;
    end for
end

This algorithm uses the trasformation techniques defined in the previous section for encoding each task goal in T in the PO planning problem phi(P). It builds up for each goal g a dummy operator op_g by means of the function *new_op*, with appropriate preconditions and effects. The dummy facts u_g are created by means of the function *new_cond.new_op* and *new_cond* are assumed to generate new unused symbol like gensym.

It is easy to see that the cost of this domain transformation is linear in the number n of the tasks present in the task network, that is the number of actions $\mathcal{A}'$ is increased by n, with respect to the number of the original actions $\mathcal{A}$, and the same relation holds between $\mathcal{I}$ and $\mathcal{I}'$, while the number of goals $\mathcal{G}'$ is exactly n.

Theoretical results for EETN planning

Also for EETN planning a similar result to the theorem stated for TN planning holds, with the restriction that only completely ordered intermediate external events can be modeled by our domain transformation black box approach.

Theorem

EETN planning is not more powerful than PO planning, in that for each
EETN planning problem $P = (\mathcal{I}, \mathcal{A}, \mathcal{T}, \mathcal{O})$ there exists a PO planning problem
$P' = \phi(P) = (\mathcal{I}', \mathcal{A}', \mathcal{G}')$ which is equivalent to P modulo ψ. ψ is similar to the
plan transformation function defined in the previous theorem, the only differ-
ence is that now ψ has to eliminate also the dummy actions op_{I_i} associated to
each intermediate state I_i, without eliminating the temporal constraints between
"true" actions and intermediate states.

The proof of this result can easily be obtained from the other proof, the main
difference is in the algorithm, where the step $\mathcal{I}' := \mathcal{I}$ has to be replaced by the
following lines

for $i \in \mathcal{I}$ **do**
    $u_i :=$new_cond$()$;
    $op_i :=$new_op$(\text{vars}(i), \neg u_i, u_i \wedge i)$;
    $\mathcal{I}' := \mathcal{I}' \wedge \neg u_i$
    $\mathcal{A}' := \mathcal{A}' \cup \{op_i\}$
    $\mathcal{G}' := \mathcal{G}' \wedge u_i$
end do

The cost of this transformation function is also linear in the number m of
the intermediate states.

6.1 Example

Consider the following example: a user wants to see a comet and suppose she/he
is in an initial state in which it is daylight, banks are open and neither telescope
nor money are available, but the user can use domain actions as **get_money**,
buy_a_telescope, **see_thru_telescope** and moreover he knows that at a given
instant **external event** it will be dark, a comet will be visible and banks will
be closed.

Although anyone can imagine an obvious solution of this problem, there is
no way to model it in HTN or TN planning, since intermediate states are not
available.

The solution plan also requires some actions to be ordered with respect to
the event **external event**, as **get_money**, which has to be executed before, and
see_thru_telescope to be executed after.

The figure 2 shows the solution plan generated by our EETN planner. Note
that **buy_a_telescope** is partially ordered with respect to **external event**.

Note the presence of the dummy fact u_1 added by the algorithm previously
described.

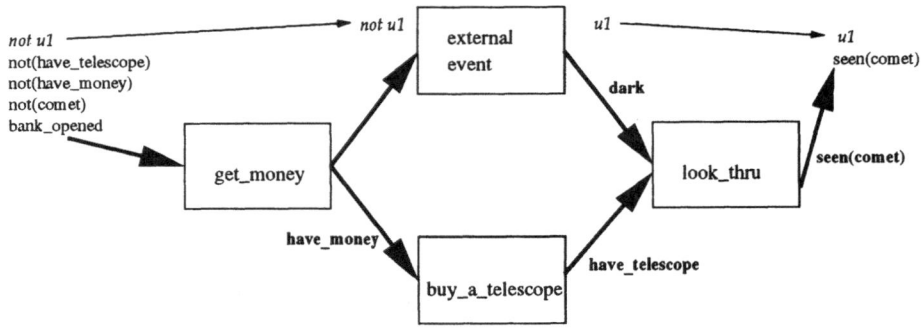

Fig. 2. Solution plan of **see the comet** problem

7   Conclusions and Implementation Issues

The result obtained for TN and EETN, and the method of domain transformation used for proving the equivalence theorem suggest an interesting technique for obtaining a EETN planner from an existing PO planner: the idea is to transform the initial domain $(\mathcal{I}, \mathcal{A}, \mathcal{T}, \mathcal{O})$ into the equivalent $(\mathcal{I}', \mathcal{A}', \mathcal{G}')$ and use the PO planner to solve the modified problem. Any solution fo PO can then easily transformed in a solution plan for EETN problem by eliminating some dummy actions and facts according to ψ.

The advantage of the approach is that the PO planner is reused as a black-box software module without any regard of its internal details. We applied this approach in implementing EETNP, a task planner based on the EETN model.

EETNP acts as a preprocessor from EETN problems to PO problems and then uses UCPOP [13] as a blackbox planner. EETNP is implemented in Common LISP and has been successfully demonstrated.

Although there is an obvious overload on the PO planner due to the presence of dummy objects, the features of software reusing, fast implementation and linear time-space cost of problem compilation are apparent advantages of the domain transformation approach. This overload can be avoided by abandoning the black box approach and operating minor modifications in the PO planner, namely the possibility of submitting a non-empty initial plan (representing the task network and containing dummy actions similar to those described in section 5), the PO planner should also be modified in order to ensure that steps and constraints of the initial plan cannot be retracted.

An EETN planner based on this approach is currently under implementation.

This latter solution however is possible only when the planner source code is available, while the domain trasformation approach is able to work with every PO planner, provided that its domain syntax is known.

The theoretical result of equivalence proved for TN, EETN and PO problems shows that using an appropriate coding of domain and decoding of solution it is possible to reach the equivalence. The equivalence result does not deny that TN and EETN formalism are still more direct and expressive for task problem, but it points out that the machinery needed to solve a TN problem is basically, with the appropriate syntactic differences, a PO planner.

References

1. A. Barrett and D. Weld. *Schema parsing: hierarchical planning for Expressive Language*. In Proceedings of AAAI-94
2. J. Blythe. *Planning with External Events*. In Proceedings of AIPS-94
3. D. Chapman. *Planning for conjunctive goals*. Artificial Intelligence 32, 1987
4. K. Erol, J. Hendler, D.S. Nau. *Semantics for Hierarchical Task-Network Planning*. Tech. rep. CS-TR-3239, Univ. of Maryland, March 1994
5. K. Erol, J. Hendler, D.S. Nau. *UMCP: A Sound and complete procedure for Hierarchical Task-network planning*. In Proceedings of AIPS-94
6. K. Erol, J. Hendler, D.S. Nau. *Complexity results for HTN Planning*. Tech. rep. CS-TR-3240, Univ. of Maryland, March 1994
7. K. Erol, J. Hendler, D.S. Nau. *HTN Planning: Complexity and Expressivity*. In Proceedings of AAAI-94
8. E.D.P. Pednault. *Synthesizing plans that contains actions with context-dependent effects*. Computational Intelligence, Vol. 4, 1988
9. S. Kambhampati. *A comparative analysis of Partial Order Planning and Task Reduction Planning*, SIGART Bull. 1995
10. S. Kambhampati, J. Hendler. *A validation structure based theory of plan modification and reuse*. Artificial Intelligence, May 1992
11. D. McAllister, D. Rosenblitt, *Systematic nonlinear planning*, In Proceedings of AAAI-91
12. E.D. Sacerdoti, *The nonlinear nature of plans*. In Proceedings of IJCAI 1975
13. J.S. Penberthy and D. Weld. *UCPOP: A Sound, Complete Partial Order Planner for ADL*. In Proceedings of KR-92, 1992.
14. Q. Yang. *Formalizing Planning Knowledge for hierarchical planning, Computational Intelligence*, Vol 6, pag. 12-24, 1990

A Hybrid Approach to Hypertext Generation

Nicola Cancedda[1], Gjertrud Kamstrup[2], Emanuele Pianta[2] and Ettore Pietrosanti[3]

[1] Dipartimento di Informatica e Sistemistica, Università di Roma "La Sapienza", via Salaria 113 - 00198 Roma, cancedda@dis.uniroma1.it

[2] IRST - Istituto per la Ricerca Scientifica e Tecnologica, Loc. Pantè di Povo - 38050 Trento, kamstrup@irst.itc.it, pianta@irst.itc.it

[3] Finsiel SpA, via G. Bona - 00100 Roma, e.pietrosanti@finsiel.it

Abstract. In this paper we present SAX, a system that generates hypertext descriptions of conceptual models designed with the SADT methodology. The combination of natural language and hypertext significantly lowers the communicative barrier between the analyst and the domain expert, thus increasing the effectiveness of conceptual model validation. The application of hybrid techniques for text generation guarantees an optimal trade-off between robustness and portability across domains on one side and text fluency on the other.

1 Introduction

Conceptual model validation is crucial in the information system development process, but this task may be difficult to accomplish if the domain expert is not acquainted with the formal language used by the *Analyst*. In such a situation the Analyst should provide the domain expert (*Reader* from now on) with additional and comprehensible documentation. Textual natural–language descriptions of the model are often suitable for this purpose. The motivation behind our work is that valuable Analyst time could be saved if these texts could be produced automatically. Furthermore, the Analyst herself may more easily detect flaws in the model by reading a natural language description of it.

In this paper we present SAX[1] (SAdt eXplain), a system that automatically generates hypertext descriptions of SADT[2] models. The input to the system is the SADT model representation adopted by the "DAFNE Tools", a CASE system developed by Finsiel SpA[3].

The Analyst can tailor the hypertext generation through parameters that select the global presentation strategy and the way specific parts of the diagram

---

[1] The SAX system is sponsored by Finsiel SpA and jointly realized by IRST, Finsiel SpA and the Computer Science Department of the University of Rome "La Sapienza".

[2] Structured Analysis and Design Technique is a trademark and copyright by Softech Inc., see [MaMc88].

[3] $DAFNE^{TM}$ is a Copyright and registered trademark (©1982, 1983, 1986, 1987, 1989-1996) of Data and Functions Networking, Finsiel Group.

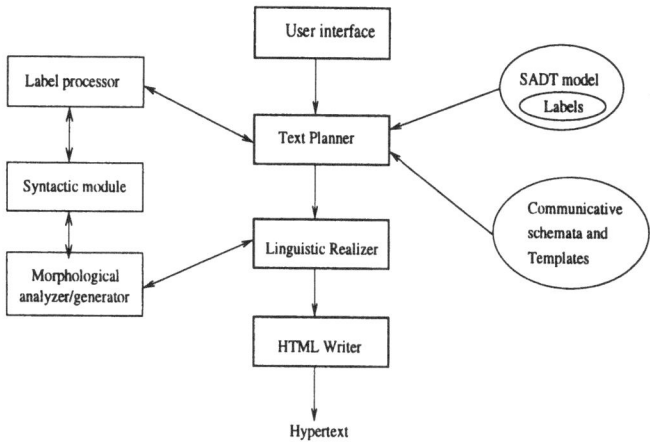

Fig. 1. SAX architecture

are described. The SAX architecture is shown in fig. 1. It includes three main components. The Text Planner is responsible for the content selection (what to say), the global textual organization (when to say what) and the sentence level template-based phrasing (how to structure sentences). The Linguistic Realizer performs morphological synthesis and phonological adjustment, while the HTML Writer translates a hypertext plan in a HTML document. SAX is implemented in Prolog and runs in the Windows environment. A first version of the system is currently under beta-testing.

When designing a text generation system, one should choose the linguistic resources which are most suitable to the task. A clear distinction is usually made between template-based approaches and deep generation based (NLG) approaches, see [Re95]. Template-based approaches are usually rated as efficient but not flexible, while deep generation is considered flexible but also inefficient and resource consuming. Also, NLG systems are usually difficult to update and require specialized support, while template-based systems can be maintained by non linguists. The distinction between these two approaches tends to become less clear-cut. On the one hand, NLG systems are beginning to use templates when deep generation is not strictly necessary. On the other hand, we think that template-based systems could become more flexible and powerful.

In SAX we have pursued the goal of integrating the two approaches. Firstly, we decided to use a classical NLG approach for the planning of the global structure of the text using a schema-like representation, while using templates at the sentence level. Secondly, we tried to enhance the flexibility of traditional static templates. The choice of a hybrid approach was motivated by system efficiency requirements. First of all the system had to *run on a PC*. Moreover, the Analyst can tailor the text generation through a graphical interface and this requires iterations of parameter setting and *on-line generation*.

1.1 The SADT Language

A SADT model is a collection of diagrams, organized in a tree structure. Each diagram is composed of *boxes*, representing activities, which are connected by *arrows*, representing flows of materials, data and informations (see fig.5). Arrow objects play different roles with regard to the activities: *inputs* (from the left), *outputs* (to the right), *controls* (constraints on the activity - from the top) and *mechanisms* (participants in the activity - from the bottom). The arrows can *branch* and *join* as shown in fig.5. *Feedback* arrows are *outputs* which go back to activities as *inputs* or *controls*. Some models are decorated with *activation rules* describing the dependencies between each arrow within an activity.

Every box and arrow is given a *label*, i.e. a natural language expression informally describing an activity (boxes) or a flow (arrows). Box labels are constrained to be infinitive verb phrases while arrow labels should be noun phrases. No other constraint on the linguistic form of the labels is imposed, apart from the fact that labels should be short, both for readability and for layout purposes. For this reason a *glossary* adding information for each label, is included in the model. Abbreviations and acronyms in the labels (like TEC, VEN and others in fig.5) are automatically expanded by the system using a table written by the Analyst.

2 A Flexible Template-Based Approach

In this section we present the hybrid approach to text generation used in SAX. During Text Planning the structure and the content of the text is computed using enhanced versions of both textual schemas and templates. *Schemas* allow to specify the global structure of a text while *templates* are used to cope with the sentence level.

2.1 Communication Schemas

To represent the global structure of the text we use *communication schemas* [NoPi95]. A communication schema is a variant of rhetorical schemas [Mc85], enhanced with the communicative intention that the corresponding presentational pattern is meant to satisfy. All the schemas in SAX have been identified through analysis of a corpus of hand-written SADT diagram descriptions. A communication schema is shown in fig.2.

The *head* slot identifies the schema. The *intentions* slot is meant to allow a free documentation string about the communicative intentions behind the schema. On the other hand, the *effect* slot describes, in a simplified but formal way, the mental state that the schema is meant to induce in the Reader[4].

---

[4] The content of the *effect* slot corresponds to what is known in the NLG literature as *communicative intention*. See [MoPa94] for the description of an application based on cycles of generation and follow-up questions, where the representation of the communicative intentions of the system plays a crucial role. In SAX communicative intentions guided the elicitation of the communication schemas, but for the moment they play no role during computation.

The *constraints* must be verified before applying the schema. The *body* slot includes a list of sub-schemas that articulate the main schema. Each *sub-schema* can be optional and its expansion can be restricted by local constraints. The *order* slot includes linear precedence constraints on sub-schemas. If no linear precedence constraint is specified, a default order is assumed. The example in fig.2 describes how to present the overall activity modeled by a SADT diagram. Observe that the body includes both a sub-schema and a template.

```
c_schema(
   head(
      main_activity(ActivityId)),
   intentions(
      'present the main activity of the diagram'),
   effect(know(reader, structure_of(ActivityId))),
   constraints(
      (sadt_parameter(strategy, forward),
       activity_topology(ActivityId, ActTopology))),
   body(
      [activity(ActivityId, forward, ActTopology),
       template(sub_activities_summary(ActivityId, forward))]),
   order([before(activity(_, _), sub_activities_summary(_))])).
```

Fig. 2. A communication schema used in SAX

2.2 The Hyper-Template Formalism

The main features of this formalism are flexibility and the ability to cope with hypertextual objects. Flexibility is given by the possibility of coping with morphological agreement and phonological adjustment. On the other hand, the formalism also allows the functional description of hyper-links and images to be inserted in the final hypertext.

A template is a declarative structure including two kinds of elements: *connectives* and *gaps*. *Connectives* are formed by preselected linguistic items, while *gaps* can be seen as variables which are instantiated by other linguistic items (fillers) during the generation process (template resolution). Both connectives and fillers may include *fixed* or *flexible* items. Flexible items are realized differently according to the context in which they occur. In the current implementation of the formalism, flexible items may undergo morphological and/or phonological variation. Here is a list of the most interesting elements that can be included in a template definition (see also fig.3):

Potential words A potential word is a word form which can undergo phonological adjustment. It is described by a term specifying the base form and its lexical category: w(noun, responsibility). Sequences of potential words are mapped onto sequences of strings by the Linguistic realization component. For example, [w(preposition, di), w(article, i), w(name, responsabili)] becomes ['dei', 'responsabili'].

Morphological bundles These are sets of morphological features that are mapped onto potential words and then on strings by the Linguistic Realization component. For example, the bundle morpho([cat=noun, pred=company, num=plur]) is mapped onto the potential word w(noun, companies) and then onto the string 'companies'.

When used in the template definitions, the values of morphological features can be variables: morpho([cat=noun, pred=company, num=Num]). Morphological variables allow to treat agreement phenomena which are difficult to handle with static templates; these variables are instantiated during the template resolution process.

Picture descriptors Templates can introduce a picture in a hypertext by specifying the absolute name of a file or a functional expression which is evaluated during template resolution.

Slots A slot fills a gap with linguistic items during template resolution. In the SAX application domain these linguistic items are selected from the labels of boxes and arrows of a diagram. Here is an example of a slot specification: slot(inputs, ActId, Agreement). This expression refers to the input labels of the activity identified by ActId (input parameter). The Agreement variable is instantiated as a result of filling the slot (output parameter).

A slot expression can be extended by a further expression specifying the syntactic elaboration that must be performed on the labels that fill the slot: slot(label, ActId) with_parse nominalization. This slot will be filled with the nominalized label(s) of the ActId activity.

Control expressions Template definitions can include conditional and disjunctive expressions. Conditional expressions bind the resolution of a subpart of the template to the satisfaction of certain constraints. Disjunctive expressions give alternative ways of expressing something, for example: or(['taking into account', 'considering']).

Formatting The template formalism allows to include any subpart of a body within the scope of one or more formatting operators such as: italic, bold, title1 etc. All HTML format operators can be used. The formalism also supports style definitions, as sets of format operators: style(my_style, [list, italic]).

Links Links are treated as a special class of format instructions. They are specified through complex terms, which refer to linked documents through absolute addresses (file name) or functional descriptors, evaluated at run time. Here is an example of a functional link description: link(to, glossary(activity,

paragraph)). This descriptor is evaluated as a link from an activity description to the corresponding entry of the activity glossary.

```
template(diagram_title(DiagId, ActId),
    [
    format([title1, title_case], /* format operator list */
        slot(label, ActId)), /* slot without syntactic elaborations */
    &newline, /* special character */
    if_then_else( /* control expression */
        ( /* constraint conjunction */
        has_father_diagram(DiagId, FatherDiagId),
        not sadt_parameter(presentation, only_text)
        ),
        /* then */
        [format(
          [picture_link(FatherDiagId)], /* parametric style */
          [picture(image, 'father.gif')]), /* absolute identifier */
        &newline],
        /* else */
        [&newline]),
    if_then_else(
        has_son_diagram(DiagId), /* simple constraint */
        /* pictures identified through functional descriptors */
        [picture(map, diagram_image(DiagId))], /* clickable image */
        [picture(image, diagram_image(DiagId))]) /* simple image */
    ]).
```

Fig. 3. A sample hyper-template definition

3 The SAX System

3.1 The Generation Process

The generation starts with a preliminary step (not shown in fig. 1) in which the input model is translated from the source language to a Prolog representation. The hypertext generation is performed in three phases: Text Planning, Linguistic Realization and HTML Writing. The Text Planning component computes the content and the structure of the text on the basis of communication schemas and templates. The Text Planner recursively expands a root schema following a top down strategy and building a text tree structure. The selection of communication schemas is guided by the topological structure of the diagram being described and by the user preferences (see sect. 3.3). When the Text Planner reaches the sentence level a template solver is called which integrates diagram labels in the text tree structure.

The output of the Text Planner is a textual tree with instantiated templates as leaves. Instantiated templates may include strings, potential words and ground morphological bundles, i.e. a subset of the elements available when defining templates. The Linguistic Realizer maps morphological bundles onto words; all possible phonological and orthographic adjustments are carried out. The HTML Writer then maps the textual tree onto a HTML document.

3.2 A Hybrid Approach to Label Transformations

In order to produce a fluent and readable text, a label processor adapts the activity and arrow labels to the context in which they are inserted. Basically, four kinds of operations are performed:

- a word can be substituted with a morphological bundle which is parametric with respect to some agreement features;
- a verb phrase can be nominalized e.g. from 'to produce ice-cream' to 'the production of ice-cream';
- when referring to an already mentioned activity, the complements of the nominalization can be left out e.g. from 'to produce ice-cream' to 'the production';
- definite or indefinite articles and prepositions can be inserted, e.g. from 'definizione prodotti' (lit. 'definition products', italian telegraphic style) to 'la definizione dei prodotti' ('the definition of the products');

The transformation of labels is performed through a special kind of syntactic analysis. During the system analysis phase two approaches to label transformation were considered. The first one is based on pattern matching, the second on a full cycle of syntactic analysis, transformation and re-generation. After some testing we realized that using pattern matching would have led to a great number of *ad hoc* rules; on the other hand using the full machinery of a text analyzer and generator seemed an overkill given the relatively simple syntactic transformations that were needed. The solution adopted in the system is again a hybrid one. The transformations are carried out by a Definite Clause Grammar which performs a shallow syntactic analysis of labels and, instead of generating a parse tree and/or a semantic representation, produces a sequence of linguistic items which can be strings, potential words or morphological bundles. These sequences are mapped onto actual sentences through morphological synthesis and phonological adjustment; given this approach deep sentence generation is unnecessary. The DCG grammar has been designed so as to guarantee at least a partial analysis/transformation of the labels.

3.3 User Preferences

The Analyst can make some choices about the text properties by setting global or local parameters. At the global level (description of the whole diagram) she can choose the description strategy i.e. how the content is linearly presented.

A thorough analysis of a corpus of human-written descriptions[5] has led to the identification of two main strategies: *forward* (for each activity the *inputs* are described first) and *backward* (the description starts from *outputs*). The Analyst can include or exclude the description of branches, joins, feedbacks and activation rules. The Analyst can also set the values of local parameters associated with single diagram elements, i.e. boxes and arrows. The current version of the system allows to set the following parameters:

- *label transformation.* The user can force or prevent any of the implemented label transformations on each label.
- *grammatical number specification.* Sometimes the grammatical number of a label is ambiguous. The user can disambiguate it by adding morphological information to the words in the label.
- *verb selection.* As the system can not perform a deep semantic analysis of the labels, it describes the relation between activities and arrows with generic verbs, e.g.: "activity x *produces* y". The user can force the system to use a more specific verb.

Both global and local parameters can be saved and re-used in subsequent generations for the same model. Given the incremental nature of the conceptual model definition this represents a clear advantage over "brute" post-editing.

4 System Output

In fig.4 the top of a hypertext description can be seen. The figure shows the clickable diagram and the first part of the text (an approximate English translation is given in fig.5). The text is generated using a *forward* strategy (see sect. 3.3). The text shows some examples of label transformations. The arrow label *"materiali"* has become *"dai materiali"* and the activity label *"definire prodotti e obiettivi di produzione"* has become *"la definizione dei prodotti e degli obiettivi di produzione"* (see also sect. 3.2). Phrases referring to activities (e.g. *"gestire la produzione dei beni industriali"*) or to arrows (e.g. *"la normativa"*) are associated with links to a glossary page where the activity or arrow is explained in more detail. These are just some of the available links: fig.6 contains a schematization of the network of links[6].

---

[5] Potential SAX users have been involved in different phases of the project. In particular, Analysts have been asked to write descriptions of SADT diagrams and to evaluate the coherence between the authomatically generated texts and the content of the diagrams.

[6] The bold boxes in the figure are hypertext pages, the grey arrows are hyperlinks, the arrow icons inside the main diagram page are hyperlink buttons, and the activity and arrow references are pieces of text with connected links. Finally, the map image is a clickable version of the SADT diagram.

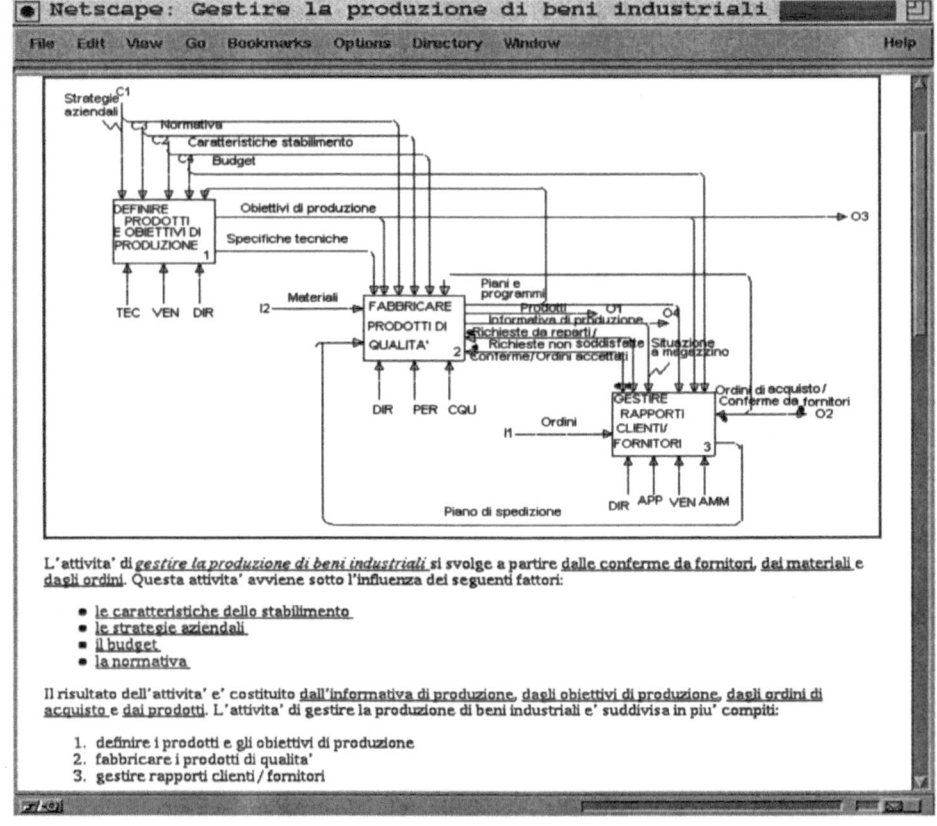

Fig.4. The first part of the diagram description with clickable image

```
The activity of managing industry production is carried out using
the materials, the orders and the customer confirmations.
This activity is influenced by the following factors:
- the budget
- the regulation
- the plant characteristics
- the company strategies
The results of the activity are the production goals, the production numbers,
the products and the purchase orders.
The activity of managing industry production can be divided into the
following subactivities:
1. the definition of products and production goals
2. the manufacturing of quality products
3. the management of customer/provider relations
```
[A description of each sub-activity follows ...]

Fig.5. Partial translation of the generated text

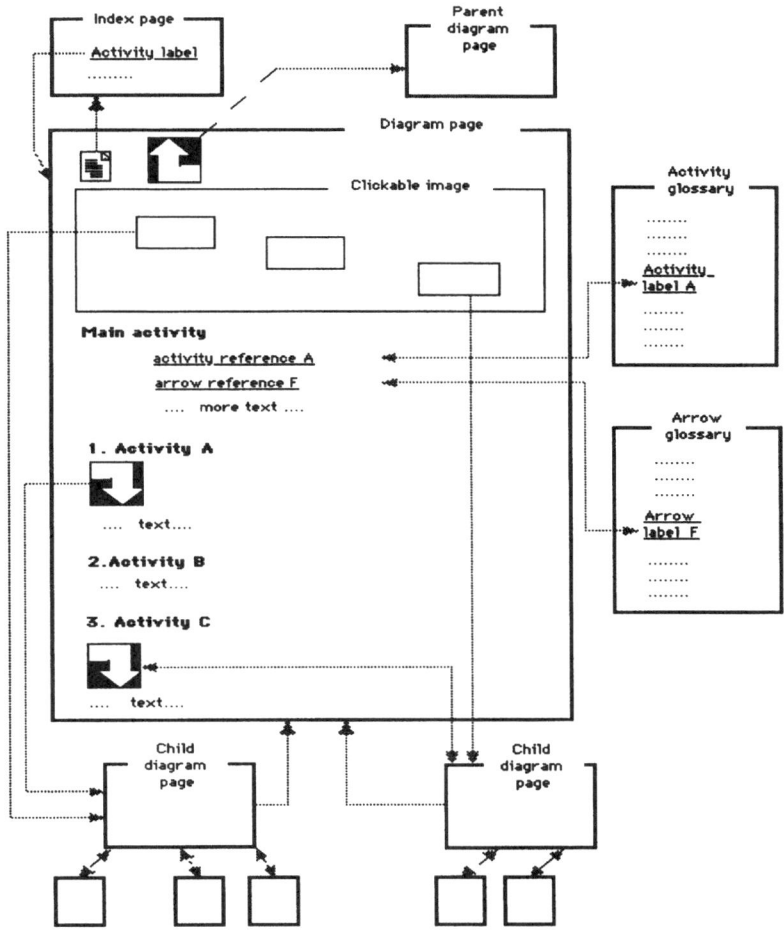

Fig.6. Page hierarchy and connecting links

5 Related Work

Text generation as a method for validating and easing the non-expert's comprehension of *conceptual models* has been treated by several researchers (see [Da92,Re94,Gu95,PaKu+96]). Many researchers also agree upon the usefulness of natural language descriptions of models for the *author* herself: the text can help her in iteratively designing the model. The above mentioned systems use full Natural Language Generation (NLG) technology and generate plain text.

Other systems presented in the literature are relevant for our purposes because they produce hypertexts, although not in the conceptual model validation domain. These systems use template-based or hybrid generation techniques to generate *dynamic hypertexts*, i.e. hypertexts that are generated in response to user requests (clicks on links), possibly taking the browsing context into account[7].

IDAS [ReMe+95] generates hypertexts concerning technical documentation. IDAS was initially designed to use pure NLG technology, but hybrid approaches were applied after a benefit-cost evaluation. Important aspects of hypertext generation are considered in ILEX [KnMe+96]. Upon request from the user, ILEX generates dynamic hypertext for simulated tours in a museum. In the system a hybrid text production approach is used: canned text is interleaved with information coming from KB entries. PEBA-II [DaMi96,MiTu+96] dynamically generates hypertext descriptions of a zoological database through an online interface. The authors argue that hypertext significantly eases the user modeling task since part of the content selection is made by the user. In both PEBA-II and ILEX discourse history is used to obtain context sensitive text. In [Ge96] a template-based approach is used both at the planning level and at the realization level. Page-templates filled with information from databases are used to generate hypertext nodes in a movie festival context.

SAX combines aspects dealt with by both these two groups of systems. The initial goal of our system is the validation of a conceptual model represented in the SADT language. The system requirements and the nature of our domain made us choose a hybrid text production approach. The result is presented as a hypertext so that the user can easily move from one diagram description to all related pages. The hypertexts include clickable images of SADT diagrams, which make the navigation in the whole model description easier.

6 Conclusions

This paper discussed the approach followed in SAX, a system for automatic generation of hypertextual descriptions of SADT models. The adopted solutions combine the advantages of hypertextual output format with those of a hybrid natural language generation architecture.

On the basis of the system efficiency requirements (PC hardware and on-line generation), a hybrid solution has been chosen for text generation: a classical NLG approach is adopted for the global text planning while flexible templates are used for sentence level generation.

The formalism devised for templates copes with morphological agreement and phonological adjustment, thus allowing the generation of flexible and fluent text. The decision to give up with traditional sentence-level generation, led to a system running on PCs, in the Windows environment, and capable of generating each diagram description in less than three seconds.

The Analyst is given the possibility to influence the output both at a global level, by stating a "description strategy" to follow, and locally, by constraining the way single diagram elements are linguistically expressed.

---

[7] The content and organization of *static hypertext* on the contrary, are completely predetermined by its authors.

SAX has been designed in a modular way in order to single out the part of the system which depends on the SADT methodology. We feel that the system is easily portable to other conceptual modeling methodologies.

References

[DaMi96]   Robert Dale and Maria Milosavljevic, March 1996. *Authoring on Demand: Natural Language Generation in Hypertext Documents*. In Proceedings of the First Australian Document Computing Conference, Melbourne, Australia.

[Da92]   Hercules Dalianis, 1992. *A method for Validating a Conceptual Model by Natural Language Discourse Generation*. In Proceedings of the Fourth International Conference on Advanced Information Systems Engineering, Springer Verlag, 425–444.

[Ge96]   Sabine Geldof, June 1996. *Hyper-Text Generation from Databases on the Internet*. In Proceedings of the second international Workshop on Applications of Natural Language to Information Systems, Amsterdam, The Netherlands.

[Gu95]   Jon Atle Gulla, 1995. *A General Explanation Component for Conceptual Modeling in CASE Environments*. ACM Transactions on Information Systems.

[KnMe+96]   Alistair Knott, Chris Mellish, Jon Oberlander and Mick O'Donnell, 1996. *Sources of Flexibility in Dynamic Hypertext Generation*. In Proceedings of the International Workshop on Natural Language Generation.

[MaMc88]   David A. Marca and Clement L. McGowan, 1988. *SADT, Structured Analysis and Design Technique*. McGraw-Hill Book Company.

[Mc85]   Kathleen McKeown, 1985. *Text Generation*. Cambridge University Press, Cambridge.

[MiTu+96]   Maria Milosavljevic, Adrian Tulloch and Robert Dale, January 1996. *Text Generation in a Dynamic Hypertext Environment*. In Proceedings of the 19th Australasian Computer Science Conference, Melbourne, Australia.

[MoPa94]   Johanna D. Moore and Cecil L. Paris, 1994. *Planning Text for Advisory Dialogues: Capturing Intentional and Rhetorical Information*. Computational Linguistics, Vol.19,4.

[NoPi95]   Elena Not and Emanuele Pianta, April 1995. *Specifications for the Text Structurer*. GIST deliverable, TST-2, LRE Project 062-09.

[PaKu+96]   Rebecca Passonneau, Karen Kukich, Jacques Robin, Vasileios Hatzivassiloglou, Larry Lefkowitz and Hongyan Jing, June 1996. *Generating Summaries of Work Flow Diagrams*. In Proceedings of the International Conference on Natural Language Processing and Industrial Applications, Moncton, Canada.

[Re94]   Ehud Reiter, 1994. *Linguistically Based Generation of Software Documentation*. Final Technical Report RL-TR-94-110, Rome Laboratory (USAF), New York, USA.

[Re95]   Ehud Reiter, 1995. *NLG vs. Template*. In Proceedings of the fifth Workshop on Natural Language Generation, Leiden, The Netherlands.

[ReMe+95]   Ehud Reiter, Chris Mellish and John Levine, 1995. *Automatic Generation of Technical Documentation*. Applied Artificial Intelligence, 9:259–287.

Generating User-Adapted Hypermedia from Discourse Plans

Berardina De Carolis, Fiorella de Rosis, Sebastiano Pizzutilo

Dipartimento di Informatica, Università di Bari
Via Orabona, 4, 70126, Bari - Italy
tel. +39-80-5443284, fax. +39-80-5443196
{nadja, derosis, pizzutil}@aos2.uniba.it

Abstract

This paper describes how hypermedia instruction manuals can be generated from a discourse plan: intentional and rhetorical knowledge in the plan tree are employed to construct the hypermedia elements, to assemble them into pages and to introduce links among them. Plan tree transformation functions are defined so as to ensure that generated hypermedia respect interface usability and Web design criteria. User adaptation is performed by parametrizing these functions: this method enables building the hypermedia according to a dynamic assessment of the user needs.

1. Introduction

The generation of complex documents is usually performed in two main steps. In the first of them, discourse planning establishes information items to be introduced in the document and their presentation order. In the second one, surface generation translates the plan into a natural language or multimedia document. Rhetorical Structure Theory (RST: Mann and Thompson,1988) plays a crucial role in the whole generation process (Hovy,1993; Moore and Paris, 1993; De Carolis et al, 1996) by ensuring coherence of the text. In user-adapted presentations, the generation strategy represented in plan operators formalizes what the Speaker believes to be important to mention in the document, as a function of hypotheses about the Addressee's knowledge, preferences and goals. When these hypotheses are incorrect, the generated text reveals to be inadequate: some systems then give the Addressee the opportunity of interacting with the Generator to require more details or to refine the text (see, e.g., Moore and Mittal, 1996).

After about ten year experiences of one-shot document generation, research is aimed, more recently, at studying whether methods developed in that context can be extended to the generation of user-adapted hypermedia. In the distribution of tasks between user and system that is proposed in this case, selection of the document subset to view is left to the user, whereas the system is responsible for arranging relevant data in a hypermedia page by organizing them in the appropriate form and language (see, for instance, Milosaljevic and Dale,1996). Methods are derived directly from those employed for one shot texts: the part of the document that the user wishes to explore is generated dynamically in one page, with links to pages with potentially interesting details.

This method is efficient when documents about concepts or objects descriptions have to be generated: most applications developed so far are in this area. In this case, it is reasonable to presume that users know which information they want to look at, and that the system is only left the task of providing this information in an adequate form. However, this idea cannot be generalized to all types of documents: in particular, to instruction manuals about how to perform some action or to use some device. Behind these documents there is, in general, a strong Instructor's intention to orient the Addressees, which is a function of their presumed level of experience. This intention is made explicit, in the document, by means of some appropriate presentation techniques and corresponds to the main communicative goal and to the way that this goal is decomposed into sub-goals.

For instance: in a manual about how to use a domestic blood pressure measurer (which is the case study that we will consider in this paper), the main purpose is to teach how to measure the pressure. To achieve this purpose, one has to teach: (i) how to prepare the device, (ii) how to connect the device to the patient and (iii) how to make the measurement. In order to teach how to prepare the device, one has to teach: (i1) how to switch it on, (i2) how to check that the device is ready for use ...and so on. This description of the goal/subgoals hierarchy is usually mirrored in a hierarchy of document Sections, Subsections and Paragraphs. According to their degree of experience, users can (i) glance non systematically at the manual to look for the Section on which to concentrate their attention, (ii) read it systematically or (iii) read the Index to find out the part of interest to them. In an adaptive hypermedia manual, one should reproduce these document-reading attitudes into different structures, and should activate the most appropriate navigation style according to the user characteristics and to the context of use. Cognitive psychology research is providing evidence for adaptation criteria. For example: 'Index navigation' is preferable for book-like hypertexts whereas 'Page navigation' gives better performance in texts whose structure is a symmetrical hierarchy (Wright and Lickorish, 1989); directed access and guidance mechanisms should be provided in 'exploratory learning' (Hammond and Allinson, 1989); browsing and searching information gathering tasks influence preference for linear vs hierarchical or network structures (De Vries and De Jong, 1997), and so on.

In the research described in this paper, we investigated how to generate a user-customized hypermedia instruction manual by studying, in particular, the following issues: which structure should such a manual have? How should this structure be adapted to the user characteristics? Is the discourse plan a suited knowledge source for this generation process? Can RST be employed successfully to this purpose, as it was for one-shot document generation? The paper answers to these questions by describing the methods developed in GeNet, an object-oriented prototype for generating hypermedia manuals on the WWW. In Section 2, we outline the main components of instruction manuals. In Section 3, we describe knowledge embodied in a discourse plan and how it is represented (Section 3.1), the hypermedia structure and generation criteria (Section 3.2) and the algorithm (Section 3.3). User adaptation methods are illustrated in Section 4. Some evaluation about results obtained so far is finally given in Section 5.

2. The case study

An instruction manual usually includes two main sections:

a. a *descriptive* section illustrates *device elements*, with the function performed by each of them, and *technical terms* employed.

b. an *instructional* section describes how to perform the action or to use the device.

In the second section, reference is frequently made to items described in the first one: separation between the two components increases the difficulty with which instructions can be followed, especially when the device structure and the role of each item are not clear. A deep integration between the two components therefore favours understanding the instruction process. This integration can be achieved by implementing the manual as a user adapted hypermedia. In this hypothesis, each component is described in a separate section, that the user can examine individually, when needed. Within the instructional component, context links may send to description of individual items, whenever they are mentioned and also according to the presumed user knowledge of each of them. We will focus, from now on, on the instructional Section of the manual.

3. Outline of GeNet

The architecture of GeNet is shown in Figure 1.

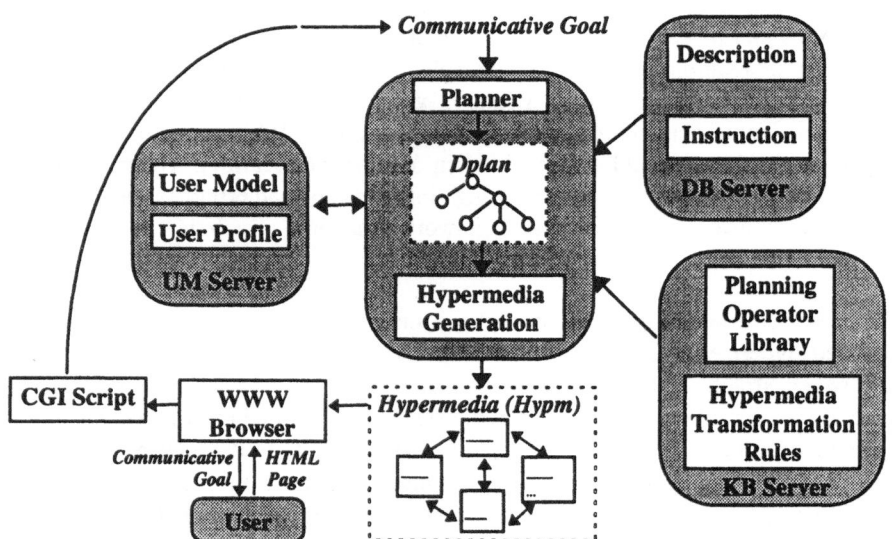

Figure 1: Architecture of GeNet

The generation process starts with the definition of a communicative goal. Starting from this goal, a discourse planner performs the task of information selection and basic organization, according to the user information needs that are represented in a stereotype-based User Model (UM). A hypermedia generation algorithm transforms the resulting discourse plan into an hypermedia structure. DB, KB and UM Servers store and provide the following information:

i)   domain knowledge: data about the descriptive and instructional parts of the manual, in textual ot pictorial form;

ii)   plan operators and hypermedia transformation rules;

iii)   stereotypes, user profiles and adaptation rules.

The last component provides various types of data about the user to the two generation components: planning takes into account the user knowledge in the domain and the task to be performed; hypermedia surface generation considers (as we will see later on) other features, such as the level of experience and the hypothesized preferences. These data are acquired explicitly from the user, through a 'user presentation' page which is displayed at the beginning of interaction. Let us now describe in more detail the system components and the methods employed.

3.1.   The discourse plan

Our planning algorithm is described in detail elsewhere (De Carolis et al, 1996); compared with other discourse planning methods, it has the following distinguishing features:

-        plan operators represent, at the same time, how a communication goal (mentioned in the Header) can be decomposed into subgoals (in the Decomposition) and which Rhetorical Relation links the discourse segments that originate from these subgoals. The subgoal which produces the RR's nucleus is denoted with an 'N'; the RR may have several satellites, all denoted with an 'S': for instance, an 'Elaboration Process Step' with a nucleus and several satellite steps is represented in a unique plan operator;

-        planning is made hierarchically according to a double adaptation: to the Speaker and to the Hearer. Data about these users are stored in two user models. A meta-level rule-based planning decides whether to further expand the plan obtained at each abstraction level, by also considering complexity of the plan generated so far. The complexity of a node in the plan tree is a function of depth and breadth of the subtree of which the node is the root, and of the type of leaves (text vs images or other).

The result of the planning step is a discourse plan (that we will call Dplan), which is represented as a tree with a set of data associated with nodes.

Def:

Dplan : $< T, Go, Db, Fo, Rr, Cc, Ro, F_d >$, where:

• T is an *ordered tree* whose nodes are denoted with $N = \{n_1, n_2, ..., n_m\}$

• Go is a set of *communicative goals*;

- Db is a set of *data* (phrase fragments or images) retrieved from a database;
- Fo is a set of *concepts or device elements* that correspond to discourse focuses;
- Rr is a set of *rhetorical relations RR* {Sequence, Joint, Contrast, ...}
- Cc is the set of *complexity classes* of a subtree {L, M, H}, which are defined as a function of its breadth and depth (L = 'low', M = 'medium' and H ='high');
- Ro is the set of *roles* that a node may have in a RR: {N, S}, (N = 'nucleus', S = 'satellite')
- *Fd*: $N \rightarrow Go \times (Db \cup \{\varepsilon\}) \times Fo \times Rr \times Cc \times (Ro \cup \{\varepsilon\})$

  is the *node description function* which associates, with each node of T
  - *the communicative goal* of the plan operator which generated the node,
  - *a phrase or an image* (if n_i is a leaf-node)
  - *the discourse focus*
  - *the rhetorical relation* among n_i' s children,
  - *the complexity class* of the subtree of which n_i is the root,
  - *the role* of n_i in the rhetorical relation associated with its father-node (N or S)

    if $n_i \neq n_1$.

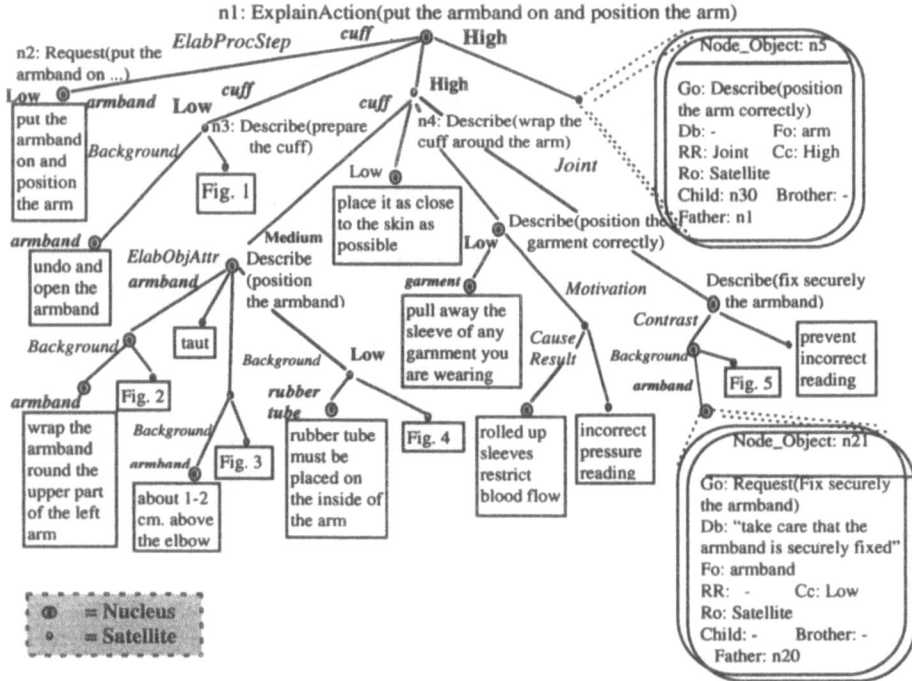

Figure 2: a portion of the discourse plan for the blood pressure measurer manual.

Figure 2 indicates part of the plan for the instructional section of a blood pressure measurer manual. This subtree illustrates, in particular, how to "put the armband and position the arm" (this is the communicative goal of root node n_1). This goal is achieved by decomposing the discourse into four segments (n_2 to n_5), which are linked by a RR of *ElaborationProcessStep* and whose goals are, respectively:

Request (put the armband onand position the arm), in n_2
DescribeAction (prepare the cuff) in n_3
DescribeAction (wrap the cuff around the arm), in n_4
DescribeAction (position the arm correctly), in n_5.

The discourse focus is 'cuff' for node n_1 and n_3, 'armband' for n_2, and so on. The complexity of the subtree from n_2 and n_3 is=Low; the complexity of n_4, n_5 is High. The RR of *ElaborationProcessStep* relates a nucleus describing the process (n_2) to satellites (n_3, n_4, n_5) that represent the steps necessary to perform the process itself. Other RRs represented in this tree are *ElaborationObjectAttribute, Motivation, Contrast* and *CauseResult*. In this example, a *Background* is used to relate a text to an image that illustrates its content. As we mentioned before, our RRs can have several satellites.

3.2. Hypermedia generation criteria

Our hypermedia (that we will call Hypm) can be represented as a graph structure: pages are associated to nodes and arcs represent links between couples of nodes, in the form of anchors, buttons or icons.

Def

Hypm: $< P, Ti, He, Bo, Ft, Bu, Hw, Co, Re >$

- P is a finite, non empty set of *pages*: $\{p_0, p_1, ...\}$; p_0 denotes the 'home page';
- Ti is a set of *titles;*
- He is a set of *heads;*
- Bo is a set of *bodies*;
- Ft is a set of *footers;*
- Co is a *page-content definition function:*
  Co: $P \longrightarrow Ti \times He \times Bo \times Ft$ which associates to each page a Title, a Head, a Body and a Footer;
- Re: $P \longrightarrow 2^P$ is a *link definition function* which associates with each page a set of related pages.

Hypm is built by an algorithm which exploits Dplan knowledge to create Hypm pages, and links among them. This algorithm performs the following functions: (i) establishing the number of Dplan nodes to be aggregated into a Hypm page, (ii) transferring into Title, Head and Body of each page information items associated with Dplan nodes; (iii) inserting anchors in the Body and Buttons in the Footer, with their URLs. In this process, Rhetorical Relations (RRs) associated with Dplan nodes play a crucial role: they establish how to structure the Body, how to insert anchors and how to compose the Footer according to the selected navigation path. This process is driven by heuristic criteria that we derived from guidelines for interface design and from Web construction manuals (Thimbleby,1991): these criteria are embedded in the generation algorithm.

a.   *page complexity control:*

Information shown in each page is the result of a compromise between two contrasting criteria: a page should contain the maximum amount of 'autoconsistent' information, so as to avoid fragmenting knowledge in Dplan into too many Hypm pages and should be displayed, if possible, in a single layout, so that it doesn't overwhelm the user. We call 'autoconsistent' the information associated with the components of a RR (nucleus and satellite): a page p_h then describes, in a synthetic or detailed way, nucleus and satellites of the RR which is associated to the node n_i from which p_h is derived. For example: a page which illustrates a discourse segment guided by a *ElaborationProcessStep* describes first the overall process; the steps necessary to perform it are described in the same page, either synthetically (if the corresponding node's complexity is 'High') or in a detailed way (if it is 'Low'): synthetic descriptions are developed in subsequent pages. Given a node n_i in Dplan and the subtree starting from n_i, the number of Dplan nodes to be aggregated into the p_h page of Hypm (only n_i and its children, or also its descendants) depends on the complexity associated to the children nodes.

b.   *consistency control:*

Consistency is insured by uniform page design: pages corresponding to 'similar' discourse segments should have a 'similar' layout; buttons and icons representing similar links in different pages should be placed in the same position and rendered with the same image or text; navigation paths among pages corresponding to similar discourse segments should be similar; same hotwords shown in different contexts should send to the same page. The similarity criterion we adopt in GeNet is based, again, on the RR which guides the discourse segment: pages originated from the same RR have a similar layout for the same navigation mode: same components and same space arrangement and presentation for each of them. The structure of links among pages is defined, as well, from RRs among discourse segments: segments guided by the same RR are described in sets of pages with similar navigation paths, suggested by similar buttons or icons. For example: 'Next item' buttons always refer to the next item of a *Sequence*; a 'Next step' to the next step of an*ElaborationProcessStep*, and so on.

c.   *navigation styles*

As we mentioned in the Introduction, the effectiveness of the navigation style is related to the user characteristics and to the task they have to perform. We included in GeNet some of the navigation modes that cognitive psychologists claim to be the most efficient for learning tasks: a *'guided tour'*, in which the Speaker's intentions are described clearly and the sequence of page presentation is rigid and a *'free'* mode, in which users are left free to select the parts of the hypermedia they want to examine; in both cases, the Speaker's intention can be either described initially and in synthesis, in an *'index'* page, or, in more detail, in a hierarchy of intention-description pages. Users should also receive a level of orientation, in their navigation, which depends on their experience in the domain and in hypertexts in general. Orientation supports may be provided in several forms; by 'connection pages', that summarize what the user has seen until that point and anticipate what he is going to see next, to describe passages from a comunicative goal to the other; and, by labels associated with buttons and icons and initial goal mapping.

4. The generation algorithm

The algorithm employes a set of micro and macro transformation functions to generate Hypm pages from Dplan .
At a **micro** level, the following elementary functions are applied:
- λ (x) is an ATN-based *linguistic transformation* that builds up a phrase, a clause or a sentence from a word, a phrase or a discourse segment or a list of words x;
- π (y) is a p*ictorial transformation* of an image; for example: zooming on a part of it, reducing its size, changing its colours;
- μ (w_1, w_2, ..., w_i) is a *combination* of sentences, images or other multimedia items; w_i can be an element of the DB or the result of application of λ (x), π (y) or μ (z_1, z_2, ..., z_i);
- α (t,p_j) selects a string or a substring t as a link anchor and associates it to a page p_j;
- β (v,p_j) selects a button v among those available, and links it to a page p_j.

At a **macro** level, functions are employed to generate the page elements, thus defining the page-content definition function *Co(p_i)*. Creating a page requires deciding, first, how Dplan nodes are to be aggregated into Hypm nodes; this process is influenced by the RR, the complexity of the information to be provided to the user for achieving the communicative goal and the selected navigation mode.

Our micro-level generation functions are, still, rather rudimentary, as we concentrated, in this phase of research, on macro-level functions (overall page organization and navigation styles); linguistic transformations are just obtained by just immersing the string associated to the 'Communication Goal' topic or to the 'Data' object-slots into a linguistic template, that is selected according to the Goal purpose and to the page Section. Multimedia combination arranges texts and pictures into a space relationship that depends on the RR. For instance: in a *Background* RR, the text is placed at the leftside of the image that illustrates it; in an *ElaborationProcessStep*, step descriptions are arranged sequentially in a numbered list,...and so on.
The following macro functions are responsible for the creation of page elements:
- Title(n_i,p_h): the title identifies the page and orients the users in the navigation history; this function composes the title of page p_h by applying a linguistic transformation to the Goal associated to the plan node n_i.
- Header(n_i,p_h) : the header cues the user to the page purpose; this function composes the header of page p_h by combining linguistic transformations of the Goals associated to the plan node n_i and to its father (if n_i is not the plan root).
- Body(n_i,p_h) : this is the most complex section of the page, as it is in this section that the discourse tree nodes are aggregated and structured. The discourse

tree is visited in pre-order, and nodes are aggregated according to: i) the RR associated to the root of the examined subtree, ii) the complexity of its children and iii) the selected navigation mode.

- in the *indexed* mode, a home page is generated from n_1 and all its children of high complexity. The body of this page shows a list of items which are developed in child pages; navigation in these pages can be 'linear' or 'hierarchical';

- in the *free* and the *guided* modes, the intentional structure of the manual is mirrored in a hierarchy of pages. In the free mode, links to lower-level pages is produced by a set of anchors that are produced by applying the alpha micro-function, as well as links to the descriptive part of the manual. In the guided mode, buttons send to the next page to visit.

- Foot(p_h, n_i, p_j): the footer allows creating links in the *guided* navigation mode; this function selects a set of buttons according to the RR and associates to each button a link to a page p_j, by the micro function β (v, p_j). If, as in the previous example, the RR is an ElaborationProcessStep, the footer buttons indicate the possibility for the user to go to the "Next Step" or to the "Previous Step", while in the case of a Sequence this link will be indicated as "Next Item" or "Previous Item". This can be viewed as a form of cognitive orientation support for the user who is navigating in the hypermedia; the level of support can be strenghtened by mentioning, in the button label, the name of next step or item.

We show, in Figure 3, an example of generation of a page from the subtree starting from node n_1 in Figure 2, in the *guided* and the *free* navigation modes.

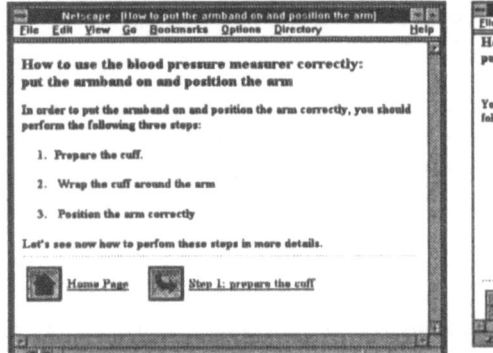 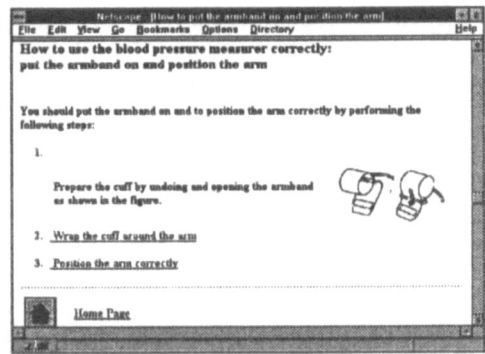

Figure 3: An example of page layouts

The main RR is an Elaboration Process Step: the nucleus describes the process and the satellites the individual steps. The page Header is obtained by a linguistic transformation function that inserts the Goal topic of the tree root, which is out of Figure 2 (item1: 'use the blood pressure measurer correctly') and the Goal topic of n_1 (item2: 'put the armband on and position the arm') into the simple linguistic template 'How to <item1> : <item2>'. The Body is obtained by a function that combines a linguistic transformation of the process (data associated to object n_2) with an ordered list of step descriptions. In the *free navigation mode* (rightside), the first step description is obtained by a multimedia combination of items associated to children of n_3 (whose complexity is 'Low'); anchor links are inserted in case of the description of steps 2 and 3 to enable the user to have further details if needed, because nodes n_4 and n_5 are of 'High' complexity. In the *guided mode* (leftside), a button sends the user to the page that describes the first step: the label of this button orients the user, by anticipating the content of that page.

4.   User-adaptation

In hypermedia, dynamic adaptation can be provided at two levels:

- at the *presentation* level, by customizing the node content and layout (text, media allocation, information selection, etc.);
- at the *navigation* level, by customizing the navigational support and paths (link hiding, reordering of links, adapted guided tours, etc.). Unexperienced users are guided in examining the manual systematically, so as that they learn all aspects of instruction and understand the purpose of any piece of information; experienced users are left more free in examining the manual so that they can concentrate on aspects they are not familiar with. Users also receive orientation support, while navigating, which depends on their experience in the domain and in using hypertexts in general.

Although the two levels of adaptation are conceptually different, in GeNet, they are strictly related. Adapting at both levels is done by exploiting knowledge about the user's preferences in the user model; our user model is a simple stereotype that is triggered by age, educational level and experience in the application domain and hypermedia. As micro and macro generation functions are parametrized, user model settings are employed to set up the following Hypm features:

- details to be included in a page (how many Dplan nodes to aggregate in a Hypm page);
- page layout (how to generate Title, Header and Body). For example, linguistics transformations of information items can be performed by employing terms with which the user is familiar;
- anchor and button links;
- level of orientation support;
- checking of whether the user skipped information items that are supposed to be relevant in the instruction process.

Figure 4 shows an example of navigation mode for the Dplan in Figure 2 for a aged user, with low domain and hypermedia experience, and willing to see figures. GeNet, then, selects in this case a guided navigation mode with strong orientation, medium fonts and provides high level of detail.

After the first page (describing the process 'put the armband on and position the arm'), the user is guided to see pages corresponding to steps 1 (in detail) and 2 (in synthesis). Details of step 2 are described in the three subsequent pages ('position the armband ', 'position the garment' and 'fix securely the armband'). Description of step 2 is now finished and description of step 3 ('position the arm correctly') can begin: the user is oriented about the instruction phase to which the system has come, by a 'connection page' which synthetizes the goals of the completed step and of the next one.

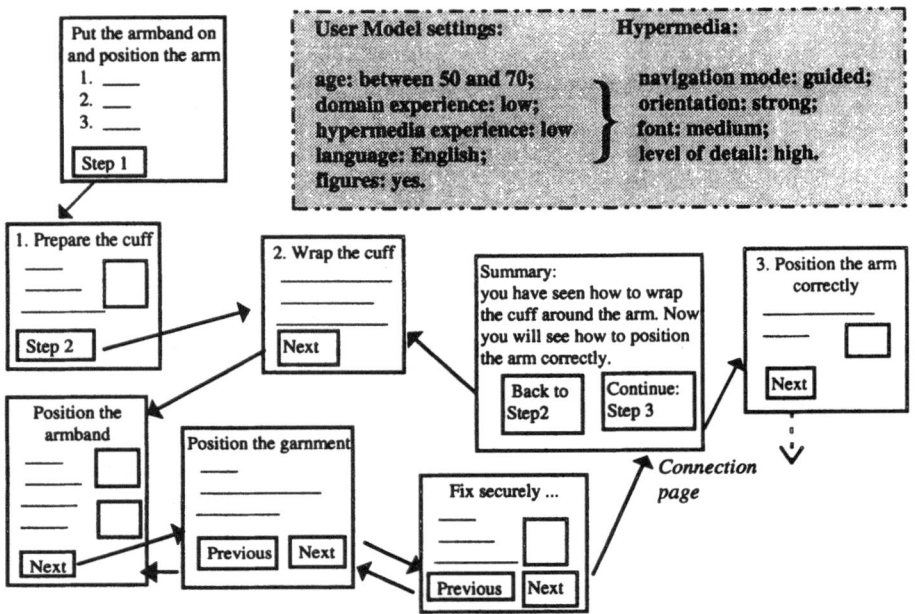

Figure 4: an example of adaptation in the navigation style

5.   Conclusions

Generation of user-adapted hypermedia can go beyond crude filtering of raw Web material if an appropriate knowledge base and refined multimedia generation methods are employed (Inder and Oberlander, 1995; Brusilovsky et al, 1996). In the generation of concept descriptions, this KB can be a hierarchy of concepts or a semantic network of items to be described. We proved that, in the case of instruction manuals, knowledge contained in a RST-based discourse plan and in the user model can be employed effectively to build hypermedia by ensuring internal consistency of pages and global consistency of the entire document. Our algorithm enables producing several navigation paths and page presentations from a unique discourse plan; the advantage is that, after text planning, one may decide whether to generate a one-shot document, a hypermedia or both. One can also generate several hypermedia from the same plan at the same time, each tailored to a specific user category.

Our future work aims studying how to improve dynamic presentation of information items by refining media allocation and integration methods and at verifying, through a set of evaluation studies in cooperation with experimental psychologists, which combination of media, which navigation modes are the most effective in reaching the desired goal, according to the user characteristics and preferences. The results of these experiments will be employed to verify whether the three modes and the page presentation that are generated with the present algorithm are effective from the instructional viewpoint, and how user acceptance of the generated hypermedia can be achieved best.

References

P Brusilovsky, E Schwarz and G Weber (1996). A Tool for developing adaptive electronic textbooks on WWW. In *Proceedings of WebNet96*, World Conference of the Web Society, june 1996, Boston, Ma, AACE; pp.64-69.

B De Carolis, F de Rosis, F Grasso, A Rossiello, D Berry and T Gillie (1996). Generating recipient-centered explanations about drug prescription. *Artificial Intelligence in Medicine*, 8, 123-145.

E De Vries and T De Jong (1997). Using information systems while performing complex tasks: an example from architectural design. *Int.J Human-Computer Studies*, 46, 31-54.

J Eklund and R Zeiliger (1996). Navigating the Web: possibilities and practicalities of adaptive navigational support. Proceedings of *AUSWEB'96*, Gold Coast, Australia.

N Hammond and L Allinson (1989). Extending hypertext for learning: an investigation of access and guidance tools. In A Sutcliffe and L MacCaulay (Eds), *People and Computers V, HCI 89*. Cambridge University Press, 293-304

E H Hovy (1993). Automated discourse generation using discourse relations. *Artificial Intelligence*, 63,341-385.

R Inder and J Oberlander (1995). Using discourse to aid hypertext navigation. In *Proceedings of HCI International, Yokohama*, July.

W C Mann and S A Thompson (1988). Rhetorical Structure Theory, towards a functional theory of text organization. *Text*, 8, 3, 243-281.

M Milosavljevic e R Dale (1996). Text generation and User Modeling on the Web. Proceedings of the Workshop on User Modelling for Information Filtering on the World Wide Web, *5th International Conference on User Modelling*, Hawaii, january.

J D Moore and C Paris (1993). Planning text for advisory dialogues: capturing intentional and rhetorical information. *Computational Linguistics*, 19, 4, 651-694.

J D Moore and V O Mittal (1996). Dynamic generation of follow up question menus: facilitating interactive natural language dialogues". *IEEE Computer*, Special Issue on Interactive Natural Language Processing, July.

H Thimbleby (1991). User Interface Design. *ACM Press,Frontier Series*.

P Wright and A Lickorish (1989). An empirical comparison of two navigation systems for two hypertexts. In *Proceedings of Hypertext 2 Conference*, York.

WORDNET for Italian and Its Use for Lexical Discrimination

Alessandro Artale, Bernardo Magnini and Carlo Strapparava

IRST, I-38050 Povo TN, Italy

e-mail: {artale|magnini|strappa}@irst.itc.it

Abstract. We present a prototype of the Italian version of WORDNET, a general computational lexical resource. Some relevant extensions are discussed to make it usable for parsing: in particular we add verbal selectional restrictions to make lexical discrimination effective. Italian WORD-NET has been coupled with a parser and a number of experiments have been performed to individuate the methodology with the best trade-off between disambiguation rate and precision. Results confirm intuitive hypothesis on the role of selectional restrictions and show evidences for a WORDNET-like organization of lexical senses.

1 Introduction

WORDNET is a thesaurus for the English language based on psycholinguistics principles and developed at the Princeton University by George Miller [Miller, 1990]. It has been conceived as a computational resource, so improving some of the drawbacks of traditional dictionaries, such as the circularity of the definitions and the ambiguity of sense references. Lemmas (about $130,000$ for version 1.5) are organized in synonyms classes (about $100,000$ synsets).

The more evident problem with WORDNET is that it is a lexical knowledge base for English, and so it is not usable for other languages. Here we present the efforts made in the development of the Italian version of WORDNET [Magnini and Strapparava, 1994; Magnini et al., 1994], a project started at IRST about one year ago in the context of ILEX [Delmonte et al., 1996] a more general project aiming at the realization of a computational dictionary for Italian[1].

A second problem with WORDNET is that it needs some important extensions to make it usable for effective parsing. In particular, parsing requires a powerful mechanism for lexical discrimination, in order to select the appropriate lexical readings for each word in the input sentence. In this paper we also explore the integration of *"selectional restrictions"*, a traditional technique used for lexical discrimination, with Italian WORDNET. Selectional restrictions provide explicit semantic information that the verb supplies about its arguments [Jackendoff, 1990], and should be fully integrated into the verb's argument structure.

Although selectional restrictions are different in different domains [Basili et al., 1996] we are interested in finding common invariants across sub-languages. It

---

[1] The ILEX consortium includes the Computer Science Department of the University of Torino, the University of Venezia, and the branch of the University of Torino at Vercelli.

is our intention to build a very general instrument that can be afterwards tuned to particular domains by identifying more specific uses. The main motivation is to have both a robust and a computational efficient natural language system. On one hand, robustness is emphasized because sentences that are syntactically correct, but which are not successfully analyzed in the specific application domain, can have a valid linguistic meaning. On the other hand, we are able to filter the sentence meanings on a linguistic basis. This phase discards the unplausible readings pruning the search space by looking for compatibility semantic relations. This kind of discrimination can be realized with computationally effective algorithms by exploiting the lexical taxonomy of WORDNET, postponing more complex and expensive computations to the domain specific analysis.

The paper is structured as follow. Section 2 describes the Italian prototype of WORDNET; while section 3 shows how selectional restrictions has been added to verb senses. Section 4 shows how Italian WORDNET has been coupled with the parser, both for describing lexical senses and as a repository for selectional restrictions. Section 5 reports a number of experiments that has been performed to individuate the methodology design with the best trade-off between disambiguation rate and precision. Finally section 6 provides some conclusive remarks.

2 The Italian WORDNET Prototype

The Italian version of WORDNET is based on the assumption that a large part of the conceptual relations defined for English (about $72,000$ ISA relations and $5,600$ PART-OF relations) can be shared with Italian. WORDNET can be described as a lexical matrix with two dimensions: the lexical relations, which hold among words and so are language specific, and the conceptual relations, which hold among senses and that, at least in part, we consider independent from a particular language. The Italian version of WORDNET aims at the realization of a multilingual lexical matrix through the addition of a third dimension relative to the language. Figure 1 shows the three dimensions of the matrix: (a) words in a language, indicated by W_j; (b) meanings, indicated by $\mathcal{M}_i$; (c) languages, indicated by $\mathcal{L}_k$. From an abstract point of view, to develop the multilingual matrix it is necessary to re-map the Italian lexical forms with corresponding meanings ($\mathcal{M}_i$), building the set of synsets for Italian (making explicit the values for the intersections $\mathcal{E}_{ij}^I$). The result will be a complete redefinition of the lexical relations, while for the semantic relations, those originally defined for English will be used as much as possible.

An implementation of the Multilingual lexical matrix has been realized which allows a complete integration with the English version and the availability of all the translations for the Italian lemmas. The architecture is easily extendible to other languages. The integration with the computational lexicon ILEX is under development: it will make the access to other levels of lexical information, such as morphological classes, syntactic categories and sub-categorization frames available. The Italian version of WORDNET, in December 1996, included about $10,000$ lemmas ($7,000$ nouns, 700 verbs, $1,500$ adjectives, 600 adverbs).

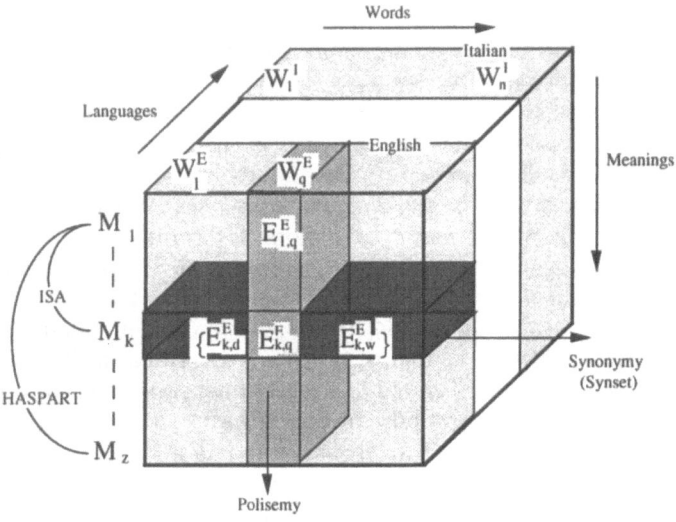

Fig. 1. Multilingual lexical matrix

Till now, data acquisition has been mostly manual, with the help of a graphical interface; however a basic goal of the project is the experimentation of techniques for the (semi)automatic acquisition of data. Algorithms for the resolution of the ambiguities in the coupling with the English WORDNET have been developed. Versions automatically created are then tested against manually acquired data, with the aim of incrementally improve the precision level. A final manual check is performed for all the data automatically acquired. It is also foreseen the use of corpora to extract contextual information to be used during the disambiguation process.

3 Adding Selectional Restrictions to Verbs

A number of steps have been followed to add selectional restrictions to Italian WORDNET. First, Italian verb senses were extracted from a paper version of an Italian dictionary and checked against a corpus of generic Italian texts. Each verb sense has been then coupled with one or more English WORDNET synsets[2]. This phase has been performed manually with the help of a graphical interface (see figure 2) that includes four integrated working tools: (i) a bilingual dictionary with more than 30,000 lemmas; (ii) a graph that allows the visualization of the coupling with the English WORDNET; (iii) the bilingual WORDNET, that behaves exactly like the English version with the additional possibility to browse the Italian semantic network; (iv) finally, the working cards allow the insertion,

---

[2] As for figurative uses, they can also be coupled with WORDNET provided that an appropriate synset does exist.

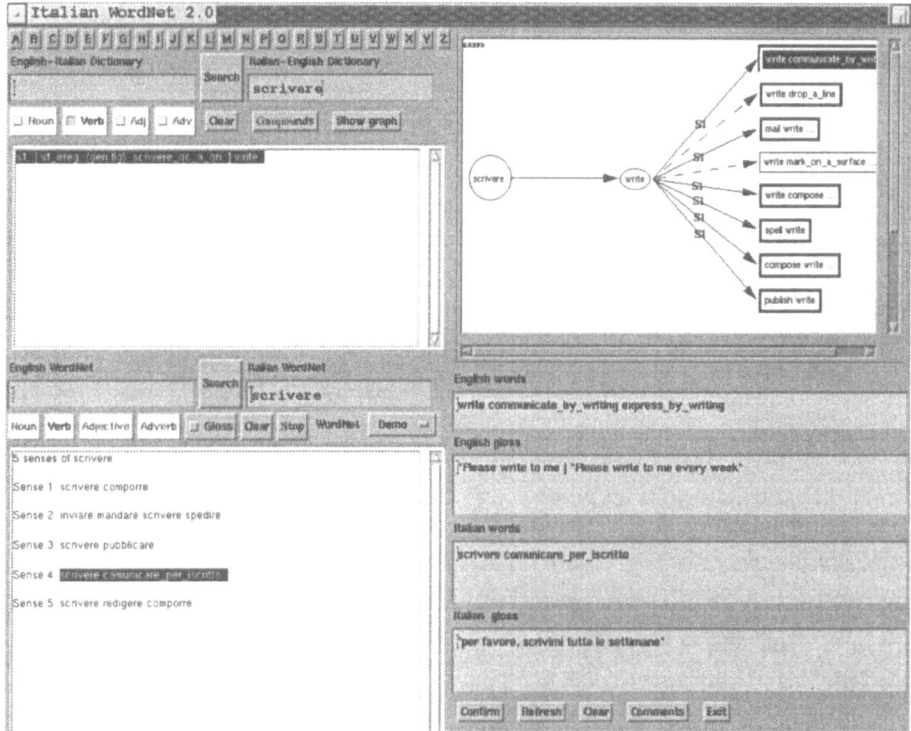

Fig. 2. The Italian WORDNET interface.

modification and check of the data for a synset. The result of this phase is the extension of the English WordNet with the Italian synsets. Figure 3 shows the correspondence between English and Italian synsets for the verb **Scrivere** (**Write**).

The next step is the definition of the sense subcategorization frame. This includes both syntactic information (i.e., argumental positions, prepositions on indirect objects, category type) and semantic information, such as thematic roles and selectional restrictions. Syntactic information are associated to single verbs, while semantic information are associated to the whole synset, i.e., semantic participants are shared among all the verbs belonging to the synset.

We built selectional restrictions using the synsets of the noun hierarchy. Two different possibilities for defining selectional restrictions are considered:

1. Selectional restrictions obtained from the frames currently provided by WORD-NET.
2. Selectional restrictions obtained from the whole WORDNET noun hierarchy.

As far as the first hypothesis is concerned, WORDNET describes all the English verbs resorting to a set of 35 different syntactic frames, which in turn

Synset Label	Italian Synset	English Synset
Write	{scrivere redigere comporre}	{write compose pen indite}
Write-Music	{scrivere comporre}	{compose write write_music}
Write-Communicate	{scrivere comunicare_per_iscritto}	{write communicate_by_writing}
Write-Publish	{scrivere pubblicare}	{publish write}
Write-Send	{inviare mandare scrivere spedire}	{mail write post send}

Fig. 3. Correspondences between Italian and English synsets for the verb '*scrivere*' (write).

include only two restrictions, that is *Something* and *Somebody*. For example, the frames provided for the verb **Write** in the synset {**Publish, Write**} are given in the form of patterns, where the dots can be substituted by the verb stem:

`Somebody...s`

`Somebody...s Something`

The problem arising in using these two restrictions is that they are completely uncorrelated to the noun synsets, then, they have to be matched with the proper synsets in the noun hierarchy. The concept **Somebody** includes not only the synset **Person** but also all the synsets denoting group of people that could hold the agent thematic role. We defined **Somebody** using the following boolean combination of synsets:

$$\text{Somebody} \doteq \text{Person} \vee \text{People} \vee \text{People-Multitude} \vee$$
$$(\text{Social-Group} \wedge \neg(\text{Society} \vee \text{Subculture} \vee$$
$$\text{Political-System} \vee \text{Moiety} \vee \text{Clan}))$$

Something is defined as the complement of **Somebody**.

In the second hypothesis selectional restrictions are taken from the whole noun hierarchy. As an example, figure 4 illustrates the senses for the Italian verb **Scrivere (Write)** found in Italian WORDNET. For each sense we report a conventional name – which unambiguously identifies the synset – and the argumental positions admitted for that sense, with the indication of the selectional restrictions. The appropriate combination of synsets for an argumental position has to be both enough general to preserve all the human readings, and enough restricted for discriminating among different senses of both verb and noun.

A problem is posed by those verb usages in which the argumental position is filled by a synset higher in the hierarchy than the selectional restriction, as in *Cosa hai scritto? (What did you write?)*. For these cases two alternative solutions are possible: (i) extending the simple subsumption check to a more comprehensive "double subsumption" check, in which or the filler is subsumed by the restriction, or the restriction is subsumed by the filler. This approach has been successfully experimented in a number of prototype systems developed at Irst. (ii) considering such high level fillers as pronouns, which stand for a noun satisfying the verb selectional restrictions.

Finding the appropriate selectional restrictions revealed itself difficult and time consuming. The process required a deep search into the WORDNET noun hierarchy. In order to achieve a good trade-off between discrimination power and precision level we adopted an empirical process with successive steps of refinement. We started with general selectional restrictions and then we validate them against experimental results. This iterative process ended with complex selectional restrictions for verbs, as the figure 4 shows.

The WORDNET verb taxonomy is based on the *troponymy* relation, which is defined as the co-occurrence of both lexical implication and temporal co-extension between two verbs. We would note that, every time a troponymy relation between two verbs holds, an ISA relation between the correspondent selectional restrictions holds, too.

WORDNET Synset	Subject	Object	Indirect-Object
Write	Somebody	Written-Material∨ Symbolic-Repres ∨ Saying∨ Correspondence ∨ Sentence∨ Message ∨ Message-Content∨ Code ∨ Symbol ∨ Date∨ Language-Unit ∨ Property∨ Address-Speech ∨ Print-Media	--
Write-Music	Person	Music	--
Write-Communicate	Somebody	(Written-Material ∧ ¬Section)∨ Symbolic-Repres ∨ Saying∨ Sentence ∨ Name∨ Message ∨ Message-Content∨ Code ∨ Date ∨ Property	Somebody
Write-Publish	Somebody	Written-Material∨ (Print-Media ∧ ¬Section)	Print-Media∨ Publishing-House
Write-Send	Somebody	Correspondence ∨ Message∨ Letter-Missive	Somebody

Fig. 4. Lexical entries for Scrivere (Write).

4 Coupling WORDNET and a TFS Parser

In this section we describe the architecture we used for checking WORDNET usability in parsing. Italian WORDNET has been used in two different phases of the linguistic analysis. On a first phase, we use Italian WORDNET as a lexicon repository to carry on lexical analysis. During the semantic analysis Italian WORDNET is used as a kind of Knowledge Base (KB) exploiting the structural relationships among synsets. In particular, we used the supertype/subtype-like hierarchy of synsets during the parsing process in order to discard unplausible constituents on a semantic base.

The parser used is a CYK chart parser embedded in the GEPPETTO environment [Ciravegna *et al.*, 1996], and coupled with a proper unification algorithm. GEPPETTO is based on a Typed Feature Logic [Carpenter, 1992] for the specification of linguistic data. The GEPPETTO environment allows to edit and debug grammars and lexica, linking linguistic data to a parser and/or a generator, integrating various form of KBs, and using specialized processors (e.g., morphological analyzers). In particular, we integrated the hierarchical structure of WORDNET as an external KB, while an IsA function uses the WORDNET hierarchy in order to check subsumption relationships between WORDNET synsets.

The grammar is written adopting a HPSG-like style, and each rule is regarded as Typed Feature Structure (TFS). For the current experiment the grammar coverage is limited to very simple verbal sentences formed by a subject, a main verb together with its internal arguments and, possibly, an adjunct phrase. Observe that, the syntactic analysis does not take into account the pp-attachment case. We excluded the possibility to capture these complex nominal phrases. Indeed, the object of the experiment is to disambiguate among WORDNET senses of both verbs and nouns on the basis of the lexical semantic restrictions for the arguments of the verb and the lexical semantic associated to the noun.

A condition for using WORDNET coupled with the GEPPETTO environment is to bring it in a format effectively usable. The exploited idea was to rebuild the WORDNET hierarchy in CLOS, the object-oriented part of COMMON LISP. The advantages of this approach is the possibility to implement a fast and flexible access to the synsets hierarchy and, in particular, an efficient IsA functionality as required for the semantic checking during the parsing. The arguments to IsA function may be a complex boolean combination of synsets (e.g., see selectional restrictions in figure 4).

The parser controls the overall processing. Whenever it tries to build a (partially recognized) constituent it incrementally verifies the admissibility of the semantic part of such a constituent, using the WORDNET hierarchy. In particular, whenever a noun is associated with a verbal argument the IsA function is triggered to check whether the synset of the noun is subsumed by the selectional restriction of the corresponding verbal argument. Due to the large number of analyses, it is useful to discard unplausible constituents as soon as possible to cut the search space. This has been obtained interliving the syntactic and semantic processes: as soon as the semantic test fails the constituent is rejected.

Word	WORDNET SynsetLabels
Regina (Queen)	Queen-Insect,Queen-Regnant,Queen-Wife, Queen-Card,Queen-Chess
Articolo (Article)	Article-Artifact,Article-Clause, Article-Grammar,Article-Document
Lettera (Letter)	Letter-Missive,Letter-Alphabet
Libro (Book)	Book-Publication,Book-Section,Book-Object

Fig. 5. Lexical entries for nouns.

5   Experiments and Results

In this section we describe the empirical results obtained by coupling a WORDNET based lexicon with a parser. In our intention, the experiment should bring evidences for the following aspects:

– Plausibility of WORDNET senses for describing lexical entries;
– Usability of WORDNET for carrying out lexical discrimination.

The experiment has been carried out on 60 sentences with 1201 different readings, and formed by using seven verbs (*write, eat, smell, corrode, buy, receive, associate*) coupled with fifty common nouns and two proper nouns. In the general experimental setting a sentence is given to the parser in a situation characterized by multiple lexical entries for each single word (one for each WORDNET sense). The analyses produced by the parser are compared with the set of interpretations given by a human.

As far as nouns are concerned, a lexical entry includes all the senses found in Italian WORDNET. Some of the nouns used in the experiment are shown in figure 5. As for verbs, we started from the Italian WORDNET senses and then we faced to the problem of individuating the proper selectional restrictions for each argumental position of the verb subcategorization frame as seen before. So we build a small number of lexical entries, by means of which we composed the sentences of the experiment. We experimented the two hypotheses on selectional restrictions presented in section 3, i.e., the one with general WORDNET frames and the other with more refined selectional restrictions.

As an example, figure 6 shows the output of the parser for the sentence *"La regina scrisse una lettera a Giovanni"* (*"The queen wrote a letter to John"*). As a convention, internal arguments are represented by the symbol '/', while a '//' denotes a verbal adjunct. This sentence was selected because it produces an high number of readings (40) among the test suite sentences. This is due to both the verb sense ambiguity (**write** has five senses) and to the noun ambiguities (**queen** has five senses, and **letter** two). Note that the parser excludes the

| Sentence | La regina scrisse una lettera a Giovanni |
| | (THE QUEEN WROTE A LETTER TO JOHN) |

| Restrictions | No semantic discrimination |
| Number of readings | 40 |

| Restrictions | Discrimination with WORDNET Frames (I exp. setting) |
| Number of readings | 16 |

Restrictions	Discrimination with WORDNET Full Hierarchy (II exp. setting)
Number of readings	8
Readings	$(1, 2, 3, 4, 5, 6)$

$$\text{Queen-Wife/Write/Letter-Alphabet//John} \tag{7}$$
$$\text{Queen-Regnant/Write/Letter-Alphabet//John} \tag{8}$$

Human Judgment	
Number of readings	6
Readings	

$$\text{Queen-Regnant/Write-Communicate/Letter-Missive/John} \tag{1}$$
$$\text{Queen-Wife/Write-Communicate/Letter-Missive/John} \tag{2}$$
$$\text{Queen-Regnant/Write-Send/Letter-Missive/John} \tag{3}$$
$$\text{Queen-Wife/Write-Send/Letter-Missive/John} \tag{4}$$
$$\text{Queen-Regnant/Write/Letter-Missive//John} \tag{5}$$
$$\text{Queen-Wife/Write/Letter-Missive//John} \tag{6}$$

Fig. 6. An example of sentence

sense **Write-Publish** since the indirect object must be introduced by the Italian prepositions *"su"* or *"per"* (in English *"on"* or *"for"*), while in this example we have the preposition *"a"* (*"to"*).

Let us first consider the results obtained in the second experimental setting, which best approximates the human judgment. Out of the eight interpretations accepted, two are implausible for a human reader. This is caused by the contemporary presence of the sense **Letter-Alphabet** and of the proper noun **John** as, respectively, patient and beneficiary of the **Write** verb sense. Note that, each of these senses are, per se, valid arguments since they satisfy the selectional restrictions.

In the first experimental setting, the presence of weaker selectional restrictions (just *Somebody, Something*) yields more spurious readings. As a matter of fact, the more evident problem is that in many cases argumental positions are not properly filled. For example, a reading is allowed in which "a **Queen-Regnant** can **Write-Music** a **Letter-Missive**" (i.e., a kind of correspondence).

Figure 7 reports the quantitative results of the experiment. They are preliminary since they have been obtained on a limited number of sentences (60). For each experimental setting the number of total readings produced by the parser, the discrimination rate (i.e., the rate of the rejected readings: $(1201 - x)/1201$), and the precision (i.e., the rate of correct readings: $122/x$) are shown. These results have to be interpreted considering that the focus of the experiment is on selectional restrictions, which of course is just one among the various kinds of information occurring during lexical discrimination. It is worth mentioning here some other crucial information sources: (i) world knowledge (e.g., it is very strange to **Write** an **Article-Clause** on a **Newspaper-Periodic**); (ii) aspectual properties of the verb (e.g., it is very difficult to interpret *La regina sta scrivendo un articolo sul gionale* (*The queen is writing an article on the newspaper*) with the **Write-Publish** sense, because publishing is a culminative process).

Experimental Setting	# of readings	Discrimination Rate	Precision
Without discrimination	1201	0%	10%
Discrimination with WordNet Frames	688	43%	18%
Discrimination with the WordNet Full Hierarchy	164	86%	74%
Human Judgment	122	90%	100%

Fig. 7. Quantitative results obtained on 60 sentences

6 Conclusions

In this paper we presented the approach underlying the Italian WORDNET, a general computational lexical resource. A prototype has been realized which implements a multilingual lexical matrix. In light of the concrete use of Italian WORDNET we propose the integration of selectional restrictions into the verbal taxonomy. The acquisition of selectional restrictions for the present experiment has been manual with the help of a graphical interface. For the future it will be necessary to consider the possibility of automatically extract selectional restrictions from corpora by means of already known techniques (e.g. [Basili *et al.*, 1996]).

The empirical verification which has been performed confirms the intuitive hypothesis that selectional restrictions crucially affect lexical disambiguation and that the discrimination rate improves as far as they are more detailed. Some general suggestions can be drawn in order to individuate a trade-of between the effort necessary for describing selectional restrictions and the lexical disambiguation obtained. Although the definition of detailed selectional restrictions was highly time consuming, our experience shows that this approach obtains good results both in the discrimination rate and in the precision.

The experiment also brings evidence for a WORDNET like sense organization. In fact, different selectional restrictions apply to different senses allowing to discriminate among different readings. However, an important drawback in WORDNET is the lack of relations among related senses of the same word. This is particularly crucial for the *logical polysemy* cases [Pustejovsky, 1995], when a sense can be generated from another in a predictable way, and, in general, to treat the so called "verb mutability effect" as discussed in [Gentner and France, 1988].

References

[Basili *et al.*, 1996] R. Basili, M.T. Pazienza, and P. Velardi. Integrating general-purpose and corpus-based verb classification. *Computational Linguistics*, 22(4), 1996.

[Carpenter, 1992] B. Carpenter. *The logic of typed feature Structures*. Cambridge University Press, Cambridge, Massachusetts, 1992.

[Ciravegna *et al.*, 1996] F. Ciravegna, A. Lavelli, D. Petrelli, and F. Pianesi. The GEPPETTO environment, Version 2.0.b. User Manual. Technical report, IRST, 1996.

[Delmonte *et al.*, 1996] R. Delmonte, G. Ferrari, A. Goy, L. Lesmo, B. Magnini, E. Pianta, O. Stock, and C. Strapparava. ILEX - un dizionario computazionale dell'italiano. In *Proc. of 5 th Convegno Nazionale della Associazione Italiana per l'Intelligenza Artificiale*, Napoli, September 1996.

[Gentner and France, 1988] D. Gentner and I.M. France. The verb mutability effect: Studies of the combinatorial semantics of nouns and verbs. In S. Small, G.W. Cottrell, and M.K. Tanenhaus, editors, *Lexical Ambiguity Resolution*. Morgan Kaufman, San Mateo, California, 1988.

[Jackendoff, 1990] Ray Jackendoff. *Semantic Structures*. Current Studies in Linguistics. The MIT Press, Cambridge, Massachusetts/London, England, 1990.

[Magnini and Strapparava, 1994] B. Magnini and C. Strapparava. Costruzione di una base di conoscenza lessicale per l'italiano basata su WordNet. In *Proc. of the 28 th International Congress of the Società Linguistica Italiana*, Palermo, Italy, Ottobre 1994.

[Magnini *et al.*, 1994] B. Magnini, C. Strapparava, F. Ciravegna, and E. Pianta. Multilingual lexical knowledge bases: Applied WordNet prospects. In *The Future of Dictionary - Workshop sponsored by Rank Xerox European Research Centre and ESPRIT Project Acquilex II*, Grenoble, France, October 1994.

[Miller, 1990] G. A. Miller. WordNet: "An on-line lexical database". *International Journal of Lexicography (special issue)*, 3(4):235–312, 1990.

[Pustejovsky, 1995] J. Pustejovsky. *The Generative Lexicon*. The MIT Press, Cambridge, Massachusetts, 1995.

Efficient Support for Reactive Rules in Prolog*

Mauro Gaspari

Dipartimento di Scienze dell'Informazione, University of Bologna
Via Mura Anteo Zamboni, 7, 40127 Bologna, Italy
E-mail: gaspari@cs.unibo.it

Abstract. FW_rules is a Prolog library which provides efficient support for forward (reactive) rules in Prolog. The library is based on an indexing mechanism to achieve efficiency, it supports interoperability between the forward chaining language and the underlying Prolog engine, and it can be embedded in any Prolog application. The implementation is based on a runtime support written in C to perform indexing efficiently, and it relies on Prolog for the evaluation of rules. In this paper we describe the library, the compiler and the indexing mechanism. Finally, we compare FW_rules with other approaches to the implementation of production rules in Prolog and with other public-domain production systems, presenting a set of benchmarks.

1 Introduction

Prolog is one of the most successful AI languages since it supplies built-in mechanisms such as unification, backward chaining search, backtracking and dynamic database handling. Several AI tools have been built using Prolog such as Flex [14]. These tools provide a set of high level knowledge representation mechanisms and a set of associated deduction methods. But, in general they luck of features supporting a data driven reactive behaviour. This limitation is caused by the fact that Prolog is goal oriented and it does not embody low level mechanisms to support data driven computations. Thus, even thought Flex provides a forward chaining engine the performance of it is not satisfying.

FW_rules is a Prolog library designed to overcome these limitations. The library consists of a compiler which exploits a non-state saving approach coupled with an indexing mechanism on the contents of the working memory to achieve efficiency. The implementation is based on a runtime support written in C, which allows us to exploit special purpose mechanisms when the fixed search strategy of Prolog in not adequate. FW_rules provides a set of basic matching mechanisms to support the implementation of forward rules in Prolog which can be embedded in any Prolog application. Thus, it is different from Flex [14], KORE/IE [17] or from the extension of Prolog presented in [11], which are programming environments

---

* The author would like to thank Steve Wallis for providing the OPS code of the cycle1000 and nocycle1000 programs. This paper has been partially supported by the Italian Ministry of Universities (MURST) and by CNR Progetto Coordinato Programmazione Logica.

(shells) based on production systems. On the other hand, FW_rules is a low level library which can be used to build data driven reactive agents and forward chaining engines in Prolog.

In this paper we describe the library, the compiler and the indexing mechanism. Finally, we compare FW_rules with other approaches to the implementation of production rules in Prolog and with other public-domain production systems, presenting a set of benchmarks.

2 FW_rules

FW_rules provides a simple extension to Prolog supporting the matching phase for production (reactive) rules. The initial working memory is specified by Prolog facts, for instance the fact **man(socrates)** is a WM element representing a man named socrates. Facts on the working memory are not necessarily ground.

Production rules have the following format: **LHS then RHS**. LHS is a sequence of tests on the contents of the working memory, Prolog goals and Prolog built-in predicates. RHS is a sequence of **assert**, **retract** and **erase** operations on the working memory and of Prolog goals which may include also WM update operations. Tests on the working memory are templates of WM elements including variables, which are bound during the matching phase exploiting unification. For instance, given a WM containing the fact **man(socrates)** and the rule:

r1: man(X) then assert(mortal(X)).

X is bound to **socrates** and **mortal(socrates)** is added to the WM. As in OPS5 [8], it is possible to retrieve the reference of a WM element performing a test. This is obtained including in braces a template of a WM element and a variable. After the matching phase the variable will be bound to the reference to the WM element. The variable can be used in the RHS of a rule to access or erase the WM element. As an example the following rule:

r2: {man(X),Ref},dead(X) then erase(Ref).

allows us to delete a man from the WM if he is dead.

The names and the arities of all the facts appearing in the working memory must be declared, defining the predicate **wm**. Thus if we have a program composed of rules *r1* and *r2*, we must include the following declaration at the beginning of the program.

wm man/1, mortal/1, dead/1.

The forward chaining engine is activated issuing a goal **run** which can be included in a Prolog predicate. This starts a recognize-act cycle which terminates successfully when no rules are satisfied; **run** is a deterministic predicate. Another instance of the activation predicate is **run(fact)** which terminates successfully when fact is asserted into the WM otherwise, if no productions are satisfied, it fails.

The library is based on a simple conflict resolution strategy which takes the first recognized rule as the next rule to be fired. As a consequence of this, the porting of an OPS5 program into FW_rules is not immediate. In particular, if we want to port an OPS5 program in FW_rules, we must consider the following issues:

- The problem of multiple firing of the same rule on the same WM elements must be handled explicitly: for instance if we consider rule r1, to avoid an infinite loop we must add the test not mortal(X) to the LHS of the rule.
- The rules must be ordered carefully: a good heuristic is to put more specific rules (i.e., rules with a larger LHS) at the beginning of the file.

More complex conflict resolution strategies are not supported in the library, but they can be defined by the user providing an adequate preprocessor which modifies the order of rules.

To solve the problem of multiple activation of rules the compiler provides an all-solutions execution mode option. When the all-solution mode is on, the recognize-act cycle avoids multiple execution of the same rule on the same set of WM elements. Moreover, when a rule fires all the instances of the rule which match the WM are executed and then the rule is discarded. To avoid loops, this optimization is only applied to rules which do not add LHS elements in the RHS. For instance, if we consider the program composed of rules 1 and 2 presented above and a WM containing the facts man(socrates) and man(aristotel), the standard recognize-act cycle loops forever, because rule r1 is always satisfied, while the all-solution cycle asserts on the WM mortal(socrates) and mortal(aristotel) and terminates.

As an additional benefit, FW_rules supports interoperability between forward chaining and backward chaining (Prolog) engines, since terms in the working memory are represented as Prolog facts.

Example 1. As an example of production rules, we consider a toy expert system performing the diagnosis of an electric circuit taken from [4]. The FW_rules solution is presented in Figure 1. This program can be executed in the normal execution mode because we have added explicit tests to verify that the RHS of rules has not already been asserted, for instance the test not proved(broken(Device)) in the first rule of Figure 1. If we remove such tests, we must exploit the all-solution execution mode to run the expert system correctly.

Example 2. As an example of a reactive agent consider the agent presented in Figure 2, filtering e-mail. Suppose that Daniel is the editor of the AI journal, he receives submitted papers by e-mail and he immediately needs to send an acknowledge message and to store the submission that will be considered at the end of the week (this is modelled by rule m1). Daniel is also the Chair of ECAI98 and he wants to answer to these messages urgently (this is modelled by rule m2). Finally Daniel do not want to see messages concerning making easy money with the internet (this is modelled by rule m3). The incoming message is represented by the fact *message(M)*. We assume predicates *subject*/2, *from*/2, *body*/2 which respectively return the subject, the sender, and the body of the message. We also assume the following predicates: *send_ack_message(X)* sends an acknowledgment message to X; *in(B, X)* returns true if X occurs in B; and

```
wm on/1, connected/2, working/1, device/1, proved/1, samefuse/2.

device(heater).    on(light1).    connected(heater,fuse2).
device(light1).    on(light2).    connected(light1,fuse1).
device(light2).    on(heater).    connected(light2,fuse1).

on(Device),device(Device),not working(Device),
not proved(broken(Device)),connected(Device,Fuse),proved(intact(Fuse))
    then assert(proved(broken(Device))).

connected(Device,Fuse),working(Device),not proved(intact(Fuse))
    then assert(proved(intact(Fuse))).

connected(Device1,Fuse),on(Device1),
not working(Device1),samefuse(Device2,Device1),
not proved(failed(Fuse)),on(Device2),not working(Device2)
    then assert(proved(failed(Fuse))).

connected(Device1,Fuse),connected(Device2,Fuse),
not samefuse(Device1,Device2),different(Device1,Device2)
    then  assert(samefuse(Device1,Device2)).

different(X,Y):-\+(X = Y).
```

Fig. 1. A Diagnosis Expert System

```
wm urgent/1, subject/2, from/2, auto_answer/1, delete/1.

urgent(ecai98).
auto_answer('aij submission').
ignore('make easy money').

m1: {message(M),R},subject(M,X),auto_answer(X),from(M,Y)
        then send_ack_message(X),assert(submission(M)),erase(R).

m2: {message(M),R},subject(M,X),urgent(X)
        then notify(M),assert(save(M)).

m3: {message(M),R},body(M,B),ignore(X),in(B,X)
        then erase(R).

send_ack_message(X):-...
notify(M):-...
in(B,X):-...
```

Fig. 2. A Mail Filtering Agent

notify(M) immediately notifies the message to the user. To execute this agent we need to call *run.* whenever a new message is received.

3 Compilation

The implementation technique, we describe in this paper, concerns mainly the match phase of the recognize-act cycle. The match algorithms for production systems can be divided in two categories: the state-saving algorithms which store intermediate results from previous recognize-act cycles; and the non-state saving algorithms which perform the match from scratch every cycle.

The rete match algorithm [9] and other conventional approaches to speeding up the performance of rule based systems [13] are based on state-saving techniques. They store the results of executing match from previous recognize-act cycles, so that only the changes made to the WM by the most recent rule firing are executed every cycle; the conflict set, the working memory elements, and the intermediate results are all stored into network nodes. These approaches are appropriate when the working memory change slowly, i.e., when the fraction of the working memory which changes every cycle is very small [12]. These conditions are not always satisfied in all application domains: as an example in real time systems, where the working memory contains continuously changing sensor data, the close world assumption about data constancy is violated [6]. Thus, it is necessary to devise new techniques in order to deal with this eventuality in applications.

We have designed a runtime support based on a non-state saving technique to overcome these limitations. We compile production rules into Prolog and we provide an efficient indexing mechanism implemented in C, which uses the contents of the working memory to select a set of *candidate rules* which potentially might match the WM. The main advantage of implementing the runtime support in C is that no extra memory is needed in the indexing phase, we need just a loop of bitwise machine operations, without resorting to function calls and dynamic memory allocation. The same efficiency cannot be achieved exploiting bitwise Prolog built-in operations on bignums, because the size of Prolog bignums cannot be determined a priori. Basically, each bitwise operation on Prolog bignums requires a function call which determines the length of the numbers involved, it performs the bitwise operations, and it returns a canonical representation of the result.

A production rule LHS_i *then* RSH_i is translated into a Prolog clause with the following form: $p(i) : -LHS_i, !, RHS_i$, where p is a new predicate symbol of arity 1, which is not appearing in the original production rules. The working memory is implemented as a database of Prolog unit clauses; since it is frequently updated, it is implemented as dynamic code, namely by **assert** and **retract** built-in predicates. This is not a drawback because compilative techniques have been studied extensively for Prolog dynamic code, and most of the modern Prolog implementations provide mechanisms to efficiently manage dynamic data areas. Finally, the evaluation of the rule with respect to the working memory is performed executing the body of the Prolog clause.

Following this translation schema it is easy to build a recognize-act loop as follows:

```
run:-
    repeat,
    p(N),
    N==end,
    write('No production true').
```

The predicate p(N) is used to retrieve production rules, if the LHS of a rule succeeds N is bound to an integer and the test N==end fails, Prolog backtracks executing the predicate **repeat** which starts the cycle again.

The resulting production system satisfies the interoperability requirement and provides a good speed-up with respect to an interpreter for production rules written in Prolog, but, it still suffers of efficiency problems. Since the LHSs of rules are evaluated left to right, it may happen that a failure occurs because one of the last elements of the LHS does not match a fact in the WM. Moreover, rules are attempted sequentially one after the other without considering the contents of the working memory: all the LHS patterns may be compared against all the WM elements for every rule on each cycle. This is a drawback if the number of rules and the medium size of the LHSs of rules are large.

3.1 Indexing

The indexing mechanism we have developed is based on a bitmap representation of the working memory and of the preconditions of rules. Bitwise operations are used to select candidate rules. We consider an abstract representation of rules and of the working memory (WM). The abstract WM and the abstract rules are represented by sets of abstract terms. Given a term, the corresponding abstract one is represented by its name, and its arity, for instance $a(X,Y)$ is represented as $a/2$. As an example, if the WM contains the following facts: $a(1)$, $a(2)$, $b(X)$ the corresponding abstract WM is $\{b/1, a/1\}$, and the abstract LHS of the rule precondition $a(X), b(1), not(f(X))$ is $\{a/1, b/1\}$.

Let $R = \{1, 2, 3, \ldots\}$ be a set of index associated to production rules, let WMI be the initial working memory, and let LHS_i $i \in R$ be a rule left hand side. To implement indexing we add to the Prolog representation of the working memory and rules a set of bitmaps, one (WMB) stores the presence of facts in the WM and the others ($LHSB_i$ $i \in R$) store the presence of conditions in rules. Let AWMI be the abstract working memory, and let $ALHS_i$ $i \in R$ be the abstract rules. Let $\Sigma = (\bigcup_{i \in R} ALHS_i) \cup AWMI$ be the union of all the abstract sets. We define a mapping ϕ from $\aleph_{|\Sigma|}$ to Σ which associates an element of Σ to each natural number in the interval $[0, |\Sigma|]$. The bitmaps WMB and $LHSB_i$ $i \in R$ are defined below.

$$WMB(j) = \begin{cases} 1 \text{ if } \phi(j) \in AWMI \\ 0 \text{ otherwise} \end{cases}$$

$$LHSB_i(j) = \begin{cases} 1 \text{ if } \phi(j) \in ALHS_i \\ 0 \text{ otherwise} \end{cases}$$

We say that a rule $i \in R$ is a candidate rule if its precondition bitmap $LHSB_i$ satisfies the test:

$LHSB_i \ \& \ WMB = LHSB_i$

where $\&$ is the bitwise *and* operation. This means that for each position j in the bitmap of a rule i, if the bitmap is set at position j, also WMB must be set at position j. In other words, all the elements in the LHS of the rule (considering name and arity) must be also in the WM. Note that in order to apply this technique it must be possible to statically calculate the set Σ.

Given a file containing production rules the compiler generates a Prolog program which also includes the initialization of the bitmaps WMB and LHSB. To

```
:- module(user).
:- dynamic on/1, connected/2, working/1, device/1, proved/1, samefuse/2.

device(heater).    on(light1).    connected(heater,fuse2).
device(light1).    on(light2).    connected(light1,fuse1).
device(light2).    on(heater).    connected(light2,fuse1).

p(0):- on(Device),device(Device),\+ working(Device),\+ proved(broken(Device)),
        connected(Device,Fuse),proved(intact(Fuse)),
        !,assert(proved(broken(Device))),upd(4).
p(1):- connected(Device,Fuse),working(Device),\+ proved(intact(Fuse)),
        !,assert(proved(intact(Fuse))),upd(4).
p(2):- connected(Device1,Fuse),on(Device1),\+ working(Device1),
        samefuse(Device2,Device1),on(Device2),\+,proved(failed(Fuse)),
        \+ working(Device2),!,
        assert(proved(failed(Fuse))),upd(4).
p(3):-connected(device1,Fuse),connected(Device2,Fuse),
        different(Device1,Device2),\+ samefuse(Device1,Device2),
        !,assert(samefuse(Device1,Device2)),upd(5).

different(X,Y):-\+ (X = Y).

fw_rules:init_system:-!,fw_rules:c_set_wm(3),fw_rules:c_set_oc(3,5),
        fw_rules:c_set_wm(0),fw_rules:c_set_oc(0,3),fw_rules:c_set_wm(2),
        fw_rules:c_set_oc(2,3),fw_rules:c_set_wm(1),fw_rules:c_set_oc(1,5),
        fw_rules:c_set_rg(0,0),fw_rules:c_set_rg(0,3),fw_rules:c_set_rg(0,1),
        fw_rules:c_set_rg(0,4),fw_rules:c_set_rg(1,1),fw_rules:c_set_rg(1,2),
        fw_rules:c_set_rg(2,1),fw_rules:c_set_rg(2,0),fw_rules:c_set_rg(2,5),
        fw_rules:c_set_rg(3,1).
```

Fig. 3. Rules compilation.

illustrate the compilation technique, we consider a diagnosis expert system presented in figure 1. The **wm** declaration has two effects: first, it defines the mapping ϕ which follows the order of the predicates in the declaration; secondly, it generates a Prolog directive (:- dynamic ...), which identifies dynamic predicates. The predicate **different/2** is an example of how it is possible to integrate Prolog code in the of rules: it does not appear in the **wm** declaration.

The Prolog code which is the result of the compilation of the diagnosis expert system, is presented in Figure 3. The **upd/1** predicate is part of the runtime support, it updates the WM bitmap in the given position. Rules are translated into clauses for a predicate **p/1**. We associate an index to each rule (a natural number) in order to exploit Prolog indexing. The bitmaps in the example are initialized as follows:

WMB	=110100	Working Memory
$LHSB_1$	=110110	Rule 1
$LHSB_2$	=011000	Rule 2
$LHSB_3$	=110001	Rule 3
$LHSB_4$	=010000	Rule 4

3.2 The Recognize-Act Loop

The recognize-act cycle is performed by a C routine which repeatedly executes tests on bitmaps to individuate candidate rules. The schema of the main loop follows:

```
c_run()
{ ... OOP:i=0; notfound=1;
        while (notfound && i < MAXRULES) {
        if TESTWM(rule(i),WM) {
            notfound = prolog_call(i); ...
        } i++;...}}
```

The tests on bitmaps TESTWM(rule(i),WM) are executed sequentially, and only when a test succeeds a Prolog call is executed; the clause, representing the candidate rule, is selected exploiting Prolog indexing. If the Prolog call succeeds the recognize-act loop restarts from scratch. Finally, when no rules are satisfied, the execution terminates. The size of the bitmap used depends on the cardinality of Σ. The bitmap is represented as a 32 bit integer; but large bitmaps are also supported, when $|\Sigma| > 32$ the bitmap is stored in a vector of integers; the size of the vector is determined at compile time.

The operations on bitmaps are defined as macros which are built at compile time depending on the size of the bitmap. As an example the macro `TESTWM(m,n)` where m and n are bitmaps is expanded at compile time into the following test: `m[0] & n[0] == m[0]`. This allows to perform indexing very efficiently executing only bitwise machine operations without introducing a function call. The macro expansion depends on the size of the bitmaps, for instance if $32 < |\Sigma| < 64$ the macro is expanded into `(m[0] & n[0] == m[0]) && (m[1] & n[1] == m[1])`. The same mechanism is adopted for all the primitives of the runtime support involving bitmaps.

The implementation of the all-solutions execution mode is based on a modified recognize-act loop. A tag is introduced to avoid multiple execution of rules: when a rule fires the tag is set, and it is restored only when a WM element, appearing in the LHS of the rule, is asserted. Rules, which do not modify LHS elements in the RHS, are compiled in order to execute a failure driven loop. As an example, rule 2 of the example in 1 is compiled as follows:

```
p(1):-connected(Device,Fuse),working(Device),
    assert(proved(intact(Fuse))),upd(4),fail.
```
The cut is removed and a explicit **fail** is inserted at the end of the rule.

4   Related Work

In KORE/IE [17] Shintani proposed a compilation technique for forward rules in Prolog which translates rules into a uniform Prolog program which is executed by an inference engine performing conflict resolution. The translated program consists of LHS clauses and RHS clauses which implement respectively the LHS and RHS of production rules. The compiler exploits indexing based on the working memory contents, but the approach is based on a state-saving technique. The

Shintani compiler generates a set of clauses for each production rule. More precisely, it generates as many clauses as the conditions which appear in the LHS of each rule, such that the head of each clause can be used to perform indexing. Thus, candidate rules are those in which at least one condition in the LHS match the WM. This is the main difference between the Shintani and our approach, because we perform indexing on all the conditions of a rule LHS using only the functors and the arities. FW_rules has several advantages with respect to KORE/IE if we need to include forward rules into a Prolog application: first, the syntax in our system is more Prolog-like while KORE/IE introduces a program notation similar to OPS5; second, we are proposing a library which can be easely used in any Prolog application, while KORE/IE is a full expert system shell, thus it requires that the application is written according to its structure.

Furukawa et al. [10] described an approach based on partial evaluation of meta-programs. They considered a simple working memory driven interpreter for production systems without conflict resolution and they developed a compiler equivalent to Shintani's by the combination of the production system interpreter and partial evaluation. The compiler generates Prolog code for a production system exploiting the same indexing technique of Shintani, but working memory elements are not represented as Prolog facts. This implies that the approach still requires an interpretation phase to evaluates LHS elements with respect to the WM (which is represented as a list), thus, the interoperability with the underlying Prolog system is not supported.

Coyle and Tanik investigated the use of rule-based programs in real-time embedded systems environments [6]. Their work is based on the distinction between first order and propositional rules; they developed an optimization technique based on partial evaluation of propositional production systems. The compilation technique they used is based on decision trees which can be used to reason about bounds on processing time in the case of propositional rules. FW_rules works nicely with propositional rules because in this context only the test on bitmaps is needed to fire a rule; thus, in this case the LHS is omitted in the Prolog code.

Several indexing algorithms for speeding Prolog execution have been presented in the literature [18, 15, 7, 16]. The aim of these methods is to reduce the number of clauses on which unification will be performed. The main difference with respect to our technique is that in our case we need to consider tuples of conditions in the matching phase where backtracking can occur, while these algorithms have been designed to match the clause heads and the goal in Prolog.

5   Benchmarks

We present tree different benchmarks which allow to evaluate different aspects of the system: the impact of indexing on the match phase; the measure of the speed of firing rules; and a comparison with other public domain production systems.

The first benchmark is oriented to evaluate the impact of the proposed indexing technique. We tested three different production system implementations in Prolog: a naive interpreter, a naive compiler, and our compiler which exploits indexing. This benchmark is executed on a Sun SparcStation 5. The results are summarized in the following table.

Indexing	Interpreter	Compiler	FW_rules
Sec	309.3	79.8	28.1
rule-fire/sec	64.6	250.6	711.7
wme-ch/sec	258.6	1002.5	2846.9

The program used is composed of 22 rules with 10 terms in the precondition, 4 wme updates for each rule. The execution of the programs involves 20000 rule firing with three candidate rules on each execution cycle. The speed-up achieved with the indexing technique is good considering that the program is composed of just 22 rules. We obtained a performance improvement of 10.5 times with respect to the naive interpreter and of 2.8 times with respect to the naive compiler. The program, we reported in this paper is similar to the toy program developed by Shintani [17] to test indexing, which consists of n rules with one candidate rule on each execution cycle. FW_rules uses the Sicstus Prolog compiler compiling in bytecode abstract instructions. The compilation in native machine instructions does not provide a great benefit; this is due to the extensive use of dynamic code and to conversion problems in the Sicstus interface with C.

The second benchmark compares two versions of FW_rules one running on Sicstus Prolog 2.1p9, and another running on Sicstus Prolog 3p5, with other production systems measuring the speed of firing rules by means of two simple examples [2]: cycle1000 (cycle) which fires 1000 instances of the same rule in a cycle; and nocycle1000 (nocycle) which fires 1000 instances of the same rule without a cycle. In particular, we report the performance of the following production systems: the Lisp OPS5 interpreter; SDML [2], a declarative production system and CParaOPS5 [1], a parallel production system running on a single processor mode. This benchmark is executed on a Sun SparcStation 5. The results are summarized in the following table where we report also rule firing per second. FW_rules runs twice faster on Sicstus Prolog 3p5 with respect to Sicstus Prolog 2.1p9. This fact depends from the new foreign functions interface which has been completely redesigned in the new version of Sicstus Prolog, indicating that such mixed-programming technology is becoming mature.

System	cycle	firing/sec	nocycle	firing/sec
FW_rules 2.1p9	0.59	1669.4	16.63	60.1
FW_rules-All 2.1p9	0.61	1639.3	0.35	2857.1
FW_rules 3p5	0.27	3703.7	11.82	84.6
FW_rules-All 3p5	0.28	3571.4	0.13	7692.3
Lisp OPS5	0.93	1075.2	11.37	87.9
SMDL	1.78	561.7	0.67	1492.5
CParaOPS5	0.92	1086.9	3.43	291.5

The time of `nocycle1000` is obtained by subtracting the time of `cycle1000`; thus it is just the time taken executing the second rule. The performance of FW_rules is not good executing the `nocycle1000` program. This depends on conflict resolution: in fact is not possible to build all the basic conflict resolution mechanisms by preprocessing rules and exploiting different instances of the assert predicate, such as asserta or assertz. In particular, it is difficult in this context to implement conflict resolution strategies which avoid loops caused by multiple firing of the same rule on the same WM elements To solve this problem in the public domain version of FW_rules we must insert an explicit test in the LHS, as an example the last rule: `test(X), not test1(X) then asserta(test1(X))`. But, the resulting program is not efficient because the program must perform about 500 tests for each firing. Conversely, if we exploits the all-solution execution mode (FW_rules-All) the performance obtained is really good.

The last benchmark aims to compare the two versions of FW_rules with other available production system implementations: KORE/IE running on Quintus Prolog release 3.1, the public domain OPS5 interpreter written in Common Lisp running on EcoLisp [3]. The benchmark is executed on a Sun SparcStation 2. We report the execution time of the extended version (27 rules) of the monkey and banana example. Although the problem is not well suited for FW_rules since the structure of the LHS of rules is uniform, our system provides better performance with respect to other public domain implementations. The results are summarized in the following table.

Production System	Monkey and Banana
FW_rules 2.1p9	0.113
FW_rules 3p5	0.056
Lisp OPS5	0.135
KORE/IE	0.320

6 Conclusion

We have described a Prolog library (FW_rules) which allows the user to embed efficient data driven rules into Prolog. The library exploits a non state-saving approach coupled with indexing, it is based on a runtime support written in C to implement indexing, while it relies on Prolog for the evaluation of production rules. The main advantage of this runtime support is that the indexing phase can be implemented as a loop of bitwise machine operations, without resorting to function calls and dynamic memory allocation. This efficiency cannot be achieved exploiting bitwise Prolog built-in operations on bignums, because the size of these numbers cannot be determined a priori. The library has been implemented in Sicstus Prolog [5] a complete, widely-used, efficient and well-supported Edinburgh Prolog implementation, using the foreign language interface to C and bitwise C operations. FW_rules is a public domain library, and it is available for experimentation (ftp.cs.unibo.it:pub/gaspari/fw_rules). We are testing the library in more complex applications to provide more significant benchmarks.

References

1. A. Acharaya and M. Tambe. Collection oriented match. In *Proc. IJCAI-93 Workshop on Production Systems and their Innovative Applications*, Chambery France, August 1993.
2. D. W. ans S. Moss. Efficient forward chaining for declarative rules in a multi-agent modelling language. Technical Report CPM 004, Centre for Policy Modelling, Manchester Metropolitan University, October 1994.
3. G. Attardi. The embeddable Common Lisp. In *Fourth International Lisp Users and Vendor Conference*, Berkeley, 1994.
4. I. Bratko. *Prolog Programming for Artificial Intelligence*. Addison-Wesley, 1986.
5. M. Carlsson, J. Widen, J. Andersson, S. Andersson, K. Boortz, H. Nilsson, and T. Sjoland. *SICStus Prolog User's Manual version 2.1 #9*. Swedish Institute of Computer Science, April 1994.
6. F. Coyle and M. Tanik. Rule Compilation and Optimization for Embedded Systems with Periodic Sensor Data. In A. Cohn, editor, *ECAI94 the 11th European Conference on Artificial Intelligence*, pages 324–328. John Wiley and SonsLtd, 1994.
7. B. Demoen, A. Marien, and A. Callebaut. Indexing Prolog Clauses. In *Proc. North American Conf. on Logic Programming*, pages 1001–1012. MIT Press, Cambridge, MA, 1989.
8. L. B. E. K. Farrel and N. Martin. *Programming Expert Systems in OPS5*. Addison Wesley, 1985.
9. C. Forgy. Rete: A fast Algorithm for the Many Patterns/Many Objects Pattern Match Problem. *Artificial Intelligence*, 19(1):17–37, September 1982.
10. K. Furukawa, H. Fujita, and T. Shintani. Deriving an Efficient Production System by Partial Evaluation. In E. Lusk and R. Overbeek, editors, *Proc. North American Conf. on Logic Programming*, pages 661–674. MIT Press, Cambridge, MA, 1989.
11. M. Gaspari. Extending Prolog with Data Driven Rules. In *Proc. 6th Int. Conf. on Artificial Intelligence and Information-Control Systems of Robots*, pages 277–282, Bratislava, 1994.
12. A. Gupta. *Parallelism in Production Systems*. Pitman, 1987.
13. D. Miranker. *TREAT: A New and Efficient Match Algorithm for AI Production Systems*. Research Notes in Artificial Intelligence. Pitman-Morgan Kaufmann, 1990.
14. Quintus Corporatio. *Quintus Flex 1.21, Reference Manual*, 1991.
15. K. Ramamohanarao and J. Shepherd. A Superimposed Codeword Indexing Scheme for Very Large Prolog Databases. In *Proc. Int. Conf. on Logic Programming*, volume 225 of *Lecture Notes in Computer Science*, pages 569–576, London, 1986.
16. R. Ramesh, I. Ramakrishnan, and D. Warren. Automata-Driven Indexing of Prolog Clauses. *Journal of Logic Programming*, 23(3), 1995.
17. A. Shintani. A Fast Prolog-Based Production System KORE/IE. In R. Kowalski and K. Bowen, editors, *Proc. 5th Int. Conf. and Symp. on Logic Programming*, pages 26–41. MIT Press, Cambridge, MA, 1988.
18. M. Wise and D. Powers. Indexing Prolog Clauses via Superimposed Code Words and Field Encoded Words. In *Proc. Int. Symposium on Logic Programming*, pages 203–211, Atlantic City, USA, 1984. MIT Press, Cambridge, MA.

Reasoning with Behavioural Knowledge in Application Domain Models

Ernesto Compatangelo[1], Francesco M. Donini[2], and Giovanni Rumolo[3]

[1] Istituto di Informatica della Facoltà di Ingegneria, Università di Ancona
[2] Dipartimento di Informatica e Sistemistica, Università di Roma "La Sapienza"
[3] Dipartimento di Informatica ed Automazione, Università di Roma TRE

Abstract. This paper describes an analyst-oriented approach to conceptual knowledge representation and reasoning based on description logics. The approach is introduced to model and analyse the static part of behavioural concepts used in application domains. Behaviours are captured in a parametric way with respect to the description logic which corresponds to the structural modelling language. Structural concepts are classified according to the usual ISA hierarchy, while behaviours are organised into a hierarchy based on countervariance. Reasoning about the domain model is performed in terms of subsumption and consistency in the adopted description logic, and complexity results carry over. The proposed approach is used to formalise and reason on process schemes introduced in the engineering of computer-based and information systems, as well as in enterprise modelling.

1 Introduction

The adoption of knowledge representation and reasoning techniques in application domain modelling is not a new idea. At the beginning of the eighties, research work on requirements specification [2] first pointed out the importance of an explicit representation of knowledge captured before the beginning of systems development. Since then, several languages and systems have been proposed to capture and manage this kind of conceptual (domain) knowledge [12, 11, 19]. However, most of them focus on the representation of structural aspects only. Moreover, those modelling approaches which deal with the representation of behavioural aspects are quite always implicitly unbalanced towards procedural details. This is the case of both Structured Data Flow (SDF) [8] and Object Modelling Technique (OMT) [13]. The observed unbalancement towards procedurality means that behavioural models often fail to support the "what vs. how" distinction, which is ubiquitous in conceptual modelling and analysis. The actual problem with most existing behavioural models is that domain knowledge should not contain any reference to the internal structure and behaviour of domain elements [11]. A domain description should give a coherent intensional image of what composes a domain with no reference to extensional individuals composing it. Data should be thus described as intensional classes, while processes should be described as black boxes with no transfer function.

A new kind of approach should be thus adopted to support domain modelling and analysis in different application areas. This approach should be explicitly conceived to formalise domain models, providing at the same time automated reasoning support which depends on the considered model as well as on the purposes of domain analysis. Formalisation is needed to avoid an ambiguous interpretation of domain concepts. Automated support is needed to deal with the high number of concepts in real-world application domain models, where manual analysis is unpractical and ineffective.

This paper describes a modelling approach based on Description Logics (DLs), which are a family of representation languages designed to model rich hierarchies of classes (concepts) [21, 15]. A DL is a subset of first-order logic with equality that contains only unary and binary predicates. It is endowed with a set of *constructors* that determines the language in which class properties can be specified. Much of the research in DLs concentrated on algorithms for reasoning about concepts. The computational and expressive properties of DLs have been extensively studied [9, 15, 1, 5].

While other approaches based on DLs [18, 5] deal with the structural component of domain knowledge only, we use DLs also to formalise some relevant aspects of the static part of behavioural domain modelling (i.e. process descriptions). Although the DL used in this paper is $\mathcal{ALN}$ [9], behaviours are captured in a parametric way with respect to the adopted DL. In fact, the only requirement we impose on a DL to be used in structural modelling is that it contains the conjunction of concepts. This means that the structural part could have been modelled using a very simple DL, such as $\mathcal{FL}^-$, as well as a much more expressive DL such as $\mathcal{CATS}$ [10]. In our approach, structural concepts are classified according to the usual ISA hierarchy, while behaviours are organised into a hierarchy based on countervariance. In fact, we propose a distinct hierarchy-forming rule for behavioural concepts instead of the well-known subsumption rule used for structural concepts. We use a DL to formalise the flow assertion between two behavioural concepts, which is a relevant domain-dependent constraint. Reasoning about the domain model is performed in terms of subsumption and consistency in the adopted DL. Moreover, we show that we only need a linear number of consistency concept checking with respect to the size of the domain model. Therefore, results about the complexity of reasoning in the adopted DL imply the same results about the complexity of reasoning in the domain model.

The presentation is organised as follows. Section 2 introduces a real-world domain fragment in order to point out some main features of our approach. Section 3 shows the set-theoretic semantics of the modelling language as well as the properties of the related deduction problems. Differences between our consistency checking and countervariant functional typing are also shown. Finally, Section 4 summarises our approach and outlines how it captures some relevant properties of conceptual models in different application domains.

2 Representing Domain Behaviours: An Example

In order to point out the main features of our approach, we present a modelling example derived from the healthcare enterprise domain. The example is first introduced using a textual description and then modelled using the analyst-oriented language $\mathcal{EDDL}_{DP}$ (Epistemological Domain Description Language for Data and Processes) presented in [7]. Each $\mathcal{EDDL}_{DP}$ statement can be translated into a finite set of expressions belonging to the $\mathcal{ALN}$ description logic.

A set of Physiological Data about a patient (Blood Pressure, Temperature, Pulse Frequency) is periodically read from different devices, formatted and successively registered in a Chronologically Ordered List. Every time a data set is read, the value of each element of the set is compared with a fixed range of corresponding Normal Physiological Values. If at least one element is outside its normal range, an alarm condition is signalled. A Patient Monitoring Report containing a chronologically ordered subset of the last N data taken from the previously cited list is issued whenever requested by the Medical Staff.

The corresponding $\mathcal{EDDL}_{DP}$ description is given in Tables 1, 2, 3 and 4. In this section, an intuitive meaning is outlined for the $\mathcal{EDDL}_{DP}$ description, while a formal semantics for $\mathcal{EDDL}_{DP}$ statements is deferred to the next section. Here and in the following, terms in bold denote reserved words, terms in small capital with first letter in capital denote concept names while terms all in small capital denote attributes. If present, an L : U declaration, where L and U are both natural numbers, denotes the cardinality of attributes and channels. In both cases, U ≥ L and we use the special symbol "M" to denote an unbounded value for U (infinite). When considering channels, L ≥ 1 must hold. For instance, let us consider the $\mathcal{EDDL}_{DP}$ description of PHYS-DATA shown in Table 1. This data concept has the meaning of a set (class) of domain elements with an attribute PRES of type BLOOD-PRES, an attribute FREQ of type PULSE-FREQ and an attribute TEMP of type MEAN-TEMP. All these attributes are functional mandatory ones, i.e. upper and lower cardinality constraints have unit value.

Following a well-known semantical distinction introduced in description logics [21], each new data concept can be defined as being either **equals** to or included **in** its description structure composed of already-existing data concepts. For example, T-PHYS-DATA is defined as a structure with the same properties as FMT-PHYS-DATA plus another attribute SAMPLING-TIME. The definition entails that all the individuals belonging to T-PHYS-DATA also belong to FMT-PHYS-DATA. Moreover the **equals** operator asserts that for each new data it is sufficient to define it with the four attributes TEMP, PRES, FREQ and SAMPLING-TIME to infer that it is subset of T-PHYS-DATA. Instead, when we choose the **in** operator for each new data defined in terms of the same four properties, we cannot infer that it is a T-PHYS-DATA. In this case, the definition of attributes only states necessary but not sufficient condition. The T-DATABASE concept, which represents the set of all individuals that have one or more elements of class T-PHYS-DATA, is neither a subset nor a superset of T-PHYS-DATA.

In this DL framework the ISA relationship has the meaning of set containment, i.e. a concept *subsumes* another when the former is included in the lat-

Table 1. Data descriptions in a patient monitoring domain

---

data

% Atomic concepts

CONTROL ;

TIME ;

PHYS-VALUE ;

PERSON-NAME ;

FAMILY-NAME ;

DISEASE ;

FMT-VALUE ;

% Primitive concepts

REPORT-REQUEST in CONTROL ;

ALARM-CONDITION in CONTROL ;

BLOOD-PRES in PHYS-VALUE ;

PULSE-FREQ in PHYS-VALUE ;

MEAN-TEMP in PHYS-VALUE ;

FMT-BLOOD-PRES in
(FMT-VALUE **and** BLOOD-PRES) ;

FMT-PULSE-FREQ in
(FMT-VALUE **and** PULSE-FREQ) ;

FMT-MEAN-TEMP in
(FMT-VALUE **and** MEAN-TEMP) ;

% Defined concepts

PHYS-DATA **equals**
structure where
PRES **is** PHYS-VALUE
TEMP **is** PHYS-VALUE
FREQ **is** PHYS-VALUE ;

FMT-DATA **equals**
structure where
PRES **is** FMT-VALUE
TEMP **is** FMT-VALUE
FREQ **is** FMT-VALUE ;

FMT-PHYS-DATA **equals**
structure where
PRES **is** FMT-BLOOD-PRES
TEMP **is** FMT-MEAN-TEMP
FREQ **is** FMT-PULSE-FREQ ;

T-PHYS-DATA **equals**
FMT-PHYS-DATA
and structure where
SAMPLING-DATE **is** TIME ;

PERSON **equals**
structure where
NAME **is** PERSON-NAME
SURNAME **is** FAMILY-NAME
BIRTHDAY **is** TIME ;

PATIENT **equals**
PERSON **and structure where**
PATHOLOGY **is** 1 : M DISEASE
TREATED-BY **is** PHYSICIAN-DATA ;

PHYSICIAN **equals**
PERSON
and structure where
SPECIALIST-IN **is** DISEASE
PATIENTS **is** PATIENT-DATA ;

T-DATABASE **equals**
structure where
ELEMENT **is** 1 : M T-PHYS-DATA ;

PATIENT-REPORT **equals**
structure where
PATIENT **is** PATIENT-DATA
HISTORY **is** T-DATABASE ;

NORM-PHYS-RANGES **equals**
structure where
N-BLOOD-PRES **is** FMT-BLOOD-PRES
N-MEAN-TEMP **is** FMT-MEAN-TEMP
N-PULSE-FREQ **is** FMT-PULSE-FREQ ;

Table 2. Data constraints in a patient monitoring domain

---

data constraints

disjoint DISEASE, PHYS-VALUE, TIME, CONTROL, STRING ;

disjoint ALARM-CONDITION, REPORT-REQUEST ;

disjoint PULSE-FREQ, MEAN-TEMP, BLOOD-PRES ;

---

ter. For example, FMT-PHYS-DATA can be automatically classified under both PHYS-DATA and FMT-DATA since it is *subsumed* by these two parent concepts.

The formalisation of processes using DLs is the innovative feature of our approach which was introduced to capture some static aspects of behaviours. Each process definition in the $\mathcal{EDDL}_{DP}$ language is given by the corresponding I/O context, i.e. I/O channels together with their domains (see Table 3). Although this resembles the declaration usually given in a structured data flow schema, the formal semantics of DLs makes automatic deduction possible.

Table 3. Process descriptions in a patient monitoring domain

---

processes

COLLECT **has**
input structure where
PRES **is** BLOOD-PRES
FREQ **is** PULSE-FREQ
TEMP **is** MEAN-TEMP
output structure where
RESULT **is** PHYS-DATA ;

SAMPLING **has**
input structure where
DATA **is** FMT-DATA
output structure where
SAMPLED-DATA **is** T-PHYS-DATA ;

COMPARISON **has**
input structure where
CURRENT-VALUES **is** FMT-PHYS-DATA
REF-VALUES **is** NORM-PHYS-RANGES
output structure where
STATUS **is** ALARM-CONDITION ;

REPORT-GENERATION **has**
input structure where
REQUEST **is** REPORT-REQUEST
REP-DATA **is** 1 : M T-DATABASE
REP-PATIENT **is** 1 : M PATIENT
output structure where
REPORT **is** 1 : M PATIENT-REPORT ;

UPDATE **has**
input structure where
MOST-RECENT-DATA **is** T-PHYS-DATA
OLD-DATA-STORE **is** T-DATABASE
output structure where
UP-DATA-STORE **is** T-DATABASE ;

Table 4. Flow descriptions in a patient monitoring domain

process constraints	**flow** INSERTION **from** SAMPLING . FMT-DATA **to** UPDATE . MOST-RECENT-DATA ;
flow SAMPLE **from** COLLECT . RESULT **to** SAMPLING . DATA ;	**flow** REGISTRATION **from** UPDATE . UP-DATA-STORE **to** UPDATE . OLD-DATA-STORE ;
flow MONITORING **from** SAMPLING . SAMPLED-DATA **to** COMPARISON . CURRENT-VALUES ;	

In the case of the SAMPLING and COMPARISON processes, the flow assertion MONITORING (see Table 4) states that the output resulting from the SAMPLING process has to be transferred to the COMPARISON process. The intuitive meaning of flow assertions is that the output of the source process is the same as the input of the target process, i.e. the sets denoted by the two concepts are equal. This interpretation gives rise to three possible situations involving the output of the source process, i.e. $Out(P_1)$ and the input of the target process, i.e. $In(P_2)$.

1. If $Out(P_1) \cap In(P_2) = \emptyset$ an inconsistency can be automatically detected.
2. If $Out(P_1) \subseteq In(P_2)$ then the flow assertion is consistent and we can infer new constraints in the domain model. For example, the flow MONITORING is consistent because FMT-PHYS-DATA subsumes T-PHYS-DATA. Moreover, we can infer that the process COMPARISON actually has the same restricted concept T-PHYS-DATA as its input instead of FMT-PHYS-DATA.
3. If $Out(P_1) \not\subseteq In(P_2)$ but $Out(P_1) \cap In(P_2) \neq \emptyset$ we can infer new constraints for both source and target processes. For example the flow SAMPLE imposes that both $Out(\text{COLLECT}) = \text{PHYS-DATA}$ and $In(\text{SAMPLING}) = \text{FMT-DATA}$ are constrained to (PHYS-DATA **and** FMT-DATA). This concept can be automatically classified, discovering that it coincides with FMT-PHYS-DATA. When reported to the analyst, this derived property can change his/her understanding of the domain.

It is very important to note that our interpretation of the flow assertion differs from the composition of functions. More specifically, if a process P_1 were to be considered as a function $P_1 : Range_1 \rightarrow Domain_1$ and a process P_2 were to be considered as a function $P_2 : Range_2 \rightarrow Domain_2$, then functional composition would have required $Domain_1 \subseteq Range_2$. Conversely, in our approach we only require that $Domain_1 \cap Range_2 \neq \emptyset$, warning the analyst that the output of process P_1 has to be constrained to $Domain_1 \cap Range_2$ in order to guarantee flow coherence. We reconsider this aspect in the next section, after the definition of a formal semantics for $\mathcal{EDDL}_{DP}$.

3 Reasoning with Domain Behaviours

All expressions in our $\mathcal{EDDL}_{DP}$ language can be given a set-theoretic semantics as follows. An interpretation $\mathcal{I}$ is defined as a triple $(\varepsilon[\cdot], \Delta_C, \Delta_P)$, where Δ_C and Δ_P are two disjoint sets of elements and $\varepsilon[\cdot]$ is a mapping. $\varepsilon[\cdot]$ assigns to each atomic data concept C a subset $\varepsilon[C]$ of Δ_C (i.e., classes are interpreted as sets), to each attribute ATT a subset $\varepsilon[\text{ATT}]$ of $\Delta_C \times \Delta_C$ (i.e. an attribute is interpreted as a binary relation), to each process P an element of Δ_P and to each channel CH a subset $\varepsilon[\text{CH}]$ of $\Delta_P \times \Delta_C$. From the interpretation of the above atomic names, the intepretation of more complex constructs can be defined as follows. Let C and D be two concepts, ATT be an attribute. Conjunction of structures is interpreted as set intersection, i.e. $\varepsilon[(\text{C and D})] = \varepsilon[C] \cap \varepsilon[D]$. We denote the cardinality of a set S as $\sharp S$. Moreover, given an element $x \in \Delta_C$ and an attribute ATT, we denote with $\varepsilon[\text{ATT}](x)$ the set $\{y \in \Delta_C \mid (x, y) \in \varepsilon[\text{ATT}]\}$.

The semantics of a structure is as follows.

$\varepsilon[\textbf{structure where } \text{ATT } \textbf{is } \text{L}:\text{U C}] =$

$$= \{x \in \Delta_C \mid \text{L} \leq \sharp\varepsilon[\text{ATT}](x) \leq \text{U and } \forall y \in \varepsilon[\text{ATT}](x) : y \in \varepsilon[C]\} \quad (1)$$

A concept C is *satisfiable* if there exists an interpretation $(\varepsilon[\cdot], \Delta_C, \Delta_P)$ such that $\varepsilon[C] \neq \emptyset$. Moreover, a concept C *subsumes* a concept D if for every interpretation $(\varepsilon[\cdot], \Delta_C, \Delta_P)$ it holds $\varepsilon[D] \subseteq \varepsilon[C]$. Given a concept name C and a complex concept D, we say that an interpretation $\mathcal{I} = (\varepsilon[\cdot], \Delta_C, \Delta_P)$ satisfies the definition of a concept (C **equals** D ;) if $\varepsilon[C] = \varepsilon[D]$. Similarly, $\mathcal{I}$ satisfies the introduction of a primitive concept (C **in** D ;) if $\varepsilon[C] \subseteq \varepsilon[D]$. $\mathcal{I}$ satisfies a data constraint (**disjoint** $C_1, \ldots, C_n,$;) if for all $i, j \in \{1, \ldots, n\}$ and $i \neq j$, it holds $\varepsilon[C_i] \cap \varepsilon[C_j] = \emptyset$. The interpretation $\mathcal{I}$ satisfies the description of a process (P **has input** C **output** D ;) if

$$\varepsilon[P] \in \varepsilon[C] \cap \varepsilon[D] \quad (2)$$

where C and D are two structures interpreted in the same way as in (1), except that to each channel is assigned a subset of $\Delta_P \times \Delta_C$.

We turn now to the interpretation of flow assertions, which is a key feature in our approach. An interpretation $\mathcal{I}$ satisfies a flow assertion from a source process P_s through its output channel OUT_s to a target process P_t through its input channel IN_t, i.e. **flow** F **from** P_s . OUT_s **to** P_t . IN_t ; if all the elements which are output of P_s through OUT_s are input of P_t through IN_t. In formulae, $\{x \in \Delta_C \mid (\varepsilon[P_s], x) \in \varepsilon[\text{OUT}_s]\} = \{y \in \Delta_C \mid (\varepsilon[P_t], y) \in \varepsilon[\text{IN}_t]\}$.

Finally, an interpretation satisfies a domain description if it satisfies all parts of the description, i.e., data descriptions and constraints, process and flow descriptions. We call such an interpretation a *model* of the description. We say that a description is *satisfiable* if it has a model.

Checking the satisfiability of a description, i.e. checking that it admits at least one model is a considerable support tool in domain analysis. We can give necessary and sufficient conditions for the satisfiability of a description as follows.

Theorem 1. *A domain description is satisfiable if and only if:*

1. *for each process description* P **has input** C **output** D ;
   concepts C *and* D *are satisfiable;*
2. *for each flow assertion* **flow** F **from** P_s . OUT$_s$ **to** P_t . IN$_t$;
   (a) source process P_s *contains in its output*
   structure where OUT$_s$ *is* L$_s$: U$_s$ C$_s$*;*
   (b) target process P_t *contains in its input*
   structure where IN$_t$ *is* L$_t$: U$_t$ D$_t$*;*
   *(c) cardinalities of source and target channels are compatible, i.e., the two
   integer intervals* [L$_s$, U$_s$] *and* [L$_t$, U$_t$] *have the non-empty intersection*
   [max(L$_s$, L$_t$), min(U$_s$, U$_t$)]*;*
   (d) the concept (C$_s$ **and** D$_t$) *is satisfiable.*

   □

Proof. (sketch)

Only-if part: if condition 1 is not met, then there exists a process description for which every interpretation assigns to either C or D the empty set. Hence, no interpretation can satisfy that process description according to Formula (2). A similar conclusion holds if one of the conditions in 2 is not met.

If part: The proof makes use of the following property (see [4]): given an interpretation $\mathcal{I}$ of the domain description, one can always build another interpretation $\mathcal{I}'$, defined as the disjoint union of many copies of $\mathcal{I}$ (i.e., the union of interpretations which are the same as $\mathcal{I}$ but renaming with new names all elements in Δ_C, Δ_P). In this way, if $\mathcal{I}$ assigns to a concept C a non-empty set, containing at least one element $x \in \Delta_C$, $\mathcal{I}'$ assigns to C a set containing many copies of x, i.e. new elements having exactly the same properties as x. Suppose that for a given flow assertion, condition (2d) holds. Then there exists an interpretation $\mathcal{I} = (\varepsilon[\cdot], \Delta_C, \Delta_P)$ such that $\varepsilon[(C_s \textbf{ and } D_t)]$ is non-empty. If $\sharp\varepsilon[(C_s \textbf{ and } D_t)] < max(L_s, L_t)$, then a new interpretation $\mathcal{I}' = (\varepsilon'[\cdot], \Delta_{C'}, \Delta_{P'})$ can be defined as disjoint unions of $\mathcal{I}$ such that now $\sharp\varepsilon'[(C_s \textbf{ and } D_t)] \geq max(L_s, L_t)$. From $\mathcal{I}'$, one can build another interpretation $\mathcal{I}''$, which interprets concepts in the same way as $\mathcal{I}'$, and assigns to channels OUT$_s$ and IN$_t$ a number of elements which is inside the interval [max(L$_s$, L$_t$), min(U$_s$, U$_t$)]. Now $\mathcal{I}''$ satisfies the flow assertion, and also the part of the descriptions of P_s and P_t regarding OUT$_s$ and IN$_t$, respectively, appearing in conditions (2a) and (2b). This operation can be iterated for each flow assertion, yielding a model of the domain description. □

The above theorem shows that to check the satisfiability of a domain description, one mainly needs to perform a number of satisfiability checkings which is linear in the number of process and flow descriptions. Hence, the complexity of satisfiability checking of a domain description is linearly related to the complexity of concept satisfiability in the underlying DL chosen for the data descriptions and constraints. For the DL used in this paper, which is a syntactic variant of the description logic $\mathcal{ALN}$, satisfiability checking of a concept of size n is a problem solvable in $O(n \log n)$ [3, 20], hence the satisfiability of a domain description of size n can be checked in $O(n \log n)$. We remark that the above theorem does not hold for DLs admitting the ONE-OF constructor—which allows classes to be described as explicit enumeration of their elements—since for such DLs the property of building new interpretations by disjoint unions does not hold.

Automated reasoning about processes is performed computing a process hierarchy based on functional type replacement. Following a well-known approach, we say that a process P is a *subtype* of a process P' when the input context of P subsumes the input context of P', and the output context of P is subsumed by the output context of P'. The subtype relation is a well established notion for programming languages. It was developed to guarantee the safe replacement of a function inside a composition of functions, where by "safe" we mean that the function resulting from the composition is always defined. In our framework, this notion is slightly extended. In fact, we not only check a safe process composition but we also individuate possibly more restrictive constraints that have to be imposed to processes in order to obtain a safe composition.

Let us consider the case represented in Table 5. In our framework the flow P_1-INTO-P_2 is satisfiable if and only if the intersection of input domain of P_2 has a non-empty intersection with the output domain of P_1. Let us recall that $In(Q)$ and $Out(Q)$ are the input and the output of process Q respectively. Then, the flow is satisfied in the following situations:

1. $Out(P_1) \subseteq In(P_2)$, i.e. there exists an inclusion between the output domain of P_1 and the input domain of P_2
2. $Out(P_1) \not\subseteq In(P_2)$, and $Out(P_1) \cap In(P_2) \neq \emptyset$, i.e. there only exists an intersection between the output domain of P_1 and the input domain of P_2

Note that the former represents the usual condition for functions composition while the latter represents our extension and in both the situations we consider both $Out(P_1)$ and $In(P_2)$ satisfiable. Moreover, while the former situation implies the latter, it isn't true the contrary. The same considerations are applied in the case of the flow P_2-INTO-P_3. Therefore, the process P_2' can replace the process P_2 iff: (i) P_2 is a subtype of P_2', (ii) the input domain of P_2' still has a non-empty intersection with the output domain of P_1 and (iii) the input domain of P_3 still has a non-empty intersection with the output domain of P_2'.

When (a) $Out(P_1) \subseteq In(P_2)$ and (b) $Out(P_2) \subseteq In(P_3)$ are true before the process replacement, from the countervariance subtype relation we infer: (i) $In(P_2) \subseteq In(P_2')$ and (ii) $Out(P_2') \subseteq Out(P_2)$ and therefore we conclude that: (c) $Out(P_1) \subseteq In(P_2')$ and (d) $Out(P_2') \subseteq In(P_3)$. This situation represents the usual safeness for function composition.

More interesting considerations apply when just (a) $Out(P_1) \cap In(P_2) \neq \emptyset$ or (b) $Out(P_2) \cap In(P_3) \neq \emptyset$ are true before process replacement. Let us consider the case (b): the countervariant subtype relation is not sufficient to infer that (d) $Out(P_2') \subseteq In(P_3)$. Hence, the composition of P_2' and P_3 is not safe. However, if $Out(P_2') \cap In(P_3) \neq \emptyset$ the composition is possible, with the further restriction that the *actual* output of P_2' is in $Out(P_2') \cap In(P_3)$. This additional restriction on P_2' is reported to the analyst when he/she tries to substitute P_2 with P_2'. In this way we extend the correct type checking for process composition in those cases where it is possible to add new constraints to obtain a safe process

Table 5. Abstract flow descriptions for the composition of processes

P_1 **has**	P'_2 **has**
input structure where IN **is** I_1	**input structure where** IN **is** I'_2
output structure where OUT **is** O_1 ;	**output structure where** OUT **is** O'_2 ;
P_2 **has**	**flow** P_1-INTO-P_2
input structure where IN **is** I_2	**from** P_1 . OUT **to** P_2 . IN ;
output structure where OUT **is** O_2 ;	**flow** P_2-INTO-P_3
P_3 **has**	**from** P_2 . OUT **to** P_3 . IN ;
input structure where IN **is** I_3	
output structure where OUT **is** O_3 ;	

composition. The rationale for this less restrictive process composition follows. In our framework channels define the requirements perceived by the analyst about the process parameters. In a true functional interpretation channels do not exist and the only relevant requirements are function domain and co-domain definitions. the domain analyst does not perceive However, as in the case of an SDF schema, the analyst does not perceive a process as a true function; he/she only defines the class of the input/output parameters. The flow assertion not only states the process composition but should also constrain the communication between processes. This means that the analyst is interested in discovering which constraints — if any — allow information transfer through the flow.

4   Summary and Discussion

We presented a treatment of behavioural aspects which encompasses a wide number of behavioural concepts such as data transformations, physical or conceptual input/output relations and generic processes. The $\mathcal{EDDL}_{DP}$ (i.e. $\mathcal{ALN}$) concept language adopted in this paper is a subset of the CLASSIC language [21], for which there is a corresponding implemented system [16]. In this way, an implementation of our approach is straightforward. The main features of behavioural descriptions in the $\mathcal{EDDL}_{DP}$ language are:

- *input and output contexts*, i.e. the signature of a black-box transformation function;
- *multiple inheritance of input and output contexts* using the **and** operator;
- *automated classification* of both processes and input/output contexts. These are separately classified according to the subsumption relation;
- *channels*, i.e. process properties which define the input and output contexts of the process itself in terms of their cardinality and data constraints;
- *flow assertions*, i.e. constraints imposing that an output of a source process equals an input of a target process.

Our formalization of behaviours is potentially useful in the following three areas.

Behaviours as functions are ubiquitous in Information Systems Engineering (ISE), where they represent data processing elements. Behaviours as processes are the essence of SDF modelling [8]. In SDF schemes, black-box transformers are connected into a network by way of conceptual or material flows. Our DL-based approach is able to capture SDF schemes. In particular, it models functions in a way which is similar to (but more expressive than) SDF processes, introducing an explicit distinction between function, input, output and flow concepts. More details are shown in [6]. Behaviours are also used in object-oriented modelling approaches such as Object Modelling Technique (OMT, [13]) to represent the functional part of the object model. In our approach, concepts correspond to OMT classes, instances to OMT objects and processes to functions in the functional model Moreover, the structural part and the behavioural one are integrated in a unique scheme. However, our approach does not capture the so-called OMT "dynamic model".

Behaviours are widely used in Enterprise Modelling (EM) [14], to provide a representation of enterprise functions. The enterprise domain is defined in terms of a set of "domain processes" which fulfil these objectives. Domain processes can be decomposed into a hierarchy of business processes or enterprise activities. The corresponding knowledge contents are easily described using our approach. We allow the construction of business process hierarchies based on functional typing. Moreover, the classification of process contexts let analysts find out the relation between processes that share common input or output elements.

Behaviours are used in the Parameter-Based (PBR, [17]) model for representing domain knowledge in the Engineering of Computer-Based Systems (ECBS). They can be captured as "functions with mechanisms" in our approach. In fact, a "mechanism context component" built using the same input and output context constructors can be easily added to our processes, giving rise to a new kind of behavioural entity. Moreover, given two functions with the same inputs and outputs but with different mechanisms, the first one is a subtype of the second one if and only if the context mechanism of the former subsumes the context mechanism of the latter. Similar relations hold in the other cases.

Acknowledgements

This research has been partially supported by ASI, CNR (Progetto SARI) and MURST 60% (Linguaggi per la modellazione concettuale dei requisiti).

References

1. A. Borgida and P. F. Patel-Schneider. A Semantics and Complete Algorithm for Subsumption in the CLASSIC Description Logic. *Journal of Artificial Intelligence Research*, 1:277–308, 1994.
2. A. Borgida and S. Greenspan and J. Mylopoulos. Knowledge Representation as the basis for Requirements Specification. *IEEE Computer*, pages 82–91, Apr. 1985.

3. B. Nebel. Computational Complexity of Terminological Reasoning in BACK. *Artificial Intelligence Journal*, 34(3):371–383, 1988.
4. B. Nebel. *Reasoning and Revision in Hybrid Representation Systems*. Number 422 in Lecture Notes In Artificial Intelligence. Springer-Verlag, 1990.
5. D. Calvanese and M. Lenzerini and D. Nardi. A Unified Framework for Class-Based Representation Formalisms. In J. Doyle and E. Sandewall and P. Torasso, editor, *Proc. of the 4th Int. Conf. on the Principles of Knowledge Representation and Reasoning (KR-94)*, pages 109–120. Morgan Kaufmann, 1994.
6. E. Compatangelo and G. Rumolo. Modelling Domain Knowledge with $\mathcal{EDDL}_{DP}$. In A. Sutcliffe and D. Benyon and F. van Assche, editor, *Proc. of the IFIP Joint Working Conference on Domain Knowledge for Interactive System Design (DKISD'96)*, pages 134–148. Chapman & Hall, 1996.
7. E. Compatangelo and G. Rumolo. $\mathcal{EDDL}_{DP} + \mathcal{TDDL}_{DP} = $ a double-level approach to Domain Knowledge Modelling. In H. Kangassalo and J. F. Nilsson, editor, *Information Modelling and Knowledge Bases VIII*. IOS Press, 1997.
8. E. Yourdon. *Modern Structured Analysis*. Prentice-Hall, 1989.
9. F. M. Donini and others. The Complexity of Concept Languages. In J. Allen and R. Fikes and E. Sandewall, editor, *Proc. of the 2nd Int. Conf. on the Principles of Knowledge Representation and Reasoning (KR-91)*, pages 151–162. Morgan Kaufmann, 1991.
10. G. De Giacomo and M. Lenzerini. What's in an Aggregate: Foundations for Description Logics with Tuples and Sets. In *Proc. of the 14th Int. Joint Conf. on Artificial Intelligence (IJCAI-95)*, pages 801–807, 1995.
11. H. Kangassalo. COMIC: A system and methodology for conceptual modelling and information construction. *Data & Knowledge Engineering*, 9:287–319, 1992/93.
12. J. Mylopoulos and others. Telos: Representing Knowledge About Information Systems. *ACM Transactions on Information Systems*, 8(4):325–362, Oct. 1990.
13. J. Rumbaugh and others. *Object-Oriented Modelling and Design*. Prentice-Hall, 1991.
14. K. D. Tham. CIM - OSA: Enterprise Modelling. Technical report, Enterprise Integration Laboratory, University of Toronto, 1996.
15. M. Buchheit and F. M. Donini and A. Schaerf. Decidable reasoning in terminological knowledge representation systems. *Journal of Artificial Intelligence Research*, 1:109–138, 1993.
16. P. F. Patel-Schneider and others. The CLASSIC Knowledge Representation System: Guiding Principles and Implementation Rationale. *SIGART Bulletin*, 2(3):108–113, 1991.
17. S. A. Friedenthal and H. Lykins. Parameter-Based Representation for Modelling Complex Systems 2. In *IEEE Symposium and Workshop on Engineering of Computer-Based Systems*, pages 65–71. IEEE Computer Society Press, 1996.
18. S. Bergamaschi and C. Sartori. On Taxonomic reasoning in conceptual design. *ACM Transactions on Database Systems*, 17(3):385–422, 1992.
19. S. Bergamaschi and S. Lodi and C. Sartori. The E/S Knowledge Representation System. *Data & Knowledge Engineering*, 14:81–115, 1994.
20. S. Salomone. An $O(n \log n)$ algorithm for Subsumption in $\mathcal{FL}^-$. In A. Marchetti Spaccamela and P. Mentrasti and M. Venturini Zilli, editor, *Proc. of the 4th Italian Conference on Theoretical Computer Science*, pages 125–139. World Scientific Publishing Co., Oct. 1992.
21. W. A. Woods and J. G. Schmolze. The KL-ONE Family. *Computers and Mathematics with Applications*, 23(2-9):1–50, 1992.

How to Solve Qualification and Ramification Using Dijkstra's Semantics for Programming Languages[*]

Ewa Madalińska-Bugaj
Institute of Informatics, Warsaw University
Banacha 2, 02-097 Warsaw, POLAND
email: ewama@mimuw.edu.pl

Abstract

In this paper we consider two aspects of reasoning about action and change: qualification and ramification problems in the context of domain constraint axioms. It was pointed out that the same axiom may cause qualification and ramification. The reason that we distinguish these two cases lies in the semantics of concerning fluents. To distinguish whether a given constrain axiom involves qualification or ramification additional information, namely *influence relation*, which define how fluents can possibly affect each other, must be provided.

To formalize effects of actions, we use Dijkstra's semantics, originally developed for reasoning about programs. In this paper we propose a method for solving the qualification and ramification problem and show how using the influence relation to distinguish between them.

1   Introduction

In this paper we consider some aspects of reasoning about action and change: qualification and ramification problems in the context of domain constraint axioms.

Consider the action *walk* which makes the turkey walking. Assume additionally that we have a constraint axiom: *walking ⊃ alive*. This axiom must be satisfied both before and after the action *walk* is performed. After the action *walk* is executed, we conclude by this axiom that the turkey is *alive*. But if it is dead before, this conclusion is unintended. In such a case, it is impossible to perform the action. Thus, being alive is executability condition of the action *walk* in the context of the above axiom. Obviously, this condition is not required if the axiom is absent. The problem described above is referred to as *qualification* problem in the AI literature.

[*]This research was supported by KBN grant 8 T11C 035 11.

The second problem we consider, i.e. *ramificatiom* problem, is strictly connected with the law of inertia. This law allows to specify effects of an action in isolation. It states that all fluents which are not explicitly mentioned in an action description remain unchanged after the action.

The presence of domain constraint axioms disturbs the law of inertia. If the action changes values of some fluents appearing in the axiom, some other fluents must be changed implicitly to make the axioms satisfied after the action.

Consider the action *shoot*. It makes the gun unloaded and the turkey dead, provided that the gun was loaded before, and does nothing otherwise. Assume now, that we have the same axiom as before, i.e. *walking* $\supset$ *alive*. After performing the action *shoot* with the gun loaded the turkey is dead. Using the axiom we conclude that it is not walking even if it was walking before. Thus, the fluent *walking* must be released from the inertia.

All these changes are dependent on the context, i.e. on domain constraint axioms imposed on the world under consideration, thus they should not be included in the description of the action. We rather need a mechanism for modelling such side effects of the action with regard to the given constraints. This is referred to as *ramification* problem in the AI literature.

It was pointed out in [12] that some constraints, instead of causing ramifications, affect the executability of an action. As the considered examples show, the same axiom may cause qualification (the first example), and ramification (the second one). The reason that we distinguish these two cases lies in the semantics of concerning fluents. We agree that *alive* may influence *walking* but not vice versa. To distinguish whether a given constrain axiom involves qualification or ramification additional information, namely *influence relation*, which define how fluents can possibly affect each other, must be provided.

The language which distinguishes between qualification and ramification has been presented in [2]. The solution to the ramification problem in the context of STRIPS-like systems has been proposed in [19]. The method described there requires completely specified situations and fails when the domain constraint axiom involves qualification, whereas our solution deals with such cases.

In this paper, to formalize effects of actions, we use Dijkstra's approach, originally developed for reasoning about programs [3, 4]. The strength of Dijkstra's proposal is its effectiveness, when compared with other approaches [18, 10, 11]. In our earlier papers [13, 14] we have employed Dijkstra's methodology to provide a general framework formalizing conventional forms of inference about action and change. In this paper we extend this approach and complete it by dealing with qualification and ramification. Although in [14] we have proposed a method for solving the ramification problem, this solution was not fully correct[1]. The method presented here is quite different and solves this problem correctly. We also show how using the influence relation to distinguish between qualification and ramification.

The paper is organized as follows. Section 2 is a brief introduction to Dijkstra's semantics for a simple programming language. In section 3 we present

---

[1] This was observed by V. Lifschitz during the presentation of [14].

formally the problem to solve and section 4 provides the solution method and a detailed algorithm of qualification and ramification. In section 5 we illustrate this method by considering a number of examples. We end in section 6 by conclusions.

Proofs of all stated results can be found in the full version of this paper.

2 Introduction to Dijkstra's semantics

In [4] we are provided with a simple programming language whose semantics is specified in terms of formula trasformers. More specifically, with each command S there are associated two formula transformers, called the *weakest precondition* and the *strongest postcondition*, denoted by wp and sp, respectively. Before providing the meaning of these transformers we introduce some terminology[2].

First of all, we assume here that the programming language under consideration contains one type of variables only, namely Boolean variables. This assumption may seem overly restrictive, but as a matter of fact no other variables will be needed for our purpose.

An *assertion language* over a set V of Boolean variables, denoted by $\mathcal{L}(\mathcal{V})$, is the set of all formulae constructable in the usual way from members of V, sentential connectives ($\neg, \supset, \wedge, \vee, \equiv$) and quantifiers ($\forall, \exists$).[3] In what follows, the term 'formula' refers always to a formula of some fixed assertion language. A formula α is said to be a *Boolean expression* if it contains no quantifiers. If β is a formula, $\alpha_1, \ldots, \alpha_n$ are Boolean expressions and $x_1, \ldots, x_n$ are variables, then we write $\beta[x_1 \leftarrow \alpha_1, \ldots, x_n \leftarrow \alpha_n]$ to denote the formula which obtains from β by simultaneously replacing all free occurrences of $x_1, \ldots, x_n$ by $\alpha_1, \ldots, \alpha_n$, respectively. A formula of the form $\exists x.\alpha$ is an abbreviation for $\alpha[x \leftarrow T] \vee \alpha[x \leftarrow F]$.

The formula transformers mentioned above are to be understood as follows. For each command S and each formula α:

- $wp(S, \alpha)$ is the formula whose models are precisely all states such that execution of S begun in any one of them is guaranteed to terminate in a state satisfying α.

- $sp(S, \alpha)$ is the formula whose models are precisely all states such that each of them can be reached by starting execution of S in some state satisfying α.

2.1 List of commands

The considered language consists of *skip* command, *assignment* to simple variables, *alternative* command and *sequential composition* of commands[4]. Semantics

---

[2] We ignore the *weakest liberal precondition* transformer, considered in [4], because it will not be used in the sequel.

[3] Note that quantifiers can be applied to Boolean variables only.

[4] The original Dijkstra's language contains *abort* and *iterative* commands as well, but they are not needed for our purpose.

of these commands is specified in terms of formula transformers defined above.

1. **The *skip* command.** This is the "empty" command in that its execution does not change the computation state. The semantics of *skip* is thus given by

$$wp(skip, \alpha) = sp(skip, \alpha) = \alpha.$$

2. **The *assignment* command.** This command is of the form $x := e$, where x is a (Boolean) variable and e is a (Boolean) expression. The effect of the command is to replace the value of x by the value of e. Its semantics is given by

$$wp(x := e, \ \alpha) = \alpha[x \leftarrow e].$$

$$sp(x := e, \alpha) = \exists y.((x \equiv e[x \leftarrow y]) \wedge \alpha[x \leftarrow y]). \tag{1}$$

If the variable x does not occur in the expression e, the equation (1) can be simplified. In this case

$$sp(x := e, \alpha) = (x \equiv e) \wedge \exists x.\alpha \tag{2}$$

In the sequel we shall often deal with assignment commands, $x := e$, where e is T or F. In this case the equation (2) can be replaced by

$$sp(x := e, \alpha) = \begin{cases} x \wedge \exists x.\alpha & \text{if } e \text{ is } T \\ \neg x \wedge \exists x.\alpha & \text{if } e \text{ is } F \end{cases} \tag{3}$$

3. **The *sequential composition* command.** This command is of the form $S_1; S_2$, where S_1 and S_2 are any commands. It is executed by first executing S_1 and then executing S_2. Its semantics is given by

$$\begin{aligned} wp(S_1; S_2, \alpha) &= wp(S_1, wp(S_2, \alpha)); \\ sp(S_1; S_2, \alpha) &= sp(S_2, sp(S_1, \alpha)). \end{aligned}$$

4. **The *alternative* command.** This command is of the form

$$\textbf{if} \quad B_1 \rightarrow S_1 \quad \| \quad \cdots \quad \| \quad B_n \rightarrow S_n \quad \textbf{fi} \tag{4}$$

where $B_1, \ldots, B_n$ are Boolean expressions and $S_1, \ldots, S_n$ are any commands. $B_1, \ldots, B_n$ are called *guards* and expressions of the form $B_i \rightarrow S_i$ are called *guarded commands*. In the sequel, we refer to the general command (4) as IF. The command is executed as follows. If none of the guards is true, then the execution aborts. Otherwise, one guarded command $B_i \rightarrow S_i$ with true B_i is *randomly* selected and S_i is executed.[5] The semantics of IF is given by

$$wp(\text{IF}, \alpha) = \bigvee_{i=1}^{n} B_i \wedge \bigwedge_{i=1}^{n} (B_i \supset wp(S_i, \alpha))$$

$$sp(\text{IF}, \alpha) = \bigvee_{i=1}^{n} (sp(S_i, B_i \wedge \alpha)).$$

---

[5]Note that when more than one guard is true, the selection of a guarded command is nondeterministic.

3 Formalization

In the AI literature actions are usualy defined as satisfying the specification $\{Pre\}\ A\ \{Post\}$, where Pre is a precondition of an action, $Post$ – a postcondition, and A is an action symbol. This precondition is treated as a condition of receiving the result represented by $Post$. If a precondition is not needed, i.e. $Pre \equiv T$, it may be empty. Sometimes an action may have more than one specification. In such a case their meaning is that according to preconditions the action produces different effects. The action A specified as $\{Pre\}\ A\ \{Post\}$ with nonempty Pre, may be represented in Dijkstra language as alternative command if $Pre \rightarrow S(A)\llbracket\neg Pre \rightarrow skip$ fi, where $S(A)$ is a command realizing the effect represented by $Post$. If we have several specifications $\{Pre_1\}\ A\ \{Post_1\},...,$ $\{Pre_n\}\ A\ \{Post_n\}$, the action A is represented in Dijkstra language as alternative command if $Pre_1 \rightarrow S(A_1)\llbracket...\llbracket Pre_n \rightarrow S(A_n)\llbracket\neg(Pre_1 \wedge ... \wedge Pre_n) \rightarrow$ $skip$ fi, where $S(A_i)$ are commands realizing the effect of $i-th$ specification of A. Thus, the action represented in Dijkstra language does not require to impose the precondition explicite, because it is embeded in its body. Its external specification is $\{T\}\ A\ \{Post'\}$[6]. In the sequel, we assume that the precondition of an action is empty, i.e. T, and by an action we mean its translation into Dijkstra language.

Let DCA be a domain constraint axiom. We require that DCA holds both before and after executing A. In general, an action A does not satisfy this condition. To satisfy it the action requires some modification or an extra condition must be imposed on its executability.

Assume next that we are provided with additional information on fluents, represented by *influence relation*. It is a transitive relation $\mathcal{I} = \{(f_i, g_i)|i = 1,...,n$, where f_i, g_i are fluents$\}$. Its meaning is that any change of the fluent g_i (called a *successor*) may influence the fluent f_i (called a *predecessor*).

Formally, we would like to solve the following task:
Assuming that $\{T\}\ A\ \{Post\}$ holds and $Post \wedge DCA \not\equiv F$,

1. modify (if possible[7]) the definition of an action A into A^R in such a way that the specification $\{DCA\}A^R\{Post \wedge DCA\}$ holds

or, if (1) is impossible,

2. impose the additional precondition Pre^Q for the action A such that the specification $\{Pre^Q \wedge DCA\}\ A\ \{Post \wedge DCA\}$ holds.

Remark 1
In the case of the modification (1) the only fluents which may be modified are those which are not affected by A, more precisely, which are not assigned new values by A, since the postcondition $Post$ must hold. The relation $\mathcal{I}$ points fluents to modify.

---

[6]The postcondition of an action A is now a suitable combination of $Post_i$, $1 \leq i \leq n$, and of an empty effect if no Pre_i holds before A.

[7]The possibility of modification(1) strictly depends on the influence relation $\mathcal{I}$.

Remark 2

Applying the alternative command notation as above, we may move a precondition Pre^Q into an action and to get an action A^Q: **if** $Pre^Q \rightarrow A \| \neg Pre^Q \rightarrow$ *skip* **fi** and A^Q satisfies $\{DCA\}\ A^Q\ \{Post \wedge DCA\}$.

4 Solution method

As we said in the previous section, the goal we want to reach is to modify an action definition in such a way that it preserves the domain constraint axiom DCA. To check whether DCA holds after performing an action A, we calculate $sp(A, DCA)$ and next, we check if $sp(A, DCA) \vdash DCA$. If the answer is positive, the action requires no modification, it preserves DCA. Otherwise, we need to generate a command (called *postfix* of A) in Dijkstra language which starting in the state satisfying $sp(A, DCA)$ ends in the state satisfying DCA. If it may be realized, we have the case of ramification. If not, we have qualification. To determine which case takes place, we use the influence relation which points fluents that can be modified. If each conjunct of DCA not implied by $sp(A, DCA)$ contains any of these fluents, their values may be modified in such a way that DCA holds. If not, all we may do is to impose an extra condition on executability of A. To find this condition we need to calculate $wp(A, DCA)$.

Before formulating the detailed algorithm we introduce some terminology.

By *clause* we mean a formula of the form $l_1 \vee \ldots \vee l_n$, $n \geq 1$, where l_i is a fluent or negation of a fluent.

Definition 1

Let $\beta \not\equiv T$ be a clause such that all fluents occuring in it are different. The command realizing a clause β, written $S(\beta)$ is obtained as follows. (Here f denotes a fluent.)

1. $n = 1$:
   $$S(l_1) \text{ is } \begin{cases} f := T \text{ if } l_1 \equiv f \\ f := F \text{ if } l_1 \equiv \neg f \end{cases}$$

2. $n > 1$:
   $S(l_1 \vee \ldots \vee l_n)$ is **if** $T \rightarrow S(l_1) \| \ldots \| T \rightarrow S(l_n)$ **fi**;
   if $T \rightarrow S(l_1) \| T \rightarrow skip$ **fi**;...; **if** $T \rightarrow S(l_n) \| T \rightarrow skip$ **fi**. ∎

We say that a clause α *absorbs* a clause β if α is a subformula of β. For instance, the clause a absorbs the clause $a \vee l$. Let α be a formula in conjunctive normal form. We write $ABS(\alpha)$ to denote the formula obtained from α by deleting all absorbed clauses. Clearly, α and $ABS(\alpha)$ are equivalent. Suppose that two clauses, α and β, have exactly one opposition. Then the *resolvent* of α and β, written $res(\alpha, \beta)$, is the clause obtained from the disjunction $\alpha \vee \beta$ by deleting the opposed fluents as well as any repeated fluents. For example, $res(\neg a \vee l, a \vee d)$ is $l \vee d$. Let α be a formula. The *canonical form of* α, written $CF(\alpha)$, is the formula obtained from α by the following construction.

1. Let β be the conjunctive normal form of α.

2. Repeat as long as possible:
   if β contains a pair δ and γ of clauses whose resolvent exists and no clause of β is a subformula of $res(\delta, \gamma)$, then $\beta := \beta \wedge res(\delta, \gamma)$.

3. Take $ABS(\beta)$. This is $CF(\alpha)$.

Theorem 1
Let α be a formula. $CF(\alpha)$ is a conjunction of all minimal clauses implied by α. ∎

Let $\mathcal{I}$ be an influence relation and A an action symbol. The *canonical form of α wrt A and $\mathcal{I}$*, written $CFI(\alpha, A, \mathcal{I})$, is the formula obtained from α by the following construction.

1. Let γ be $CF(\alpha)$.

2. Transform each conjunct of γ into the form of implication to get $\gamma = (\gamma_1 \supset \beta_1) \wedge \ldots \wedge (\gamma_n \supset \beta_n)$, where $\beta_1, \ldots, \beta_n$[8] are built of predecessors wrt fluents from A in relation $\mathcal{I}$, and $\gamma_1, \ldots, \gamma_n$ contain other fluents.

We say that DCA satisfies *an independence condition* iff $CFI(DCA, A, \mathcal{I}) = (\gamma_1 \supset \beta_1) \wedge \ldots \wedge (\gamma_n \supset \beta_n)$ satisfies the condition: if there exist i, j ($i \neq j$) such that clauses β_i and β_j have at least one opposition then either β_i and β_j are one-literal clauses or γ_i is inconsistent with γ_j[9]. This condition guarrantees that subsequent commands realizing conjuncts of DCA does not disturb results obtained by previous ones.

Algorithm 1
Let A be an action symbol, $\mathcal{I}$ an influence relation and DCA a domain constraint axiom which satisfies an independence condition.

1. Calculate $\alpha = sp(A, DCA)$.
   If $\alpha \vdash DCA$, then $A^D = A$, STOP (A preserves DCA) otherwise go to 2.

2. Transform DCA into $\gamma \equiv CF(DCA)$.

3. Cluster conjuncts of γ into three groups, some of them possibly empty, $\gamma = \gamma^Q \wedge \gamma^R \wedge \gamma^{DCA}$ such that

   (a) γ^{DCA} is the maximal subformula of γ satisfying $\alpha \vdash \gamma^{DCA}$;

   (b) no conjunct of γ^Q contains predecessors of fluents from A in the sense of relation $\mathcal{I}$;

   (c) each conjunct of γ^R contains at least one predecessor of some fluent from A in the sense of relation $\mathcal{I}$.

---

[8] If a conjunct does not contain predecessors we put $\gamma_i \supset T$.

[9] The above restriction is stated only for simplify the command realizing ramification. Omitting this limitation requires more complicated command in the case mentioned above while most of DCA satify this condition.

4. If $\gamma^Q \not\equiv T$, then (*qualification*) calculate $\beta = CF(wp(A, \gamma^Q))$ otherwise go to 8.

5. Relocate conjuncts of β receiving $\beta \equiv \beta^Q \wedge \beta^{DCA}$ such that

   (a) β^{DCA} is the maximal subformula of β satisfying $DCA \vdash \beta^{DCA}$

   (b) no conjunct of β^Q contains predecessors of fluents from A in the sense of relation $\mathcal{I}$;

6. Put A^Q: **if** $\beta^Q \rightarrow A \| \neg\beta^Q \rightarrow skip$ **fi**.

7. If $\gamma^R \equiv T$ then $A^D = A^Q$, STOP otherwise proceed in the following way

   (a) Calculate $\alpha = sp(A, DCA \wedge \beta^Q)$ and perform p. 3 and 8a, 8b of algorithm to receive A^R.

   (b) If $A \neq A^R$ (*a composition* of ramification and qualification) put $A = A^R$ to receive $A^D = (A^R)^Q$, STOP.

8. (*Ramification*) If $\gamma^R \equiv T$ then put $A^R = A$ else go to 8a.

   (a) (We generate a postfix A^* for the action A. $A^R = A; A^*$.)
   Create $CFI(\gamma^R, A, I) = (\gamma_1 \supset \beta_1) \wedge \ldots (\gamma_n \supset \beta_n)$

   (b) Put A^* as **if** $\gamma_1 \rightarrow S(\beta_1) \| \neg\gamma_1 \rightarrow skip$ **fi**; $\ldots$; **if** $\gamma_n \rightarrow S(\beta_n) \| \neg\gamma_n \rightarrow skip$ **fi**

   (c) Put $A^D = A^R$

The action A^D is a modified form of A. ∎

Theorem 2
Let the assumptions of algorithm 1 be satisfied and the action A satifies $\{T\}A\{Post\}$. The action A^D resulting from algorithm 1 satisfies $\{DCA\}A^D\{Post \wedge DCA\}$. ∎

In the next section we present some examples illustrating the presented method.

5 Examples

Example 1
The Yale Shooting scenario consists of fluents: l (*loaded*), a (*alive*), w (*walking*), and actions *load* defined as $l := T$ and *shoot* as **if** $l \rightarrow l := F; a := F \| \neg l \rightarrow skip$ **fi**. $DCA = (w \supset a)$. The scenario is $YSS = [w]load; shoot[T]$. The intended conclusion is that in the final situation $\neg w$ holds. We are provided with the relation $\mathcal{I} = \{(w, a)\}$. We calculate, for the action *load*

$$\beta = sp(load, DCA) = l \wedge (w \supset a).$$

$\beta \vdash DCA$, so *load* preserves DCA and hence does not require a modification. And for *shoot*

$$\beta = sp(shoot, DCA) = \neg l.$$

$\beta \nvdash DCA$ but $CF(DCA) \equiv (\neg w \vee a)$ contains the fluent (w) which is a predecessor in relation $\mathcal{I}$ with regard to the fluents affected explicitly by *shoot*. So, we have ramification. A postfix *shoot** is: **if** $\neg a \to w := F \llbracket a \to$ *skip* **fi**.

To reason about the final situation we need to consider the modified scenario $[w \wedge (w \supset a)]load; shoot^D[DCA]$. By Theorem 4 in [14] the description of the final state of $SC = [\alpha]A_1, \ldots, A_n[\beta]$, written $DS_n(SC)$, is the formula given by

$$DS_n(SC) = \beta \wedge sp(A_1; \ldots; A_n, \alpha)$$

Accordingly, the description of the final state of YSS is

$$
\begin{aligned}
DS_2(YSS) &= sp(load; shoot^D, w \wedge (w \supset a)) \wedge (w \supset a) \\
&\equiv sp(shoot; shoot^*, l \wedge w \wedge a) \\
&\equiv sp(shoot^*, \neg l \wedge \neg a \wedge w) \\
&\equiv \neg l \wedge \neg a \wedge \neg w.
\end{aligned}
$$

As we easily see, $DS_2(YSS) \vdash \neg w$. ∎

In the next examples we only show how to modify actions under consideration.

Example 2
We have three fluents: $sw1$, $sw2$, *light*, standing for positions of switch1, switch2 and the state of the light bulb, respectively. The action *toggle1* is defined by: $sw1 := \neg sw1$. The domain constrain axiom $DCA = (light \equiv (sw1 \equiv sw2))$. The influence relation is $\mathcal{I} = \{(light, sw1), (light, sw2)\}$.
To check whether DCA holds after *toggle1* we calculate

$$
\begin{aligned}
\beta = sp(toggle1, DCA) &= & (\neg light \vee sw1 \vee sw2) \\
& \wedge & (\neg light \vee \neg sw1 \vee \neg sw2) \\
& \wedge & (light \vee \neg sw1 \vee sw2) \\
& \wedge & (light \vee sw1 \vee \neg sw2) \\
& \equiv & \neg light \vee (sw1 \equiv \neg sw2) \\
& \wedge & light \vee (sw1 \equiv sw2)
\end{aligned}
$$

$CF(DCA) \equiv (\neg sw1 \vee sw2 \vee \neg light) \wedge (\neg sw2 \vee sw1 \vee \neg light) \wedge (sw1 \vee sw2 \vee light) \wedge (\neg sw1 \vee \neg sw2 \vee light)$

No conjunct of DCA is implied by β but each of them contains the fluent $(light)$ which may be affected by the fluent $sw1$ (see relation $\mathcal{I}$), so it is ramification. The implicational form of DCA is

$$DCA \equiv (sw1 \equiv \neg sw2) \supset \neg light \wedge (sw1 \equiv sw2) \supset light$$

We obtain a postfix *toggle1** as: **if** $(sw1 \equiv \neg sw2) \to light := F \llbracket (sw1 \equiv sw2) \to light := T$ **fi**. ∎

Example 3
The fluents, the influence relation and DCA are as in the example 1. Consider the action *walk* defined as $w := T$. Let's calculate

$$\beta = sp(walk, DCA) = w$$

$\beta \not\vdash DCA$. $CF(DCA)$ does not contain predecessors of w – the only fluent affected by $walk$. Thus, it is qualification. In order to calculate the qualification condition we calculate

$$\alpha = wp(walk, DCA) = a.$$

$walk^Q$ is realized as: **if** $a \to walk \| \neg a \to skip$ **fi**. ■

Example 4

The fluents are: l, a, w, h (standing for *hidden*). The action *shoot* is as before (ex.1). $DCA = (w \supset a) \wedge (w \equiv h)$. The relation $\mathcal{I} = \{(w, a), (w, h)\}$.

$$\beta = sp(shoot, DCA) = \neg l \wedge (\neg w \vee h) \wedge (\neg h \vee w)$$

The $CF(DCA) \equiv (\neg w \vee a) \wedge (\neg w \vee h) \wedge (\neg h \vee w) \wedge (\neg h \vee a)$. The second and the third conjuncts are implied by β, the first one contains predecessor w, so it may be realized as ramification. But the last conjunct does not contain predecessors. Thus, we have qualification and we need to calculate

$$
\begin{aligned}
\alpha &= wp(shoot, \neg h \vee a) = (\neg l \vee \neg h) \wedge (l \vee \neg h \vee a) \\
&\equiv (\neg l \vee \neg h) \wedge (l \vee \neg h \vee a) \wedge (\neg h \vee a) \\
&\equiv (\neg l \vee \neg h) \wedge (\neg h \vee a)
\end{aligned}
$$

The second conjunct is implied by DCA. $\alpha^Q \equiv (\neg l \vee \neg h)$. We have qualification with respect to $(\neg l \vee \neg h)$. $shoot^Q$: **if** $\neg l \vee \neg h \to shoot \| l \wedge h \to skip$ **fi**. To check whether the ramification is still needed we calculate $sp(shoot, DCA \wedge \alpha^Q)$.

$$
\begin{aligned}
\beta' &= sp(shoot, DCA \wedge \alpha^Q) \\
&= \neg l \wedge (\neg w \vee h) \wedge (\neg h \vee w) \wedge (\neg w \vee a)
\end{aligned}
$$

$\beta' \vdash DCA$, the ramification is not needed. ■

In the next examples we consider nondeterministic actions.

Example 5

Consider now nondeterministic action $walk$: **if** $T \to w := T \| T \to w := F$ **fi**. $DCA = (w \supset a)$. We are provided with the relation $\mathcal{I} = \{(w, a)\}$. Calculate

$$\alpha = sp(walk, DCA) = T$$

Since $\alpha \not\vdash DCA$ and $CF(DCA) = \neg w \vee a$ contains no fluent to modify, we have qualification. We need to calculate

$$\beta = wp(walk, DCA) = a$$

A^Q is **if** $a \to walk \| \neg a \to skip$ **fi**. There are no more conjuncts to realize. ■

Example 6

We have fluents: l, a, u (standing for *usable*), d (*demaged*). The action *spin* is defined as: **if** $T \to l := F; \| T \to l := T$ **fi**. $DCA = u \equiv l \wedge \neg d$. The relation $\mathcal{I} = \{(u, l), (u, d)\}$

We calculate

$$\alpha = sp(spin, DCA) = \neg u \vee \neg d$$

$CF(DCA) = (\neg u \vee l) \wedge (\neg u \vee \neg d) \wedge (u \vee \neg l \vee d)$. The second conjunct of DCA is implied by α. The remaining ones contain fluent to modify. We have ramification and A^* is **if** $\neg l \to u := F \| l \wedge \neg d \to u := T \| l \wedge d \to skip$ **fi**. ■

6 Conclusions

In this paper we have presented how to solve the qualification and ramification problems with respect to domain constraint axioms in the process of reasoning about action and change using Dijkstra's semantics for programming languages. The method provided here essentially differs from the most other methods in AI literature. Our approach is based on modification of an action definition while in the other methods one modifies the state resulting after an execution of an action. The advantage of our approach is that this modification is performed once for each action and not for each execution of an action.

Although our approach is similar to that presented in [19], we do not need that the initial state is completely specified and we admit nondeterministic actions. In contrast to the above paper, where the method fails when the domain constraint axiom involves qualification, our method properly deals with this problem. This leads to the conclusion that qualification and ramification cannot be solved separately.

Applying Dijkstra's semantics allows us to calculate precisely the executability condition for an action and also to generate a command for realizing ramification.

Acknowledgements
I would like to thank Witold Lukaszewicz for his helpful comments.

References

[1] A. B. Baker. Nonmonotonic Reasoning in the Framework of Situation Calculus, *Artificial Intelligence*, **49**, 1991, 5-23.

[2] C. Baral. Reasoning about actions: Non-deterministic effects, Constraints, and Qualification, in *Proc. IJCAI-95*, 1995, 2017-2023.

[3] E. W. Dijkstra. *A Discipline of Programming*, Prentice Hall, 1976.

[4] E. W. Dijkstra, C. S. Scholten. *Predicate Calculus and Program Semantics*, Springer-Verlag, 1990.

[5] R. E. Fikes, N. J. Nilsson. STRIPS: A New Approach to the Application of Theorem Proving to Problem Solving, *Artifficial Intelligence*, **2**, 1971, 189-208.

[6] M. Gelfond, V. Lifschitz, A. Rabinov. What Are the Limitations of Situation Calculus?, *AAAI Symposium of Logical Formalization of Commonsense Reasoning*, Stanford, 1991, 55-69.

[7] S. Hanks, D. McDermott. Nonmonotonic Logic and Temporal Projection, *Artificial Intelligence*, **33**, 1987, 379-412.

[8] J. Jabłonowski, W. Łukaszewicz, E. Madalińska-Bugaj. Reasoning about Action and Change: Defeasible Observations and Actions with Abnormal Effects. In *Proc. of 20th German Conference on Artificial Intelligence*, Springer-Verlag, Lecture Notes on Artificial Intelligence,

[9] G. N. Kartha, V. Lifschitz. Actions with Indirect Effects (Preliminary Report), in: *Proc. KR-94*, Bonn, Germany, Morgan Kaufmann Publishers, San Francisco, 1994, 341-350.

[10] V. Lifschitz. Formal Theories of Action, in: *Readings in Nonmonotonic Reasoning*, M. Ginsberg (ed.), Morgan Kaufmann Publishers, Palo Alto, 1988, 35-57.

[11] V. Lifschitz, A. Rabinov. Miracles in Formal Theories of Action, *Artificial Intelligence*, **38**, 1989, 225-237.

[12] F. Lin, R. Reiter. State constraints revisited, in: *Journal of Logic and Computation*, **4(5)**, 1994, 655-678.

[13] W. Łukaszewicz, E. Madalińska-Bugaj. Program Verification Techniques as a Tool for Reasoning about Action and Change, in: *KI-94: Advances in Artificial Intelligence, Proceedings of 18th German Conference on Artificial Intelligence*, Springer-Verlag, Lecture Notes in Artificial Intelligence, **861**, 226-236, 1994.

[14] W. Łukaszewicz, E. Madalińska-Bugaj. Reasoning about Action and Change Using Dijkstra's Semantics for Programming Languages: Preliminary Report, in *Proc. IJCAI-95*, 1995, 1950-1955.

[15] W. Łukaszewicz, E. Madalińska-Bugaj. Reasoning about Action and Change: Actions with Abnormal Effects, in: *KI-95: Advances in Artificial Intelligence, Proceedings of 19th German Conference on Artificial Intelligence*, Springer-Verlag, Lecture Notes in Artificial Intelligence, **981**, 209-220, 1995.

[16] J. McCarthy, P.J. Hayes. Some Philosophical Problems from the Standpoint of Artificial Intelligence, in: B. Meltzer and D. Michie (eds.), *Machine Intelligence* **4**, 1969, 463-502.

[17] E. Sandewall. The Range of Applicability of Nonmonotonic Logics for the Inertia Problem, in: *Proc. IJCAI-93*, 1993, 738-743.

[18] E. Sandewall. *Features and Fluents: The Representation of Knowledge about Dynamical Systems*. Oxford Logic Guides, **30**, Oxford Science Publications, 1994.

[19] M. Thielscher. Computing Ramifications by Postprocessing, in: *Proc. IJCAI-95*, 1995, 1994-2000.

[20] R. Waldinger. Achieving Several Goals Simultaneously, in: *Machine Intelligence* **8**. E. Ellock and D. Michie (eds.), 1977, 94-136.

Towards a Qualitative Representation of Linguistic Negation of Nuanced Properties

Daniel Pacholczyk

LERIA, Université d'Angers, 2 Boulevard Lavoisier,
F-49045 Angers Cedex 01, France

Abstract. In this paper, we focus our attention on Representation of Linguistic Negation of Nuanced Properties in Knowledge-Based Systems. Our Approach is based upon a Similarity Relation between Nuanced Properties through their corresponding Fuzzy Sets. By using an interactive Choice Strategy, the User can explain the intended meaning of Linguistic Negations. This Model improves the abilities in Knowledge Management in that a premise or conclusion of a Classical Rule can include Linguistic Negations.

1 Introduction

In this paper, we focus our attention on the Representation of Linguistic Negation of Imprecise Information in Knowledge-based Systems. Desmontils & Pacholczyk have proposed ([3], [4]) a System based upon Zadeh's Fuzzy Set Theory [18] and, dealing with *Affirmative Information* encoded in a Qualitative way. So, the User can refer to an assertion like « the weather is *really very* dry » . This Model is briefly presented in Section 2. Our purpose here is to improve its abilities in such a way that the User can also express Knowledge using *Negative Information*. That is to say, he can also assert that «the weather is *not* wet». In such a case, he may refer to the Fuzzy Complement Property «not wet», but very often he intends to mean another Property like «*very* dry» or «*really very* wet». Several authors (see Muller [9], Ladusaw [7], Ducrot & Schaeffer [5], Horn [6], Culioli [2], Lenzen [8], Pearce [11], Pearce & Wagner [12]) have developed methods dealing with Negation of a precise Property. In Section 3, we present the main ideas concerning these Approaches to Negation in Linguistics. Within the Fuzzy Context, some similarities could be found between our Approach and the one proposed by Torra [16].

In many cases, « x is not A » seems to have an affirmative translation of the form « x is P », where the fuzzy Property P is defined in the same domain as A, but has a *weak similarity* to A. Several authors have defined *Similarity Relations* (see Tversky [17], Baldwin & Pilsworth [1], Zadeh [20], Ruspini [14], Pacholczyk [10]). We have chosen the weakly transitive Similarity Relation proposed by Pacholczyk [10]. In Sections 4.1 and 4.2 we present the basic notions leading to the Concept of θ_i-*similarity of Fuzzy Sets*. We generate (§ 4.3) a set of ρ-*plausible Linguistic Negations* in the domain. In Section 5 we propose to the User an *Interactive Choice Strategy* of « x is P » as interpretation of « x is not A ». We give in Section 6, some Common sense Properties of our Linguistic Negation. Finally, Section 7 is devoted to the Interpretation of Rules containing Linguistic Negations.

2 The Representation of Affirmative Information

In this Section, we briefly describe the Symbolic Representation of Affirmative Information proposed by Desmontils & Pacholczyk ([3], [4]). The Discourse Universe is characterized by a finite number of concepts C_i. A set of Properties P_{ik} is associated with each C_i, whose Description Domain is denoted as D_i. The P_{ik} are said to be the *Basic Properties* connected with C_i.

A finite set of *Fuzzy Modifiers* m_α allows to define new Properties, denoted as « $m_\alpha P_{ik}$ », whose membership L-R function simply results from P_{ik} by using a translation and a contraction. We can select the following set (Fig. 1): $M_7=\{$extremely little, very little, rather little, moderately ($\emptyset$), rather, very, extremely$\}$.

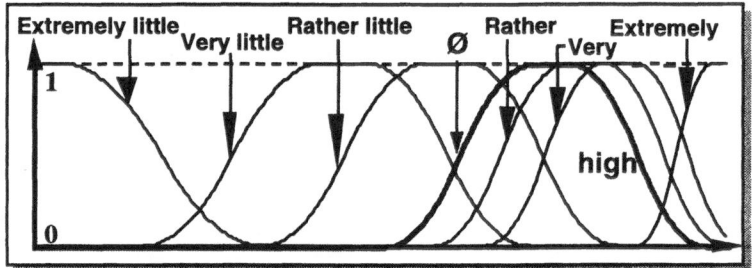

Fig. 1. Application of Fuzzy Modifiers to the Property « high »

In order to modify the Precision or Imprecision of each « $m_\alpha P_{ik}$ », we use a finite set of *Fuzzy Operators* f_α defining new Properties « $f_\alpha m_\beta P_{ik}$ ». Their membership L-R functions simply result from the ones of « $m_\beta P_{ik}$ ». The following set F_6 gives a possible choice of Fuzzy Operators (Fig. 2):

$F_6=\{$vaguely, neighboring, more or less, moderately ($\emptyset$), really, exactly $\}$.

Given a Basic Property P_{ik}, a property such as «$f_\alpha m_\beta P_{ik}$» which requires for its expression the list of linguistic terms (f_α, m_β) can be called a *Nuanced Property*.

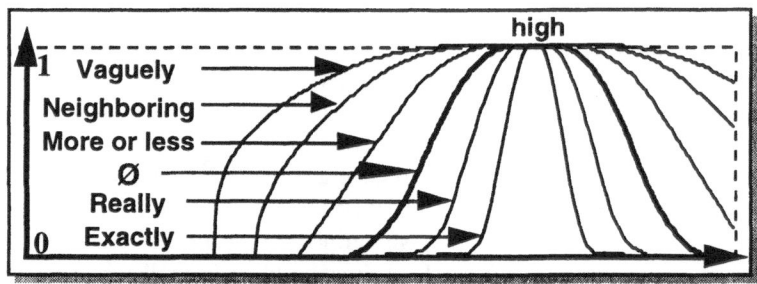

Fig. 2. Application of Fuzzy Operators to the Property « high »

So, this basic Model deals with Affirmative Information having the standard Representation presented in the Figure 3. Note that a large part of Information can be translated in this form.

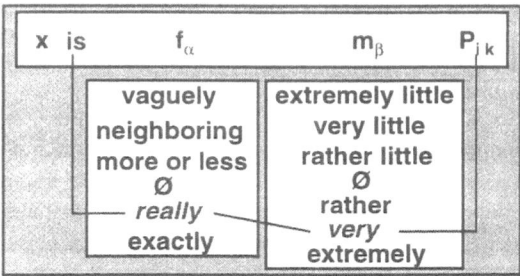

Fig. 3. Representation of Affirmative Information

3 About the Negation in Linguistics

In this Section we present the fundamental aspects resulting from the Analysis of Negation proposed in Linguistics (see Muller [14], Culioli [4], Horn [11], Ducrot and Schaeffer [7]).

3.1 Characterization of Linguistic Negation

As pointed out by previous Linguists, the Negation must be defined within a *Pragmatic Context*. More precisely, saying that « x is not A », the Speaker characterizes as Negation *i)* the *judgement of rejection* and *2)* the *semiologic means* exclusively used to notify this rejection. In other words, « x is A » is not in Adequation with Discourse Universe, but « x is not A » does not necessarily imply its Adequation with this Universe. It can only be a step in the outcome of this precise Adequation by the Speaker.

3.2 Different Interpretations of « x is not A »

We have chosen some characteristic cases to present the argumentation of previous linguists leading to the interpretations of « x is not A ». Note that we have immediately extended these results within the Fuzzy Context.

A simple rejection of « x is A ».

Saying that « John is not tired », the Speaker can *only reject* the fact « John is tired ». So, we progress weakly with the adequation of « x is not tired » to Reality.

Reference to logical ¬A.

The interpretation of the assertion « my hat is not black » is « my hat has another colour than black ». So, « x is not A » means that « x is P (colour) » with P ≠ A. The Property P is exactly ¬A. We can note that between P and A, no similarity can exist.

Linguistic Negation based upon A.

Saying that «John is not tall », the Speaker does not deny a certain height, he simply denies that his height can be high. So, his precise Adequation to Reality can be « John is *extremely little* tall ». In this case, the Speaker refers to the same Property and expresses a weak agreement between « tall » and « *extremely little* tall ».

Marked and not marked Properties.

Let us suppose that three Properties « thin », « big » and « enormous » are associated with the basic concept « weight » (Fig. 4). Then, « x is not thin » can mean that the speaker *1)* rejects « x is thin » and *2)* refers to « x is enormous » or « x is *really* big », but not to « x is *vaguely* big ». On the other hand, asserting that « x is not big » generally means that « x is thin », that is to say, the affirmative Interpretation is precise and unique. So, linguists distinguish a *marked* property like « thin » from a *not marked* property such as « big ». This distinction is important *since the Negation of not marked Property is explicitly defined.*

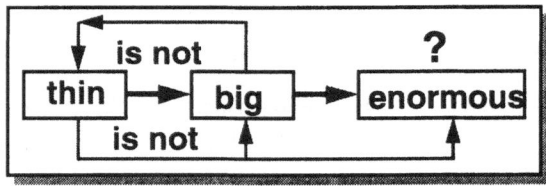

Fig. 4. Negations of Properties associated with the concept « weight »

A new property denoted as « not-A ».

When the Speaker asserts that « the tourist season is not bad », it looks like a *Negation* but it is in fact an *affirmative reference* to the new Property « not-bad ». So, the Negation of « A » can introduce *a new Basic Property* denoted as « not-A ».

4 A new Approach to Linguistic Negation

4.1 Interpretations of « x is A » and « x is not A »

As already pointed out by Scheffe [15], linguistically speaking, the statement «x is A» implies a lot of related statements. So, applying this result to Nuanced Properties, «x is A» may be interpreted as one of the statements: «x is $\varnothing$ A», «x is really A» or «x is more or less A». As an example, basic Properties such as «low», «average» and « high » can be associated with the particular concept «number of intersection points» (Fig. 5). Then, the statement « x is low » corresponds to one of the following statements: «x is $\varnothing$ low», « x is *really* low » and « x is *more or less* low ». In F_6, we can put: G_1={more or less, $\varnothing$, really } and G_2 ={vaguely, neighboring, exactly}. So, more formally we have : « x is A »$\Leftrightarrow$ { « x is f_α A » with $f_\alpha \in G_1$}.

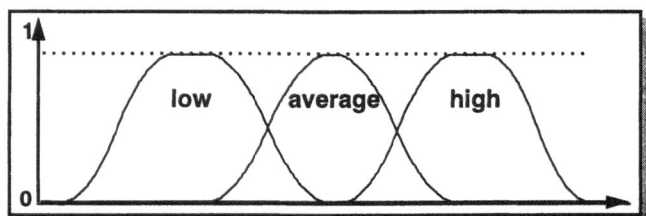

Fig. 5. Basic Properties associated with the Concept « number of intersection points »

Then, the Negation of « x is A », denoted as « x is not A », can receive the following meaning: the speaker *rejects* all previous interpretations of «x is A» and *refers to* a Nuanced Property P having a weak agreement with A and in such a way that «x is P» is equivalent to the statement « x is not A». The main difficulty is then due to the fact that P is not explicitly given.

4.2 Nuanced Similarity of Fuzzy Sets

In the following, we propose to the User a *Choice Strategy* based upon the notion of Nuanced Similarity of Fuzzy Sets. Let us recall Lukasiewicz's Implication: $u \rightarrow v = 1$ if $u \leq v$ else $1 - u + v$, where the values u and v belong to [0, 1]. The *neighborhood relation* $\mho_\alpha$ is defined in [0, 1] as follows.

Definition 1. u and v are α-*neighboring*, denoted as $u \mho_\alpha v$, if and only if, Min $\{u \rightarrow v, v \rightarrow u\} \geq \alpha$.

So, we can define the Similarity of Fuzzy Sets.

Definition 2. The Fuzzy sets A and B are said to be α-*neighboring*, and we denote this as $A \approx_\alpha B$, if and only if, $\forall x, \mu_A(x) \mho_\alpha \mu_B(x)$.

In order to define the Linguistic *Nuanced Similarity of Fuzzy Sets*, we have introduced a totally ordered partition of the interval [0, 1]:
$\{I_1, I_2, ..., I_7\} = [0] \cup]0, 0.25] \cup]0.25, 0.33] \cup]0.33, 0.67[\cup [0.67, 0.75[\cup [0.75, 1[\cup [1]$.

We have defined a one-to-one correspondence between these intervals and a *totally ordered set of Linguistic Expressions*: $\{\theta_1, ..., \theta_7\} = \{$not at all, very little, rather little, moderately (or $\varnothing$), rather, very, entirely$\}$.

Finally, we put the following definition of θ_i-similar Fuzzy Sets.

Definition 3. A and B are said to be θ_i-*similar* if and only if, $\alpha \in I_i$ knowing that $\alpha = $Max $\{\delta | A \approx_\delta B\}$.

4.3 ρ-plausible Linguistic Negations

Definition 4. Let ρ be a real such that $0.33 \geq \rho \geq 0$ and P a property defined in the same domain as A. If P satisfies the following properties:
[P1] : P and A are θ_i-similar with $\theta_i <$moderately (or $\varnothing$),   (Global Property)
[P2] : $\forall x, ((\mu_A(x) = \xi \geq 0.67 + \rho) \Rightarrow (\mu_P(x) \leq \xi - 0.67))$,   (Local Property)
[P3] : $\forall x, ((\mu_P(x) = \xi \geq 0.67 + \rho) \Rightarrow (\mu_A(x) \leq \xi - 0.67))$,   (Local Property)
then « x is P » is said to be a ρ-*plausible Linguistic Negation* of « x is A ».

Remark: Note that the values 0.33 and 0.67 are not arbitrarily chosen. The Neighborhood degree is weak if its value is less than 0.33, and strong if its value is greater than 0.67 (§ 4.2). Moreover, the Fuzzy Operators have been defined in such a way that: $\forall f_\alpha \in G_1$, P and $f_\alpha A$ will be θ_i-similar with $\theta_i \geq$moderately. So, any ρ-plausible solution rejects all previous interpretations of « x is A ».

5   An Interactive Choice Strategy

5.1   Construction of the Sets of ρ-plausible solutions

Initially, we ask the Speaker for the Possibility of Negation based upon A and we determine a value of ρ satisfying this condition. If he does not make a Choice, we include Negation based upon A by putting ρ=0.3. Thus, we can define and structure the *set of ρ-plausible Linguistic Negations* of A, denoted as **Neg**(A,ρ), by using successively the following Rules.

Simplicity Principle.

We define the set **Neg**(A,ρ) of ρ-plausible linguistic Negations P based upon *at most two Nuances of a Basic Property.*

Increasing Similarity.

For each degree θ_i with θ_i<moderately, we define the subset S_i of **Neg**(A,ρ) whose elements P are θ_i-*similar* to A.

Increasing Complexity extent.

We constitute a partition of each S_i in subsets $S_{i\,P}$ where P is a Basic Property defined in the same Domain as A. The last subset will be $S_{i\,A}$. Moreover, each $S_{i\,P}$ is reorganized in such a way that its elements appear ordered to an increasing *Complexity extent*, that is to say, the number of Nuances (different from ∅) required in their construction.

Example. The concept being «the number of intersection points», and the associated properties being « low », « average » and « high » (Fig. 5), the Choice Strategy suggests among the elements of **Neg**(low, 0.3) the solutions having 1 as Complexity collected in Figure 6.

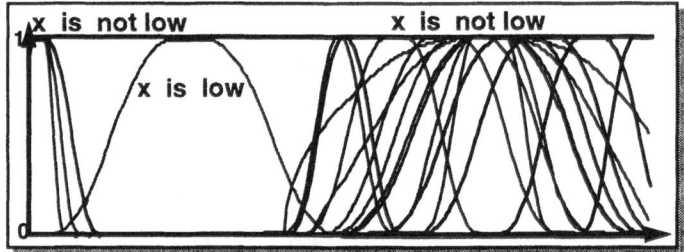

Fig. 6. Linguistic Negations of « x is low » having 1 as Complexity

Remark: For any Property A, the function of ρ is to increase (or not) the number of Nuanced Negations and to accept (or to reject) some Negations based upon A. A first Choice is made among 20 interpretations of « x is not low » when ρ= 0.3, and among 10 interpretations when ρ=0.1. So, the User can choose, for any ρ, solutions as « high », « extremely high », « exactly average », « really average », and in addition, « extremely low », « really extremely low » and « exactly extremely low » for ρ= 0.3.

Remark: The function of the *mark* i, defined in the following section, is then to select the subset of pertinent solutions.

5.2 The intended Meaning of a Linguistic Negation

The Choice Strategy, based upon the following Rules denoted **M[i]**, allows the User to explain his interpretation of a *particular occurrence* of the assertion « x is not A ». Each occurrence of « x is not A » being explained with the aid of a particular Rule **M[i]**, we associate the *mark* **i** to this particular occurrence.

An interactive Process proposes to the User the following ordered Rules.

M[0] : If the Negation is in fact the *logical Fuzzy Negation* $\neg A$, then :
- if $\neg A$ is a Property defined in the same domain as A, we propose $\neg A$,
- if not, for any P such that $P \subset (\neg A)$, we propose a Choice among the solutions of S_{iP}, i=1,2, ...

M[1] : If the Negation *is based upon* A, we propose a Choice among the solutions of S_{iA}, i=1,2, ...

M[2] : If the Negation *is based upon only one P different from A*, we ask the User for its basic Negation P. Then, his Choice has to be made among the solutions of the previous sets S_{iP}, i=1,2, ...

M[3] : If the Negation can be *based upon B* and C *different from A*, then the User has to retain his interpretation among the solutions of S_{iB} and S_{iC} where i=1,2, ...

M[4] : If the Negation can be *based upon one of all the basic properties*, his interpretation is one of plausible solutions of S_{iP} where i=1,2, ... , for any P.

M[5] : If the Negation *is in fact a New basic Property denoted as not-A*, we must ask the User for its membership L-R function.

M[6] : If the Negation is *simply the rejection* of « x is A », then any element of **Neg(A, ρ)** is a potential solution but he does not choose one of them.

M[7] : If the Negation requires a *Combination based upon two basic Properties B and C*, we ask the User for the Linguistic Operator. So, we propose a Choice among the Combination solutions of S_{iB} and S_{iC}, i=1, 2, ...

M[8] : If no Choice is made with rules **M[0]-M[4]** or **M[7]** then the System proposes a *Default Choice*.

Remark: The solutions are always proposed by increasing Complexity.

Remark: Using rule **M[6]**, no Choice is made. But, « x is not A » (without explicit translation) is however less than moderately similar to A. Then, an Inference Process based upon Similarity can deduce a conclusion when a Rule contains such an hypothesis. This aspect will be developed in a subsequent paper.

Remark: A lot of work on Linguistic Negation have already been achieved. Among these, the papers by Trillas, Lowen, Ovchinnokov and Esteva are not quoted here since very different points of view are considered. In the recent paper by Torra [16], one will find a closer point of view. First, we can give their common aspects. Our Set **Neg(A, ρ)** of ρ-plausible Linguistic Negations and the Torra Negative Function have been conceived within a Fuzzy Context in such a way that they lead to results consistent with those intuitively expected in the chosen Domain. In both cases, by using the Torra terminology, this is a function Neg from L to $\mathcal{P}(L)$, where L is a given set of Fuzzy Properties (or Linguistic Labels) and $\mathcal{P}(L)$ the set of parts of L. Note that our set **Neg**(A, ρ) takes the place of Neg(x). Moreover, in both Approaches the Torra Condition C2 holds, that is to say, if x∈ Neg(y) then y∈ Neg(x). We can now point out some essential differences. Indeed, the Model of Torra concerns the sets of totally ordered Linguistic Labels. In our Approach, we refer to Fuzzy Properties for which an order relation is of no importance. This point is enforced by the fact that the Use of Fuzzy Operators and Modifiers in the combinations of the Basic Properties creates difficulties in making a total Order. Note that our Nuanced Properties being automatically defined, the User has not to define their L-R membership functions. He has only to supply the L-R membership functions of the Basic Properties associated with each Concept. In other words, the Context of our Analysis seems to be more general that the one of Torra. We can now examine the Torra Conditions C0 and C1. Linguists have pointed out that in some cases a Linguistic Negation may be simply the rejection of « x is A ». In other words, Neg(x) can be an empty Set. Moreover, the Basic Properties, associated with the concept « height », being « low », « medium » and « high », linguists accept that Neg(medium)={low, high} (in our System Nuanced Properties based upon these Basic Properties). In this case, Neg(x) is not a Convex Function. So, our analysis based upon Natural Language does not require the Torra Condition C0. We can also recall that a Linguistic Negation can induce a new Basic Property. So, the set of Linguistic Labels cannot be considered as completely defined, and it is not sure that the order can be preserved. By using the previous Basic Properties, The Linguistic Analysis accepts the following results: Neg(medium)={low, high} and Neg(low)={medium, high}. Then, if we add the following order: low<medium<high, it is obvious that the condition C1 fails in this case. So, the Contexts of both Analyses are basically different, and the Concept of Negation of Torra, fulfilling more restrictive conditions, can be viewed as a particular restriction to ordered Labels of our Concept of Negation.

6   General Properties of the Linguistic Negation

We point out the fact that our Linguistic Negation satisfies some Common sense properties of Linguistic Negation.

Proposition 1. *Given a Fuzzy Property A, « x is A » does not define the Knowledge about « x is not A ».*

Proof. This property results directly from our construction Process of Linguistic Negation. Knowing exactly A does not imply, as does the Logical Negation, precise Knowledge of its Negation, since most of them require complementary information, as the mark of the property, and a Choice among pertinent interpretations. □

Proposition 2. *Given a Fuzzy Property A, its double Negation does not lead to A.*

Proof. Using Figure 4, the User can choose « x is thin » as the interpretation of « x is not big », and « x is enormous » as the negation of « x is thin ». □

Proposition 3. *If « x is P » is a ρ-plausible Linguistic Negation of « x is A », then « x is A » is a ρ-plausible Linguistic Negation of « x is P ». Moreover, « x is A » is a ρ-plausible double Negation of « x is A ».*

Proof. This properties result from the definition of ρ-plausible Negation. □

Proposition 4. *Given the Rule « if « x is A » then « y is B » », we can deduce that « if « y is not B » then « z is A' » » where A' is a ρ-plausible Negation of A.*

Proof. This property results from the definition of ρ-plausible Linguistic Negation. □

Remark: Our Approach to Linguistic Negation gives us a *Pragmatic Model* leading to results consistent with those intuitively expected, and this, within the Context of Nuanced Fuzzy Properties. Its integration in Many-valued Predicate Logics is actually being examined. Our objective is to define a new Adequate Fuzzy Negation Operator having Properties like the one proposed in a logical Approach to the Negation of Precise assertions (see Lenzen [8], Pearce [11], Pearce & Wagner [12]). At this point, we can point out that Propositions 1-4 give us the first results as the Basis of a possible formalization within a Many-valued Logics.

7   Dealing with Linguistic Negation

In this Section, we suppose that the Knowledge Base is the one collected in Figure 7. It is clear that a classical Deductive Process, based upon affirmative assertions, cannot deduce conclusions by using the current Facts and Rules. But, it is easy to show that our interpretation of Linguistic Negations appearing in Facts and Classical Rules does not generally modify the use of the existing Deductive Process, since all Information can receive Affirmative translations.

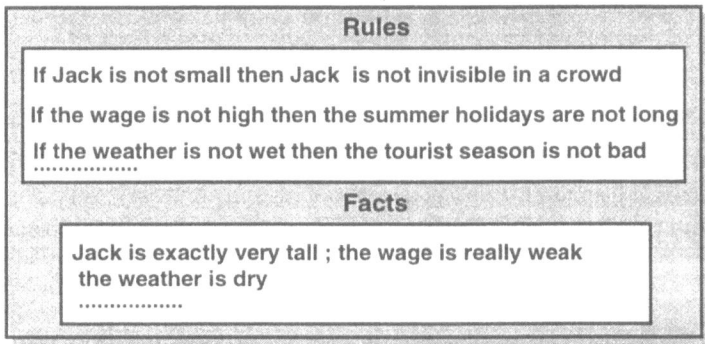

Rules

If Jack is not small then Jack is not invisible in a crowd

If the wage is not high then the summer holidays are not long

If the weather is not wet then the tourist season is not bad

Facts

Jack is exactly very tall ; the wage is really weak
the weather is dry

Fig. 7. A Knowledge Base

Let us now analyse this Knowledge Base in different situations. Please note that in the following Figures 8-11, the lines specify the direction of the plausible Negations and the angles stand for subsets of Nuanced Properties. Moreover, the User Choices leading to the intended Meanings of Linguistic Negations appear in Brackets.

The Intended Meaning of the Rule I

This Rule refers to the concepts « height » and « appearance ». The associated properties have been collected in Figure 8. The User Choices lead to an equivalent Rule only using Affirmative Information. Finally, knowing that the first Fact is true, a classical Modus Ponens Rule (see Zadeh [19]) allows us to deduce that « Jack is extremely visible in a crowd ».

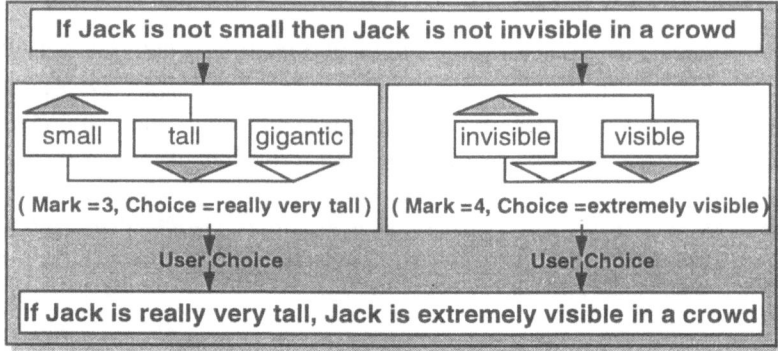

Fig. 8. User Choices for the Rule I

Different Interpretations of the Rule II

In the same way, the User Choices can lead to the intended Meaning of the Rule II (see Fig. 9). But, in this case, the previous Deductive Process cannot lead to a Deduction expressed in terms of a Nuanced Property based upon a precise Basic Property.

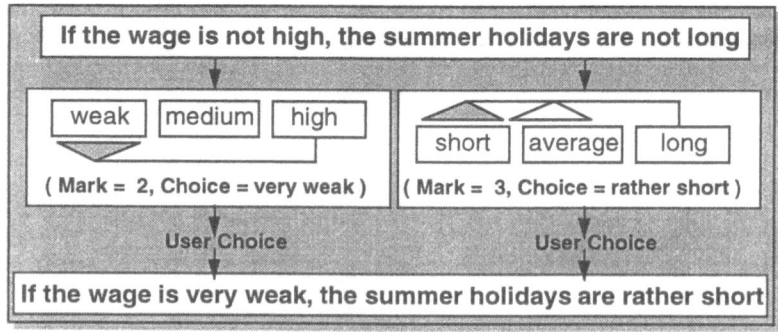

Fig. 9. User Choices for the Rule II

Let us now illustrate the actual implementation of the *Default Choice Strategy* proposed by the System. It defines as Intended Meaning of a Linguistic Negation, a disjunction of the basic Properties having the lowest Complexity Degree. So, because the User has not chosen explicit Interpretations, the System creates the Rule (equivalent to the Rule II) appearing in Figure 10. However, knowing that the « the wage is really weak » is true, we can deduce in this case that « the summer holidays are short or average ».

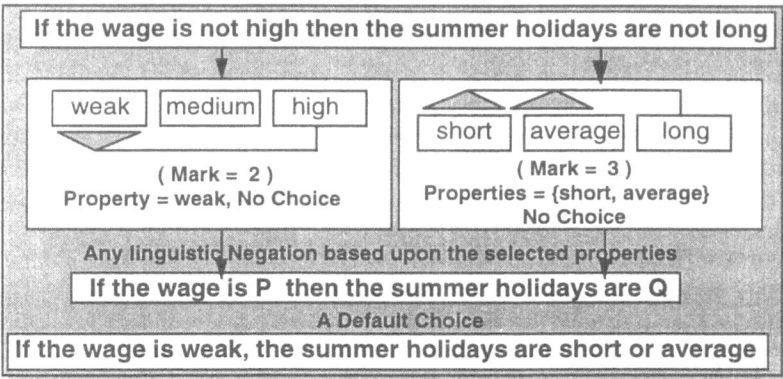

Fig. 10. Default Choices

Definition of a New Basic Property though the Rule III

This example illustrates the particular case leading to the definition of a new Basic Property (Fig. 11). Initially, the User has only associated the Basic Properties « bad » and « good » to the Concept « tourist season ». The User Choices mean that « not bad » is not a Linguistic Negation. So, he has to define the L-R Representation of the Basic Property « not-bad ». This being done, knowing that the fact « the weather is dry » is true, the System can deduce that « the tourist season is not-bad » is also true.

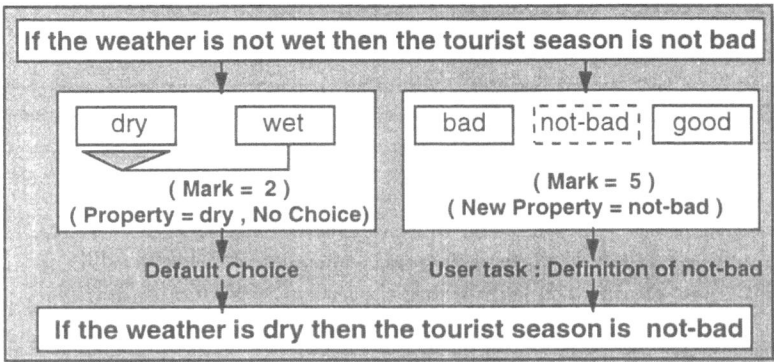

Fig. 11. A new Basic Property

Remark: The previous examples point out that information does not necessarily correspond with the Premise of Rules. In other words, a Deductive Process founded upon some Generalized Modus Ponens Rule (like Zadeh's [19]) creates difficulty in making useful Deductions in terms of the Basic Properties of the Discourse Universe. Note that we are actually achieving a variant of Zadeh's deductive Process *via* the previous Similarity of Nuanced Properties.

Remark: It seems that our Approach to Linguistic Negation can be applied to Default Reasoning (Reiter [13]). This point is also actually on Study.

8 Conclusion

We have presented an Approach to Negative Information based upon a Similarity Relation. So, the User can refer to Linguistic Negations, since a Choice Strategy allows him to explain their intended meanings. This Model improves the abilities in the Management of a Knowledge Base in that a premise or a conclusion of a classical Rule can include Linguistic Negations.

References

1. Baldwin J. F., Pilsworth B. W.: Axiomatic approach to implication for approximate reasoning with fuzzy logic. Fuzzy Sets and Systems **3** (1980) 193-219
2. Culioli A.: Pour une linguistique de l'énonciation: Opérations et Représentations. Tome 1 Ophrys Eds. Paris (1991)
3. Desmontils E., Pacholczyk D.: Apport de la théorie des ensembles flous à la modélisation déclarative en Synthèse d'images. Proc. LFA'96 Nancy (1996) 333-334
4. Desmontils E., Pacholczyk D.: Modélisation déclarative en Synthèse d'images: traitement semi-qualitatif des propriétés imprécises ou vagues. Proc. AFIG'96 Dijon (1996) 173-181
5. Ducrot O., Schaeffer J.-M. et al.: Nouveau dictionnaire encyclopédique des sciences du langage. Seuil Paris (1995)
6. Horn L.R.: A Natural History of Negation. The Univ. of Chicago Press (1989)
7. Ladusaw W.A.: Negative Concord and « Made of Judgement ». Negation, a notion Focus. H. Wansing, W. de Gruyter eds. Berlin (1996) 127-144
8. Lenzen W.: Necessary Conditions for Negation Operators. Negation, a notion in Focus. H. Wansing, W. de Gruyter eds. Berlin (1996) 37-58
9. Muller C.: La négation en français. Publications romanes et françaises Genève (1991)
10. Pacholczyk D.: Contribution au traitement logico-symbolique de la connaissance. Thèse d'Etat Paris 6 (1992)
11. Pearce D.: Reasoning with negative information II: Hard Negation, Strong Negation and Logic Programs. LNAI **619** Berlin (1992) 63-79
12. Pearce D., Wagner G.: Reasoning with negative information I: Hard Negation, Strong Negation and Logic Programs, Language, Knowledge, and Intentionality: Perspectives on the Philosophy of J. Hintikka. Acta Philosophica Fennica **49** (1990) 430-453
13. Reiter R.: A Logic for Default Reasoning. Artificial Intelligence **13** (1980) 81-132
14. Ruspini E. H.: The Semantics of vague knowledge. Rev. int. De Systémique **3:4** (1989) 387-420
15. Scheffe P.: On foundations of reasoning with uncertain facts and vague concepts. Fuzzy Reasoning and its Applications (1981) 189-216
16. Torra V.: Negation Functions Based Semantics for Ordered Linguistic Labels. Int. Jour. of Intelligent Systems **11** (1996) 975-988
17. Tversky A.: Features of Similarity. Psychological Review **4** (1977)
18. Zadeh L.A.: Fuzzy Sets. Inform. and Control **8** (1965) 338-353
19. Zadeh L.A.: PRUF-A meaning representation language for natural languages. Int. J. Man-Machine Studies **10:4** (1978) 395-460
20. Zadeh L.A.: Similarity relations and Fuzzy orderings. Selected Papers of L. A. Zadeh **3** (1987) 387-420

CBET: A Case Base Exploration Tool*

Paolo Avesani, Anna Perini and Francesco Ricci

Istituto per la Ricerca Scientifica e Tecnologica
Via Sommarive
38050 Povo (TN)
Italy
{avesani,perini,ricci}@irst.itc.it

Abstract. CBET is a software tool for the interactive exploration of a case base. CBET is an integrated environment that provides a range of browsing and display functions that make possible knowledge extraction from a set of cases. CBET is motivated by an application to training firemen. Here cases describe past forest fire fighting interventions and CBET is used to detect dependencies between data, acquire practical planning competences, visualize complex data, clustering similar cases. In CBET well rooted Machine Learning techniques for selecting relevant features, clustering cases and forecasting unknown values have been adapted and reused for case base exploration.

1   Introduction

This paper describes CBET (Case Base Exploration Tool), a system grown from the results of CHARADE, a decision support system for controlling environmental emergencies. A demonstrator based on the CHARADE platform was developed for managing forest fires emergencies [8]. A major component of the CHARADE demonstrator is a Case-Based Reasoning system for planning first interventions to forest fires. Case-Based Reasoning is a general problem solving methodology that searches for a solution of a problem by first retrieving a similar problem stored in a memory of cases and then adapting the solution found to the new problem [1]. When a forest fire is detected CHARADE retrieves similar emergencies from the memory and builds a plan through an interactive process where the user makes strategical choices and the system checks and propagates domain constraints.

An extensive evaluation of the system showed that, in this application domain, users are not keen to accept the system solutions even if those proposals can be even completely changed by user interaction. We were forced to reconsider the usefulness of the CHARADE case base. Rather that using it inside a program for building *solutions* we realized that the user needs a tool for *learning* how to plan first interventions and acquire knowledge from the data stored in the case base. For that reason we moved from a strict CBR paradigm to a

---

* This work has been partially supported by the EspritIV project CARICA #20401 (Cases Acquisition and Replay in Fire Campaign Ambiance).

KDD system [5]. Knowledge Discovery in Database (KDD) refers to the overall process of discovering useful knowledge from data, mapping low-level data into other forms, more compact, more abstract and more useful. A case base, a product of the CBR methodology, is a rich source of information that can be reused outside a strict CBR paradigm, it can be "mined" with KDD techniques. CBR tools can be used for that goal, but some changes are needed. For instance, the retrieval algorithm, the primary component of a CBR system, must discover similar case, but similarity must be redefined query by query according to the the target information searched by the user.

Case bases store knowledge combining numerical and symbolic data and often they adopt case representations based on complex structures (graph, semantic net) [3]. In our domain, for example, graphics is largely used to describe both the assessment of the emergency situation and the reaction plan. A set of icons displaced on a map illustrate the deployment of the resources and the activity they are engaged to. We argue that a rich description, plus a large collection of cases, become a real obstacle to the process of learning from the past experience contained in a case base.

In this paper we show how combining case-based reasoning and knowledge-discovering techniques can help significantly both teachers and students to acquire the knowledge contained in a case base. In our application, cases record the forest fire emergencies occurred in a department of the Southern France. Manipulation, browsing and enquiring tools enable users to directly extract knowledge in the form of: feature mutual dependencies; clusters and prototypes existing in the case base; feature statistical descriptors; results of CBR queries. In fact, the major focus of the system is retrieval for learning, that is addressed by using both CBR and KDD techniques. So for example retrieval based on a Nearest Neighbor algorithm, a standard techniques in CBR [2], can be supported by a selection of relevant features, performed with statistical and information theory algorithms [15]. CBET supports the user from the definition of the data structures, to the modification and maintenance of the case base.

The paper is organized as follow. Section 2 presents the main CBET functions by following an example in the forest fire domain. Section 3 reviews the techniques implemented in CBET for case retrieval, feature weighting, clustering and plotting. We end the paper with a discussion of the main contributions of CBET and future developments.

2 An Example: Fire Fighting

In this Section we illustrate the CBET functions by going through a typical interaction with the system.

2.1 Case Base Loading

Cases bases are stored in two different formats. The first, (raw) is a flat text file used mainly to import data from other systems. The second (qbe) is a richer

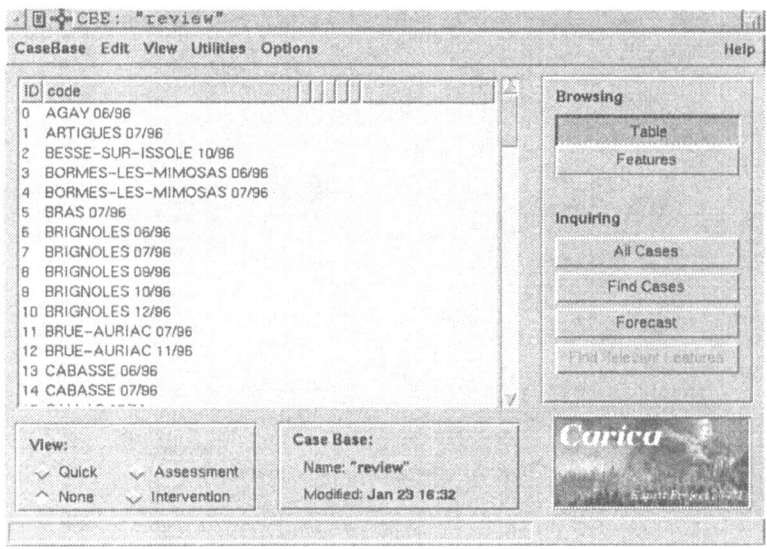

Fig. 1. The table browsing modality.

format that stores both data and info on data, e.g. feature relevance, feature distribution, etc. We shall refer to a case as a vector of feature values (e.g. `case1 = <id = 10232, hour = 15, risk-index = 5, .... >`), where a feature denotes a property of cases.

Many case bases can be loaded simultaneously, enabling parallel exploration of different knowledge sources. CBET supports editing actions like deleting a feature or creating a new feature whose values are obtained by the application of an arbitrary user defined function.

2.2 Case Base Browsing

A case base can be browsed in two modalities: table and features. The *table* modality shows a table where the columns display features (values) and the rows are cases (in Figure 1, "ID" and "code" features are shown). The user can select the features to show and the order in which they must appear on the table. That enables a simple customization of the interface.

In the second modality all the feature descriptors are listed. This provides another perspective to the information contained in the case base, which would help, for example, in selecting the most appropriate features to show in the *table* modality. A closer look to a feature is provided by another panel that shows summary information on the feature: maximum value, minimum value, type, the presence of missing values, mean, median, etc.

The system can also show summary information on a selected case (see Figure 2). In the Forest Fire application this panel shows a simple map of the zone

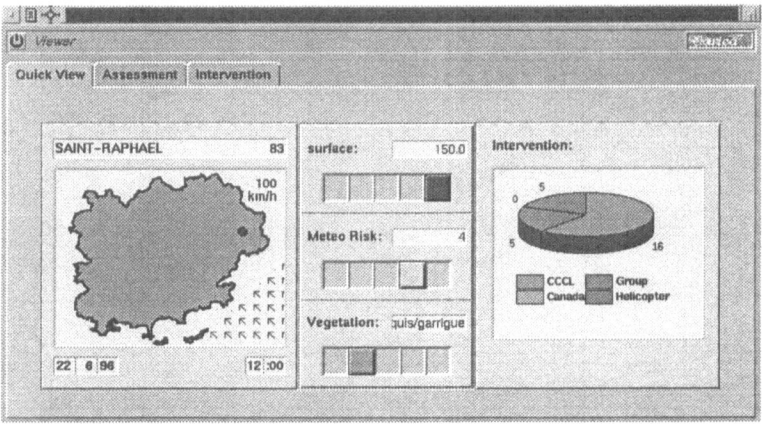

Fig. 2. The quick view panel.

surrounding the fire with the location of the fire and the description of the wind direction and speed. It also shows the values of the "surface", "meteo risk" and "vegetation" features and a pie chart of the types of resources used in the intervention.

A fire emergency is normally *assessed* by people in a control center by running mathematical models that forecast the fire evolution and by checking the state of the resources (human, aerial and ground means). That information and the description of the intervention made are described in other application oriented panels.

2.3 Plotting

Many different types of plots can be showed with CBET. For example, simple feature histograms can be shown for assessing the distribution of both numerical and symbolic features. Two dimensional plots of numerical features can also be showed. When one of the two features to plot has symbolic values CBET shows the distributions (histograms) of the numeric feature values conditioned to the different values of the symbolic feature. It results a set of histograms (one for each different value of the symbolic feature) that show the influence of the symbolic feature on the distribution of the numeric feature. Finally if two numeric features are plotted a third symbolic feature can be shown by using different icons.

2.4 Finding Relevant Features

CBET can show dependencies between data contained in a case base, i.e. how the variation of a feature impact on another. The user must select the target feature (the feature he/she is interested in) and the algorithm to be used for evaluating the relevance of the other features in describing the behavior of the

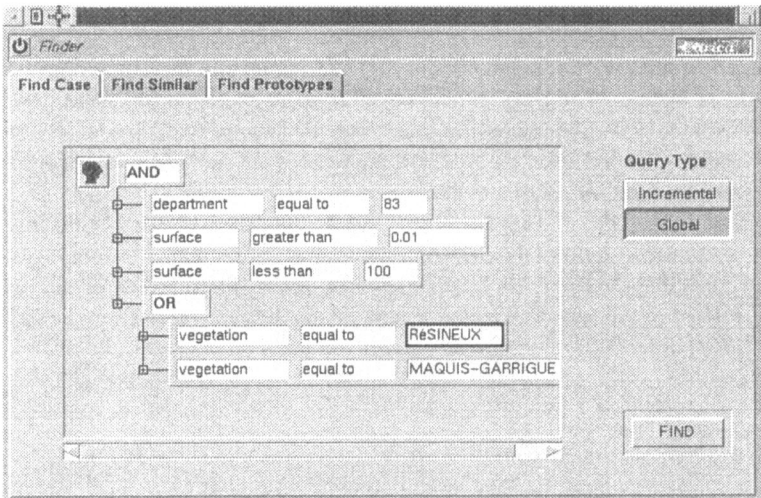

Fig. 3. A query by example.

target. The result can be viewed in two ways: as an ordered list of features, or with a plot showing for each feature the precise value of the relevance. The evaluation of the relevance of features can be also stored in the case base, so next time these data can be only retrieved from the information stored in the case base. [2]

In a similar way the relevance of pairs of features can be estimated. This provides an heuristic for deciding what pairs of features produce the most clear and effective plots.

2.5 Searching the Case Base

CBET searches a case base in two ways: the classical query by example and the case base search. Queries by example like that depicted in Figure 3 can be easily composed.

A second type of search is the "fuzzy" search performed by a nearest neighbor algorithm with feature relevance computed as described before. Every case can be selected as probe to search for similar cases. Some feature values of the selected case and feature relevance can also be modified, therefore building a completely new case (probe).

---

[2] This a very general technique: one can always store the result of the the most computational expensive algorithms and access them afterwards without recomputing it.

2.6 Finding Prototypes and Forecasting Values

Searching for prototypes is another important function supported by CBET. A prototype is a case that have a cluster of similar cases in the case base. These similar cases can be described by referring to this prototype. The prototypes created can be loaded and the partition of cases in the clusters represented by prototypes can also be shown to the user.

The last collection of functions in CBET are those related with forecasting of unknown feature values. In order to solve this problem a classifier is built and then the classifier is used for evaluating the most likely value of the unknown feature. CBET supports the many types of classifiers, including: k-NN and IB family, ID3, C4.5, NGE.

3 Techniques

In this Section we describe the major groups of techniques used in CBET. As we have shown in Section 2 they can be grouped in five classes: retrieval; feature selection; clustering; graphics; value forecasting. In this paper we concentrate on the first three.

3.1 Retrieval

Case-Base retrieval is a central activity for knowledge acquisition and learning from a case-base. Case-base retrieval consists of looking for a set of cases that are in the case-base and are similar to a given partially described case (probe). Case-base retrieval relates to Information Retrieval and DBMS querying. In fact, new approaches are trying to integrate CBR and Information retrieval [11]. CBET provides both ways to case retrieval: query by example (QBE) and nearest neighbor (NN).

QBE is one traditional approach to query a data base. CBET allows this type of query: the user provides ranges for a set of features and the system returns those cases that satisfy the given constraints. The result of a QBE is a new case base and can be further queried by QBE or NN, or can be used for other studies supported by CBET.

Nearest Neighbor is a common algorithm in Pattern Recognition [4] and Case-Based Reasoning[1]. Given a set of cases $X = \{x_1, \ldots, x_n\}$ and a probe case y, NN searches in X for the k most similar cases to y. Similarity is defined by means of a distance function, $(\sum_{i=1}^{m} w_i d_i(x_{ij}, y_i)^2)^{1/2}$, where $d_i(x_{ij}, y_i)$ is the distance between the $i-$th feature values, x_{ij} is the value of the i-th feature of the j-th case, m is the number of features, w_i is a weight used for balancing feature relevance.

- **The feature distance.** Feature values are compared by using the feature distances d_i. If the $i-$th feature is numeric then $d_i(x_{ij}, y_i) = |x_{ij} - y_i|/r_i$, where r_i is the range of the $i-$th feature values. Otherwise $d_i(x_{ij}, y_i) = 0$ if $x_{ij} = y_i$ and $d_i(x_{ij}, y_i) = 1$ if $x_{ij} \neq y_i$. If x_{ij} or y_i are missing then

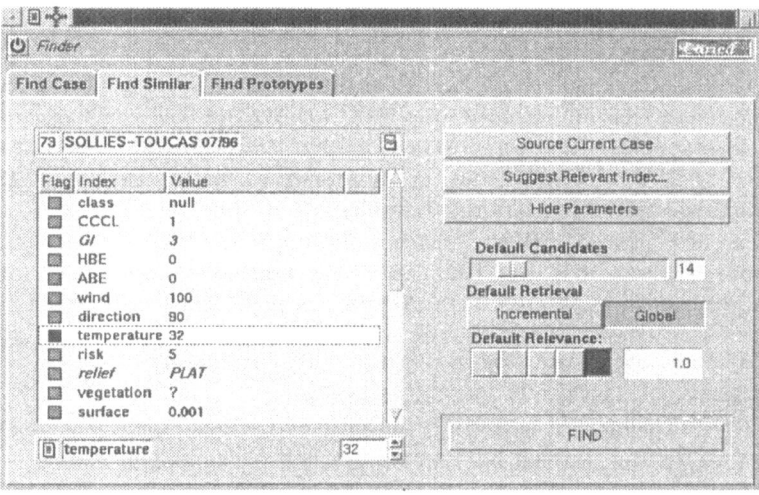

Fig. 4. Changing the relevance the "temperature" feature in searching for a similar case.

$d_i(x_i, y_i) = 0.5$. Missing values originates from missing information in the case base or from the fact that the probe y is normally only partially defined, i.e., some features' values are not specified.

- **The feature relevance.** The contribution to the total distance given by the i-th feature value distance is weighted by the positive constant w_i. There is a vast literature on feature weighting [15] and a number of different distance functions can be defined by varying the weights. Case bases are often used for classification tasks, i.e. a symbolic feature f_T (class) in the probe is unknown and the f_T feature value of the nearest neighbor provides a prediction of f_T in the probe. In nearest neighbor classification weights are chosen in such a way that the classification accuracy is maximized (learning weights).

CBET retrieval has not been primarily designed for classification, even if that can be supported. Retrieval, generally speaking, must satisfy user's information needs. For that reason we have developed a number of different approaches to feature weighting that are targeted to the satisfaction of the user information needs when a query is executed by the system. We describe these techniques in the next section.

3.2 Feature Selection and Weighting

Cases are described by a set of numeric and symbolic features. A central problem in Machine Learning relates to the identification of those features that provide predictive or descriptive value for a given target feature [7]. In CBET feature selection and more in general feature weighting [15] has two types of applications. First, in retrieval, when features are to be balanced in computing the similarity function. Second, when data are to be visualized we must identify the most relevant dimensions along which to plot data.

Feature selection and weighting algorithms can be divided into two general classes: filter models and wrapper models [7]. Filter models selects relevant features before applying the chosen induction algorithm. Conversely wrapper models search for a good subset using the induction algorithm itself as part of the evaluation function. Even if wrapper models seem more accurate as the bias of the feature selection algorithm matches the induction algorithm they are not easily applicable to CBR. In CBET, feature weighting is mainly used inside the retrieval process where there is no reasonable definition of classification accuracy with respect to adapt the weights. Therefore, filter models seem more appropriate to CBET, moreover they are computationally cheaper and are based on some general theory of data correlation and relevance.

We have implemented in CBET weighting methods based on Information Theory. Assume that the user is *focussed* on a feature f_T, and he/she is interested in discovering what features may account for the behavior of f_T. Let us assume first that f_T is discrete and finite (symbolic features), in this situation we have borrowed some ideas from the theory of top down induction of decision trees (TDIDT) for classification [14]. A decision tree recursively selects a feature and partitions the data set into many subsets as the number of possible values of the chosen (discrete) feature. A central problem in TDIDT is therefore selecting features in such a way that the associated partition maximize a given "purity" objective function.

We hypothesize that the features that maximize the "purity" objective functions used for TDIDT can be also valuable for evaluating the relevance of feature when the user is generally interested in judging what are the most important features for understanding the behavior of f_T. We present in the following the functions used in CBET for evaluating feature relevance.

The *info* of the distribution of the f_T values is defined as:

$$Info(f_T) = -\sum_{j=1}^{k} p(j) \log_2(p(j)) \tag{1}$$

where $p(j)$ is the probability of value j among the possible values of f_T [9]. The information brought by a feature f_d with values $\{x_{d1}, \ldots, x_{dm}\}$ is defined:

$$Entropy(f_d) = -\sum_{j=1}^{k}\sum_{i=1}^{m} p(x_{di})p(j|x_{di}) \log_2(p(j|x_{di})) \tag{2}$$

where $p(x_{di})$ is the probability of observing x_{di} given that f_d is not unknown, i.e. given that $x_{di} \neq ?$. In TDIDT test on continuous features are usually performed by selecting a threshold and dividing the cases into those whose value of feature f_d is greater of the threshold and those whose value is less than the threshold

[9]. We have followed a different approach, we discretize the feature f_d into a finite number of values and then we apply the above definitions. [3]

A first index of the relevance of feature f_d in describing feature f_T is given by the Information Gain [9]:

$$Gain(f_T, f_d) = (1 - p(f_d =?))(Info(f_T) - Entropy(f_d)) \qquad (3)$$

where $p(f_d =?)$ is the probability that feature f_d has unknown value. So features f_d that have high information gains provide more knowledge to the understanding of the behavior of f_T. It is well known that the Gain criterion tend to favor features with many outcomes. The Information Gain Ratio has been introduced for overcoming that problem.

$$GainRatio(f_T, f_d) = \frac{Gain(f_T, f_d)}{SplitInfo(f_d)} \qquad (4)$$

where SplitInfo is

$$SplitInfo(f_d) = - \sum_{i=1}^{m+1} p'(x_{di}) \log_2(p'(x_{di}))$$

and $p'(x_{di})$ is the a priori probability of x_{di} (unknown is treated as another possible value of f_d). SplitInfo is the information generated by dividing the case base into as many subsets as the number of possible values of f_d.

CBET uses also another index for evaluating features, namely the Calinski-Harabasz. This index has been used in clustering for evaluating how well the classes (different values of f_T), regarded as clusters, are separated in a dataset[12]. In our application, clusters are defined by grouping cases having equal values of the feature f_d (continuous features are dealt with discretization). The Index is defined as:

$$CH(f_T, f_d) = (TraceB/(g - 1))/(TraceW/(n - g)) \qquad (5)$$

Where $Trace$ is the trace of the matrix (the sum of the diagonal elements); W and B are the within-class covariance matrix and the between-classes covariance matrix respectively [10]; n is the number of cases and g is the number of different values of f_d

In case of f_T is numeric more classical statistical indices of correlation are used. We describe here only the use made in CBET of the Mean Squared Error. The MSE is given by the following:

$$MSE(f_T, f_d) = \sum_{i=1}^{g} p_i \sigma^2(X_i) \qquad (6)$$

where $\bigcup_{i=1}^{g} X_i = X$ is a partition of the case base X, $p_i = |X_i|/|X|$ and σ^2 is the variance of the feature f_T in X_i. The sets X_i are produced by splitting

---

[3] Many alternative discretization algorithms can be selected through the CBET user interface.

a continuous feature f_d in g equally spaced bins, or by grouping together the values of f_T that are paired with equal values of f_d (i.e. $X_i = \{x_T \; : \; x_d = i\}$). The littler the MSE the better correlation between features f_d and f_T.

So, resuming the process, when the user want to retrieve cases, the focus of the user is acquired, i.e. the target feature f_T. For example if the planning techniques for forest fire fighting are the focus, the number of firemen involved or the total area burned can be the target feature. The other features are then weighted with one of the methods described above. The weights are computed and fed into the distance definition used for Nearest Neighbor retrieval to finally run the search.

3.3 Clustering

Usually case base systems do not provide any indication about the distribution of cases in the features' space. Exploring a new case base this information can help focusing on a smaller subset of "significantly" different cases. The same problem occurs when we examine the result of some query to a case base: if the answer is represented by a wide collection of cases we need to identify quickly the variability of cases. Moreover, it could be useful to summarize the answer replacing similar cases by a barycentric prototype.

Clustering means grouping together cases that possess strong internal similarity. In order to cluster data we must be able to decide if a given case is more similar to the examples in one cluster rather than those in another. That yields two issues: first, defining a similarity measure between cases; second, a partitioning criteria to divide a set of examples into two clusters.

In CBET we have borrowed two methods: COBWEB [6] and RPCL (Rival Penalized Competitive Learning) [17], they are based on unsupervised and supervised learning techniques respectively [14].

COBWEB organizes the examples into a hierarchy using four kind of operators: *incorporate* when an examples fits well into an existing cluster; *create* when an examples has very different characteristics from any existing example in the current cluster; *merge* when the hierarchy is overly branched and combining two clusters provides a better one; *split* when the hierarchy contains a cluster that is too general and therefore less accurate than breaking it into two clusters. COBWEB scores alternative operators to apply to a case with an evaluation function called *category utility*. This function is defined as follows:

$$CU = 1/n(\sum_{k=1}^{n} P(C_k) \sum_i \sum_j P(f_j = x_{ij}|C_k)^2 - \sum_i \sum_j P(f_i = x_{ij})^2)$$

where $P(C_k)$ is the probability of occurrence of a particular cluster C_k, $P(f_j = x_{ij}|C_k)$ is probability of observing a particular feature value x_{ij} in the cluster C_k, and $P(f_i = x_{ij})$ is the a priori probability of observing the feature value x_{ij}.

The first sum represents the probability to correctly guess the feature values given the cluster membership, the second one the probability to correctly guess the feature values without any cluster knowledge. Category utility gives a high score to partitions which maximize similarity among cluster examples (intra-cluster similarities) and dissimilarity between examples of different clusters (inter-cluster dissimilarities). This function trades off the *predictiveness* of each feature value (the probability of an example to be a member of a cluster given its feature value) and the *predictability* of the value (the probability of the value, given that an example is a member of a cluster).

RPCL algorithm is an adaptive version of the classical *k-means* clustering algorithm. RPCL addresses and solves a limitation of *k-means*, i.e. the need to hypothesize, before starting clustering, the right number of clusters. RPCL starts by randomly choosing a set of k, p_i for $i = 1, \ldots, k$, candidate prototypes. Then an iterative procedure executes the following three steps:

Step 1: randomly take a case x in the case base and select the closest prototype p_c to x (Euclidean metric).

Step2: if $f_T(x) = f_T(p_c)$ then update the selected candidate prototype $p_c := p_c + \alpha_c(x - p_c)$

Step3: if $f_T(x) = f_T(p_c)$ and also the second closest prototype p_s has $f_T(x) = f_T(p_s)$ then update also $p_s := p_s - \alpha_r(x - p_s)$.

α_c and α_r are two positive (< 1) constants called learning rates for the winner and rival respectively. While p_c moves towards x the second closest is moved far from x. The rival penalized mechanism tries to prevent that two prototype move both towards the center of the same cluster. At the same time when the number of the initially selected prototypes is larger than the number of clusters in the given case base, the RPCL algorithm automatically selects the correct number of prototypes.

The prototype candidates are abstract representations of cases. They don't really belong to the case base but could be considered as a generalization of all the examples in the cluster represented by a prototype. The final set prototypes used by CBET are then obtained replacing each prototype with its nearest neighbor case.

4 Conclusions

In this paper we have presented CBET a tool aimed at the exploration of rich and complex sources of knowledge (case bases). CBET is based on the application of a range of Machine Learning techniques including: feature weighting, clustering, classification. We have illustrated the application of CBET to a real problem: acquiring competence in fire fighting techniques.

CBET has been integrated with another tool for knowledge acquisition (not described here) that makes simple the acquisition of cases in the fire fighting domain. In this way CBET completes the learning cycle, from case acquisition to knowledge discovery. Our primary future objective is a thoroughly evaluation with the user. The goal is to score alternative algorithms for feature weighting and clustering according to the user evaluation and to compare that results with more abstract (Machine Learning) indicators.

We also aim to introduce a better metric for dealing with symbolic features. That will mimic the VDM metric [13] and could be integrated with other metrics on numerical features following the approaches proposed in [16].

References

1. Agnar Aamodt and Enric Plaza. Case-based reasoning: foundational issues, methodological variations, and system approaches. *AI Communications*, 7(1):39–59, 1994.
2. David W. Aha, Dennis Kibler, and Mark K. Albert. Instance-based learning algorithms. *Machine Learning*, 6:37–66, 1991.
3. L. K. Branting. Techniques for the retrieval of structured cases. In *Working Notes of the AAAI Spring Symposium on Case-Based Reasoning*, Palo Alto, CA, 1990.
4. B. V. Dasarathy, editor. *Nearest neighbor (NN) norms: NN pattern classification techniques*. IEEE Computer Society Press, Los Alamitos, CA, 1991.
5. Usama Fayyad, Gregory Piatetsky-Shapiro, and Padhraic Smyth. From data mining to knowledge discovery in databases. *AI Magazine*, pages 37–54, fall 1996.
6. Douglas H.Fisher. Knowledge acquisition via incremental conceptual clustering. *Machine Learning*, 2:139–172, 1987.
7. G. John, R. Kohavi, and K. Pfleger. Irrelevant features and the subset selection problem. In *Proceedings of the Eleventh International Machine Learning Conference*, pages 121–129, New Brunswick, NJ, 1994. Morgan Kaufmann.
8. Anna Perini and Francesco Ricci. An interactive planning architecture. In M. Ghallab and A. Milani, editors, *New directions in AI Planning*, pages 273–283. IOS Press, 1996.
9. J. R. Quinlan. *C4.5: Programs for machine learning*. Morgan Kaufmann, San Mateo, CA, 1993.
10. B. D. Ripley. *Pattern recognition and neural networks*. Cambridge U.P., 1996.
11. E.L. Rissland and J.J. Daniels. Using cbr to drive ir. In *Proceedings of the Fourteenth International Joint Conference on Artificial Intelligence (IJCAI-95)*, pages 400–407, Montreal, Canada, 1995.
12. David B. Skalak. Prototype and feature selection by sampling and random mutation hill climbing algorithms. In *Proceedings of the Eleventh International Machine Learning Conference*, pages 293–301, New Brunswick, NJ, 1994. Morgan Kaufmann.
13. Craig Stanfill and David Waltz. Toward memory-based reasoning. *Communication of ACM*, 29:1213–1229, 1986.
14. Sholomon M. Weiss and Casimir A. Kulikowski. *Computer Systems that Learn*. Morgan Kaufmann, 1991.
15. Dietrich Wettschereck, Takao Mohri, and David W. Aha. A review and comparative evaluation of feature weighting methods for lazy learning algorithms. *AI Review Journal*, 11:273–314, 1997.
16. D. Randall Wilson and Tony R. Martinez. Improved heterogeneous distance functions. *Journal of Artificial Intelligence Research*, 11:1–34, 1997.
17. Lei Xu, Adam Krzyzak, and Erkki Oja. Rival penalized competitive learning for cluster analysis, RBF net, and curve detection. *IEEE Transaction on Neural Networks*, 4(4):636–649, 1993.

Learning Feature Weights for CBR: Global versus Local[1]

Andrea Bonzano, Pádraig Cunningham
Artificial Intelligence Group
Trinity College Dublin
Ireland
{Andrea.Bonzano,cnnnghmp}@tcd.ie

Barry Smyth
Department of Computer Science
University College Dublin
Ireland
bsmyth@cslan.ucd.ie

Abstract

k-Nearest Neighbour is a popular case retrieval technique in Case-Based Reasoning. It has the disadvantage that its accuracy depends strongly on the weights assigned to the case features. This problem can be addressed by using Introspective Learning to discover appropriate values for feature weights. The basic idea with Introspective Learning (IL) is to examine cases that are similar in order to discover which features are important and which are not. The only problem with this idea is that there are a myriad of ways in which weights can be updated based on this kind of analysis. There are several different cues that can trigger a weight change; there are several ways in which the weights can be changed and there is the added complication that weights can be global or local. In this paper we report some analysis of IL in a CBR system for conflict resolution in Air Traffic Control. We show that local weights are best in this particular domain and we show which update cues are most effective. We also show that overfitting can be a problem with IL and we discuss how it can be avoided.

1. Introduction

When a k-Nearest Neighbour (k-NN) technique is used for case retrieval in Case-Based Reasoning (CBR) accuracy depends on the weights assigned to the features. Recent research in Machine Learning and Case-Based Reasoning has shown that Introspective Learning (IL) of feature weights can improve accuracy (Saltzberg, 1991; Fox & Leake, 1995; Wetterschereck & Aha, 1995; and Ricci & Avesani, 1995; Muñoz-Avila & Hüllen, 1996). In this context IL involves examining similar cases in order to determine which features are important and which are not. It has been pointed out that this is a complex area and much research remains to be done (Wettschereck, Aha & Mohri, 1997).

In a recent paper we have shown that IL improves retrieval in ISAC a CBR system for Air Traffic Control (Bonzano, Cunningham & Smyth, 1997). However there are many ways in which feature weights can be adjusted and it is difficult to

---

[1] This research was carried out with the support of Eurocontrol Experimental Centre at Paris, the European centre for research and simulation in Air Traffic Control.

discover which are the best policies in a given application. There are three criteria to be considered:-

- What cues should drive learning?
- How should weights be adjusted?
- Should weights be local or global?

In this paper we evaluate the merits of learning local versus global weights in ISAC. Local weights are appropriate when the importance of the features is context sensitive. On the other hand, because there will be so many more local than global weights, the learning information may be spread thin when learning local weights. When training data is scarce one might have more confidence in global weights.

In the next section we review feature weight learning and discuss the learning cues that may drive this introspective learning process. The possible global and local weight update policies are presented in section 3 and the combination of these alternatives are evaluated in section 4. In addition, we show how overfitting can be a problem and how it can be avoided. The paper finishes with a conclusion and some directions for future work.

2. Learning Feature Weights

Since k-NN is so sensitive to feature weights there has been much research on learning feature weights (see Wettschereck, Aha & Mohri (1997) for a review. Since the importance of features can be context sensitive there has also been much research on learning local weights that can reflect context. Atkeson, Moore and Schall (1997) have done some work on locally weighted learning but this is not so relevant here because they concentrate on local weights in linear regression systems. Of more relevance to us this the work of Aha and Goldstone (1992) and Ricci and Avesani (1995). Aha and Goldstone developed GCM-ISW a k-NN system that uses a combination of local and global weights in assessing similarity. The importance of the local weight increases as the difference between instances decreases. They show that this models well the behaviour of humans on context sensitive classification tasks. Ricci and Avesani present a local weighting system that is asymmetric and local. Their system has the unusual feature that the weight varies with direction - i.e. the weight is different depending on whether the query feature value is greater or less than the feature value with which it is being compared. They show that this approach works well with standard test data sets.

In this paper we extend this work by evaluating different policies for driving weight update in the ISAC domain. We also compare the effectiveness of global versus local weights in this domain and show that overfitting to training data can be a problem and how it can be avoided.

2.1 Learning Policies

There are four distinct cues that can drive learning (i.e. that trigger the change of a feature weight). These differ depending on whether the retrieved case from the case base has the same solution as the target from the training set and if the parameter's value of the case is matching the parameter's value of the target.[*]

By changing the weights, we move the cases in the case space. We want the cases that led to a correct solution to be "pulled" closer to the target and the cases that were retrieved incorrectly to be "pushed" away from the target. There are four possible learning policies; two cause a "push" and two cause a "pull":

- GUM, Good Up Matching: the case retrieved from the case base has the same solution as the target in the training set (Good retrieval). We increase (Up) the weights of the parameters that have the same value as the target (Matching values). By doing this we increase even more its activation, i.e. we "pull" the case towards the target.
- GDU, Good Down Unmatching: the case retrieved from the case base has the same solution as the target in the training set (Good retrieval). We decrease (Down) the weights of the parameter that have a different value from the target (Unmatching values). The non-matching parameters decrease the case activation even if we want this case to be retrieved, so by decreasing their weights we again "pull" the case towards the target.
- BUU, Bad Up Unmatching: the case retrieved from the case base has a different solution from the target (Bad retrieval) and the weights of the parameters that have a different value from the target (Unmatching values) are increased (Up). By doing this we "push" the case away from the target because we reduce even more the activation of the case.
- BDM, Bad Down Matching: the case retrieved from the case base has a different solution from the target (Bad retrieval) and the weights of the parameters that have the same value as the target (Matching values) are decreased (Down) because these weights contributed too much to the activation that we want to be low. So we are again "pushing" the case away from the target.

A spreading activation mechanism is used in ISAC to determine case similarity. If a symbolic feature of a case in the case-base matches exactly with that feature in the target case the activation of that case is increased by the weight of the feature. This weight can either be a global weight for that feature or a local weight stored with the case in the case-base. The same principle is used with numeric features with the activation being proportionate to the closeness of the numeric features - see (Bonzano, Cunningham & Smyth, 1997). Any combination of the above updating policies should increase the performance of the system. In the evaluation section we show that different combinations have different effects.

Another perspective on these policies is that the cues derived from bad retrievals (BUU and BDM) represent failure driven learning. It is quite clear in the evaluation shown in 4.1 that these are the most useful in the ISAC domain.

---

[*] In our training process the available cases are divided into a case-base and a training set. The cases in the training set are presented to the case-base as target cases.

3. Weight Update Policies

In section 2 we have described the four cues that can drive weight update. The manner in which the weights can be updated based on these cues is the next issue to be considered. The first fundamental question concerning weight update is whether there should be a global weight for each feature or a local weight in each case for each feature. (It is also possible to have specific weights for each feature value (Wettschereck, Aha & Mohri, 1997) but that was not found useful in ISAC). If the importance of individual features is believed to be context sensitive then local weights make sense. However, this has the disadvantage that the amount of information contributing to each weight is drastically reduced because of the large number of weights to be decided.

3.1. Local weights

In learning local weights we found the update decay policy described by Muñoz-Avila and Hüllen (1996) to be very useful. The idea is that the amount by which a weight is adjusted should reduce the more often a case is retrieved correctly. So we count the number of correct retrievals K_c and the number of faulty retrievals F_c and adjust weights as follows:

If the weight is to be increased: $\quad w_{ik}(t+1) = w_{ik}(t) + \dfrac{F_c}{K_c}$

If the weight is to be decreased: $\quad w_{ik}(t+1) = w_{ik}(t) - \dfrac{F_c}{K_c}$

Where w_{ik} is the weight on the ith feature of the kth case.

When all the weights in a case have been updated it is important they are normalised so that the maximum activation remains the same after the updating. This is important to prevent a popular case becoming a strong attractor in the case-base. This is done as follows:-

$$w_{ik} = w_{ik} \frac{Number\ of\ Features}{\sum w_{ik}}$$

Other local weight update policies were evaluated in ISAC (Bonzano, Cunningham & Smyth, 1997) but this particular policy was found to be the most effective.

3.2. Global weights

In the evaluation we present here we compare this local update policy with four global update policies:-

1. Each global weight is updated by adding/subtracting the quantity λ:

   If the weight is to be increased: $\; w_i(t+1) = w_i(t) + \lambda$

   If the weight is to be decreased: $\; w_i(t+1) = w_i(t) - \lambda$

This strategy does not use a decay function, so it is necessary to keep the increment small, otherwise a case that is retrieved too often will have very big weights (we chose $\lambda = 0.1$ after some experimentation).

2. Each global weight is updated by adding/subtracting the quantity $\dfrac{F_c}{K_c}$

$$\text{If the weight is to be increased:} \quad w_i(t+1) = w_i(t) + \frac{F_c}{K_c}$$

$$\text{If the weight is to be decreased:} \quad w_i(t+1) = w_i(t) - \frac{F_c}{K_c}$$

   Note that K_c and F_c belong to the single cases and not to the parameter.

3. Each global weight is the average of all the corresponding local weights after they have been trained with the policy shown in section 3.1. All the weights are considered to calculate the average, even the weights that have not been updated (i.e. weights that remain as initialised at 1).

4. Each global weight is the average of all the corresponding local weights, as in strategy 3, but the average is calculated without considering the weights that have not been changed during learning.

The last two strategies are time consuming because a previous training of the local weights is necessary, but are useful to test if the global weights can carry as much information as the local.

4. Evaluation

The IL algorithm trains the weights of the case base by working on a set of cases called the training set and the error is calculated on a different set of cases called the test set (Bonzano, Cunningham & Smyth, 1997). The first step is to evaluate the initial error on the test set, called E_{ts}, when all the weights are equal to one because IL has not yet changed any weight.

We then start training the case base by solving the cases in the training set and by updating the weights of the case base according to the chosen updating policy. The loop solve-update-evaluate is repeated several times until some stopping criterion is reached. The error on the training E_{tr}, is calculated on each iteration. Because of the potential of the weight learning to overfit to the training set it would not be sensible to try to minimise E_{tr}. In practice some of the training data can be held back from the training process and used as a validation set to determine when overfitting starts to occur. If there are not enough data to dedicate cases to a validation set then it is possible to use cross validation to determine when to stop training.

For all the experiments we used a case base of 126 cases coming from the ATC domain, a training set of 40 cases and a test set of 27 cases. Each case has 23 parameters, of which 19 symbolic and 4 numeric. The system iterated 20 times on the training set to extract the best weights. The points in the graphics are the average of 50 experiments with different combinations of test set and training set.

4.1. Learning Policies

We worked on eleven different combinations of learning policies:

- *All Four* (GUM + GDU + BUU + BDM) where learning is driven by all the four policies;

- *onlyBad* (BUU + BDM) where learning is driven only by the badly retrieved cases (failure driven);

- *onlyGood* (GUM + GUU) where learning is driven only by the correctly retrieved cases;

- *onlyGUM* (GUM) and *onlyGDU* where learning is driven only by the cases that are correctly retrieved;

- *withoutGUM* (GDU + BUU + BDM) and *withoutGDU* (GUM + BUU + BDM) where the learning is driven by all the policies except from respectively GUM and GDU;

- *onlyBUU* and *onlyBDM* where the learning is driven only by the cases that are badly retrieved;

- *withoutBUU* (GUM + GDU + BDM) and *withoutBDM* (GUM + GDU + BUU) where the learning is driven by all the policies except from respectively BUU and BDM.

We tested the effectiveness of learning on local weights with the combinations of the updating policies that we introduced previously; the results are shown in Table 1.

Table 1. Performance on the *Test* Set.

Learning Policy	Before Learning	After Learning
Without GUM	47.2	22.1
Without GDU	47.2	23.7
Without BDM	47.2	26.7
Only BDM	47.2	29.7
Without BUU	47.2	29.9
Only Bad	47.2	31.8
All Four	47.2	31.9
Only BUU	47.2	32.7
Only Good	47.2	37.9
Only GDU	47.2	42.1
Only GUM	47.2	42.4

All the 11 updating policies showed a performance increase. The best increase of performance was recorded with the combination "Without GUM". On average, it seems that the combinations where the failure driven policies are predominant are more effective than the combinations where cues come from successful retrievals. To test the robustness of the learning we also initialised the local weights with random values from 0.5 to 1.5 instead of having the starting weights all equal to 1. The performance increase was the same.

4.2. Local v's Global

We repeated the same experiments with the global weights and the four different strategies presented in 3.2. We were expecting an increase in performance not as big as the one with the local weights. This was true on average, but, sometimes for the strategy 1 the performance was better than the local weights. The results are shown in Figures 1 and 2.

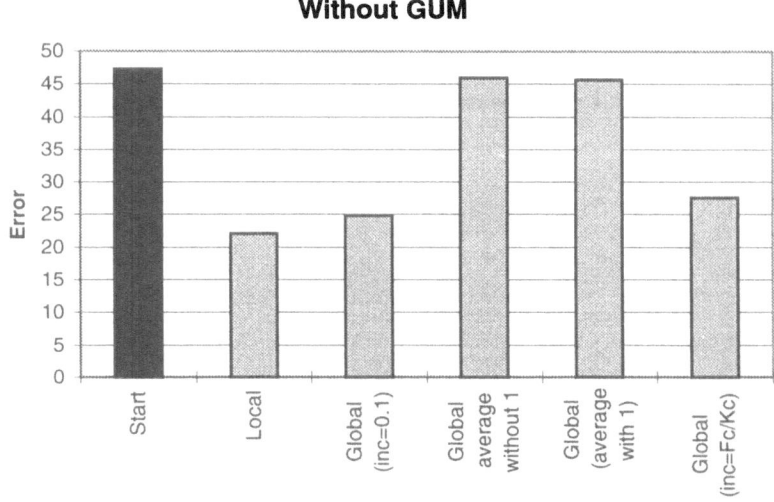

Figure 1: performance of global and local weights for the "withoutGUM" combination.

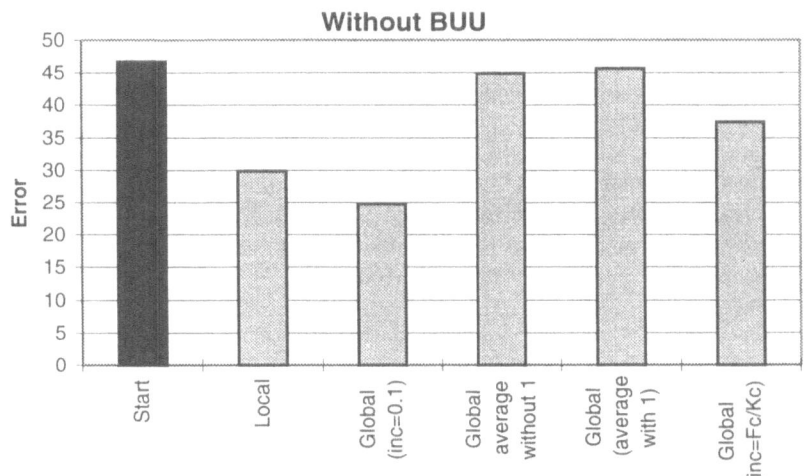

Figure 2: performance of global and local weights for the "Without BUU" combination.

So our best results occur with the "Without GUM" learning policy for local weights. This reduces the error from 47% to 22%. The best result with global weights is the 25% shown in Figure 2. We would expect the difference between the best local result and the best global result to be greater as more data comes available for training.

4.3. Overfitting

The overfitting phenomenon happens when the weights become too specialised for the training set and they loose the generality needed to solve the test set. The error on both the training set and the test set decreases during the first iterations, but the more the case base learns about the training set, the more it gives specific solutions, so the error on the training set keeps decreasing, but the error on the test set starts increasing again.

This phenomenon had been found on both local and global weights but only with some policies.(e.g., the combination "Without GUM" shown in Figure 3).

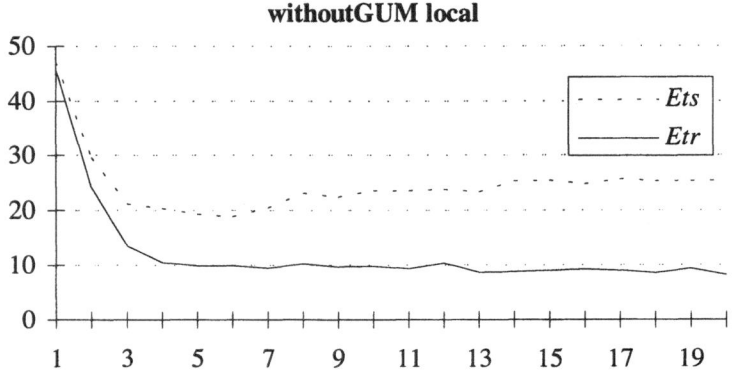

Figure 3: E_{tr} and E_{ts} for the "Without GUM" policy for local weights.

The graph shows that this is a well behaved learning process but there is evidently a need to stop learning early. In practice this can be achieved using a separate validation set as mentioned already.

In Figure 4 we show the behaviour of the case base when the global weights are updated with the strategy 1: after a few iterations, the global weights saturate and the error increase because there is no update decay. In Figure 5 we show the same behaviour with strategy 2: it can be seen that the saturation process is slightly less strong because of the presence of the decay function.

withoutGUM global

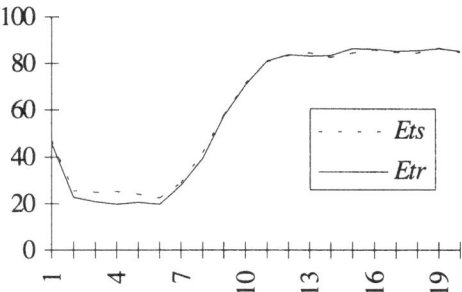

Figure 4 E_{tr} and E_{ts} for the combination "Without GUM" (global weights).

withoutGUM global with Fc/Kc

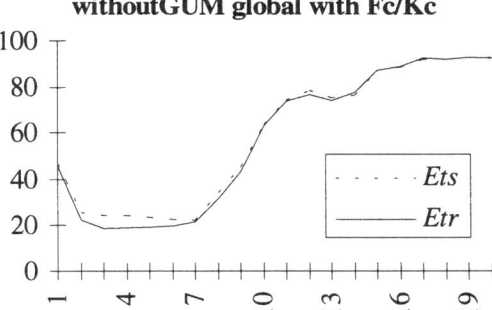

Figure 5. E_{tr} and E_{ts} for the combination "Without GUM" (global weights) but using update decay.

5. Conclusions

We have shown the solution to the feature weight learning problem in ISAC a CBR system for conflict resolution in Air Traffic Control. Our central conclusions are:-

- Because of the context sensitivity of features local feature weights are more effective than global weights.

- Failure driven learning is most effective and the best policy is 'Without GUM'.

- The learning process can overfit to the training set so an early stopping policy is needed. A validation set can be used to achieve this.

It is not clear how these findings will generalise to other domains so we now propose to repeat this evaluation in other problems. We also propose to explore any variation in performance between global and local weights as the size of the case-base increases.

References

Atkeson, C.G., Moore, A.W., Schaal, S., (1997) Locally Weighted Learning, To appear *in Artificial Intelligence Review.*

Bonzano A., Cunningham P., Smyth B., (1997) Using introspective learning to improve retrieval in CBR: A case study in air traffic control, to be presented at *International Conference on Case-Based Reasoning,* Providence Rhode Island, 1997.

Fox, S. & Leake, D. B. (1995) Using Introspective Reasoning to Refine Indexing. *Proceedings of the 14th International Joint Conference on Artificial Intelligence*, pp. 391-397.

Hansen L.K., Larsen J., Fog T., Early Stop Criterion from the Bootstrap Ensemble, *Proceedings of ICASSP'97*, Munich, Germany, April 1997.

Muñoz-Avila, H., Hüllen, J. (1996) Feature Weighting by ExplainingCase-Based Planning Episodes. Advances in Case-Based Reasoning (Ed.s I. Smith & B. Faltings), Proceedings of the Third European Workshop on Case-Based Reasoning, pp. 280-294, Springer-Verlag.

Ricci, F., Avesani P., (1995) Learning a Local Similarity Metric for Case-Based Reasoning. (Ed.s M. Veloso & A. Aamodt), Proceedings of *The 1st International Conference on Case-Based Reasoning*, pp301-311, Springer-Verlag.

Saltzberg, S. L. (1991) A Nearest Hyperrectangle Learning Method. *Machine Learning,* **1.**

Wetterschereck, D., & Aha, D. W. (1995) Weighting Features. Case-Based Reasoning Research and Development (Ed.s M. Veloso & A. Aamodt), Proceedings of *The 1st International Conference on Case-Based Reasoning*, pp347-358, Springer-Verlag.

Wettschereck, D., Aha, D. W., & Mohri, T. (1997). A review and empirical evaluation of feature weighting methods for a class of lazy learning algorithms. To appear *in Artificial Intelligence Review.* (also available on the Web from http://www.aic.nrl.navy.mil/~aha/)

CompAss: A System for Plans of Study Compilation

Giuseppe Attardi
Antonio Cisternino
Maria Simi

Dipartimento di Informatica, Università di Pisa

Abstract

CompAss is a system which assists the students in the task of producing a plan of study. CompAss can be seen as an instance of a general tool for developing configuration applications running on the Web. Starting from a declarative description of the basic items to be chosen for the configuration and of the configuration constraints, the tool generates the HTML files for user guidance and the Java code for constraints checking.

1. Introduction

CompAss (COMPilazione ASSistita di piani di studio) is a system which assists students in the task of producing a plan of study. CompAss and its associated support tools have been developed in the context of a pilot project for the Faculty of Letters and Philosophy of the University of Pisa. Plans of study approval is a time consuming job for all the courses of study in the faculty, due to the high number of submissions each year (around 3000) and the high rate of incorrect submissions. One of the initial requirements was that students could use any computer located in the various departments of the faculty to compile plans of study; data had to be collected in one single place for archival. The Java solution was the obvious choice and offers additional advantages such as the possibility of using the system from home.

The task of producing a plan of study can be seen as a simple configuration application where the basic items are the courses offered by the faculty and the constraints are the rules for plan of study formation. A configuration is a legitimate plan of study, i.e. a list of courses which a student plans to take, fulfilling all the requirements imposed by the faculty.

The official submission of the plan must be done on paper because it requires a signature by the student. Our current solution is that the plan is printed locally, after completion and verification by CompAss, and automatically sent to the server and registered in a temporary area. When the student submits the plan to the secretary office, the plan is retrieved and transferred to the archive of submitted plans. CompAss saves a lot of work for secretaries who previously had to manually input the plans from the paper forms submitted by students and eliminates most of the work of the faculty committees which had to verify and approve the plans.

The plan of study manager running on the server accepts communications from several CompAss clients, receives data from plans of study, generates HTML pages, stores data in a database, and gathers statistics on the number of users and on the pattern of use of the system.

In this paper we briefly describe the main ideas behind the implementation of CompAss and argue that a general tool for developing specific configuration assistants running on the Web can evolve from the approach we have followed.

CompAss is at the Web address: "omega.di.unipi.it/local/Compass/start.html".

2. The User Interface

The Web page of CompAss is vertically divided in two parts. The right part contains the *navigation frame* with related title bar and navigation buttons, the *help frame*, and the *documentation frame*. The left part contains the *configuration frame* and an *application specific tool bar* (see figure 1).

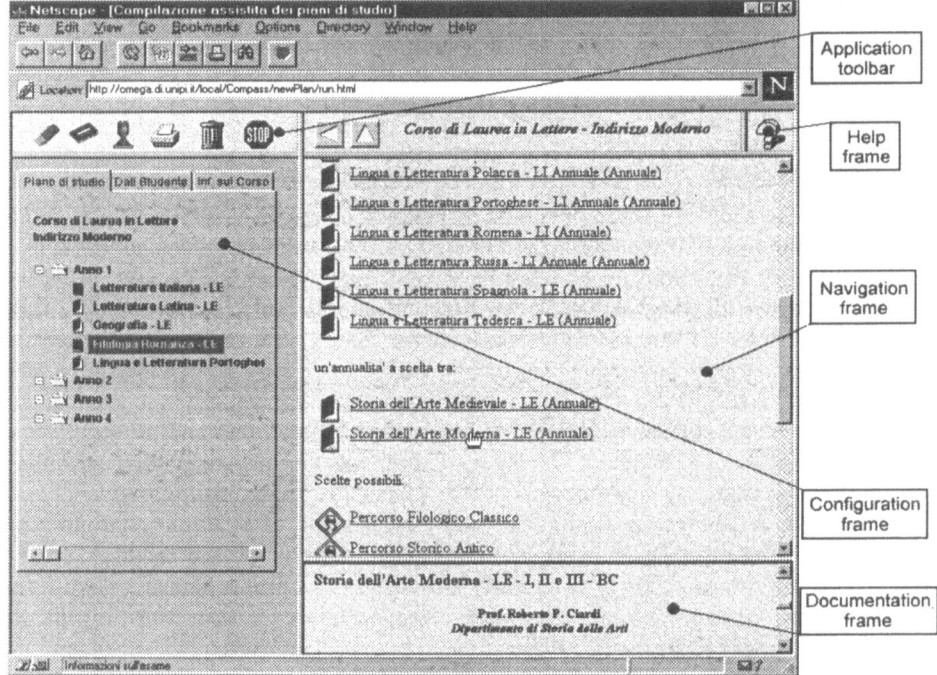

Fig. 1. The user interface of CompAss

The navigation frame displays a HTML document, which presents the available choices and informative text deemed useful to guide the user during the configuration process. Choice points and configuration items are represented by icons (such as the booklet) and hyperlinks to other HTML documents; in the case of links associated to items a description appears in the documentation frame. Clicking on the icons is the way to perform configuration actions such as interrmediate choices or item selections; as a result messages are sent to the configuration program, which is a Java Applet running in the configuration frame.

The configuration frame on the left contains the Java applet which manages the configuration. The applet receives input by direct interaction in its client area (handled through events in the AWT) or by selection of special icons in other frames (the navigation frame and the tool bar frame). Whenever a configuration action is performed the applet reacts by checking the current partial configuration, accepting the change or prompting the user if any configuration constraints is violated.

Tool icons in the toolbar denote general utility or application specific actions available to operate on the partial configuration displayed in the configuration frame (i.e. item deletion, final configuration validation, abortion of the configuration process, printing or submission of the final configuration).

3. A General Approach for Building Configuration Applications

A configuration is a subset of the basic items, and a set of intermediate user choices, that match a given set of constraints. Basic constraints are represented in a directed acyclic graph called *choice graph*; each node defines a set of items required for the node; its successors correspond to alternative choices in the configuration process. A configuration is valid only if the user choices define a path from the root to a leaf, and the selected items match all the constraints associated to the nodes in the path.

To build the configuration application we have developed a declarative language for defining the various aspects of the configuration. The application is generated by using a compiler for this language; the output of the compiler is a data structure to be used by the Java applet. The Java applet depends on the configuration domain only for the item structure and a set of custom constraints functions; this elements are Java classes generated by the compiler and later combined with the rest of the applet. The applet also uses the items database and a binary representation of the configuration constraints.

The compiler is divided in two modules: the first module is needed for generating Java code and constructing the items data base; the second module takes as input a *constraint file* and generates a binary representation of the constraints and the HTML files for navigation.

The constraint file is the heart of the configuration application; in fact the validator module of the application interprets the constraints defined in this file to check the configuration. The constraints are defined in a special declarative language designed for this purpose, which closely reflects the structure of the choice graph.

4. Communication with the server

For implementing persistency we use a special server on the Web host that listens to a given TCP port: the applets open sockets to this server on the specified port and use the server for saving data. The server itself is written in Java, thus exploiting the language facilities for communicating via sockets and object serialisation.

The server allows different kinds of clients: configuration clients but also server console clients. The server console clients are Java standalone applications that allow remote monitoring of the server. Through the server console the user can monitor in real-time configuration clients, displaying the Internet hosts with open configuration connections, and save statistics on the use of the system.

The server also provides local printing capabilities generating HTML pages in the required form with the data provided by the client.

5. Towards a General Tool for Building Configuration Assistants

Configuration systems are a subclass of design systems, whose task is to synthesise a set of objects that satisfy a given set of problem specific constraints [1]. Examples of configuration problems are computer equipment (XCON [2]) and software configuration, timetables generation and scheduling. A configuration task is generally rather complex since it involves coping with many interacting design decisions, whose consequences cannot readily be assessed, and constraints of different nature. Configuration problems are a challenging domain for expert system technologies.

For simpler configuration tasks we can envision interactive *configuration assistants* which operate by guiding the user step by step through the available design decisions by exploiting their knowledge of the domain constraints and of the constraints deriving from previous choices. Configuration tasks that are amenable to this simplified vision, in addition to plan of study compilation, are the assembling of any coherent system built from a catalogue of components, like a complex piece of furniture (a kitchen furniture for instance) or a personal computer.

Configuration assistants of this kind running on the Web have potential in the field of electronic commerce since important advantages of the Java solution are portability, wide availability and the possibility of remote access and use. Moreover all the constraints checking can be done at the client's side by downloading the necessary Java code; communication with the server can be reduced to tasks such as user validation, statistics gathering or archiving.

The strategy we have adopted for CompAss can be profitably be extended to other configuration applications. More experimentation is however needed to exactly define the range of applications and to come out with a general enough configuration language. Future plans are to enhance the configuration language by including a language-level specification for the display of items both in the applet and in the HTML files. The specification for the applet determines in which manner items are displayed in the configuration frame, since the topology of the configuration partially depends on the application domain.

6. Acknowledgements

We thank prof. M. Tavoni of the Faculty of Letters and Philosophy of the University of Pisa for sponsoring the project, dr. P. Pisanti, technical director of the CISIAU (the computing centre of the Faculty) for the technical support, prof. C. Letta and prof. S. Scalfati who helped us to understand the rules for plans of study.

7. References

1. F. Hayes-Roth, D. A. Waterman, D. B. Lenat (ed.). *Building Expert Systems*, Addison Wesley Publishing Company, Reading, Ma, 1983.

2. V. E. Barker, D. E. O'Connor. Expert Systems for Configuration at Digital: XCON and beyond. *Communications of the ACM*, 32(3):298-318, 1989.

3. Arnold, J. Gosling. *The Java Programming Language*. Addison Wesley Publishing Company, Reading, Ma, 1996.

A Prototypal System for Data-Validation

Ing. A. Balderi*, Ing. M. Solimano**

* ENEL SpA-CRT, Via Andrea Pisano, 120 - 56122 Pisa
e-mail Balderi@crt.enel.it; fax 0039-50-535521
** ORSI AUTOMAZIONE S.p.a., Corso Europa 799 - 16148 Genova (I)
fax 0039-10-380309

This paper describes a prototypal system able to solve the data validation problem. The knowledge representation used is rather general and can be extended to any plant fitted with a supervising and data-acquisition system. The prototype has been realized in a G2 environment (expert system shell) and therefore it is an application that can work on many hardware platforms (P.C., Unix Workstation, VMS mainframe). The basic idea of the application is to break down the data validation function into *components* and each component into the *logical phases* of *verification, computation and interpretation*. A three-level network is developed which visually describes the rules by which data are worked out. It is also possible to monitor the elaboration during the debug, step by step.

1. The problem of data validation

In any data acquisition system from a process there is a *physical system* which is the process housing and which we shall call *"field"*, and a set of instruments for measuring the physical quantities of the process which we shall call *"sensors"*; finally, there is a data acquisition system, which collects the performed measurements. The functions of a supervising system very seldom provide more than basic indications of the measurements as to availability and reliability. The acquired data can be considered as validated, only if they satisfy the congruence conditions derived from physical or empirical laws.

2. Applied method and implementation

The approach stems from observing that not all quantities are equally important and that quantities and physical relations can be grouped into subsystems. The computation has been broken down into components. Each component represents a quite isolated entity; that is a subset of quantities and physical relations having few connections among each other. The components are a representation of the subsystems of the specific process. For each component, the input quantities to be validated are defined as well as the output quantities already validated or calculated according to a specific scheme. Each scheme can be represented by the composition of three types of phase: *verification, computation and interpretation* (the second level network).

The *verification phase*, evaluates the 'field values' of the quantities selected as input quantities. These values may be bound to some conditions. The *computation phase* contains physical and empirical relations which allow to calculate the computed quantities or to recalculate more congruent values of the input quantities. The calculations may be influenced by the current status and may trigger a cascade recall of secondary calculations or even external routines. The *interpretation phase* allows to compare the results of the verifications and calculations already carried out and to decide if they can be accepted or not. At the third level of the network, for each phase, we can define the basic operations. The method representation is based on three hierarchical levels and for each level some objects have been defined: component, phase, operation. Each object has its own graphic representation as well as specific attributes.

I. Component representation

At the first level, the component together with its connections to others, are explicitly represented bearing in mind, when defining the components, that the interactions among components must be the exception rather than the rule, so as to understand where, when and why a quantity is recalculated. Each component has the following attributes:

- Maximum time available for carrying out the operations
- The state of the component, namely: under examination, correctly completed, not completed

The connections among components imply an activation signal which allows to establish a preferential order of component analysis and consequently to guide the computation at a high level, during the analysis evolution, simply by observing the graphic representation of the components.

II. Phase representation

At the second level, the various types of phases together with their connections to the other phases belonging to the same component, are explicitly represented. Each phase contains the information on its state of completion; this state is represented by a symbol associated with a colour for the graphic interface, according to the following table:

colour	green	red	yellow
state	OK	any other symbol	under examination

The connections between one phase and the other indicate their activation sequence and are of two types:

- phase-OK-connection: connects the phase under examination with the phases which must be executed if its state is OK;
- phase-notOK-connection: connects the phase under examination with the phases which must be executed if its state is not OK.

III. Operation representation

The most flexible way to do these operations is to directly use the tools provided by G2: rules, formulas, procedures. The user is allowed to insert the knowledge relevant to an operation without having to explicitly specify the invocation algorithm. However, it was decided to define a certain number of operations having their own graphic representation while conditions for their activation are made explicit through connections. The invocation output of each operation is of the logic type; the operation is explicitly represented by an object assuming different colouring depending on its state as shown in the table below:

colour	state	description
green	true	if the operation was definitely successful
red	false	if the operation has definitely failed
rose	intermediate	an intermediate value of certainty in between

The operations may be correlated; in this case the connections indicate the constraints between operations. The following classes of operations were defined:

conditions

They include elementary conditions (namely verifications of logical expressions) and logical operators (and, or, not). The elementary conditions may be connected to logical operators. A logical operator acquires a value according to connected input conditions.

constraints

A constraint contains the indication of the correlated measurement; once verified, this measure is assumed as correct and so it is used for calculating the others. There might be some conditions connected to each constraint. A constraint is verified only if all connected input conditions are verified. A constraint has the following subclasses: ever-verified-constraint and never-verified-constraint, which always contains, respectively, the 'true' and 'false' values.

calculations

A calculation is the application of one or more mathematical relations for re-computing the value of one or more quantities. Some conditions may be associated to a calculation object; in this case the calculation may be applied if all input conditions are verified. The calculations are used in the calculation phase.

A final-calculation may invoke the execution of other calculations contained in the same phase; hence, the calculation phase consists of the analysis of all final calculations specified in it. The attributes of a calculation are:

- *calculation:* a text indicating the calculation to be executed;
- *message:* a text (optional) which is communicated to the operator once the calculation is performed;
- *precondition:* a logical variable whose value, if true, allows the activation of the calculation (by default, the precondition of a calculation is true if all associated input conditions are true or if there are no connected conditions);
- *error-type:* (only for final calculations) a symbol indicating the type of error in the phase under examination, if the calculation is not verified.

A calculation is verified if the mathematical relation expressed by it is true.

interpretations

They are divided into OK-interpretation and not-OK-interpretation; they are used in the phase of result interpretation. The attributes of an interpretation are:

- *formula:* logical expression verifying the interpretation;

- *message*: a text (optional) which is communicated to the operator, once the interpretation has been verified;
- *error-type:* (only for the not-OK-interpretation) a symbol indicating the type of error in the phase under examination, if the not-OK-interpretation is verified.

If the formula attribute is empty, an interpretation is verified if all connected input conditions are verified or there are no connected conditions. If all OK-interpretations are verified, the phase assumes the OK value; if any not-OK-interpretation is verified, the phase assumes the state of error specified in the error-type attribute of the not-OK-interpretation.

IV. Control system

It is necessary to define a control cycle which regulates the executions of the analyses at the various levels of knowledge representation; this cycle shall be repeated for each acquisition of the data set received from the supervising system. During each cycle, the following actions are carried out:

- Copying the values measured by the sensors to the local quantity data base;
- Carrying out, in order, the analysis of all the connected components;
- Performing a global verification of the results, and, if necessary, re-analyzing some components;
- Copying the reconciled quantity values to the output files;
- Waiting for the next data acquisition

The analysis of a component is carried out in this way:

a) Executing the first specified phase
b) If the state is OK, executing the connected phase through the phase-OK-connection
c) If the state is not OK, executing the connected phase through the connection phase-not-OK-connection
d) Back to a)

The analysis of a component is completed when one of the following conditions is satisfied:

- All executable phases have been analyzed (OK state of the component)
- The analysis performance time has expired
- Some phases conclude that the component state is not OK.

A phase execution consists in the activation of the proper operations which can conclude its state.

3. Conclusions and results

It has been shown that human experience and intelligence are extensively used during the phase of measurement validation and therefore an approach for representing them seems to be promising. The tests performed so far demonstrate an overall resolution capacity higher than mathematical approaches, more strict formally, but less easy to be mastered by the expert, though a quantitative and systematic comparison with other methods has not yet been made so far.

ODB-Tools: A Description Logics Based Tool for Schema Validation and Semantic Query Optimization in Object Oriented Databases

Sonia Bergamaschi[1,2], Claudio Sartori[2], Domenico Beneventano[1], Maurizio Vincini[1]

e_mail: {dbeneventano, sbergamaschi, csartori}@deis.unibo.it
vincini@dsi.unimo.it

[1] Dipartimento di Scienze dell'Ingegneria, Università di Modena,
Via G. Campi 213/B, I-41100 Modena
[2] Dipartimento di Elettronica, Informatica e Sistemistica
CSITE - CNR Viale Risorgimento 2, I-40136 Bologna

Abstract.
ODB-Tools is a integrated environment for the object oriented database (OODB) validation, preserving taxonomy coherence and performing taxonomic inferences, and semantic query optimization. Semantic query optimization uses problem-specific knowledge (e.g. integrity constraints) for transforming a query into an *equivalent* one (i.e. with the same answer set) that may be answered more efficiently. The approach of the tool is based on two fundamental ingredients. The first one is the *OCDL* description logics proposed as a common formalism to express class descriptions, a relevant set of *integrity constraints* rules (IC rules) and queries. The second one are Description Logics inference techniques, exploited to evaluate the logical implications expressed by IC rules and thus to produce the *semantic expansion* of a given query. The optimizer tentatively applies all the possible transformations and delays the choice of beneficial transformation till the end. ODB-Tools is a ODMG 93 [1] compliant tool, both for the schema definition (ODL language) and for the query language (OQL); The tool is available in internet at http://sparc20.dsi.unimo.it and supports an on-line graphical interface developed in Java language.

1 The approach

Let us briefly explain the main ingredients of our approach [2, 3].

OCDL: a description logic (DL) for database schema with integrity constraints

OCDL (Object Constraints Description Language) is a new description logics [4], extending the expressiveness of traditional description logics languages (derived from the KL-ONE model [5]) in order to represent the semantics of complex object data models. Its main characteristics are: a distinction between *values* and *objects* with identity and, thus, between *value types* and *class types* (briefly called classes); type constructors, such as *tuple, set* and *sequence* recursively used to define complex objects. In particular, *quantified path types* and *integrity constraints*

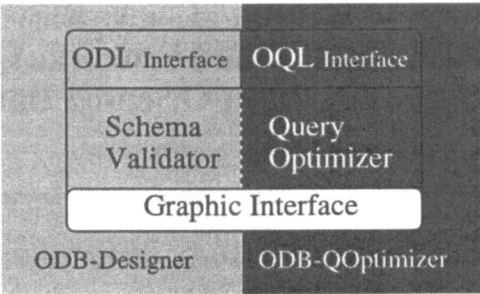

Fig. 1. ODB-Tools

rules have been introduced. Paths, which are essentially sequences of attributes, represent the central ingredient of OODB query languages to navigate through the aggregation hierarchies of classes of a schema. Quantified paths are paths existentially and universally quantified. Integrity constraints (IC) rules are *if then rules* whose antecedent and consequent can be expressed as *OCDL virtual* types (i.e. *defined* type descriptions expressing a set of sufficient and necessary conditions) and allow the declarative formulation of a relevant set of integrity constraints. A *generalized database schema* definition can be thus introduced which perfectly fits the usual database viewpoint.

Query Optimization by DLs inference techniques

A relevant set of queries, that is the ones referred to a target class and to the navigation through its composition hierarchy, can be expressed as *virtual OCDL* types. Description Logics inference techniques such as subsumption computation, incoherence detection and canonical form generation can be used to produce the *semantic expansion* of an *OCDL* query. It is a transformed query which incorporates any possible restriction which is not present in the original query but is *logically implied* by the query and by the overall schema (classes + value types + IC rules). Following the approach of [6] for semantic query optimization, but exploiting subsumption computation to evaluate logical implication, we perform the semantic expansion of the types included at each nesting level in the query description.

2   ODB-Tools Architecture

ODB-Tools, whose architecture is shown in Fig. 1, provide a *user-friendly* integrated environment based on the ODMG-93 standard, with the following features:

Schema validation and classification (ODB-DESIGNER): The user inserts a DB schema, using ODL language, and the system performs the coherence validation and the classification, i.e., for each class, the system determines the right place of the class in the inheritance hierarchy between its most specific generalizations and its most generalized specializations. The result is shown by a graphic representation of the schema inheritance and aggregation hierarchies.

Semantic Query Optimization (ODB-QOPTIMIZER): now the user can insert a query, using ODL language, related to the given schema and the system executes the semantic query optimization. The result is the semantic expansion of the query shown by a new OQL description and by a graphic representation of the classification of the query with respect the schema.

ODB-Tools is composed of five main modules:

- **ODL Interface**: the schema acquisition module that accepts a schema description in ODL language and translate it into a *OCDL* schema. ODL syntax has been extended to provide the IC Rules descriptive capability.
- **OQL Interface**: the query input (output) interface module that receives a query in OQL language and translates it into *OCDL* syntax (and vice-versa).
- **Schema Validator**: the schema validation module which automatically builds the class taxonomy and preserves the coherence with respect to the inheritance and aggregation hierarchies.
- **Query Optimizer**: the module which executes the semantic expansion of the query (by using the Schema Validator).
- **Graphic Interface**: the module which visualizes the schema inheritance and aggregation hierarchies.

ODB-Tools is available on Internet at http://sparc20.dsi.unimo.it. The interfaces, validation and optimization modules are realized using C language (gcc 2.7.2 compiler, flex 2.5 and bison 1.24 generator), while the graphic module is developed by Java language (JDK 1.1 compiler).

3   The Storage domain example

In order to illustrate our approach, let us introduce the Storage domain example which describes part of the organizational structure of a company in an extended (integrity rules have been added) ODMG-93 syntax (see table 1). The involved classes are: Material and its subclass SMaterial, Storage and its subclass SStorage, Manager and its subclass TManager. Note that the class Storage description is quite complex: departments stocking materials all of quantity between 10 - 300 of a given category.

Let us briefly describe the IC rules of table 1:

Rule R_1 says that managers with a level from 5 to 10 must have a salary from 40K to 60K.

R_2 says that, having a risk greater equal to 10, is a sufficient condition for a material to be an smaterial.

R_3 constrains storages, with a "B4" category, to be managed by a tmanager.

Let us give a simple query optimization example using OQL syntax.

Q: "Select storages storing *all* materials having a risk ≥ 15"
select * **from Storage**
where for all x **in stock** : $(x.\text{item.risk} \geq 15)$

The applicable rules are R_2, R_3, leading to the semantic expansion of Q:
select * **from SStorage**
where for all x **in stock** : $(x.\text{item in select } y$
                                          from   SMaterial **as** y
                                          where risk $\geq 15)$

```
interface Material () {                          interface SMaterial:Material()
  attribute string name;                         { };
  attribute int risk;
  attribute set<string> feature;  };

interface Manager ()  {                          interface TManager:Manager(){
  attribute string              name;            attribute range{8, 12} level;};
  attribute range {40000, 100000} salary;
  attribute range{1, 15}        level;  };

interface  Storage ()  {                         typedef struct t_stock
  attribute string       name;                     { Material item;
  attribute string       category;                 range {10, 300} qty;
  attribute Manager      managed_by;             } t_stock;
  attribute set<t_stock> stock; };
interface SStorage:Storage ()  { };

rule R1 forall X in Manager: ( X.level >= 5 and X.level <= 10 )
  then X.salary >= 40000 and X.salary <= 60000 ;
rule R2 forall X in Material: ( X.risk >=  10 ) then X in SMaterial ;
rule R3 forall X in Storage: ( forall X1 in X.stock: ( X1.item in SMaterial ))
  then X in SStorage ;
```

Table 1. The Storage Domain Schema

In this way, the query is optimized as we obtained the *most specialized generalization* of the classes involved in the query SStorage and SMaterial.

References

1. R.G.G. Cattell. *The Object Database Standard: ODMG-93, Release 1.1.* Morgan Kaufmann Publishers, Inc., 1994.
2. D. Beneventano, S. Bergamaschi, S. Lodi, and C. Sartori. Using subsumption in semantic query optimization. In A. Napoli, editor, *IJCAI Workshop on Object-Based Representation Systems - Chambery, France*, August 1993.
3. S. Bergamaschi and B. Nebel. Acquisition and validation of complex object database schemata supporting multiple inheritance. *Journal of Applied Intelligence*, 4:185–203, 1994.
4. D. Beneventano, S. Bergamaschi, and C. Sartori. Semantic query optimization by subsumption in oodb. In *Int. Workshop on Flexible Query Answering Systems*, Roskilde, Denmark, May 1996.
5. R.J. Brachman and J.G. Schmolze. An overview of the KL-ONE knowledge representation system. *Cognitive Science*, 9(2):171–216, 1985.
6. M. Siegel, E. Sciore, and S. Salveter. A method for automatic rule derivation to support semantic query optimization. *ACM Transactions on Database Systems*, 17(4):563–600, December 1992.

Processing Paper Documents with WISDOM

Donato Malerba Floriana Esposito Giovanni Semeraro Luca De Filippis

Dipartimento di Informatica, Università degli Studi di Bari
via Orabona 4, 70126 Bari, Italy
{malerba | esposito | semeraro}@lacam.uniba.it

Abstract. WISDOM is a paper-computer interface that can transform printed information into a symbolic representation. This is done into four distinct steps: Document analysis, document classification, document understanding, and text recognition with an OCR. Machine learning tools and techniques are used in the first three steps to easily customize the interface on the exigencies of different users.

1 Introduction

The idea of building distributed digital libraries that would cover the globe is no longer a dream but the great challenge of the information technology community. Unfortunately, most of the documents still exists only in printed forms, thus it is important to develop systems for the transformation of data presented on paper into a computer-revisable form.

In this demo we present WISDOM (Windows Interface System for DOcument Management), a paper-computer interface that can transform printed information into a symbolic representation. This transformation process is performed into four distinct steps: Document analysis, document classification, document understanding and, finally, text recognition with an optical character recognizer (OCR) [1]. In the first three steps WISDOM uses a knowledge base automatically built using machine learning tools and techniques. This allows the system to be quickly customized on the exigencies of different users, provided that they are able to supply a collection of training documents whose layout components and semantic labels have already been defined.

2 Functional architecture of WISDOM

The functional architecture of WISDOM is given in Figure 1. Initially a single-page document is scanned with a resolution of 300 dpi and thresholded into a binary image, which takes 1.1Mb for an A4 page size. Since the segmentation algorithm used in the system is sensitive to skew, it is necessary to pre-process the image in order to correct its skew. Deskewing is accomplished by evaluating a horizontal projection profile, which will have sharply-rising peaks with widths equal to the character height when text lines spans horizontally, while it will show smooth slopes when the skew angle is large.

The study of the horizontal projection profile allows WISDOM to estimate the *complexity* of the document. This parameter is computed as the ratio of the mean distance between peaks and the peak width. It is greater than (lower than) 1.0 for simple (complex) documents. Complexity is used to compute one of the three smoothing parameters considered in the subsequent segmentation phase. The page is segmented by means of the Run Length Smoothing Algorithm (RLSA) [6]. In order to speed up the segmentation process, the RLSA operates on a reduced document image with a resolution of 75 dpi.

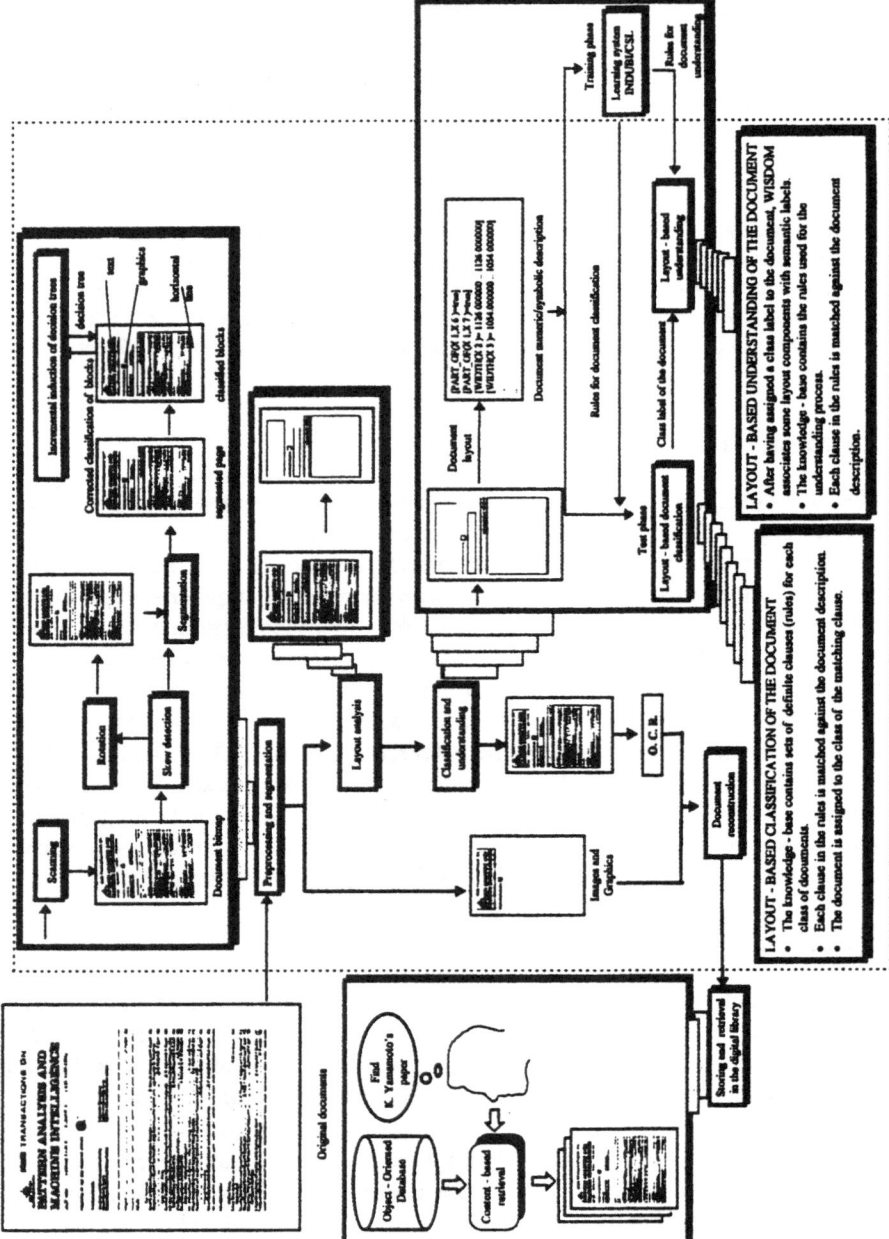

Figure 1. Functional architecture of the document processing system. Functions available in WISDOM are inscribed in a dotted square.

The result of the segmentation process is a list of rectangular blocks, enclosing either textual or non-textual content portions. Textual information present within the digitized document must be separated from the graphics so that subsequent processing stages may operate on the appropriate type of information (e.g., an OCR will be applied only to textual components). This separation problem can be reformulated as a classification problem, where the classes are *text, horizontal line, vertical line, picture* and *graphics*. In WISDOM, a decision tree is used for this task. It is induced from a set of training examples of the five classes. Features used to describe each example are: Height, length, area, eccentricity, total number of black pixels in the reduced bitmap, total number of black pixels in the segmented block, number of white-black transitions in the reduced bitmap, percentage of black pixels in the reduced bitmap, percentage of black pixels in the segmented block, and mean horizontal length of the black runs of the reduced bitmap.

In a first release of the system, we used a decision tree induced from a set of 5473 examples of pre-classified blocks taken from 53 documents of various kinds. The best result we observed featured an average accuracy above 97% [2]. However, this approach operates off-line: It is not possible to revise the decision tree when some blocks are misclassified, unless a new tree is generated from scratch using an extended training set. Furthermore, some blocks can be considered text for some users and graphics for others, as in the case of a logo. Therefore, we felt the exigency to give the user the possibility of on-line training the system. To answer this need we integrated ITI [5], a system for the incremental induction of decision trees, in a second release of WISDOM. In the *normal* operation mode, ITI guarantees to build the same decision tree independently of the order in which examples are presented. Unfortunately, in this operation mode ITI creates a file of 10Mb when trained on the set of 5473 instances used in the previous experiment. This space inefficiency can be contained (about 1.5Mb) in the *error-correction* operation mode, although the independence of the induced tree from the order of presentation of training instances is no longer guaranteed. Luckily, we noticed that a single user can obtain satisfying results with a lower number of training instances, since printed documents managed in a specific application often show a similar layout.

The segmentation process produces a description of the document that is still too detailed. Generally, we do not need so much information for the subsequent phases of document classification and understanding. *Layout analysis* is the perceptual organization process that aims to detect structures among blocks. The result is a hierarchy of abstract representations of the document image, called the *layout structure* of the document. At the lowest level of this abstraction hierarchy we have the blocks produced by RLSA, while at the higher levels we have some layout components (called *frames*) that have a logical meaning. An ideal layout analysis process should produce frames at the highest level such that each of them can be associated with a different semantic label (e.g., title and author of a scientific paper). However, it is considered equally good a layout structure in which it is still possible to distinguish the logical meaning of distinct frames.

The approach adopted for the layout analysis is knowledge-based [3]. Indeed, generic knowledge and rules on typesetting conventions are used to group basic blocks together into frames. This knowledge is independent of the particular class of processed documents and turns out to be appropriate for a range of problems. The layout analysis is performed into two steps: First, a *global* analysis of the document image determines possible areas containing paragraphs, sections, columns, figures and tables, then a *local* analysis groups together blocks which possibly fall within the same area.

The result of the layout analysis process is a file describing the hierarchy of layout components, made up of blocks (at the bottom), lines, sets of lines, first frames and second frames (at the top). Each layout component is associated with one of the following type: text, horizontal line, vertical line, picture, graphics and mixture. More precisely, when the constituent blocks of a logical component are homogeneous, the same type is inherited by the logical component, otherwise the associated type is set to 'mixture'.

Once the layout structure of a document has been extracted, WISDOM generates a numeric/symbolic description of the page layout. More precisely, only the most abstract level of the layout hierarchy is described in terms of *attributes*, such as height and width of a frame, and *relations*, such as *part-of*, *on-top*, *to-right* and relative alignment [1].

Document descriptions can be matched against rules of a knowledge base in order to classify or understand the document. Rules used in this labelling process are automatically learned from a set of training documents for which the user has already provided the correct class and frame labels. The learning system used to generate the rules for WISDOM is INDUBI/CSL, recently extended to deal with both numeric and symbolic attribute/relations [4]. The learning process is currently performed off-line, since its computational complexity is considered out of the reach of medium-sized PC.

Finally, WISDOM allows the user to set up the text extraction process by selecting the labelled frames that have to be passed to the OCR. In this way, the application of an OCR can be limited only to those (textual) layout components that are of interest for the application. The result of the document processing is a text file with extension *.lay* that contains all the relevant information on the original document image (namely, the heading of the original TIFF file), on the layout structure, on the class and frame labels, as well as on the text read by the OCR in some labelled frames.

The current release of WISDOM (2.1) has been implemented in C and runs in Windows 3.1 on a PC with processor 486 and a RAM of at least 8Mb. The average time for document analysis, classification and understanding is less than one minute.

References

[1]   F. Esposito, D. Malerba, and G. Semeraro. Multistrategy learning for document recognition. *Applied Artificial Intelligence*, vol. 8, no. 1, pp. 33-84, 1994.

[2]   F. Esposito, D. Malerba, and G. Semeraro. A comparative analysis of methods for pruning decision trees, *IEEE Transactions on Pattern Analysis and Machine Intelligence*, vol. 19, no. 5, pp. 476-491, 1997.

[3]   D. Malerba, G. Semeraro, and E. Bellisari. LEX: A knowledge-based system for the layout analysis. *Proceedings of the Third International Conference on the Practical Application of Prolog*, pp. 429-443, 1995.

[4]   D. Malerba, F. Esposito, G. Semeraro, and S. Caggese. Handling continuous data in top-down induction of first-order rules. *Proceedings of the 5th Congress of the Italian Association for Artificial Intelligence*, Rome, Italy, September 1997.

[5]   P.E. Utgoff. An improved algorithm for incremental induction of decision trees. *Proceedings of the Eleventh International Conference on Machine Learning*, San Francisco, CA: Morgan Kaufmann, 1994.

[6]   K.Y. Wong, R.G. Casey, and F.M. Wahl. Document analysis system. *IBM Journal of Research Development*, vol. 26, no. 6, pp. 647-656, 1982.

REGAL3.2: FOL Concept Learning by Cooperative Genetic Algorithms

Filippo Neri
Dipartimento di Informatica
Università di Torino,
Corso Svizzera 185
10149 TORINO (Italy)
neri@di.unito.it

Requirements for Demo: REGAL3.2 has been developed in C language using the PVM3.3 library; it runs on a cluster of workstations running SUNOS 4.1.3 or Solaris operative systems. The remote demonstration of the system is possible without graphical interface; a local demostration will also include the description of the graphical interface. Only one workstation is needed for a demo. REGAL3.2 is available at ftp://ftp.di.unito.it /pub/MLprog/REGAL3.2/regal3.2.tar.Z.

1 The System REGAL3.2

This paper describes REGAL3.2[Giordana and Neri, 1995; Neri, 1997], a distributed genetic algorithm-based system, designed for learning First Order Logic disjunctive concept descriptions from examples. The system is a hybrid between Pittsburgh's and Michigan's approaches, as the population constitutes a redundant set of partial concept descriptions, each evolved separately. REGAL3.2 is specifically tailored to cope with the task of concept learning from examples; hence, REGAL3.2 is *task-dependent,* but, on the other hand, *domain-independent.* The system proved to be particularly robust with respect to parameter setting across a variety of different application domains.

REGAL3.2 's main features are: a task oriented selection operator, called Universal Suffrage operator [Neri and Saitta 1996a], provably allowing the population asymptotically converge, in average, to an equilibrium state, in which several species coexist; and a cooperative distributed architecture.

The system has been tested on several complex real-world and artificial domains, in order to show its power, and to analyze its behaviour under various conditions [Neri and Saitta, 1996b]. The results obtained so far suggest that genetic search may be a valuable alternative to other logic-based approaches to learning concepts.

2 REGAL3.2's Language: First Order Logic Formulas with Internal Disjunctions

The concept description language **L**, used by REGAL3.2, is a First Order Logic language, intermediate between VL_2 and VL_{21} [Michalski, 1983]. More precisely, **L** is a Horn clause language, in which terms can be variables or disjunctions of constants, and negation occurs in a restricted form. Internal disjunction has been widely used in concept learning because it allows compact inductive hypotheses to be expressed. An example of an atomic expression containing a disjunctive term is "color(x, yellow ∨ green)", which is semantically equivalent to "color(x, yellow) ∨ color(x, green)", but is more natural. In REGAL3.2, an atomic formula of arity m+1 has the syntactic form $P(x_1, x_2, ..., x_m, K)$, where $x_1, x_2, ..., x_m$ are variables and the term K is a disjunction of constant terms, denoted by $[v_1, v_2, ..., v_n]$, or the negation of such a disjunction, denoted by $\neg [v_1, v_2, ..., v_n]$.

2.1 The Definition of the Hypothesis Space

All learning algorithms use some kind or other of *bias* (i.e a set of implicit or explicit constraints) to restrict the inductive hypothesis space. REGAL3.2 limits the hypothesis space by means of a *Language Template* Λ ($\Lambda \in L$). Given a language template Λ, the search space explored by REGAL3.2 is restricted to the set $H(\Lambda)$ of formulas that can be obtained by deleting some constant from the terms occurring in Λ. Any formula, obtained by dropping some constants from Λ, is more specific than Λ itself. A formal definition of the language template can be found in [Giordana and Neri, 1995].

2.2 The Representation of an Individual: mapping FOL Formulas to Bitstrings

An inductive hypotheses φ, belonging to the space $H(\Lambda)$, corresponds to the body of an implication rule $\varphi \rightarrow h$, being h the name of a target concept. Formulas in $H(\Lambda)$ can be easily represented on a fixed-length bit string $s(\Lambda)$. By keeping adjacent the bits corresponding to literals that are adjacent in the template, each completed predicate will correspond to a specific substring and, hence, decoding a bit string is straightforward (see fig. 1). Since a bitstring univocally characterizes an inductive hypothesis φ, a bitstring is the information processed by the genetic algorithm.

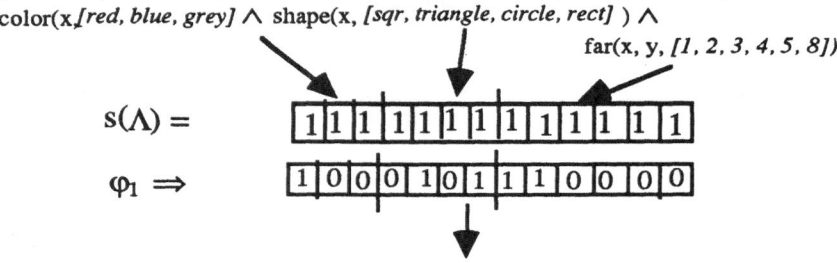

Figure 1 – Bit strings corresponding to a template Λ and to a formulaa φ_1.

3. The Selection Operator and the Fitness Function

Only the *Universal Suffrage* (US) selection operator [Neri and Saitta, 1996a] and the fitness function will be described due to lenght limitation.

3.1 The Universal Suffrage Selection Operator

The basic idea underlying the *Universal Suffrage* (US) selection operator [Neri and Saitta, 1996a] can be explained through a metaphor. Conjunctive formulas are "candidates" to be elected in a parliament (the population), whereas the positive training examples are the voters; an example can vote for one of the formulas that cover it. The main departure of the US operator from the others proposed so far resides in the fact that the individuals to be mated are not chosen directly from the current population, but, instead, indirectly through the selection of an equal number of positive examples, as we will now describe.

Let the population $A(t)$ at generation t be a multiset of cardinality M; $A(t)$ contains m different individuals (i.e. conjunctive formulas of the description language L), each one occurring with multiplicity $x_j(t)$ ($1 \leq j \leq m$). Let $COV(\varphi_j)$ be the subset of E covered by φ_j. Informally, the selection procedure works as follows. At each generation t, a number $g * M \leq M$ of examples is randomly selected with replacement from the set of positive examples E. The parameter g is the *generation gap* and represents the proportion of individuals selected for mating. To each selected example ξ_k a set $R(\xi_k)$, containing the formulas belonging to $A(t)$ and covering ξ_k, is associated. The set $R(\xi_k)$ corresponds to a "roulette wheel" r_k, divided into sectors, each one associated to a $\varphi_j \in R(\xi_k)$. The extension of the sector associated to φ_j is proportional to the ratio between φ_j 's total fitness (i. e. the fitness of φ_j multiplied by φ_j's multiplicity $x_j(t)$ in $A(t)$) and the sum of the total fitness values of all the formulas occurring in $R(\xi_k)$. For each spin of the wheel r_k the winning formula is chosen.

3.2 Fitness Function

In concept learning the criteria employed to evaluate solutions have traditionally been completeness, consistency ($w(\varphi)$) and simplicity. In the case of REGAL3.2, a computational definition of simplicity $z(\varphi)$ has been adopted, corresponding to the number of tests which has to be done by the matcher in order to verify whether a formula is satisfied by an example. More precisely, we use the function

$$f(\varphi) = f(z, w) = (1 + A z) e^{-w}$$

where, the parameter A is user-tunable and its current value is $A = 0.1$. We observe that $f_{Max} = 1.1$ and $\lim_{w \to \infty} f(z, w) = 0$.

4 REGAL3.2's Architecture

REGAL3.2 is based on a distributed architecture in which the US selection is distributed across the network in order to preserve, or even increase, the survival chances of the (small) disjuncts. REGAL3.2's implementation consists of a network of *Nodal Genetic Algorithms* (NGAs) coordinated by a *Supervisor*. Each NGA v performs the US selection on an assigned subset E_v of the learning set E, which, in general, differ from one to another. The *Supervisor* dynamically assigns the sets to the NGAs according to a long-term strategy aimed at promoting cooperation among different species on different nodes in order to reduce the genetic pressure of the large disjuncts on the small ones. From another perspective, each NGA can be seen as a niche needed for the survival of a species or for a group of species. The *Supervisor* distributes the examples of the learning set according to the emerging species, thus identifying NGAs with niches, where specific species, or groups of them, can grow up. Moreover, the *Supervisor* iteratively extracts the evolving concept descriptions from the distributed population, as long as the evolution proceeds.

4.1 The Supervisor Cooperative Strategy

In order to develop cooperation among the NGAs, the *Supervisor* monitors the activity of the NGAs on the basis of a status report it periodically receives from all of them. A status report from a node v contains a copy of the best solution $\varphi_{best}(v)$ which it has currently found in order to cover the assigned set E_v. The choice of $\varphi_{best}(v)$ is made according to a local measure $\pi(\varphi)$ depending on φ's completeness and consistency on E_v; the measure currently used is simply the product $\pi(\varphi) = P\, f(\varphi)$, being P the number of positive examples in E_v covered by φ. Any formula covering at least one positive example in E, with fitness higher than any other one previously received, is recorder by the *Supervisor*.

From all recorded formulas, a disjunctive concept description, which becomes the current best solution, is assembled. The algorithm used to this aim is quite simple. First, the set COVER(t) is constructed as the union of the positive examples covered by all the formulas received up to the generation t. Then, the formulas are sorted in decreasing order according to $\pi(\varphi)$ (re-evaluated on the whole set E) and the first K-best ones able to cover the entire set COVER(t) are selected as current best concept description BEST(t).

As said before, the *Supervisor* focuses the search of the NGAs by assigning specific subsets E_v of learning examples to each node v; this is done in concomitance with the extraction of the global solution BEST(t). The Supervisor remembers the BEST(t) available the last time t the subsets E_v have been assigned. When, a new description BEST(t') is found at time t' > t it estimates the improvement with respect to BEST(t). If it is significant (above an assigned threshold), the sets E_v are modified in order to distribute the task of improving BEST(t') among the nodes. Roughly, this is done by distributing the formulas in BEST(t') to the nodes and defining the generic set E_v as the union of the positive examples covered by the formulas assigned to the node v and the examples not covered by any formula in BEST(t').

The *Supervisor* stops the genetic search when the current solution BEST(t) doesn't not improve for an assigned number of consecutive generations, or when a maximum generation limit is exceeded.

5 References

Giordana A. & Neri F. (1995). "Search–Intensive Concept Induction". *Evolutionary Computation* , MIT Press (Cambridge, MA), vol. 3 (4), pp. 375-419.

Michalski R. (1983). "A Theory and Methodology of Inductive Learning". In R. Michalski, J. Carbonell & T. Mitchell (Eds.), *Machine Learning: An AI Approach, Vol. I.* Morgan Kaufmann, pp. 83-134.

Neri F. (1997). "First Order Logic Concept Learning by means of a Distributed Genetic Algorithm". PhD Thesis, University of Torino, Italy. Available at http://www.di.unito.it/-neri/phd/thesis.ps.gz.

Neri F. and Saitta L. (1996a). "An Analysis of the Universal Suffrage Selection Operator". *Evolutionary Computation* , MIT Press (Cambridge, MA), vol. 4 (1), pp. 87-107.

Neri F. and Saitta L. (1996b). "Exploring the Power of Genetic Search in Learning Symbolic Classifiers". *IEEE Transactions on Pattern Analysis and Machine Intelligence*, **PAMI** 18, 1135-1142.

IDL: A Prototypical Intelligent Digital Library Service

Giovanni Semeraro   Floriana Esposito   Donato Malerba

Nicola Fanizzi   Stefano Ferilli   Pasquale Lops

Dipartimento di Informatica - Università degli Studi di Bari
Via E. Orabona 4 - 70126 Bari, Italy
{semeraro, esposito, malerba, nico, ferilli, lops}@lacam.uniba.it

Abstract. This paper presents IDL (Intelligent Digital Library), a prototypical digital library. It integrates machine learning tools and techniques in order to make effective, efficient and economically feasible the process of capturing the information that should be stored and indexed by content in the digital library.

1 Introduction

A digital library is *"a distributed technology environment which dramatically reduces barriers to the creation, dissemination, manipulation, storage, integration and reuse of information by individuals and groups."* [3]. Three are the main functions of a digital library [2]: *Collection*, which includes techniques that allow to detect those information sources that are useful to a client population; *organization* and *representation*, which require that the information resources are classified and indexed according to criteria relevant to their potential users; *access* and *retrieval*, which involve the design and organization of materials within a physical space in order to retrieve effectively information items, when the user requires them.

Building an effective and efficient digital library is the task of a project that we started recently, as the natural evolution of an early project on electronic document processing [1]. Since the beginning, it has been clear that the key issue of the project lies in the role that learning systems can play for *information capture* and *semantic indexing*.

By *information capture*, we mean the task of setting information items free of the physical medium on which they are stored. It involves the problem of converting data from a paper format into a digital one. This has given raise to the birth of new research areas dealing with the automated recognition of the components of documents, such as the analysis of the overall physical structure of a document (*document analysis*), the classification of the whole document (*document classification*), and the analysis of the overall logical structure of a document (*document understanding*). All these problems aim at the high-level understanding of the semantic content of the document, which is the *conditio sine qua non* we can index the information in the library according to its content.

This paper presents IDL, a prototypical intelligent digital library service that integrates learning systems for document analysis, classification and understanding.

2 The Architecture of the Digital Library

A major bottleneck in developing technologies for digital libraries is the transformation of data presented on paper into an effective electronic representation. A solution to this problem could come from the application of document processing techniques [4]. Since the pixel representation of a document image is far from being considered *effective*, it is necessary to process the bitmap in order to extract an abstract representation of the content of the document itself. Information capture through document processing can take place at several levels of abstraction. At the lowest level, called *document analysis*, it aims at extracting the *geometric* (or *layout*) structure of a document, that is, a hierarchical organization of layout areas with contents of different categories (text, image or graphics). After detecting the layout structure, the logical constituents of the document, such as title, authors, sections of a paper, can be identified. This high level process is called *document understanding*, since logical constituents are much closer to semantics than the layout components. The logical objects can be arranged in another hierarchical structure, which is called *logical structure*. The document understanding process can be viewed as a mapping from the layout into the logical structure. When documents to be stored have a variety of layout and logical structures, it becomes difficult to find such a mapping. In this case, the problem can be simplified by *classifying* the documents into a set of distinct classes characterized by certain standard layout and logical structures (*document classification*).

The accomplishment of the three tasks of document analysis, classification and understanding can actually benefit by the application of machine learning techniques. The learning systems that perform these tasks constitute three *application enablers* in the system architecture of IDL. Indeed, a *digital library service* is a set of modules that can be classified as either resource managers or application enablers. A *resource manager* is a program that represents the only access path to the data contained in a *protected resource* and is accessible to multiple concurrent clients. Intuitively, a protected resource is a data collection. An *application enabler* is a software that allows a class of users to make application programming easy and quick or to avoid it completely.

The architecture of IDL is shown in Fig. 1. The *Repository* is a protected resource containing the actual collection of data that constitutes the digital library. Usually, it consists of highly structured items. Here, we use the word *database* rather than *information collection* because in IDL it is a commercial object-oriented database management system, namely ObjectStore 2.0 by Object Design, Inc. Thus, the Repository is actually a set of objects. More precisely, these objects constitute an instance of an ObjectStore conceptual scheme, that we designed purposely for the digital library. The *document object model* is the conceptual schema according to which documents are stored and (internally) represented in both the layout and the logical structure.

The portion of the object model that allows us to store (and retrieve) the objects related to the layout structure of a document is given in Fig. 2a. For our purposes, we defined a hierarchy of five distinct classes corresponding to the levels of objects in the layout tree (other than Page), called BasicBlock, LineBlock, SetOfLineBlock, FirstFrameBlock, and SecondFrameBlock. Each level corresponds to an internal representation of the layout structure of a document at a different level of granularity (levels are listed starting from the coarsest

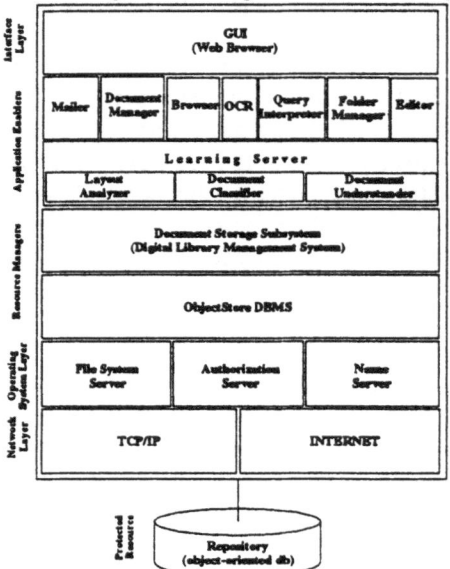

Fig. 1. The architecture of IDL.

one - BasicBlock - to the finest one - SecondFrameBlock) and every object at a level is made up of objects at a lower level. All the objects at any level have the same basic structure, since they are instances of the class Block (in Fig. 2a), as well.

The information about the type of document is stored in the portion of the document object model depicted in Fig. 2b. Specifically, each class of documents in a digital library is defined as an instance of the object DocClass. In fact, defining each class of documents as an instance of a meta-level class - DocClass - allows us to achieve a greater flexibility when the digital library needs to be updated (by adding/deleting a new class of documents, through the methods InsertClass, DeleteClass of the class DigitalLibrary). Moreover, each class of documents is associated with a set of meaningful types of logical objects, called *logical labels*, thus adding a new class of documents requires the introduction of a set of new logical labels. This is performed by creating a new instance of the class Attribute for each logical label (Fig. 2b).

With reference to Fig. 1 again, above the protected resource there is the digital library software. It consists of five layers. The lower layers are those more related to the machinery used to implement the digital library service and ignore the semantics of the repository, since they do not need to know the format of the data stored in it. Specifically, the *Network Layer* allows remote access to a library via Internet, while the *Operating System Layer* makes available all the functions of the operating system and controls that the users who required an access to the repository have proper access rights. In detail, it maps names of the users that issued the request to the proper locations by means of the *Name Server*, and limits each user to what the administrator of the digital library service permits by means of the *Authorization Server*.

The layer of the *Resource Managers* mainly deals with the management of documents, viewed at different levels of abstraction. The lower box in this layer - *ObjectStore DBMS* - is a database management system. The upper box contains the *Document Storage Subsystem*, that is to say, the document storage and access software. It is involved in both storing and retrieving items to and from the library collection and updating and searching

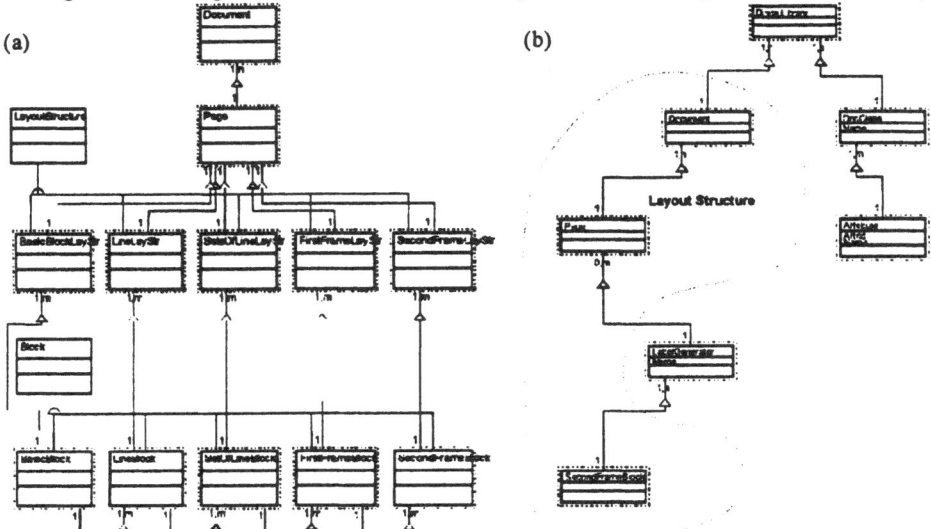

(a)   (b)

Fig. 2. The object models of IDL: (a) the layout structure, (b) the logical structure .

the library catalogs. Its scope is limited to aspects that are independent of the meaning and the internal representation of information items in a digital library. It is implemented as a client-server tool.

The layer of the *Application Enablers* makes available several functionalities to the end users of the libraries. This layer hides operating system and machine differences. The lower layer of application enablers is a *Learning Server*, that is to say, it provides a *suite* of learning systems that can be exploited concurrently by multiple *clients* in order to perform document layout analysis, classification and understanding. These tools are used by the library's custodian to recognize patterns and layout/logical structures of the documents in the library, with the aim to create search indexes automatically. Conversely, at the upper layer there are the tools developed for the end users of the library. The *Mailer* enabler implements a standard electronic mailing system. The *Document Manager* is in charge of helping end users with their special kinds of documents, mainly as regards their presentation and manipulation. The *Query Interpreter* is the inference engine that allows the user to formulate any query concerning the objects in the library by a first-order logic language. The *Browser* enabler is a tool that allows the user to navigate into a digital library. It is intended to be exploited by people who do not know the organization of the library. It produces *on the fly* an HTML file corresponding to the document required by the user. The *Folder* enabler is used to create new folders, add a document to a folder, delete an existing folder. The *Editor* enabler is activated when a user wants to change a document. This is possible on local copies of a document, unless the user is the library's custodian. The *OCR* enabler is a classical OCR system, integrated into the digital library service with the aim of *reading* the content of all and only those layout blocks of a document that are considered useful to the semantic indexing and retrieval by content of the document itself. The *Interface Layer* implements the applications that actually interface the users of the library. Currently, a unique GUI based on any Web browser allows three categories of IDL users to create/delete a library (*IDL Administrator*), manage a specific library, provided that he/she possesses the proper access rights (*library's custodian*), choose a specific library and query/browse it on the ground of the content of its documents (*end user*). The GUI is designed around a state-transition model, with each state representing an HTML page. All the HTML pages are dynamically generated by Common Gateway Interface (CGI) scripts (in C language) in order to reflect the current content of a library.

3 Conclusions and Future Work

Future work will concern the extension of the digital library tools and services to different kinds of documents, such as topographic maps for applications like geographic information systems, and technical documents for applications that support project development.

References

1. Esposito, F., D. Malerba, and G. Semeraro (1994). Multistrategy learning for document recognition. *Applied Artificial Intelligence: An International Journal*, vol. 8, no. 1, 33-84.
2. Gladney, H. M., Z. Ahmed, R. Ashany, N. J. Belkin, E. A. Fox, and M. Zemankova (1994). Digital library: Gross structure and requirements (report from a Workshop). *Proceedings of the Workshop on On-line Access to Digital Libraries*, Los Alamitos: IEEE Computer Society.
3. Lesk, M. (1993). The Digital Library: What is it? Why should it be here? *Source Book on Digital Libraries*, TR 93-35, Virginia Tech, Dept. of Computer Science, Blacksburg, VA. Edited Volume (Ed. E. A. Fox).
4. Tang, Y. Y., C. D. Yan, and C. Y. Suen (1994). Document processing for automatic knowledge acquisition. *IEEE Transactions on Knowledge and Data Engineering*, vol. 6, no. 1, 3-21.

An Object-Oriented Architecture for the DRS Scheduling Problem

Paolo Bazzica[1], Gianni Casonato[1] and Amedeo Cesta[2]*

[1] Corso di Laurea in Ingegneria Informatica
Università di Roma "La Sapienza", Rome, Italy
[2] IP-CNR, Consiglio Nazionale delle Ricerche
Viale Marx 15, I-00137 Rome, Italy
amedeo@pscs2.irmkant.rm.cnr.it

1 Problem Description

The Data Relay Satellite (DRS) System is an European Space Agency program aimed at providing a data relay service between Low Earth Orbiting (LEO) satellites and their ground terminals. Actually this program is in the last step of development, and it will be operative within 1999. The DRS infrastructure consist in a constellation of two satellites and in a set of ground stations that allow: (a) almost total coverage area; (b) strong reduction of the LEO's ground terminal network; (c) reduction in data-distribution problems; (d) reduction of required on-board data storage capacity for LEO satellites.

The scheduling problem of DRS consists in the production of a mission plan that allows the customers to access in the transmission service. The access requests are supposed to be in high numbers, with temporal specifications that exceed the total transmission time available, introducing conflicts that have to be solved following some quality objectives. For the technical characteristics of the DRS system, the crucial aspect in the production of the plan is the management of the link between the DRS and the LEO satellites, while the links between DRS and ground stations are less problematic. Such a link imposes the fulfillment of physical constraints of the DRS's antennas, temporal constraints of the requests, and specifics of priority, commercial value and allocation preference. This problem is a scheduling problem, and more specifically is an open-shop problem, in whose is possible to identify: (a) *resources:* the three antennas on the DRS satellite; (b) *operations:* transmission requests, with priority, physical and temporal constraints, and preference specifications; (c) *constraints:* technological (supplied bands) and physical (processing capacity) limits of the antennas. The production of the mission plan is supposed to follow an iterative process repeated three times, and that involves two kinds of users:

- commercial operators at the Mission Control Center: negotiates with the clients the sale of the free transmission spaces, and inserts in the plan the related activities;

* This research is part of a joint project supported by ASI – Agenzia Spaziale Italiana. Members of the project are: Dipartimento di Informatica e Sistemistica dell'Università di Roma "La Sapienza", Dipartimento di Informatica ed Automazione della Terza Università di Roma, and Reparto di Intelligenza Artificiale, Modelli Cognitivi e dell'Interazione, IP-CNR, Roma.

- spacecraft engineers at the Operation Control Center: modifies the plan inserting in some special activities for the maintenance of the system operativity, and requests with a special character of urgency.

These two operational profiles follow different and potentially conflicting objectives (maximum satisfaction of requests vs. DRS's resources saving). Those objectives have to be integrated together in a complete automated scheduling system.

2 The O-OSCAR Architecture

The Artificial Intelligence techniques provide an approach at the scheduling which identifies three fundamental aspects: (a) representation of the domain; (b) generation of optimal solution; (c) interaction with the user. These three aspects, typical of the symbolic approach, can increase the project complexity for a system that supply all these characteristics. This problem has been addressed using the tools provided from the object-oriented analysis and design techniques. Following this objectives a scheduling architecture has been designed and implemented named O-OSCAR (Object-Oriented SCheduling ARchitecture). After having defined a base-level architecture, a specialization for addressing the full DRS problem has been obtained. For lack of space in the following we describe just the main functionalities developed for the different users.

2.1 The Commercial Profile

This version of the sequencer is directed to the user of the Mission Control Center. The main screen consists of two windows, the main window and the Gantt chart window. In the main window there are three lists with the information about the service requests proposed to the system, the requests accepted by the system and the requests refused by the system. The system allows loading and saving of partial schedules on the disk, the possibility to input a new request interactively via a dedicated mask and the capability to load a set of request from a disk file. The scheduling process consists on the selection of a request set and in the successive attempt to schedule it through the selection of the button Process. The interesting key points of this profile are: (a) attempt to abstract from the technical detail of the task; (b) simplified vision of the scheduling task; (c) exclusive instruments to trade with the clients about the parameters of the requests refused by the system. Regarding the last point this version of the sequencer provides the capability to select a set of requests from the refused requests list and the management for each request of the relative conflicting parameters. At this purpose is useful to use the Gantt chart to be able to directly the availability of the temporal parameters. The Gantt window allows the selection of each box associated with a request to have access to the relative detailed parameters. The successful trading of a request causes the apparition of the relative box in the Gantt chart.

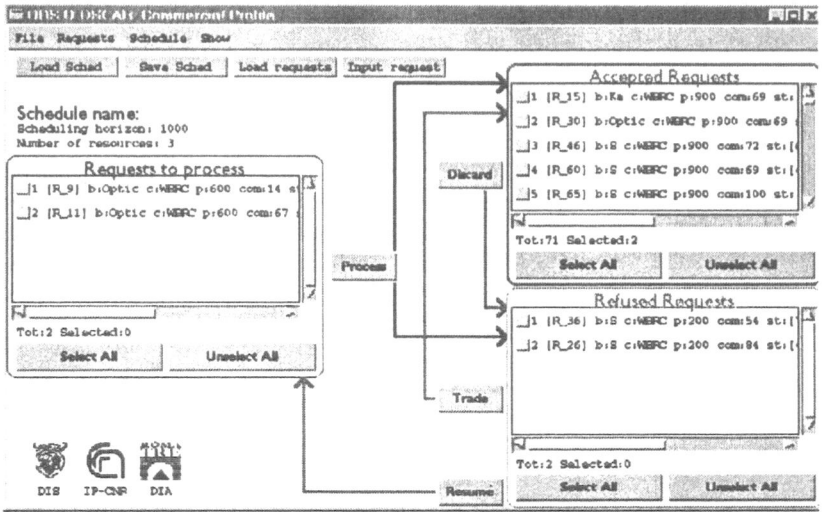

Fig. 1. The interface for the commercial user

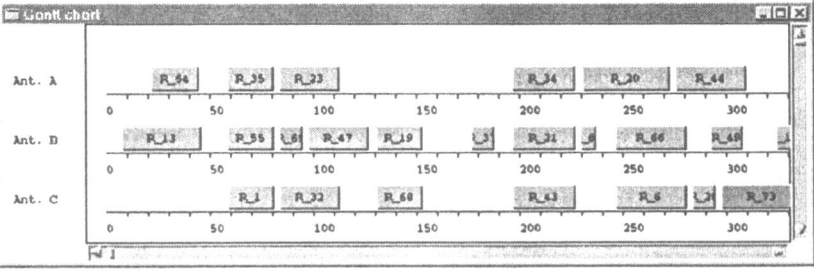

Fig. 2. Current solution representation through a Gantt chart

2.2 The Operative Profile

The operative version of the sequencer has the objective to incorporate in the partial plans created by the Mission Control Center the requirements that allow the operativity of the orbiting platform (e.g. orbital shifts, maintenance of antennas), manage the available resources (e.g. excluding a broken antenna from the schedule) and allow the input of "last minute" requests (e.g. emergency operations). The need to minimize the effects of those operations claims full access to the available scheduling strategies provided from the system. When the program is started the screen shows the next window and the Gantt. In the main window appear in each moment: (a) the global state of the schedule. (b) the total number of requests proposed to the system. (c) the total number of rejected requests. The details relatives to each of these aspects are accessible by the "More Info..." buttons. The Gantt chart window is the same provided from the commercial profile sequencer. The key points of this profile are: (a) the chance to alter the scheduling domain by removing an antenna; (b) the ability to change the heuristic used to schedule the selected requests; (c) the direct management of the backtracking. As far as the last point is concerned the user has the capability to choose directly the activities to remove in case they are in conflict with the selected activity. In this way the modifications due to the backtracking are under the direct control of the user, allowing the minimum side effect of the reactive phase on the existent partial schedule.

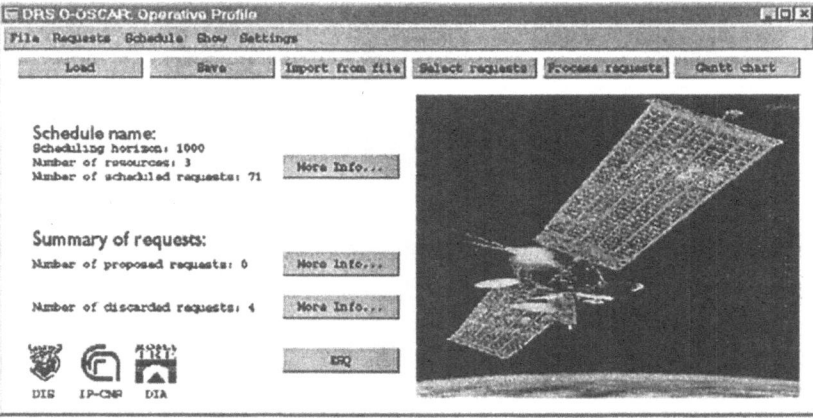

Fig. 3. The interface for the operative user

3   System Performances

The system has been implemented in C++ and uses the Amulet libraries, from CMU, for developing portable graphical interfaces. The two Users Profiles are able to exchange partial solutions in an intermediate file format allowing a complete management of the schedule in the workspace. The system has been tested with the DRS problem simulator developed independently by a research effort of the National Research Council (CNR). A typical daily DRS problem consists in 75 requests and it is integrally processed by the system in times compatible with the interactive use of the software. The 75 requests problem requires approximately 1 minute on the Windows 95 version of the sequencer with a Pentium at 75 MHz. The times on a typical UNIX workstation are reduced by one half.

MASMA: A Personal Assistant for Meetings Management

Rodolfo Brancaleoni[1]*, Amedeo Cesta[2] and Daniela D'Aloisi[1]

[1] Fondazione Ugo Bordoni
Via B. Castiglione 59, I-00142 Rome, Italy
gheo,dany@fub.it
[2] IP-CNR, National Research Council of Italy
Viale Marx 15, I-00137 Rome, Italy
amedeo@pscs2.irmkant.rm.cnr.it

1   Problem Overview

This paper presents a general overview of a multi-agent meeting scheduler called Masma (Multi-Agent System for Meeting Automation).

Organizing meetings generally requires a massive organizational effort, complex negotiation strategies and a huge numbers of communication acts, e.g., e-mail messages, phone calls, faxes, etc. A significant reference problem is the so-called *secretaries' nightmare* since generally are the secretaries who find a compromise among the different users' constraints, the availability of the resources and the need of satisfying their bosses. An efficient and optimal scheduling process could bring benefits in term of saving time and costs and of optimizing the information flow.

The problem can be seen as a particular application domain of distributed scheduling among a set of agents (Distributed Task Scheduling). In this context the tasks are the appointments to be fixed and the resources are the participants. To each resource (person) an agent is associated managing his agenda and organizing meetings by negotiating with other agents. It knows the user's preferences concerning the available dates, the information to be exchanged with the others, the agents to negotiate with, the user's interests and so on. Each meeting is organized by an agent, involves a number of other agents and is characterized by a set of constraints. The organizer agent—the *host*—leads the negotiation process proposing a set of possible time intervals, gathering the invitees' answers and figuring out a common solution. If necessary the process is repeated until an agreement is reached.

The meetings can be reserved to a precise set of users (closed meetings) that are specifically invited or be open to anyone. In the last case, the topic(s) of the event can be used to select the persons the announce is sent to.

All the users are connected to a network even if they can be located anywhere. A centralized management of the resources—in the sense of sites and instruments—is applied.

---

* Now at Datamat S.p.A., Via Laurentina 760, I-00142 Rome, Italy

2 Masma's Architecture

Masma consists of four agents that cooperate to accomplish the user's task. Inherently distributed problems are faced in a distributed way and centralized problems are faced in a centralized way. The approach followed in designing the different agents starts with the definition of a skeletal agent that contains all the functionalities (the infrastructure) that are common to all the agent instances. Then the designer specializes some parts or add new capabilities to create a particular class dedicated to solving specific problems.

Masma's architecture consists of a personal assistant for each user, called *Meeting Agent*, and other three agents that are shared among a community. The Masma's agents are the *Meeting Agent*, the *Server Agent*, the *Resource Agent* and the *Travel Agent*.

- *Meeting Agent.* This agent is associated to each user and behaves as a personal assistant specialized in meeting organization. It has two main tasks: managing the user's profile and taking part in the meeting organization. The profile contains information concerning the personal agenda and the preferences of the user on how to perform the tasks. The preferences mainly regards the meeting, e.g., time availability and particular attitudes toward attending people, but can also concern general social rules. In the present version, preference values—from *nil* to *high*—can be assigned to the different dates and times through a graphical interface. The profile contains also a part about user's general interests. In the organizational process the agent represents the user according to his profile.

The other three agents work as specialized knowledge servers to which some common services have been delegated. They could also perform their job autonomously without any connection with the Meeting Agents.

- *Server Agent.* It is in charge of managing the network addresses since in an "open world" it is quite difficult that everyone knows all the addresses of everybody. The chosen solution is a specialized management in which a single agent maintains a knowledge base with the users' addresses: in the case of new users, it can get the addresses by querying an external server. In Masma it also manages a database containing the interest areas that users have made public in order to receive free announcements on the network. This is related to an additional service consisting in user being notified of workshops, seminars and similar events by their personal agents and having the possibility of quickly reserving time on their own agendas. The Server Agent is in charge of selectively spreading announces out without bothering all the connected users. It also gathers the subscriptions in case of open meetings with registration.
- *Resource Agent.* The Congress Centers or Universities or other similar sites are crucial resources in a meeting organization. Masma adopts a centralized administration of these common resources to avoid conflicts in selecting one of them. The *Resource Agent* maintains the databases and furnishes to the

Meeting Agent a list of structures satisfying the problem constraints. When a decision is taken, the agent carries out the operations necessary to reserve the place.

- *Travel Agent*. The user can also wish to mechanize the last step in organizing a meeting, the lodging and travel decisions. The *Travel Agent* can help the user is choosing the best path or the less expansive ticket or the most luxurious hotel. The agent can connect the user to train and flight timetable, decide the best path between to places, inform him about prices, show a list of possible hotels. It could also furnish a reservation service.

This structure can be made complex in several ways. At present it is worth noting that the two basic classes of an applied multi-agent system are present in Masma: personal agents and information (or service) agents. Moreover the system structure is flexible enough to easily accept agent additions of both types.

3   Interaction Control in Masma

Masma is a personal assistant devoted to solve tedious tasks. In such a system there are several aspects in which the control of the interaction is relevant. It should be noted that here are at least three different types of interaction: human user *vs* (personal) meeting agent, meeting agent *vs* meeting agent, meeting agent *vs* service agent.

The approach followed for distributing the initiative and the devised solutions are characterized both by the specific application and by general issues related to delegating a task to an agent.

Task driven control of the initiative: the negotiation protocol followed by the agents to reach an agreement about a meeting actually establishes activity turns between the user, his agent and the other agents. The protocols influence the degree of interaction between the actors and delineate the initiative strategy.

User centered control through personalization: the possible personalization of agents' behavior in meeting scheduling can represent an indirect means of constraining the interactions. In order to mechanize the decision process and to limitate the interaction with the user, the agent maintains a user's profile with his availability and preferences and supplies tools to define and update the profile itself. The profile influences the interaction user-agent.

Mechanisms for the user to take the control: the user can inspect what the agent is doing. In order to increase its possibility of acceptance, an agent-based system should be endowed with an inspection mode about its activities: that will involve a major level of trust by the user. Moreover the user should contemporary be able to modify values and parameters to influence the current state of affairs: this would be a way of constraining the dynamic behavior, a "dynamic" possibility of influence. MASMA allows in its main dialogue window to verify the status of the agent, and then to inspect the details of the current activity.

Heuristics to give the initiative back to the user: general strategies about *how* and *when* to interact with the user are relevant to this issue. Concerning *how*: the agents dialogue with their users by means of simple and effective windows that are adapted to the current needs and that hide the complexity of the system. Concerning *when*: the procedure that manages the shift of control allows the meeting agent interrupts its user only for the most important—in user's view—decisions. It is the user who decides when to leave decisions to the agent.

4 Conclusions

We have briefly presented Masma, a particular approach to the meeting scheduling problem. Masma is a complete running system written in Common Lisp, that uses the KQML Kapi routines developed at Lockheed to exchange messages among agents and the Garnet tool to develop the user interface. A Masma agent can reside on any machine able to understand and interpret the languages. An upgraded version—written in Java—is under development that will incorporate suggestions and coming from the use.

Aspects related to our agent's architetture are described in [2] and [3], a longer description of Masma can be found in [1], the interaction issues are presented in [4].

Acknowledgments

Daniela D'Aloisi and Rodolfo Brancaleoni carried out their work in the framework of the agreement between the FUB and the Italian PT Administration. Amedeo Cesta's work is partially supported by CNR Committee 12 on Information Technology (Projects SARI and SCI*SIA).

References

1. R. Brancaleoni, A. Cesta, and D. D'Aloisi. MASMA: A Multi-Agent System for Scheduling Meetings. In *Proceedings of Second International Conference on The Practical Application of Intelligent Agents and Multi-Agent Technology (PAAM 97)*, 1997.
2. A. Cesta and D. D'Aloisi. Building Interfaces as Agents: A Case Study. *SIGCHI Bulletin*, 28(3):108–113, July 1996.
3. A. Cesta, D. D'Aloisi, and R. Brancaleoni. Mixed-Initiative Agenda Management with Software Agents. In *Proceeding of the First International Conference on Autonomous Agents,* February 1997.
4. D. D'Aloisi, A. Cesta, and R. Brancaleoni. Mixed-initiative aspects in an agent-based system. In *AAAI Spring Symposium on "Computational Models of Mixed-Initiative Interaction"*, 1997.

Author Index

Springer
and the
environment

At Springer we firmly believe that an international science publisher has a special obligation to the environment, and our corporate policies consistently reflect this conviction.

We also expect our business partners – paper mills, printers, packaging manufacturers, etc. – to commit themselves to using materials and production processes that do not harm the environment. The paper in this book is made from low- or no-chlorine pulp and is acid free, in conformance with international standards for paper permanency.

Springer

Lecture Notes in Artificial Intelligence (LNAI)

Lecture Notes in Computer Science